Eugenio Coseriu

Eugenio Coseriu

―

Past, Present and Future

Edited by
Klaas Willems and Cristinel Munteanu

DE GRUYTER

This publication was printed with the financial support of "Danubius" University of Galaţi (Romania) and the Linguistics Department of Ghent University (Belgium).

ISBN 978-3-11-126341-0
e-ISBN (PDF) 978-3-11-071239-1
e-ISBN (EPUB) 978-3-11-071241-4

Library of Congress Control Number: 2021937869

Bibliographic information published by the Deutsche Nationalbibliothek
The Deutsche Nationalbibliothek lists this publication in the Deutsche Nationalbibliografie; detailed bibliographic data are available on the Internet at http://dnb.dnb.de

© 2023 Walter de Gruyter GmbH, Berlin/Boston
This volume is text- and page-identical with the hardback published in 2021.
Cover illustration: photo Coseriu in younger years: © 2021 Eugenio Coseriu-Archiv Tübingen; photo Coseriu in later years: Universiteitsarchief Gent, © UGent, foto Hilde Christiaens; logo: © 2021 Eugenio Coseriu-Archiv Tübingen
Printing and binding: CPI books GmbH, Leck

www.degruyter.com

Table of Contents

Contributors —— IX

Klaas Willems (Ghent) and Cristinel Munteanu (Galați)
Introduction —— 1

Part I: Philosophy of language

Jürgen Trabant (Berlin)
The essence of language: on Coseriu's philosophy of language —— 47

Ana Agud (Salamanca)
Eugenio Coseriu's approach to language and linguistics: building a 'philosophically sustainable' linguistics —— 63

Part II: History of the language sciences

Gerda Haßler (Potsdam)
Coseriu as a historiographer of linguistics in relation to his linguistic ideas —— 81

Viggo Bank Jensen (Copenhagen)
Coseriu's Hjelmslev —— 97

Lorenzo Cigana (Copenhagen)
Coseriu and glossematics: an uncompleted dialogue —— 115

Part III: Theory and practice of Integral Linguistics

Mircea Borcilă (Cluj-Napoca)
Integral Linguistics as a cultural science —— 137

Göran Sonesson (Lund)
Considerations on the subtle art of integrating linguistics (and/or semiotics) —— 151

Jörn Albrecht (Heidelberg)
Eugenio Coseriu and the primacy of history —— 165

Pierre Swiggers (Leuven)
At the roots of linguistic change: the historicity of language —— 181

Ioan Milică (Iași)
Coseriu's journey to the realm of linguistic change —— 197

Angela Schrott (Kassel)
Eugenio Coseriu and pragmatics —— 211

Johannes Kabatek (Zürich)
Eugenio Coseriu on immediacy, distance and discourse traditions —— 227

Andreas Widoff (Lund)
System, norm and meaning —— 245

Dagobert Höllein (Kassel)
Coseriu, significative semantics and a new system of semantic roles —— 261

Wolf Dietrich (Münster)
Coseriu's approach to word formation as an illustration of his theory of meaning —— 279

Brenda Laca (Montevideo)
The categories of the Romance verb —— 295

Elena Faur (Cluj-Napoca)
The crux of metaphor: between Cognitive and Integral Linguistics —— 311

Thomas Belligh (Ghent)
Language as activity, linguistic knowledge and cognitive psychology: a Coserian perspective —— 327

Bibliography —— 345

Author Index —— 379

Subject Index —— 385

Johannes Kabatek
Erratum to: J. Kabatek, Eugenio Coseriu on immediacy, distance and discourse traditions —— 393

Contributors

Ana Agud (PhD 1976) is professor emeritus of Indo-European linguistics at the Universidad de Salamanca. She was born in San Sebastián (Spain), where she visited the German School. She studied classical philology at the University of Salamanca and earned her PhD under the supervision of Eugenio Coseriu with a thesis on case theory. She continued her training in linguistics and oriental studies with Bernfried Schlerath (Berlin), Jürgen Untermann (Colonia) and the members of the Indological Department in Bonn, where she worked after receiving a Humboldt Grant. She studied philosophy with Josef Simon in Tübingen and Bonn. She specialised in oriental Indo-European languages (Slavic, Iranian and Indian) and devoted her main research and teaching activity to indological subjects (Vedic and Classical Sanskrit philology, Indian philosophy and linguistics, Indian aesthetics). She also published extensively on critical philosophy of language and linguistics, including the relation of language with music and aesthetics. She has translated many philosophical and poetic texts from ancient languages, German and other languages into Spanish and German and has published several articles on translation theory. Her main publications include *Historia y teoría de los casos* (1981), *La ciencia del brahman. Once Upanishad antiguas* (2000), *Los poemas del ser y el no ser y sus lenguajes en la historia* (2017) and the forthcoming monograph *Critical philosophy of language and linguistics: a humanistic, historical and comparative approach*. Ana Agud can be reached at anaagud@usal.es.

Jörn Albrecht (PhD 1970) was born in Berlin and grew up in Swabia. He studied German, Romance languages and literature, and General linguistics in Tübingen and Berlin. He was Eugenio Coseriu's assistant at the University of Tübingen from 1973 until 1978. He taught in Tübingen, Le Mans, Florence, Würzburg and Mainz-Germersheim, before becoming full professor of Translation studies at the University of Heidelberg. After his retirement he has continued to teach, but to a limited extent. His main fields of research are: contrastive linguistics and translation studies, sociolinguistics, text linguistics, the history of translation. His most important monographs are: *Le français langue abstraite?* (1970, PhD dissertation), *Europäischer Strukturalismus* (1988, third edition 2007), *Übersetzung und Linguistik* (2005, second edition 2013) and *Europäische Übersetzungsgeschichte* (with Iris Plack, 2018). With René Métrich he co-edited *Manuel de traductologie* (2016). He has edited two series of lectures by Eugenio Coseriu: *Textlinguistik* (1994, fourth edition 2007) and *Geschichte der Sprachphilosophie* (2 volumes, 2015). He also served as a co-editor, with Jens Lüdtke and Harald Thun, of the three-volume Festschrift for Eugenio Coseriu *Energeia and Ergon* (1988). Jörn Albrecht can be reached at joern.c.albrecht@web.de.

Viggo Bank Jensen is a postdoctoral researcher at the Department of Nordic Studies and Linguistics (NorS) at the University of Copenhagen. His interest in the history of linguistics dates from 2008. After doing research on eighteenth and nineteenth-century Italian linguists – Melchiorre Cesarotti (2009, 2011), Francesco Soave (2013), Alessandro Manzoni (2014) and Graziadio Ascoli (2014) – he turned to Danish linguists from roughly the same period: Rasmus Rask (2015, 2016, 2018), Niels Matthias Petersen (2014, 2017) and Kristoffer Nyrop (2018). His interest in Eugenio Coseriu was triggered by Coseriu's role in diffusing the various "dia"-concepts and their connection to Scandinavian linguists (2012, 2015). His interest in structuralism also includes Hjelmslev (2017). He recently edited the book *From the early years of phonology. The Roman Jakobson – Eli Fischer-Jørgensen correspondence (1949–1982)* (with Giuseppe D'Ottavi; Copenhagen, 2020). He is currently a researcher in the "Infrastructuralism" project, whose aim is to establish an open-source infrastructure that provides the international academic community access to correspondences and manuscripts from the archives of Louis Hjelmslev and other Danish structuralist linguists in a digitalized and commented form. He has participated in the establishment of the Italian network CISPELS ("Inter-society coordination for the history of linguistic and semiotic thought") since its inception in 2014. Viggo Bank Jensen can be reached at vbj@hum.ku.dk.

Thomas Belligh (PhD 2021) is a researcher at the General linguistics section of the Linguistics Department at Ghent University. At Ghent University, he obtained a PhD in linguistics, a master's degree in linguistics and literature, a bachelor's degree in law and a bachelor's degree in theoretical and experimental psychology. His main research interests are information structure, the semantics-pragmatics interface, the relation between linguistics and cognitive psychology, and the epistemology of the language sciences. His research is currently focused on the study of information structure phenomena on the semantics-pragmatics interface in contemporary Dutch and Italian. His approach to the study of information structure is inspired by insights taken from Coseriu's 'Integral Linguistics' as well as other contemporary theories of language. His publications include several articles that have appeared in journals such as *Language Sciences*, *Journal of Pragmatics* and *Studies in Language*. Thomas Belligh can be reached at thomas.belligh@ugent.be.

Mircea Borcilă (PhD 1980) is a senior associated professor at the Faculty of Philology, "Babeș-Bolyai" University of Cluj-Napoca. His main concern with Coseriu's work has been initiated and grounded during his research period as a Visiting Lecturer at the University of Washington in Seattle (1972–1974) and Ohio State University in Columbus (1981–1985). He is the founder of a first *Center for Integralist Studies "Eugenio Coseriu"* at his home university (1988), with a group of students and scholars from various backgrounds, working in connection with the Department of General Linguistics and Semiotics he chaired. His first research area includes editing and interpreting major Romanian contributions in the tradition of historical philology, especially Vasile Bogrea: *Pagini istorico-filologice* [Historical-philological writings] (1971), *Sacra via* (1973), *Opere alese* [Selected writings] (1998). A second research area includes studies on contemporary linguistics and related disciplines: *Studii de stilistică, poetică, semiotică* (1980), *Poetica Americană. Orientări actuale* [American poetics. Current trends] (1981) (with a postscript by Richard McLain), *Semiotică și poetică* (1992). A third research area is Coseriu's legacy and "integralist studies", on which he published several articles. A comprehensive anthology of his contributions on Coseriu is forthcoming: *Eugeniu Coșeriu. Bazele integralismului lingvistic* [Eugenio Coseriu. The foundations of linguistic integralism], coordinated with Elena Faur (to appear this year at the Romanian Academy's Publishing House). Mircea Borcilă can be reached at icaborcila@yahoo.com.

Lorenzo Cigana (PhD 2014) is a postdoctoral researcher at the Department of Nordic Studies and Linguistics (NorS) at the University of Copenhagen. Since his PhD on Louis Hjelmslev's theory of markedness he has been working on structural linguistics, with a particular focus on Danish theoretical linguistics, glossematics and the theory of language developed by L. Hjelmslev and H. J. Uldall in the 1930s. His main research interests include the issue of form and formalisation in linguistics, the epistemological underpinnings and historical evolution of linguistic ideas, the interconnections between linguistics, French semiotics, the philosophy of language, ethno-anthropology, phenomenology and *Gestalt* psychology, and the notions of opposition and markedness. His publications include *Louis Hjelmslev. Écrits choisis* (sdvig.-press, forthcoming) and *Elmar Holenstein, Phenomenological philosophy of language: collected papers* (with S. Aurora, forthcoming). He is currently a researcher in the "Infrastructuralism" project, whose aim is to establish an open-source infrastructure that provides the international academic community access to correspondences and manuscripts from the archives of Louis Hjelmslev and other Danish structuralist linguists in a digitalized and commented form. He can be reached at lorenzo.cigana@hum.ku.dk.

Wolf Dietrich (PhD 1971) is professor emeritus of Romance linguistics, Westfälische Wilhelms-Universität Münster. He is an associate member of the Academia Brasileira de Filologia (Rio de Janeiro) and of the Academia de la Lengua Guaraní (Asunción, Paraguay). He has taught at the University of Münster from 1973 to 2006, at the Universidad de Navarra (Pamplona, Spain) in 1973 and at the University of Bucarest (Rumania) in 2000. His main research interests are grammatical categories such as tense and aspect, modality, syntax, word formation, historical linguistics in Romance languages (French, Spanish, Portuguese, Italian, and Rumanian), in Latin and Greek (old and modern) and in South American indigenous languages, mainly in Tupi-Guarani languages. He was co-director (with Harald Thun and Haralambos Symeonidis) of the *Atlas Lingüístico Guaraní-Románico* project. His books include *Der periphrastische Verbalaspekt in den romanischen Sprachen* (1973) (revised Spanish translation: *El aspecto verbal perifrástico en las lenguas románicas*, 1983), *Bibliografia da língua portuguesa do Brasil* (1980), *El idioma chiriguano. Gramática, textos, vocabulario* (1986), *More evidence for an internal classification of Tupi-Guarani languages* (1990), *Einführung in die spanische Sprachwissenschaft* (together with Volker Noll, seventh edition 2019), *Einführung in die französische Sprachwissenschaft* (together with Horst Geckeler; fifth edition 2012), *Griechisch und Romanisch. Parallelen und Divergenzen in Entwicklung, Variation und Strukturen* (1995), *Atlas lingüístico Guaraní-Románico* (ALGR), Tomo I: *Léxico del cuerpo humano* (together with Haralambos Symeonidis, 2009), Tomo II: *Léxico del parentesco* (together with Guido Kallfell and Harald Thun, 2015). He edited Eugenio Coseriu, *Geschichte der romanischen Sprachwissenschaft*. Vol. 2: *Die Epoche des Humanismus* (2020) and co-authored Eugenio Coseriu, *Geschichte der romanischen Sprachwissenschaft*. Vol. 3: *Das 17. und 18. Jahrhundert*, Teil I: Italien – Spanien – Portugal – Katalonien – Frankreich (2021). Wolf Dietrich can be reached at dietriw@uni-muenster.de.

Elena Faur (PhD 2013) is a scientific researcher at the Romanian Academy – The Institute of Linguistics and Literary History "Sextil Pușcariu" Cluj-Napoca. Her interests in Integral Linguistics and Cognitive Linguistics date from the 2000s. Other research interests include cognitive and anthropological poetics, stylistics, cognitive semiotics, lexical semantics, discourse analysis, corpus linguistics, and metaphor theory. Her publications include: *Semantica cognitivă și emergența studiilor elocuționale* [Cognitive semantics and the emergence of elocutional studies] (PhD thesis), "The metaphors for death and the death of conceptual metaphors in poetry. An analysis based on Emily Dickinson's poem 'Because I could not stop for death'" (2012), "Integral semantics and conceptual metaphor: rethinking conceptual metaphor within an integral semantics framework" (2013), "Eugeniu Coșeriu și noua direcție în studiile cognitiviste" [Eugenio Coseriu and the new direction in cognitive studies] (2019). She is a co-author of *Dicționarul Limbii Române* [The Romanian Language Dictionary], Vol. V (2008) and Vol. III (Serie Nouă) (2010). Elena Faur can be reached at faur.elenacarmen@gmail.com.

Gerda Haßler (PhD 1978) is full professor at the Institute of Romance Studies, University of Potsdam. She is an associate member of the research groups Modèles Dynamiques Corpus UMR 7114 (Université Paris Nanterre), Laboratoire de Recherche sur le Langage (Université Clermont Auvergne), and Descriptive Grammar and Historiography of Spanish Grammar (Universidad de Salamanca). Her main research interests in the history of linguistics and in cognitive and functional linguistics date from the 1970s, when she started investigating the early history of the concept of linguistic relativity in Europe. She has been studying linguistic theories of the Enlightenment, the notion of 'organism' in nineteenth-century linguistics and the reception of Saussure's theory of language in Europe. Her focus of attention is on aspect, modality and evidentiality in Romance languages, collocations and discourse traditions, and polyphony in written language. Her books include *Sprachtheorien der Aufklärung zur Rolle der Sprache im Erkenntnisprozeß* (1984), *Der semantische Wertbegriff in Sprachtheorien vom 18. bis zum 20. Jahrhundert* (1991), *Lexikon sprachtheoretischer Grundbegriffe des 17. und 18. Jahrhunderts* (with Cordula Neis, 2009), *Temporalität, Aspektualität und Modalität in romanischen Sprachen* (2016), *Manuel des modes et modalités* (2021). She is a co-editor of the journal *Beiträge zur Geschichte der Sprachwissenschaft*. Gerda Haßler can be reached at hassler@uni-potsdam.de.

Dagobert Höllein (PhD 2017) is a postdoctoral researcher at the Department of German Studies at the University of Kassel. His PhD on semantic roles of prepositional objects was published by De Gruyter in 2019: *Präpositionalobjekt vs. Adverbial: Die semantischen Rollen der Präpositionalobjekte*. His research interests are syntactic theory (construction grammar and valency theory), historical linguistics, grammaticalization, valency change, significative semantics, argument structure constructions, corpus linguistics and cultural studies. He is currently a lecturer at the Department of German Studies at the University of Kassel and a researcher at the DFG [German Research Foundation] supported project "Syntaktische Grundstrukturen des Neuhochdeutschen. Zur grammatischen Fundierung eines Referenzkorpus Neuhochdeutsch [Basic syntactic structures in New High German]", whose aim is to establish a reference corpus for New High German. He can be reached at d.hoellein@uni-kassel.de.

Johannes Kabatek (PhD 1995) was born in 1965 in Stuttgart. He studied Romance philology, Political science and Musicology in Tübingen and Málaga. From 1993 until 1999 he was assistant professor at the universities of Paderborn and Tübingen. From 2000 until 2013 he held professorships at the universities of Erfurt, Freiburg im Breisgau and Tübingen. Since September 2013 he has been full professor (chair) for Ibero-Romance linguistics at the University of Zurich. He has held visiting professorships in the USA, Brazil, Chile, Italy and Spain. He is a corresponding member of the Royal Galician and the Royal Spanish Academy. He holds an honorary doctorate from the University of Suceava (2016). He currently serves as the president of the Societas Linguistica Europaea (2020–2021). His main research areas are Romance linguistics (French and Ibero-Romance languages), language contact, minority languages; Medieval Spanish, Galician, Catalan and Brazilian Portuguese; historical linguistics, historical syntax, spoken and written language. He is editor-in-chief of *Revista Internacional de Lingüística Iberoamericana* and *Energeia. Online journal for linguistics, language philosophy and* *history of linguistics*. He is the author of numerous publications on Eugenio Coseriu. He has been the director of the Coseriu Archive since 2005 and host of www.coseriu.com. Johannes Kabatek can be reached at kabatek@rom.uzh.ch.

Brenda Laca (PhD 1984) is full professor at the Institute of Linguistics of the Universidad de la República in Montevideo, Uruguay. She previously held a full professorship for linguistics at the University Paris 8 for two decades, from which she retired in 2018. Her research concentrates on the Romance languages. Her main research interests lie in the semantics of grammatical categories. She has done work on the semantics of word formation, on determiners, noun phrases and quantification, on nominal and verbal plurality and on tense, aspect and modality. She has (co-)edited several books on aspect, among them *Temps et aspect: de la morphologie à l'interprétation* (2002) and *Layers of Aspect* (2011), and she has published a number of book chapters and journal articles on tense, aspect and modality. She has been a guest professor at several European and Latin American universities and has acted as a co-editor for the series *Sciences du Langage* and *Recherches Linguistiques de Vincennes* at Presses Universitaires de Vincennes. Brenda Laca can be reached at brendalaca@gmail.com.

Ioan Milică (PhD 2007) is associate professor at the Department of Romanian Studies, Faculty of Letters, "Alexandru Ioan Cuza" University of Iași, Romania. His main research interests are theoretical linguistics and the history of linguistics, with a particular focus on the intellectual legacy of Saussurean semiology. He has also published a number of articles devoted to linguistic creativity, more specifically such phenomena as the use of slang and other unconventional forms of expression, the history of naive and expert botanical terminologies, as well as the appeal to proverbs, maxims and idioms in various spoken and written contexts. His books include *Expresivitatea argoului* [Expressiveness of slang] (2009), *Lumi discursive* [Worlds of discourse] (2013) and *Noțiuni de stilistică* [Notions of stylistics] (2014). He has taught Romanian at the University of Konstanz, Germany. He has also been a visiting scholar at the University of Bergen, Norway, Saarland University, Germany and the Catholic University of Leuven, Belgium. He is co-editor of the journal *Diacronia* (www.diacronia.ro) and board member of several other Romanian journals: *Text și discurs religios* (Iași), *Limba Română* (Chișinău, Republic of Moldova), *Argotica* (Craiova) and *Language and Literature – European Landmarks of Identity* (Pitești). Ioan Milică can be reached at mioan@uaic.ro.

Cristinel Munteanu (PhD 2006 and 2018) is currently full professor at "Danubius" University of Galați (Romania) and director of the Center for Hermeneutics "Symbols and Texts" at the same university. He earned his first PhD (in philology) in 2006 with a thesis on phraseological synonymy in Romanian and his second PhD (in philosophy) in 2018 with a thesis on John Dewey's "theory of inquiry" considered as a *sui generis* type of hermeneutics. His main research interests lie in phraseology, text linguistics, hermeneutics, semiotics, philosophy of language and the history of linguistic ideas, with a special focus on Eugenio Coseriu's Integral Linguistics. His books include *Sinonimia frazeologică în limba română din perspectiva lingvisticii integrale* [Phraseological synonymy in Romanian from the perspective of Integral Linguistics] (2007), *Lingvistica integrală coșeriană. Teorie, aplicații și interviuri* [Coserian Integral Linguistics. Theory, applications and interviews] (2012), *Frazeologie românească. Formare și funcționare* [Romanian phraseology. Formation and functioning] (2013), *Tradition and innovation in language and linguistics. A Coserian perspective* (2017), *Problema sensului la John

Dewey. Premise pentru constituirea unei hermeneutici integrale [The problem of meaning in John Dewey. Premises for the establishment of an integral hermeneutics] (2019). He has published over 150 articles and also edited texts by Tobias Peucer, Bogdan P. Hasdeu and Eugenio Coseriu. He is the editor-in-chief of *Acta Universitatis Danubius. Communicatio* (Galați) and a member of the editorial board of journals such as *Fonetică și Dialectologie* (Bucharest) and *Limba română* (Chișinău). Cristinel Munteanu can be reached at munteanucristinel@yahoo.com.

Angela Schrott (PhD 1996) has been a full professor of Romance linguistics at the University of Kassel since 2007. She received her PhD in Romance linguistics from the Ludwig-Maximilians-University in Munich with a study on tense and aspect in contemporary French and completed her "Habilitation" on historical pragmatics at the University of Bochum in 2006. Her current research focuses on the interconnectedness of text linguistics and discourse traditions, discourse analysis and text complexity. She is also still interested in historical pragmatics, especially in verbal politeness, and in tense and aspect, particularly in their interplay with narrative structures. A major current focus is her involvement in the Maria Sibylla Merian Center for Advanced Latin American Studies (CALAS). She is a member of the CALAS Steering Committee and conducts research in the field of discourse linguistics (e. g., discourses on crisis and social inequalities in Latin America). At the University of Kassel, she is the founding director of the Latin America Research Center (CELA). She has held several visiting professorships in Latin America: at the Universidad de Buenos Aires, the Universidad Nacional de Cuyo/Mendoza, the Universidad Nacional de Córdoba, and the Universidad de la República Montevideo. Between 2015 and 2017 she was Vice President, from 2017 to 2019 President of the *Deutscher Romanistenverband*. Her recent publications address the categorization of discourse traditions, the connections between discourse analysis and traditions of speaking, and the concepts of text complexity between linguistics and didactics. Angela Schrott can be reached at angela.schrott@uni-kassel.

Göran Sonesson (PhD in linguistics in Lund and in semiotics in Paris, both 1978) is professor emeritus at the section for Cognitive Semiotics, Centre for Language and Literature, Lund University. After initially being concerned with language and gesture in a phenomenological and semiotic framework, he later concentrated on pictorial and cultural semiotics, recently extending his interest to epistemology and evolutionary theory. Within pictorial semiotics, he has focused on the notion of iconicity and the constituents of pictures, especially photographs and rhetorical pictures. His contributions to the semiotics of culture at first involved a more differentiated analysis of the relations between cultures, but increasingly came to include a historical and an evolutionary approach. In epistemology, he has been concerned with similarities and differences between the natural sciences and the semiotic (human and social) sciences. In addition to three books: *Pictorial concepts* (1989), *Bildbetydelser* (1992) and *Human Lifeworlds* (2016), he has published numerous papers in journals such as *Semiotica, Cognitive Semiotics, Cognitive Development, Sign System Studies, Degrés, Signa, Signata, Sign and Society, Versus* and *Frontier of Psychology*. Apart from editing several thematic issues of these journals, he has also been a co-editor of, among others, the *Encyclopaedia of Semiotics* (1998) and *Meaning, mind and communication: Explorations in cognitive semiotics* (2016). He was one of the founders of the *Association internationale de sémiotique visuelle* (1989) and of the *International Association for Cognitive Semiotics* (2013). Göran Sonesson can be reached at goran.sonesson@semiotik.lu.se.

Contributors — XV

Pierre Swiggers (PhD 1981) is Senior Research Director of the Flemish Science Foundation (FWO-Vlaanderen) and Professor at KULeuven and ULiège. He is the Director of the "International Centre for General Dialectology" and co-founder of the Leuven "Centre for the Historiography of Linguistics". His research interests are in the historiography and methodology of linguistics, historical-comparative linguistics, dialectology and onomastics, and the philosophy of language. He is currently involved in projects on ancient grammar, Romance etymology and missionary linguistics. He has edited bio-bibliographical studies on J. Larochette, G. Straka, M. Lejeune, J.-C. Chevalier, E. M. Uhlenbeck, J. Perrot, E. F. K. Koerner, H. B. Rosén and H. Seiler. His books include: *Abbé Gabriel Girard: Les vrais principes de la langue françoise* (1982), *Les conceptions linguistiques des Encyclopédistes. Étude sur la constitution d'une théorie de la grammaire au siècle des Lumières* (1984), *Frege's "Over betekenis en verwijzing"* (1984), *Grammaire et méthode au XVIIe siècle* (1984), *La langue française au XVIe siècle: Usage, enseignement et approches descriptives* (1989, edited with W. Van Hoecke), *Bibliographie sélective de linguistique romane et française* (with W. Bal, J. Germain, J. R. Klein, 1991, 2nd edition 1997), *De la grammaire comparée à la sémantique. Textes de Michel Bréal publiés entre 1864 et 1898* (1995, with P. Desmet), *Histoire de la pensée linguistique. Analyse du langage et réflexion linguistique dans la culture occidentale, de l'Antiquité au XIXe siècle* (1997), *De Tékhnê Grammatikê van Dionysius Thrax: De oudste spraakkunst in het Westen* (1998, with A. Wouters), *Taal en teken. Een historisch-systematische inleiding in de taalfilosofie* (2000, with W. de Pater), *Grammaire et enseignement du français, 1500–1700* (2000, edited with J. De Clercq and N. Lioce), *The Collected Works of Edward Sapir, vol. I: General linguistics* (2008), *Trois linguistes (trop) oubliés: Antoine Meillet, Sylvain Lévi, Ferdinand Brunot* (2010, edited with C. Ravelet), *De Tuin der Talen. Taalstudie en taalcultuur in de Lage Landen, 1450–1750* (2013, edited with T. Van Hal and L. Isebaert), *Karl Jaberg: Linguistique romane, géographie linguistique, théorie du langage* (2015, edited with A. Fryba-Reber), *Language, grammar, and erudition: from antiquity to modern times* (2018). Pierre Swiggers can be reached at pierre.swiggers@kuleuven.be.

Jürgen Trabant (PhD 1969) is professor emeritus of Romance linguistics, Freie Universität Berlin. He taught at the Universities of Tübingen, Bari, Rome, Hamburg and FU Berlin and was a visiting professor at Stanford University (1988–1989, 1991), Leipzig (1992), the University of California Davis (1997), EHESS Paris (1998, 2003), Limoges (2003), Naples (2005, 2007), Bologna (2008), Brasília (2013), Milan (2013), Shanghai (2017) and at the Istituto Croce Napoli (2018, 2019). He was a professor for European plurilingualism at Jacobs University Bremen (2008–2013) and a member of the research group "Bildakt und Verkörperung" at the Humboldt University (2010–2014). His fields of interest include French and Italian linguistics, semiotics (especially literary semiotics), the history of European linguistic thought, the philosophy of language, historical anthropology, language politics and the relationship between language and image. His books include *Elemente der Semiotik* (1976, third edition 1996; translated into Japanese, Portuguese, Italian and Korean), *Apeliotes oder Der Sinn der Sprache. Wilhelm von Humboldts Sprach-Bild* (1986, translated into French), *Traditionen Humboldts* (1990, translated into Korean, French and Japanese), *Neue Wissenschaft von alten Zeichen: Vicos Sematologie* (1994, translated into Italian and English), *Artikulationen. Historische Anthropologie der Sprache* (1998), *Der Gallische Herkules. Über Sprache und Politik in Frankreich und Deutschland* (2002), *Mithridates im Paradies. Kleine Geschichte des Sprachdenkens* (2003), *Europäisches Sprachdenken. Von Platon bis Wittgenstein* (2006), *Cenni e voci. Saggi di sematologia vichiana* (2007), *Was ist Sprache?* (2008), *Die Sprache* (2009),

Weltansichten (2012), *Globalesisch oder was?* (2014), *Giambattista Vico – Poetische Charaktere* (2019), *Sprachdämmerung. Eine Verteidigung* (2020) and *Wilhelm von Humboldt. Menschen Sprachen Politik* (2021). Jürgen Trabant can be reached at trabant@zedat.fu-berlin.de.

Andreas Widoff (PhD 2018) is a postdoctoral researcher at the Centre for Languages and Literature, Lund University. Previously, he has taught courses in Swedish and linguistics at Kristianstad University and Lund University. His dissertation *Hermeneutik och grammatik* investigates topics of interpretation and structure and presents a phenomenological defence and account of the distinction between language as a technique and language as speech. This account is in part influenced by Coseriu's work. His main research interests include Scandinavian languages, semantics, pragmatics, phenomenology of language and epistemology of linguistics. Currently, he is engaged in work in prepositional semantics, pursuing a line of research where prepositional sense variation is accounted for in terms of general meanings and particular senses. Andreas Widoff can be reached at andreas.widoff@nordlund.lu.se.

Klaas Willems (PhD 1992) is professor of General linguistics at Ghent University. After his German and Scandinavian Studies in Ghent and Freiburg im Breisgau he earned his PhD in 1992 with a thesis on Husserlian phenomenology and the theory of meaning. Following a research stint at the University of Tübingen and a postdoctoral fellowship of the Flemish Research Foundation (FWO-Vlaanderen), he was appointed at the Linguistics Department of Ghent University, where he has been at the helm of the General Linguistics section since 1997. He has published widely on various subjects at the interface of grammar and the theory of language. His main research interests lie in semantics, syntax (in particular case theory), linguistic theory and epistemology, the historiography of the language sciences, philosophy of language and their mutual relationships. He has focused in his research on theoretical and methodological synergies between complementary frameworks, with a constant concern to integrate Coseriu's Integral Linguistics into corpus-based investigations. His books include *Sprache, Sprachreflexion und Erkenntniskritik* (1994), *Eigenname und Bedeutung* (1996), *Kasus, grammatische Bedeutung und kognitive Linguistik* (1997), *Geschichte und Systematik des adverbalen Dativs im Deutschen* (with Jeroen Van Pottelberge, 1998) and *Naturalness and iconicity in language* (edited with Ludovic De Cuypere, 2008). He has also been a co-editor of *Historiographia Linguistica* since 2011. Klaas Willems can be reached at klaas.willems@ugent.be.

Klaas Willems (Ghent) and Cristinel Munteanu (Galaţi)
Introduction

This volume brings together eighteen articles, by as many authors, that deal with the scholarly work of Romanian linguist Eugenio Coseriu (1921–2002). The volume commemorates the 100th anniversary of his birth and is the first volume devoted to Coseriu's legacy to appear entirely in English. There are several reasons why such a volume is of interest. Coseriu's work is wide-ranging and varied but less well-known internationally than might be expected on intrinsic grounds. Although his fame has been well-established among linguists in the Spanish-speaking world (and, albeit to a lesser extent, in other areas of the Romance-speaking world as well as Germany), Coseriu's publications have not in equal measure found their way into linguistic circles in the English-speaking world. This is in large part due to the fact that few of Coseriu's publications have appeared in English (see Section 4 for an overview). However, Coseriu's work stands apart from much contemporary scholarship also with respect to its content and scope, which makes it a treasure trove for both theoretical and empirical linguists. This volume seeks to advance the exploration and understanding of this work, in particular with regard to a broader international community of scholars.

In this Introduction we first provide a condensed CV of Coseriu (Section 1) before outlining the key features of his 'Integral Linguistics' approach (Section 2). We then summarize the eighteen articles of the volume and contextualize them in the broader perspective of Coseriu's scholarly work (Section 3). In the next two sections, we provide bibliographical information about the few publications by Coseriu that have hitherto appeared in English (Section 4) and draw up a list of the festschrifts, commemorative volumes and conference proceedings that have been dedicated to Coseriu and his work (Section 5). The final section is devoted to editorial remarks which serve to supply the reader with information regarding references, terminology and translation issues (Section 6).

1 Coseriu's career in brief

Eugenio Coseriu (alternatively: Eugen Coşeriu; original spelling: Eugeniu Coşeriu) was born on 27 July 1921 in Mihăileni, a small Romanian town in Bessarabia that today lies in the Republic of Moldova. After starting studying Modern philology and Law at the University of Iaşi (Romania) from 1939 to 1940, he went to Italy and studied Romance and Slavic studies at the University of Rome from 1940 to 1944. In 1944, he earned a degree in literature ("Laurea in lettere") in Rome with a thesis entitled "Su gli influssi della poesia epica francese medievale sulla poesia epica popolare degli Slavi meridionali" [On the influences of medieval French epic poetry on the popular epic poetry of the southern Slavs]. He went on to study philosophy at the University of Padua in 1944 and at the University of Milan in 1945. In Milan, he earned a second degree in philosophy ("Laurea in filosofia") in 1949 with a thesis entitled "L'evoluzione delle idee estetiche in Romania" [The evolution of aesthetic ideas in Romania]. After being, among other things, a lecturer of Romanian at the University of Milan and a collaborator of the *Enciclopedia Hoepli* from 1947 to 1950, he became professor of General and Indo-European linguistics at the University of Montevideo (Uruguay) in 1951 and head of the Linguistic Department. At the same time he was appointed professor of linguistics (General linguistics, Romance and Spanish) at the Instituto de Profesores Artigas in Montevideo. It is in the 1950s that Coseriu developed the foundations and core concepts of his theory of language. At first he focused on the development of a comprehensive approach to language which was not only informed by structural linguistics but by the history of the language sciences overall. In many of his early studies he critically deals with structuralism, including Ferdinand de Saussure, whose theory of language and linguistics he modified and complemented by drawing on Wilhelm von Humboldt, Georg Wilhelm Friedrich Hegel and Aristotle, among others. Coseriu's publications of this period already show his abiding ambition to go beyond a structural approach to language and adopt a much wider-ranging perspective on language, including, e.g., a theory of text linguistics (Coseriu 1955–1956). In 1961, Coseriu went to Germany, at first to Bonn and Frankfurt am Main. In 1963 he was appointed professor of Romance linguistics at the University of Tübingen, where in 1966 he became professor of Romance philology and General linguistics. From the 1970s onwards, Coseriu's "Tübingen School" became particularly influential in Romance linguistics, not only in Germany but throughout Europe. His work had considerable impact even beyond Romance studies, especially regarding general linguistics and the philosophy of language, but also in such disciplines as Germanic and Slavic linguistics. Coseriu retired as a professor in 1991. He died on 7 September 2002 in Tübingen. (For further details, see www.coseriu.com, the website of the Eugenio Coseriu Archives in Tübingen.)

2 'Integral Linguistics'

> I am willing to recognize that everything of value in my writings and in my conceptions and in the methods I follow is the fruit of dialectical reworking of the reflections and of the elaborations that may be found in other linguists and philosophers of language. The ever-present touchstone in this process is the reality of language – the reality that reveals itself through reflective observation and hermeneutic meditation. (Coseriu 1995a: 187–188)

2.1 A striking feature of Coseriu's scholarly work is that he aimed, from the very beginning of his academic career, at elaborating a comprehensive and unitary theory of language which according to his own account was conceived and had to be developed in accordance with the complex reality of language itself. In hindsight, Coseriu's œuvre seems to follow a certain rule, or maxim, which can be described as follows: by the way a scholar treats one specific linguistic topic, it is possible to infer the way he would treat another. Based on a linguist's specific conception of semantics, it is possible – or even necessary – to assess what his or her ideas imply, e. g., for phonetics and phonology, syntax, word formation, linguistic change, linguistic typology, the theory of translation, text linguistics etc. (Kabatek and Murguía 1997: 139–140). It therefore comes as no surprise that Coseriu's own publications contain many assertions and suggestions which can serve as starting points to further develop his approach. They help us understand and anticipate in what way he would have treated certain linguistic matters which he only touched upon in the course of his long academic career. Looked at from this angle, a number of his early studies that appeared in the 1950s are particularly important because of the wealth of observations and the often ground-breaking insights they contain; these studies include *Sistema, norma y habla* [System, norm and speech] (1952), "Determinación y entorno. Dos problemas de una lingüística del hablar" [Determination and setting. Two problems of a linguistics of speaking] (1955–1956) and *Sincronía, diacronía e historia. El problema del cambio lingüístico* [Synchrony, diachrony and history. The problem of linguistic change] (1958). The article "Determinación y entorno" deserves to be especially mentioned in this regard; it contains, according to many specialists of Coseriu's work, the core of his 'Integral Linguistics' approach in a very concise, if clearly articulated, form.

In his first studies Coseriu tried to determine the accomplishments and limitations of Saussure's linguistic framework, and already there he emphasized that *langue*, the subject matter Saussure sought to delimit within the complex phenomenon that is language, does not refer to language without further qualification but to a 'functional language'. For Coseriu, a 'functional language' is a homogeneous language from a syntopic, synstratic and synphasic point of view (cf. the articles by **Jensen**, **Cigana** and **Kabatek**, this volume). It corresponds, in Coseriu's terminology, to a 'system', i.e. that level of a language which only comprises language-specific functional distinctions ("oppositions") and, consequently, the 'possibilities' of a language, but not the usual realisations of a language formed by tradition (the 'norm'). For Coseriu, delineating the object of study in this manner entails a radical reduction within the subject matter of investigation: when Saussure states that we should take *langue* as the 'measure' for all the other manifestations of speech (Saussure 1968 [1916]: 30; 1975 [1916]: 25), then he does not actually refer to a 'historical language' with all its dynamic features and internal variation, but only to an underlying system. However, if linguistics as a science is to live up to its commitment of being a comprehensive science of language, then it is the analysis of historical languages and not only functional languages that must be the goal of linguistics.

However important they may be, structures only represent a part of language. One of Coseriu's lasting achievements is that he provided a plausible and coherent account of what an authentic 'structural linguistics' can be. Given his insistence on treating this topic in the 1960s and 1970s, he came to be considered a structuralist linguist himself, which is only partly correct. When asked how to characterize his relationship with structuralism, Coseriu preferred to call himself a "Humboldtian structuralist". This label aptly summarizes his aim to reconcile the Saussurean perspective on language systems with Wilhelm von Humboldt's visionary, and much more encompassing, conception of language as *enérgeia* (Humboldt 1963 [1836]: 418; 1988 [1836]: 49; cf. **Trabant**, **Agud** and **Albrecht**, this volume). Building on Humboldt's seminal contributions to the language sciences (in particular with regard to the philosophy of language, the theory of language, linguistic anthropology, linguistic typology and variational linguistics), Coseriu argues – in contrast to Saussure – that linguists should not take *langue* but the activity of speaking (Sp. *hablar*) as the point of departure of their analyses. Accordingly, Coseriu's Integral Linguistics approach deals, first of all, with identifying language in terms of an integral object, that is, language in all its manifold manifestations and malleability and with due attention paid to all the aspects and dimensions of variation and change. It is in this sense that Coseriu's frequent reference, especially since the 1980s, to the way structuralism should be integrated and preserved but at the same time surpassed (G. *aufheben* 'sublate', to use Hegel's term, cf. Hegel 1970 [1832–1845], Vol. 5, *Wissenschaft der Logik I*: 113–114) has to be understood: it is imperative to go beyond structuralism in linguistic research (in French: *au-delà du structuralisme*, Coseriu 2001 [1982]); cf. also Kabatek (2021).

No less noteworthy is that Coseriu also rejected Saussure's concept of 'diachrony', proposing instead the concept of 'history' (cf. Oesterreicher 2001: 1555–

1556). He later acknowledged that Hermann Paul's provocative statement – viz., that "Sprachwissenschaft ist Sprachgeschichte" – is essentially correct (Coseriu 1979 [1978]: 129 and 1980: 145). The elaboration of a coherent conception of history with regard to language is one of the main subjects of Coseriu's first book, actually the only book he ever conceived and completed as a monograph, the already mentioned *Sincronía, diacronía e historia* (Coseriu 1978 [1958]). Accordingly, he defined his 'Integral Linguistics' as language history (cf. **Albrecht**, this volume). This entails that, in order to be coherent, description must refer to one functional language only, which is conceived of as a homogeneous system. By contrast, language history encompasses all aspects of language, even to the level of the language of a single speaker, since any speaker knows, as a rule, more than one functional language (Coseriu 1996: 73–75).

2.2 Coseriu assessed the importance of Saussure's legacy as follows:

> "My" Saussure is therefore the Saussure who, in his *Cours*, established the fundamental distinctions that subsequently determined the development and the progress of linguistics in this century. (Coseriu 1995a: 189)

Much in the same vein as Coseriu considered Saussure as the author of "fundamental distinctions", Coseriu himself considered introducing distinctions as a prime feature of his scientific work. It should be emphasized that his many distinctions are *distinctiones rationis*, not *disiunctiones*. Distinctions concern different levels of analysis and do not contradict the claim that it is possible to analyse the whole of language from an integrationalist perspective. To 'distinguish' is different from to 'separate': objects can be separated but concepts are distinguished. In this respect, Coseriu is an avowed Hegelian: truth lies in the whole (Hegel 1970 [1832–1845], Vol. 3: *Vorrede* to *Phänomenologie des Geistes*), yet to meet the scientific challenges such a guiding principle poses, the infinite variations of human actions, and of the products they bring about, are explained as manifestations of a unitary and all-embracing consciousness (cf. **Agud**, this volume).

Many of Coseriu's distinctions actually pertain to different but complementary disciplines: philosophy of language, philosophy of science (or epistemology of linguistics), theory of language, general linguistics and the various fields of empirical linguistics (phonetics and phonology, semantics, syntax etc.). Coseriu attached great importance to the internal consistency of an approach to language that should be all-encompassing and driven by the reality of language itself. A first level is constituted by the philosophy of language. Its aim is to determine the 'essence' of language and the place language occupies in our lives and its relation to all other human activities (cf. **Trabant**, this volume). Language is a form of culture (such as art, science and philosophy, religion and mythology), but it stands out among human cultural manifestations because it is, according to Coseriu, also the basis of culture itself: language underlies all other forms of culture. To the extent that it is essentially a cultural object, language belongs to the world of freedom and purposiveness, and not to the world of necessity and causality (a distinction already stressed by Immanuel Kant). Language is moreover neither an exclusively formal object (as Coseriu stressed in his discussion of L. Hjelmslev's approach, cf. **Cigana**, this volume), nor a natural object, which is governed by causes and necessary conditions. Moreover, language must be studied, according to Coseriu (1992 [1988]: Chapters 3–5), from a perspective that takes an intermediate position between anti-positivism and positivism. He thus establishes, at the level of epistemology, the raison d'être of linguistics along with its role and place among the sciences of man (cf. **Belligh**, this volume).

Once the status of language among the human activities and the role and place of linguistics as a science are determined, it is necessary to establish how the various fields of linguistics are related to each other and in what ways they can mutually inform and benefit one another. R. Jakobson's famous assertion, *linguista sum: linguistici nihil a me alienum puto*, is very much true of Coseriu as well. It is one of the express purposes of 'Integral Linguistics' not to neglect any orientation or trend in the language sciences, and it insists that all of them contribute, in one way or another, to an overall understanding of language as an activity in which all human beings partake. Admittedly, Coseriu remained unconvinced of many efforts in such disciplines as psycholinguistics and neurolinguistics. He was especially critical of their claim to be the objective foundation of all other aspects of language, a claim he considered reductionist and resulting in an illusory objectivity. To his mind, this followed from their deliberate conflation of the language-specific content of linguistic expressions and the non-language-specific designation of what these linguistic expressions refer to, subsumed under the single heading of an undifferentiated 'meaning' (see Section 2).

2.3 Coseriu defined his 'Integral Linguistics' succinctly as follows (cf. **Albrecht** and **Sonesson**, this volume):

> What is Integral Linguistics? It is the linguistic approach that aims to take into account the knowledge the speaker puts to work when speaking (Sp. *saber que el hablante pone en obra al hablar*), with the purpose of organizing the facts conceived of in this way within a homogeneous and unitary framework (Sp. *un marco homogéneo y unitario*). (Coseriu 1984: 37)

Coseriu attached a lot of importance to the definition of language that underpins his Integral Linguistics approach. This definition, which stands out among other approaches for being at the same time multi-layered and multi-perspectival, reads as follows:

> Language is a *universal* human activity that is realized *individually*, but always according to *historically* determined techniques ("languages", Sp. *"lenguas"*). (Coseriu 1999 [1981]: 265; 1992 [1988]: 250; italics in the original)

Not only can the distinction between the universal, historical and individual level in language be intuitively understood, but the three levels are moreover not mutually reducible. On the contrary, they must be distinguished and are to some extent autonomous from the point of view of analysis (Coseriu 1985: xxviii; 1999 [1981]: 266; 1992 [1988]: 251; cf. Oesterreicher 2001: 1558–1559). However, they do not represent functionally encapsulated subsystems. The challenge is precisely to show how they are interconnected in multiple ways.

Being aware of the contribution of every linguistic (sub)discipline within Integral Linguistics involves, in turn, recognizing the importance of a number of 'fundamental distinctions' regarding language and linguistics. Coseriu proposed a complex matrix, in which different 'levels of language' are combined with different 'perspectives on language' in view of the study of linguistic competence (Coseriu 1955–1956, 1985, 2007 [1980], 2007 [1988]). Various authors in the present volume discuss (aspects of) this matrix (see in particular the contributions by **Albrecht**, **Schrott** and **Kabatek**). We therefore here confine ourselves to a brief presentation.

There are, on the one hand, three levels of language that differentiate the linguistic competence of language users: the universal non-language-specific (G. *allgemein-sprachliche*) competence which concerns linguistic activity in general (*Sprechen im Allgemeinen*), the historical language-specific (*einzelsprachliche*) competence which distinguishes one language from another (*historische Einzelsprache*), and the individual text- and discourse-specific competence (*Textkompetenz*) which comprises both universal and language-specific properties. To acknowledge the fact that language includes a universal level (of 'linguistic activity in general'), a historical level (of specific languages) and an individual level (of discourse or text), entails that it is imperative not to confuse these levels and to observe the division of labour between three linguistic disciplines, viz. a linguistics of linguistic activity in general, a linguistics of languages and a linguistics of text (text linguistics). Furthermore, considering the fact that language is characterised by both internal variation (on account of creativity) and homogeneity (on account of intersubjectivity), it is possible to define a number of different disciplines. On the one hand, since internal variation is threefold (viz. 'diatopic', 'diastratic' and 'diaphasic'), there are three corresponding disciplines:

dialectology, sociolinguistics and idiomatic stylistics. On the other hand, there is structural linguistics or 'grammar', whose subject-matter is language-specific structures in a homogeneous system.

The aforementioned three levels of language cross-cut with three points of view. Drawing on Humboldt's philosophy of language, Coseriu stresses the importance of viewing language, in its essence, as a productive activity. In the case of productive activities, as we already learnt from Aristotle, three aspects have to be taken into consideration: activity in itself (*enérgeia*), knowledge or 'technique' (*dýnamis*) and the product of linguistic activity (*érgon*). *Enérgeia* is, rationally or logically, prior to any *dýnamis*; it is creativity in itself. Thus, language is *enérgeia*, functioning according to an acquired knowledge or technique, but precisely because it is a creative activity, it also, and constantly, surpasses the acquired knowledge or technique. As a result, language as a whole comprises these three aspects, which are present simultaneously – and only – in discourses (or texts), because that which is realized (i.e. "produced" in spoken or written form) is always and necessarily a specific language (German, Romanian, English, Spanish, Japanese etc.).

Coseriu's insistence on drawing attention to necessary distinctions does not end here. First of all, there are three levels of linguistic content that correspond to the aforementioned three levels of language: non-language-specific 'designation' (reference to things, states and events in the extra-linguistic reality, G. *Bezeichnung*, and the corresponding 'elocutional' knowledge), language-specific 'signifieds' which are the meanings of linguistic signs in a particular language (G. *Bedeutung* and the corresponding 'idiomatic' knowledge) and the content of a text, a speech act or unity of discourse (G. *Sinn* and the corresponding 'expressive' knowledge) (Coseriu 2007 [1988]: Chapter 2; cf. also Coseriu 1978c). Importantly, these three levels of linguistic content can be observed in every speech act (Coseriu 1985: xxx).

Secondly, Coseriu also distinguishes three types of norms, each operating at one of the following three different levels: (i) at the universal level, 'congruence' corresponds to the general laws of thinking as well as linguistic activity in general and knowledge of the world; (ii) at the historical level, 'correctness' is ensured by the system of speech traditions that hold in a community; (iii) at the individual level, 'adequacy' (Aristotle's *tò prépon*, i.e. what is fitting, appropriate) is obtained in accordance with the knowledge that refers to the communication in certain situations or regarding the elaboration of discourses/texts. The norm of adequacy can annul the other two, while the norm of correctness can annul that of congruence (Coseriu 1985, 2007 [1988]).

The conceptual distinctions thus drawn are summarized in Table 1. We introduced two terminological changes, viz. the English translations of G. *Bedeutung* and G. *Sinn*, respectively, for the sake of clarity (cf. the editorial remarks in Section 6 below).

Levels	Points of view			Content	Judgments
	Activity (*enérgeia*)	Knowledge (*dýnamis*)	Product (*érgon*)		
Universal	Speaking in general	Elocutional knowledge	Totality of utterances	Designation (*Bezeichnung*)	Congruent/incongruent
Historical	Concrete particular language	Idiomatic knowledge	(Abstracted particular language)	Signified (*Bedeutung*)	Correct/incorrect
Individual	Discourse	Expressive knowledge	Text	Text meaning (*Sinn*)	Appropriate/inappropriate

This matrix, Coseriu writes, has been

> a helpful epistemological frame of reference for the interpretation not only of the various linguistic problems ranging from that of linguistic change to that of translation and of linguistic correctness, but also of the structure of the linguistic disciplines themselves and of recent developments in linguistics. (Coseriu 1985: xxv)

2.4 Another series of distinctions is called for when Saussure's *langue* is the object of enquiry. A coherent analysis requires that the following distinctions are observed (Coseriu 1966): (1) knowledge of language and knowledge of 'things'; (2) primary language and metalanguage; (3) synchrony and diachrony; (4) free technique and 'repeated discourse'; (5) 'structure' (functional language) and 'architecture' (historical language). Whereas a historical language ('architecture') is characterized by internal variation ('diatopic', 'diastratic' and 'diaphasic'), it is necessary to establish the 'type', the 'system', the 'norm' and the 'speech' with regard to a functional language ('structure') (Coseriu 1992 [1988]: Chapter 12) (cf. **Jensen** and **Kabatek**, this volume). Coseriu applied these distinctions to great effect, in addition to proving their practical utility, in his study of the verbal system in Romance languages (Coseriu 1976 [1968–1969]) (cf. **Laca**, this volume). They have moreover been successfully applied in various other fields of linguistic research by scholars who adopt the Coserian framework. However, despite Coseriu's clear writing style, the conceptual and terminological foundations of his framework may occasionally be difficult to grasp, precisely due to the numerous distinctions, and applying the framework may seem like a daunting task. Nevertheless, the distinctions are imposed by the complexity of language itself, and there is no denying that the sustained search for coherence that characterizes Coseriu's lifework requires at least a similar effort in interpretation and understanding on the part of the reader.

Finally, in addition to developing a new, comprehensive approach to language, Coseriu identified a number of epistemological principles that served as guidelines in his research (Coseriu 2000 [1992]; compare Coseriu 1977b). The 'principle of objectivity' requires that one has "to say things as they really are". This guideline, which echoes Plato's *Sophist* (cf. Kabatek and Murguía 1997), applies to any science but it has a special status with respect to a cultural science such as linguistics. This special status relates to the second principle, the 'principle of humanism'. It says that the basis of cultural sciences, including linguistics, is a preliminary or hermeneutical 'original knowledge' which human beings possess as creators of culture. More specifically, linguistics as a science taps into intuitive knowledge with regard to what is universal in language, i.e. shared by all human beings as speakers. Moreover, this intuitive knowledge is the inevitable starting point in a linguist's research, i.e. he starts from what he already knows, not from hypotheses that are alien to that knowledge (compare the phenomenological concept of *Vorbekanntheit* or *Vorwissen*, Husserl 1939: 26–27). An important corollary is that theory and empirical investigations are intrinsically tied together and must form a unity. The third 'principle of tradition' is an invitation to pay heed to the history of the language sciences. It is important, according to Coseriu, to study and understand this history and to acknowledge the observations of interest found in the work of predecessors. The distinction between modern, scientific and old, pre-scientific language studies we are accustomed to, is otiose and unnecessary in light of this third principle. The principle is closely related to the next 'principle of antidogmatism', which demands that theories and claims of other scientists cannot be simply dismissed out of hand, but have to be interpreted with a critical but constructive mindset, precisely because other scientists too start from their intuitive knowledge. The result of paying attention to this principle is not, according to Coseriu, eclecticism but "critical rationalism" (cf. **Agud**, this volume). Finally, the 'principle of public utility or responsibility' entails that scholars should treat questions of laymen regarding language and speech as significant and important. They concern issues that are of potential interest to all speakers, including matters of translation, language learning and teaching, language planning and multilingual awareness.

3 The structure of the volume

Each article in the present volume is preceded by a quotation from one of Coseriu's publications which is particularly appropriate with respect to the article's main subject. Taken together, the quotations provide a revealing, if brief and incomplete, introduction to Coseriu's scholarship 'in his own words'. The quotations highlight claims and assumptions that are noteworthy for a variety of reasons, which often go beyond the remit of a single article. All quotations have been translated into English for ease of read (as a general rule, translations were provided by the authors, often in collaboration with the editors; see Section 6 for further editorial remarks).

The articles are grouped into three main sections: 1) Philosophy of language, 2) History of the language sciences, and 3) Theory and practice of Integral Linguistics.

3.1 Philosophy of language

The first section of the book consists of two articles. Their common denominator is Coseriu's lifelong pursuit of a comprehensive framework in which all branches of the study of language can find their proper place. This objective betokens a general 'philosophical' mindset towards the study of language and languages that is itself rooted in the study, and reappraisal, of the history of Western philosophy. With his ideal of Integral Linguistics, Coseriu was probably among the last representatives in a long tradition of thought according to which a grand unified conception of science is not only possible but also desirable, in particular with regard to culture. In this respect, Coseriu continues a tradition initiated by Aristotle which was subsequently represented by such scholars as Giambattista Vico, Gottfried Wilhelm Leibniz, Immanuel Kant, Georg Wilhelm Friedrich Hegel, Wilhelm von Humboldt, Edmund Husserl, Ernst Cassirer, John Dewey, Robin G. Collingwood, Wilbur M. Urban, among others – all of them thinkers Coseriu regularly referred to in his work. Several contributions in the present volume address questions regarding the remit and scope of Coseriu's Integral Linguistics project.

For Coseriu, a main challenge was to develop the philosophy of language, the theory of language and linguistic methodology in such a way as to bring out their interdependence and synergies. Meeting such a challenge entails that the philosophy of language must at the same time be able to establish a general epistemological foundation of the language sciences. No empirical investigation or methodological decision can dispense with considerations about the nature of the subject under study, just as theoretical considerations are in turn inseparable from the philosophical enquiry into the nature of language, as language happens to be both the object and instrument of study. This approach of the philosophy of language sets Coseriu apart from other approaches with partly similar objectives developed in the recent past. Some of them either tend to integrate linguistic methodology and empirical enquiry from a mainly logical point of view, effectively restricting their scope to a primarily formal account of language (compare the tradition of analytic philosophy and the 'linguistic philosophy' that goes with it; e.g. Devitt and Sterelny 1999, Lepore and Smith, eds. 2008), or they pursue an integration of empirical and theoretical linguistics under the guiding principles of cognitive psychology, adopting such notions as 'prototype', 'Gestalt', 'embodiment', 'mental imagery' and 'cognitive archetype' without much recourse to philosophy altogether (e.g. Langacker 1987, 1991, Lakoff 1987, Turner 1996, Taylor 2002; but see also Johnson 1987 for a more philosophical account). By contrast, Coseriu rejects the pervasive logicism in analytically-based accounts of language (as well as its counterpart, anti-logicism) (Coseriu 1973 [1956]), just as he finds fault with approaching language as a psychological entity (Coseriu 2000 [1990]).

In his article "The essence of language: on Coseriu's philosophy of language", **Jürgen Trabant** takes stock of some of the central notions of Coseriu's philosophy of language and traces their origin and mutual relations in Coseriu's representative scholarly work. **Trabant** draws particular attention to the major studies that were first published between 1952 and 1957 and subsequently collected into the volume *Teoría del lenguaje y lingüística general. Cinco estudios* (Coseriu 1973 [1962]). Among the other milestones are *Sincronía, diacronía e historia. El problema del cambio lingüístico* (Coseriu 1978 [1958]), the two volumes of the *Geschichte der Sprachphilosophie* (Coseriu 2015) and *Textlinguistik* (Coseriu 1994 [1980]), besides a plethora of smaller studies and essays. All of these publications contribute to elucidating Coseriu's philosophical view of what he considered to constitute the 'essence of language', hence to answering the question what language is in an ontologically constitutive sense. Such an objective may be disconcerting to those who favour a relativist or radically pragmatic stance towards language and the study of language. But it is necessary to understand that for Coseriu it is indeed imperative to ask oneself "qué son y cómo existen realmente las lenguas" (Coseriu 1978 [1958]: 29), "was die Sprachen sind und wie sie wirklich existieren" (1978 [1958]: 23), that is, what languages are and how they really, or actually, exist. From a Coserian point of view, there is nothing mistakenly essentialist to this question. Coseriu's answer can be summarized as follows: the essence of language is the individual but intersubjective activity of speaking that creates meaning. As pointed out already in Section 2, the English word 'meaning' makes for a notoriously elusive term in linguistics and further qualifications are needed to explain the particular aim of Coseriu's overall 'semantic' approach to language.

The complex matrix introduced in Section 2 demonstrates the importance Coseriu attaches to an approach to language that accommodates various types of meaning. This focus on meaning is imbedded in a complex framework that rests, as **Trabant** shows, on Coseriu's philosophy of language. Coseriu has himself described the main tenets of his philosophy of language by drawing on a number of basic notions: formativity or creativity (language is a specifically human creative activity, *enérgeia*), semanticity (the purpose of language is the creation of meaning, i.e. the formation of thought *qua* language-specific meanings, in German: *Bedeutungen*), alterity (language is always directed from one subject to another, or several others, in the original sense of intersubjectivity, of which communication in dialogue is one instantiation) and historicity (language is realised in the diversity and variation of the languages of the world). Within Coseriu's work, these notions are informed by encyclopaedic investigations of philosophical accounts of language from the Presocratics to Wilhelm von Humboldt, along with a systematic review of a representative selection of language studies from the end of the Middle Ages to nineteenth and twentieth century linguistics. Coseriu's synthetic treatment at the same time aspires to presenting itself as the unfolding of the universal 'idea' of language, in accordance with the legacies of both Humboldt's and Hegel's versions of German idealism, which also underpins Coseriu's stance on the relation between language-specific and universal categories of language (cf. Willems 2016).[1] **Trabant** outlines what the unfolding of the 'idea' of language in Coseriu's reasoning amounts to. He also asks why Coseriu did not engage in a serious effort to address modern philosophy of language from the middle of the nineteenth century onwards, in particular the successful philosophy of language usage developed by Ludwig Wittgenstein and his followers. **Trabant** links Coseriu's uncompromising refutation of Wittgenstein to Coseriu's no less significant disagreements with authors such as Noam Chomsky and Martin Heidegger.

Ana Agud further elaborates on the importance of Coseriu's philosophy of language for a coherent epistemological foundation of linguistics in her article "Eugenio Coseriu's approach to language and linguistics: building a philosophically sustainable linguistics". According to **Agud**, Coseriu was acutely aware of

---

[1] It may be worthwhile to point out that while subscribing to Humboldt's philosophy of language, Coseriu was very critical of the so-called 'Sapir-Whorf hypothesis', which he qualified as exaggerated, simplistic and ill-founded (Coseriu 1982: 274–276).

the oversimplifications in post-war structuralism and the need to overcome them, without throwing overboard some of the important and lasting contributions of structuralism to linguistics altogether. Methodological, theoretical and philosophical discussions are omnipresent in Coseriu's own research from the very beginning, but they are mostly part of empirical investigations of a large number of concrete linguistic issues and problems. Of particular importance in this regard is Coseriu's monograph *Sincronía, diacronía e historia* (Coseriu 1978 [1958]). In this book, which to this day merits close attention (cf. **Swiggers**, this volume), many important theoretical and methodological issues are addressed in an unusually clear and precise fashion. Coseriu's discussion of the fallacies that beset structuralist accounts of linguistic change are evidence that simply calling Coseriu a structuralist is deceptive (cf. Willems 2003 and 2019). This may partly be due to Coseriu's Hegelian approach to the history of the language sciences, which is characterized by the wish to discuss shortcomings in previous research but at the same time preserve its achievements (see Section 2). Coseriu's objective was to provide linguistics with a solid grounding in both the philosophy of language and the epistemology of the language sciences (referred to as the 'critical' approach by **Agud**). This entailed, first and foremost, stressing that language is not a static object, but an ongoing historical practice in which individuals perpetually create and 're-create' language. As a consequence, linguistic change is not something that 'happens to' language, but creating language in the activity of speaking *is* linguistic change. How then is it possible to 'speak about speaking' in an objective, epistemologically consistent way, **Agud** asks. She argues that Coseriu's discussions of the various linguistic concepts, methods and frameworks which he encountered in the existing literature and tried to integrate in his own approach contain many clues that help us understand how linguistics can be made a philosophically, theoretically and methodologically coherent enterprise. They all point to the importance of a principled hermeneutical conception of linguistics. This conception acknowledges the general validity of the sceptics' warning that speaking truthfully about language cannot itself be language-independent or, for that matter, independent from previous discourses about language (and in this sense 'external' to language). This should not be misunderstood as a restriction or as reflecting a negative attitude towards linguistics, because the intention of truthfulness in any discourse about language is itself a standard of its – however partial – trustworthiness and veracity. Coseriu has expressed this attitude in a succinct way when specifying his understanding of hermeneutics, the 'sense' (G. *Sinn*) making of texts: apart from the obligation to be 'objective' (the first hermeneutical principle), Coseriu explains a second hermeneutical principle as follows:

According to the second principle of hermeneutics, in either case [static objectivity and dynamic objectivity towards predecessors] a sympathetic interpretation (G. *Auslegung*) is required. This means that, with regard to what a person one is interpreting has said, one must try to determine in what sense it is nonetheless correct, what the 'truth' is of what he said, under the assumption that no mistake ever is only a mistake, but that mistakes are due to the partitioning of, or the deviations from, an originally correct intuition. (Coseriu 1995b: 73; cf. Coseriu 2000 [1992]: 113)

3.2 History of the language sciences

The second section of the book consists of three articles that deal with one of Coseriu's bedrock convictions already mentioned in Section 2. Linguistics, like any other discipline in the field of cultural sciences, has itself a history which is pertinent to its objective of being a full-fledged science in its own right. (We here continue to use 'language sciences' rather than 'linguistics' as a cover term so as not to exclude relevant branches of 'scientific' discourse on language, in particular philosophical accounts). Thus, the recognition that every language has a history – and, concomitantly, that every language is a historical object of research with individual historical traits – is reflected in the fact that the science of language, too, has its history. All facts of language can ultimately only be adequately accounted for in view of their historical coming into being (cf. **Albrecht**, this volume), and so does linguistics as a science build on a complex and diverse history of reflexion and research. Here again Coseriu is an avowed Hegelian: the development of a science is the historical instantiation of a rational, cultural and social process, the course of which should not fall into oblivion lest we forget its very origins in the object of study itself. On this view, engaging in the history of the language sciences, broadly construed (which means: including the philosophy of language as well as, ideally, all pre-modern approaches of language), is an indispensable part of the discipline: all thoughtful accounts of language, or some linguistic feature, that have been truthfully provided in the past, no matter how remote in time, are worthy of interest from a historiographical point of view. Like modern endeavours, these past accounts, too, are ultimately rooted in the intuitive knowledge all human beings possess, however dimly, of language. To the extent that all sciences are part of human culture understood as a historical process of preserving and developing knowledge (itself an instance of the dynamics of creation and re-creation Humboldt identifies as the core property of language conceived as *enérgeia*), passing on this knowledge from one generation to the other is therefore also a moral obligation, according to Coseriu (2005b: 112; cf. 2000 [1992]). Publications such as the *Geschichte der Sprachphilosophie* (Coseriu 2015) and the no less monumental *Geschichte der ro-*

manischen Sprachwissenschaft (Coseriu 2003–2021), of which the first three volumes have been published, provide eloquent testimony to the importance Coseriu attached to this part of his scholarly work.

Ascertaining, at any point in time, the importance of the history of the language sciences for current linguistics is a challenging task that faces several potential pitfalls. Some of the difficulties are related to the object of study, others to its aims. With regard to the object of study, Coseriu is adamant in his intent to not just registering historical facts but presenting historical scientific developments in the language sciences in such a way that they 'make sense' against the background of the history of the humanities and cultural sciences as a whole. For Coseriu, limiting an account of the history of the language sciences to a disengaged accumulation and enumeration of factual issues would be like running an antique store. What Coseriu proposes is in accordance with Hegel's credo in the *Vorlesungen über die Philosophie der Geschichte* (Hegel 1970 [1832–1845], Vol. 12: 23): the historiographer is not a passive observer of the past but, on the contrary, a scholar who reviews history – the accomplishments and limitations, or, in Coseriu's words, the "Leistung und Grenzen", "alcances y limites" of previous scholarship – by interpreting publications of the past through the lens of one's own philosophical, theoretical and methodological assumptions, whose categories in turn are clarified and deepened in and through the historiographical account. Such a stance on how to conceptualize the object of study is obviously closely linked to the aims of linguistic historiography. The purpose of studying the history of the language sciences is emphatically not to find one's own ideas and convictions about language in the work of previous scholars. Coseriu was among the first to criticize, in the 1960s – and thus, for the record, years before the history of the languages sciences gradually became a respected subdiscipline in the large enterprise we nowadays refer to as 'language sciences' – Noam Chomsky's search for 'predecessors' in the latter's influential *Cartesian Linguistics* (1966), which Trabant (2015 [2003]) aptly called a "legenda aurea" of Generative Grammar (see also Coseriu 1992 [1988]: 138). Coseriu not only pointed to Chomsky's biased interpretation of Humboldt and other philosophers of the past, explaining its possible reasons and motivations, but he also showed that the "Cartesian" perspective Chomsky sought to promote entails a view of the mind that ultimately abstracts away from language, thus emphasizing the deeper antagonism between Descartes and Humboldt that Chomsky had glossed over (Coseriu 1970; cf. **Borcilă**, this volume). However, there is a significant difference between projecting one's own ideas and convictions into the writings of previous scholars and reading them with a disposition to find the insights and intuitions that have led the way in the historical development of the language sciences. In the latter sense, there is no harm, according to Coseriu, in reconstructing claims proffered by scholars in the – recent or more remote – past as a history of precursors, or better still: as a history of anticipation, under the condition that historiographical awareness is observed at every stage of the analysis. This entails that insightful claims, while being integrated, must be taken from within their original historical contexts and areas of application to form part of a more comprehensive, historically motivated, integrationalist account that goes beyond the claims' original purview. All must be understood and explained in such a way that they are eventually merged into a synthesis – *aufgehoben* 'sublated' – on a higher level and in a new explanatory framework.

This basically three-pronged, Hegelian approach advocated by Coseriu in conducting the history of the language sciences has occasionally led to misunderstanding and poor dialogue, in particular when confronted with the tradition of linguistic historiography in which scholars' biographies tend to play a more significant role. It is against this background that **Gerda Haßler**, in her contribution "Coseriu as a historiographer of linguistics in relation to his linguistic ideas", explores how Coseriu's lifelong preoccupation with the history of the language sciences interacted with his scholarly work as a theoretical linguist (a 'language theorist') and an empirical linguist. According to **Haßler**, Coseriu's treatment of the history of linguistics neither represents a search for predecessors nor is it a reverence for earlier ideas that have been forgotten. Rather, it draws on paradigms of thought whose building blocks and potential effects are potentially timeless with regard to scientific practice, which is why they can – at least in part – be revived under new conditions. **Haßler** highlights landmarks in the history of the language sciences such as Coseriu's *Geschichte der romanischen Sprachwissenschaft* (2003–2021) and the *Geschichte der Sprachphilosophie* (2015), both monumental overviews which pay testimony to the painstaking research of Coseriu as a historiographer. By way of example, **Haßler** discusses Coseriu's seminal article "L'arbitraire du signe. Zur Spätgeschichte eines aristotelischen Begriffes" (Coseriu 1967a), in which Coseriu shows that the language sciences did not need to wait until Ferdinand de Saussure in order to realize that linguistic signs are arbitrary pairings of expression and meaning. The concept of arbitrariness in language has a history of over 2,000 years, starting with Aristotle, and increasingly attracted the attention of philosophers since the seventeenth century.

A further issue touched upon in **Haßler**'s contribution, and one that has loomed large in recent historiography, is the extent to which one scholar's thoughts are influenced by those of another scholar, either directly (e.g., when someone attends lectures of someone else or is educated in a specific milieu) or indirectly, in particular through publications. 'Influence' is a notoriously problematic concept in the history of the language sciences. Moreover, against the background of the rational development of a science in the course of history, questions of such influences may not have the importance commonly attributed to them. However, Coseriu contributed to this type of historiographical research as well, particularly in the 1960s. Apart from the aforementioned article on the concept of arbitrariness (Coseriu 1967a), one is reminded of the detailed exposition of the terminological influence Georg von der Gabelentz exerted on a number of notions that subsequently became influential through Saussure's *Cours de linguistique générale* (1916) (Coseriu 1967b). **Haßler** furthermore draws attention to a small-scale study in which Coseriu reassessed a semantic analysis that dates back to the nineteenth century in terms of structural paradigmatic relations, which showcases Coseriu's intent to uncover groundbreaking insights in accounts whose objectives are emphatically not those of later accounts with which they are compared (Coseriu 1967c). Coseriu's claims about specific threads of influences were variously met with criticism by other scholars. Colleagues did not altogether question the purport of unearthing such influences and occasionally even the supposed borrowing of specific terminological distinctions, but often came up with alternative putative influences considered more important than those suggested by Coseriu (on the Gabelentz controversy, see in particular Ezawa, Hundsnurscher and von Vogel, eds. 2014). No attempt is made in the present volume to revisit comparisons of this kind, which are fraught with complications due to differences in assumptions and perspectives; they have, moreover, suffered on both ends by paying too little attention to the transformations certain insights, concepts and terminological distinctions usually undergo in the process of adoption and assimilation in subsequent frameworks. Instead, two articles aim to shed light on an important, and itself unquestionable, influence on Coseriu: the writings of Louis Hjelmslev (1899–1965).

Coseriu has on several occasions explicitly acknowledged his indebtedness to Hjelmslev, stressing the importance of Hjelmslev not only for his own theory of language but for the language sciences in general. Important concepts in Coseriu's work such as "norm", "commutation test", "invariant", language understood as an open system of "possibilities" (or "virtualities") etc. are informed by Coseriu's (critical) reception of Hjelmslev's work. There are several reasons for Coseriu's high regard of Hjelmslev. One that deserves special mentioning is the fact that Coseriu not only credited Hjelmslev for continuing the work of Saussure but also of W. von Humboldt (Coseriu 1962 [1954]: 175). In his article "Coseriu's Hjelmslev", **Viggo Bank Jensen** traces the complex relationship between Coseriu's developing thought, from the 1950s onwards, and several key concepts of Hjelmslev's abstract but fascinating theory of language. Four issues stand out in the article. There is, firstly, Coseriu's mixed interpretation of Hjelmslev's famous distinction between form and substance. While the distinction is readily applicable to the level of expression and of central importance to Coseriu's theoretical foundation of phonology, Coseriu initially did not adopt it with regard to the level of content. A second point of contention is the connection between concepts revolving around language variation and the 'architecture of language' (the 'diasystem'), which Coseriu adopted from the Norwegian linguist Leiv Flydal (1904–1983), and their partly obscured relationship to Hjelmslev's notion of connotative semiotics. A third matter of interest is Coseriu's overall assessment of Hjelmslev's contribution to structural semantics, of which Hjelmslev is generally considered one of the founding pioneers. Finally, due attention should be paid, according to **Jensen**, to the influence of Hjelmslev that is already apparent in Coseriu's first major contribution to linguistics, *Sistema, norma y habla* [System, norm and speech] (Coseriu 1952; 1973 [1952]), even though at the time Coseriu's reception of Hjelmslev's writings was incomplete and partly indirect. **Jensen**'s article shows that Hjelmslev has been a lifelong source of inspiration for Coseriu and the scaffold of Hjelmslev's theoretical building served as a reference that allowed Coseriu to establish the demarcation points for his own theory of language.

Lorenzo Cigana's article "Coseriu and glossematics: an uncompleted dialogue" complements the previous contribution and addresses yet another central part of Coseriu's theory of language, viz. his theory of linguistic change, against the backdrop of some of the key concepts of Hjelmslev's theory of linguistic change. While Coseriu's approach to the history of language and linguistic change takes pride of place within his Integral Linguistics project (cf. **Agud, Albrecht** and **Swiggers**, this volume), Hjelmslev's account of linguistic change has often been overlooked. **Cigana** draws attention to a number of correspondences, similarities and divergences between the approaches of the two scholars which according to the author are neither coincidental nor unrelated. The article's main focus is on the concepts of 'markedness' and 'teleology' (i.e. purposiveness, Sp. *finalidad*, G. *Finalität*) as well as on the assumption that language is instantiated under the form of multiple sub-systems along the lines of Hjelmslev's notion of 'connotation'. By examining the particularities of Coseriu's reading – or 'misreading' – of Hjelmslev's publications, **Cigana** argues, it is not only possible to arrive at a better understanding of Coseriu's approach, but such an analysis is in turn also instrumental in illuminating the main tenets of Hjelmslev's approach. In the final analysis, and notwithstanding Coseriu's occasional criticism of some of Hjelmslev's claims, Coseriu's and Hjelmslev's points of view can be approached synergistically, according to **Cigana**. Both can eventually be reframed in such a way as to create a common ground on which their partly converging, partly diverging assumptions about linguistic change can be made fruitful for future research in historical linguistics. If successful, the author predicts, a synthesis of Coseriu's and Hjelmslev's points of view on linguistic change might even lead to a new, more appreciative, interpretation of Hjelmslev's formalist stance in an updated form of 'structuralist' historical linguistics.

3.3 Theory and practice of Integral Linguistics

The third section of the book consists of the remaining thirteen articles of the volume. The authors either focus on basic theoretical and empirical claims of Coseriu's Integral Linguistics approach or on Coseriu's treatment of particular linguistic phenomena. Several authors also discuss the compatibility of Coseriu's approach with current linguistic accounts and identify avenues that contribute to a better understanding of theoretical and empirical challenges that linguistic research currently faces, often providing possible solutions for these challenges that are informed by Coseriu's scholarly work.

Mircea Borcilă presents in his article "Integral Linguistics as a cultural science" five reasons why he considers Coseriu to be the most consistent advocate of a thoroughly Humboldtian approach in modern linguistics. First of all, Coseriu has taken great care to expose the ontological and epistemological foundations of linguistics as a discipline that is central to the humanities (cf. **Agud**, this volume). For Humboldt as well as Coseriu, linguistics is ultimately equivalent to linguistic anthropology. The study of language is the avenue of choice to understand what makes human beings what they essentially are: historical beings endowed with language. Secondly, Coseriu succeeded in developing an approach to the study of language, Integral Linguistics, that is unlike any other because it not only defines linguistics as a cultural science of prime importance, but is characterized by a radical reversal of 'perspective' in the investigation of language: rather than accounting for the facts of speech and discourse from the point of view of some abstract underlying system, the activity of speaking is firmly established, in Coseriu's framework, as the point of departure on which all linguistic enquiries are dependent. (Here and elsewhere, 'activity of speaking' is used in a modality-neutral way and also comprises writing; on the difference between spoken and written language, cf. **Kabatek**, this volume). Thirdly, Coseriu identifies meaning, the 'signifying function of language', in such a manner that no linguistic subdiscipline can count as phenomenologically adequate or internally coherent if it does not position itself vis-à-vis meaning. The creation of meaning is, as also **Trabant** explains (this volume), the aim of all linguistic activity. This entails that 'linguistic competence' has to be determined in a way that does justice to its complex and multi-faceted nature, which reflects its origin in man's historical life and consciousness. This, fourthly, in turn requires that a framework for the study of all relevant aspects of language as a cultural object is created. Coseriu's project of Integral Linguistics establishes a comprehensive approach to language, both with regard to the objectives it sets itself and the domains of investigation and linguistic subfields it focuses on. Finally, **Borcilă** points out that Coseriu's list of publications, which during his lifetime already covered a time span of 50 years and since Coseriu's death has been steadily growing due to posthumous editions, re-editions, translations etc., testifies to his scholarly productivity and his competence in a great number of languages and domains of the language sciences.

In "Considerations on the subtle art of integrating linguistics (and/or semiotics)", **Göran Sonesson** traces the recent history of the label 'Integral Linguistics'. Coseriu laid claim to this label since the 1970s. For instance, a course he gave in Mexico in 1975 was entitled "Hacia una lingüística integral" [Towards an integral linguistics]. Coseriu considered this label particularly appropriate to characterize his framework which aims at a comprehensive study of all aspects of language in terms of a cultural science. In hindsight, it is astonishing to what degree Coseriu managed to develop the foundations of the framework in barely a decade, from 1951 to 1961, when he began to publish studies and parts of extensive manuscripts in Montevideo. The framework not only allocated a place to every linguistic subdiscipline recognized at the time, but tied them together in a principled way that was both highly innovative and respectful of tradition. Probably more than any other linguist at the time, Coseriu felt from the very start of his scholarly career the need to determine and circumscribe the basic concepts and assumptions for such a project in order for it to be internally consistent, empirically feasible and compliant with the philosophical and epistemological standards he had set for himself. As pointed out by **Agud** (this volume), Coseriu's orientation on 'the whole' as the inalienable goal of his scientific project in the sense of Hegel is not something that gradually developed over the years to satisfy a growing interest in ever more phenomena or problems in linguistics, but it was the original motivation for developing the 'Integral Linguistics' project in the first place, which only later was identified by means of this convenient label.

In his article, **Sonesson**'s main focus is on an important part of Coseriu's project, viz. the complementarity of investigations into the three different levels of language, which according to Coseriu must take pride of place in the framework: the study of 'speaking in general', the study of particular languages and the study of texts and discourses (see Section 2; cf. also **Albrecht** and **Schrott**, this volume). Incidentally, the same label 'Integral linguistics' – or similar ones such as 'integrational linguistics' – was also used by other scholars around the same time, including Helmut Gipper, Hans-Heinrich Lieb, Roy Harris, and **So-**

nesson himself. While most scholars apparently did not intentionally borrow the label from Coseriu or from each other, **Sonesson** raises the question whether using such a label points to a shared underlying concern. He finds a common ground in the rejection of some of the basic assumptions of Chomsky's Generative Grammar, in particular the formalist – and reductionist or, better still, restrictivist – stance Generative Grammar takes on language.[2] **Sonesson** goes on to explain that there are many routes to an 'integral' approach to language. Coseriu insisted that linguistics is a cultural science. Hence neurology (including neurolinguistics) was not a part of his Integral Linguistics, even if neurological findings may prove helpful, if only obliquely, in additionally clarifying findings and observations that surface in the study of language as a cultural object (cf. **Belligh**, this volume). Similarly, it is possible to make statements about, e.g., the physical nature of the formal schemata in which languages are expressed, even though these do not, strictly speaking, concern language in the full meaning of the term (see Coseriu 1978 [1958]). However, while **Sonesson** sides with Coseriu in grounding linguistics in philosophy and phenomenology, they conceive of the relation between language and semiotics differently.

Sonesson's project of a 'cognitive semiotics' subsumes the study of language under semiotics, in line with the dominant trend in semiotics which takes a broad perspective on signs. By contrast, for Coseriu the study of language (i.e. 'natural language', though with regard to Coseriu 'historical language' is more appropriate, see Section 2) occupies a special place vis-à-vis semiotics. Rather than considering linguistics part of a broad science of signs in the wake of Saussure, Coseriu subscribes to Humboldt's and Hjelmslev's more radical view that language is a special and ultimately unique form of semiosis. According to this view, linguistic signs are imperfectly described and understood if they are characterized in terms of the traditional core phrase of semiotics *aliquid stat pro aliquo*. Importantly, "language is the semiotic system into which all other semiotic systems can be transferred, but which cannot be transferred as a whole into any other semiotic system" (Coseriu 1992: 6). Only language is a "se-

---

[2] Differences between the various 'integrationalist' approaches may nevertheless prevail. It suffices, e.g., to compare Coseriu's Integral Linguistics with Toolan's (1996) "integrational approach" (based on R. Harris) or Agha's (2007) more influential "integrationist-expansionist-and-collaborative" approach. Coseriu and Toolan would seem to disagree on virtually every theoretical issue (even leaving aside Toolan's almost complete disregard of the history of the language sciences). By contrast, Agha's account of the work of Saussure, Bloomfield and Chomsky illustrates an approach that does not assume the aforementioned guiding principles of tradition and antidogmatism (see Section 2), which entails, e.g., that Agha's approach cannot integrate, in a spirit of synthesis (*Aufheben* 'sublation'), such Saussurean concepts as *langue* and *signifié*.

mantic system" properly speaking, i.e. a system of signs with a signifier (Fr. *signifiant*) and a signified (Fr. *signifié*, Coseriu 1992: 16–19), all other systems of signs are "systems of designation". Because linguistic signs are the only signs that are not merely interpreted but both intended and interpreted as signs with signifieds of their own, the study of language informs and underpins semiotics in general, according to Coseriu: language is the "very basis of the historicity of mankind" (1973 [1957]: 255) and thus of all signs that people recognize, use and create as historical beings.

In "Eugenio Coseriu and the primacy of history", **Jörn Albrecht** attempts to resolve a seeming paradox in Coseriu's writings on linguistic change. In the 1950s, Coseriu considers Hermann Paul's famous claim according to which the study of language is ultimately identical to language history as "partly rhetorical" and "obviously a reduction" (Coseriu 1978 [1958]: 21). Two decades later, Coseriu (1980) concedes that Paul's claim is reasonable and acceptable, under the condition that it is clearly stated how synchronic and diachronic linguistics are related to one another. **Albrecht** argues that there is no contradiction between the two positions Coseriu defended over time. According to Coseriu (1980: 144–145), synchronic linguistics is not ahistorical but itself a partial, provisional history of that part of language that has been instantiated at a specific point in time, even if such a partial account entails that it is not possible to explore the full array of the 'possibilities' of a language. Thus, for Coseriu the description of the many facets of a language at any particular point in time does not contradict its history, all the more so because the term 'language' applies both to a 'functional language' and a 'historical language' (see Section 2). While 'functional language' refers to the units, rules and procedures of a specific, more or less unitary language system (a 'structure'), which also includes its typological properties, the term 'historical language' refers to a series of functional languages, viz. the whole of 'diatopic', 'diastratic' and 'diaphasic' variation that makes up a language's multidimensional diasystem or 'architecture' (Coseriu 1964: 139; 2008 [1964]: 140).[3] Language description and language history should be consistent with one another, because ultimately it is language history that encompasses the descriptions of a language's consecutive stages, and not the other way round. **Albrecht** takes this tension between the seamless historical development of a language and the manifold historical manifestations in which it is realised in the course of time as a starting point for an enquiry into the basic assumptions

---

3 The terms 'architecture', 'diatopic' and 'diastratic' are adopted from Flydal (1952) and cover varieties as well as variants: dialects (regional varieties, 'diatopic'), social variation (with regard to profession, age, gender etc., 'diastratic') and variation in style or register ('diaphasic') (Coseriu 1998 [1981], 1998, 2005b, 2007 [1980]); cf. also Cigana and Kabatek (this volume).

of Coseriu's consistently 'historical' approach to synchronic linguistics. In the second part of his article, he discusses a number of areas of linguistic research which emerge as important tasks for the future if Coseriu's Integral Linguistics project is taken forward. With regard to future priorities, **Albrecht** stresses, among other things, the importance of a historical linguistics of texts and discourses (and the corresponding 'expressive knowledge' of speakers), the study of metalanguage (itself an object with a complex history), the study of intertextuality across different languages, historical stylistics and the study of changing normal language use. Barely paved roads of research lie ahead of us, but Coseriu's work will hopefully inspire future generations of linguists to continue to make significant contributions to a form of language science (G. *Wissenschaft*) in which the 'scientific dignity' of history in general, and of specific historical investigations in particular, take pride of place.

In "At the roots of linguistic change: the historicity of language", **Pierre Swiggers** provides a detailed explanatory overview of the theory of linguistic change Coseriu developed in his early monograph *Sincronía, diacronía e historia* (Coseriu 1978 [1958]). Even if **Swiggers** is clear from the outset that he cannot deal in a short article with all the issues Coseriu raises in this book, the reader is likely to understand why the author still considers it a must-read both for historical linguists and theoretical linguists (cf. also **Agud**, this volume). After outlining the book's main theoretical concepts and assumptions, **Swiggers** demonstrates how these concepts and assumptions are put into practice in Coseriu's account of the emergence of the so-called 'periphrastic' future in Vulgar Latin. This account draws on a wide range of types of evidence, not just observations regarding systematic features of language and language use but also philosophical concepts and considerations pertaining to cultural history. **Swiggers** then goes on to explain the rationale of Coseriu's model of 'innovation' and 'adoption' which drive linguistic 'change', while at the same time emphasizing that a language is not, in Coseriu's account, conceived as something that is being changed but as the historical manifestation of a continuous process of creation by speakers/hearers who instantiate the units, rules and procedures of a specific language system; see Coseriu (1973 [1955–1956]: 288): *langue* is "el momento históricamente objetivo del hablar". To conclude his article, **Swiggers** raises the question why *Sincronía, diacronía e historia* has not received the attention it deserves. He points out a number of possible reasons, including the general neglect of language history and historical-comparative linguistics by theoretical linguists, the muddled relation between Romance linguistics and language theory, and the fact that initially the book has long been available only in Spanish and in a Russian translation, whereas no English translation has ever been published (the German translation did not appear until 1974, the French translation has been available since 2007).

Coseriu reiterated and further explained the key pillars of his theory of linguistic change, which he had developed early on in his career, on many occasions and in many publications throughout his scholarly life. It arguably comprises the components Coseriu treasured most in a comprehensive theory of language: the focus on linguistic activity which has precedence over the language system, the creativity of speakers, intersubjectivity in the twofold sense of communication and alterity (the foundational connection with the *alter ego*), the essential intentionality of creating and re-creating language-specific meanings, the conscious processes of innovation and adoption in the historical development of languages, the permanent and, in the final analysis, unpredictable interaction between universal, language-specific and individual factors that eventually determine the outcome of what speakers/hearers realize when they engage in language. It is therefore probably no exaggeration when **Agud** (this volume) calls the publication of *Sincronía, diacronía e historia* in 1958 a revolutionary moment in twentieth-century linguistics despite its ill-fated reception brought up by **Swiggers.** As with other aspects of his Integral Linguistics project, Coseriu was also eager to confront his theory of linguistic change with subsequent developments in the theory of language and historical linguistics. In particular, he demonstrated that from his Humboldtian perspective, explaining linguistic change through the workings of an 'invisible hand' (Keller 1990; 1994) amounts to an unacceptable attempt to reduce an innumerable series of intentional speech acts to an unrecoverable chain of allegedly causal events (Coseriu 2005a: 78; cf. Kabatek 2005). However, controversies such as these have not prevented that the 'invisible hand' theory has remained popular in the literature on linguistic change to this day, despite the circularity involved.

One of **Swiggers'** points of criticism regarding Coseriu's theory of linguistic change is that Coseriu adheres to the view that linguistic change is abrupt rather than gradual. It might be more precise, according to **Swiggers**, to say that languages evolve rather than change. According to Coseriu only natural objects 'evolve'; he considers 'evolution' an inconvenient and inadequate term to designate the "historical development" cultural objects undergo in the course of time (Coseriu 1978 [1958]: 181). In "Coseriu's journey to the realm of linguistic change", **Ioan Milică** casts additional light on this matter. **Milică** contrasts Coseriu's approach to linguistic change in terms of "language in the making" (Sp. *hacerse sistemático de la lengua*, Coseriu 1978 [1958]: 271) with approaches that seek to explain change by appealing to methods and concepts borrowed from the natural sciences. Such approaches were popular at the time *Sincronía, diacronía e historia* appeared and they still are (compare, e.g., Croft 2000). Explanations of linguistic change in terms of natural or biological causes are unacceptable to Coseriu, whose theory of linguistic change focuses instead on the dynamics of discourse and the interplay between the speech acts of individual speakers in diverse historical settings. To understand the basic assumptions of Coseriu's theory, **Milică** argues, it is necessary to reconstruct the historical context in which it was developed. This also entails a historical and conceptual analysis of the notion 'evolution'. 'Evolution' has assumed pride of place in modern history of sciences since Charles Darwin, but it might have a considerably larger scope than Coseriu was willing to accept.

Set at the crossroads of philosophy and linguistics, Coseriu's theory of linguistic change primarily draws on Aristotle and Wilhelm von Humboldt, but Coseriu also positions himself, e.g., vis-à-vis F. de Saussure (**Milică** points out that differences between the 'historical Saussure' and the published *Cours de linguistique générale* (1916) must be observed). Humboldt advanced the idea of 'development' (G. *Entwicklung*), which he linked with his views on the 'organism of language'. According to Coseriu, the main fallacy of modern theories of linguistic change is that they approach language as a mechanical communicative 'product' allegedly shaped by largely blind laws of change, instead of regarding language as a uniquely human creative activity. The free and creative activity of speaking shapes any given language as a historical and cultural entity. It is in the light of adaptive discourse traditions that natural languages must be described not as static, but as dynamic systems of signs. Because languages are permanently being created and re-created by virtue of the speakers' communicative abilities and expressive needs, languages display a dynamic though fragile equilibrium between what has just been said and what is about to be said. No language should consequently be viewed as a phenomenon shaped by external causes and law-like generalities, but as an infinitely diversified flow of speech acts created within the communicative possibilities systematically entailed in each language. Hence, linguistic change and the creation of language are, strictly speaking, one and the same (cf. also **Albrecht**, this volume).

Albrecht, in his contribution to the volume, makes the observation that Coseriu's theory of language is to some extent 'anti-pragmatist' by its very nature. Yet, **Angela Schrott** demonstrates in "Eugenio Coseriu and pragmatics" that Coseriu's work can be approached differently. Coseriu's multi-layered account of linguistic competence (G. *Sprachkompetenz*, cf. Coseriu 1973 [1955–1956], 1985, 2007 [1988]) can be read, according to **Schrott**, as an attempt to come to terms with many of the challenges modern linguistic pragmatics is concerned with. In spite of appearances to the contrary, **Albrecht** and **Schrott** do not contradict each other. They draw attention to different aspects of language and linguistic activity from different points of view. These do not exclude one another.

Albrecht highlights Coseriu's often-repeated remark that communication is not the primary function of language but only one among several functions (Coseriu 1985 [1956]). Moreover, communication does not simply consist, according to Coseriu, in 'using' language, because this would entail that language is a fixed set of units, rules and procedures that await to be applied by speakers. This would contradict Coseriu's guiding principle that creating and re-creating, rather than 'using', language is what characterizes linguistic activity (a differentiation that must also be kept in mind when one resorts to the ubiquitous term 'language use'). Moreover, most of what is commonly called 'pragmatic' in language in the linguistic literature of the past half century is not 'historical' when examined from Coseriu's multi-layered and multi-perspectival approach to linguistic competence, but either pertains to the universal level of 'speaking in general' or to the strictly individual level of context-specific utterances (**Kabatek**, this volume).[4]

Schrott, on her part, focuses on the potential of Coseriu's matrix for the study of linguistic competence (see Section 2) with regard to carrying out fine-grained pragmatic analyses of discourse processes and the layered historical traditions that underpin them. One of the main appeals of Coseriu's model is that it allows linguists to approach the many components that together make up linguistic competence from a multitude of angles which are complementary and mutually supportive of each other. Unlike traditional pragmatics, Coseriu's matrix is based on the assumption that every part of linguistic competence relates to what Coseriu calls the 'essence of language': the activity of speaking that creates meaning grounded in the ability to express oneself in a particular language (cf. **Trabant**, this volume). Thus, while linguistic competence encompasses much more than the activity of speaking a particular language and the corresponding 'idiomatic knowledge' required to do so and also includes abilities and skills that are not language-specific and not even all of a verbal nature, linguistic competence is inconceivable without it being grounded in the historicity of particular language systems.

In her article, **Schrott** indicates what pragmatic aspects of language use might fall within each of the levels and points of view between which Coseriu's matrix draws distinctions. Taking verbal politeness as an example, she shows that certain strategies of polite interaction are not language-specific but universal tendencies, which therefore are the subject of universal pragmatics. Converse-

---

4 Harald Weydt circumscribes the type of meaning that corresponds to the third, individual level of language, G. *Sinn*, as "pragmatic meaning" (G. *pragmatische Bedeutung*) or "speech act meaning" (G. *Sprechaktbedeutung*) (Schlieben-Lange and Weydt 1979: 69).

ly, aspects of polite verbal interaction that pertain to specific linguistic communities in space and time should be dealt with as language-specific features, whereas the various discourse traditions of verbal politeness are those that individual speakers selectively draw upon depending on the expressive needs of specific discourse requirements. This differentiation opens up, according to **Schrott**, a horizon for wide-ranging historical as well as comparative pragmatic research, e.g. as when polite requests by means of indirect interrogative sentences can be shown to be a relatively recent development in a number of Romance languages as compared to the frequent use of direct imperatives in older stages of these languages. However, indirect interrogative sentences, although widespread in many modern cultures, are not universally used for polite requests and hence qualify as culture-specific discourse traditions, which in turn transcend the level of language-specific rules and procedures.

While **Schrott** emphasizes the compatibility of Coseriu's matrix of linguistic competence with issues in current (historical and comparative) pragmatics, **Johannes Kabatek**'s article "Eugenio Coseriu on *immediacy, distance* and *discourse traditions*" zeros in on variational linguistics from a different perspective. His focus is on concepts that are in part based on Coseriu's layered model of linguistic competence and that have loomed large in Romance linguistics in the past few decades. In 1985, Peter Koch and Wulf Oesterreicher presented an influential proposal that combines Coseriu's notion of the 'architecture' (Flydal 1952) of a 'historical language' with Ludwig Söll's (1985) distinction between the linguistic 'medium' (written or spoken language) and 'conception' (a continuum along which language is realized). Koch and Oesterreicher introduced 'immediacy' and 'distance' (G. *Nähesprache* and *Distanzsprache*) as the two poles of the continuum, on which a variety of 'discourse traditions' (G. *Diskurstraditionen*) (Koch 1987) can be situated. **Kabatek** first traces the history of these concepts in Koch's and Oesterreicher's writings. While acknowledging the importance of Coseriu's matrix, the authors found fault with Coseriu's allegedly too rigid distinction between the 'historical' level of the lexicon and grammar of specific languages and the 'individual' level of utterances in particular settings. They emphasize that utterances, too, display features that are historical because utterances never are entirely new but draw on previous or already established forms of language use, e.g. when someone writes a letter or gives a scholarly lecture or when two people are engaged in a telephone call. Assuming that such discourse traditions cross-cut with variables like written language and spoken language or 'distance' and 'immediacy', Koch (1987) argues that Coseriu's historical level of specific languages should not only encompass the rules of language but also the knowledge of previously produced texts and discourses, which are partly repeated and partly altered on any one occasion of language use. **Kabatek** then goes on to discuss Coseriu's response to Koch and Oesterreicher's proposal. He shows that the way Oesterreicher and Koch elaborated Coserian distinctions is of great importance. He also demonstrates that the specifications and differentiations the authors added to Coseriu's matrix are fully anticipated by Coseriu. **Kabatek** draws on an unpublished manuscript by Coseriu (*El problema de la corrección idiomática*, ms. 1957) of which a fragment was published in German translation (Coseriu 1988 [1957]; cf. also **Albrecht**, this volume). This manuscript moreover presents, if summarily, an even more complex picture of Coseriu's three-levelled approach to language. The differentiation between the universal, historical and individual level not only applies to different levels of language but also to the level of individual discourse itself. The expressive knowledge of speakers/hearers that corresponds to the production and reception of utterances in context must not be narrowed down, according to Coseriu, to an individual's competence, but it encompasses aspects that are themselves either historical (knowledge of various discourse traditions people share) or universal (e.g. knowledge pertaining to differences between written and spoken language or to the differentiation between 'immediacy' and 'distance' in language).

Kabatek's appraisal of one of Coseriu's as yet largely unknown studies demonstrates that already at an early stage Coseriu's framework accommodated many of the considerations that have only later been made explicit by other scholars – a finding that is likely to sound familiar to those who have taken Coseriu's theory of language as a starting point or source of inspiration for own, subsequent research projects. **Kabatek**'s account also reminds us of the fact that there still are manuscripts by Coseriu that remain to be published (cf. Kabatek 2002), apart from *El problema de la corrección idiomática* (1957) in particular the extensive manuscript *Teoría lingüística del nombre proprio* (Montevideo 1955), from which such important studies as Coseriu (1973 [1955–1956]), Coseriu (1973 [1957]), Coseriu (1973 [1955]) and Coseriu (1972 [1955], 2004 [1972]) were drawn and published separately (cf. Willems 1996 and 2020).

Andreas Widoff's article "System, norm and meaning" deals with one of Coseriu's probably best-known conceptual distinctions, viz. the distinction between the system of a language (Sp. *sistema*, G. *System*, Fr. *langue*), linguistic norm or 'normal language use' (Sp. *norma*, G. *Norm*, Fr. *norme*) and speech or discourse (Sp. *habla*, G. *Rede*, Fr. *parole*). This tripartite distinction, which was proposed in Coseriu's first major study, *Sistema, norma y habla* (Coseriu 1952; 1973 [1952]), is informed by similar conceptual distinctions proposed by Louis Hjelmslev (cf. Jensen 2015a and **Jensen**, this volume) and Prague structuralist phonology (Trubetzkoy 1958 [1939]: 11). Coseriu developed the distinction in a way that is consistent with his overall theory of language, which – unlike his structuralist predecessors – takes its starting point not in the language system but in the activity of speaking and the traditions that are handed down, and historically constituted, in specific discourse contexts. Coseriu elaborated his account of system, norm and speech as a result of the observation that the dichotomous Saussurean distinction between *langue* and *parole* leaves many facts unaccounted for, in particular those that cannot simply be assigned to one of the two levels. A third, intermediary level is called for. In Coseriu's approach, *langue* comprises all the units, rules and procedures of a language whose values are defined by language-specific functional oppositions. The system thus corresponds to what Coseriu commonly refers to as the 'idiomatic knowledge' speakers possess of a particular language (Coseriu 1985, 2007 [1988]). Conversely, *parole* consists of the innumerable realisations speakers create in every-day speech acts, which are based on their idiomatic knowledge of a particular language but always involve many other types of knowledge as well. However, not everything in *parole* is entirely new or unique, both with regard to expression and meaning. Much of *parole* is conventional, traditional and in this sense 'regular', even though it cannot be identified by virtue of language-specific functional oppositions in the *langue*. This is what Coseriu calls 'norm', which thus constitutes a level between *langue* and *parole*, even though it is, in terms of analysis, a particular modality of *parole*, viz. its conventional, traditional part (Coseriu 1973 [1952]: Chapters 4 and 5). One consequence of Coseriu's definition of norm is that it goes beyond *langue*, given that normal language use contains additional specifications and differentiations in expression and meaning that are not found in the functional oppositions of any particular language, which are unspecified and undifferentiated (Coseriu 1973 [1952]: 95). On the other hand, *langue* also goes beyond norm, and for precisely the same reason: the functional oppositions of a particular language only delimit what is possible in speech; *langue* is an open system of possibilities which virtually contains more than is – or ever can be – realized in *parole*, including those realisations that are not – or not yet – part of normal language use (Coseriu 1973 [1952]: 97–98; cf. Kabatek 2020, who also discusses Coseriu's notion of 'exemplary' norms). Languages, Coseriu argues, are "not static systems of already created or ready-made things, but systems of virtualities, systems of methods to speak, not just spoken systems" (Coseriu 2000 [1992]: 112).

Coseriu's concept of norm was adopted by a number of other scholars in the 1970s and 1980s, e.g. by Bartsch (1985, 1987), who interpreted the concept in a narrower sense than Coseriu, effectively restricting 'norms' to guidelines of communication in accordance with her overall pragmatic theory of language which was partly developed as an alternative to Chomsky's theory of language. Other scholars sought to align Coseriu's account of norms with the upcoming concept of 'prototype' which was gaining foothold in various linguistic subdisciplines in the 1980s and 1990s (e. g., Snell-Hornby 1988; for a similar assessment of norms in terms of prototypes, see Hanks 2013). Coseriu's tripartition system–norm–speech is also echoed in such frameworks as Levinson's influential three-levelled approach to 'sentence meaning', 'utterance type meaning' and 'utterance token meaning', albeit without any reference to Coseriu or any other structuralist forebears (cf. Levinson 2000). **Widoff** interprets the distinction between system and norm in the sense that a language cannot be characterized as a uniform structure that unambiguously prescribes and proscribes certain expressions given that the language system permits more than what is found in the norm. The distinction is particularly useful, according to the author, in accounting for the different modes in which various linguistic manifestations are nevertheless part of a language, broadly construed. According to **Widoff**, Coseriu himself has illustrated the importance of the distinction mainly with regard to phonology and morphology, whereas it has less often been applied to syntax and semantics, or more specifically, to the interpretation of expressions. In his article, the author discusses and illustrates the distinction against the backdrop of Coseriu's assumption that all lexical items of a language have general unitary, language-specific signifieds, including function words such as prepositions. He draws on Coseriu's well-known account of the German preposition *mit* or the French preposition *avec* in terms of an underspecified signified (Coseriu 1989: 20), which Coseriu paraphrases as 'copresence' or 'concomitance' (Coseriu 1970 [1969]: 117; 1987: 8; 1989: 9). Other authors have proposed similar paraphrases. Coseriu's account was primarily directed, in the 1970s, against the pervasive confusion between the signified (G. *Bedeutung*) of a linguistic sign and its designation (G. *Bezeichnung*) in Generative Grammar, which also led to the assumption of rampant polysemy. At the same time, Coseriu's account was inspired by the semantic analysis of the English conjunction *but* Leibniz had proposed in his *Nouveaux essais sur l'entendement human* (1703–1705, published posthumously in 1765) in critical response to Locke's earlier analysis of this function word. Whereas Locke listed several senses of *but* which at first glance might seem to be mutually exclusive, Leibniz stressed that the conjunction can be substituted, in every context, by a general paraphrase which captures the word's unitary meaning ('et non pas davantage', 'non plus ultra'; cf. Coseriu 2015, I: 212–213). **Widoff** compares a range of uses of four similar prepositions in four languages (Engl. *with*, G. *mit*, Sw. *med* and Fr. *avec*) and finds subtle differences between the languages regarding what can be considered 'normal' usages. His conclusion is that an efficient distinction between system and norm should also accept overgeneralised unitary meanings of function words. A monosemic account of the prepositions in the four languages not only reveals language-specific semantic differences that account for the differences in distributions, but also, according to the author, that systemically defined abstract meanings license possible uses that do not fall within the scope of an established norm and in this respect can be qualified as 'deviant'. However, this does not contradict the monosemic account, quite the contrary.

In "Coseriu, significative semantics and a new system of semantic roles", **Dagobert Höllein** addresses a concept which has played a central role in the development of modern syntactic theory: 'semantic role'. **Höllein**'s focus is on the theoretical foundations and the empirical operationalisibility of semantic roles in syntactic analyses. Shortly after Fillmore published *The case for case* (1968) and long before the limitations of case grammar became obvious, Coseriu published a series of articles in German (Coseriu 1970 [1969], 1970, 1972 [1971]) in which he takes issue with Fillmore's account. The key problem is associated with the use of a single English term, 'meaning', to refer to two entirely different types of linguistic content that must be carefully distinguished: the signified (G. *Bedeutung*) and designation (G. *Bezeichnung*) (see Section 2). A linguistic sign consists of a language-specific expression, the signifier, and a language-specific content, the signified. By contrast, designation is the reference to an extralinguistic entity (or that entity itself) which speakers convey by applying a linguistic sign in a specific discourse or text. Thus, whereas the signified corresponds language-internally to a signifier, designation is not language-specific yet based on the pairing of a signifier and a signified. However, no entity is simply language-external since "each language delimits and structures reality in its own manner" (Coseriu 2004 [1972]: 50). Coseriu (1970 [1969]: 109) illustrates the importance of the distinction by discussing some of Fillmore's well-known examples (Fillmore 1968: 22). According to Fillmore, *John* is an AGENT in a sentence such as *John broke the window*, whereas *a hammer* is an INSTRUMENT in a sentence such as *A hammer broke the window*. Coseriu counters this analysis by pointing out that the difference between AGENT and INSTRUMENT obviously stems from the designation of the words *John* and *hammer* by virtue of their lexical meanings, but not from the subject function which is exactly the same in both sentences: both sentences instantiate the transitive construction with the verb *break* and code the same semantic role of 'AGENT' (G. *Handlungsträger*) as the subject of the sentences. Fillmore's analysis is inconclusive even from a language-external point of view, given that "it is possible to break a window with John as an instrument" (Coseriu 1970 [1969]: 109). Hence the lexical meaning of the subject NP does not determine the semantic role, on the contrary, it is precisely because both are different types of signified that they must be kept apart in a semantics-based syntactic analysis. The fact that Coseriu's critical account of Fillmore's 'denotative roles' has been largely ignored in current theories of syntax (compare the treatment of roles in Generative Grammar and cognitive Construction Grammar, to name only two currently popular models) is all the more regrettable because Coseriu's alternative analysis can form the basis of a theory of semantic roles that does not run into the same difficulties as Fillmore's approach. In his article, **Höllein** outlines the methodology and objectives of a model of semantic roles he and other colleagues have developed as an alternative to the traditional assumptions of case grammar. **Höllein** first shows to what extent an analysis based on denotative roles leads to inconclusive findings once naturally-occurring sentences drawn from corpora are analysed. He then proposes an analysis of the same data based on 'significative-semantic roles', which shows that semantic roles have to be established in terms of signifieds, hence for each language separately, and not as putative universal roles of designation, in line with Coseriu's criticism 50 years ago. It is noteworthy that the model of semantic roles **Höllein** maps out does not follow Coseriu blindly. The model adopts, e.g., the concept of prototype from Cognitive Linguistics, which according to Coseriu (2000 [1990]) is alien to the level of signifieds in language and pertains to the realm of designation.

In "Coseriu's approach to word formation as an illustration of his theory of meaning", **Wolf Dietrich** demonstrates how Coseriu's theory of word formation accommodates the various types of compounds and derivations in accordance with his central claim that every branch of linguistics must first and foremost acknowledge that linguistic signs are created by speakers with a specific "meaning intentionality" (Sp. *intencionalidad significativa*, Coseriu 1957: 15; 1973 [1957]: 250; G. *Bedeutungsintentionalität*, 1975 [1957]: 223). Coseriu's approach to word formation is remarkable because it leaves the trodden paths of traditional word formation – so much so that it has not received the attention it deserves in modern linguistics. It is thus far the only approach that takes a radically semantic stance on word formation, which entails that the boundaries between the categories of compound words and derivations are defined differently compared to traditional accounts. Coseriu is anxious to avoid the mixture of morphological categories (e.g. prefixation and suffixation) and semantic categories (e.g. diminutive, 'nomen agentis' etc.). He instead proposes strictly semantic categories such as 'modification' and 'development', on the one hand, and 'composition', on the other. The former categories entail that a given primary word is either modified or developed into a new, complex word by adding a syntactic function which is either predicative or attributive. Conversely, composition is not only the combination of two lexemes, as in traditional accounts, but also the combination of a lexeme and an element with a generic meaning such as 'someone' or 'something'; for example, *teach-er* is semantically a generic compound.

The input of word formation processes (or procedures, G. *Verfahren*) is the 'primary' lexicon of a language, which gets transformed in a process of 'grammar making' (Coseriu 1977a: 52) to yield new, semantically complex words. For Coseriu (1989: 5–6), observing the distinction (known since antiquity) between the 'naming' function of words (ὀνομάζειν) and the 'saying' function of grammatical constructions (λέγειν) is a matter of principle. Accordingly, it is a fallacy to assert that the primary units of the lexicon of a language ('words') are themselves constructions, as is assumed, e.g., in current constructionalist approaches (cf. Goldberg 2003). Words in natural languages are no names for extralinguistic things but for intuitively conceived essences (*quidditates*). Hence the 'signifieds' of words are, in Hegel's parlance, general ideas (G. *allgemeine Vorstellungen*) created by man's *Zeichen machende Phantasie* [imaginative ability to create signs] (Hegel 1970 [1832–1845], *Enzyklopädie der philosophischen Wissenschaften III*, Vol. 10: 457). Coseriu writes:

> For the words of historical languages, at least those of the primary and purely linguistic lexicon, name – in an immediate manner – not 'things' but intuitions of *quidditates* that are intuitively apprehended. Each primary expression of 'natural' languages originally corresponds to a νόησις τῶν ἀδιαιρέτων (*apprehensio simplex* or *indivisibilium intelligentia*) and not to a clearly delimited class of objects or facts. (Coseriu 1976c: 19; italics in the original)

Equally important is that word formation processes constitute a distinct subsystem of language, according to Coseriu (1977a: 52–53). The products of these processes exhibit internal relations which are "grammatikähnlich", i.e. similar but not identical to those found in syntactic constructions (G. *Konstruktionen*, 1977a: 52). For example, it is perfectly legitimate to paraphrase the meaning of Fr. *beauté* as 'le fait d'être beau/belle' [the fact of being beautiful], but it has to be kept in mind that this paraphrase is an analytical, metalinguistic circumlocution of the word formation's signified: *fait* represents the implied nominalisation and *être* the attributive predication, while *beau/belle* designates the primary unit which is the lexical input of the word formation process. However, the complex word *beauté* is not itself the outcome of a "transformation" of this paraphrase.

Given that the purpose of word formation, its 'function' in language-specific terms, is of a semantic nature, it is imperative to establish a framework that provides the necessary tools to make the distinction between different types of meaning possible. Like **Widoff** in his article on the meaning of prepositions and **Höllein** in his article on semantic roles, **Dietrich** concentrates on the distinction between signified (G. *Bedeutung*) and designation (G. *Bezeichnung*), which is, unsurprisingly, also of central importance to Coseriu's account of word formation processes. In the context of word formation, designation is the relation between a language-specific complex word and its reference to an extralinguistic object or concept. This relation is very often mediated by conventions of normal language use. Conversely, the inherent meaning of the language-specific complex word itself is a signified of a different nature, which has to be accounted for in its own terms. **Dietrich** provides a wealth of examples from Spanish, French and English that show the extent to which Coseriu's distinction between underspecified (or 'indeterminate', G. *unbestimmt*, cf. Willems 1994b) signifieds and the contextually enriched meanings in specific discourse contexts embodies a coherent unified account of different word formation processes.

In her article "The categories of the Romance verb", **Brenda Laca** zooms in on probably one of Coseriu's boldest and most original empirical analyses, viz. his account of the verbal system in Romance languages. Published in 1976 under the title *Das romanische Verbalsystem* by a student of Coseriu, Hansbert Bertsch, who edited a series of lectures Coseriu gave mainly in Tübingen at the end of the 1960s, Coseriu's account remains noteworthy for a number of reasons. First of all, despite Coseriu's emphasis on the importance of analysing each language in its own terms, here we have a comprehensive account of a particular grammatical subsystem that treats the Romance languages as a language type of its own and with a number of common properties, on a level above that of the individual languages which nevertheless exhibit considerable cross-linguistic variation (cf. also Coseriu 1988 [1971]). Secondly, Coseriu's account stands out because it approaches the observable cross-linguistic variation in the temporal domain in Romance languages first and foremost in terms of the expression of aspect and its relation to tense. According to **Laca**, contemporary work on tense and aspect has endorsed key features of Coseriu's account, in particular the claim that Romance imperfect morphology expresses a particular modal-temporal category which Coseriu identifies as 'non-actuality'. No less important is Coseriu's claim that some periphrastic expressions in Romance languages are best analysed as syncretic forms which correspond to different layers of aspect. Contemporary, more formal approaches, appear to dovetail with much of Coseriu's early account, according to **Laca**, even though they no longer subscribe to the structuralist notions typical of the 1960s and 1970s which Coseriu draws upon in his analysis.

In "The crux of metaphor: between Cognitive and Integral Linguistics", **Elena Faur** brings to our attention a somewhat neglected aspect of Coseriu's theory of language, viz. his observations on metaphorical language. Coseriu devoted considerable attention to metaphor at the beginning of his career but he did not frequently return to it in subsequent work. **Faur** demonstrates that Coseriu's study "La creación metafórica en el lenguaje" (Coseriu 1956; 1985 [1956]) is a highly interesting contribution to metaphor studies, which to her mind makes it the ideal touchstone for the development of the theory of metaphor that also pays attention to current cognitive approaches, in particular Conceptual Metaphor Theory (Lakoff and Johnson 2003 [1980], Lakoff 1987, Johnson 1987, Gibbs 2017b). **Faur** notes a number of convergences between the two approaches, in particular regarding the conception of metaphor as a dynamic form of enactive cognition by means of creative language use. There are also important differences, which should be addressed, according to the author, because they clarify the conditions under which figurative speech occurs in natural language. This is the goal of a research program at the Babeş-Bolyai University in Cluj-Napoca (Romania). It aims to develop an 'integralist' framework for the study of language based on Coseriu's Integral Linguistics (cf. also **Borcilă**, this volume). One important difference between Coseriu's observations on metaphors and Conceptual Metaphor Theory relates to the way notions such as 'image schema' and 'emotion' are treated. Whereas in the cognitive framework these notions refer to pre-verbal phenomena, in the integralist framework they stand for genuinely semantic phenomena that emerge in discourse and are directly associated with the lexical meaning of words. The latter claim, **Faur** argues, is an essential part of a full-fledged theory of metaphor which does not construe figurative language as a secondary figure of speech or a rhetorical device that relies on an implicit comparison of referents, but as a genuine, original resource of creative language use (see also Coseriu 1995b, with reference to Giambattista Vico, Benedetto Croce and Antonino Pagliaro).

Finally, in "Language as activity, linguistic knowledge and cognitive psychology: a Coserian perspective", **Thomas Belligh** takes recent advances in the philosophy of cognitive science as a starting point for a comparison of Integral Linguistics and Cognitive Linguistics (regarding the latter, the author focuses on what he refers to as 'Mainstream Cognitive Linguistics'). Both frameworks aspire to contribute to our understanding of the role language plays in human cognition. However, because the definition of the nature of language differs considerably in both frameworks, their objects of study are different as well. The primary aim of investigations from the perspective of Integral Linguistics is to describe and explain linguistic activity along with the implicit knowledge that underpins this activity. In accordance with the conceptualization of language as a creative human activity and the foundation of linguistics as a cultural science, Integral Linguistics takes speakers' intuitive knowledge of language to be conscious, if largely implicit. Accordingly, the goal of linguistics is to make explicit what speakers implicitly know, "das *Bekannte* zum *Erkannten* zu machen" (Coseriu 2005b: 111; emphasis in the original). By contrast, according to **Belligh**, the declared object of enquiry in Cognitive Linguistics is to a large extent unconscious computational mechanisms, which are assumed to constitute the conditions for conscious language use. The focus on mechanisms that allegedly operate below the level of consciousness poses an epistemological challenge regarding scientific consistency and rigour: the study of unconscious mechanisms that nevertheless find their fulfilment in conscious language use faces the classical problem that the explanandum is ill-defined. Building on two lines of arguments from the philosophy of cognitive science, **Belligh** explains why central claims in Cognitive Linguistics regarding the unconscious level of cognition are problematic, whereas Integral Linguistics does not run into similar problems by virtue of its self-imposed restriction not to engage in the analysis of an object of investigation that falls outside the purview of a cultural science. Cognitive Linguistics would therefore be well-advised, according to the author, either to adopt some of the basic assumptions on which Integral Linguistics is founded in order to develop an epistemologically more coherent approach to language, or else to solve the outstanding epistemological and methodological challenges with which an up-to-date scientific enquiry of subpersonal computational mechanisms is confronted, so that Cognitive Linguistics can live up to its promise of providing explanations of cognitive processes which traditional linguistics has not been able to provide.

4 Coseriu in English

This section lists the texts by Coseriu that have been published in English.

4.1 Theory of Language / Integral Linguistics

1971 [1973]. "The situation in linguistics". In: *Collection of papers commemorating the 50th birthday of the Korean Language Research Society*, 483–492. Seoul. English translation of: Coseriu, Eugenio. 1973. *Die Lage in der Linguistik*. Innsbruck: Institut für Sprachwissenschaft der Universität Innsbruck.

1977 [1974]. "Linguistic (and other) universals". In: Adam Makkai, Valerie Becker Makkai and Luigi Heilmann (eds.), *Linguistics at the crossroads*, 317–346. Padua & Lake Bluff, Ill.: Liviana & Jupiter Press. English translation of: Coseriu, Eugenio. 1974. "Les universaux linguistiques (et les autres)". In: Luigi Heilmann (ed.), *Proceedings of the Eleventh International Congress of Linguists*. Vol. I, 47–73. Bologna: il Mulino.

1983. "Linguistic change does not exist". *Linguistica nuova ed antica. Rivista di linguistica classica medioevale e moderna* 1, 51–63. Also in: *Studi di linguistica e filologia* II, 2. Charisteria Victori Pisani oblata. Edited by G. Bolognesi and C. Santoro, 167–179. Galatina: Congedo.

1985. "Linguistic competence: what is it really?" The Presidential Address of the Modern Humanities Research Association. *The Modern Language Review* 80:4, xxv–xxxv.

2000 [1992]. "The principles of linguistics as a cultural science". *Transylvanian Review* 9:1, 108–115. English translation of: Coseriu, Eugenio. 1992. "Principiile lingvisticii ca știință a culturii". *Apostrof* (Cluj) III: 11, 11 & 14. New version (transcript) in: *Omul și limbajul său. Studia linguistica in honorem Eugenio Coseriu* (= *Analele științifice ale Universității "Al. I. Cuza" din Iași (Serie nouă), Secțiunea III.e.* Vol. 37–38. *Lingvistică, 1991–1992*), 11–19.

4.2 History of Linguistics

1968. "General perspectives". In: Robert Lado, Norman A. McQuown and Sol Saporta (eds.), *Current trends in linguistics*. Vol. IV: *Ibero-American and Caribbean Linguistics*, 5–62. The Hague: Mouton.

1974 (with Horst Geckeler). "Linguistics and semantics". In: Thomas A. Sebeok (ed.), *Current trends in linguistics*, Vol. 12, 103–171. The Hague & Paris: Mouton.

1981 [1974] (with Horst Geckeler). *Trends in structural semantics*. Tübingen: Narr (new version of Coseriu and Geckeler 1974, with updated References).

1983. "Adam Smith and the beginnings of language typology". *Historiographia Linguistica* 10:1/2, 1–12. English translation of: Coseriu, Eugenio. 1968. "Adam Smith und die Anfänge der Sprachtypologie". In: Herbert E. Brekle and Leonhard Lipka (eds.), *Wortbildung, Syntax und Morphologie. Festschrift zum 60. Geburtstag von Hans Marchand am 1. Oktober 1967*, 46–54. The Hague: Mouton.

1994. "My Pagliaro". In: Tullio de Mauro and Lia Formigari (eds.), *Italian studies in linguistic historiography*, 39–44. Münster: Nodus.

1995. "My Saussure". In: Tullio de Mauro and Shigeaki Sugeta (eds.), *Saussure and linguistics today*, 187–191. Roma: Bulzoni.

4.3 Semantics

1967 [1966]. "Lexical structure and the teaching of vocabulary". In: *Linguistic theories and their applications*. Strasbourg: The Council of Europe. English translation of: Coseriu, Eugenio. 1966. "Structure lexicale et enseignement du vocabulaire". In: *Actes du Premier Colloque International de Linguistique Appliquée*, 175–217. Nancy: Annales de l'Est.

2000 [1990]. "Structural semantics and 'cognitive' semantics". *Logos and Language* 1:1, 19–42. English translation of: Coseriu, Eugenio. 1990. "Semántica estructural y semántica cognitiva". In: *Homenaje al Profesor Francisco Marsá / Jornadas de Filología*, 239–282. Barcelona: Universidad de Barcelona.

2004 [1972]. "On parts of speech (word categories, 'partes orationis')". *Logos and Language* 5:2, 47–61. English translation of: Coseriu, Eugenio. 1972 [1955]. "Sobre las categorías verbales ('partes de la oración')". *Revista de lingüística aplicada* [Concepción/Chile] 10, 7–25.

2008 [1964]. "Towards a structuralist diachronic semantics". In: Patrick Hanks (ed.), *Lexicology. Critical concepts in Linguistics*. Vol. 2: *Lexical semantics and structures*,

140–193. London: Routledge. English translation of: Coseriu, Eugenio. 1964. "Pour une sémantique diachronique structurale". *Travaux de linguistique et de littérature* (Strasbourg) 2:1, 139–186.

4.4 Miscellaneous

1952 (with Washington Vásquez). "For the unification of the phonic sciences: a provisionary scheme". Universidad de la República, Facultad de Humanidades y Ciencias, Departamento de Lingüística. Montevideo. English translation of: Eugenio Coseriu and Washington Vásquez. 1953. "Para la unificación de las ciencias fónicas (Esquema provisional)". Universidad de la República, Facultad de Humanidades y Ciencias, Departamento de Lingüística. Montevideo. Also in: *Revista de la Facultad de Humanidades y Ciencias* (Montevideo) 10, 183–191.

1954. "'Form' and 'substance' in the sounds of language (Summary)". Universidad de la República, Facultad de Humanidades y Ciencias, Departamento de Lingüística. 75–77. Montevideo. Also in: *Revista de la Facultad de Humanidades y Ciencias* (Montevideo) 12, 215–217.

2017. "On cross-linguistic equivalences". *Acta Structuralica* 2, 153–156. English translation of: Coseriu, Eugenio. 1977 [1962]. "Sobre equivalencias interidiomáticas". In: Coseriu, Eugenio. 1977. *El hombre y su lenguaje: estudios de teoría y metodología lingüística*, 170–171. Madrid: Gredos.

5 Festschrifts, commemorative volumes and conference proceedings

This section presents an overview of edited volumes in honour of Coseriu and of proceedings of conferences devoted to Coseriu's scholarly work.

5.1 Festschrifts

1981. *Logos semantikos. Studia linguistica in honorem Eugenio Coseriu 1921–1981*. Edited by Horst Geckeler, Brigitte Schlieben-Lange, Jürgen Trabant and Harald Weydt. Madrid: Gredos and Berlin & New York: Walter de Gruyter. 5 volumes. Vol. I: *Historia de la filosofía del lenguaje y de la lingüística*. Vol. II: *Teoría y filosofía del lenguaje*. Vol. III: *Semántica*. Vol. IV: *Gramática*. Vol. V: *Historia y arquitectura de las lenguas*.

1981. *Hommage au professeur Eugenio Coseriu* (= *Dacoromania. Jahrbuch für östliche Latinität* 5). Edited by Paul Miron. Freiburg & München: Karl Alber.

1988. *Energeia und Ergon. Sprachliche Variation – Sprachgeschichte – Sprachtypologie. Studia in honorem Eugenio Coseriu*. Edited by Jörn Albrecht, Jens Lüdtke and Harald Thun. Tübingen: Narr. 3 volumes. Vol. 1: *Schriften von Eugenio Coseriu (1965–1987)*.

Vol. 2: *Das sprachtheoretische Denken Eugenio Coserius in der Diskussion* (1). Vol. 3: *Das sprachtheoretische Denken Eugenio Coserius in der Diskussion* (2).

1992. *Omul și limbajul său. Studia linguistica in honorem Eugenio Coseriu* (= *Analele științifice ale Universității "Al. I. Cuza" din Iași*, Serie nouă, Secțiunea III, e, Lingvistică, Tomul XXXVII-XXXVIII, 1991–1992). Iași: Editura Universității "Al. I. Cuza".

2002. *Un lingvist pentru secolul XXI: Materiale ale Colocviului Internațional "Filologia secolului XXI" organizat cu prilejul a 80 de ani din ziua nașterii Prof. Eugeniu Coșeriu* (Bălți, 18–19 mai 2001). Edited by Gheorghe Popa. Chișinău: Știința.

2002. *Sprache und Welt: Festgabe für Eugenio Coseriu zum 80. Geburtstag*. Edited by Adolfo Murguía. Tübingen: Narr.

5.2 Commemorative volumes and special issues (selection)

2001–2002. *Fonetică și dialectologie* 20–21. Special issue. In memoriam Eugeniu Coșeriu.

2002. *Limba română. Revistă de știință și cultură* 12, nr. 10. Special issue. *In memoriam Eugen Coșeriu*.

2003. *Eugenio Coseriu in memoriam*. Edited by Jesús Martínez del Castillo. *Odisea. Revista de estudios ingleses* 3 (Numero extraordinario). Almería: Universidad de Almería.

2004. *Studi in memoria di Eugenio Coseriu*. Edited by Vincenzo Orioles. Supplement to *Plurilinguismo. Contatti di lingue e culture* 10. Udine: Forum.

2005. *Eugenio Coseriu in memoriam* (II). Edited by Jesús Martínez del Castillo. Granada: Método.

5.3 Conference proceedings

2015. *Eugenio Coseriu aujourd'hui. Linguistique et philosophie du langage*. Edited by Christophe Gérard and Régis Missire. Limoges: Éditions Lambert-Lucas. [Proceedings of the 1st International Conference on Eugenio Coseriu, Aix en Provence/France, 17.9.–19.9.2007.]

2013–2014. *Coseriu: Perspectives contemporaines. Actes du deuxième Colloque International d'études cosériennes: CoseClus 2009: 23–25 septembre, Cluj-Napoca, Roumanie*. Edited by Eugenia Bojoga, Oana Boc and Dumitru-Cornel Vîlcu. Cluj-Napoca: Presa Universitară Clujeană. 2 volumes (Vol. I: 2013, Vol. 2: 2014). [Proceedings of the 2nd International Conference on Eugenio Coseriu, Cluj/Romania, 23.9.–25.9.2009.]

2012. *Eugenio Coseriu (1921–2002) en los comienzos del siglo XXI*. Edited by Jesús Martínez del Castillo (= *Analecta Malacitana* 86). Málaga: Universidad de Málaga. 2 volumes. [Proceedings of the 3rd International Conference on Eugenio Coseriu, Almería/Spain, 5.10.–7.10.2011.]

2015. *Oltre Saussure. L'eredità scientifica di Eugenio Coseriu / Beyond Saussure. Eugenio Coserius scientific legacy*. Atti del IV Congresso Internazionale Università degli Studi di Udine, 1–2 ottobre 2013 / Proceedings of 4th International Congress University of Udine, 1–2 October 2013. Edited by Vincenzo Orioles and Raffaella Bombi (= *Quaderni della Rassegna* 106). Firenze: Cesati. [Proceedings of the 4th International Conference on Eugenio Coseriu, Udine/Italy, 1.10.–2.10.2013.]

2017. *Kompetenz – Funktion – Variation / Competencia – Función – Variación. Linguistica Coseriana V.* Edited by Thomas Stehl and Gerda Haßler. Frankfurt a. M.: Peter Lang. [Proceedings of the 5th International Conference on Eugenio Coseriu, Potsdam/Deutschland, 8.10.–10.10.2015.]

Forthcoming. *Actualidad y futuro del pensamiento de Eugenio Coseriu.* Edited by Carlos Garatea and Jorge Wiesse. Lima: Fondo Editorial de la Pontificia Universidad Católica del Perú / Fondo Editorial de la Universidad del Pacífico. [Proceedings of the 6th International Conference on Eugenio Coseriu, Lima/Peru, 2.8.–4.8.2017.]

6 Editorial remarks

Throughout the volume, care has been taken to unify references to Coseriu's œuvre as much as possible. This proved challenging given the tortuous path of many of Coseriu's publications. A large number of texts have appeared in several versions and several languages, many of them have moreover been translated into various languages. Some of the translations were supervised by Coseriu himself or delivered in consultation with him, e.g. the collection of articles in *L'homme et son langage* (Coseriu 2001), to mention just one example. In other translations Coseriu was not directly involved. At present less than twenty English texts or translations exist (see Section 5). The number of publications listed on the website of the Eugenio Coseriu Archives based in Tübingen (www.coseriu.com) currently amounts to almost 400 entries. Their publication history is often complex and so is the translation history of some of the articles (slightly revised translations exist of several articles). In the present volume, the date of the original publication is provided for a number of recurring references, e.g. Coseriu (1978 [1958]), which refers to the third edition (with Gredos in Madrid) of *Sincronía, diacronía e historia. El problema del cambio lingüístico*, originally published in Montevideo in 1958.

In the present volume, all quotations from Coseriu's publications are supplied in English translation. Translations were initially provided by the authors and, occasionally, revised in consultation with the editors. Terms and parts of the original are occasionally given between brackets in addition to the English translations, in order to ensure as much transparency and terminological consistency as possible. The editors would like to thank Pierre Swiggers, Johannes Kabatek, Jeroen Van Pottelberge, Renata Enghels, Jörn Albrecht and Jürgen Trabant for their help with terminology and translation issues, in particular regarding Spanish and German quotations.

The editors have also strived to make terminology consistent across contributions with regard to some of the concepts that are central to Coseriu's theory of language and linguistic research. First of all, Coseriu makes a distinction between 'speaking' (Sp. *hablar*, G. *Sprechen*) and 'speech' (Sp. *habla*, G. *Rede*). Whereas 'speaking' designates the activity of speaking in general (*enérgeia*), 'speech' can also be used to encompass the product of this activity; the term 'speech' is therefore more comprehensive (if potentially ambiguous).

Of particular importance is Coseriu's well-known distinction between G. *Bedeutung* and *Bezeichnung* (Sp. *significado* and *designación*, Fr. *signifié* and *désignation*), which is rendered by means of the English terms 'signified' and 'designation' throughout the volume (see Section 2). This terminological distinction figures prominently in a number of contributions in the volume. The English term 'designation' does not pose any difficulties and readily lends itself as a translation of G. *Bezeichnung*, Sp. *designación*, Fr. *désignation*. Coseriu preferred these terms over the more common term 'reference' (which he occasionally also used), partly because of the transparent association with 'sign' (G. *Zeichen*, Sp. *signo*, Fr. *signe*). 'Designation' highlights that it takes place on the basis of 'linguistic signs' that combine a *signifié* and a *signifiant*, whereas any reference can more generally be achieved by means of signs that are no such bilateral combinations (recall Husserl's pure *Anzeichen*, Husserl 1980 [1913], II/1: 23; cf. also Coseriu 1992a: 6–9). 'Signified' is now commonly used as the English translation of the Saussurean term *signifié*, with which Saussure referred to the language-specific, 'encoded', content of a linguistic sign, which in turn always consists of a *signifié* and a *signifiant*. Coseriu frequently used Fr. *signifié* as well, even in German publications, albeit with the additional qualification that a signified does not merely hinge on a differential 'value' (Fr. *valeur*) in the sense of Saussure and subsequently Hjelmslev (Coseriu 2007 [1980]: 138–143), but also constitutes a unitary meaning that is intuitively known to speakers (cf. Belligh and Willems 2021). In this respect, Coseriu's approach is obviously at variance with Hjelmslev's emphasis on considering language "merely as a pattern of mutual relations" (Hjelmslev 1947: 73).

The terminology in the texts that exist in English translation is not consistent. For example, in Coseriu (1985: xxx), *signifié/Bedeutung* is simply rendered as "meaning", which seems inconvenient because "meaning" is a general term used in a variety of ways in the linguistic literature and therefore requires further qualification (cf. Section 2 and **Albrecht**, this volume). In other texts, e.g. Coseriu (1971 [1973]: 3) and Coseriu and Geckeler (1974: 141), *signifié/Bedeutung* is rendered as "signification". However, this term, too, is liable to create confusion. In some of Coseriu's publications on lexematics and the theory of meaning, Fr. *signification* and *signifié* are clearly distinguished. Whereas the signified (*signifié*) is the language-specific, unitary meaning of a bilateral linguistic sign (*signifiant* + *signifié*) which speakers intuitively apprehend, signification (Fr. *signification*) refers to the relations (Fr. *rapports*) that obtain between signifieds of different linguistic signs which contrast with one another within one and the same language, thus mutual delimiting their functional ranges and, hence, domains of applicability (see, e.g., Coseriu 1992 [1988]: 188, 216). Compare the following diagram taken from Coseriu (1968: 3):

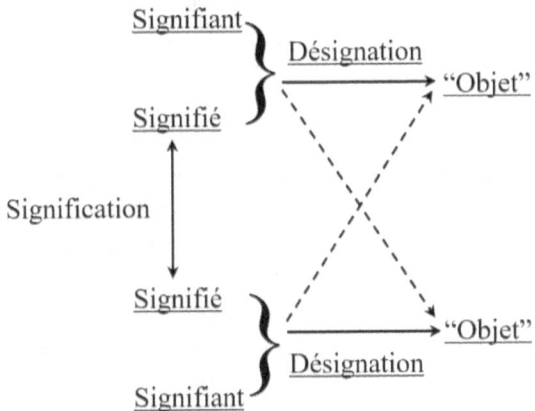

Figure 1: The distinction between signifier (*signifiant*), signified (*signifié*), signification and designation

Finally, Coseriu distinguished a third layer of content, next to the signified and designation, viz. G. *Sinn*, Sp. *sentido*, Fr. *sens*. This layer regards the meaning of a text (G. *Textinhalt*, Coseriu 2007 [1980]: 63), which Coseriu also circumscribes as the "*signifié* der Textzeichen", the "signified of textual signs" (2007 [1980]: 65). To further clarify what is meant, Coseriu draws on Bühler's Organon model of communication (Bühler 1933 and 1934), but complements it with the notion of 'evocation', which in turn is inspired by Hjelmslev's theory of 'connotation' (Hjelmslev 1961 [1943]: Chapter 22). Coseriu emphasizes that the study of *Sinn* requires an all-encompassing approach that takes into account every aspect of texts as units of discourse:

> *Sinn* arises from the combination of Bühler's functions – i.e. representation (G. *Darstellung*), expression (*Kundgabe*) and appeal (*Appell*) – and evocation. (Coseriu 2007 [1980]: 137)

For 'evocation', Coseriu relies on the work of Urban (1939). A comprehensive account of *Sinn* not only entails a bottom-up approach to linguistic signs as parts of texts in terms of language-specific structures (Coseriu 2007 [1980]: 220) but also – and from Coseriu's perspective: first and foremost – a top-down approach to the content of any one particular text in terms of a separate, autonomous object of hermeneutical analysis with an ultimately irreducible individuality (Coseriu 2007 [1980]: Chapter 2; cf. Loureda Lamas 2005). It stands to reason that Coseriu's *Sinn* might easily be rendered as 'sense' in English, which in itself would be an appropriate translation (recall that Lat. *sensus* has been used in this regard since classical antiquity). However, it has to be borne in mind that 'sense' is nowadays commonly used in modern linguistics either as an alternative to the general term 'meaning', without clear differentiation, or to refer to contextually enriched meanings of words and expressions in specific utterances, as in many studies in pragmatics, linguistic anthropology, discourse analysis, variationist sociolinguistics etc. From this angle, 'senses' are specific designations (*Bezeichnungen*) rather than hermeneutically recoverable meanings of texts or discourses. In order to avoid confusion, Coseriu's *Sinn* might simply be rendered as 'meaning of a text' or 'text meaning' in English.

The eighteen articles which make up the present volume can do no more than provide an introduction to the vast body of work Coseriu produced in the half century of his scholarly activity. The articles do not remotely cover all the topics that Coseriu himself addressed, let alone do they justice to the complexity and richness of his work. The articles moreover present their authors' personal interpretations and preoccupations, not a channelling of Coseriu. We hope that the volume is a fitting tribute to a scholar of unique stature whose ideas and published work have not received, for a variety of reasons, the attention they deserve in modern linguistics and the language sciences more generally. We therefore hope that all parts of the volume taken together are reasonably representative of Coseriu's scholarship. To the extent that the volume reflects the importance the editors and the authors attach to his publications, we trust that it will attract an international readership and evoke future discussions.

Lastly, the editors would like to express their gratitude to Christine Henschel with De Gruyter, who has accompanied the project from the outset and provided indispensable professional service.

Part I: **Philosophy of language**

Jürgen Trabant (Berlin)
The essence of language: on Coseriu's philosophy of language

> Language manifests itself only in the speaking of individuals, and speaking is always speaking a particular language. The whole being of language necessarily revolves within this circle.
>
> For Humboldt, language is the first form of formativity or creativity of the human being. The human being is characterised by formativity, and at the same time formativity is both the characteristic feature and task of the human being. [...] To create language means to manifest contents of consciousness semiotically for the Other, i. e. to project them into the world. In this regard, language is form, and since language is activity, it is formativity. Language forms the contents and also manifests their material expression. It posits the contents in the world between I and Thou. [...] To create language means to create a specific language each time. [...] The particular language corresponds to the idea of language in a historical form, to its essential historicity.*

1 Introduction

The first quote, from 1958, contains Coseriu's philosophy of language in a nutshell. And the second quote, which summarises Humboldt's philosophy in Coseriu's monumental (and partially) posthumous *Geschichte der Sprachphilosophie* [History of the Philosophy of Language] (2015), is like an expansion of that sentence.[1] According to Coseriu, philosophy is concerned with the question of the "sense of the being of objects", "der Sinn ihres Seins" (2015 I: 7); hence, the philosophy of language investigates the "essence of language as such", "das Wesen

---

* "La lengua no se da más que en el hablar de los individuos, y el hablar es siempre hablar una lengua. Todo el ser del lenguaje gira necesariamente en este círculo" (Coseriu 1978 [1958]: 31). "Die Sprache ist für Humboldt die erste Form der Formativität bzw. Kreativität des Menschen. Der Mensch ist durch die Formativität charakterisiert, und zugleich ist die Formativität die charakteristische Zug und Aufgabe des Menschen. [...] Sprachliches zu schaffen bedeutet, Inhalte des Bewusstseins zeichenhaft für einen anderen zu manifestieren, d. h. sie in die Welt zu projizieren. In dieser Hinsicht ist die Sprache Form, und da sie Tätigkeit ist, ist sie Formativität. Sie gestaltet die Inhalte und manifestiert auch ihren materiellen Ausdruck. Sie stellt die Inhalte in die Welt zwischen das Ich und das Du. [...] Sprache schaffen heißt, jeweils eine bestimme Sprache zu schaffen. [...] Die Einzelsprache entspricht der Sprachidee in einer historischen Form, der Historizität schlechthin" (Coseriu 2015, II: 454–456).
1 According to Forster (2017: 165), the chapter on Humboldt also contains much of Coseriu's own philosophy of language.

https://doi.org/10.1515/9783110712391-003

der Sprache an sich" (2015, I: 13). Coseriu's work is a disclosure of his reflections on the "essence of language".

There is no other linguist in the twentieth century who was as much a philosopher of language as Eugenio Coseriu was. However, Coseriu did not write a systematic book on the philosophy of language. He wrote important philosophical papers (e. g. Coseriu 1971 [1966] and 1971 [1967]), he also lectured on the history of language philosophy, first in 1968/69 and 1970/71, and then, fifteen years later, in the winter semesters 1985/86, 1987/88 and 1988/89. These lectures were published as books: the first part in the 1970s, re-edited in 2003 (and again in 2015), and the second part in 2015, edited by Jörn Albrecht. As a "continental" scholar, deeply formed by Hegelian thought, Coseriu distinguishes the systematic and the historical perspectives (cf. 2015, II: 320), but he does not separate systematic considerations from their historical presentation. History is the unfolding of the "idea" of language, hence of his idea of language, too. And Coseriu is not only a philosopher when he speaks and writes explicitly on the philosophy of language, he is also a philosopher in his linguistic work. Or rather: his philosophical observations also aim at an epistemological foundation of linguistics. His philosophy of language is thus also a philosophy of linguistics. The development of his linguistics mirrors the most important features of his reflections in the philosophy of language. My presentation will therefore start with Coseriu's linguistics and highlight its philosophical foundations.

2 The philosophical principles of Coseriu's linguistics

Two of Coseriu's early books are commentaries on Saussure or rather on Saussurean concepts in modern linguistics. The title of the first book, *Sincronía, diacronía e historia. El problema del cambio lingüístico* [Synchrony, diachrony and history. The problem of linguistic change] (1978 [1958]), refers to Saussure's famous dichotomy between diachrony and synchrony, and the third term in the title, "history", shows the solution to the problem posed by that opposition: diachrony and synchrony do not form two different kinds of linguistics (and linguistic change is not just within the purview of diachrony), but they are two aspects of history, the dimension in which language exists. "History" is not the passing of time – as the Saussurean term "diachrony" derived from the Greek word for time, *chronos*, implies – but "history" is the world of human action, *mondo civile* in Vichian terms, that part of the world that is created by humans, as opposed to nature. Language is human action and hence essentially – *wesentlich* in German

– "historical". It manifests itself in the activities of individuals in interaction with others. Therefore it is *"ser con otro* que coincide con el *ser histórico* del hombre", "being with the Other that coincides with the historical being of Man" (1978 [1958]: 70, italics in the original). Language changes all the time because it is created by human individuals in dialogue. "Cambio linguistico", linguistic change, simply belongs to its essential historicity. "The history of language overcomes the antinomy between synchrony and diachrony", "la historia de la lengua supera la antinomía entre sincronía y diacronía" (1978 [1958]: 281). The verb *superar* is used in the sense of Hegel's *aufheben*.

The same dialectical argumentative pattern underlies some of the five studies, "cinco estudios", in Coseriu's most famous book *Teoría del lenguaje y lingüística general. Cinco estudios* [Theory of language and general linguistics. Five studies] (1973 [1962]). The title, here again, refers to Saussure's *Cours de linguistique générale*, while adding the "theory of language" (which is not the same as "general linguistics", cf. Coseriu 2015, I: 12–13). The first chapter of the volume, "Sistema, norma y habla" [System, norm and speech] alludes to the Saussurean opposition of *langue* and *parole* and argues that *langue* and *parole* are not opposed as they are in the *Cours* but belong together in the triad of system, norm and speech. The title of the study leads to the most profound opposition between Coserian and Saussurean linguistics, to the primacy of speaking: speaking – *hablar* – is the reality of language, the way in which language is in the world, whereas norm and system are layers of the rules underlying the production of speech. The activity of speaking, is the essence of language. Activity is *enérgeia* in the sense of Aristotle and Humboldt. In this perspective, the final – itself apocryphal – phrase of the *Cours*, that linguistics is about "la langue envisagée en elle-même et pour elle-même" (Saussure 1975 [1916]: 317), is a fatal postulate for linguistics. According to Coseriu, linguistics has to be "lingüística del hablar", linguistics of speaking, as it appears in the subtitle of the fifth chapter: "Determinación y entorno. Dos problemas de una lingüística del hablar" [Determination and environment. Two problems of a linguistics of speaking]. And this chapter shows also that *hablar* transcends language since linguistic activity is embedded in the human being and in the world – the "surroundings", *entornos* – to which it is related in many ways. As Coseriu always said, we do not speak with language alone.

The second chapter of Coseriu (1973 [1962]), "Forma y substancia en los sonidos del lenguaje" [Form and substance in the sounds of language], takes up another aspect of the *langue-parole* dichotomy (which of course is much older than the *Cours*) and argues against the concept of *langue* as a domain of pure form in linguistics as it was promoted by glossematics. Louis Hjelmslev radicalised Saussure's sentence that *langue* is a form not a substance, "la langue est une forme et non une substance" (Saussure 1975 [1916]: 169, 157). Coseriu shows that the forms of sounds are always "substantial" forms, i.e. linguistically formed matter, that there can be no pure forms in language that is concrete and living action.

Finally, the fourth chapter of Coseriu (1973 [1962]), "Logicismo y antilogicismo en la gramática" [Logicism and anti-logicism in grammar], directs us towards another essential feature of language and the underlying philosophy of language: language is not a form of logical thought, nor is it illogical thought or feeling, but it is a creative human activity in its own right because its specific task is to form concepts that precede logical categories. It is "das bildende Organ des Gedanken", "the formative organ of thought" (Humboldt 1903– 1936, VII: 53). However, that "thought" is specifically linguistic, a special form of cognition: *Bedeutung*. And since that formation of content coincides with its historicity, it is subject to inherent change and diversity. Language (including *Bedeutung*) is always created in the form of particular languages. The linguistic creation of thought will be Coseriu's most important field as a linguist: semantics is the centre of his descriptive work.

Thus, the aforementioned publications do not only treat subjects of linguistic theory but also – and not only implicitly – the most important questions of Coseriu's philosophy of language cited in the introductory quote: activity, formativity, semanticity, alterity ('I – Thou') and historicity. Their titles often reflect Coseriu's *forma mentis*: Coseriu's thought is triadic, not dyadic, and these triads are inspired by Hegel. The opposition of diachrony and synchrony is *aufgehoben*, i.e. mediated and overcome, in history (the two verbs Coseriu uses in his Spanish publications for Hegel's *aufheben* are *superar* and *levantar*, cf. Coseriu 1978 [1958]: 272). Language and speech are not opposed to each other: the activity of *hablar* encompasses both, the concrete appearance of language in the world as well as the rules underlying that activity which creates formed substances. And the very task of the activity of *hablar* is the creation of meaning, *Bedeutung*, which is neither "pure thought" nor a dark, irrational entity.

These remarks on his first linguistic publications are also meant to highlight the fact that Coseriu's appearance in the world of modern linguistics in the 1950s was something special. He was modern, contributing to new developments in linguistics, but at the same time he was critical of those developments, and that criticism was based on firm philosophical convictions about language and speech, or let us rather say about the "essence" (*Wesen*) of language and speech. The permanent presence of his reflections on the "essence of language", the quest for "the essence of language as such", "das Wesen der Sprache an sich" (2015, I: 13), is the very specificity of Coseriu's linguistics and also the motive for its development. Thus, not only does the production of thought (*Bedeutung*), as the very essence of linguistic activity, necessarily lead Coseriu to semantics, but the philosophical primacy of *hablar* also drives him to produce his most radical linguistic book: *Textlinguistik* [Text linguistics] (Coseriu 2007 [1980]). *Hablar* does not only constitute the material for the investigation of its underlying rules (*langue*), but the primacy of *hablar* also allows linguistics to deal with the concrete utterances themselves, the level of individual speech, in a linguistics of texts. Text linguistics for Coseriu is not only the study of transphrastic phenomena and extralinguistic things beyond the utterances (*entornos*) but also – and mainly – the study of individual utterances themselves, which necessarily involves an interpretation of these texts. Coseriu's *Textlinguistik* can therefore be considered the outcome of his philosophical insight that language is *hablar*, activity or "formativity" as he calls it in the first sentence of my introductory quote, thereby using the central term of one of his important philosophical inspirations, the Italian philosopher Luigi Pareyson (cf. Pareyson 1954). Moreover, by considering the analysis of literary texts as the task of a linguist, Coseriu very much resembles the Italian linguist Benvenuto Terracini (cf. Terracini 1966), who then, like Leo Spitzer, was somehow excluded from the community of linguists because they considered him to be a literary scholar and therefore no longer a member of the linguistic family. But dealing with the linguistic productions of an individual is the consequence of Coseriu's first philosophical thesis that language is activity, *enérgeia*, *hablar*.

3 "Das Wesen des Seins der Sprache"

In the twentieth century, there are only a few great linguists who are as close to philosophy as Coseriu. Chomsky seems to be a philosophical linguist since he wrote a book on *Cartesian Linguistics* (2009 [1966]). But there is no such thing as Cartesian linguistics, as Coseriu remarks (2015, I: 181). And Chomsky's references to Descartes and Humboldt as his most important authorities in the philosophy of language are not so much based on historical studies of these authors but fairly superficial *post festum* justifications for his own linguistics. By contrast, Coseriu's linguistic work is essentially and deeply linked to his lifelong philosophical quest. Of course, there are other important philosophical moments in modern linguistics. Roman Jakobson's "Quest for the essence of language" (1971 [1965]) is a philosophical paper. Émile Benveniste, in the wake of Saussure, certainly asks philosophical questions with his chapters on "man in language" (Benveniste 1966). Tullio De Mauro, a linguist who is at the same time a philosopher, is in many respects comparable to Coseriu. De Mauro's chair in Rome was dedicated to the "philosophy of language". His much-lauded book on Ludwig

Wittgenstein (De Mauro 1967) is as central to his work as are his countless descriptive linguistic studies. And he is also close to Coseriu in placing semantics at the very centre of his linguistic research. De Mauro shares Coseriu's conviction that the creation of *Bedeutung* is the very task of language (even if he disagrees with him on how semantics should proceed; here he sides with Wittgenstein and his semantics of language usage). He continually contributed to the history of the philosophy of language, e.g. with studies on Leibniz and Humboldt. This philosophical foundation of their linguistics might well be due to their common Italian tradition. Not only did Benedetto Croce, Italy's *maître à penser* of the first part of the twentieth century, call his *Estetica* "linguistica generale" (Croce 1902), but De Mauro and Coseriu belong to the tradition of Antonino Pagliaro (1898–1973), the great Indo-Europeanist who was also a great language philosopher (cf. Pagliaro 1930). However, not even De Mauro produced a *History of the Philosophy of Language* that covers the philosophical reflection on language from the Presocratics to Humboldt and that unfolds a philosophy of language, an investigation into the "Wesen des Seins der Sprache" that underpins the science of language.

Coseriu's monumental *Geschichte der Sprachphilosophie* (2015) deals with the following authors and epochs: the Presocratics, Plato, Aristotle, the Stoics, Saint Augustine, the Scholastics, Vives, Descartes, Locke, Leibniz, eighteenth-century Great Britain, Vico, eighteenth-century Germany, eighteenth-century France, Herder, Hamann, Fichte, Friedrich Schlegel, August Wilhelm Schlegel, Schleiermacher, Schelling, Schopenhauer, Hegel and Humboldt. As the most important contributors to the philosophy of language Coseriu highlights Aristotle, Vico, Hegel and Humboldt. This history ends in 1835, when Humboldt died. There is unfortunately no discussion of Nietzsche, Heidegger, Cassirer, nor of any author in the analytical tradition stretching from Frege and Wittgenstein to the Anglo-Americans, Quine, Putnam, Davidson and Austin. However, Coseriu's lectures on Chomsky can be regarded as an example of what he might have said about these modern forms of the philosophy of language.

Coseriu often presents his authors in close readings of their writings, but he always has in mind three fundamental features of the "Wesen des Seins der Sprache".

The first question about the essence of language concerns its place in the world: What is language, what is it for? Language is a human activity, a creative force, an Aristotelian *enérgeia*. Language is an activity of a special nature; it is not a means to something else, e.g. it is not just a means for the transport of thought, to which it was traditionally reduced, and it cannot be reduced to some other activity. It is an activity that has a finality of its own, and in this sense it is autonomous. Language is not an instrument of knowledge, it is itself a form of knowledge; language is not an instrument of thought, it *is* thought; language is a "prelogical" objectivation of thought through the activity of the imagination (2015, I: 225, 292) in a synthesis of sound and thought.

Second, language as *enérgeia* has a special finality, viz. the production of thought, of meaning (*Bedeutung*). This production of meaning is always done in the perspective of the Other, in a fundamental togetherness, i.e. not the communication *of* something to the Other, but communication *with* the Other. Humboldt's "Arbeit des Geistes" is realised in the "unalterable dualism", "unabänderlicher Dualismus", of I and Thou (Humboldt 1903–1936, VI: 26). This two-dimensional nature of language (semanticity and alterity) is its very specificity, and it distinguishes language from all other human activities, including art which is not directed towards the other but is the creative activity of an "absolute" subject.

Third, as a human activity for the production of meaning in the "unalterable dualism", language is always "historical", i.e. its appearance in the world corresponds to the essence of the human being as an individual who is a member of a specific group of humans: "being with the Other that coincides with the historical being of Man" (1978 [1958]: 70). Diversity (Humboldt's *Verschiedenheit*) is therefore an essential feature of human language. We always speak a particular determinate language, not language in general. And, as Humboldt wrote: "The diversity of languages is not a diversity of sounds and signs but a diversity of world views" (Humboldt 1903–1936, IV: 27).

As a consequence of these essential traits of language, I would like to add a crucial idea that Coseriu utters *en passant* and in brackets, but that seems to me to be extremely important in the actual semantic fights in society: language must be left behind, it is a "Provisorium", a provisional solution, something that has to be overcome (2015, II: 343, 425). It is an initial mental formation of the world, the way in which the world is given to us; but speakers have to go beyond it, they have to advance to science and forms of objective knowledge. Language is not a prison of the mind, but a first step into knowledge of the world, which, like Wittgenstein's ladder, we necessarily abandon for higher forms of knowledge. Words can become Signs, i.e. completely arbitrary signifiers for language-independent contents, but, as such, they cease to be language.[2]

These features which constitute the "essence" of language, "das Wesen der Sprache an sich", are the features Coseriu is looking for in his *Geschichte der Sprachphilosophie*. Aristotle is – according to Coseriu – the first important author

---

[2] For this Humboldtian differentiation between Word and Sign, cf. Humboldt (1903–1936, V: 427–430), a passage Coseriu (1992a) unfortunately did not discuss. Cf. Trabant (2018).

in the philosophy of language. Europe's linguistic philosophy starts with Aristotle and depends on Aristotle for centuries. He puts the issues that Europe will be struggling with on the agenda. In *De interpretatione*, Aristotle discusses language mainly in terms of scientific apophantic discourse (*lógos apophantikòs*), as a way of communicating (true) knowledge with words. Language is not yet conceived of as an autonomous activity for the production of thought. Thoughts, the famous *pathêmata tês psychês*, the "affections of the soul", are produced independently from language. Words are only "arbitrary" (*katà synthéken*) signs (*sêmeia*), communicative means, sounds that differ from language to language. The crucial insight into the autonomy of language as a special form of knowledge is attained by Vico who, in the discovery (*discoverta*) of the *universale fantastico* as the original invention of human thought, discovers linguistic meaning (Coseriu 1995b: 78). Vico grasps the specific semantic creativity of language but has not yet an adequate concept of the word. The specificity of the word – formation of thought in the inalterable dualism of I and Thou – and the essential historicity of language are clearly seen by Humboldt, who for the first time fully recognizes that the formation of thought takes place in humanity's many languages which, as such, are "Weltansichten", world views.

4 Outstanding issues

Of course, there are many questions regarding Coseriu's philosophical claims and insights. I will just mention two. First, Coseriu does not consider the structural feature of the word, phonetic articulation, and hence the "double articulation" of language, as a part of its "essence". Humboldt writes: "Die Gliederung ist aber gerade das Wesen der Sprache", "Articulation is the very essence of language" (Humboldt 1903–1936, V: 122). By contrast, Coseriu reflects on the formation of semantic units, the first articulation, but he does not regard phonetic articulation as an essential feature of the word. Yet without the wonder of the second articulation, language could arguably not be the specific activity it is. But perhaps this is not a philosophical feature but one belonging to "general linguistics"?

Second – and this is not merely a terminological question –, Coseriu does not accept Humboldt's sharp distinction between the Sign and the Word. Rather, he follows Hegel, who even takes the Word to be the Sign par excellence (Coseriu 1992a: 16–18), thus confirming Aristotle's conception of the word as a *sêmeion*. Hegel acknowledges, as Humboldt does, the specific structural properties of the Word as compared to the Image and the Symbol, but he continues the Aristotelian tradition by calling the word a "sign" and "arbitrary" (as does Saussure). In this regard, Humboldt is more precise in restricting the term "sign" to its post-linguistic "arbitrary" usage (Trabant 2018).

There are several questions as to Coseriu's choice and evaluation of the philosophers of language in the *Geschichte der Sprachphilosophie* (cf. Forster 2017). The most important question is why Coseriu did not discuss modern developments. Why did Coseriu not proceed to a presentation – and criticism – of modern philosophy of language? What we really miss is his critical assessment of authors such as Wittgenstein or Heidegger who are generally considered as the most important philosophers of language of the twentieth century.

Coseriu briefly addressed this question in his long interview with Johannes Kabatek and Adolfo Murguía (Kabatek and Murguía 1997: 221–232). Coseriu is extremely negative about Wittgenstein: "I do not consider Wittgenstein a philosopher of language and I refuse to talk about him" (Kabatek and Murguía 1997: 229). He does however add some comments: Wittgenstein never understood what meaning is, hence what language is, because he approaches language from the perspective of an artificial system of reference; and the switch to "usage" in his later philosophy does not resolve that misunderstanding of meaning. Coseriu is certainly right but I will try to say a little bit more from a Coserian perspective (cf. the chapters on Wittgenstein and Heidegger in Trabant 2003).

Of course, in the *Tractatus* (1921) Wittgenstein does not consider language as an autonomous activity of the human being. Wittgenstein, in the tradition of rationalist philosophy, considers language as a means of designating reality. With the classical enlightenment philosophy he shares, however, the discovery of natural language containing particular thoughts as well as the Baconian criticism of those "vulgar" linguistic meanings as "idola fori", as prejudices that have to be rejected and renounced (*sunt abneganda et renuncianda*) for scientific usage. In the wake of Frege's rediscovery of that language criticism, Wittgenstein notices that natural language does not depict reality correctly, and that it is a bad means to approach the world. Therefore, in the same way that Frege did, he calls for language to be fixated and become a Sign, i.e. a non-historical means of designation. Only when it is fixated and when its historical – i.e. changing, "prelogical" and particular – essence is eliminated, when it is hence eliminated as natural language, can it be used in science. This, just as Frege's criticism, is not a new philosophical insight; it is language criticism from the viewpoint of epistemology. Language is considered as a – bad – means of referring to the world and has to be reformed. The historicity of language, its particular semantics, is denounced – as it was in the seventeenth century by Bacon and Locke – as a fault of language and not celebrated as its very essence and wealth.

As far as Wittgenstein II is concerned, the insights of the *Philosophical Investigations* (1953) seem to be closer to Coseriu's essence of language. Wittgenstein abandons the very traditional investigation into the logical and scientific usage of language and "discovers" other usages of language: language games. He opens up philosophy to rhetoric and broadens its otherwise exclusive attention to scientific affirmation (apophantic discourse, *lógos apophantikòs*). Language now appears as a dialogical activity, hence its alterity is somehow recognised. But still, it is not the Humboldtian activity of I and Thou creating thought, but rather that of social interaction, a game, where language is still used as an "instrument". And as far as particular languages are concerned, Wittgenstein does not at all change his criticism of natural languages. He still thinks that particular semantics are *Verhexungen*, bewitchments (Wittgenstein 1971 [1953]: § 109), which we have to get rid of. He has no sympathy for the historicity of language. And finally, Wittgenstein has no sympathy for language without practical aims. Language has to work, it has no right to celebrate, *feiern*. But it is precisely what Coseriu calls the autonomy of language that makes this possible: "das Feiern der Sprache", the celebration of language, activity as such. Thus, it is true that there is a wide gap between Wittgenstein's and Coseriu's philosophical positions.[3]

On the other hand, Coseriu is rather friendly with Martin Heidegger. He admits that Heidegger has to say important things about language, e. g. on its quintessential alterity (*Miteinandersein*) in *Sein und Zeit* (1927) and on language as "das Haus des Seins", the "House of Being", in his later philosophy (Kabatek and Murguía 1997: 229).[4] Coseriu admires the great philosopher and, in a striking contrast to his treatment of Wittgenstein, interprets him sympathetically. But Coseriu did not appreciate Heidegger's language and the priestly approach to language. Heidegger was convinced that language manifests the essence of things – and acted accordingly. Without referring explicitly to Heidegger, Coseriu opposes such an attitude: "Man traut der Sprache zuviel zu, wenn man in ihr die Wahrheit der bezeichneten Sachen suchen will" (1971 [1967]: 152), "You give too much credit to language if you want to search it for the truth of the things it designates".

Heidegger separates language from human subjects; language becomes an independent entity outside human activity and the creation of the human mind. It does not seem to be an activity at all since it is a place, the House of Being. This house is the home of the world. Coseriu's considers Heidegger's

---

[3] For another brief but emphatic criticism of Wittgenstein, cf. Coseriu (2003: 12–13).
[4] There is also a rather dark commentary on Heidegger's "Haus des Seins" in Coseriu (1967: 141, fn. 3).

House of Being to be close to his claim that language is the formativity through which the world is given to us. But for Heidegger language *is* the world and therefore he delves into language, not into the world, to look for truth. As far as the historicity or diversity of language in different languages is concerned, we may say that the House of Being has a rather precise geographical place: the Black Forest. Thus, the Being, *das Sein*, is linked to a particular language, German. But German is not understood as a historical language since Heidegger destroys its particularity in two ways: He uses German disregarding the historical traditions of that language by creating an extremely idiosyncratic dialect, and he deletes the historicity of German (together with Greek) by universalising it as the Philosophical Language.

Coseriu certainly could not accept Heidegger's "deconstruction" of the philosophy of language in the German tradition – the heart of Coseriu's philosophy – as a progress but must have seen it as a reactionary and somehow dark and mythical regression. This philosophy of language leaves behind thousands of years of philosophical work on language. It goes back to the Presocratics, when only one language – Greek – existed for thinkers who delved into that language to find true knowledge. Coseriu says about the disciples of Heraclitus: "They follow an etymological research that looks for truth, the *étymon*, in the *onómata*" (2015, I: 29). But that wisdom had already been effectively destroyed by Plato, who analysed Greek words and created a strong sceptical attitude towards language as a source of truth. But these are my own critical observations on Heidegger from what I consider a Coserian viewpoint. We do not have a thorough analysis by Coseriu himself.

We might perhaps consider Coseriu's discussion of Chomsky's linguistics as a chapter on what he has to say about a modern philosophy of language or at least as an example of what he could have done with the other authors. What is striking in his lectures on Chomsky's Transformational Grammar (Coseriu 1970 [1968]) is the depth and fairness of that discussion. Chomsky does not write as a philosopher but as a linguist. Coseriu's opposition to Chomsky's linguistics is also a philosophical one. There are substantial differences regarding what we have put forward as philosophical essentials. First of all, for Chomsky, language is not *hablar*, the concrete activity of speaking. Chomsky reduces the material appearance of language, "performance", to the "competence" underlying it. Yet Coseriu acknowledges that Chomskyan linguistics for the first time introduces the subject of performance as an important problem in linguistics (Coseriu 1970 [1968]: 48). But, in a certain way, Chomsky is a radical believer in the last sentence of the *Cours* – that the only object of linguistics is *la langue* – and he radicalises, like Hjelmslev, *la langue* into something completely formal, without any substance. He calls *langue* "competence", later on I-language, "internal language", which is not even *langue*, a particular historical language, but *le langage*, i.e. the universal innate linguistic capacity of human beings. However, even if language is not the concrete activity of speaking, *enérgeia* in Aristotelian terms, it still is something special to human beings, as a *dýnamis*, a potentiality. Secondly, language is certainly thought, cognition, in Chomsky's view. But this does not mean that it creates "meaning", *Bedeutung*, as in Coseriu's view; it creates specific forms for the combination of mental units. This is the very centre of Chomsky's philosophical convictions: the essence of language is this somehow innate "cognitive" device of the human mind. However, the cognitive nature of language is the common feature of the philosophies of language put forward by Chomsky and Coseriu. Language is a "bildendes Organ des Gedanken" for both of them, but in Chomsky's view it is a very special kind of *Gedanke*, an ensemble of structural features that has nothing to do with Coseriu's *Bedeutung*. Moreover, as far as alterity is concerned, Chomsky's "cognitive" conception of language is not connected to the Other. It is a solipsistic inner mental disposition. Chomsky explicitly excludes the communicative dimension from the essence of language, communication is only a secondary potentiality of usage. Thirdly, as a natural innate feature of the individual biological human being, language cannot be essentially "historical". An individual's speech production is ultimately negligible "performance", and historical languages are "surface" phenomena. Language, for Chomsky, is a universal natural object.

The abyss between Coseriu's philosophy of language and Chomsky's conception of language is clear. But Chomsky's linguistics does include a "philosophical" investigation into the essence of language. And Coseriu appreciated that passionate fight for the essence of language in Chomsky, which he presents in a close and sympathetic reading of his first books.

Thus, it is a pity that Coseriu did not really discuss Wittgenstein's extension of philosophy to language games beyond the scientific discourse and his quite traditional criticism of words (dating back to Bacon and Locke) as "idola fori" or "bewitchments". And we would have appreciated a critical investigation of Heidegger's regression to pre-philosophical times as well, that strange mysterious diving into language that does not even submit language to the critical questions of Plato.

5 Conclusion

To conclude, I would like to come back to the earlier question why Coseriu did not write a "systematic" book on the philosophy of language. Coseriu is not only a philosopher but also a linguist who is looking for the disclosure of the "essential" features of his scientific object – "language" – in the history of philosophy. The two volumes of the *Geschichte der Sprachphilosophie* show that history is *at the same time* the systematic presentation of that philosophy.[5] There is hence no opposition between "systematic" and "historical", they are two aspects of history. In the Hegelian way characteristic of Coseriu's first book, *Sincronía, diacronía e historia* (1958), the essence of language unfolds historically in the development of the philosophical reflections. It is a long process, it is a difficult process, it is not a unidirectional process – it is a process of the slow discovery of the essence of language. And what is good about history is that it has no end. It is open to new insights and new developments.

Thus, it is possible that what is called "language" in the context of the current state of humanity and in the present social and cultural reality will change or even disappear. For instance, we can observe that the historicity of language is in decline, given that the diversity of human languages is decreasing dramatically. Perhaps there will be only one language at the end of this cultural process. What does that mean for the "essence" of language? Or: Certain socio-cultural changes seem to separate the cognitive and the social dimensions of language. On one side, in our modern scientific and technical world, language is severely reduced to clear and scientific denotation. On the other side, ever more people are using language only as a gregarious means of socially being-together without any "cognitive" content in their messages which are more like animal signals than dialogue. The cognitive (semanticity) and the social (alterity) dimensions of language seem to be falling apart. Again: What does that mean for the "essence" of language? Does the disappearance of languages as well as the splitting up of the "essential" dimensions of language create new techniques of developing "thought" and of acting socially? Will this result in there being no language anymore and hence no more human beings, but post-humans and other animals – with a kind of resemblance to former humans? In order to do philosophical research on those anthropological transformations, we may still need language, "Arbeit des Geistes" in its "unabänderlicher Dualismus", the work of the spirit in its unalienable dualism. There is hope for the persistence of the "Wesen des Seins der Sprache".

---

[5] Cf. Forster (2020) for a great presentation of this general characteristic of "continental philosophy".

References

Benveniste, Émile. 1966. *Problèmes de linguistique générale*. Paris: Gallimard.
Chomsky, Noam. 2009 [1966]. *Cartesian linguistics. A chapter in the history of rationalist thought* (third edition). Cambridge: Cambridge University Press.
Coseriu, Eugenio. 1970 [1968]. *Einführung in die transformationelle Grammatik*. Tübingen: Narr.
Coseriu, Eugenio. 1971 [1966]. "Der Mensch und seine Sprache". In: Eugenio Coseriu, *Sprache. Strukturen und Funktionen. XII Aufsätze*, 109–124. Tübingen: Narr.
Coseriu, Eugenio. 1971 [1967]. "Das Phänomen der Sprache und das Daseinsverständnis des heutigen Menschen". In: Eugenio Coseriu, *Sprache. Strukturen und Funktionen. XII Aufsätze*, 131–155. Tübingen: Narr.
Coseriu, Eugenio. 1973 [1962]. *Teoría del lenguaje y lingüística general. Cinco estudios* (third edition). Madrid: Gredos.
Coseriu, Eugenio. 1978 [1958]. *Sincronía, diacronía e historia. El problema del cambio lingüístico* (third edition). Madrid: Gredos.
Coseriu, Eugenio. 1992a. "Zeichen, Symbol, Wort". In: Tilmann Borsche and Werner Stegmaier (eds.), *Zur Philosophie des Zeichens*, 3–27. Berlin & New York: De Gruyter.
Coseriu, Eugenio. 1995b. "Von den *universali fantastici*". In: Jürgen Trabant (ed.), *Vico und die Zeichen – Vico e i segni*, 73–80. Tübingen: Narr.
Coseriu, Eugenio. 2003. "*Orationis fundamenta*. La plegaria como texto". In *RILCE. Revista de filología hispánica* 19:1, 1–25.
Coseriu, Eugenio. 2007 [1980]. *Textlinguistik. Eine Einführung*. Edited by Jörn Albrecht (fourth edition). Tübingen: Narr.
Coseriu, Eugenio. 2015. *Geschichte der Sprachphilosophie*. Vol. 1: *Von Heraklit bis Rousseau*. Vol. 2: *Von Herder bis Humboldt*. Edited by Jörn Albrecht. Tübingen: Narr & Francke, Attempto.
Croce, Benedetto. 1902. *Estetica come scienza dell'espressione e linguistica generale*. Milano, Palermo & Napoli: Sandrone.
De Mauro, Tullio. 1967. *Ludwig Wittgenstein. His place in the development of semantics*. Dordrecht: Reidel.
Forster, Michael N. 2017. Review of E. Coseriu, *Geschichte der Sprachphilosophie* (2015). *Historiographia Linguistica* 44:1, 165–171.
Forster, Michael N. 2020. "Philosophy, history of philosophy, and historicism". In: Efraim Podoksik (ed.), *Doing humanities in nineteenth-century Germany*, 19–39. Leiden & Boston: Brill.
Heidegger, Martin. 1986 [1927]. *Sein und Zeit* (sixteenth edition). Tübingen: Niemeyer.
Heidegger, Martin. 1959: *Unterwegs zur Sprache*. Pfullingen: Neske.
Humboldt, Wilhelm von. 1903–1936. *Gesammelte Schriften* (17 vols.) Edited by Albert Leitzmann et al. Berlin: Behr.
Jakobson, Roman 1971 [1965]. "Quest for the essence of language". In: Roman Jakobson, *Selected Writings*, Vol. 2: *Word and language*, 345–359. Den Haag & Paris: Mouton.
Kabatek, Johannes and Adolfo Murguía. 1997. "*Die Sachen sagen, wie sie sind…*". *Eugenio Coseriu im Gespräch*. Tübingen: Narr.
Pagliaro, Antonino. 1993 [1930]. *Sommario di linguistica arioeuropea*. Palermo: Novecento (reprint 1993).

Pareyson, Luigi. 1960 [1954]. *Estetica. Teoria della formatività*. Bologna: Zanichelli.
Saussure, Ferdinand de. 1975 [1916]. *Cours de linguistique générale*. Edited by Tullio De Mauro. Paris: Payot.
Terracini, Benvenuto. 1966. *Analisi stilistica. Teoria, storia, problemi*. Milano: Feltrinelli.
Trabant, Jürgen. 2003. *Mithridates im Paradies. Kleine Geschichte des Sprachdenkens*. München: Beck.
Trabant, Jürgen. 2018. "Über Humboldts Trias von Zeichen, Wort und Bild". In: *In memoriam Josef Simon. Alma Mater. Beiträge zur Geschichte der Universität Bonn*. 110. Bonn: Bouvier, 36–54.
Wittgenstein, Ludwig. 1963 [1921]. *Tractatus logico-philosophicus*. Frankfurt am Main: Suhrkamp.
Wittgenstein, Ludwig. 1971 [1953]. *Philosophische Untersuchungen*. Frankfurt am Main: Suhrkamp.

Ana Agud (Salamanca)
Eugenio Coseriu's approach to language and linguistics: building a 'philosophically sustainable' linguistics

> *Many linguists, jealous of an improper autonomy, mistrust philosophy, which is the true science of principles.*
>
> "Saying things as they are..."*

1 Introduction

At the beginning of the twentieth century a true paradigm shift took place in the scientific study of language. Or at least this is what the most prominent linguists of the period thought about themselves. From Bloomfield, Sapir, Saussure and others onward, 'modern linguists' openly declared that they were inaugurating a new era of approaching language as an autonomous object of study, no longer at the service of other disciplines such as philology but for its own sake. This conception of linguistic research was the result of a decision to replace traditional grammar as well as historical and comparative linguistics with an approach of languages as objective phenomena and scientific objects in their own right. This new science rejected any form of treating languages in terms of normative grammar and claimed to be able to describe languages as they are actually spoken and/or written.

This new beginning paralleled analogous developments of finding new foundations for other human sciences such as anthropology, psychology and sociology. Linguistics soon became like a paradigm for them, since in the recent past historical and comparative linguists had discovered regularities in the development of languages which seemed very similar to 'natural laws', or so they were initially interpreted. This had opened a new perspective on human sciences, and it fostered the hope that they could eventually compete with the exact sciences in accuracy, cogency and predictive power.

A number of new theoretical principles was generally adopted by modern linguistics. These principles constitute what is generally known as 'structural-

---

* "[M]uchos lingüistas, celosos de una autonomía impropia, consideran con desconfianza a la filosofía, que es la ciencia misma de los principios" (Coseriu 1978 [1958]: 217, n. 63). "Die Sachen sagen, wie sie sind..." (Kabatek and Murguía 1997 [title]).

ism', which soon became the most common methodological approach, developing many variants. Its approach to linguistic 'facts' was generally somewhat simplistic. A basic assumption was that language 'in itself' is a social systematic code speakers 'use' or 'apply' in order to communicate their ideas, and which can be directly observed and analysed. This perspective was not entirely new, but it is difficult to overestimate the general conviction that linguistics could be carried out like the 'proper sciences'.

In the course of the nineteenth century, when the human sciences developed in a spectacular fashion, scientists concluded that there is a fundamental difference between the human sciences and the exact sciences. This conclusion presupposes that 'nature' and 'culture' (or 'history') are opposite notions and that culture is a fundamentally different object of research as compared to natural objects. One of the most accurate and influential treatments of this subject was provided by Hermann Paul in his famous *Prinzipien der Sprachgeschichte* (Paul 1920 [1880]). 'Phonetic laws' were also soon understood as generalizations of historical processes whose occurrence cannot be predicted. By contrast, many modern linguists increasingly denied the importance of the difference between nature and culture and fantasized about the unification of all sciences under the umbrella of a basically naturalistic scientific paradigm. This ideology is commonly called 'scientism' and it still dominates the linguistic landscape today: it is now customary to find linguistic accounts based on mathematics (algorithms, formal logic, mathematical logic), statistical analysis ('big data') etc.

In the late 1950s, Eugenio Coseriu burst onto this landscape with an unusual critical attitude towards many aspects of structuralism. He was acutely aware of the shortcomings inherent in the most basic concepts of structuralism and wanted to overcome them from the very beginning. Coseriu was convinced that language only in part consists of 'structures'. His knowledge covered a wide range of ancient and modern languages and he also had an impressive command of world literature (not only Western); he had moreover thoroughly studied most grammars and linguistic theories in the Western tradition. But his most important asset was the thorough education in philosophy he had received. He was familiar with the work of all the important Western philosophers, including Hegel, and he had developed a sophisticated account of Wilhelm von Humboldt's ideas about the nature and the study of language. This also meant that Coseriu's approach to language stood in stark contrast to the approach favoured by most of his contemporaries.

Coseriu initiated a thorough revision of the linguistic concepts of both European and American structuralism. In the following decades he went on correcting naïve conceptions of language and elaborated his own approach based on partly new and coherent distinctions, concepts and heuristic categories. He also taught and gave lectures about the history of linguistics and of the philosophy of language, which were partly recorded and subsequently edited and published by students (cf., e.g., Coseriu 2015). In the early seventies, Coseriu also gave a series of lectures on Chomsky's generative grammar, which at the time was gradually becoming the new mainstream in linguistics all over the world (cf. Coseriu 1970 [1968], 1975 [1971]). His thorough criticism of Chomsky cost him dearly. Although his achievements both in theoretical and empirical linguistics were overwhelming, they were largely neglected in the dominant schools of the language sciences. It seems that Coseriu belongs to a long tradition of critical thinkers who are primarily ignored because of the difficulty of following them on their most demanding paths.

In this article, I aim to show why and how Coseriu developed his own scientific approach, which surpassed the extant ones in many respects in philosophical breadth and consistency. I argue that Coseriu intended above all to found a 'philosophically sustainable linguistics'. This task proved very difficult, since most of modern linguistics had largely ignored the advances in critical philosophy of language to which Coseriu subscribed. This meant that Coseriu's approach was – and remains – at odds with mainstream linguistics, to which it was opposed in many ways. There can be no doubt that the philosophical complexity of Coseriu's approach to the study of language is an important obstacle to its reception within a scholarly context in which reductionism and scientism continue to loom large.

2 The conceptual revolution of *Sincronía, diacronía e historia* (1958)

Coseriu was appointed as a professor of General and Indo-European Linguistics at the University of Montevideo in Uruguay in 1951. In this remote place, far from the centres of European and American linguistics, he published a monograph, *Sincronía, diacronía e historia* (1958; 1978 [1958]), for a contest at his university because he "needed the money", as he once told me (cf. Kabatek and Murguía 1997: 93). The book provides a synthesis of Coseriu's central ideas about language and linguistics which he had developed in Europe during the difficult previous years of the Second World War and its immediate aftermath. As he recounts in *"Die Sachen sagen, wie sie sind..."*, he succeeded to escape from his menaced Moldavian homeland in 1940 and then lived in Italy for several years, making a living doing all kinds of jobs (Kabatek and Murguía 1997: Ch. 1–2). He studied in Rome with prominent Italian linguists and philosophers, who were all familiar with German thought, and earned two doctoral degrees (in Slavonic linguistics in Rome and in philosophy in Milan). When he eventually started his academic position in South-America, he began what might be considered a ground-breaking career in linguistics and the theory of language.

Unlike most of his peers in Europe and America, whose linguistic research was mostly characterized by a mixture of traditional and new terminology (the latter partly borrowed from other sciences), Coseriu decidedly sided with nineteenth-century historicism and tried to reconcile the historical conception of language with the structural description of linguistic systems. However, he acknowledged the primacy of the historical treatment of language and maintained that "language history, not language description, is the authentic and 'integral' science of language, the only one which truly responds to its object of study, since only language history is able to identify and understand the dynamicity as such, with all its determinations" (Kabatek and Murguía 1997: 163). He was moreover aware of the fact that the language of professional linguists is itself historical and that an essential part of its actual meanings is also derived from their history. This is why it was important to Coseriu to not only investigate individual languages from a historical perspective, but also the history of the language sciences and the whole of its conceptual and terminological apparatus, which is a decisive part of linguistics conceived as a hermeneutic discipline (cf. Agud 1981, supervised by Coseriu and devoted to this problem).

Coseriu (1978 [1958]) opposes a widespread linguistic ideology, which divided linguistics into two opposing branches: research of the historical development of particular linguistic phenomena, on the one hand, and the description of a specific language state at a certain moment in time in terms of systematic oppositions between the elements of the 'code'. Saussure had expressed this view in his famous *Cours de linguistique générale* (1975 [1916]) in such a clear manner that it subsequently became something of a methodological and theoretical dogma for decades. The contrast between synchronic and diachronic linguistics was moreover considered to refer to an actual difference in language itself. Languages were viewed as systematic 'codes', and the evidence that they change over time thus became enigmatic and had to be explained. Linguists asked themselves "why languages change", as if properly speaking they should not.

Coseriu, following Humboldt, proposed a diametrically opposed view: language is an ongoing free activity of individual speakers, who follow the patterns of previous linguistic experience, but only as reference points which can either be confirmed or not. Since speaking occurs in a historical context among persons with different backgrounds and different expressive needs, each time the activity of speaking reinvents its models, either confirming the previous habits or introducing new ones, which in turn either remain individual initiatives or get adopted by others and eventually substitute the previous way of speaking, becoming the new model (Coseriu 1978 [1958]: 108–110). Under this view, the question is not why languages change, but rather why they do not change even more, why most models remain unaltered for a long time instead of being modified (cf. Vîrban 2020). Thus, change is the natural outcome of the historical nature of language. Relative stability of linguistic habits and models within a linguistic community is due to the general desire of speakers to ensure that what they say is understandable (and acceptable), even though there are so many things that change in the environment and in the individuals themselves that speaking habits are bound to alter in time.

Note that these ideas about linguistic change are essentially pre-scientific. They are not the result of applying any scientific method, but reflect a preliminary understanding of language that precedes language as a scientific object of enquiry. This preliminary understanding is as speculative as the alternative view of standard structuralism with which it contrasts. However, Coseriu's account of linguistic change betokens a novel philosophical approach to language and linguistics, although it does not present itself as such. It moreover forces us to re-assess the generally accepted structuralist ideology in order to find out what the underlying pre-scientific or speculative background of this ideology is like, what kind of philosophy of language and linguistics it supports.

Probably the strongest theoretical assumption of both structuralism and scientism in linguistics follows from a kind of obsession with obtaining a well-defined, autonomous object of research whose study can be approached for its own sake, from outside and at the same time by relying on immediate intuitions about its nature. Any preliminary critical reflection on human language seems to be either forgotten or rejected beforehand. This also entails the relation of language to human thinking in general, which has a long history in Western thought. The straightforward self-understanding of the old grammarians is restored instead, but their normative claims are replaced by the commitment of purely descriptive science. Coseriu strongly opposes this attitude. He maintains that linguistics needs philosophy because philosophy, unlike natural sciences and mathematics, is the "true science of principles" (Coseriu 1978 [1958]: 217, n. 63). The need for such principles guiding linguistics had already been forcefully expressed by Hermann Paul as early as 1880 (cf. also Coseriu 1980 and Albrecht, this volume). Its implications are far-reaching.

The first philosophical principle underpinning Coseriu's methodological turn is Paul's claim that language is no natural object but a cultural object, and that its study has therefore to be historical (Paul 1920 [1880]: 1 and *passim*). Coseriu adds to this claim the Kantian distinction between the 'realm of necessity' and the 'realm of liberty', and he assigns language to the domain of "liberty, intentionality, invention, free creation and adoption, whose motivations are exclusively purposive (Sp. *motivadas sólo finalísticamente*)" (Coseriu 1978 [1958]: 193). He therefore rejects any form of causal explanations in linguistic accounts:

> "The problem of linguistic change cannot and should not be treated in causal terms (Sp. *en términos causales*)" (Coseriu 1978 [1958]: 14). "Language does not belong to the *domain of causes* (Sp. *orden causal*), but to the *domain of purposes* (Sp. *orden final*)" (29). "[C]ultural and functional explanations of changes are in no way 'causal'" (178). "Language changes because language is *nothing already made* (Sp. *no está hecha*), but it *is being made* (Sp. *se hace*) all the time by linguistic activity. [...] Speaking is creative activity, free and purposive (Sp. *finalista*), and it is new each time, since it is determined by an individual, actual and unprecedented expressive purpose (Sp. *una finalidad expresiva individual, actual e inédita*)" (69) (emphases in the original).

This approach to human language builds on what has been labelled 'linguistic idealism', for which the work of Wilhelm von Humboldt is an important inspiration. Generally speaking, the idealistic conception of human language does not divide human personality into two mutually independent realms of thinking and speaking. Instead it maintains that individuals' consciousness *is* their language. Language, Humboldt (1963 [1836]: 383) writes, "is the organ of the inner being, or rather it is this very being as it arrives step by step to inner knowledge and expression" ("ist das Organ des inneren Seyns, dies Seyn selbst, wie es nach und nach zur inneren Erkenntnis und zur Aeusserung gelangt"). According to this view, human beings form their perceptions and ideas in accordance with the pathways of speaking which have been conventionalized in historical languages. Speaking is an individual act of "re-creating" (G. *Wiedererzeugung*) the results of previous patterns of speech and their constitutive parts in view of individual expressive goals. Strictly speaking, we do not 'use' words, we 'create' them more or less like on previous occasions, depending on what we aim to convey in each instance. Humboldt emphasized that each language draws around the individuals of a linguistic community "a circle we can only leave if we enter that of another language" ("einen Kreis, aus dem nur insofern hinauszugehen möglich ist, als man zugleich in den Kreis einer andren [Sprache] hinübertritt", Humboldt 1963 [1836]: 434). This entails that thinking cannot take place outside of language, according to Humboldt, we are always "inside" language. We can undoubtedly broaden the horizon of our thoughts, but then only if we enter other circles of language.

Coseriu was strongly committed to this Humboldtian philosophical approach, but it must be stressed that he also, and even primarily, was interested in 'doing linguistics', and specifically structural-functional linguistics. For this to accomplish he had to reconcile the aforementioned idealistic point of view, according to which it is impossible to step outside language and distance oneself from its cognitive purview, with the kind of scientific objectivity demanded by the language sciences. But how can a linguist be simultaneously within and outside language, remain a speaker with an individual horizon of understanding and be nonetheless a scholar who analyses language and speech in an objective manner? This, I contend, is the philosophical crux of linguistics.

3 The theoretical paradox of structuralism

Coseriu has to my knowledge never been explicit about the inherently paradoxical starting point of scientific linguistic enquiry and never developed any systematic philosophy of language and linguistics of his own. However, he was consistently concerned with such questions and provided answers to them on several occasions. He elaborated the philosophical claims put forward in *Sincronía, diacronía e historia* (1958) in many publications in which he conceptualizes language in such a way as to emphasize the difference with the reduced 'object' of structural-functional descriptions of linguistic systems. For Coseriu, a linguistic system is an ontologically real level of language: that of the common, structured patterns of speech within a particular linguistic community at a specific time. He carefully distinguished this level of language from other aspects of speech, above all from the actual speech of individuals and 'normal language use', i.e. the conventionalized instantiations of the possibilities offered by the language system (cf., in particular, Coseriu 1973 [1952]).

Modern linguistics has developed into a plethora of new disciplines such as pragmatics, sociolinguistics, discourse analysis, psycholinguistics, neurolinguistics, etc., which are largely carried out in terms of more or less autonomous approaches to language. In contrast to these disciplines, Coseriu was determined from the very beginning to apply his analytical methods to the *whole* of language, i.e. all the linguistic levels he considered relevant, with a view to laying the foundations for an 'Integral Linguistics' that addresses human language in its entirety (Kabatek and Murguía 1997: 157 ff.). In this respect, his outline of a comprehensive structural-functional approach of the processes and mechanisms of actual speech in his article "Determinación y entorno" (Coseriu 1973 [1955]) is particularly noteworthy, as is his account of the semantics of texts in his *Textlinguistik* (Coseriu 2007 [1980]). However, he always kept in mind that different objects demand different methodologies, because in language nothing is an autonomous 'object' per se. This entails that many aspects and properties of actual speech have to be excluded from a structural-functional analysis of language. They have to be identified as objects of enquiry and analysed according to the fitting methodology that is required, in each case, by the 'constitution' of the object and the 'purpose' of the corresponding analysis.

Regarding the level of 'historical systems', Coseriu (1978 [1958]: 57) maintains that every speaker knows with certainty how to speak, that is, how to express oneself in accordance to the systematic patterns shared by his or her fellow men in the language community at all levels: the phonetic, morphological, syntactic, semantic, and pragmatic level. And although speakers occasionally produce utterances that hardly qualify as systematic, they 'know' how the system works, according to which they act. In other words, they possess a 'reliable intuition' of the language system. Thus, it is true that the systematic level is only one of many levels, but it is a *real* one. Contrary to Hermann Paul (Paul 1920 [1880]: 24), for Coseriu the systematic level of language is no "abstract construction of grammarians and linguists".

The kind of linguistic knowledge speakers possess has been the subject of many discussions. For the nineteenth-century historical-comparative linguists this was essentially an 'unconscious' knowledge. Much later, Chomsky determined it not as knowledge proper, but as 'cognizing', a term intended to distinguish linguistic competence both from conscious and unconscious knowledge, thus securing that its treatment by linguists could be kept apart both from epistemology and psychology (for an epistemological criticism on Chomsky's 'cognizing', cf. Hacker and Baker 1985). Coseriu rejects the old idea that knowledge of language is an unconscious knowledge. He instead proposes to characterize knowledge of language in terms of the now more common idea of 'know-how' (Kabatek and Murguía 1997: 164, 178): speakers know how to speak, and linguistic analysis consists in raising this intuitive know-how to the level of explicit knowledge and consciousness. This view involves a series of theoretical problems relating to the very concept of 'consciousness', which has become fashionable due to recent advances in neurosciences. It is now commonly assumed that we are conscious of those contents we actually express in language. Such a view actually transposes the problems related to the concept of consciousness to the no less problematic concept of 'language'. The role of unconscious neural processes in the activity of speaking remains an open question, arguably to be approached from the perspectives of both linguistics and neurosciences. But the latter are still far from having developed adequate tools to connect basic neural research with language, while linguistics simply lacks the means of making empirical claims in this domain and is thus forced to remain a hermeneutical enterprise.[1]

---

[1] In a forthcoming book, *Critical philosophy of language and linguistics*, I further elaborate on

Coseriu has never presented a complete and detailed discussion of the concepts 'consciousness' and 'the unconscious'. He was convinced that linguistic analysis is possible without tracing linguistic phenomena back to their interior psychological sources. He relied on the phenomenological assumption that, whatever the ultimate impulses to speak may be, the activity of speaking follows in each case identifiable patterns which can be inferred from their actual realizations in actual speech (Coseriu 1978 [1958]: 50 and *passim*). This claim raises the problem how to identify those patterns with certainty and in an objective way. We are all accustomed to speaking of nouns, adjectives, verbs, morphemes, phonemes, etc., and this discourse works fine within the community of linguists, in particular with regard to Indo-European languages. But it should be borne in mind that all these concepts and terms, too, arose in history as answers to concrete questions and points of view that are themselves also part of history. Nothing guarantees that the facts to which these concepts and terms refer have an objective existence. Furthermore, virtually all concepts and terms are used in different ways by different linguists. There is no 'phoneme in itself' whose true nature we have to find out or define. Terms like 'phoneme' are verbal strategies of particular linguists in order to approach aspects of language previously unnoticed, and they become determined or defined because of the linguists' purposes of making them useful to solve some new problem. Their 'conceptual substance' is the complex of the historical circumstances that has given rise to ever new questions and that enable each linguist to answer such questions from his or her personal background and based on his or her own ingenuity and familiarity with previous scholarly work. The common use of concepts and terms within the academic community does not in itself prove that they are good answers to good questions. Ultimately, history always overtakes each individual approach or common use, because perspectives change and new questions and theoretical requirements appear.

4 Linguistic scepticism and Coseriu's way of escaping it

Viewing human language primarily as an ongoing, free historical activity or *enérgeia* leads to a form of conceptual relativism or scepticism. Linguists cannot en-

---

these ideas and present a critical approach to language and consciousness in which I draw on the European tradition of critical philosophy (mainly I. Kant, G. W. F. Hegel, W. von Humboldt and J. Simon), which is unjustly ignored in present-day cognitive sciences.

tirely rely on their own language because the words they use are formed in each case according to contingent variables, and one and the same word may refer to different things or ideas. This fact is not accounted for by simply assuming that words are 'polysemous': 'polysemy' is a linguistic concept which applies to words whose invariant meanings are already acknowledged.

Normally, utterances (above all in prose[2]) strongly suggest that their reference is entirely clear, certain and unequivocal. Conversely, 'misunderstanding' is generally considered a contingent failure of an otherwise properly working communicative system. As a matter of fact, speakers have to rely on their language because they need to believe in a reliable and stable relation between language and the environment as well as other speakers. We have to believe that our words are names of really existing things and that everybody understands them the same way as we do. However, there are many proofs to the contrary. The very fact that this belief works fine in normal situations does not prove that words in any conceivable sense mirror reality (cf. Agud, forthcoming). Misunderstandings, like beliefs that ultimately prove false, are just the outcome of the fact that our speech merely enacts behavioural patterns shared by people in their linguistic community, processed within our individual minds and brains in a subtle, non-observable way, involving our memories, recombining those patterns according to ever new situations and expressive impulses and expanding them – also metaphorically – to ever new experiences (cf. Mauthner 1982 [1901–1902]). This applies to colloquial speech and academic discourse alike. The only way we can circumvent this gap between language and reality is by applying the pragmatic strategy of formal and experimental sciences that consists in turning away from natural language and restricting the vocabulary and syntax to strictly specified 'formal languages'. Unfortunately, such a strategy cannot be applied to natural language because that would obviously be circular: it is impossible to comprehend natural language with the tools of a restricted formal language. The theory of metalanguage has long recognised that natural language is the first and 'highest' metalanguage of all more or less formalized languages.

The above observations entail that we can understand common linguistic accounts, in contrast to the terminology developed within the confines of formal languages, as a form of actual speech produced by individual scholars, in

---

[2] Authors such as Fritz Mauthner (1982 [1901–1902]) and Antonio Machado (1988) argue that poetry is free from the objectivistic delusions characteristic of prose. Poetry, the argument goes, does not suggest any conceptual cogency but presents itself directly as what language actually always is: a personal expression in accordance with specific speaking habits, yet capable of going beyond these habits by investing them with individual intuitions, sensations and feelings.

other words, as the narrative of individual linguists. We are therefore obliged to proceed hermeneutically when we enter in dialogue with other linguists, i.e. as individuals encountering other individuals: we try to intuit the issues and concerns other linguists raise and judge their success or failure from the vantage point of our own horizon of understanding. Coseriu himself acknowledged that "the whole of linguistics is hermeneutics" (Kabatek and Murguía 1997: 151). On this particular issue, Coseriu largely agrees with scholars such as Esa Itkonen (cf. López-Serena 2009).

This way of approaching natural language and of focussing on words not as reliable tools of knowledge, but as individual efforts of expressing subjective convictions and attitudes, producing narratives which cannot reach reality beyond speakers' own subjectivity, continues the sceptical tradition of thinkers such as Pyrrho, Sextus Empiricus, Fritz Mauthner, Josef Simon, among others. This sceptical tradition has never imposed itself in the history of the humanities. This is not surprising, it defies one of the most basic psychological needs of human beings, which is why it is a constantly suppressed tradition in Western thought. Coseriu rejected all forms of scepticism and relativism, but he did not ignore the deep epistemological problems raised by the aforementioned authors and he certainly acknowledged their importance. The point I would like to stress is that Coseriu laid the basis for a well-founded, coherent and singularly comprehensive approach to language despite the sceptics' warnings.

In order to avoid confusions, either derived from an uncritical attitude towards existing scholarship or from the ignorance of both the history of linguistics and the philosophy of language, Coseriu initially spent a lot of time and energy clarifying the basic concepts and terminology of both European and American structuralism, the major paradigms after World War II (cf. Kabatek and Murguía 1997: 185). Of course, this was a task he could not undertake 'from the outside', since his own language and his own horizon of understanding were in turn inherited from the linguistic and philosophical tradition in which he had been educated.

Coseriu's approach to language is conceived 'from the inside'. He adopts as a point of departure the preliminary, intuitive and original knowledge speakers possess of their own language and speech (Coseriu 1978 [1958]: 57 ff.; cf. Kabatek and Murguía 1997: 167, about the speaker's "*saber originario*"), despite the danger that speakers are deluded by language, assuming that it mirrors reality. Coseriu takes into account the actual belief of speakers that words are names of (concepts of) things, real as well as imagined. Words have specific features the linguist is able to identify through analysing texts and finding out how each element (sound, word, etc.) contrasts with other elements that might fit into the same context. The fact that Coseriu adopts the classical phonology of N. Trubetzkoj (Willems 2019) as a methodological tool to pursue this project has been levelled against Coseriu as a naïve transposition of phonological analysis onto other linguistic levels. But this criticism is unjustified: the classical phonological analysis applies to linguistic sounds because it reflects a general feature of human language, its particular 'logic', which is basically inclusive with regard to all parts of language and therefore to some extent fuzzy. Linguistic sounds contrast among themselves like words do, viz. not simply opposing *a* to *not-a*, but as far as necessary or convenient in each case within a certain "zone" of values and features (Coseriu 1992 [1988]: 215–216).

It is worthwhile to ponder what the implications are of a linguistic account from a critical epistemological perspective. How can such an account be carried out while paying attention to the sceptical warning that the linguists' language faces the same challenge of being incapable of mirroring reality as the language of normal speakers? To my knowledge, Coseriu has never explicitly addressed this question, but there are nevertheless some clues scattered throughout his work that provide important indications of how he meets this challenge. Acknowledging that linguistics is a hermeneutic activity undertaken 'from the inside' entails that linguists are aware of the fact that their words are interpretations of facts or, better still, that these words designate already interpreted facts, not 'things in themselves'. It also means that the interpretation of something as a linguistic fact, or rather as a fact interpreted in such or such a way, is an individual act in each case. Finally, and most importantly, it means that linguistic categories, like all concepts, are the results of individual efforts to subsume matters of language under one's own categorial system, for which one is therefore also responsible.

Coseriu stressed that scholars must "say things as they are", even though he acknowledged that this might be very difficult, perhaps even impossible. But "we always have to try" ("man muss sich immer anstrengen", Kabatek and Murguía 1997: 185). On the one hand, this is of course a truism: no serious person tries not to say things as they are. On the other hand, with regard to linguistics we are aware of the abovementioned linguistic delusion, we actually cannot know how things (including linguistic things) really are 'in themselves'. We only know things through the mediation of our language or languages. We necessarily identify facts from the point of view of the categorial networks of our historical and professional languages, but fortunately we are aware of those networks and we can explore their particular features. This is only possible by explicitly or implicitly comparing them with each other. I would not be able to identify the particular properties of my mother tongue Spanish if I had no experience with other languages and categorial alternatives. Coseriu did not explicitly state this, as far as I know, but based on my experience as one of his students and my interpretation of his work, I venture to characterize his methodological attitude in these terms. Coseriu conceived his scholarly work (as well as his life) from a multilingual perspective as a matter of principle, which was moreover substantially enriched by his vast knowledge of the literatures in many languages. Although he did not systematically practice comparative linguistics, he was in fact all the time comparing words, structures and concepts from the point of view of the most diverse languages and linguistic traditions.

Languages are the channels through which experiences of all kinds are made conscious through speech. Languages change in time and space, but at each moment, Coseriu assumes, they are real active structures in our minds and brains[3] which condition our speech. Languages are thus part of our individual memories. They do not determine what we say, but they strongly influence how we say things. Although the academic language of linguists is susceptible to the same changes, we assume that there are relatively stable and unitary patterns of speech at a certain time and in a certain place. It is therefore reasonable and useful to identify distinct elements within languages and subsume them under the linguist's own categories, provided – and this is decisive – that the linguist is willing to extend his own horizon of understanding as much as possible. This attitude requires a broad education: knowledge of categorial alternatives in actual as well as ancient languages, along with a broad knowledge of culture, including literature, art, philosophy and history.

Coseriu's scholarly work is not to be misunderstood as a new 'metaphysics' of language. It is more appropriately characterized as grounded in a 'negative dialectics', which consists in a critical analysis of the categories and concepts of predecessors as well as contemporaries, not only in order to identify differences and similarities but also, and primarily, with a view to – in Hegelian terms – their *Aufhebung*, i.e. 'overcoming', through Coseriu's own heuristic categories. He applied these categories in a great number of accounts of particular linguistic features, always based on real data drawn from texts, and he made a series of methodological proposals for approaching aspects of language such as actual speech and texts. Much like Aristotle, Coseriu's scholarly work bears testimony to a powerful imagination and the ability to design a highly coherent system of new categories in order to capture the defining features of the objects of analysis. That is also why Coseriu's analyses and interpretations are both innovative an thought-provoking and why others can build on them in future research.

---

3 I deliberately add the term "brain" because although Coseriu himself consistently refrained from using this term, I believe that Coseriu's approach to language is entirely compatible with most results of contemporary neurosciences. However, I cannot further develop this argument in the present article.

Many of Coseriu's conceptual distinctions are designed to avoid common confusions, in particular between the level of empirical facts and the methods used to analyse them. Basic distinctions like the important distinction between *system*, *norm* and *speech* (Coseriu 1973 [1952]) do not, properly speaking, refer to 'things' themselves but to perspectives of the linguist, since in actual speech they are intertwined, and it is often a matter of perspective if one attributes particular features to one or the other level. Similarly, the difference between synchrony and diachrony is shown by Coseriu to be a difference in analytical perspective, not one between facts (Coseriu 1978 [1958]: 14ff.). The same applies to his very useful distinction between language in general (the universal level of language), the level of the 'historical' languages and their systems, and the individual or particular linguistic know-how of speakers (Coseriu 2007 [1988]). These are all methodological distinctions that serve the purpose of integrating various empirical analyses into a larger theoretical framework, which simultaneously takes into account the limitations of each structural-functional categorization and the need to keep in mind that the only real goal of linguistics is the whole of language and speech (recall Hegel's famous dictum: "Das Wahre ist das Ganze" [true is the whole]). According to Coseriu, whenever something is given a name and turned into an object of enquiry, one's perspective is necessarily partial and one cannot but ignore the whole. As a consequence, a particular linguistic account can only claim epistemological legitimacy if it succeeds in clarifying its position relative to the whole of language, i.e. language as everyone may imagine it.

5 Conclusion

The main claim I have put forward in this article is that no linguist is able to transcend his own subjectivity and conceive language as it is 'in itself'. No linguistic theory can draw its epistemological legitimacy based on the claim that it is true because of any real *adaequatio ad rem*. The study of language has to proceed 'from the inside', and the only kind of 'objective distance' to language linguists may obtain is the *degree of consciousness* regarding the linguistic and cultural conditions they have acquired through learning several languages, through comparative and historical research of various different linguistic traditions, and through own experience, reflection and observation.

Although Coseriu certainly belongs to the tradition of European structuralism, his scholarly work is definitely not restricted to this tradition. Coseriu is perhaps the only linguist who actually justified structuralist methods through a comprehensive criticism of their theoretical assumptions and the implications of their linguistic vocabularies. His own analyses as well as the diverse methodological categories he introduced are therefore, epistemologically, particularly well substantiated. He succeeded in convincing many readers and colleagues who actually read him that he had examined in depth all the conditions of his approach, and that he did not limit himself to simply applying structural schemas to particular facts of language. Instead, he combined his analytical work with a theoretical framework that builds on the knowledge of the history of both grammar and the philosophy of language, having submitted every idea and analytic approach to thorough scrutiny. It is the verifiable broadness and complexity of this specifically cultural attitude, together with a brilliant intelligence and a nearly miraculous memory, which makes that his scholarly work stands out, in terms of a critical approach to language and linguistics, among the linguists of his time. In the final analysis, his achievements, like those of everyone else, have no other legitimacy than the quality of his individual language. It is a pity that only relatively few linguists have bothered to study this language, to share its critical level and its empirical richness, and to profit from Coseriu's lasting insights into the very nature of human language. Let's hope that this, too, will change in due course.

References

Agud, Ana. 1981. *Historia y teoría de los casos*. Madrid: Gredos.
Agud, Ana. Forthcoming. *Critical philosophy of language and linguistics: a humanistic, historical and comparative approach.*
Coseriu, Eugenio. 1973 [1952]. "Sistema, norma y habla". In: E. Coseriu, *Teoría del lenguaje y lingüística general. Cinco estudios*, 11–113. Madrid: Gredos.
Coseriu, Eugenio. 1973 [1955]. "Determinación y entorno. Dos problemas de una lingüística del hablar". In: E. Coseriu, *Teoría del lenguaje y lingüística general. Cinco estudios*, 282–323. Madrid: Gredos.
Coseriu, Eugenio. 1973 [1962]. *Teoría del lenguaje y lingüística general. Cinco estudios* (third edition). Madrid: Gredos.
Coseriu, Eugenio. 1978 [1958]. *Sincronía, diacronía e historia. El problema del cambio lingüístico* (third edition). Madrid: Gredos.
Coseriu, Eugenio. 1970 [1968]. *Einführung in die transformationelle Grammatik*. Tübingen: Narr.
Coseriu, Eugenio. 1975 [1971]. *Leistung und Grenzen der transformationellen Grammatik*. Tübingen: Narr.
Coseriu, Eugenio. 1980. "Vom Primat der Geschichte". *Sprachwissenschaft* 5, 125–145.
Coseriu, Eugenio. 2007 [1980]. *Textlinguistik. Eine Einführung*. Edited by Jörn Albrecht (fourth edition). Tübingen: Narr.
Coseriu, Eugenio. 1992 [1988]. *Einführung in die allgemeine Sprachwissenschaft* (second edition). Tübingen: Francke. (German translation of Coseriu 1981.)

Coseriu, Eugenio. 2007 [1988]. *Sprachkompetenz. Grundzüge der Theorie des Sprechens*. Edited by Heinrich Weber (second edition). Tübingen: Narr.

Coseriu, Eugenio. 2015. *Geschichte der Sprachphilosophie*. 2 vols. Tübingen: Narr.

Hacker, Peter and Gordon Baker. 1985. *Language, sense and nonsense. A critical investigation into modern theories of language*. Oxford: Blackwell.

Humboldt, Wilhelm von. 1963 [1836]. *Über die Verschiedenheit des menschlichen Sprachbaues und ihren Einfluss auf die geistige Entwicklung des Menschengeschlechts (1830–1835)*. In: *Schriften zur Sprache*. Edited by Andreas Flitner and Klaus Giel, 368–756 Darmstadt: Wissenschaftliche Buchgesellschaft.

Kabatek, Johannes and Adolfo Murguía. 1997. *"Die Sachen sagen, wie sie sind…"*, *Eugenio Coseriu im Gespräch*. Tübingen: Narr.

López Serena, Araceli. 2009. "Intuition, acceptability and grammaticality: a reply to Riemer". *Language Sciences* 31:5, 634–648.

Machado, Antonio. 1988. *Poesía y Prosa I-IV*. Ed. by Oreste Macrí. Madrid: Espasa Calpe.

Mauthner, Fritz. 1982 [1901–1902]. *Beiträge zu einer Kritik der Sprache*. 3 vols. New edition. Frankfurt am Main, Berlin & Wien: Ullstein.

Paul, Hermann. 1920 [1880]. *Prinzipien der Sprachgeschichte* (5th edition). Halle: Max Niemeyer.

Saussure, Ferdinand de. 1975 [1916]. *Cours de linguistique générale*. Edited by T. De Mauro. Paris: Payot.

Vîrban, Floarea. 2020. "Language change *versus* language non-change: the peculiar issue of language identity". Paper presented at the Coseriu conference in Cádiz, Spain, January 2020.

Willems, Klaas. 2019. "Eugenio Coserius Sprachzeichentheorie und der Prager Strukturalismus". In: Tomáš Hoskovec (ed.), *Travaux du Cercle linguistique de Prague. Nouvelle Série* 8 (*Expérience et avenir du structuralisme*), 469–503. Kanina: OPS & Praha: PLK.

Part II: **History of the language sciences**

Gerda Haßler (Potsdam)
Coseriu as a historiographer of linguistics in relation to his linguistic ideas

*You have certainly often noticed that what is new in the literature frequently turns out to be already old.**

Eugenio Coseriu's reflections on earlier epochs of thinking about language began early in his academic career. His treatment of the history of linguistics does not present itself as a hunt for predecessors or as a reference to earlier ideas that have been forgotten. Rather, it draws on paradigmatic approaches whose potential effects are timeless and can be revived under new conditions (cf. Haßler 2016). Coseriu's publications on the history of linguistics fall into two types that differ fundamentally in their format and objectives. On the one hand, there is the large-scale *Geschichte der Sprachphilosophie* based on his lectures and edited by students (Coseriu 1969–1972; 2015). On the other hand, he published several smaller historiographical studies in which he sketched the horizon of retrospection regarding the topics he dealt with in remarkable depth. In this article, I will first describe the connection between the historical and philosophical points of view in relation to Coseriu's own theory of language. I will then go on to discuss the identification of certain elements of structural semantics in the work of nineteenth-century authors, and I conclude with an analysis of a number of corrections that Coseriu proposed to traditional views of persons and terms in the history of linguistics.

1 The historical and philosophical perspective: the importance of Aristotle, Humboldt and Saussure

As we know from interviews with Coseriu in *"Die Sachen sagen, wie sie sind...": Eugenio Coseriu im Gespräch* (Kabatek and Murguía 1997), it was not at all clear at the beginning of his career that he was going to dedicate himself to linguistics. He had studied philosophy extensively, including Plato (428/427–348/347 BC) and the Pre-Socratics, but no other philosopher exerted a greater influence on

---

* "Sie haben sicher schon oft bemerkt, wie häufig das Neue in der Literatur sich gerade als schon alt erweist" (Coseriu 1967b: 30). All translations in this article are mine, G.H.

https://doi.org/10.1515/9783110712391-005

him than Aristotle (384–322 BC). It was, however, the interpretation of Aristotle by Georg Wilhelm Friedrich Hegel (1770–1831) that was particularly important to Coseriu's thinking, in addition to his own studies of Aristotle. Coseriu defends Aristotle against the common criticism that Aristotle takes a logicist position in philosophy. According to Coseriu, Aristotle assumed that language precedes logical thought and is logically indeterminate. The qualities of being right or wrong do not concern the categories of language, but are part of its use. To further substantiate this interpretation, Coseriu applies a Saussurean perspective to Aristotle's explanation.

This perspective seems to be one of the three fundamental axes of Coseriu's thinking: Aristotle, Wilhelm von Humboldt (1767–1835) and Ferdinand de Saussure (1857–1913). As a matter of fact, Coseriu applies the Saussurean perspective to several authors in the history of the philosophy of language, even to the successors of Bhartṛhari (fl. 5th century CE) in the Indian tradition, where he sees a discussion of the relationship between signifier (*signifiant*) and signified (*signifié*). He also attributes to Plato, in the *Kratylos*, a semiotic relationship between content and expression that is equivalent to the assumption of a signifier and a signified. An articulated sound is not a name (Coseriu 2015, I: 44). But a few pages later, he expresses his doubts about Pagliaro's claim (Pagliaro 1993 [1930]: 15–16) that Plato distinguished a signifier and a signified. According to Coseriu, Plato only noticed that something in the way of discussing the "correctness of names", in his time, did not work. These arguments for and against the correctness of names either concern the relationship of the signifier to the thing designated, or the relationship between signifier and signified within the sign. Coseriu considers the possibility that it might have been an intentional confusion, but finally prefers to believe that Plato did not yet make the distinction.

The presence of Saussurean terminology in the work on the philosophy of language and on the history of linguistics is evident throughout Coseriu's work, but it does not prevent him from distancing himself from too hasty conclusions and making a number of necessary distinctions. Although he does not always avoid the adverb *already*, which is very dangerous in historiography, he consistently relativizes the observation that an earlier scholar already distinguished between signifier and signified or that words were analysed down to the level of phonemes.

In attempting to study a linguistic problem over several centuries, one always runs the risk of overestimating continuity. But this law of continuity, already noted by August Friedrich Pott (1802–1887) in 1876 (I: XLI), does not necessarily lead to a description of history in terms of precursors, under the condition that one is aware of the double meaning of a word: it can either be a term that is defined by an author and potentially becomes paradigmatic or it is a designation of a historically developing problem. For instance, already the Aristotelian conception of signs, which is in agreement with the issue of the arbitrariness of linguistic signs in later theories, does not only concern the relationship between sound and the thing referred to, but also the capacity of signs to possess a semantic function (Coseriu 1967a: 87–89; see also Coseriu 2004). For medieval *modistae*, a sound (*vox*) becomes a word by its denominating function (*ratio significandi*).

Coseriu repeatedly opposed the view that Aristotle was a representative of conventionalism and that Aristotle identified logical and linguistic categories. The claim that language is logically indeterminate and that it precedes logical thought may be considered more Humboldtian, Saussurean or Coserian, but Coseriu readily attributes it to Aristotle (Coseriu 2015, I: 69). Not surprisingly, Coseriu differentiates, in the context of the philosophy of language developed by Aristotle, three relations (Coseriu 2015, I: 71):

1. the purely linguistic relationship between sound and meaning, the signifier and the signified that he situates within language;
2. the ontological relationship between the name (the word that consists of a signifier and a signified) and the thing that belongs to extra-linguistic reality,
3. the logical relationship between subject and predicate, or rather between an object represented by a name and a predicate that states something about the object.

The fourth relation, that between the sound and the thing designated, is no longer of interest to Aristotle, according to Coseriu. While the first two relations pertain to a domain prior to logic and the question of true or false, it is only the third relation that goes beyond the *lógos semantikòs*, but it is not logically determined in all cases. This model, developed from Aristotle, seems to be the semiotic basis of Coseriu's own theory of the linguistic sign. He added Humboldtian elements to it for the explanation of the functioning of a language that mainly raises the question of creativity, and Saussurean elements for the explanation of a language-specific meaning as a relative and dependent value due to oppositions in a particular language (Haßler 1991, Haßler 2006, Saussure 2003).

It is also to his interpretation of Aristotle that Coseriu owes his distinction between the signified (G. *Bedeutung*) and designation (G. *Bezeichnung*). He starts from Aristotle's idea that names and their corresponding notions are limited in number, but the number of things is unlimited. That is why a name must designate a multitude of things (Aristotle 1997, *Sophistici elenchi* 165a, 11–12). From this observation of Aristotle, Coseriu concludes that the unitary meaning of a word and the designation of an object in the use of language do not coincide (Coseriu 2015, I: 89). This distinction is reinforced, in Coseriu's theory of semantics, by the influence of the Saussurean theory which distinguishes between the value (*valeur*) and the meaning (*signifié*) of a word.

In the history of the philosophy of language up to the beginning of the nineteenth century, Coseriu sees no studies that are oriented towards language itself and that seek to explain the purpose of language as an activity of man. He took into account the writings of several earlier authors who, like John Locke (1632–1704), had dealt with words, but this was done from a perspective which is restricted to the importance of words for human cognition. Scholars such as Locke treat language as an instrument of thought, according to Coseriu, which does not justify their being classified as philosophers of language strictly speaking, even if Coseriu devotes separate chapters to scholars such as Locke in his *Geschichte der Sprachphilosophie* (Coseriu 2015). Coseriu instead ranks them among the representatives of epistemology, which he separates from philosophy, and acknowledges the importance of making epistemological observations on the philosophy of language as well. Does the process referred to by Coseriu as *Erfassung der Wirklichkeit* [apprehension of reality] not correspond to man's cognitive activities? In his history of the philosophy of language we read:

> How can the universal function of language in its objective function be made compatible with its intersubjective function, given that the second seems to relativize the first, revealing itself as historical and thus particular? Does this mean, in the final analysis, that the apprehension of reality through language is not universal, but conditioned by particular languages? Does the apprehension of reality differ from one linguistic community to another? (Coseriu 2015, I: 17).

Of course, Coseriu attributed great importance to Locke's theory, which he even classified as a precursor of modern semantics. Starting from sensualist positions, Locke, in his *Essay concerning Human Understanding* (1690), had already extended the arbitrariness of signs not only to the relationship between sequences of sounds and ideas, but also to the composition of designated ideas. Locke had explained the specific meanings of words in each language by the differences between ideas and the communicative needs of peoples (Locke 1894 [1690]: I, 384; II, 48).

Influenced by Locke, Étienne Bonnot de Condillac (1714–1780) developed in his *Essai sur l'origine des connaissances humaines* (1746) a coherent sensualist theory of the development of thought, in which he attributes a central place to the arbitrariness of the sign. The specificity of language as an analytical method, depending above all on the choice of combinations of ideas designated by particular signs, is part of the 'genius' of language. This applies to accessory ideas, which are fixed when a language is stabilised, according to the estimation of the linguistic community concerned. But for Condillac, the differences in structure in vocabularies are even more important than that. Our notions cannot be clearly determined until we have found the right signs which allow them to be fixed and which then remain available for further thought processes. Under this view, the formation of complex ideas is, in this process, absolutely linked to the existence of institutional signs (Condillac 1947–1951: I, 42–43). Since there is no extra-linguistic support for uniting ideas under a common name, there is also no unanimity among the different languages for the formation of complex notions, which in turn become a condition for the classification of things and phenomena (Condillac 1947–1951: I, 88–91). According to Condillac, the best method for understanding and describing the linguistic system is the observation of oneself and one's linguistic behaviour, because each person possesses within him or herself the system of language. The language system is already considered here as a condition for the ability to express oneself: "Le système du langage est dans chaque homme qui sait parler" [The language system is in every man who is able to speak] (Condillac 1947–1951: I, 443).

Coseriu found semantic ideas in sensualist authors that coincided with two of his favourite positions concerning semantics: the idea that each language organizes meanings in its own way and the idea that language is a system that determines the value of words. He offered a schema for Condillac's theory which explains that from a certain point on the progress of human knowledge is inseparably linked to language (Fig. 1). Language plays an important role in crossing the boundary between sensation-related operations and truly mental operations (Coseriu 2015, I: 366).

The claim that German Romanticism is the beginning of true linguistic philosophy should not be taken literally. This claim is certainly an idea that Coseriu had adopted from the histories of linguistics published before the 1970s. However, it seems impossible to draw a line between a philosophy of language and epistemology, especially if one attributes a central place in linguistic thought to Wilhelm von Humboldt, all the more so if one conceives linguistic meaning as a mental phenomenon that cannot be described by recording its different uses. Humboldt treated the question of meaning within the framework of his conception of language as an organic whole that assigns to each element its proper place. The relationship between the organism and its parts provided a new basis for the problem of value. There were several attempts to develop these ideas into a theory of semantics.

What Coseriu owes above all to Humboldt is the distinction between *érgon* and *enérgeia*. Based on Aristotle's notions, Humboldt had said that language is not, by its nature, a product (*érgon*) that is completed, but a creative activity (*enérgeia*). Aristotle sees three ways of looking at an activity, namely as *enérgeia*,

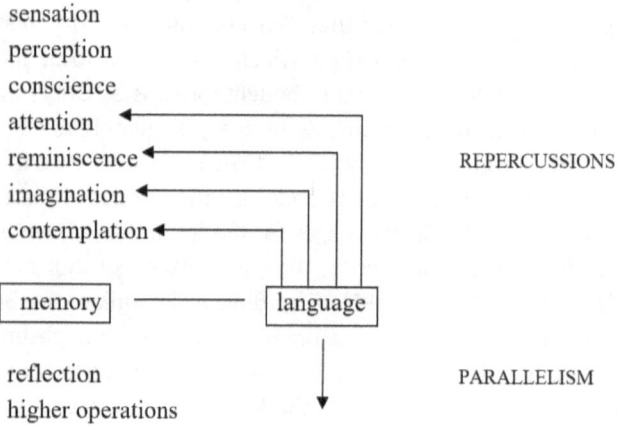

Figure 1: Coseriu's schema of Condillac's theory

as *dýnamis* and as *érgon*. *Enérgeia* means the creative and purposeful activity of creating something new, *dýnamis* is the reproductive activity and *érgon* means the product created by the activity. Consequently, no human activity can be pure *enérgeia*. Furthermore, *enérgeia* as creation precedes *dýnamis*, that is, creation precedes the reproduction of this very creation. But Coseriu is not the only one to take up these Humboldtian notions. However, the neo-Humboldtians, whose doctrine was already considered outdated when Coseriu came to Germany, did not take over the concept of *dýnamis*, applying it to language considered as a productive activity. But Coseriu does not criticize the neo-Humboldtians and he says that their most original results are to be found in lexicology. They did not develop structural semantics because they lacked the concept of opposition, according to Coseriu (1992 [1988]: 95, 161). By contrast, he severely criticizes the linguistic creativity described by Noam Chomsky, taking issue with Chomsky's instrumentalization of the history of linguistics for the creation of a basis for Chomsky's own theory in his *Cartesian Linguistics* (2009 [1966]), but he also finds inadequacies in the very concept of 'creativity'. According to Coseriu, man's linguistic creativity is expressed not only in the application of certain rules that serve to produce sentences, but also in the changing of these rules (Coseriu 1970).

It is very difficult to transform the Humboldtian notion of 'creativity' into a principle of semantic analysis. In Humboldt himself, there is a discrepancy between the theoretical claim of his notion of 'creativity' and his practical descriptions of languages (cf., e.g., Humboldt's treatises on the dual, 1827, and the language of the South Sea Islands, 1828). A similar difficulty emerges with Saussure. The manuscripts discovered in 1996 and published under the title *Écrits de linguistique générale* (Saussure 2002), raised the question whether the interpretation of his work in dichotomies can still be upheld (Bouquet 2000, Bouquet and Rastier 2002). The difficulties Saussure encountered in pinpointing what is general in linguistic signs gave him the feeling that these signs "are part of a much broader science than the 'science of language'" (Saussure 2002: 265). This confirms Saussure's hesitation regarding a form of pure linguistics and the delimitation of its object. In this perspective, Saussure argues, future linguistic research will have to rediscover the traditional objects of morphology, lexicology and syntax, but it will also include rhetoric and stylistics. This will bring together all approaches to language in a semiology that explains its subject matter on the basis of the principle of oppositions, 'negativity' and differences.

The central idea of relations and oppositions that already appears in Saussure's historical-comparative studies is common to Saussure and Coseriu. It is formulated even more clearly in the *Ecrits* (Saussure 2002) than in the *Cours* (Saussure 1968) when Saussure writes that linguistic values do not consist in forms or in meanings, nor in signs or in meanings. They are determined by the particular solution of a general relationship between signs and meanings, based on the general difference of signs, the general difference of meanings and the prior attribution of certain meanings to certain signs or vice versa. The way the identity of signs is established by means of differential oppositions is described in a very clear scheme which corrects the simplifying idea that a sign simply consists of a signifier and a signified (Fig. 2). In this scheme, Saussure draws a distinction between the systematic perspective and the perspective of the isolated sign, and he applies this distinction to the mental existence of both sides of the linguistic sign (Saussure 2002: 42; 2006: 24).

In the *Écrits* (2002), Saussure's program appears less rigid and more complex than what we were used to. The field of interest has since widened, leading to the conception of a linguistics of speech, rather than language, and bringing it closer to the development that Coseriu had given to Saussure's ideas.

2 Coseriu's work on the history of linguistics and structural semantics

In his historiographical work, Coseriu does not postulate a closed line of tradition, but he does identify certain elements of structural semantics in authors of the nineteenth century. Obviously, these elements were not to be found in posi-

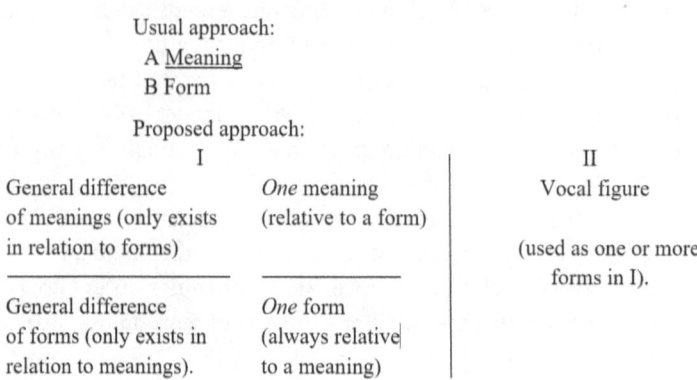

Figure 2: Saussure's correction of the simplifying concept of a sign

tivist, historical-comparative linguistics which dominated studies in German Romance linguistics in the 1960s. In 1967, Coseriu began to publish a series of studies on the history of linguistics, including a short article on the French ideologist Jean-François Thurot (1768–1832), in which he makes the following observations: "Thus, Thurot seems to have been the first grammarian to make an explicit distinction between synchronic and diachronic or language description and language history, and in this respect, he deserves to be mentioned as an important precursor of Georg von der Gabelentz and Ferdinand de Saussure in the history of linguistics" (Coseriu 1967b: 34).

According to Coseriu, the tradition in the language sciences that distinguishes between a synchronic and a diachronic approach was initiated by Thurot and later continued by Georg von der Gabelentz (1840–1893). In an article on Gabelentz' synchronic linguistics, Coseriu complains that theoretical linguistics has incomplete knowledge of history, often ignoring that earlier scholars have already developed important ideas in the past. Coseriu sees correspondences between Gabelentz' and Saussure's terms (*Rede – parole, Einzelsprache – langue, Sprachvermögen – langage*) that were already observed by other authors, and he has no doubt that Gabelentz influenced Saussure (Coseriu 1967c: 76). Coseriu's intention was not to do pure historiography. He mixed his own theoretical thoughts with those of Gabelentz, using Gabelentz's *Sprachwissenschaft* (2016 [1891/1901]) as a model for the presentation of his own theory. This becomes even clearer in his observations regarding the distinction between diachrony and synchrony, which he concludes by saying that these two approaches can indeed be found in linguistic research but in fact constitute two sides of the same thing, viz. language. Coseriu thus agrees with the theory he considers to be advanced by Gabelentz and contrasts it with Saussure's approach, which he criticises as follows:

> As a consequence, his [Gabelentz'] synchronic linguistics does not correspond to everything that is simultaneous (in fact, it only concerns that which coexists in the same system) and, on the other hand, his diachronic linguistics does not only correspond to what is successive, since it also concerns facts that are simultaneous but do not belong to the same system. Thus, the proper domain of synchronic linguistics is narrower than synchrony (simultaneity) and diachronic linguistics goes beyond diachrony (successiveness):

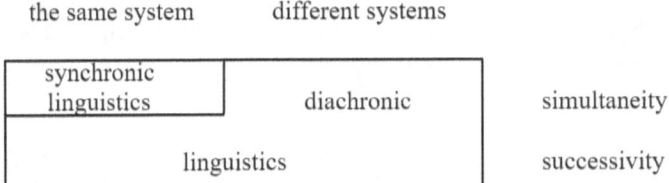

> This is perfectly legitimate from Gabelentz' point of view, who distinguishes only two different forms of linguistics, but not from Saussure's point of view, who would like to make the methodological distinction between systematic description and history coincide with a difference in nature between synchronic and diachronic facts. (Coseriu 1967c: 92–93)

In another article, also published in 1967, Coseriu describes the preceding history of structural semantics. He concentrates on Karl Wilhelm Ludwig Heyse's (1797–1855) analysis of the semantic field 'sound' and wants to incite a structural reinterpretation of the notion of 'semantic field'. He uses concepts such as 'opposition' and 'distinctive feature' while developing his own definition of the semantic field in terms of a lexical paradigm, i.e. a structure, in which lexemes that contrast with one another divide up the content. According to Coseriu, Heyse's analysis of the lexical field in his *System der Sprachwissenschaft* (Heyse 1856) provides an almost completely structural content analysis, even if it is elaborated with other aims (Coseriu 1967d: 490). Heyse did not write in his book about the structure of contents or word fields, his intention was to delimit the essence of speech sounds. To this end, he took as his starting point the use of German words and defined a series of lexemes such as *Klang* 'timbre', *Hall* 'echo', *Widerhall* 'resonance', *Geräusch* 'noise', etc. Heyse's purpose was to distinguish the meanings of these words, explicitly excluding diachronic aspects such as their etymology. Heyse describes the meaning of each word by means of certain features, such as 'continuous'/'discontinuous': "[...] that's what we call any discontinuous, tangled sound *Geräusch* 'noise'. The *Klang* 'ring', on the other hand, is what we call the continuous sound pleasant to the ear of a completely trembling body whose substance is a completely homogeneous continuum, for example the glass, the metal" (Heyse 1856: 31–32).

When Coseriu sees Heyse's procedure as an early manifestation of differential-opposite determinations of meaning, he ignores the tradition of synonymy that had begun long before and that had worked with very similar procedures (Haßler 1991). However, Coseriu is not interested in making an exact historiographical classification, but focuses on the foundations of his own method that were introduced by predecessors in the history of linguistics. Finally, he reinterprets Heyse's analysis in the sense of an explicitly structural analysis to clarify the methodological agreement with structural semantics (Fig. 3).

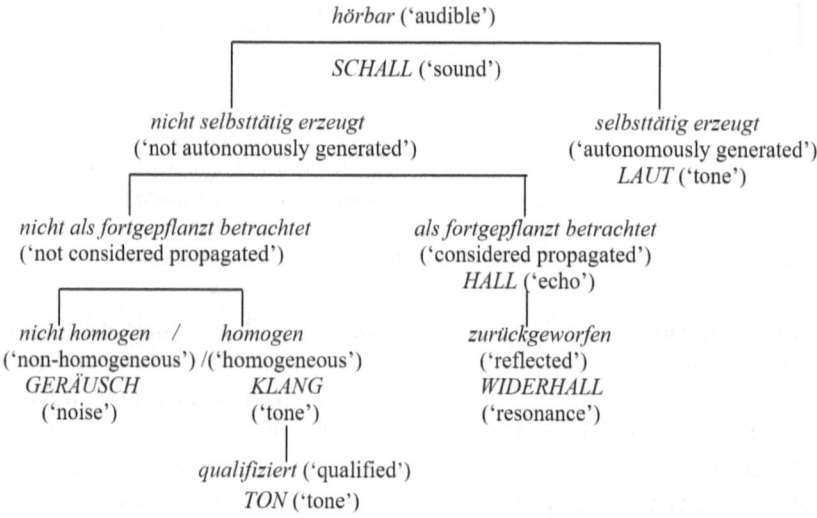

Figure 3: Coseriu's (1967d) interpretation of Heyse's semantic field *Schall* 'sound'

More such examples of support for his own theory of language can be found in Coseriu's historiographical work. They clearly show his intention to demonstrate a long tradition of structural linguistics that can be traced back long before Saussure. Like Chomsky, Coseriu's accounts of this second historiographical type do not deal with the real history of science, but with a historical perspective of research related to the prime object, viz. language. In relation to the development of structuralist positions, Coseriu focused above all on the problem of linguistic signs in the history of theories of language. However, if all aspects of his surveys are taken into account, it emerges that Coseriu's treatment of the history of linguistics cannot be regarded as a search for precursors or as a reference to obsolete earlier ideas.

3 Corrections of certain stereotypes in the historiography of linguistics

From the vantage point of his own linguistic research Coseriu also contributed to discussions among historiographers and corrected some errors. In a contribution to studies offered to Emilio Alarcos Llorach (1922–1998) entitled *Lo que se dice de Hervás* [What is said about Hervás], Coseriu 1978a), Coseriu rectifies some hagiographic and nationalist findings about the Spanish Jesuit and polymath Lorenzo Hervás y Panduro (1735–1809). In the history of linguistic theories, Hervás is one of those authors who are not so well known for the extent and complexity of their work but remembered primarily thanks to legends and prejudices. The most significant error that circulated about Hervás was that he had travelled as a missionary in America collecting information about the indigenous languages of America. This erroneous assumption is first found in a text from 1801 by Friedrich Adelung (1768–1843), a nephew of the famous author of the *Mithridates* (1806) Johann Christoph Adelung (1732–1806). According to another common opinion, Hervás wrote about forty grammars, which became over time the grammars of the indigenous languages of America. The first to speak of such grammars was Max Müller (1823–1900). This myth was also adopted in the early histories of linguistics by Theodor Benfey (1869), Wilhelm Thomsen (1927) and Manuel Mourelle-Lema (1968), among others. It is surprising that all these authors apparently did not know the biography of Hervás by Caballero (1868). Coseriu (1978a) dismissed the legend of Hervás' adventures in America and its alleged consequences for linguistic theories. However, instead of making false or debatable statements about Hervás, there are aspects of Hervás' conception of language as well as his linguistic activity that deserve careful study, according to Coseriu:

> [...] it should be pointed out in the first place: a) his peculiar conception about the "*artificio gramatical* ('grammatical artifice')" and the "structure" of languages; b) his ideas about arbitrary and non-arbitrary signs; c) his likely influence on Humboldt in two points of no small importance within the general conception of the great German linguist, namely with regard to structural analysis through literal translation and with regard to the idea of constancy and stability of linguistic systems; (d) his ideas about the relationship be-

tween language and history; his conception of the substratum. (Coseriu 1978a: 36; for the substratum, see also Coseriu 1978b).

When one considers these particular issues in Hervás' work against the background of Coseriu's own theory, it is easy to see that they correspond exactly to his linguistic interests. For Coseriu's retrospective historiography history serves as a source for modern research. The historiographical information is arranged in a teleological way, starting from up-to-date linguistic problems. With this approach, which is typical for a linguist rather than a historian of linguistics, Coseriu has nevertheless been able to correct historiographical errors.

To conclude, I will briefly discuss the origin of a concept that was virtually rediscovered by Coseriu: the arbitrariness of the linguistic sign. To understand the importance of this rediscovery, it is necessary, first of all, to take a look at the state of reception of structural linguistics in Germany in the 1960s. Information on this situation can be drawn from Ehlers' book on the promotion of linguistic research in Germany from 1920 to 1970 (Ehlers 2010), in which Ehlers analysed the reports of the National Research Foundation (*Deutsche Forschungsgemeinschaft*, DFG) on the research activities that were supported during that period and the most frequent objects of study.

Almost one third of the projects that were funded dealt with the development of dictionaries, typically long-term projects for the development of monumental publications. 115 projects, i.e. 10% of the linguistic projects, were about phonological problems, continuing the tradition of the neogrammarians, while the number of projects about grammar and syntax was negligible with 4% each (Ehlers 2010: 259). The diachronic profile of German linguistics was very strong until the 1960s and was represented by 35.3% of the selected projects (Ehlers 2010: 263). Together with dialectology (16.1% in the 1950s and 11.5% in the 1960s), diachronic and dialectological research represented a large part of the mostly very traditional research in German linguistics.

In the 1960s, many researchers moved away from diachronic studies, while motivating their new methodology with the development of structural linguistics abroad (Ehlers 2010: 264). This change in methodology was supported by the demands of educational policy that favoured modern languages and their teaching. Computational linguistics, which emerged in the 1960s, was a "modernity marker for a modern, present-oriented linguistics" (Haß 2010: 201), but quantitatively it did not play a decisive role in the projects selected by the DFG; only 3.6% mentioned the use of computers. In the 1960s, new fields gradually emerged: language acquisition, text linguistics and research of spoken language. In 1969 a central programme of theoretical training and method development for linguistics was established to "promote structural linguistics and the use of automatic data processing in linguistic research" (Bericht 1969: 20, quoted from Ehlers 2010: 266).

It is difficult to measure the astonishment of German linguists who had recently realized the importance of Saussure's work when they read the title of Coseriu's 1967 article *L'arbitraire du signe. Zur Spätgeschichte eines aristotelischen Begriffes* [The arbitrariness of the sign. The late history of an Aristotelian concept] (Coseriu 1967a, cf. also Coseriu 2004, 1–35). Attributing a long history to a notion that for them had emerged with Saussure's *Cours de linguistique générale* (1916) must have seemed confusing to most of them.

Right at the beginning of his article, Coseriu dismantled the conviction that Saussure was the first to explicitly formulate the theory of the so-called *arbitraire du signe*. Coseriu presents in a relatively disorganized way a whole series of authors in whose texts this concept had appeared much earlier and finally attributes the concept to Aristotle. While in antiquity two sides were related to the concept of arbitrariness, viz., on the one hand, the relationship not given by nature between meaning and signifier and, on the other hand, its conventional determination, in the Middle Ages the two sides were kept separate and each side was considered in terms of arbitrariness. Coseriu traces the development of this concept throughout the early modern period up to Saussure's contemporaries. He concludes his observations by stating that Saussure represents only one more stage in the interpretation of a conventional principle. All the elements of Saussure's theory of arbitrariness already appear in linguistic considerations before Saussure, who did not add a single element to the theory. However, Saussure's merit is to have made a synthesis of these elements and his originality consists in the fact that he attributes an extraordinary importance to arbitrariness. It is therefore perfectly legitimate to speak of a Saussurean principle of the arbitrariness of the linguistic sign, if one understands by this the particular interpretation of this principle and the relevance it has in Saussure's overall theory of language. On the other hand, it is completely wrong and misleading to speak of a Saussurean principle when it is the principle itself that is meant, because it is already 2300 years old, according to Coseriu (1967a: 112).

It is obvious that Coseriu, who had been appointed to a professorship in Germany only four years earlier, was overstraining his German colleagues with this combination of historical scholarship and linguistic theory. Moreover, Coseriu showed them that they had not even read Saussure's *Cours* correctly because in this work there was no claim of novelty regarding the concept of arbitrariness. As a matter of fact, Coseriu concluded his essay as follows: "Unsere Untersuchung hat also den Satz des *Cours* bestätigt: "le príncipe de l'arbitraire du signe n'est contesté par personne" [Our investigation has thus confirmed the phrase of the *Course:* "no one denies the principle of the arbitrariness of the sign"], Coseriu 1967a: 112).

With this important and philologically sound work, Coseriu showed that his colleagues had forgotten long periods of the history of linguistics. However, his type of argumentation and style – besides the fact that he rarely published in English – may have contributed to the fact that he himself has been forgotten by many linguists today.

References

Aristotle. 1997. *De Sophisticis Elenchis. Translatio Boethii, Fragmenta Translationis Iacobi, Et Recensio Guilleimi De Moerbeka (Aristoteles Latinus).* Leiden: Brill.
Bouquet, Simon. 2000. "Sur la sémantique saussurienne." *Cahiers Ferdinand de Saussure* 53, 135–139.
Bouquet, Simon and François Rastier. 2002. *Une introduction aux sciences de la culture.* Paris: Presses Universitaires de France.
Caballero, Fermín. 1868. *Noticias biográficas y bibliográficas de L. Hervás y Panduro.* Madrid: Sordomudos.
Chomsky, Noam. 2009 [1966]. *Cartesian linguistics. A chapter in the history of rationalist thought* (third edition). Cambridge: Cambridge University Press.
Condillac, Étienne Bonnot de. 1947–1951. *Œuvres philosophiques de Condillac.* Texte établi et présenté par Georges Le Roy. Paris: Presses Universitaires de France.
Coseriu, Eugenio. 1967a. "L'arbitraire du signe. Zur Spätgeschichte eines aristotelischen Begriffes". *Archiv für das Studium der neueren Sprachen und Literaturen* 204, 81–112.
Coseriu, Eugenio. 1967b. "François Thurot". *Zeitschrift für französische Sprache und Literatur* 77, 30–34.
Coseriu, Eugenio. 1967c. "Georg von der Gabelentz et la linguistique synchronique". *Word* 23, 74–100. (*Linguistic Studies Presented to André Martinet*, I).
Coseriu, Eugenio. 1967d. "Zur Vorgeschichte der strukturellen Semantik: Heyses Analyse des Wortfeldes 'Schall'". *To Honor Roman Jakobson. Essays on the Occasion of His Seventieth Birthday.* Vol. I, 489–498. The Hague & Paris: Mouton.
Coseriu, Eugenio. 1970. "Semantik, innere Sprachform und Tiefenstruktur". *Folia Linguistica* 4:1–2, 53–63.
Coseriu, Eugenio. 1969–1972. *Die Geschichte der Sprachphilosophie von der Antike bis zur Gegenwart. Eine Übersicht.* Vol. I: *Von der Antike bis Leibniz.* Edited by Gunter Narr and Rudolf Windisch. Vol. II: *Von Leibniz bis Rousseau.* Edited by Gunter Narr. Tübingen: Narr.
Coseriu, Eugenio. 1978a. "Lo que se dice de Hervás". *Estudios ofrecidos a Emilio Alarcos Llorach* III, 35–58. Oviedo: Universidad, Servicio de publicaciones.
Coseriu, Eugenio. 1978b. "Hervás und das Substrat". *Studii şi cercetări lingvistice* 29, 523–530.
Coseriu, Eugenio. 1992 [1988]. *Einführung in die allgemeine Sprachwissenschaft* (second edition). Tübingen: Francke. (German translation of Coseriu 1981.)

Coseriu, Eugenio. 2004. *Der Physei-Thesei-Streit. Sechs Beiträge zur Geschichte der Sprachphilosophie.* Edited by Reinhard Meisterfeld. Tübingen: Narr.

Coseriu, Eugenio. 2015. *Geschichte der Sprachphilosophie.* Vol. 1: *Von Heraklit bis Rousseau.* Vol. 2: *Von Herder bis Humboldt.* Edited by Jörn Albrecht. Tübingen: Narr & Francke, Attempto.

Ehlers, Klaas-Hinrich. 2010. *Der Wille zur Relevanz. Die Sprachforschung und ihre Förderung durch die DFG 1920–1970.* Stuttgart: Franz Steiner Verlag.

Gabelentz, Georg von der. 2016 [1891/1901]. *Die Sprachwissenschaft, ihre Aufgaben, Methoden und bisherigen Ergebnisse.* Edited by Manfred Ringmacher and James McElvenny. Berlin: Language Science Press.

Haß, Ulrike. 2010. "'Datenverarbeitende Maschinen' und der strukturalistische Diskurs". In: Hans-Harald Müller, Marcel Lepper and Andreas Gardt (eds.), *Strukturalismus in Deutschland. Literaturwissenschaft und Sprachwissenschaft 1910–1975*, 194–216. Göttingen: Wallstein.

Haßler, Gerda. 1991. *Der semantische Wertbegriff in Sprachtheorien vom 18. bis zum 20. Jahrhundert.* Berlin: Akademie-Verlag.

Haßler, Gerda. 2006. "Los conceptos en el período del nacimiento del estructuralismo y su transmisión en España". In: Ricardo Escavy (ed.), *Caminos actuales de la historiografía lingüística.* Vol. I, 81–114. Murcia: Universidad de Murcia.

Haßler, Gerda. 2016. "La historiografía de la lingüística en la obra de Eugenio Coseriu". In: Antonio Salvador Plans, Carmen Galán Rodríguez et al. (eds.), *La Historiografía Lingüística como paradigma de investigación*, 519–531. Madrid: Visor Libros.

Kabatek, Johannes and Adolfo Murguía. 1997. *"Die Sachen sagen, wie sie sind...": Eugenio Coseriu im Gespräch.* Tübingen: Narr.

Locke, John. 1894 [1690]. *An Essay concerning Human Understanding.* Edited by Alexander Campbell Fraser. Oxford: University of Oxford Press.

Pagliaro, Antonino. 1993 [1930]. *Sommario di linguistica arioeuropea.* Palermo: Novecento.

Pott, August Friedrich. 1876. *Ueber die Verschiedenheit des menschlichen Sprachbaues und ihren Einfluss auf die geistige Entwicklung des Menschengeschlechts, Von Wilhelm von Humboldt. Mit erläuternden Anmerkungen und Exkursen sowie als Einleitung Wilhelm von Humboldt und die Sprachwissenschaft von A.F. Pott.* Berlin: Calvary.

Saussure, Ferdinand de. 1968. *Cours de linguistique générale.* Édition critique par Rudolf Engler. Wiesbaden: Harrassowitz.

Saussure, Ferdinand de. 2002. *Écrits de linguistique générale.* Texte établi par Simon Bouquet et Rudolf Engler. Paris: Éditions Gallimard.

Saussure, Ferdinand de. 2006. *Writings in General Linguistics.* English translation of Saussure (2002) by Carol Sanders and Matthew Pires. Oxford: Oxford University Press.

Saussure, Louis de. 2003. "Valeur et signification ad hoc". *Cahiers Ferdinand de Saussure* 56, 289–310.

Viggo Bank Jensen (Copenhagen)
Coseriu's Hjelmslev

Almost everything I've done so far is related (positively or negatively) to glossematics or has been also said, in one way or another (or denied), by Mr. Hjelmslev (to whom I currently feel closer than ever).*

1 Introduction

In his 2013 inaugural address at the conference on the scientific heritage of Coseriu in Udine, Tullio De Mauro (2015: 16, see also De Mauro 2007: 11) referred to his dialogues with Coseriu in Rome in the second half of the 1950s and to Coseriu's four main points of reference concerning the history of the language sciences, i.e. Aristotle (384–322 BC), Ferdinand de Saussure (1857–1913), Antonino Pagliaro (1898–1973) and Louis Hjelmslev (1899–1965). While Coseriu discussed Aristotle at considerable length (Coseriu 2015, I: Chapter 6) and devoted papers to both Saussure and Pagliaro (Coseriu 1995a and 1994), he never actually provided an overall presentation of his views on Hjelmslev, which seems remarkable in light of the above quote.

In this article, I discuss Coseriu's reception of Hjelmslev's linguistic theory and the concepts and terminology that form part of it. I shall focus on four subject matters which span almost thirty years of Coseriu's scholarly work. Section 2 deals with Coseriu's discussion of Hjelmslev in "Forma y sustancia en los sonidos del lenguaje" [Form and substance in the sounds of language] (Coseriu 1954; cf. also Coseriu 1973 [1954]). In Section 3, I discuss Coseriu's adoption of the concepts 'architecture of language', 'diatopic' and 'diastratic' variation from the Norwegian linguist Leiv Flydal and their relationship to Hjelmslev's concept of 'connotative semiotics' (Coseriu 1981 [1958], 1967 [1966], 2007 [1980]). Section 4 is devoted to Coseriu's (and Hjelmslev's) views on structural semantics (various papers by Coseriu from 1957 to about 1976). In Section 5, I investigate the possible influence of Hjelmslev's linguistic theory on Coseriu's first major work in linguistics, entitled *Sistema, norma y habla* [System, norm and speech] from 1952 (cf.

---

* "Presque tout ce que j'ai fait jusqu'à présent est en rapport (positif ou négatif) avec la glossématique ou bien a été dit aussi, d'une façon ou d'une autre (ou nié), par M. Hjelmslev, (auquel à présent je me sens plus proche que jamais)". Letter from Coseriu to the Danish general linguist and phonetician Eli Fischer-Jørgensen, March 24, 1962, Royal Danish Library, cf. Jensen 2015a (my translation, V.B.J.).

also Coseriu 1973 [1952]), with a particular focus on concepts that may have their origin in Hjelmslev's analysis of the Saussurean concept of *langue*.[1]

With regard to the issues I will discuss in the first three sections, it is possible to reconstruct a direct line of influence from Hjelmslev to Coseriu based on Coseriu's own references to Hjelmslev's publications. Things become more complex, with regard to Section 5. In Coseriu (1952) there is no reference pointing directly to any of Hjelmslev's publications, even though Hjelmslev has a rather a prominent role in Coseriu's study. Therefore, defying chronology, I have decided to save the discussion of this issue for the end of the article.

In Coseriu (1992 [1988]: 124) a number of terms widely used by structuralists are said to have been coined by Hjelmslev, including 'paradigmatic', 'commutation', 'expression plane', 'content plane'. In Coseriu (1995a: 187 ff.), Hjelmslev is mentioned with regard to the distinctions between *langue* and *parole* and between the 'architecture' of a language and a linguistic variety. In the Hjelmslev Archive at the Royal Danish Library in Copenhagen, there is a letter from Coseriu to Hjelmslev, dated October 23, 1951. Based in his new position in Montevideo, Coseriu writes that it would be an honor for him to establish and maintain contact with Hjelmslev and have the possibility of receiving suggestions and advice from a professor with such a wide experience. Coseriu also proposes exchanging books and journals. I have not found any sign of an answer from Hjelmslev in the archive. In the Royal Library's book section, however, there is a copy of *Forma y sustancia en los sonidos del lenguaje* (Coseriu 1954), with a dedication to Hjelmslev: "Al ilustre Prof. L. Hjelmslev, respetuoso homenaje, Eugenio Coseriu". The above mentioned letter indicates that already in 1951 Coseriu privately paid homage to the illustrious Hjelmslev.

Coseriu's desire to exchange books points to an important issue in the analysis of the sources of his early work. It is likely that, while Coseriu was writing *Sistema, norma y habla* (1952), he did not have direct access to Hjelmslev's central work, published in Danish, *Omkring Sprogteoriens Grundlæggelse* (1943). He might, however, have become familiar with it before leaving Europe for Montevideo (see Section 5.2).

---

[1] Louis Hjelmslev's reception of Saussure was based on the *Cours de linguistique générale* (1916; second edition 1922; cf. Saussure 1975 [1916]). He did not live to see the discussion on Saussure's allegedly true intentions; cf. Joseph (2012).

2 *Forma y sustancia en los sonidos del lenguaje* [Form and substance in the sounds of language] (1954)

This early study features the most comprehensive discussion Coseriu has devoted to Hjelmslev. Chapter five, which discusses form and substance in Hjelmslev's theory, comprises twenty-two pages, about thirty percent of the study.

2.1 Hjelmslev on 'form' and 'substance'

From 1928 onwards, Hjelmslev elaborated the idea of separating form from substance, hypothesizing that *langue* can be analyzed without involving 'substance'. During the 1930s, Hjelmslev also introduced the concepts 'expression plane' and 'content plane', both of them featuring a form and a substance. He suggested that the two planes be analyzed in a parallel fashion but underlined that they are not 'conformal', and each of them may therefore be described on the basis of their own form. In particular, Hjelmslev's approach that it is possible to disregard the substance of expression caused a lively debate, partly because it was seen as an attack on the phonology of the Linguistic Circle of Prague (Jensen 2020: 21 ff.).

2.2 Coseriu on the relation between form and substance in Hjelmslev's theory

The aim of Coseriu's study (1954: 75) is to "justify a reunification of the phonic sciences". According to Coseriu, the fundamental problem of establishing phonetics as a scientific discipline "can be posed and resolved with consistency only starting from a Hjelmslevian position" (Coseriu 1954: 38). Also the problem of the object of phonology "implies a stance towards the Hjelmslevian distinction between 'form' and 'substance'" (Coseriu 1954: 38–39).

Coseriu argues in detail why it is not possible to analyze the expression plane[2] without paying attention to the substance of expression in the study of 'language' as a historical or functional language. According to Coseriu, glossematicians can only disregard 'substance' because they study "language as an

---

[2] For form and substance at the content plane, see Jensen (2015b: 124–125).

idea". For Coseriu, the early and most rigid glossematic formulations reveal "that glossematics is not located at the same abstraction plane as linguistics: glossematics is not a science of concrete or historical realities, but a science of possibilities" (Coseriu 1954: 55). Coseriu criticizes Hjelmslev's "Platonic" claim that "language *is* a network of functions" and maintains that in Hjelmslev's approach the levels of theory and application do not coincide. For Coseriu, Hjelmslev's theory is structured on the "Platonic" level of pure forms, whereas it should be possible for the *corresponding* method to be applied to the "Aristotelian" level of forms that are elaborated on the basis of experience in the world of entities. According to Coseriu, the contradiction in Hjelmslev's theory lies in confirming, on the one hand, that *langue* is a form independent of linguistic activity and, on the other hand, that *langue* reveals itself in the "text" (*parole*) or is deduced only from its manifestations (Coseriu 1954: 63).

While for Hjelmslev it is important to derive a description of the linguistic *form* following theoretically based procedures of description, Coseriu expresses his skepticism about the results of the glossematic procedures. In particular, he doubts whether it is possible to arrive, on the basis of these procedures, at the *same form* as when the form is deduced from its manifestation. Coseriu himself focuses on the latter point, i.e. the close relationship between *form* and its manifestation, and he stresses the speaker's (and the linguist's) preliminary knowledge of language, 'language intuition'. Conversely, he is less explicit regarding the procedures how to get to the description of language in a systematic way (see also Rasmussen 1992: 344 f.).

3 Diasystems and language architecture: Coseriu, Flydal and Hjelmslev

From 1958 onwards (cf Coseriu 1981 [1958]: 3 and 32, note 48), Coseriu played an important role in promoting and complementing the variational concepts suggested by the Norwegian linguist Leiv Flydal: 'diatopic', 'diastratic' and 'language architecture' (Flydal 1952). In two articles, Harald Völker (2009 and 2013, see also Jensen 2012) argues that there is a connection between these terms and Hjelmslev's account of 'connotative semiotics' (Hjelmslev 1953 [1943]: Chapter 22; cf. Hjelmslev 1961 [1943]). As a matter of fact, even though there are no references in Flydal's article to Hjelmslev (1943), a letter from Flydal to Hjelmslev from December 14, 1951 indicates Flydal's awareness of Hjelmslev's influence:

[...] it was encouraging for [me] that you found the two articles I sent you interesting. When I had finished writing the article on language and style [Flydal 1952] last summer, I thought I had mastered the subject, and then re-read Chapter 22 of [your book, Hjelmslev 1943] – which I had carefully avoided opening during the work itself – then I found it true that all of it was pretty banal. (Letter from Flydal to Hjelmslev, December 14, 1951; my translation, V.B.J.)

This suggests that Flydal, when taking a closer look at a work he had deliberately not consulted, found that what he had written could already be found in Hjelmslev's book. A comparison of Flydal's and Hjelmslev's texts seems to confirm this direct influence, e. g. the use of the word "solidary": Flydal (1952: 245) describes the architecture of language as a "systematic whole formed by solidary parts". Compare Hjelmslev (1953 [1943]: 74): "Stylistic form, style, value-style, medium, tone, vernacular, national language, regional language and physiognomy are solidary categories".³

Coseriu has always explicitly credited Flydal for inventing the terms 'diatopic' and 'diastratic'. It is noteworthy that in his *Textlinguistik* (2007 [1980]), Coseriu also connects the dia-concepts to Hjelmslev's 'connotative semiotics'. In Coseriu (2007 [1980]: 98–105 and 138–140) there are two long passages referring to this theory. Hjelmslev assumes that every linguistic sign functions in two ways: the content of a sign refers to a reality, the denotation, but it also takes part in a system of signs to which it belongs, hence the connotation. In Coseriu's interpretation of Hjelmslev's account, this 'connotation' – 'evocation' in Coseriu's terminology, a term he borrowed from Urban (1939) – can be very effective within a 'historical language', i. e. across the boundaries between the various 'functional languages' that make up the 'historical language' according to regional, social and situational variation (Coseriu 2007 [1980]: 103–104). Here, rather than referring to Hjelmslev's notion of the 'schema' of a particular 'functional language', Coseriu is inspired by Hjelmlev's remarks on the 'architecture' of language.

---

3 While Flydal expresses his indebtedness to Hjelmslev's ideas in a rather unclear way in 1951, he goes to Copenhagen in 1954 to study with Hjelmslev and also publishes a series of articles that explicitly draw on the glossematic approach.

4 Structural semantics

4.1 Coseriu's contributions to structural semantics

Geckeler (1981b) discusses the Coserian model of structural semantics and lists all the texts by Coseriu on the subject up until then (Coseriu 1964, 1966, 1967e, 1968, 1973, 1976a, b, and Coseriu and Geckeler 1974). Coseriu (1964; cf. 2008 [1964]) already provides the pivotal concepts of his 'structural semantics', including 'conceptual field' (later 'lexical field'), 'commutation test' and 'distinctive feature'. From this text onwards it is easy to see a gradual 'unfolding' of Coseriu's theory of structural semantics. However, Coseriu had already given a brief contribution to structural semantics as early as 1957 (published as Coseriu 1958 [1957]). If we take this contribution as point of departure, the development seems less gradual. Before moving on to a comparison of Coseriu and Hjelmslev, I shall first have a look at three examples taken from Hjelmslev.

4.2 Hjelmslev's analysis of the content plane

In his main work, Hjelmslev (1953 [1943]) illustrates how it is possible to proceed with the analysis of the content plane in the same way as the expression plane, viz. by using the commutation test (in the first quote called "exchange test") that yield minimum invariants. Below, I shall refer to this example as 'Hjelmslev 1':

> If, for example, a mechanical inventorying at a given stage of the procedure leads to a registration of the entities of content 'ram', 'ewe', 'man', 'woman', 'boy', 'girl', 'stallion', 'mare', 'sheep', 'human being', 'child', 'horse', 'he', and 'she' – then 'ram', 'ewe', 'man', 'woman', 'boy', 'girl', 'stallion', and 'mare' must be eliminated from the inventory of elements if they can be explained univocally as relational units that include only 'he' and 'she' on the one hand, and 'sheep', 'human being', 'child', 'horse' on the other. Here, as in the expression plane, the criterion is the exchange test, by which a relation is found between correlations in each of the two planes. [...] 'Ram' = 'he-sheep' will be different from 'ewe' = 'she-sheep', just as *sl* will be different from, say, *fl* [...] The exchange of one and only one element for another is in both cases sufficient to entail an exchange in the other plane of the language. (Hjelmslev 1953 [1943]: 44)

At the Eighth International Congress of Linguists in Oslo (1957), Hjelmslev acted as chair of the session organized to discuss the question: "To what extent can meaning be said to be structured?" He gave the introductory report on the possibilities of establishing a structural semantics and attaches great importance to the use of the commutation test. Hjelmslev (1958: 645–646) provides the following example ('Hjelmslev 2', my translation, V.B.J.):

> Similarly, considering only the non-compound signs, the four semantic elements 'elder brother', 'younger brother', 'elder sister', 'younger sister' are all mutually commutable in Chinese and Hungarian, while in most European languages there is substitution between 'elder' and 'younger'; Malay, on the other hand, presents a substitution at the same time between 'elder' and 'younger' and between 'brother' and 'sister':

	Hungarian	French	Malay
'elder brother'	bátya	frère	sudarā
'younger brother'	öcs		
'elder sister'	néne	sœur	
'younger sister'	húg		

Hjelmslev (1958: 668) goes on to remind us that the lexicographic method used in monolingual dictionaries "has prepared the way for plerematic analysis of the smaller units, and in particular the semantemes". He adduces the following example from French ('Hjelmslev 3'):

	A	B
a	père	mère
b	frère	sœur
c	fils garçon	fille

Hjelmslev explains that the decomposition makes it possible to define each unit as composed of a unit from the vertical column a, b, c and a unit from the horizontal row A, B, which thus gives: $père = aA$, $mère = aB$, $frère = bA$, etc.

4.3 Coseriu and structural semantics: comparison with Hjelmslev

In a comment on Hjelmslev's report at the conference in Oslo, Coseriu (1958 [1957]) expresses doubts about the relevance of the commutation test with regard to the content plane. He takes issue with the commutation example reported in 'Hjelmslev 2' because, Coseriu argues, you can only know significations by means of other significations. This is different from the expression plane, where you are able to recognize a 'substitution' because you know the phonemic substance not only as phonemes but also as 'variants':

> And, in this regard, I must express my doubts with regard to the commutation test in the domain of content. We can identify a 'substitution' in the expression plane because we know, e.g., the phonic 'substance' otherwise than as phonemes (we know it also in the form of 'variants'). But we do not know significations otherwise than as significations. We can say that Fr. *frère* includes the significations 'frère aîné' [elder brother] et 'frère cadet' [younger brother] (between which there would be 'substitution'), but, as soon as it is thought and named, the signification 'frère aîné' is also *another unitary signification* and not simply a 'variant' of 'frère cadet', to which it is no longer substitutable from the moment it is expressed (Coseriu 1958 [1957]: 698).

Another point of contention is how to recognize parts of 'substance of the content' without giving it an expression. In Coseriu's contribution to the discussion, he does not mention anything in favour of using the commutation test in analyzing the content, nor does he refer to 'Hjelmslev 3'.

In Coseriu (1964), he explains on the first page that he prefers the Hjelmslevian terms 'expression' and 'content' to the Saussurean terms 'signifiant' and 'signifié' and proposes to make a diachronic study of the structure of the 'content plane'. At the same time, Coseriu expresses reservations against Hjelmslev's theoretical foundations (Coseriu 1964: 139). Later in the text, Coseriu also distances himself from Hjelmslev's comprehensive semantic project, i.e. Hjelmslev's endeavour to establish the 'minimal' functional elements of the lexical content of an entire language and to reduce *all* the 'open' classes of the lexicon to 'closed classes'. According to Coseriu, it is better to start more modestly by establishing partial systems; he refers to the theory of *Begriffsfelder* ('conceptual fields') which from that point will play a central role in his theory, as "lexical fields" (Coseriu 1964: 149). According to Coseriu, the conceptual fields correspond to Hjelmslev's 'small closed classes', and Coseriu remarks that "it is curious to note that Hjelmslev, in his report on the structure of the lexicon, held at the VIII Congress of Linguists, in which he also refers to other theories, does not mention the only one that so far has produced positive results in this regard [...] i.e. that of the *Begriffsfelder*" (Coseriu 1964: 155).

Coseriu (1964) also introduces the notion of 'distinctive features' into the field of semantics, and he combines their role with the commutation test: "We also believe that the theory of conceptual fields must be combined with the functional theory of linguistic oppositions [...] and that the commutation test should be applied equally to lexical relationships, not to identify the units, which are given, but to establish the distinctive features that characterize them, and thus the content oppositions within which the units themselves function" (Coseriu 1964: 157). In a note, Coseriu repeats his criticism of 'Hjelmslev 2', but the now explicit approval of the use of the commutation test in structural semantics is new. With the introduction of the concept of distinctive features, he apparently found a new domain for the commutation test. In another note, Coseriu (1964: 152) maintains that the content of lexical units ('words') is analogous to phonemes; as a consequence, differential semantic features are analogous to distinctive features in phonology. In this passage he refers to 'Hjelmslev 3' as a possible example of a similar way of interpreting a lexical unit.

Coseriu (1967 [1966]) discusses the relationship between "technique of discourse" and "repeated discourse" and introduces the issue of how to treat 'the functional level' in semantic analysis. In Coseriu's account of the two methods in the structural analysis of the lexicon (1966: 217, 1967 [1966]: 51), i.e. commutation and the distributional method, he maintains that commutation is the more basic method.

In Coseriu and Geckeler (1974: 127) we find a general assessment of Hjelmslev's contribution to the development of structural semantics. According to the authors, Hjelmslev's approach suffers from two limitations, viz. its elimination of semantic substance and its lack of a clear "separation between the lexical and the grammatical sphere". On the other hand, Coseriu and Geckeler acknowledge that Hjelmslev has "laid the foundation for the possibility of a structural semantics, with his idea that the content-level of language can be analyzed in a way analogous to the level of expression" (1974: 127). The previously criticized example 'Hjelmslev 2' is no longer addressed, but referring to 'Hjelmslev 1', the authors write: "While he considers, on the level of expression, already the phonemes as *figurae*, his *content figurae* correspond at least in part to what we now call *distinctive content features* or *semes*" (Coseriu and Geckeler 1974: 128). They then go on to discuss the role of the commutation test:

> The commutation test serves first of all to identify the functional units, the invariants, within a paradigm. However, this service is not necessary for content analysis, since the units are here given as already identified, if one disregards homophony and polysemy. On the other hand, however, the commutation test forms the instrument for the delimitation of the functional level and for the analysis of lexemes into distinctive features [...] (Coseriu and Geckeler 1974: 128).

The use of the commutation test is thus considered a characteristic property of the Coserian approach to structural semantics, and a direct relationship between Hjelmslev's theory and Coseriu's theory is explicitly acknowledged (Coseriu and

Geckeler 1974: 129). In a footnote (Coseriu and Geckeler 1974: 114, fn. 44), the authors moreover contend that both Hjelmslev and Coseriu consider lexicographical work already done as an important starting point for the practical realization of content analysis, while other linguists, e.g. Bernard Pottier and Uriel Weinreich, are said to have been mainly concerned with the weak theoretical bases of existing dictionaries.

In summary, in 1957 Coseriu does not yet acknowledge the relevance of the commutation test for semantics. He disagrees with 'Hjelmslev 2' and does not yet mention the concept of 'lexical field' nor 'distinctive semantic features'. In 1974, Coseriu uses (his own version of) the commutation test as a characteristic property of his own theory of meaning. He also regards 'Hjelmslev 1' as a precursor of the concept of 'distinctive semantic features' and emphasizes the mutual agreement regarding the value of previous lexicographical results. Hence, when Coseriu's claims in 1957 are taken into account, the development of Coseriu's structural semantics appears considerably less straightforward than suggested in Geckeler (1981b).

5 *Sistema, norma y habla* [System, norm and speech] (1952)

Hjelmslev is given a rather prominent place in Coseriu's first major publication. On the very first page, Hjelmslev is mentioned alongside John Lotz (1913–1973) because of their tripartition of the Saussurean dichotomy between *langue* and *parole*, i.e. their 'schema, established norm, *parole*' (hereafter referred to as the Hjelmslev/Lotz-tripartition). Two pages later, Coseriu argues that a tripartite division like Hjelmslev's (Coseriu has not introduced other examples of tripartition, so it is likely that he is still referring to the Hjelmslev/Lotz-tripartition) is useful, but it has to be made on a different basis and described in other terms. Hjelmslev is thus introduced as a starting point for Coseriu's own account. But is Hjelmslev also a direct inspiration? This is not easy to assess, as Coseriu does not include references to any text by Hjelmslev. There are only two indirect references along with a quote credited to Hjelmslev but with no precise bibliographic reference.

In this section, I shall follow a suggestion of T. De Mauro. According to De Mauro (2009), Coseriu's starting point was the theoretical ideas elaborated by Saussure and Hjelmslev as can be seen in Coseriu (1952) and (1954), later summed up by De Mauro (2009: 329) as follows: "Language is the concrete realization of specific utterances (*parole*). At the same time language is an abstract system of potentialities and limits". In what follows, I focus on Coseriu's concept of 'system'. Coseriu's 1952 study provides clues of Hjelmslevian inspiration, albeit in a rather indirect way. In the following two subsections, I distinguish between the Hjelmslev/Lotz-tripartition and Hjelmslev's tripartition. It is also important to note that, in accordance with the examples provided by Hjelmslev and Coseriu, Hjelmslev's 'norm' more or less corresponds to Coseriu's 'system', and Hjelmslev's 'usage' to Coseriu's 'norm' (Jensen 2015a: 30).

5.1 Hjelmslev's tripartition

Hjelmslev presents examples of a tripartite division on different occasions. For example, in his work on case (Hjelmslev 1935: 88ff.), he distinguishes between 'system', 'norm' and 'usage':

> The system is defined as an abstract and virtual reality. The system immediately reveals itself in the *norm*, which fixes, by rules, the possible latitude of variations in execution through speech. *Usage*, defined as the execution of the language by the majority of its speakers in a given environment, is different from norm. Usage constitutes the adopted mode, the set of preferred ways of execution of the language [...]. By making use of these distinctions we can say that the system is a set of possibilities among which usage makes a certain choice (my translation, V.B.J.).

The most important explanation of a tripartite division is to be found in Hjelmslev (1942). Hjelmslev here introduces the term 'schema' and adds in a footnote that he himself sometimes used 'system' instead of 'schema' in previous accounts. According to Hjelmslev, Saussure's *langue* covers all the three elements in this tripartition (schema, norm, usage), albeit rather vaguely, whereas *parole* refers to what is also known as the speech act. Hjelmslev (1942) rejects the concept of norm as superfluous, arguing that it is really something we only infer from usage. In Hjelmslev's treatise on case (1935), norm had been a key concept, and returning to semantic problems in Hjelmslev (1958), he again refers to norms in order to determine the semantic range of words. In the intervening period he dropped the concept completely, which also enabled him to reject the Prague School's conception of the phoneme (Fischer-Jørgensen 1995 [1975]: 123–124). At the point in time when Coseriu introduced his tripartite division, i.e. in 1952, the level referred to by Coseriu as 'system' (which corresponds to Hjelmslev's 'norm') was obviously neglected in Hjelmslev's publications. What remains to be answered is, however, a fundamental question regarding Coseriu (1952): why does he not quote Hjelmslev's aforementioned well-known tripartite division from 1942? Fischer-Jørgensen raised this question in 1955 in a letter to Coseriu, but Coseriu apparently never answered (Jensen 2015a).[4]

5.2 The 1951 Nice conference as a background for Coseriu's tripartition

The Hjelmslev/Lotz tripartite division 'schema, established norm, *parole*' mentioned in Coseriu (1952) is taken from a short account by Devoto (1951) of a conference on semantics in Nice organized by Émile Benveniste. However, in the Hjelmslev/Lotz-tripartition, the distinction which Hjelmslev had made in his own accounts (most comprehensively in 1942) between 'norm' and 'usage' (Coseriu's 'system' and 'norm') is blurred. The main reason is that the Hjelmslev/Lotz-tripartition presented in Nice is, for Hjelmslev, a compromise with the other participants (see, e.g., some of Hjelmslev's comments pointing out problems in the discussion as reproduced in the proceedings of the conference, Benveniste 1951: 87).

Coseriu establishes two critical points of difference between his tripartition and the ones of Hjelmslev and Hjelmslev/Lotz. Firstly, Coseriu considers Saussure's *langue* to be a concept related to historical linguistics, unlike Hjelmslev, for whom *langue* pertains to theoretical linguistics, according to Coseriu (1952: 5). Secondly, the concept 'system' in Coseriu, in contrast to the concept 'schema' in Hjelmslev, includes the substance of the sounds (Coseriu: 1952: 60). However, there are also indications in Coseriu's account that his 'system' nevertheless bears the mark of Hjelmslev to some extent. Coseriu (1952: 14 and 21) introduces the notion *réseau de fonctions* ('network of functions'), explicitly referring to it as stemming from Hjelmslev, and on page 58 Coseriu writes: "As a matter of fact, the *system* presents itself, from this point of view, as an abstract entity, 'a network of functions' [...]". There is again no specific reference to a publication by Hjelmslev, but the 'system' is unambiguously associated with Hjelmslev, and in the following paragraph the system is defined as "a system of possibilities". Coseriu mentions the constraints due to the system, but at the same time he emphasizes that the system is associated with the "freedom" implied in the possibility of infinite realizations which only require that they are not in conflict

---

[4] A comparison of Coseriu's and Hjelmslev's terms yields the following chart:

Hjelmslev:	Schema	Norm	Usage	
Coseriu:		System	Norm	Speech

In this schematic presentation, I only include the terms that are most relevant for the discussion in this article.

with the functional conditions of the language. This arguably resembles Hjelmslev's reasoning.

Although Coseriu's 'system' thus definitely possesses a Hjelmslevian flavour, it seems important for Coseriu to draw a distinction between his 'system' and Hjelmslev's 'schema'. However, if Coseriu had compared the conceptual content of his 'system' with the Hjelmslevian concept of 'norm' (from 1935 or 1942), he would have found it much more difficult to demonstrate a substantial difference between both accounts and their corresponding terminologies.

As pointed out above, it is possible to find in Coseriu (1952) a kind of text-documented line of thought which goes from Hjelmslev to 'system' (in the Coserian sense) and further to a 'system of possibilities'. It is, however, not possible to find a direct text reference to a specific passage in one of Hjelmslev's texts. In this regard, Martinet's famous review of Hjelmslev (1943) is of primary importance (Martinet 1946). Coseriu quotes Martinet (1946) twice (Coseriu 1952: 5, 39–40[5]), and it is quite clear that he has studied the review in depth. Coseriu could also have found "Hjelmslev's possibilities" by reading Martinet (1946: 24), who twice describes how the aim of Hjelmslev's theory, once constituted, is to make it possible to predict "all the imaginable linguistic possibilities" ("toutes les possibilités linguistiques pensables"). This passage is not directly quoted in Coseriu (1952). As mentioned above, Coseriu might quite well have had access to Hjelmslev (1943) while still staying in Europe. At any rate, in 1954, when Coseriu had the possibility to directly quote from Hjelmslev (1953 [1943]) (in the English translation), he explicitly calls glossematics a "science of possibilities": "[...] the level on which glossematics is situated is not the same level of abstraction as linguistics; glossematics is not a science of concrete reality or history, but the science of possibilities" (Coseriu 1954: 55). Coseriu thus assigns the 'possibilities' to the level of the 'schema' in Hjelmslev's theory, whereas Coseriu (1952) himself assigns them to the level of the 'system' (the 'norm' in Hjelmslev's terms). This means that Coseriu attributes the 'possibilities' to a less abstract level compared to Hjelmslev and then combines it with an emphasis on the constraints that the (Coserian) norm imposes on the possibilities in the language community. In so doing, Coseriu manages to give the concept of 'possibilities' a place in his theory which seems more easily applicable to the analysis of 'functional languages', as Coseriu calls them. On the other hand, the methodological instructions for telling us how to analyse and describe an en-

---

5 In the latter case, Coseriu gives a reference to Hjelmslev (1943) but without pagination, and the passage is almost identical to a passage in Martinet (1946: 31). It is therefore probable that Coseriu draws on Martinet's review rather than Hjelmslev's original publication.

tire system are less clear. Coseriu often explains his ideas by means of concrete examples which are very convincing. However, unlike Hjelmslev, he does not provide precise procedural instructions. At any rate, much work remains to be done with regard to the material harboured in the Coseriu Archive if we wish to reconstruct in detail the inspiration Coseriu found in Hjelmslev.

6 Conclusion

Hjelmslev's scholarly work undoubtedly played a major role in Coseriu's development as a scholar, albeit in various ways. As for the relation between form and substance, Hjelmslev is the orthodox representative of the Saussurean theory of language who is at the centre of Coseriu's critical account, in which Coseriu defines his own position to a large extent in opposition to that of Hjelmslev. With respect to this subject matter, Coseriu's relationship to Hjelmslev's work is quite stable. With regard to variational linguistics, Coseriu adopts some of Leiv Flydal's concepts early on, but it is not until later that he acknowledges that these concepts have their origin in Hjelmslev's chapter on connotative semiotics. Regarding structural semantics, we saw that Coseriu's relationship to Hjelmslev's theory is more complex. In 1957, Coseriu emphasizes above all the divergences to Hjelmslev's proposals, while from 1963–1964 onwards he expresses support for some of Hjelmslev's central ideas and terminological distinctions, albeit partially changing their content.

Finally, Hjelmslev's influence on Coseriu's first major publication *Sistema, norma y habla* (1952) is more difficult to assess. The 'relocation' of 'possibilities' from the 'schema' level to the 'system' level shows that Coseriu can use Hjelmslev's theory not only as a source of inspiration, but also as a demarcation point for his own theory. First of all, Hjelmslev can be interpreted as probably the most orthodox, or consistent, follower of Saussure, so in distancing himself from Hjelmslev, Coseriu can also distance himself from Saussure. Secondly, Hjelmslev is trying to develop a 'minimal, formalist, theory' at a very abstract level, according to Coseriu on a higher level than linguistics proper and with a focus on the central parts of a general semiotic theory. This part of Hjelmslev's project is readily acknowledged by Coseriu, but it is not Coseriu's own project, so everything else is left open to Coseriu's 'Integral Linguistics'. These two 'demarcation points' may explain why it seems more important for Coseriu to deal with the theories proposed by Hjelmslev than with those proposed by Roman Jakobson. However, in many respects – in particular regarding phonology – Coseriu seems closer to Jakobson than to Hjelmslev.

References

Benveniste, Émile (ed.). 1951. *Actes de la conférence européenne de sémantique (Nice 26–31 mars 1951)*. Paris: Société de linguistique de Paris.

Coseriu, Eugenio. 1952. *Sistema, norma y habla*. Montevideo: Universidad de la República, Facultad de Humanidades y Ciencias. (Reprint: Coseriu 1973 [1952].)

Coseriu, Eugenio. 1954. *Forma y sustancia en los sonidos del lenguaje*. Montevideo: Universidad de la República, Facultad de Humanidades y Ciencias. (Reprint: Coseriu 1973 [1954].)

Coseriu, Eugenio. 1958 [1957]. "Discussion". In: *Actes du Huitième Congrès International des Linguistes (1957)*, 697–699. Oslo: Presses Universitaires d'Oslo.

Coseriu, Eugenio. 1964. "Pour une sémantique diachronique structurale". *Travaux de linguistique et de littérature* (Strasbourg) 2:1, 139–186.

Coseriu, Eugenio. 1966. "Structure lexicale et enseignement du vocabulaire". In: *Actes du Premier Colloque International de Linguistique Appliquée*, 175–217. Nancy: Annales de l'Est.

Coseriu, Eugenio. 1967 [1966]. "Lexical structure and the teaching of vocabulary". In: *Linguistic theories and their applications*. Strasbourg: The Council of Europe (English translation of 1966).

Coseriu, Eugenio. 1967e. "Lexikalische Solidaritäten". *Poetica* 1, 293–303.

Coseriu, Eugenio. 1968. "Les structures lexématiques". In: Wilhelm Theodor Elwert (ed.), *Probleme der Semantik* (Zeitschrift für französische Sprache und Literatur, Neue Folge, Beiheft 1), 3–16. Wiesbaden: Steiner.

Coseriu, Eugenio. 1973 [1952]. "Sistema, norma y habla". In: Eugenio Coseriu, *Teoría del lenguaje y lingüística general. Cinco estudios*, 11–113. Madrid: Gredos.

Coseriu, Eugenio. 1973 [1954]. "Forma y sustancia en los sonidos del lenguaje". In: Eugenio Coseriu, *Teoría del lenguaje y lingüística general. Cinco estudios*, 115–234. Madrid: Gredos.

Coseriu, Eugenio. 1973 [1962]. *Teoría del lenguaje y lingüística general. Cinco estudios* (third edition). Madrid: Gredos.

Coseriu, Eugenio. 1973. *Probleme der strukturellen Semantik*. Edited by Dieter Kastovsky. Tübingen: Narr.

Coseriu, Eugenio. 1976a. "Die funktionelle Betrachtung des Wortschatzes". In: Hugo Moser (ed.), *Probleme der Lexikologie und Lexikographie. Jahrbuch 1975 des Instituts für deutsche Sprache*, 7–25. Düsseldorf: Schwann.

Coseriu, Eugenio. 1976b. "L'étude fonctionelle du vocabulaire. Précis de lexématique". *Cahiers de lexicologie* 29, 5–23.

Coseriu. Eugenio. 1981 [1958] "Los conceptos de 'dialecto', 'nivel' y 'estilo de lengua' y el sentido propio de la dialectología". *Lingüística española actual* 3:1, 1–32.

Coseriu, Eugenio. 1992 [1988]. *Einführung in die allgemeine Sprachwissenschaft* (second edition). Tübingen: Francke. (German translation of Coseriu 1981.)

Coseriu, Eugenio. 1994. "My Pagliaro". In: Tullio de Mauro and Lia Formigari (eds.), *Italian studies in linguistic historiography*, 39–44. Münster: Nodus.

Coseriu, Eugenio. 1995a. "My Saussure". In: Tullio de Mauro and Shigeaki Sugeta (eds.), *Saussure and linguistics today*, 187–191. Roma: Bulzoni.

Coseriu, Eugenio. 2007 [1980]. *Textlinguistik. Eine Einführung.* Edited by Jörn Albrecht (fourth edition). Tübingen: Narr.
Coseriu, Eugenio. 2008 [1964]. "Towards a structuralist diachronic semantics". In: Patrick Hanks (ed.), *Lexicology. Critical concepts in Linguistics.* Vol. 2: *Lexical semantics and structures,* 140–193. London: Routledge (Englisch translation of Coseriu 1964).
Coseriu, Eugenio. 2015. *Geschichte der Sprachphilosophie.* Vol. 1: *Von Heraklit bis Rousseau.* Vol. 2: *Von Herder bis Humboldt.* Edited by Jörn Albrecht. Tübingen: Narr & Francke: Attempto.
Coseriu, Eugenio and Horst Geckeler. 1974. "Linguistics and Semantics". In: Thomas A. Sebeok (ed.), *Current Trends in Linguistics,* Vol. 12, 103–172. The Hague & Paris: Mouton.
De Mauro, Tullio. 2007. "Prefazione". In: Eugenio Coseriu, *Il linguaggio e l'uomo attuale. Saggi di filosofia del linguaggio,* ed. by Christian Bota, Massimo Schiavi, Giuseppe Di Salvatore and Lidia Gasperoni, 9–16. Verona: Edizioni Centro Studi Campostrini.
De Mauro, Tullio. 2009. "Eugenio Coseriu". In: Harro Stammerjohann (ed.), *Lexicon Grammaticorum. A bio-bibliographical companion to the history of linguistics* (second edition), 327–330. Tübingen: Niemeyer.
De Mauro, Tullio. 2015. "Indirizzo di saluto di Tullio De Mauro". In: Vincenzo Orioles and Raffaella Bombi (eds.), *Oltre Saussure: L'eredità scientifica di Eugenio Coseriu. Atti del IV Convegno Internazionale Università degli Studi di Udine* (1–2 ottobre 2013), 15–18. Firenze: Franco Cesati.
Devoto, Giacomo. 1951. "Cronaca". *Archivio glottologico italiano* 36, 82–84.
Fischer-Jørgensen, Eli. 1995 [1975]. *Trends in phonological theory until 1975. A historical introduction.* (Travaux du Cercle Linguistique de Copenhague, 27.) København: Akademisk Forlag.
Flydal, Leiv. 1952. "Remarques sur certains rapports entre le style et l'état de langue". *Norsk Tidsskrift for Sprogvidenskap* 16, 241–258. (Occasionally cited as 'Flydal 1951' due to offprints of the article dated 1951.)
Geckeler, Horst. 1981b. "Progrès et stagnation en sémantique structurale". In: Horst Geckeler, Brigitte Schlieben-Lange, Jürgen Trabant and Harald Weydt (eds.), *Logos semantikos. Studia linguistica in honorem Eugenio Coseriu 1921–1981,* Vol. III, 53–69. Berlin & New York: Walter de Gruyter.
Hjelmslev, Louis. 1935. *La catégorie des cas. Étude de grammaire générale.* Première partie. *Acta Jutlandica* 7:1. Aarhus: Universitetsforlaget.
Hjelmslev, Louis. 1942. "Langue et Parole". *Cahiers Ferdinand de Saussure* 2, 29–44. Reprinted in: Louis Hjelmslev. 1959. *Essais linguistiques.* Vol. I, 69–81. (Travaux du Cercle Linguistique de Copenhague 12.) København: Nordisk Sprog- og Kulturforlag.
Hjelmslev, Louis. 1943. *Omkring sprogteoriens grundlæggelse.* København: Festskrift udgivet af Københavns Universitet.
Hjelmslev, Louis. 1953 [1943]. *Prolegomena to a theory of language.* Translated by Francis J. Whitfield. Baltimore: Waverly Press.
Hjelmslev, Louis. 1961 [1943]. *Prolegomena to a theory of language.* Translated by Francis J. Whitfield (second edition). Madison: The University of Wisconsin Press.
Hjelmslev, Louis. 1958. "Dans quelle mesure les significations des mots peuvent-elles être consideréés comme formant une structure, rapport par Louis Hjelmslev". In: *Actes du Huitième Congrès International des Linguistes (1957),* 636–654, "Discussion",

666–669, "Conclusion", 704. Oslo: Presses Universitaires d'Oslo. Reprinted as "Pour une sémantique structurale" in: Louis Hjelmslev. 1959. *Essais linguistiques*. Vol. I, 96–112. (*Travaux du Cercle Linguistique de Copenhague* 12.) København: Nordisk Sprog- og Kulturforlag.

Hjelmslev Archives, Royal Danish Library, Acc. 1992/5. See also the site https://cc.au.dk/en/infrastructuralism/about-project-infrastructuralism/

Jensen, Viggo Bank. 2012. "Eugenio Coseriu, Scandinavian linguists and variational linguistics". *Dacoromania. Serie nouă* 17:2, 154–162.

Jensen, Viggo Bank. 2015a. "Eli Fischer-Jørgensen, Eugenio Coseriu et Louis Hjelmslev: Quelque points d'une correspondance". *Cahiers Ferdinand de Saussure* 68, 27–45.

Jensen, Viggo Bank. 2015b. "Il ruolo della "Scuola di Copenaghen" nel "rimodellamento" coseriano degli assiomi saussuriani". In: Vincenzo Orioles and Raffaella Bombi (eds.), *Oltre Saussure: L'eredità scientifica di Eugenio Coseriu. Atti del IV Convegno Internazionale Università degli Studi di Udine* (1–2 ottobre 2013), 121–132. Firenze: Franco Cesati.

Jensen, Viggo Bank. 2020. "Introduction". In: Viggo Bank Jensen and Giuseppe D'Ottavi (eds.), *From the Early Years of Phonology. The Roman Jakobson – Eli Fischer-Jørgensen correspondence (1949–1982)*, 11–84. Copenhagen: Det Kongelige Danske Videnskabernes Selskab.

Joseph, John Earl. 2012. *Saussure*. Oxford: Oxford University Press.

Martinet. André. 1946. "Au sujet des "*Fondements de la théorie linguistique de Louis Hjelmslev*"". *Bulletin de la société linguistique de Paris* 42, 19–42.

Rasmussen, Michael. 1992. *Hjelmslevs sprogteori*. Odense: Odense Universitetsforlag.

Saussure, Ferdinand de. 1975 [1916]. *Cours de linguistique générale*. Edited by Tullio De Mauro. Paris: Payot.

Urban, Wilbur Marshall. 1939. *Language and Reality*. London: Macmillan.

Völker, Harald. 2009. "La linguistique variationnelle et la perspective intralinguistique". *Revue de Linguistique Romane* 73, 27–76.

Völker, Harald. 2013. "The diasystem and its role in generating meaning: Diachronic evidence from Old French". In: Deborah Artaega (ed.), *Research on Old French: the state of the art*, 187–204. Dordrecht: Springer.

Lorenzo Cigana (Copenhagen)
Coseriu and glossematics: an uncompleted dialogue

> For we are convinced that glossematics marks a decisive point in the history of linguistics. It cannot be passed over, or regarded simply as a 'deviation' from the course of the language sciences proper, since it actually – and despite what Hjelmslev himself claims – takes up and continues a tradition that can be traced back to the founder of general linguistics, Wilhelm von Humboldt.*

1 Introduction

The importance of Louis Hjelmslev's ideas for the writings of Eugenio Coseriu has been emphasized by many researchers (Trabant 1987, Völker 2009, Jensen 2012, among others). Given the highly abstract view on language that glossematics endorses, as well as Coseriu's sceptical remarks on such 'mathematical' approaches, one might expect a maximal distance between Hjelmslev's and Coseriu's positions. Hjelmslevian radical formalism would inevitably seem to clash with Coseriu's Humboldtianism. Yet despite the appearance, philological evidence has been provided that rather points towards Coseriu's appraisal of Hjelmslev's thought, in particular regarding crucial points such as the distinctions between system, norm and usage, the relation between form and substance, and commutation (cf. Jensen 2012, 2015b).

In this article, I intend to substantiate Coseriu's claim quoted above by examining the proximity between the two views on language, paying special attention to three different issues – purposiveness (Sp. *finalidad*), markedness and connotation – that are linked by their being conditions for linguistic change. The relation between Coseriu and Hjelmslev regarding the first two aspects has been highlighted by Andersen (1990) and De Backer (2009). As a matter of fact, given Coseriu's remarks on teleology, the proximity between the two approaches is far from self-evident and deserves a more detailed epistemological analysis. As regarding the third aspect, while Coseriu's interest in Hjelmslev's

---

* "En efecto, estamos convencidos de que la glosemática representa un momento esencial en la historia de la lingüística, que no puede ignorarse ni considerarse simplemente como una "desviación" del camino propio de la ciencia del lenguaje, porque, en realidad – y a pesar de lo que afirma el mismo Hjelmslev –, ella retoma y continúa una tradición que puede hacerse remontar hasta el fundador de la lingüística general, W. von Humboldt" (Coseriu 1973 [1954]: 175).

concept of connotation via Leiv Flydal is well established (cf. Völker 2009; Jensen 2012), the issue of connotation itself has rarely been addressed in the light of the distinction between synchrony and diachrony.

The comparison will be carried out in counterpoint. Section 2 deals with Coseriu's perspective which is subsequently contrasted in Section 3 to Hjelmslev's. In Section 4, I argue that the synergy between Coseriu and Hjelmslev on several points should not be simply read as evidence of Coseriu's critical reception, but exploited as a promising avenue for reframing various claims of both authors. Ideally, this would lead to a better understanding of the divergences and similarities between both as well as a renewed interpretation of the ill-reputed formalist stance of structuralism.

2 Coseriu on linguistic change

One of Coseriu's main aims was to resolve (G. *aufheben*) Saussure's antinomy between synchrony and diachrony. He explicitly intended to challenge some assumptions concerning the separation between language and its synchronic constitution on the one side and diachronic change on the other, aiming to integrate Saussure's views with Humboldt's concept of ἐνέργεια. Throughout Coseriu's work, such *Aufhebung* takes the form of extensive discussions of both the conceptual and the terminological architecture of various theories in order to disclose their epistemological underpinnings as well as exposing their naturalistic, mechanistic or organicist premises.

Most of Coseriu's criticisms address "diachronic structuralism" (Coseriu 1978 [1958]: 210), especially insofar as it bears traces of the Neogrammarian account, which describes a (sound) change in terms of a tautological replacement of one unit or state by another unit or state. Structuralism, too, runs the risk of reducing change to a mere substitution between two successive states, systems or structures ('mutation', cf. Coseriu 1978 [1958]: 220–222; 1968 [1965]: 288), which however can only take place within language conceived of as as ἔργον, i.e. a static collection of phenomena, according to Coseriu (1978 [1958]: 97–98). Yet the coexistence of alternative possibilities in a state – or even the coexistence of different states concerning a single variant, both representing the proper historical process of changing – inevitably gets lost in such an approach.

Insofar as structuralism tries to make linguistic laws more precise and stringent in order to grasp the evolution of a linguistic state, it still incurs the same fallacy of the Neogrammarian approach and can be said to continue its mechanical, causal framework (Coseriu 1978 [1958]: 201). The point is not to improve the concept of necessity, in the vain attempt to rank linguistics among the exact sciences, but to discard it altogether: admitting exceptions on linguistic laws is not a consequence of any incomplete knowledge of how language works, Coseriu (1978 [1958]: 233) argues, but an inbuilt feature of language itself, because language at work is the realisation of potentialities. Linguistic laws are thus not laws of necessity but laws of possibility: they do not concern causes but rather general conditions for change. Accordingly, the interpretation of change as a projection of synchronic features into a second, abstract dimension has to be rejected. Change is not a collection of phenomena to be observed under a specific angle, but rather the intrinsically dynamic process in which linguistic tradition consolidates itself on different levels, hence language in its own making (Coseriu 1978 [1958]: 108–109). Yet even adopting the distinction between synchrony and diachrony as a distinct methodological perspective rather than a realistic separation of actual phenomena (Coseriu 1968 [1965]: 273) might not be sufficient, as change cannot be approached from one perspective at the expense of the other. Being the *factum* of language, change demands to be grasped in its integrity, as *enérgeia*, i.e. as ongoing systematization through which linguistic facts are established and codified.

Coseriu suggests that the issue of change be tackled on three distinct levels (Coseriu 1978 [1958]: 56; cf. Andersen 2006: 63)[1]: the universal level, which is concerned with the problem of 'mutability' of languages and the only real 'cause' behind it, viz. human freedom; the general level, on which the conditions for linguistic change can be provided; and the historical level, which concerns the actual context of change for a given language. Within this framework, three more issues can be identified on which Coseriu's theory of linguistic change is built:

1) a stratified view of language based on the intersection of two distinctions: one, hierarchical, between the functional layers of language (type, system and norm), and a second, variational, between historical and functional language leading to different subsystems (cf. Section 2.1);
2) the distinction between causality and purposiveness concerning the direction of change: the so-called 'causes' of linguistic change are rather conditions than motivations for change, whose only proper cause is human freedom (cf. Section 2.2);

---

[1] It seems that Andersen (2006: 63, n. 4) came closest to formulating Coseriu's distinction in terms comparable to Hjelmslev's repartition of linguistic theory into "universal", "general" and "particular" components (Hjelmslev 1975: Df. 1, 2, 65) – the first level consisting of the defining features allowing a language to be described as such, the second level concerning the network of possibilities each language consists of, and the third level consisting of the actualized configuration of a given language.

3) the idea that the functional layer (the system) is organized in terms of inclusive oppositions, so that change is described as a reconfiguration in the network of such oppositions (cf. Section 2.3).

2.1 The 'polysystematic' nature of language

The first issue pertains to the hierarchical distinction of three functional strata, namely 'type', 'system' and 'norm' (Coseriu 1968 [1965]: 276–278; Coseriu 1983: 61 ff.). This distinction echoes a similar one advocated by Hjelmslev, as Eli Fischer-Jørgensen pointed out in a letter she wrote to Coseriu (cf. Fischer-Jørgensen 1995 [1975]: 124; on this, cf. in particular Jensen 2015a: 29–32, 43–44). Change is rendered in terms of actualization, in a given stratum, of means and possibilities set on a higher stratum (Coseriu 1968 [1965]: 278, 280), so that the diachronic movement (Sp. *movimiento*) of each stratum – consisting of the punctual acts of selection by speakers – coincides with the synchronic functioning (Sp. *funcionamiento*) of the superordinate stratum: "for in reality there is diachrony in the norm within synchrony – functioning – of the system, and diachrony of the system within synchrony of the language type" (Coseriu 1983: 62). It is worth noticing that within such a framework movement presupposes functioning, and functioning is essentially conceived of as *systematization*. This means that a language does not function because it is a system. It is rather the other way round: a language functions *as* a system.

Such a system is far from monolithic. Through the second distinction, borrowed from Flydal (1952) (and indirectly from Hjelmslev, cf. Völker 2009, Jensen 2012), the diatopically, diastratically and diaphasically heterogeneous 'historical language' is distinguished from the 'functional language', understood as a complex stratification of a plurality of (syntopic, synstratic or symphasic) homogenous systems. In these terms, a historical language results from the interaction of all these layers, thus corresponding to a functional language provided with (possibly multiple) traditions of speaking. This can account for the facts that 1) different norms may correspond to a single system (Coseriu 1968 [1965]: 277) and 2) a single norm may include realizations that are seemingly contrary to one given system (Coseriu 1978 [1958]: 131). However, both 1) and 2) can be explained by assuming the intervention of partial systems (Coseriu and Geckeler 1981: 51) within the overarching architecture of a functional language (the so-called 'diasystem'). While entailing the coexistence of such partial systems, the diasystem does not necessarily imply that these move at the same pace or according to the same rules. Rather, each one of the partial systems functions on its own accord, having its own 'synchrony' (cf. Coseriu 1966: 194): such 'polysystematicity' (Coseriu 1973 [1954]: 77; 1964: 140) thus serves as an essential requisite if we want 1) to understand the purposiveness (i.e. direction) of change (cf. Andersen 1990: 13, 14) and 2) to describe the internal organization of a given system in terms of oppositions, as oppositions can only be established within a homogeneous domain (Coseriu and Geckeler 1981: 53).[2]

2.2 Causality and purposiveness

The second issue concerns a finalistic view of language, which recasts the role of the speakers. Speakers are not perceived as mere "users" (Willems 2003: 7), but rather in Humboldtian terms as those who re-create language from within, re-enacting its structure through conscious selection and actualization of linguistic resources (possibilities) according to each one's own practical and expressive goals. Language as a whole, then, is an intrinsically instable, internally articulated totality, resulting from multiple discrete and individual acts and moving at different paces along the vectorial average of all its components. Direction of change thus relies on the finalistic nature of speakers' acts, through which virtual possibilities encoded on a 'lower' layer are selected and actualized.

According to Coseriu, it must be possible to capture those movements in a methodologically sound, objective way while avoiding their reification, which would result from unduly abstracting them from the speakers (Coseriu 1978 [1958]: 228, 229–230). For the most part, diachronic structuralism fails to keep these two aspects apart. For instance, Anton Marty's and Otto Funke's idea of *tastende Auslese* ('fumbling selection') as well as Henri Frei's concept of unconscious purposiveness are well suited to account for both linguistic stability and oscillations (Coseriu 1978 [1958]: 198, 225), especially as they reflect the "intuitively made interpretation" of the speakers (Coseriu 1983: 62). However, resorting to the unconscious is merely a way to justify the regularity of change by relocating causality outside the speakers' consciousness, ultimately disregarding their freedom. Such an approach, then, is just a reiteration of the old mechanistic view of linguistic change. The same holds, according to Coseriu (1978 [1958]: 226), for Edward Sapir's and Otto Jespersen's idea of drift, the multiple variants of the 'tendency' (Antoine Meillet, Maurice Grammont) towards conservation, simplicity (André Martinet) or harmony (Nikolai Trubetzkoy, but also for Hjelm-

---

[2] Note that 'homogenous' does not mean 'regular' (cf. Coseriu 1964: 156).

slev's notion of dispositions.³ All these notions imply the risk of a fallacious hypostatical approach *à la* Durkheim (cf. Coseriu 1978 [1958]: 32ff.), according to which speakers conform to a system and to its evolution because of the imperative pressure of the system on the speakers.

Reification is singularly problematic insofar as it supports the unfounded claim of external, independent causation. From Coseriu's perspective, any causal explanations have to be rejected and replaced by explanations that draw on purposiveness, which is the hallmark of "any individual act of adoption of linguistic means" (Coseriu 1978 [1958]: 224). A further distinction must be made between subjective and objective purposiveness (Coseriu 1983: 63; Sp. *finalidad* is there translated as 'finality'). Subjective purposiveness explains both the intentional and the local nature of speakers' behaviour, i.e. the fact that speakers select and actualize specific means, viz. those that match their specific expressive needs. Thus, speakers' behaviour intervenes only on partial sections of the system. By contrast, objective purposiveness reflects the fact that linguistic resources are tapped collectively and that individual freedom is conditioned in a twofold manner: by concomitant actions of different subjects but also by the range of communicative techniques encoded in the system. Objective purposiveness is valid if it refers to norms of the speakers' activity, according to Coseriu (1983: 63; 1978 [1958]: 229), but not if it refers to disembodied forces that allegedly act upon the subjects from outside. Concepts such as 'simplicity', 'economy', 'system pressure', etc. must consequently be understood as objective conditions (to be referred to as 'motivations') of change, not as impersonal causes: "these norms tell us not why but how linguistic change occurs; and not absolutely and necessarily, but how ἐπί τὸ πολύ: in most cases" (Coseriu 1983: 63). Markedness is possibly the most important among these norms.

2.3 Markedness and inclusive oppositions

Markedness can account for how possibilities are chosen and actualized in relation to the paradigmatic organization of a given system. It is not surprising that Coseriu's interest in this aspect of language was bound to increase over time. As a matter of fact, Coseriu incorporated Hjelmslev's terminology relating to markedness into his framework (cf. Coseriu 1964: 151 and *passim*; Coseriu 1976 [1968 –

---

3 Even if not explicitly mentioned by Coseriu, the reference applies to Hjelmslev, too. The observation that change does not result from an "internal logic" (Coseriu 1978 [1958]: 227, 230), which inevitably leads to a "mysticism of the system" (Coseriu 1978 [1958]: 212), is consistent with Coseriu's critical reception of Hjelmslev's approach.

1969]: 59; cf. De Backer 2009) and in 1988 he recognized markedness (properly speaking: 'neutralisation', cf. De Backer 2009, 2013) as an essential element of linguistic theory (Coseriu 1992 [1988]: 225). Considering the extensive discussion that the principles of linguistic oppositions between marked ('extensive') and unmarked ('intensive') terms receive in Hjelmslev's *La catégorie des cas* (1935, 1937), it is possible that Coseriu's re-edition of this work in 1972 (Hjelmslev 1972b) was due to a renewed interest in Hjelmslev's approach. An account of the general development of Coseriu's approach on this topic lies beyond the scope of this paper (for this, see De Backer 2009, 2010, 2013), instead I will only discuss it in connection with linguistic change and Hjelmslev's thoughts on the subject.

Assumed to be an inbuilt property of language, inclusive oppositions can explain typical 'irregularities' to be found within a given state (Coseriu 1964: 156) such as neutralisations, ambiguity and the asymmetrical distribution of units. Hence their importance (cf. Coseriu 1992 [1988]: 212–231). Moreover, it is thanks to inclusive oppositions, rather than commutation, that a semantic configuration of a lexical field becomes a proper "linguistic structure" (Coseriu 1964: 157; cf. Coseriu and Geckeler 1981: 57). And if linguistic structure is overall perceived as intrinsically dynamic, then it seems consistent to assume that inclusive oppositions represent the 'schema' for linguistic change, even more so as they were indeed conceived in terms of objective teleology (see Section 2.2).

These assumptions form the basic tenets of Coseriu's diachronic structural semantics (Coseriu 1964; cf. 2008 [1964]): functional change (called 'modification') is explained in terms of the "appearance or disappearance of a distinctive feature and, thus, constitution or dissolution of an opposition" (Coseriu 1964: 159–160, 173 ff.; cf. Coseriu and Geckeler 1981: 65) within each partial system that belongs to a single level or 'plane'. One of the most striking features of Coseriu's proposal is that modifications are typologically classified on a combinatory base, according to the structure of linguistic oppositions. Such a typology is only meaningful if not all combinations are possible, that is to say: only if some directions of change can be pinpointed. According to Coseriu, an opposition can be simple (between two terms only) or complex (involving more than two terms), neutralisable or non-neutralisable (Coseriu 1964: 176). This last feature strictly depends on the structure of the opposition encoded in the system, i.e. whether the opposition occurs between marked *and* unmarked terms (thus being in principle neutralisable) or only between marked terms (thus being non-neutralisable). The case of an opposition consisting only of (two or more) unmarked terms is excluded a priori.

Accordingly, the 'constitution' of an opposition is said to always involve the appearance of a marked term (Coseriu 1964: 175), which follows from the as-

sumption that an opposition is introduced within a previously given term, by excising, as it were, a portion in the initially broader meaning of the latter. This originally marked term can become unmarked or marked, in turn leaving room for another unmarked term or 'locking' the opposition as non-neutralisable. The 'dissolution' of an opposition, on the other hand, involves a more complex combination. Within simple oppositions,
(1) the unmarked term can eliminate the marked one,
(2) the marked term can eliminate the unmarked one,
(3) one marked term can eliminate another marked one (thus dissolving the non-neutralisable opposition as such).

Conversely, within complex oppositions,
(4) the unmarked term can eliminate a marked one,
(5) the unmarked term can eliminate all the marked ones,
(6) one marked term can eliminate another marked one,
(7) a marked term can eliminate all the marked ones.

Examples for such cases are provided in Coseriu (1964: 175 ff.) and occasionally discussed in the literature (compare, for instance, Coseriu's example of the relationship between G. *Tag* 'day' and *Nacht* 'night' discussed in De Backer 2010: the unmarked word *Tag* can be used to refer to 'day' *and* 'day and night' whereas the marked word *Nacht* can only be used to refer to 'night'). We need not go into detail here, as it is quite clear that a modification is said to occur through elimination of a term by incorporation (of the marked by the unmarked), substitution (of a marked by another marked) or rarefaction (the unmarked term tends to dissolve progressively becoming more rare, see no. 2). In all these cases, the new term inherits the features of the suppressed term or terms, as indeed the change – at least when it comes to simple oppositions – always leads to the constitution of a new 'unmarked' (neutral) term (Coseriu 1964: 176). Despite some difficulties of this approach (especially regarding no. 2),[4] the underlying type of calculus shows to what extent, in Coseriu's view, change can be systematically parametrized on the basis of markedness patterning, and more specifically of unidirectional neutralisability (cf. De Backer 2010; Coseriu 1992 [1988]: 220). This "immanent stance" (De Backer 2014: 7) fits in with Coseriu's early claim that "structures can surely be conceived as dynamic structures" (Coseriu 1978 [1958]: 211, n. 54) –

---

4 This seems to be the most problematic case, because of the discrepancy between frequency and semantic values, in the two Latin terms *ater* (unfrequent but unmarked) and *niger* (frequent but marked), cf. Coseriu (1964, 176, n. 50).

an assumption that is not only very structuralist in nature, but also quite Hjelmslevian.

3 Hjelmslev on change

Hjelmslev's ideas on change mostly transpire in texts that have remained peripheral in the receiving literature, such as *Sprogsystem og Sprogforandring* (1972a, originally a series of lectures held in 1934) and *La catégorie des cas* (1972a [1935–1937]). The starting claim in both texts is that Saussure's antinomy between synchrony and diachrony must be neutralized (*udligne*, 1972a: 18) in order to be resolved (*ophæve*, cf. Hegel's and Coseriu's *aufheben*, 1972a: 158) into a higher synthetic unit. From this perspective, change can be explained through system, as indeed change belongs to the life of language, and system be explained through a teleologically directed change. To accomplish this, diachrony must be set aside, as it deals with singled-out units (linguistic substance), and replaced by metachrony (Hjelmslev 1972a: 110; initially called pandiachrony in Hjelmslev 1928). Metachrony represents change in functional terms via the establishment of a relationship between different synchronies (cf. Coseriu 1968 [1965]: 288). Moreover, Hjelmslev distinguished change in the system that can be accounted for by means of an 'internal' method, as opposed to change in the norm and usage that cannot be so accounted for. Any external form of change requires further analysis because of the socio-historical complement of the internal type of change, which is indispensable to provide the positive factors bearing on the realisation of the possibilities that are available in the system (Hjelmslev 1972a: 147–148, 150 ff.). This amounts to saying that change is not conceived of as an external property, but rather as an inbuilt feature of language (Hjelmslev 1972a: 159), to be reconstructed by integrating various levels of description and explanation.

The claim regarding an intrinsic dynamicity of language was put forward as early as 1928. In his *Principes de grammaire générale*, Hjelmslev takes a stance against the terminological substitution of 'synchrony' with 'static' suggested by Albert Sechehaye, arguing with Humboldt that in language nothing is static but everything is dynamic (Hjelmslev 1928: 56):

> Le synchronique n'est rien que la langue en fonctionnement, le jeu des oppositions entre signes. Le synchronique est une activité, une ἐνέργεια. La synchronie est la théorie des procédés linguistiques. La δύναμις est le principe le plus élémentaire du langage; on n'y échappe pas, quel que soit le point de vue adopté. (Hjelmslev 1928: 56)

This Humboldtian background marks a major point of consonance between Hjelmslev and Coseriu. This is even more relevant considering that the *Principes* form the basis of Hjelmslev's theory of language (Swiggers 2005: 50) and most of the claims therein were carried on in its subsequent developments. Glossematics itself can be seen as a reformulation of these insights into a fully dependency-based model of linguistic analysis. In this framework, change was reinterpreted as the realisation of possibilities within a given system and described by taking into account that any unit is realised in a context of occurrence. Any unit is thus envisaged as realisable under a specific set of conditions (Hjelmslev 1970b [1939]: 131).

At no point Hjelmslev puts forward the claim that a system has to be taken *en bloc*. In order to describe the structural character of language, Hjelmslev's distinction of 'schema' ('system'), 'norm', 'usage' and 'act' was certainly the most important step, yet not the only one: the introduction of connotation marks another decisive step towards a fully-fledged conception of language in terms of an intrinsically dynamic 'system of systems' (Section 3.1). This conception is entirely compatible with Coseriu's perspective. Firstly, linguistic form – language's proper 'engine' – is less of a static mould between two substances than an organising "principle of formation" (Hjelmslev 1961 [1943]: 76;[5] cf. Coseriu 1978 [1958]: 267, n. 91), i.e. an activity of systematisation based on objective teleology (Section 3.2). Secondly, Hjelmslev's objective teleology relies on a finely chiselled system of "optima" (Hjelmslev 1935: 109), essentially points of evolution toward which each subsystem strives. Those optima in turn depend on the organisation of each system in terms of oppositions, i.e. on markedness patterns (Section 3.3) which in Hjelmslev's view defines the δύναμις of language.

---

5 "On a oublié de se demander comment il faut expliquer le fait incontestable que, bien que soumise à des altérations constantes, une langue conserve toujours la faculté de former système" (Hjelmslev 1973a: 63, § 14).

3.1 Subsystems, multiple synchronies and connotation

Language is not one language, but many (Hjelmslev 1973b: 115).

The reason for introducing connotation was to qualify the basic distinction of schema/norm/usage/act in order to accommodate collateral, variational subsystems. Hjelmslev recognized as early as 1940 the necessity of accounting for "different kinds of linguistic states (ancient and modern, common and regional, stylistically neutral or not, etc.)". The complexity of language can only be grasped synthetically, through multiple analyses of all its varieties (Hjelmslev 1973a: 95, § 85). The distinction between denotation and connotation involves two levels: the semiotic level and the methodological level. The first level concerns the abstract structure of a language: denotation represents the basic structure of any sign, while connotation occurs when denotation itself is made an expression for a new content (e.g. with regard to different corpora of literary works, dialects, stylistic norms, etc.). However, denotation and connotation are no separate semiotic moments, but different dimensions of analysis. Connotation in particular is no ancillary element: from the point of view of a concrete object (an actual language), connotation belongs to its very structure.

According to Hjelmslev, a particular historical language is not just linguistically but also semiotically heterogeneous (cf. Coseriu 2007 [1980]: 103): any linguistic text may incorporate elements from different semiotic systems (verbal or written languages, gesture, etc.), as speakers do not have to stick to a single semiotic structure. They are able to 'get off trouble' in practical situations by resorting to different systems (on this point, compare Coseriu 2007 [1980]: 104). Moreover, even within a single semiotic system, a text is usually an amalgamation of different norms that need not be completely aligned, as language always contains remnants of the old and seeds of the new (Hjelmslev 1970d: 102). In fact, all those levels correspond to different subsystems, with each one having its own temporal features (Hjelmslev 1970c: 99; Hjelmslev 1970d: 102; compare Coseriu 1964: 156). These subsystems can be distinguished on the basis of connotation, as each linguistic unit comes along with a 'connotator', i.e. an element that links the linguistic unit, as an expression, to the extralinguistic context to which it belongs (a concrete corpus of literary works, a given society or community of speakers, a specific period or a particular geographical area, etc.) and which is conceived of as a *content*. For instance, with respect to lexemes such as *fanciullo*, *ragazzo* and *guaglione*, all denoting 'young boy', the resp. connotators [literary], [neutral] and [dialectal] (cf. Di Girolamo 1978: 12) as well as [Italian] (valid for all three) can be identified.[6] By virtue of these connotators, the lexemes are expressions for a specific variational content, viz. a specific corpus of 'high' usages, a standard variation of a national language and a south-Italian dialect, respectively.

Historically speaking, the link between the linguistic units and their context is always present and active, even if not always "actualised" (cf. Coseriu 2007 [1980]: 99). In other words, any linguistic unit is connotatively coloured. Analytically speaking, connotation demands a tiered approach: once the denotational structure of any sign analysed, connotators must be registered and singled out, their analysis constituting a separate step in the analysis. By subtracting the connotators from the actual signs, the latter are turned into variants (Hjelmslev 1970c: 98) of a single unit that belongs to a single overarching system. For instance, when the connotators of *fanciullo*, *ragazzo* and *guaglione* are subtracted, these units become variants amenable to be analysed as belonging to Italian and denoting 'young boy'. The description of their specific variational properties is postponed to another step in the analysis, when the connotators themselves are analysed in terms of specific norms.

The subtraction of connotators serves as a factor that homogenises the analysis, similar to the level of a 'functional language' in the Coserian approach: subtraction is a temporary procedure in, and part of, a step-by-step analysis. Units are thus described in a coordinated twofold way: (1) as belonging to an overarching system and (2) as obeying a particular set of rules (a subsystem) that specifies/modifies the set of rules that governs the overarching system. Since each subsystem is supposed to possess its own genetic dimension, linked to all the others' through unilateral determination (Hjelmslev 1970c: 99), any chronological consideration is reinterpreted as the realization of possibilities from a superordinate layer onto one or several subordinated layers. Within such a framework, linguistic change is described in terms of a network between two or more macrosystems, each one containing different subsystems that function according to their specific 'synchronies'.

To properly account for such a multi-layered articulation, linguistic theory has to account for all possible types of semiotic structures, through a step-by-

---

[6] More connotators can of course be added to the list, including such very specific labels as [oral] vs. [written language], [low register], [high register], [Latinism], etc. They constitute a set of coordinates identifying the object in its chronological, social, cultural and even individual context. Connotators may even include single physiognomies, thus referring to micro-systems as well, or even 'singletons' (one-unit sets): for instance, a segment of handwritten text could include connotators such as [elegant style] (for some letters), [italic] (for some words), etc., ideally leading to the identification of an individual handwriting (e.g. [John Smith's handwriting]).

step approach (Hjelmslev 1970d: 102; Hjelmslev 1961 [1943]: 106). This Hjelmslevian approach clearly resonates in Coseriu's approach: since each language may include different systems and manifest itself through different substances, the analysis must be tailored to each specific case (Coseriu 1966: 203; cf. Coseriu and Geckeler 1981: 53). In Hjelmslev's terms, there is no universal procedure, there are only universal principles of analysis.

This is also important when it comes to understanding the relationship between written and spoken language. Interestingly, this was the subject of a debate between Eli Fischer Jørgensen (who conveyed Hjelmslev's view) and Coseriu (Jensen 2015a: 34 ff.). Strictly speaking, Hjelmslev suggested that the semiotic relationship between written and spoken language cannot be qualified once for all, as the circumstances may differ greatly for each case. In some languages, he argued, there may be conformity between sounds and graphemes, which will then turn out to be a single system manifested by two different substances. In other languages, there may be non-conformity, so that written and spoken language are two distinct systems, each having its specific form (Hjelmslev 1973 [1957]: 272–273).

3.2 System and teleology

We saw that Coseriu rightly pointed out Hjelmslev's recourse to objective teleology, along with its pitfall (Section 2.2). In fact, Hjelmslev endorsed the idea of 'purpose' in linguistic change "that proves particularly important in its metachronic aspect [...], where the change of the system itself is supposed to be caused by an inherent drift" (Hjelmslev 1946 [1940]: 3). Further evidence of this is easy to provide, as Hjelmslev's theory of systematic change includes notions such as 'dispositions' and 'optima' (Hjelmslev 1972a: 21–22, 74–75, 104 ff. and *passim*; 1935: 109; cf. Andersen 1990: 8, 15 and Cigana 2014b: 54–55). By means of these notions it is possible to outline the immanent configuration of a system, e.g. a particular morphological category, considered in its evolution toward an ideal state. Such an ideal state is assumed to depend on the oppositional structure of the system; for instance, the optimal configuration for inflectional (called "fundamental") case is said to consist of four terms – viz. two extensive and two intensive terms (without regard to their content-substance, cf. Hjelmslev 1972a: 108) – so that a language featuring morphologically marked cases will always try to reorganise itself in order to reach that configuration, *ceteribus paribus*.

Again, we are here dealing with a level of abstraction that is obviously quite remote from the *sentiment du sujet parlant*, and Coseriu strongly condemned the idea of an inherent drift that is separated from the speakers. Yet aspects such as drift, disposition and optima can still be conceived of as connected with speakers by motivating them cognitively – much like markedness has been, cf. for instance Andersen (2001: 45 ff.) – as schemata for action (Cusimano 2012: 72; cf. Coseriu 1983: 63 and Section 2.2). Such an account poses no particular problems within Hjelmslev's framework, even more so as he rejected the very notion of an unconscious mind being conditioned by linguistic rules. While stressing the need to keep the theory clearly distinguished from the subjective intuitions of speakers, he actually linked the system of language not to unconscious but to the "subconscious" of speakers (cf. Hjelmslev 1928: 21, 24, 45–46 and *passim*). With this term, Hjelmslev referred to an activity which is always potentially conscious. Under this view, to suppose either a conscious will or a purely passive conformity ends up being futile, since the speaker is not meant to comply with a set of rules imposed from above but to stabilize language as such, imparting a specific pace to its intrinsic pulse, using language as a means to shape and share experiences. There is thus no need to admit that the interventions of the speakers 'distort' the linguistic system, on the contrary, they constantly re-enact it, tapping into its possibilities which are themselves conceived of as a set of resources for their expressive needs.

3.3 Oppositions and the functioning of language

It is not surprising that markedness plays a crucial role in Hjelmslev's theory. With the system being one of the hallmarks of a structuralist approach (Van de Walle et al. 2006), it is only natural that Hjelmslev tried, as early as 1929, to determine the principle according to which a system "functions" as such (see Hjelmslev 1973a: 57). This principle was identified as oppositions, similar to what was maintained by the representatives by the Prague School and Geneva School, equally inspired by Saussure. In contrast to Prague phonology, Hjelmslev argues that linguistic oppositions are inclusive ("participative") by definition, i.e. grounded on the "general law of participation" (Hjelmslev 1970a [1939]: 87) whose form, "A vs. A + non-A" (Hjelmslev 1935, 102) was explicitly adopted by Coseriu (1992 [1988]: 218–219; cf. De Backer 2010). Hjelmslev also claimed that any binary assumption necessarily leads to a hierarchic distribution of features, which he rejected. As a closed paradigm of units, a system can consist of only a limited number of features; to the extent that they form a cohesive totality, all units behave correlatively in respect to those same features. For instance, the general category of inflectional case is said to consist of up to three main oppositions, viz. 1) proximity-distance, 2) coherence-incoherence and 3) objectivity-subjectivity, in respect to which any case morpheme in a given language can be defined. The metachronic evolution of a category is then described as an internal reorganization: any increase or reduction in the number of morphemes involves the appearance or disappearance of the three main distinctive oppositions, and vice versa, as well as a complete redefinition of each term in the system. Hence the need to establish a nuanced, non-binary set of six different markedness values: a simple-intensive α, a simple-extensive A, a contrary-intensive β, a contrary-extensive B, a contradictory-intensive γ, and a contradictory-extensive Γ (Cigana 2014b: 52).

Correlations such as these are specific to Hjelmslev's approach (Cigana 2014a: 192–193). They have three main features: 1) Since they only define the value of a unit in opposition to all other units, they are purely formal and encoded in the system, while phenomena such as neutralisation or suppression (cf. Hjelmslev 1970a [1939]: 88) are said to manifest those correlations on a different level of analysis and according to specific patterns. For instance, neutralisations are always said to occur between an intensive (α, β or γ) and an extensive term (A, B or Γ). But another configuration is also possible, viz. when either term may include the other (so-called "contensive" terms). 2) They are said to be exclusively 'homoplane', which means that they define the relationships between *figurae*, i.e. elements of one level or plane that have been identified and separated from their counterpart on the corresponding level or plane via commutation. 3) Correlative terms occur in a closed array of combinations, one leading to the other according to its intrinsic form. Such evolutive patterns, which basically reproduce intensive-extensive relations, are typologically described by virtue of a calculus, which is comparable to Coseriu's account of the dissolution of an opposition discussed in Section 2.3. There are further points of convergence: both Coseriu and Hjelmslev consider oppositions to be the only factor that explain "which of the terms of an opposition is the unmarked term and which one the marked term" (De Backer 2014: 180; cf. Coseriu 1992 [1988]: 214) and both Coserian 'neutralisability' and Hjelmslevian 'participation' depend on the inclusion of the marked term within the unmarked, rather than defective distribution (De Backer 2014: 153). There are also important differences. For example, Hjelmslev's account of 'extensive terms' does not imply any bifunctionality (or 'duosemy') of units, contrary to what Coseriu assumes for unmarked terms. Moreover, Hjelmslev's theory seems better suited to account for bidirectional neutralisation, which remains a major problem in Coseriu's rendering of asymmetrical oppositions (De Backer 2010). Conversely, Coseriu rightly pointed out that lexical opposition need not always be inclusive; Hjelmslev's claim that any two-term linguistic opposition is assumed to be a simple participation (α-A) could however be modified accordingly, by admitting other oppositional couples (β-B, γ-Γ) as valid in particular domains (such as the lexical level), thus making the theory more widely applicable.

The extent to which Coseriu's theory is consistent with some of Hjelmslev's basic assumptions regarding the oppositional organisation of linguistic systems may have become clear. This agreement on basic assumptions can be found behind each one of the four senses of 'structure' discussed by Coseriu (1964: 150–153), viz. as an "organised delimitation of a substance into functional units" (structure$_1$), resulting from a network of "distinctive oppositions" (structure$_2$) through which these units can be fully analysed into differential elements (structure$_3$) that can occur in different systems (structure$_4$).

4 Conclusion

The prime aim of the above comparison was to show the theoretical convergence between Coseriu and Hjelmslev with regard to the specific domain of linguistic change. This convergence, of course, at the same time attests to Coseriu's critical reception and further development of Hjelmslevian structuralism. However, in my opinion this connection should not be read unidirectionally, but rather seized as an opportunity to examine the extent to which a glossematic framework can be called into question *and* expanded in the light of Coseriu's remarks, and vice versa. Further investigations might focus on issues such as the following: In what sense could Hjelmslev's idea of a markedness-based organisation of connotators (Hjelmslev 1975: 226 ff.) entail a functional evolution of their architecture? Or in what way could Hjelmslev's model of marked and unmarked terms, including the possibility of having two "contensive" terms (Hjelmslev 1975: 46, Df 118), serve to overcome some difficulties in Coseriu's model of neutralisation? Confronting the way Hjelmslev's theory was received and reinterpreted by Coseriu with the real convergences and differences that can be found between their two approaches would help dissolve many long-lasting preconceptions, such as the static and monolithic conception of the linguistic system or the alleged rejection of history that only seemingly characterizes Hjelmslev's formalist approach to language.

The notion of connotation in particular may prove to be a fruitful ground for conducting the comparison between the two authors from a new perspective, especially if one considers the implications it has on the relation between language and its description. In this respect, Coseriu's claim that a description of a particular language is a moment in the history of that very language (Coseriu 1978 [1958]: 279) does not seem alien to a basic tenet of glossematics, viz. the peculiar circularity taken to obtain between language and metalanguage:

> As soon as we have said that linguistic theory is a language, we have in addition opened the door to an interesting perspective: Linguistic theory must be capable of being analysed and described by means of its own method; linguistic theory must be susceptible of being made its own object. (Hjelmslev 1973b: 106–107)

Since connotation represents the link between the signs of a language and their corresponding context of occurrence, any sign belonging to a specific metalanguage (a grammar, a concrete linguistic description) is susceptible to connote, among other things, the language in which that theory is expressed. Connotators themselves ('literary', 'dialectal', etc.) are part of the vocabulary of a given natural language and must be described accordingly. Moreover, a linguistic description does not just reflect a specific usage of language, but a scientific ideology and eventually an entire mentality. On this basis, a particular grammar of a language may be simultaneously understood as a concrete product of a given language (connoting that very language in a phase of its institutionalization) and as an attempt to codify it (connoting the scientific ideology behind that very attempt). This is no cursory remark, as glossematics itself builds upon the idea that a linguistic description is a moment in the functioning of language.

In view of these observation, it is not surprising that Coseriu felt the need to incorporate Hjelmslev's account of connotation into his own framework (Coseriu 2007 [1980]: 99, 102–104, 138–143; see also Jensen, *this volume*): as Coseriu himself pointed out, "like Humboldt, Hjelmslev sees the possibility of comprehending all cultural and human problems from the vantage point of language" (Coseriu 1973 [1954]: 175).

References

Andersen, Henning. 1990. "The structure of drift". In: Henning Andersen and Ernst Frideryk Konrad Koerner (eds.), *Historical Linguistics 1987. Papers from the 8th International Conference on Historical Linguistics*, 1–20. Amsterdam & Philadelphia: John Benjamins.
Andersen, Henning. 2001. "Markedness and the theory of linguistic change". In: Henning Andersen (ed.), *Actualization*, 21–57. Amsterdam & Philadelphia: John Benjamins.
Andersen, Henning. 2006. "Synchrony, diachrony, and evolution". In: Ole Nedergaard Thomsen (ed.), *Competing models of linguistic change*, 59–90. Amsterdam & Philadelphia: John Benjamins.
Cigana, Lorenzo. 2014a. "La notion de 'participation' chez Louis Hjelmslev: un fil rouge de la glossématique". *Cahiers Ferdinand de Saussure* 67, 191–202.
Cigana, Lorenzo. 2014b. "*Sprogsystem og Sprogforandring*: il dinamismo del sistema". In: Lorenzo Cigana and Romeo Galassi (eds.), *Strutturalismo, strutturalismi e loro forme* (Janus, Quaderni del Circolo Glossematico, 13), 45–63. Treviso: ZeL Edizioni.

Cigana, Lorenzo. 2016. "La forma del mondo. L'analisi glossematica del contenuto tra linguistica e filosofia". *Rivista italiana di Filosofia del Linguaggio* 1, 22–36.

Coseriu, Eugenio. 1964. "Pour une sémantique diachronique structurale". *Travaux de linguistique et de littérature* 2:1, 139–186.

Coseriu, Eugenio. 1966. "Structure lexicale et enseignement du vocabulaire". In: *Actes du premier colloque international de linguistique appliqué*, 175–217. Nancy: Faculté des Lettres et des Sciences humaines de l'Université de Nancy.

Coseriu, Eugenio. 1968 [1965]. "Sincronía, diacronía y tipología". In: Antonio Quilis, Ramón Blanco Carril and Margarita Cantarero (eds.), *Actas XI Congreso International de Lingüística y Filología Románicas (Madrid 1965)*. Vol. I, 269–281. Madrid: Revista de Filología Española.

Coseriu, Eugenio. 1973 [1954]. "Forma y sustancia en los sonidos del lenguaje". In: Eugenio Coseriu, *Teoría del lenguaje y lingüística general. Cinco estudios*, 115–234. Madrid: Gredos.

Coseriu, Eugenio. 1976 [1968–1969]. *Das romanische Verbalsystem*. Tübingen: Narr.

Coseriu, Eugenio. 1978 [1958]. *Sincronía, diacronía e historia. El problema del cambio lingüístico* (third edition). Madrid: Gredos.

Coseriu, Eugenio. 1983. "Linguistic change does not exist". *Linguistica nuova ed antica. Rivista di linguistica classica medioevale e moderna* 1, 51–63.

Coseriu, Eugenio. 1992 [1988]. *Einführung in die allgemeine Sprachwissenschaft* (second edition). Tübingen: Francke (German translation of Coseriu 1981).

Coseriu, Eugenio. 2007 [1980]. *Textlinguistik. Eine Einführung*. Edited by Jörn Albrecht (fourth edition). Tübingen: Narr.

Coseriu, Eugenio. 2008 [1964]. "Towards a structuralist diachronic semantics". In: Patrick Hanks (ed.), *Lexicology. Critical concepts in Linguistics*. Vol. 2: *Lexical semantics and structures*, 140–193. London: Routledge (Englisch translation of Coseriu 1964).

Coseriu, Eugenio and Horst Geckeler. 1981. *Trends in structural semantics*. Tübingen: Narr.

Cusimano, Christophe. 2012. *La sémantique contemporaine. Du sème au thème*. Paris: Pups.

De Backer, Maarten. 2009. "The concept of neutralization outside the field of phonology". *Indogermanische Forschungen* 114:1, 1–59.

De Backer, Maarten. 2010. "Lexical neutralisation: a case study of the lexical opposition 'day'/'night'. *Language Sciences* 32:5, 545–562.

De Backer, Maarten. 2013. "Neutralisation and semantic markedness: an inquiry into types of lexical opposition in German". *Sprachwissenschaft* 38:3, 343–382.

De Backer, Maarten. 2014. *Lexical neutralisation: theoretical and empirical perspectives*, Ghent, Belgium: Ghent University. Faculty of Arts and Philosophy.

Di Girolamo, Edoardo. 1978. *Critica della letterarietà*. Milano: Il Saggiatore.

Fischer-Jørgensen, Eli. 1995 [1975]. *Trends in phonological theory until 1975. A historical introduction* (Travaux du Cercle Linguistique de Copenhague, 27). København: Akademisk Forlag.

Flydal, Leiv. 1952. "Remarques sur certains rapports entre le style et l'état de langue". *Norsk Tidsskrift for Sprogvidenskap* 16, 241–258. (Occasionally cited as 'Flydal 1951' due to offprints of the article dated 1951.)

Hjelmslev, Louis. 1928. *Principes de grammaire générale*. Copenhague: Bianco Lunos Bogtrykkeri.

Hjelmslev, Louis. 1935. *La catégorie des cas. Étude de grammaire générale.* Première partie. *Acta Jutlandica* 7:1. Aarhus: Universitetsforlaget.
Hjelmslev, Louis. 1937. *La catégorie des cas. Étude de grammaire générale.* Deuxième partie. *Acta Jutlandica* 9:2. Aarhus: Universitetsforlaget.
Hjelmslev, Louis. 1941. "Et par sprogteoretiske betragtninger". *Årbog for nordisk målstræv* 4, 81–88.
Hjelmslev, Louis. 1961 [1943]. *Prolegomena to a theory of language.* Translated by Francis J. Whitfield (second edition). Madison: The University of Wisconsin Press.
Hjelmslev, Louis. 1970a [1939]. "Note sur les oppositions supprimables". *Travaux du Cercle Linguistique de Prague* 8, 51–57. Also in: Louis Hjelmslev. 1970. *Essais linguistiques* (second edition) (Travaux du Cercle Linguistique de Copenhague 12), 82–88. København: Nordisk Sprog- og Kulturforlag.
Hjelmslev, Louis. 1970b [1939]. "La structure morphologique". *Cinquième congrès international des linguistes. Rapports*, 66–93. Bruges: Imprimerie Sainte Catherine. Also in: Louis Hjelmslev. 1970. *Essais linguistiques* (second edition) (Travaux du Cercle Linguistique de Copenhague 12), 113–138. København: Nordisk Sprog- og Kulturforlag.
Hjelmslev, Louis. 1970c. "Observations de L. Hjelmslev (23.04.42)". *Bulletin du Cercle Linguistique de Copenhague 1941–1965*, 8/31, 96–99. Copenhague: Akademisk Forlag.
Hjelmslev, Louis. 1970d. "Language and system (19.09.46)". *Bulletin du Cercle Linguistique de Copenhague 1941–1965*, 8/31, 101–102. Copenhague: Akademisk Forlag.
Hjelmslev, Louis. 1972a. *Sprogsystem og sprogforandring* (Travaux du Cercle Linguistique de Copenhague 15). København: Nordisk Sprog- og Kulturforlag.
Hjelmslev, Louis. 1972b. *La catégorie des cas. Étude de grammaire générale.* Edited by Eugenio Coseriu. München: Fink.
Hjelmslev, Louis. 1973a. "Structure générale des corrélations linguistiques". In: Louis Hjelmslev (ed.), *Essais linguistiques II* (Travaux du Cercle Linguistique de Copenhague 14), 57–98. Copenhague: Nordisk Sprog- og Kulturforlag.
Hjelmslev, Louis. 1973b. "A causerie on linguistic theory". In: Louis Hjelmslev (ed.), *Essais linguistiques II* (Travaux du Cercle Linguistique de Copenhague 14), 101–117. Copenhague: Nordisk Sprog- og Kulturforlag.
Hjelmslev, Louis. 1973 [1957]. "Introduction à la discussion générale des problèmes relatifs à la phonologie des langues mortes, en l'espèce du grec et du latin". *Acta Congressus Madvigiani. Proceedings of the Second International Congress of Classical Studies.* Vol. 1: *General Part*, 31–33. København: Munksgaard. Also in: Louis Hjelmslev (1973), *Essais linguistiques II* (Travaux du Cercle Linguistique de Copenhague 14), 267–278. Copenhague: Nordisk Sprog- og Kulturforlag.
Hjelmslev, Louis. 1975. *Résumé of a theory of language* (Travaux du Cercle Linguistique de Copenhague 16). Copenhagen: Nordisk Sprog- og Kulturforlag.
Holt, Jens. 1946. *Rationel semantik (pleremik).* København: Munskgaard.
Holt, Jens. 1967. "Contribution à l'analyse fonctionnelle du contenu linguistique", *Langages* 6, 59–69.
Jensen, Viggo Bank. 2012. "Eugenio Coseriu, Scandinavian Linguists and Variational Linguistics". In: *Report from 2011: 6th International Conference on Languages, E-learning Studies and Romanian Studies, 3–5 June, Isle of Marstrand, Sweden.* Available online at http://nile.lub.lu.se/ojs/index.php/elears/article/view/5458.

Jensen, Viggo Bank. 2015a. "Eli Fischer-Jørgensen, Eugenio Coseriu et Louis Hjelmslev: Quelque points d'une correspondance". *Cahiers Ferdinand de Saussure* 68, 27–45.
Jensen, Viggo Bank. 2015b. "Il ruolo della 'Scuola di Copenaghen' nel 'rimodellamento' coseriano degli assiomi saussuriani". In: Vincenzo Orioles and Raffaella Bombi (eds.), *Oltre Saussure: L'eredità scientifica di Eugenio Coseriu. Atti del IV Convegno Internazionale Università degli Studi di Udine* (1–2 ottobre 2013), 121–132. Firenze: Franco Cesati.
Meillet, Antoine. 1921. *Linguistique historique et linguistique générale*. Paris: Honoré Champion.
Morpurgo Davies, Anna and Giulio Ciro Lepschy. 2016. *History of linguistics*. Volume IV: *Nineteenth-century linguistics*. London: Routledge.
Swiggers, Pierre. 2005. "Formes, fonctions at catégories linguistiques: les *Principes de grammaire générale* de Louis Hjelmslev". *Linguistica* 45:1, 41–52.
Trabant, Jürgen. 1987. "Louis Hjelmslev: Glossematics as General Semiotics". In: Martin Krampen, Klaus Oehler, Roland Posner, Thomas A. Sebeok and Thomas von Uexküll (eds.), *Classics of semiotics*, 89–108. New York & London: Plenum.
Van de Walle, Jürgen, Klaas Willems and Dominique Willems. 2006. "Structuralism". In: Jan-Ola Östman and Jef Verschueren (eds.), *Handbook of pragmatics*, 1–36. Amsterdam & Philadelphia: John Benjamins.
Völker, Harald. 2009. "La linguistique variationnelle et la perspective intralinguistique", *Revue de linguistique romane* 73, 27–79.
Willems, Klaas. 2003. "Eugenio Coseriu. Versuch einer Würdigung". *Leuvense Bijdragen* 92, 1–25.

Part III: **Theory and practice of Integral Linguistics**

Mircea Borcilă (Cluj-Napoca)
Integral Linguistics as a cultural science

> [E]very philosophy of language worthy of the name and also any linguistics conscious of its task should insist in particular on linguistic creativity (which, on the other hand, also pervades the techniques of speaking, which are essentially open techniques). And as regards the techniques themselves, at least their three levels should be adequately investigated.*

In his *Lecciones de lingüística general* (1999 [1981]), Coseriu writes that establishing the theoretical foundations of linguistics "as an authentic science of culture, coherent in all its aspects, remains the task of the present and the future" (Coseriu 1999 [1981]: 100). I myself have challenged this judgement in a series of articles (Borcilă 1988, 1997, 2001, 2002, 2016)[1] to the extent that an essential part of this challenging task has already been accomplished precisely in and through Coseriu's own life-long scholarly efforts. I would like to argue that, if Coseriu's legacy is considered as a whole,[2] it is possible to identify its general significance regarding the 'ideal' of building linguistics as a cultural science, and moreover as the central discipline of the humanities along the lines of W. von Humboldt. In this article, I briefly present five main reasons why Coseriu can be considered the most consistent advocate of this Humboldtian approach in the entire post-Humboldtian era. These five reasons can be summarized as follows:

(1) Coseriu provides, maybe for the first time, a coherent account of the ontological and epistemological foundations of linguistics as the central discipline of the humanities;

(2) on this basis, Coseriu develops an integralist program for defining, in terms of a conceptual (re-)construction, linguistics as a cultural science, which takes its starting point in a radical reversal of the 'perspective' of linguistic investigations;

Acknowledgements: I am sincerely grateful to the editors and an anonymous reviewer and deeply appreciate their help in substantially improving the quality of this text.

* "[T]oda filosofía del lenguaje digna de este nombre y también una lingüística consciente de su tarea deberían insistir de modo particular en la creatividad lingüística (la cual, por otra parte, impregna de sí también las técnicas del hablar, que son esencialmente técnicas abiertas). Y en lo que concierne a las técnicas mismas, deberían, por lo menos, estudiarse en medida adecuada sus tres niveles" (Coseriu 1999 [1981]: 270).
1 The present contribution mainly follows the line of reasoning proposed in Borcilă (2002).
2 Coseriu himself insisted on the relevance of such an approach; cf., e. g., Kabatek and Murguía (1997: 263), where he mentions Borcilă (1988) in this regard.

(3) a crucial aspect of Coseriu's approach is that he identifies the 'signifying function of language' as the object of linguistics and, accordingly, determines the scope of 'linguistic competence' in a new manner;
(4) against the background of what Coseriu defines as the object of linguistic enquiry, his 'Integral Linguistics' establishes a comprehensive approach both of the objectives and the major domains of investigation of linguistics as a science;
(5) along these lines, Coseriu has himself made a number of significant contributions to solving some of the central problems in modern linguistics.

Taken together, these five reasons testify to the singular importance of Coseriu's work in establishing linguistics as a cultural science. However, an adequate understanding of their range and scope is only possible if considered 'from within'. I will therefore elaborate on a number of aspects that I consider essential for a cogent and fruitful interpretation of each of the five reasons in turn.

1 The ontological and epistemological foundations of linguistics

Delineating the ontological foundations of linguistics and securing, on this basis, the scientific status of the discipline represents, in my understanding, the most important step of the entire Coserian project. In a brief account, we must start from the historical fact that in the second half of the twentieth century only two linguists – first Eugenio Coseriu and then Noam Chomsky – have fully assumed the difficult but important task of systematically reconstructing the ontological and epistemological foundations of their discipline. And of the two solutions elaborated by these scholars, only the one proposed by Coseriu pursues in a coherent way a principled foundation of linguistics as *a cultural science*. The rank and value of Coseriu contribution in this regard can be revealed along two main coordinates: (a) the reconstruction of a phenomenological-hermeneutical approach to language against the background of the entire history of linguistic thought; (b) the systematic elaboration of a body of principles designed to ground linguistics on a firm scientific basis.

Coseriu's historical reconstruction of the foundations of linguistic theory (in particular in his *Geschichte der Sprachphilosophie*, Coseriu 2015)[3] represents per-

---

[3] Cf. also Coseriu (1995 [1984/1986]), a transcript of lectures Coseriu delivered on the history of the language sciences, which hitherto has not yet been published.

haps the most thorough philosophical account of its kind in the literature, if one takes into account that Coseriu stops his overview in the nineteenth century (cf. Trabant, this volume). Coseriu takes a broad 'phenomenological' approach, with a focus on language and speech as a symbolic activity in the history of European culture. Coseriu's account leads, first of all, from Aristotle's treatment of language, conceived as 'semantic logos', to Hegel's philosophy of culture, which Coseriu held in particularly high esteem, especially because Hegel considers language as a fundamental dimension of human beings. To this line of thinking, Coseriu added the systematic completion of the phenomenological approach itself at the beginning of the twentieth century, viz. Husserl's epistemology. However, it must be pointed out that Coseriu combines this global 'phenomenological' approach with a focus on the 'hermeneutical' approach to language and culture, starting with its anticipation in the work of G. B. Vico, through the Kantian revolution, and subsequently articulated, for the first time in all its breadth and multiple dimensions, in W. von Humboldt's 'linguistic philosophy'. It is also in relation to W. von Humboldt, whose writings on language he considered the decisive moment in the historical development of the sciences of mankind, that Coseriu proposes to valorise two centuries of efforts towards establishing the foundation of humanities, i.e. *Geisteswissenschaften*.

It is worthwhile to briefly compare Coseriu's approach of the history of linguistics with Chomsky's position. Although Coseriu always acknowledged the significance of Chomsky's contribution to linguistics (cf. Coseriu 1970 [1968], 1992b and particularly 1996: 143–148), the differences between their two foundational projects are substantial. Whereas Coseriu takes into account the whole history of the humanities from Antiquity until the nineteenth century, Chomsky and the generative movement have done nothing of the kind. Apart from his early considerations in *Cartesian linguistics* (Chomsky 2009 [1966]), Chomsky and his followers offer nothing comparable in their exploration of linguistics, which would allow them to clarify and 'justify' their approach from a historical perspective. As a matter of fact, Coseriu's historical reconstruction shows that the theoretical retreat to the positions of Cartesian rationalism actually amounts to endorsing an obsolete reductionist epistemology which had already been surpassed by Kant's philosophy (see, for example, Chomsky 1980 and Chomsky 1986). It would seem, then, that Chomsky's decision to abandon the Vichean line of thought for a Cartesian approach amounts to throwing overboard many of the valuable insights that contributed to establishing the human sciences in the last centuries.

Coseriu's contribution to the epistemological foundations of linguistics as a cultural science also encompasses a systematic elaboration of basic linguistic concepts. Early publications such as Coseriu (1978 [1958]) and Coseriu (1973

[1962]) are particularly important in this respect. Coseriu provides a penetrating critique of the – often implicit – philosophical assumptions and prevailing positivist perspective in the then dominant currents of modern linguistics, including European and North-American (Bloomfieldian and post-Bloomfieldian) structuralism, which presented themselves from various perspectives, if deceptively, as 'purely empirical' linguistics. By contrast, Coseriu (1978 [1958]) demonstrates that it is impossible to ground any scientific study of language without a preliminary clarification of the 'nature' of the object of enquiry. At the same time, he provides a coherent phenomenological and hermeneutical basis for the study of language understood as an essentially creative activity (Humboldt's *enérgeia*) and developed against the specific backdrop of history. Coseriu has also confronted this conceptual basis directly with Chomsky's alternative approach (cf. Coseriu 1970 [1968] and 1975 [1971]) and subsequently developed it into a comprehensive corpus of principles in several publications (cf. in particular Coseriu 1991 [1977], 1999 [1981] and and 2001). Further landmarks in the elaboration of what might be called the 'principles of linguistics as a cultural science' are Coseriu (1987 [1978]) and (1992b). I cannot here discuss these principles in detail, but it bears pointing out that e.g. Bernardo (1995) has described Coseriu's approach in terms of the "construction" of a comprehensive "anti-positivist epistemological paradigm" in linguistics, which Bernardo appropriately identifies with the "construction of linguistics" itself as a cultural science. This is not the place to further discuss the Chomskyan alternative, but it is perhaps significant to point out that erstwhile prominent supporters of the generative approach have abandoned it in favour of Coseriu's approach (cf., e.g., Ruwet 1991). Moreover, current trends in linguistics such as 'second generation' cognitive linguistics have positioned themselves explicitly as 'anti-chomskyan' and 'anti-formalist' and appear to share at least some of the theoretical assumptions with Coseriu's integralist stance (cf. Johnson 1987: 175–176, Lakoff and Johnson 1999: 89), despite differences regarding the definition of the specific object of enquiry and the corresponding objectives of linguistic research (see Sections 2 and 3 below).

2 Coseriu's radical change of perspective in linguistics

The key moment in Coseriu's comprehensive program to provide a firm foundation of the language sciences that is both historically informed and theoretically coherent consists in establishing a radical change of perspective in linguistics. The main – and, as Coseriu later repeatedly pointed out, decisive – argument for this change is already put forward in detail in "Determinación y entorno" (Coseriu 1973 [1956]). According to Coseriu (1992b: 73), "linguistics has always been linguistics of particular languages". From this viewpoint, the well-known Saussurean focus on *langue* as opposed to *parole* was "not in opposition to traditional, historical linguistics" but, quite on the contrary, "in agreement with" that tradition. It meant that the focus of enquiry was seriously biased and only on the systematic, synchronically hypostasized dimension of languages which were construed as the "unique and integral object of linguistics". Conversely, Chomsky explicitly argues that linguistics is not concerned with the activity of speaking (see Section 1). Against this background, Coseriu maintains that "it is an error to study speech from the viewpoint of language" and instead argues that a "radical reversal of perspective" is called for. The basic assumption that underpins this reversal is as simple as it is foundational: it is not speech (*parole*) that has to be explained from the viewpoint of language (*langue*) in the Saussurean sense, or from the viewpoint of *competence* in the Chomskyan sense, but on the contrary, languages (*langues*) and the whole of linguistic competence can only be explained on the basis of the activity of speaking: "we have to situate ourselves from the outset at the level of speaking (Sp. *el hablar*) and consider it as the norm for all other manifestations of language, including '*langue*'" (Coseriu 1973 [1962]: 287–288, cf. Coseriu 1992b: 74).

The many implications and consequences of this "radical change of perspective" could easily be pinpointed in terms of extending the object of linguistic investigations. The immediate corollary of Coseriu's proposal is indeed that of a much more comprehensive approach to language, since clearly "speech is broader than language: while language is entirely contained in speech, speech is not entirely contained in language" (Coseriu 1973 [1962]: 287). Under this view, linguistics can accommodate all aspects of speech which are rightfully within its purview as a science but had been largely excluded from it. In particular, Coseriu paved the way for the study of what he called 'elocutional knowledge', i.e. the domain of designation, on the one hand, and the study of 'expressive knowledge', i.e. the domain of the 'sense' of texts (G. *Sinn*, Sp. *sentido*), on the other (cf. Coseriu 1985 for a succinct overview). It is this extension of the scope of linguistics that warrants 'Integral Linguistics' as an appropriate name for Coseriu's approach.

There is more to Coseriu's program than a mere extension of the object of linguistic investigations. Less well understood so far is the comprehensive dimension involved in Coseriu reversal of perspective, which actually provides for the authentic and profound sense of his approach. This consists in considering speech, or more precisely: the 'act of speaking' in the Humboldtian sense of *enérgeia*, as the only concrete form of language and, moreover, as representing the very essence of the linguistic phenomenon (cf. Agud, this volume, and Trabant, this volume). The novelty of Coseriu's approach lies, therefore, in the fact that the change of perspective he advocates also implies a different view on the very nature of language, a dimension which is unfortunately often neglected even by those scholars who claim to adopt Coseriu's approach, in particular with regard to the linguistic investigation of particular languages and text linguistics (see Section 4). However, as Colette Laplace rightly observed, what Coseriu calls "speaking", i.e. *parole* understood in the sense of "parler" (G. *das Sprechen überhaupt*), is of "a fundamentally different nature" than "what Saussure and Chomsky called parole or performance", i.e. "a simple realisation of the linguistic system" (Laplace 1994: 107). The essential feature of Coseriu's definition of 'speaking' lies in the emphasis on its creative dimension, as 'activity of the subject'. Laplace rightly stresses the 'Copernican revolution' Coseriu thus introduces in linguistics, which also situates the discipline *ab initio* in a completely distinct tradition compared to the traditions of Saussure and Chomsky, viz. the philosophical tradition going back to Aristotle, Hegel and Humboldt already mentioned in Section 1. Furthermore, a major achievement of Coseriu's approach – and probably its true originality – is that he succeeded in revealing what until then remained implicit in the way the nature of the object of linguistic enquiry was defined, while at the same time urging for a radical reversal of the point of view. Any attempt to identify Coseriu's role in the modern history of linguistics in terms of the 'mediating' or 'conciliatory' nature of his contribution with regard to the main currents of twentieth-century linguistics runs the risk to overlook the importance of this achievement for the further development of the language sciences. I am therefore in agreement with Laplace's conclusion that we are dealing, strictly speaking, with a radically new conception of language and linguistics, which is undoubtedly to be considered one of "the most pertinent" of all linguistic theories that have so far been elaborated (Laplace 1994: 108).

3 Defining the object of enquiry in linguistics

I now turn to the way Coseriu defines the object of linguistics according to his radically new approach. After the initial structuralist enthusiasm of the 1940s, during which linguistics was declared a 'pilot discipline' among the humanities precisely because it allegedly succeeded in defining its own object of enquiry and in establishing an appropriate methodology, a half century of devastating criticism followed in which structuralism was rightly criticised from the perspective of the theoretical justification of its object of study. Among these criticisms, let us only recall Paul Ricœur's incisive criticism that structuralist linguistics actually eliminated the "primary function" of language from its object of study. There is no room here to go into the details of this debate, but I believe that Coseriu's definition of the "signifying function of language", as presented in "L'homme et son langage" (Coseriu 2001 [1968]; cf. Coseriu 1991 [1977], 2001) and in several later texts, puts an end to this crisis of the 'foundations of linguistics'.

Coseriu's definition of the 'signifying function of language' has been the subject of several investigations, such as Caamaño (1993). It remains a central issue of all studies in the wake of Coseriu's integralist program. Coseriu's contribution can best be summarized in terms of a 'fusion' of two distinct components, which were independently profiled in twentieth-century European linguistics and in the philosophy of language:
(1) on the one hand, the Aristotelian 'semantic logos' (cf. Coseriu 2015, I: chapter 6), which Coseriu revived by imbuing it with the essential dimension of 'creativity'; creativity is in this context taken in its original sense related to the concept of *enérgeia*, i. e. as a "free" purposeful activity, in which "the creative act [...] is [ideally] prior to its *dýnamis*" or potential (cf. Coseriu 1996: 64; Di Cesare 1988);
(2) on the other hand, the 'dialogical' component of language, i. e. the specific historical relation between speaking subjects or, better still, 'alterity' in the sense of an essential, constitutive 'intersubjectivity' of language; this view was pioneered by W. von Humboldt but revived and consolidated by Coseriu in general accordance with his most important philosophical sources (G. W. F. Hegel, M. Heidegger and J. Dewey, among others) (see Borcilă 1988).

While these two components traditionally stand in opposition to one another, Coseriu shows that they actually form a dialectical unity. This synthesis is achieved in Coseriu's approach by including, and simultaneously overcoming, both the 'idealistic' and the 'positivist' (including structuralist) assumptions in the preceding history of linguistics. Moreover, the merging of both components into a single, unified concept enabled Coseriu to resolve some of the main aporias with which the history of linguistics is fraught.

The notions of 'semantic logos' and 'alterity' are to some extent contradictory. In Coseriu's approach they are unified under the Humboldtian principle of creativity, yielding the definition of the 'essence of language' in terms of the 'signifying function' of language. The constitutive function of language is consequently defined as the 'free creation of verbal signs' and, more precisely, as the 'free creation of significant contents', in the broad but specifically linguistic sense of G. *Bedeutung* (Sp. *significado* 'signified'). Coseriu's approach thus integrates disparate elements from previous 'semiotic' accounts in the history of the language sciences and the 'idealistic' theory of linguistic creativity under a unified framework, yet it goes beyond these sources and provides a new horizon for the scientific study of language.

It is important to point out that already in Coseriu's first systematic treatise, "Sistema, norma y habla" (Coseriu 1973 [1952]), the signifying function of language is expressly correlated with "linguistic knowledge" (Sp. *saber lingüístico*) – years before 'linguistic knowledge' emerged as a key notion in the generative paradigm initiated by Noam Chomsky, who would approach 'linguistic knowledge' from a different epistemological point of view and through the lens of a different conception of 'linguistic competence'. Indeed, for Coseriu and Chomsky, 'linguistic competence' means two entirely different things. While Chomsky restricts competence to the purely combinatorial (or 'computational') capacity to produce language, including the creative capacity of language, Coseriu approaches competence in a much more comprehensive way. Coseriu (1992b) defines competence as "intuitive technique", viz. the "intuitive knowledge" speakers possess with a view to create meaningful content. Moreover, contrary to Chomsky, linguistic competence has nothing to do with the biological conditioning of a supposedly computational faculty. For Coseriu, it represents, in the final analysis, the deep internal dimension of the signifying function understood as "free creation of verbal signs", whose specific content, even though it corresponds to the general level of the 'signifieds' of a language, emerges only in and through the intuitive spontaneity of the (inter-)subjectivity of speakers within every single act of speaking. Coseriu's competence therefore underpins the 'cultural activity of speaking' as well as being part of the broader cultural capacity of 'acquiring' meaningful content. Not surprisingly, the way Coseriu defines the nature of the object of linguistic enquiry, including the linguistic-cultural specificity of competence, converges in some respects with the approach advocated by a number of American semanticists and semioticians who developed in the post-Chomsky era the currently influential framework of 'cognitive linguistics' (cf., e.g., Johnson 1987, Lakoff 1987, Lakoff and Johnson 1999).

4 The 'integral' approach to language

In Integral Linguistics, three domains of investigation are identified: 'elocutional knowledge' (speaking in general), 'idiomatic knowledge' (speaking a particular language) and 'expressive knowledge' (the individual speech in specific acts of discourse) (cf. Coseriu 1992b: chapter 2). It is in this threefold distinction that the originality and significance of Coseriu's approach to language perhaps become most apparent. The three domains are directly accessible to descriptive research and readily localisable in the vast and diversified research field of language studies. As Di Cesare (1997: 11) observed, the "individualisation" of the individual domains has its roots in "the reflection on the nature of language" and in the way of defining the object of study. Coseriu's delimitation of three levels is also based on a real dissociation of different layers of content and, consequently, of three corresponding levels of linguistic competence. As a result, the Coserian tripartite division imposes itself independently of whether or not one accepts the underlying theoretical assumptions discussed in the previous sections, because the distinction depends on a heuristic exigency that refers to the homogeneity of the three domains of investigation thus identified. Viewed from this angle, it does not come as a surprise that Coseriu (1985: xxv) himself once said that he considered his distinction between the three levels of linguistic knowledge and the corresponding three domains of enquiry his "main contribution to the understanding of language and consequently to the foundation of linguistics". Because of the distinction's pivotal role in the Coserian framework, some final clarifications are in order.

It has been pointed out that Coseriu's division between three clearly defined domains of investigation offers the possibility to incorporate many different strands of research of the past. For example, historical and structural linguistics can be appropriated into the study of the language-specific domain of idiomatic knowledge, whereas the gist of what models such as generative linguistics and cognitive semantics examine pertains to the elocutional domain, and the field of 'literary stylistics' relates to the textual, expressive domain. It is important to emphasize that integrating the procedures and findings of previous research does not amount to simply adopting them in their original form. Coseriu's 'integral' approach necessitates that they are re-interpreted in an altogether new perspective. For example, the version of structural semantics known as 'lexematics' (G. *Lexematik*), which has become associated with the 'Tübingen school' Coseriu founded in the 1960s, is not simply a return to Saussurean structuralism, given that Coseriu had rejected Saussure's theory of language already in the first decades of his scholarly activity, in particular in Coseriu (1978 [1958]) and the studies from the 1950s collected in Coseriu (1973 [1962]) (cf. Sanchez de Zavala 1982). Crucially, we are dealing with a 'reinterpretation' of some 'Saussurean motives' in the spirit of W. von Humboldt, in other words, with a recuperation of the specific structuralism of Saussurean origin from the perspective of the much more comprehensive historical-anthropological 'pre-structuralist' concepts that can be found in Humboldt's writings.⁴ Thus, the method of establishing the language-specific signifieds of words based on the functional principle of intra-systemic oppositions applied in lexematics pursues the objective of capturing the signifying contents of a language in their dimension of primal intuitive contents of a historically determined activity of speaking and not simply as a series of 'differences of ideas' of an abstract and reified 'system' as in Saussure's approach. This change of focus is essential to integral investigations into the semantic structure of languages. Similarly, the Coserian notion of 'sense' of a text (G. *Sinn*, Sp. *sentido*, 'text meaning') does not refer to an *érgon*, i.e. a layer of content given as such and simply approachable through a formal description and/or logically explainable by means of a 'deep' structural analysis of the kind proposed in contemporary studies of textual mythology (for example, in the work of C. Lévi-Strauss and his followers). On the contrary, the singular achievement of Coseriu's Integral Linguistics approach to this level of content resides in the vindication of central insights of contemporary hermeneutics. As a matter of fact, Coseriu's contribution to text linguistics constitutes a distinctive *linguistic* "introduction to the hermeneutics of sense" (Coseriu 1997 [1980]; Di Cesare 1997: 11–24). In Coseriu's approach, 'sense' is conceived as primarily evolving from a 'core act' of semantic textual creativity, in which the signifieds of the language and their potential designations are dynamically and convergently activated in the projection of an emerging ('possible') world. This approach to texts has a solid conceptual framework in Coseriu's definition of "modes of discourse" and in his original theory of "universes of discourse" (cf. Coseriu 2002). Important work has already been done over the last years in which Coseriu's approach has been applied to different cultural contexts; see, for example, Tămâianu's (2001) investigation of textual typologies in Romanian and Japanese texts.

5 Concluding remarks

Coseriu's major contributions to linguistics, in which he consistently applied the principles outlined in the preceding sections, cannot be reviewed in the present article. Suffice it to say that they make up a formidable body of research, covering a wide array of topics and domains and different levels of language: from the history of linguistics over studies in semantics, syntax and language typology and extensive investigations of all Romance languages (a primary area of interest

---

4 Note that Coseriu always referred to the Saussure of the *Cours de linguistique générale* (Saussure 1975 [1916]), not the 'authentic' Saussure (cf. Albrecht, this volume).

in Coseriu's œuvre), to studies of a wide area of literary, scientific and philological texts. I would like to conclude this article by emphasizing that most of Coseriu's investigations reveal their true value only in the light of the profound changes his approach has brought about regarding the horizons of linguistics that they implicitly or explicitly illustrate. For example, Bojoga (1999) demonstrates how the reception of the Russian translation (published in 1963) of *Sincronía, diacronía e historia* (Coseriu 1978 [1958]) suffered from a number of misinterpretations due to the fact that Russian linguistics was at that time dominated by a theoretical framework for which Coseriu's monograph did not provide any support, even if Russian linguists agreed with some of Coseriu's ideas and solutions to "the problem of linguistic change". This assessment seems valid, *mutatis mutandis*, for most of Coseriu's descriptive, historical and comparative investigations in the broader perspective of the development of linguistics in the twentieth century (cf. Faur 2013a; this volume).

I am convinced that Coseriu's seemingly disparate contributions prove their importance if one is willing to read them with the deep conceptual unity of his work in mind, which testifies to what in my view is best described as 'linguistic-cultural integralism'. If we interpret Coseriu's historical observation in the *Lecciones de lingüística general* (1999 [1981]), which I quoted at the beginning of this article, against this background, then it seems to me that the requirement of "founding contemporary linguistics as a science of culture" has come a long way thanks to Coseriu's own ground-breaking accomplishments, so that it only in part remains for us "the task of the present and the future".

References

Bernardo, José Maria. 1995. *La construcción de la lingüística. Un debate epistemológico.* Valencia: Universitat de Valencia.
Bojoga, Eugenia. 1999. *Receptarea operei lui E. Coșeriu în fosta U.R.S.S.* Universitatea Babeș-Bolyai: Cluj-Napoca (PhD Dissertation).
Borcilă, Mircea. 1988. "Eugeniu Coșeriu și orizonturile lingvisticii". *Echinox* 5:1, 4–5.
Borcilă, Mircea. 1997. "Între Blaga și Coșeriu. De la metaforica limbajului la o poetică a culturii". *Revista de filosofie* 1–2, 147–163.
Borcilă, Mircea. 2000. "Eugenio Coseriu and the new horizons of linguistics". *Transylvanian Review* 9:1, 103–107.
Borcilă, Mircea. 2001. "Eugeniu Coșeriu și bazele științelor culturii". *Academica* 9:7–8, 22–23.
Borcilă, Mircea. 2002. "Eugeniu Coșeriu, fondator al lingvisticii ca știință a culturii". *Limba Română* 10, 48–55.

Borcilă, Mircea. 2016. "Eugeniu Coșeriu și problema temeiului epistemologic al științei lingvistice". In: Cornel Vîlcu, Eugenia Bojoga and Oana Boc (eds.), *Școala coșeriană clujeană. Contribuții*. Vol. I, 19 – 28. Cluj: Presa Universitară.

Caamaño, Antonio V. 1993. *Lógica y lenguaje en Eugenio Coseriu*. Madrid: Gredos.

Chomsky, Noam. 1980. *Rules and representations*. New York: Columbia University Press.

Chomsky, Noam. 1986. *Knowledge of language: its nature, origin, and use*. New York: Praeger.

Chomsky, Noam. 2009 [1966]. *Cartesian linguistics. A chapter in the history of rationalist thought* (third edition). Cambridge: Cambridge University Press.

Coseriu, Eugenio. 1970 [1968]. *Einführung in die transformationelle Grammatik*. Tübingen: Narr.

Coseriu, Eugenio. 1973 [1952]. "Sistema, norma y habla". In: Eugenio Coseriu, *Teoría del lenguaje y lingüística general. Cinco estudios*, 11 – 113. Madrid: Gredos.

Coseriu, Eugenio. 1973 [1962]. *Teoría del lenguaje y lingüística general. Cinco estudios* (third edition). Madrid: Gredos.

Coseriu, Eugenio. 1975 [1971]. *Leistung und Grenzen der transformationellen Grammatik*. Tübingen: Narr.

Coseriu, Eugenio. 1978 [1958]. *Sincronía, diacronía e historia. El problema del cambio lingüístico* (third edition). Madrid: Gredos.

Coseriu, Eugenio. 1987 [1978]. *Gramática, semántica, universales. Estudios de lingüística funcional* (second edition). Madrid: Gredos.

Coseriu, Eugenio. 1985. "Linguistic competence: what is it really?" *The Modern Language Review* 80:4, xxv-xxxv.

Coseriu, Eugenio. 1991 [1977]. *El hombre y su lenguaje: estudios de teoría y metodología lingüística*. Madrid: Gredos.

Coseriu, Eugenio. 1992b. *Competencia lingüística. Elementos de una teoría del hablar*. Madrid: Gredos. (Spanish translation of Coseriu 2007 [1988].)

Coseriu, Eugenio. 1995 [1984/1986]. *Die Sprachwissenschaft im 20. Jahrhundert. Theorien und Methoden*. Transcript by Peter Fink and Heinrich Weber. Unpublished manuscript. University of Tübingen.

Coșeriu, Eugeniu. 1996. *Lingvistica integrală*. Interviu cu Eugeniu Coșeriu realizat de Nicolae Saramandu. București: Editura Fundației Culturale Române.

Coseriu, Eugenio. 1997 [1980]. *Linguistica del testo. Introduzione a una ermeneutica del senso*. Translated by Donatella Di Cesare. Roma: La Nuova Italia Scientifica.

Coseriu, Eugenio. 1999 [1981]. *Lecciones de lingüística general* (second edition). Madrid: Gredos.

Coseriu, Eugenio. 2001 [1968]. "L'homme et son langage". In: Eugenio Coseriu, *L'homme et son langage*. Edited by Hiltrud Dupuy-Engelhardt, Jean-Pierre Durafour and François Rastier, 13 – 30. Louvain: Peeters.

Coseriu, Eugenio. 2001. *L'homme et son langage*. Edited by Hiltrud Dupuy-Engelhardt, Jean-Pierre Durafour and François Rastier. Louvain: Peeters.

Coseriu, Eugenio. 2002. "Prolusione: Orationis fundamenta. La preghiera come testo". In: Giuseppe De Gennaro (ed.), *I quattro universi di discorso. Atti del Congresso Internazionale "Orationis Millenium"*, 24 – 47. L'Aquila: Libreria Editrice Vaticana.

Coseriu, Eugenio. 2007 [1988]. *Sprachkompetenz. Grundzüge der Theorie des Sprechens*. Edited by Heinrich Weber (second edition). Tübingen: Narr.

Coseriu, Eugenio. 2015. *Geschichte der Sprachphilosophie*. Vol. 1: *Von Heraklit bis Rousseau*. Vol. 2: *Von Herder bis Humboldt*. Edited by Jörn Albrecht. Tübingen: Narr & Francke: Attempto.

Di Cesare, Donatella. 1988. "Die aristotelische Herkunft der Begriffe ἔργον und ἐνέργεια in Wilhelm von Humboldts Sprachphilosophie". In: Jörn Albrecht, Jens Lüdke and Harald Thun (eds.), *Energeia und Ergon. Sprachliche Variation – Sprachgeschichte – Sprachtypologie. Studia in honorem Eugenio Coseriu*. Vol. 2: *Das sprachtheoretische Denken Eugenio Coserius in der Diskussion (1)*, 29–46, Tübingen: Narr.

Di Cesare, Donatella. 1997. "Introduzione". In: Eugenio Coseriu. 1997 [1980]. *Linguistica del testo. Introduzione a una ermeneutica del senso*, 11–24. Roma: La Nuova Italia Scientifica.

Faur, Elena. 2013a. "Integral Semantics and Conceptual Metaphor: rethinking Conceptual Metaphor within an Integral Semantics framework". In: Riccardo Fusaroli and Simone Morgagni (eds.), *Cognitive Semiotics. Conceptual Metaphor Theory: thirty years after*, 108–139. Berlin & Boston: Mouton de Gruyter.

Johnson, Mark. 1987. *The body in the mind. The bodily basis of meaning, imagination, and reason*. Chicago: University of Chicago Press.

Kabatek, Johannes and Adolfo Murguía. 1997. *"Die Sachen sagen, wie sie sind…". Eugenio Coseriu im Gespräch*. Tübingen: Narr.

Lakoff, George. 1987. *Women, fire, and dangerous things: what categories reveal about the mind*. Chicago: The University of Chicago Press.

Lakoff, George and Mark Johnson. 1999. *Philosophy in the flesh. The embodied mind and its challenge to Western thought*. New York: Basic Books.

Laplace, Colette. 1994. *Théorie du langage et théorie de la traduction: les concepts – clefs de trois auteurs: Kade (Leipzig), Coseriu (Tübingen), Seleskovitch (Paris)*. Paris: Didier Érudition.

Ruwet, Nicolas. 1991. "À propos de la grammaire générative. Quelques considérations intempestives". *Histoire Épistémologie Langage* 13:1, 109–132.

Sánchez de Zavala, Victor. 1982. *Funcionalismo estructural y generativismo*. Madrid: Alianza.

Saussure, Ferdinand de. 1975 [1916]. *Cours de linguistique générale*. Edited by T. De Mauro. Paris: Payot.

Tămâianu, Emma. 2001. *Fundamentele tipologiei textuale. O abordare în lumina lingvisticii integrale*. Cluj-Napoca: Clusium.

Göran Sonesson (Lund)
Considerations on the subtle art of integrating linguistics (and/or semiotics)

> *What is Integral Linguistics? It is the linguistic approach that aims to take into account the knowledge the speaker puts to work when speaking, with the purpose of organizing the facts conceived of in this way within a homogeneous and unitary framework.**

Whether or not it was Saussure or his posthumous editors (see Joseph 2012) who claimed that the proper study of linguistics is "la langue envisagée en elle-même et pour elle-même" (whatever that means), it remains true that, for more than a century, under the sway of structuralism as well as that of generative grammar, a bare bone approach has prevailed in linguistics, and later on also in semiotics. There can hardly be any doubt that for a time this reduction of the object of linguistics (but more dubiously that of semiotics) constituted a useful methodical device, but, in the long run, it could only bring about an impoverishment of the object of study, and an increasing irrelevance of its results to the ordinary *Lifeworld*. It is not surprising, then, that a number of proposals for integrating linguistics have been forthcoming, one of which is due to Eugenio Coseriu. But what does it mean to integrate linguistics? Should it be integrated into semiotics, cognitive science, or cognitive semiotics? Should it be integrated into the human and social science generally, if we take that to be something different? Or should different perspectives on language be integrated with each other? In other words, is linguistics the subject or the object of the process of integration? Or perhaps both? Or is something entirely different meant?

1 Coseriu's Integral Linguistics

It has become customary to refer to Coseriu's conception of linguistics as 'Integral Linguistics'. Or, to be more exact, it seems that the usage of this label has been an ingrained habit in Romania for a long time already, while even addicted

---

* "¿Qué es la Lingüística Integral? Es aquella Lingüística que se propone dar cuenta del saber que el hablante pone en obra al hablar, proponiéndose ordenar los hechos comprobados a este respecto en un marco homogéneo y unitario" (Coseriu 1984: 37).

readers of Coseriu's work only discovered the term rather recently.¹ In a lecture given in Bucharest in 1996 (Academia Română 2004: 65–140), Coseriu declared:

> Quite late in my life, I have decided to term my linguistic conception 'Integral Linguistics'. I first used this term in a course held in 1981, at the University of San Juan, in Argentina, and the course has been published in 1982 with exactly this title: *La lingüística integral*.²

It seems that these lectures were actually published, but under the title "Más allá del estructuralismo" (not identical to Coseriu 2001 [1982] which bears the same title in French). According to the review by Borcilă (1986: 102), this publication "represents a significant moment for contemporary linguistics. Thirty years after the first outline of 'a unitary and coherent vision of language as creative activity' (in his already 'classic' study "Sistema, norma y habla", Coseriu 1973 [1952]), the linguist presents here for the first time, in a systematic manner, the principles and the research domains that together, from his perspective, constitutes 'Integral Linguistics'". Borcilă also remarks that the book is a "quasi-literal transcription" of the lectures given by Coseriu at the time, and that a revised version is expected to be published by Gredos. This didn't happen.³

In another lecture, held at the Babes-Bolyai University in Cluj-Napoca, Romania, Coseriu said: "I proposed this name ['Integral Linguistics'] very late, around 1982, with the specific intention to designate the way of doing linguistics of which I am an exponent".⁴ This kind of linguistics, he claims, has no place in contemporary linguistics, because it spans the whole field of the different approaches to linguistics currently existing. This is because he favours a threefold approach to language.

---

1 Vîlcu (2014) is a testimony to the surprise felt by a Romanian linguist, who had studied under Coseriu's follower, Mircea Borcilă, when discovering that this label was not familiar outside of Romania. It is a pity that I did not know this article when writing my text, since it contains several of the relevant references which I had to search out in more convoluted ways.

2 I owe the information about this lecture, as well as the English translation, and all other translations from Romanian, to Elena Faur. I also want to take this opportunity to thank her for all the relevant information she has forwarded to me, as well as her comments on an earlier version of this article.

3 According to Loureda Lamas and Meisterfeld (2007) and Maldonado García (2015), there is a manuscript of a lecture given by Coseriu at UNAM, Mexico D.F., in 1975, which now will probably be at the Coseriu Archive in Tübingen, and it is indeed listed on one of the pages as manuscript A XIV, 3 (http://www.romling.uni-tuebingen.de/coseriu/klassif.htm), but not available for download. Kabatek (2018b), who has a lot to say about what integral linguistics is, does not refer to this manuscript but only to Kabatek and Murguía (1997).

4 I want to thank Mircea Borcilă for authorising me to refer to this text, which will form part of a volume of Coseriu's work which he is currently editing.

There is, however, a paper (not a course) which Coseriu gave at a linguistic conference in San Juan, Argentina, in 1981, the title of which contains the mention of Integral Linguistics (Coseriu 1984: 37). Integral Linguistics, Coseriu writes, "aims to take into account the knowledge the speaker puts to work when speaking, with the purpose of organizing the facts conceived of in this way within a homogeneous and unitary framework". He goes on to recount an anecdote about the problems Spanish speakers have to understand the relentless German custom for saying thanks, which very much suggests the kind of linguistics which he later on repudiates in the work of Harris (see Section 2). In the later part of the paper, however, Coseriu (1984: 45) writes:

> We would then have three levels: elocutionary knowledge, idiomatic knowledge and expressive knowledge. Since these three types of knowledge exist and have different contents and different values (even on the part of the speakers), it is necessary for there to be also three different linguistics to study them. We therefore need a linguistics of speaking, a linguistics of languages and a linguistics of discourse or text. They should form, respectively, a linguistics of designation, of meaning (within a particular language) and of sense (within each text, or at least within a series of analogous discourses).

It is clear, then, that for Coseriu the integration which takes place in Integral Linguistics is the integration of three perspectives, which, as it happens, take in more or less of the environment, but which are basically characterized by the shift of perspective. This is classical Coseriu, as we know him from some of his books (e.g. Coseriu 1973 [1962], 1992b). This interpretation is confirmed by what Coseriu says in the section about Integral Linguistics in Kabatek and Murguía (1997: 157 ff.). Integral Linguistics, Coseriu says:

> are actually three linguistics, 'three times linguistics' – linguistics of speaking, of languages and of the text. In general, one recognizes only one linguistics and reduces the other two to the one which is accepted or recognized. One also does linguistics of speaking in general or of texts within the linguistics of languages. Or one tries to do a linguistics of speaking in general and then present it as a linguistics of languages or of a language. For example, if you do general pragmatics and present it as the pragmatics of German; in reality it is pragmatics of speaking with German examples. (Kabatek and Murguía 1997: 159–160).

We here recognize some of the themes broached by Coseriu (1973, 1992b) in earlier publications, where he does not use the term 'Integral Linguistics'. All in all, this suggests that, to Coseriu, the integration of linguistics involves maintaining the same object of study while looking at it from different perspectives.

2 What Coseriu's Integral Linguistics is not

In the sources to which I have referred above, Coseriu also has a lot to say about what he does not want the term 'Integral Linguistics' to mean, in particular by contrasting his view with those of Helmut Gipper and Roy Harris. Thus, in the lecture at Babes-Bolyai University in Cluj-Napoca, Coseriu says:

> In a homage to me, [Gipper] directly adopted the term 'Integral Linguistics'. This form of Integral Linguistics aims to be linguistics and, at the same time, to integrate the neurophysiological basis of language. It is in this sense that it is 'integral'. Personally, I do not agree with this mode of understanding and considering language, because I believe that linguistics is exclusively a cultural science and that the material bases of language do not belong to this discipline as such, though, of course, when needed for explaining certain linguistic aspects one can also refer to them [and] to other disciplines, as auxiliary disciplines to linguistics.

Coseriu here seems to have a false memory of Gipper's contribution to his *Festschrift* (Gipper 1981). After some courteous remarks about Coseriu's importance to linguistics, Gipper does not mention Coseriu again, except once, in passing, in a paper which is concerned with the interpretation of Wilhelm von Humboldt's work. Moreover, if we consult the introduction to the *Festschrift* dedicated to Gipper, which bears the title *Integrale Linguistik* (Bülow and Schmitter, eds., 1979), we discover, not only that Gipper apparently used this term for a workshop organized already in 1972, but also that his conceptual horizon was much wider than what Coseriu indicates: his notion of linguistics is said to be as comprehensive as that of Roman Jakobson (1990 [1969]) in the latter's paper dedicated to Claude Lévi-Strauss. This is the paper in which Jakobson places linguistics firmly within semiotics, itself part of the even wider domain of the sciences of communication.

This fits nicely with Gipper's purpose in defining such a linguistics, as summarized by the editors, according to which Gipper wanted to expand the traditional approach to semantics, especially so as to include the question about the conditions of possibility of linguistic meaning-making. They go on to suggest that Gipper was interested in the neural and biochemical structures of the brain corresponding to language and thought, linguistic works of art, language acquisition and the use of language, and the lexical, semantic and syntactic structures of his own language as well as that of, for instance, Hopi, an Uto-Aztec Indian language of southwestern North America (Bülow and Schmitter, eds. 1979: XII). These examples would seem to go beyond semiotics, in Jakobson's (limited) understanding, to the other sciences of communication, perhaps not economics, but certainly sociology and anthropology.

Coseriu probably only mentions Gipper's interest in the neurophysiological basis of language because it goes directly beyond his own understanding of linguistics as a cultural science, no doubt in the sense of Ernst Cassirer (1942), i.e. in the sense of the social and human sciences, which is also what Luis Prieto (1975a, b) termed the semiotic ("semiological") sciences (see Section 5). Meanwhile, this suggests that the term 'Integral Linguistics' was used by Gipper before Coseriu took it up. Nevertheless, we learn from the same editorial introduction to Gipper's *Festschrift* that Coseriu in the Winter semester of 1966–1967 gave a series of lectures in Tübingen, where he used the term "integrale sprachliche Betrachtung" ('integral linguistic considerations') to designate an understanding of linguistics that not only studies the systematic character of language, as in classical structuralism, but also its creativity and historicity (Bülow and Schmitter, eds. 1979: XI). However, the published version of these lectures (Coseriu 1973) is precisely the book Coseriu (1981 [1977]: 7) qualifies as being the result of students' notes, and which therefore "also contains statements, interpretations and formulations which are not my own".

In the same talk, Coseriu also rejects Roy Harris' notion of 'integrational linguistics', which, in his view, "pretends to be an explanation of speaking by means of all its determinations, one of which is language". Coseriu claims that while "all the other circumstances of speaking can be absent to some degree, the only determination that cannot be absent in order for that act to be language is certainly this determination, and not only language, but a particular historical language". If you peruse one of Harris' (1981: 167) books, there is a passage at the beginning which should speak to Coseriu's Humboldtian heritage: that integrational linguistics should establish "that language is continuously created by the interaction of individuals in specific communication situations". However, when Harris (1981: 165) goes on to claim that it should "recognize that human beings inhabit a communicational space which is not neatly compartmentalized into language and non-language", it is easy to agree with Coseriu's dismissal. In fact, rather than integrating linguistics, Harris seems intent on dissolving it, and with it any other possible semiotic study.

3 Other brands of Integral Linguistics

Coseriu could not know Subbiondo's (2017) endeavour to bring together more or less all the human and social sciences, more inspired, he claims, in Darwin than in Descartes, in an attempt to resolve the old puzzle of linguistic relativity under the banner of 'integral linguistics'. It is more curious that Coseriu apparently was unaware of Hans-Heinrich Lieb's (2020) forage into 'integrational linguistics', initiated already in 1964, in particular because, in spite of Lieb's tongue-in-cheek admittance that linguistics is part of semiotics, like Coseriu Lieb is primarily concerned with internally integrating linguistics. Interestingly, Lieb was also anxious to distinguish his approach from that of Harris, but, unlike Coseriu, he does not mention Gipper. Nor does Lieb mention Coseriu.

As the reader might have suspected by now, I have a personal stake to defend, or at least to account for. In my doctoral thesis (Sonesson 1978), reacting to the domineering paradigm of generative grammar, I suggested that language could be better understood by placing it within the general framework of semiotics. The following year, at the 5th Conference of Scandinavian Linguistics, probably in order to render my message more palatable to linguists, I summarized my thesis in a lecture bearing the title "A plea for integral linguistics" (Sonesson 1981). At the time, I had hardly heard about Coseriu, whose work I got to know and appreciate some years later, when I taught semantics at the School of Anthropology in Mexico City. Even so, the notion of 'integral linguistics', as used by Coseriu or anybody else but myself, was unknown to me until a few years ago.

Meanwhile, I have not returned to the notion of 'integral linguistics' until now. This is largely because circumstances made me abandon the original idea of studying language within a semiotic framework, opting instead for delving deeper into other semiotic resources. Nevertheless, I kept a broad perspective, which, in my case, meant to bring about a true integration of linguistics into semiotics. In the programmatic phrases of my dissertation, "the context is another text, but the world is inexhaustibly contextual". This was a recipe not only for abandoning the autonomy of linguistics, but also that of semiotics. The dissertation made abundant use of psychology as well as phenomenology, as has all my later work. Indeed, in these publications, I made use of a lot of experimental results, even if, until recent years, I did not design experiments which were specifically geared to answer semiotic questions (see Sonesson 2019a). Thus, my integral linguistics became semiotics, and later on, cognitive semiotics. In this way, my integral linguistics parted company with that of Coseriu.

In another way, however, I have kept company with Coseriu all along, as I have done with a few other scholars who have dedicated themselves to clarifying the nature of language. It is easy to say that linguistics is part of semiotics (although most linguists have found it difficult to do so), but this only makes sense once you have spelled out what language is, so that it becomes comparable to other semiotic resources, of which we know much less. In spite of their formalist *profession de foi*, Louis Hjelmslev and Luis Prieto certainly contributed to such an approach, but Coseriu (1978 [1958]; 1973 [1962]; 1987 [1978]; 1991 [1977]; 1992b) did so much more extensively, in part because he explicitly embedded his discussion not only within the earlier linguistic traditions (something which has become ever rarer since the incipit of the Chomskyan era), but also within a broader philosophical framework (which sometimes also includes Edmund Husserl).

4 Integration one way or other

I do not aspire to answer, in this article, all the questions which I formulated at the beginning. But, let us at least try to cast some light on the difference (and the similarity, as I will go on to suggest) between understanding integral linguistics as being about integrating different perspectives on language and integrating linguistics into some wider domain, whether this is semiotics or "the cultural sciences" (as Coseriu also suggested in the speech referred to in note 2; cf. Kabatek and Murguía 1997: 159 f.). It might perhaps be said, very summarily, that Lieb, like Coseriu, sets as his aim to integrate different approaches to the study of language, while Gipper (at least if the claims of the editors of his *Festschrift* are taken seriously), Subbiondo, and I put the emphasis on the integration of linguistics into a wider domain. I do not pretend to understand how Harris' vision of integrating linguistics fits in with any of the two interpretations I have delineated. Harris, it seems to me, is rather out to dissolve linguistics (at the level of theory) as well as any other conceivable scientific approach. But, in this long second half of the twentieth century, self-described as the postmodernist era, he is not alone (far from it, I am afraid) in trying to pursue a scientific endeavour, while declaring it impossible from the start.

To summarize, then, many scholars have used the term 'integral linguistics' in spite of having different aims. None of them, as far as I can judge, has been successful in establishing the term beyond a specific community (which is the case of the followers of Coseriu) as a brand, contrary to what was the case, most notably, with Noam Chomsky, whose approach was initially known as 'transformational grammar' and, later, when transformations were more or less dispensed with, as 'generative grammar'. As I have observed in earlier publications, when Saussure claimed that the place of semiotics (his "sémiologie") had been prepared beforehand, his argument was entirely rational, but in this wretched world not even the division of the sciences depend on purely rational arguments. It is rather a question of successful propaganda, as was clearly the case with 'generative grammar' (see Sonesson 2006, 2007, 2009, 2010, 2012, 2016, 2018). In a rationally ordained world, by contrast, (cognitive) semiotics should have been generally accepted as a major division of the sciences all over the world, and Coseriu (although he probably would not have liked it) would have been accepted as a "a pioneer, or rather a backwoodsman, in the work of clearing and opening up that which I call semiotic" (Peirce 1931–58, V: 335).

Still, it is possible to distil out a common core in all these attempts (except perhaps that of Harris) to integrating linguistics (and later on semiotics). In his original discussion of "Sistema, norma y habla", Coseriu insists that the three points of view on language he discusses, are distinct but intimately connected (Coseriu 1973 [1952]: 11 ff.). Put more crudely, as expressed by Loureda Lamas and Meisterfeld (2007: 270) and Maldonado García (2015: 2), linguistic structuralism is a valid approach to language, but we have to go beyond it by including other perspectives, which incorporate insights gained all the way from Aristotle to Hegel, and in particular from Humboldt.[5] If we try to capture this epistemological position in more general terms, we might say that when shifting the perspective to the object of study, we inevitably expand and/or reduce the latter, but we should retain a certain overlap. Changes of perspective thus entail some form of displacement of the domain studied. In other words, each perspective takes in a little more, or a little less, context (Sonesson 1978, 2012). The study of language as a system is the most comprehensive in taking in all potentialities, but it is also the most restricted with regard to its connection to the Lifeworld in which it is spoken. Once you consider language in terms of norms, you leave all the potentialities behind, but you also extend the object studied to encompass at least some elementary amount of sociability. Finally, the speech act can hardly be considered without reference to sociability, but it must in particular comprise the here and now, i.e. the *I-here-now* dimension.[6] This is an operation applied to the field of consciousness, in the sense of the phenomenologist Aron Gurwitsch (1964), rebaptized "the sphere of attention" by the psychologist Sven Arvidson (2006): a change in the theme selected as point of focus within consciousness brings about a modification of the thematic field, and possibly also of the margins, which, unlike the thematic field, coexist with the theme in the here and now, without sporting any obvious meaningful link. The necessities of our concrete study may then easily force us not only to take in a wider thematic field, but also to modify the theme of the field, which is where we may leave linguistics behind and enter semiotics. Norms and other constraints on sociability are present also outside of language and can be made into a new theme. The subject in

---

[5] In Coseriu (2001 [1982]), where the term 'Integral Linguistics' is not mentioned, these very words are used, but Coseriu's primary aim is to further clarify the "plan du système fonctionnel de la langue".
[6] Further differentiation, as suggested by Coseriu (1973 [1952]: 101), is of course always possible.

one's 'here and now' is present not only in language, and not only in other semiotic systems, but also in the immediate Lifeworld.

Still, there might in the end be a limit to the possibility of expansion, once we encounter the border between the human (semiotic) sciences and the natural sciences.

5 The objectivity of the semiotic sciences

When I stated in Sonesson (1978), long ago, that the world is inexhaustibly contextual, I did not, in spite of the phenomenological framework, specify that the world I was referring to was the world as experienced, or, in Husserl's terms, the Lifeworld, also known, in Alfred Schütz' terms, as "the world taken for granted", and, at least with reference to its basic structure, in James Gibson's phrase, "the world of ecological physics" (cf. Sonesson 1989, 2007, 2010, 2016). If our experience always takes place within the Lifeworld, our access to its structures is in some sense more immediate than anything we can get to know about the natural world (except as it appears in the Lifeworld, 'ecologically', in Gibson's terms, not as in the natural sciences). As Husserl points out, the natural sciences are forced to cover the world as experience with a clothing of ideas.

This conception appears to dovetail with what Giambattista Vico (1988 [1710]) termed the *Verum-Factum* principle. According to this principle we as human beings have access to the truth about anything we, or other human beings, have created, i.e. culture in the wide sense and all specific cultures. If we try to formulate this principle in our terms, it would be something like this: We, as human beings, can understand that which we, as human beings, have, or could have, created. In Kabatek and Murguía (1997: 167), Coseriu observes that

> the cultural sciences are the real 'exact sciences' because they have their origin in the *saber originario*, the primal knowledge of human beings, i.e. that which human beings know with regard to themselves and with regard to their free activities.

Coseriu (2015, I: 278, 282–305) discusses at length the way Vico extends this principle from mathematics, where others had characterized it, to the cultural sciences.

Apparently unaware of this precedent, Luis Prieto formulated much the same idea, suggesting that, contrary to the reigning positivist epistemology, our access to the subject matter of the human and social sciences (which he terms 'semiotic sciences') is direct, whereas our access to the subject matter of the natural sciences can only be indirect. The sound, as a material object, may have innumerable properties, Prieto (1975a: 140 ff., 1975b: 215 ff.) observes, but the phoneme, which is defined by its functional relations to the other plane of the sign, has a limited number of clearly defined features. Linguistics is concerned with the phoneme and everything erected on this basis (not on the sounds as such), hence with the subjective point of view of the language user. Therefore, linguistics, and the semiotic sciences generally, can be objective in the description of the subjective point view, whereas the natural sciences are subjective from the start, because they aim to account for physical reality, which as such is indifferent. Prieto's use of the term 'subjective' no doubt sounds outlandish to us today. However, the general idea is no different from Husserl's (1954) conception of natural science as being made up of different theories (*Ideenkleider*) cast upon the Lifeworld, which serve to connect a series of isolated observations, often made in an indirect way by means of some kind of instrument. According to another formulation, linguistics, and the semiotic sciences at large, produces knowledge about knowledge, not, as the natural sciences, about the material world (Prieto 1975a: 140 f.).

Nevertheless, as I have argued elsewhere (Sonesson 1989: 26 ff., 2018, to appear), the *Verum-Factum* principle can only have a partial application. Any scientific explanation is bound to carry us to layers below what is directly given to consciousness, whether these can be phenomenologically recuperated or only hypothetically posited, as in the natural sciences. Even if the phonemes form part of the experience of the speakers of a language, the distinctive features may not, and even if they do, we can proceed to the formants, etc. Put in the traditional terms of hermeneutics, we may say that, after coinciding with the user in his or her understanding of the phoneme, the semiotician goes on to explain the conditions of possibility of this understanding on the level of distinctive features, sound waves, etc. If so, semiotics involves the knowledge of the user but also something more. As Coseriu (2015, I: 280 ff.) rightly observes, Vico does not only reverse Leibniz' scale of knowledge going from 'cognitio obscura' to 'cognitio clara distincta adaequata' in a value perspective, but he treats them as distinct types of knowledge. He goes on to explain this different evaluation in terms of an attention, in Aristotelean terms, to final, rather than efficient, causes. It is the former which, to Vico, should attain 'cognitio clara distincta adaequata'. But a real scholarly understanding may also have to reach a Leibnizian 'cognitio clara distincta adaequata' of Vichean knowledge, that is, a clear understanding of that which is inherently obscure.

Somewhat along these lines, I suggest that in the semiotic sciences there are basically two procedures, one of which is particular to the semiotic sciences, as suggested by Vico and Prieto, and another one which is identical to the only one available to the natural sciences. The really fundamental question, however, is how we are able to attain this knowledge which, according to Prieto, is not given directly to the user of the semiotic resources. I call the first procedure an 'iconic operation', and the second one an 'indexical operation'. These terms are used here in Peirce's sense, in which they do not basically designate kinds of signs in any ordinary sense of the term, but something more general. According to my meta-analysis of Peirce's different phenomenological characterizations of iconicity (Sonesson 2013), it basically stands for the idea of 'something being there', that is, a direct perceptual experience. Indexicality, according to the same meta-analysis, involves something being added to what was first perceived, by some more indirect means.

Since nature is necessarily opaque to us, we can only gain knowledge about it by applying 'indexical operations'. In the semiotic sciences, however, we have a choice of using 'iconic operations', which go beyond first appearances, while staying at the level of appearance, that is, within the Lifeworld; or employing 'indexical operations', otherwise characteristic of the natural sciences, as when having recourse, e.g., to spectrograms or fMRI scanning. To clarify the idea of iconicity beyond the first impression while staying within the Lifeworld, we may make use of the Husserlean notion of 'sedimentation'. According to Husserl (1954: 152, 249, 373), all acts of consciousness (including those which have an external manifestation) are only possible because they take for granted the passive synthesis of earlier experience, building on numerous other acts of consciousness, some of which took place in our earlier life (genetic sedimentation) while others resulted from the experience of earlier generations of human beings (generative sedimentation). Since the sedimented results of these acts are what helps to make sense of our current interactions, we may be able to reactivate these acts, using the procedures of phenomenology. Combining Husserlean and Peircean phenomenology could open up an avenue for delving deeper into iconicity. We could also describe this, in Coseriu's (1995b: 73) terms, as going from the static principle of objectivity in hermeneutics (i.e. what the interpreter really says) to the dynamic principle (what he 'really' did mean to say), but applying these principles to the self at difference stages of interpretation.

Within the Lifeworld, there are only indexical references to the world described by the natural sciences, which have to be explained by means of hypothetical models. In the same Lifeworld, there is an iconic experience ('pure iconicity') of the subject matter of the semiotic sciences. But the indexical approach is also necessary in the semiotic sciences, because large batches of human work are presently reified, in Feuerbach's sense made famous by Marx. We can conceive reification as something which offers resistance to the reanimation of that which is sedimented. In this sense, economics and parts of sociology are reduced to using indexical procedures and construct hypotheses (which often prove wrong) on this basis. That is why they are, in Prieto's sense, as subjective as the natural sciences.

5 Conclusion

It is a moot question who first used the expression 'integral linguistics' or its cognates, in particular because those who used the term clearly meant different things. As I have demonstrated elsewhere (Sonesson 2019a), more or less the same has recently happened with the term 'experimental semiotics'. I stand by my original choice (in an existentialist sense), according to which integral linguistics is not only about integrating different perspectives on language, but more pertinently about integrating linguistics into semiotics – and, more specifically, into Cognitive Semiotics (Sonesson 2009; 2016). In spite of Coseriu's own restricted understanding of the term, however, he has given an immense contribution to integral linguistics, also in the wider sense of the term, because his approach is firmly rooted in philosophy (cf. Agud, this volume). Using both hermeneutics and phenomenology, Coseriu has probed into the nature of language in a way that is of lasting importance for anyone who aims to do the same for any other semiotic domain.

References

Academia Română, Institutul de lingvistică "Iorgu Iordan – Al. Rosetti". 2004. *In memoriam Eugenio Coseriu*. Extras din "Fonetică și Dialectologie", XX-XXI, 2001–2002. București: Editura Academiei Române.
Arvidson, Sven. 2006. *The sphere of attention: context and margin*. London: Kluwer Academic.
Borcilă, Mircea. 1986. Review of Eugenio Coseriu, *Más allá del estructuralismo, Tomo I* (San Juan, 1982). *Cercetări de lingvistică – Recherches de linguistique* 31:1, 102–103.
Bülow, Edeltraud and Peter Schmitter (eds.). 1979. *Integrale Linguistik: Festschrift für Helmut Gipper*. Amsterdam & Philadelphia: John Benjamins.
Cassirer, Ernst. 1942. *Zur Logik der Kulturwissenschaften: Fünf Studien*. Gothenburg: Göteborgs Högskolas Årsskrift.
Coseriu, Eugenio. 1973 [1952]. "Sistema, norma y habla". In: Eugenio Coseriu, *Teoría del lenguaje y lingüística general. Cinco estudios*, 11–113. Madrid: Gredos.
Coseriu, Eugenio. 1978 [1958]. *Sincronía, diacronía e historia. El problema del cambio lingüístico* (third edition). Madrid: Gredos.
Coseriu, Eugenio. 1973 [1962]. *Teoría del lenguaje y lingüística general. Cinco estudios* (third edition). Madrid: Gredos.

Coseriu, Eugenio. 1973. *Probleme der strukturellen Semantik*. Edited by Dieter Kastovsky. Tübingen: Narr.
Coseriu, Eugenio. 1981 [1977]. *Principios de semántica estructural*. Madrid: Gredos.
Coseriu, Eugenio. 1984. "Fundamentos y tareas de la lingüística integral". In: *Segundo Congreso de Nacional de Lingüística (16 al 19 de Setiembre de 1981)*. Tomo III, Actas I, 37–53. San Juan: R. Argentina.
Coseriu, Eugenio. 1987 [1978]. *Gramática, semántica, universales: estudios de lingüística funcional* (second edition). Madrid: Gredos.
Coseriu, Eugenio. 1991 [1977]. *El hombre y su lenguaje: estudios de teoría y metodología lingüística*. Madrid: Gredos.
Coseriu, Eugenio. 1992b. *Competencia lingüística. Elementos de una teoría del hablar*. Madrid: Gredos. (Spanish translation of Coseriu 2007 [1988].)
Coseriu, Eugenio. 1995b. "Von den *universali fantastici*". In: Jürgen Trabant (ed.), *Vico und die Zeichen – Vico e i segni*, 73–80. Tübingen: Narr.
Coseriu, Eugenio. 2001 [1982]. "Au-delà du structuralisme". In: Eugenio Coseriu, *L'homme et son langage*, 109–115. Louvain, Paris & Sterling, Virginia: Peeters.
Coseriu, Eugenio. 2015. *Geschichte der Sprachphilosophie*. Vol. 1: *Von Heraklit bis Rousseau*. Vol. 2: *Von Herder bis Humboldt*. Edited by Jörn Albrecht. Tübingen: Narr & Francke: Attempto.
Gipper, Helmut. 1981. "Schwierigkeiten beim Schreiben der Wahrheit in der Geschichte der Sprachwissenschaft. Zum Streit um das Verhältnis Wilhelm von Humboldts zu Herder". In: Horst Geckeler, Brigitte Schlieben-Lange, Jürgen Trabant and Harald Weydt (eds.). *Logos semantikos. Studia linguistica in honorem Eugenio Coseriu, 1921–1981*. Vol. 1: 101–115. Madrid: Gredos and Berlin: Walter de Gruyter.
Gurwitsch, Aron. 1964. *The field of consciousness*. Pittsburgh: Duquesne University Press.
Harris, Roy 1981. *The language myth*. London: Duckworth.
Husserl, Edmund. 1954. *Die Krisis der europäischen Wissenschaften und die transzendentale Phänomenologie: eine Einleitung in die phänomenologische Philosophie* (Husserliana VI). The Hague: Martinus Nijhoff.
Jakobson, Roman. 1971 [1969]. "Linguistics in its relation to the other sciences". In: R. Jakobson, *Selected Writings*. Vol. II: 655–696. The Hague & Paris: Mouton.
Joseph, John Earl. 2012. *Saussure*. Oxford: Oxford University Press.
Kabatek, Johannes. 2018b. "Lingüística coseriana, lingüística histórica y tradiciones discursivas". *Anadiss* 25, 255–258.
Kabatek, Johannes and Adolfo Murguía. 1997. *"Die Sachen sagen, wie sie sind ...": Eugenio Coseriu im Gespräch*. Tübingen: Narr.
Lieb, Hans-Heinrich. 2018. "Integrational Linguistics: The approach". Available online (Consulted on 27/3, 2020): https://www.integrational-linguistics.science/inteling/introAppr
Loureda Lamas, Óscar and Reinhard Meisterfeld. 2007. "Eugenio Coseriu y su legado científico". *Estudis romànics* 29, 269–277.
Maldonado García, María Isabel. 2015. "Eugenio Coseriu y su contribución a la lingüística". *Eurasian Journal of Humanities* 1:1, 1–11.
Peirce, Charles Sanders. 1931–1958. *Collected Papers I-VIII*. Edited by Charles Hartshorne, Paul Weiss and Arthur Burks. Cambridge, MA: Harvard University Press.
Prieto, Luis. 1975a. *Essai de linguistique et sémiologie générale*. Genève: Droz.

Prieto, Luis. 1975b. *Pertinence et pratique*. Paris: Minuit.
Sonesson, Göran. 1978. *Tecken och handling*. Lund: Doxa.
Sonesson, Göran. 1981. "A plea for integral linguistics". In: *Papers from the 5th Scandinavian Conference of Linguistics*, II, 151–166. Stockholm: Almqvist & Wiksell.
Sonesson, Göran. 1989. *Pictorial concepts. Inquiries into the semiotic heritage and its relevance for the analysis of the visual world*. Lund: Aris/Lund University Press.
Sonesson, Göran. 2006. "The meaning of meaning in biology and cognitive science. A semiotic reconstruction". *Sign Systems Studies* 34:1, 135–214.
Sonesson, Göran. 2007. "From the meaning of embodiment to the embodiment of meaning". In: Tom Ziemke, Jordan Zlatev and Roslyn M. Frank (eds.), *Body, language and mind*. Vol 1: *Embodiment*, 85–128. Berlin & New York: Mouton De Gruyter.
Sonesson, Göran. 2009. "The view from Husserl's lectern. Considerations on the role of phenomenology in Cognitive Semiotics". *Cybernetics and Human Knowing* 16:3/4, 107–148.
Sonesson, Göran. 2010. "Semiosis and the elusive final interpretant of understanding" *Semiotica* 179:1/4, 145–258.
Sonesson, Göran. 2012. "Semiotics inside-out and/or outside-in: How to understand everything and (with luck) influence people". *Signata* 2, 315–348.
Sonesson, Göran 2013. "The natural history of branching: approaches to the phenomenology of Firstness, Secondness, and Thirdness". *Signs and Society* 1:2, 297–326.
Sonesson, Göran. 2016. "Epistemological prolegomena to the Cognitive Semiotics of evolution and development". *Language and Semiotic Studies* 2:4, 46–99.
Sonesson, Göran. 2018. "Beyond the 'tragedy of culture'. In-between epistemology and communication". *The American Journal of Semiotics* 33:3/4, 141–180.
Sonesson, Göran. 2019a. "The Psammetichus Syndrome and beyond: five experimental approaches to meaning-making". *The American Journal of Semiotics* 35:1/2, 11–32.
Sonesson, Göran. To appear. "Nothing human is alien to me – except some of it. From Integral Linguistics to Cognitive Semiotics by way of phenomenology". *Zeitschrift für Semiotik*.
Subbiondo, Joseph. 2017. "The history of linguistics matters: linguistic relativity and integral linguistics". *US-China Foreign Language* 15:4, 215–221.
Vico, Giambattista. 1988 [1710]. *On the most ancient wisdom of the Italians, unearthed from the origins of the Latin language*. Ithaca & London: Cornell University Press.
Vîlcu, Dina. 2014. "Pleading for 'Integral Linguistics'". In: Eugenia Bojoga, Oana Boc and Dumitru-Cornel Vîlcu (eds.), *Coseriu: Perspectives contemporaines*. Vol. 2, 165–173. Cluj: Presa Universitară Clujeană.

Jörn Albrecht (Heidelberg)
Eugenio Coseriu and the primacy of history

> *By the way, for Hermann Paul grasping a structure as such was not something that is independent of the historical explanation of the structure itself. This explains his famous, and partly rhetorical, identification of linguistics and language history, which is obviously a reduction.*
>
> *In this sense, one can only agree with Hermann Paul's statement: linguistics really is language history.**

1 Introduction

The above two quotations are taken from publications Coseriu wrote at different stages in his career. Both refer to a famous assertion by Hermann Paul:

> I have briefly to justify my choice of the title 'Principles of the *history* of Language' (G. *Prinzipien der Sprachgeschichte*). It has been objected that there is another view of language possible besides the historical. I must contradict this. What is explained as an unhistorical and still scientific observation of language is at bottom nothing but one incompletely historical. (Paul 1888 [1886]: xlvi; italics in the original; German original: Paul 1920 [1880]: 20)

According to Guitarte (1988: 498), this is one of the rare cases in which Coseriu abandoned (or rather modified) a once-held opinion. The title of Coseriu (1983) is: "Linguistic change does not exist". Coseriu writes: "Language [...] does not have an organic continuity independent of the consciousness of its speakers" (Coseriu 1983: 54).

In what respects does Coseriu's position differ from that of other linguistic 'schools'? This can best be demonstrated by a brief comparison with traditional historical-comparative linguistics on the one hand and European structuralism on the other.

In the nineteenth century, when the humanities were struggling for their right to exist in the face of the triumphal march of the natural sciences, a species of linguistic naturalism developed in the field of historical linguistics. The most impressive testimony to this development is the famous "Sendbrief" (open letter)

---

* "Por cierto Paul no vio que el aprehender una estructura como tal es algo independiente de la explicáción historica de la estructura misma. De aquí su famosa, y en parte retórica, identificación entre *Sprachwissenschaft* y *Sprachgeschichte*, que es, evidentemente, una reducción" (Coseriu 1978 [1958]: 21; italics in the original). "In diesem Sinn muss man wohl dem Satz von Hermann Paul zustimmen: Sprachwissenschaft ist tatsächlich Sprachgeschichte" (Coseriu 1980: 145).

from the Jena linguist August Schleicher to his friend, the zoologist Ernst Häckel, in which Schleicher claimed with regard to languages precisely the kind of "organic continuity independent of the consciousness of its speakers" Coseriu would later oppose:

> Languages are organisms of nature; they have never been directed by the will of man: they arose, they grew according to definite laws, they developed and then in turn grew old and died out [...]. The science of language (G. *Glottik*) is consequently a natural science. (Schleicher 1977 [1863]: 88)

A number of handbooks on linguistics insist that structuralism neglected the historical dimension of language; some even mention a general "hostility to history" on the part of structuralism. However, this is an unacceptable generalization. Ferdinand de Saussure is considered by many to be the founder of structuralism and the major figure intent on 'abolishing' historical linguistics. This is plainly wrong. Saussure was not a 'structuralist', he even did not know this term, and throughout his life he remained a representative of historical linguistics: "All the work Saussure published in his lifetime was historical, as nearly all the manuscript material he left behind" (Joseph 2018: 203).[1] But he was one of those who claimed "that there is another view of language possible besides the historical". Nor was the structuralism of the Prague School "hostile to history". The Copenhagen School was quite different. In the preface to the first issue of *Acta Linguistica*, the publication organ of the circle, Viggo Brøndal, one of the leading members of the Copenhagen Linguistic Circle, spoke of time as "ce grand obstacle à toute rationalité [the great obstacle to all rational thought] (Brøndal 1939: 8).

In this article, I argue that Coseriu was willing to exclude the historical dimension in the description and analysis of linguistic phenomena, but only provisionally, so to speak. He accepted such an approach only as a reduction for methodological reasons. For Coseriu, languages are historical objects that cannot be adequately accounted for by a "science of genera and species" (cf. Section 2). In this respect, Coseriu agrees with Robin George Collingwood, a scholar who had a strong influence on Coseriu.[2] In *The idea of history*, Collingwood begins by discussing the differences between the nomothetical and the historical sciences:

---

[1] Cf. Milner (2002: 18): "le structuralisme n'avait pas tort de se croire issu du *Cours*, mais il n'est pas dans le *Cours*".

[2] Albrecht (1988: xxvi). According to Munteanu (2013a), Collingwood had a confirmative rather than formative influence on Coseriu.

> Historical thought has an object with peculiarities of its own. The past, consisting of particular events in space and time which are no longer happening, cannot be apprehended by mathematical thinking, because mathematical thinking apprehends objects that have no special location in space and time, and it is just this lack of peculiar spatio-temporal location that makes them knowable. [...] Theories of knowledge designed to account for mathematical and theological and scientific knowledge thus do not touch on the special problems of historical knowledge; and if they offer themselves as complete accounts of knowledge, they actually imply that historical knowledge is impossible. (Collingwood 1993 [1946]: 5)

Interestingly, Coseriu (2000 [1992]) refers to both Leibniz' treatise "Meditationes de cognitione, veritate et ideis" (1965 [1684]) and Collingwood and reaches a similar conclusion:

> Original knowledge applies only to whatever is universal. Namely, original knowledge makes us understand what language is, what its function is, what a linguistic unit is, but we shall not know what they [its function and the respective unit] are in each case. However, it is for this very reason that, both in interpreting particular facts and in interpreting historical facts, the same original knowledge man has about himself is the basis for interpretation. People believe all too often that the historical interpretation of facts, for instance, is an interpretation that is not filtered by the subject and the subject's intuition. In reality, each and every interpretation in this field – where there are no other hypotheses than those we can conceive with regard to ourselves – is an explanation *from my viewpoint*. (Coseriu 2000 [1992]: 110; italics in the original)

2 Coseriu's three types of *Wissenschaft*

Coseriu's *Geschichte der Sprachphilosophie* starts off with a discussion of three types of *Wissenschaft* (Coseriu 2015, I: 1–11; cf. Munteanu 2013b). The German term *Wissenschaft* has no exact equivalent in English. It encompasses humanities, social sciences, natural sciences and formal sciences as areas of enquiry that are based on different questions, which are moreover asked, discussed and answered in different academic disciplines. The most important questions in this context are the following:
1. the *historical* question about the being of an object ("ipseity"); i.e. historical investigations concerning individuals;
2. the *general* scientific question about the being of classes of objects and "states of affairs" (G. *Sachverhalte*); i.e. scientific disciplines in the normal sense of the term, which are concerned with species and genera;
3. the *philosophical* question that deals with the "sense of the being of objects", "der Sinn ihres Seins" (Coseriu 2015, I: 7) (cf. Trabant, this volume).

In what follows, I will restrict the discussion to the first question. Coseriu regards it the pertinent question with regard to the study of particular languages (in the plural), which Coseriu refers to as "historical languages". For Coseriu, a particular language is an "individual". It therefore belongs to the field of the historical sciences in the broadest sense. Wilhelm von Humboldt had already emphasized – and Coseriu never tires of pointing this out – that the various languages are to be regarded as individuals, they do not represent genera (or "classes"):

> The particular languages are different not as genera but as individuals, their character is not generic but individual. The individual, considered in this way, always constitutes a class in itself. (Humboldt 1963 [1829]: 189)

Coseriu calls languages that are designated by means of proper names, such as *Spanish*, *English*, *German* etc., "historical languages", adopting the term "lingue storiche" from Terracini (1957: 116). This term has often been misunderstood. Of course, it does not refer to dead languages or older states of a language. With "historical" Coseriu refers to any phenomenon that has an individual character, which can be identified by its own name, something contingent that cannot be derived from general laws, in short, anything that has a history. The Italian philosopher Giambattista Vico spoke in this context of the *mondo civile* or *mondo delle nazioni*.

Like Wilhelm Dilthey, who coined the somewhat unfortunate but still widely used term *Geisteswissenschaft* (the English expression 'humanities' is more appropriate), Coseriu aimed at restoring the historical disciplines to their inherent dignity at a time when only nomothetic disciplines were taken seriously among the supporters of the 'hard core' sciences. He counters the criticism that such an approach necessarily leads to losing a view of the whole by saying:

> While it is true that history is the science of the individual (G. *Wissenschaft vom Einzelnen*), its 'individual facts' are not necessarily details (any language system, historical language, or language family, too, are 'individuals' for history), and history considers each fact with all its determinations [...]. This is not because history is a 'hybrid' science, but because history is, in the case of language as in all other cases, the integral science of the particular fact. (Coseriu 1980: 140)

What is usually called "linguistic change" is for Coseriu nothing else than "the historical objectification of the creative character of language" (Coseriu 1988 [1979]: 5). The Saussurean distinction between 'synchrony' and 'diachrony' is an approach to language: it concerns linguistics, not language (Coseriu 1980: 138). Historical enquiries are about purposes ("what for"), not causes ("why").[3] Language is not an object of nature in which being can be separated from becoming, but an object of culture in which becoming belongs to being (Coseriu 1980: 142–143). Coseriu is aware of the fact that all this is bound to encounter widespread incomprehension. He explicitly mentions the "oddity" of his background when he first presented his views in the late 1950s, "especially in the English-speaking world" (Coseriu 1983: 51–52). An author like Raimo Anttila, who writes in English and lives in California, agrees with Coseriu's position on some important points: "meaning is when history is, [...] mental activity is the product of history", or "this of course makes history the primary ingredient in language, although it goes against the maxim taken to be Saussure's" (Anttila 1993: 53). In a long self-quotation, which cannot be entirely reproduced here, Anttila paraphrases Coseriu's position and concludes with the following words:

> In short, only historical linguistics does justice to our real experience with language and the essence of language. This does of course not deny synchrony. A synchronic-structural treatment of a given language state is the only reasonable one for description, although the description of a cultural object belongs to a phase in its becoming. There is no contradiction between description and history. As Hermann Paul said, linguistics is really historical linguistics (Anttila 1993: 54).

Coseriu develops his position against the background of – and partly in polemical opposition to – Ferdinand de Saussure's *Cours de linguistique générale* (Saussure 1975 [1916]). In contrast to Anttila, whose reference to "the maxim taken to be Saussure's" makes it clear that he distinguishes between the author of the *Cours* and the "true Saussure", Coseriu categorically refrains from taking recourse to the authentic sources that have become known in the meantime. According to Coseriu, only the 1916 *Cours* has been important for the history of linguistics, not the "authentic" Saussure (Coseriu 1980: 126, footnote 4). To what extent this stance is (un)justified cannot be examined here. In his evaluation of Saussure, Coseriu is strongly influenced by his teacher Antonino Pagliaro:

> I would describe my conceptions as essentially an attempt to reconcile – while keeping a firm eye on the reality of language – Saussure with Humboldt and Pagliaro [...]. (Coseriu 1995a: 188)

---

3 Recall that Aristotle distinguishes four 'causes': *causa efficiens, causa materialis, causa formalis* and *causa finalis*. The latter concerns the purpose, the goal of an action (cf. Albrecht 1988: xxv).

In the next section, I turn to the question to what extent a linguistic approach that understands itself as a historical, non-nomothetic discipline can claim to be 'scientific', in the broadest sense of the term.

3 Coseriu's 'Integral Linguistics'

Especially after his move to Germany in the early 1960s, Coseriu was perceived as a structuralist linguist focused on the study of language systems. Influential representatives of comparative linguistics mostly reacted skeptically to his work, if not dismissively. This can best be explained by the attention his publications on lexical semantics received. Their reception is to a large extent based on misunderstandings, more specifically on a confusion between a 'systems linguist' and a 'systematic linguist' (Willems 2003: 4). Coseriu always stressed that the analysis of the systematic features inherent to every 'technique of speaking' is only one aspect of the 'scientific' description of a language. Without such systematic features, speaking would not be possible at all, if only for mnemotechnical reasons. However, what he envisaged was a linguistics that takes into account everything a speaker must know in order to express himself in a particular language, viz. an 'Integral Linguistics':

> What is Integral Linguistics? It is the linguistic approach that aims to take into account the knowledge the speaker puts to work when speaking, with the purpose of organizing the facts conceived of in this way within a homogeneous and unitary framework. (Coseriu 1984: 37)

We need hardly point out that Coseriu could only outline many components of such an extensive program (cf. Willems 2003: 6). At a time when the dominant influence of a few 'schools' or 'paradigms' seem to have weakened and Paul Feyerabend's maxim "anything goes" (Feyerabend 1970) has fallen on fertile ground, the conditions for an appropriate reception of Coseriu's works may in the meantime have improved. It will be the task of the 'third generation' of Coseriu's disciples to elaborate and expand on the ideas Coseriu outlined (cf. Albrecht 2003). In what follows, I put forward a number of suggestions that are more or less closely related to the 'primacy of history'.

Coseriu's plea for an Integral Linguistics which subscribes to the 'primacy of history' can perhaps best be appreciated if we consider three characteristics of his personality as a researcher, two of them *ex negativo*, one of them positively.

Coseriu was 'anti-naturalist' and 'anti-pragmatist', and he was a philologist in the traditional sense of the term, although he drew on the technically advanced methods of modern linguistics. He rejected any attempt to grant language some kind of natural autonomy. This anti-naturalist aspect of his approach has already been discussed in the previous sections. Coseriu's anti-pragmatism regarding his conception of the nature of language is no less important. Coseriu does not consider language primarily as a system of communication. Of course, language can also be used to communicate, i.e. to communicate something to someone (G. *jemandem etwas mitteilen*) or to confide in someone (G. *sich jemandem mitteilen*) (Coseriu 1968 [1966]: 78; Coseriu 2007 [1980]: 82). But language is first of all the source of what can be communicated: the goal of language (not to be confused with the goal of individual speech acts) is meaning. Self-expression that goes beyond mere gestural expression is manifested by meaning, and the creation of meanings is a never-ending historical process (cf. Boc 2007: 272). In this regard, Coseriu pursues a famous and often-quoted remark by Wilhelm von Humboldt in a more precise and complete way than many other scholars:

> *Language*, regarded in its real nature, is an enduring thing, and at every moment a *transitory* one. [...]. In itself it is no product (*Ergon*), but an activity (*Energeia*). Its true definition can therefore only be a genetic one. For it is the ever-repeated *mental labour* of making the *articulated* sound capable of expressing *thought*. (Humboldt 1988 [1836]: 49; German original: Humboldt 1963 [1836]: 418; emphasis in the original)

Coseriu's commitment to the 'primacy of history' appears in connection with the two *ex negativo* characterizations, anti-naturalism and anti-pragmatism, but only in an abstract manner. It manifests itself much more tangibly if one sees in Coseriu a philologist for whom a language is an integral part of a historical community. For him, linguists have to approach a language understood in this way with the questions posed by ancient rhetoric and classical philology. The questions remain largely unaltered, but the methods and techniques with which they have to be investigated have been adapted in the course of time.

Coseriu, one of the pioneers of linguistic structuralism in Italy and Germany, a philologist? The strongest arguments in support of this claim can be found in his career. He repeatedly affirmed that he learned many languages primarily in order to be able to read poems in the original languages. His first philological doctoral thesis was on the influence of Old French epic poetry on the popular epics of Yugoslavia. This was followed by a philosophical dissertation on the development of ideas on aesthetics in Romania (Albrecht 2018: 13–14). In addition, it suffices to leaf through an index of Coseriu's writings to realize how great his interest in historical-philological questions was. The volume *Lateinisch-Romanisch* (Coseriu 2008) edited by Hansbert Bertsch some years after Coseriu's death deserves special mention in this context. It contains many lectures and essays on so-called Vulgar Latin, the influence of Greek on Vulgar Latin, and the emergence of the Romance languages – many of them previously unpublished.

It is no exaggeration to say that the originality of Coseriu's contribution to linguistics lies precisely in his ability to reconcile the technicity of modern linguistics with a philological and historical perspective on language. He emphasized something that all speakers are intuitively aware of, namely that a 'historical language' – such as Spanish, English or German – is a highly variable entity, not one system but rather a conglomerate of similar systems (a 'diasystem'). Only within a homogeneous speech technique (Coseriu's term is 'functional language') are there structures that can be described with structuralist methods. A 'functional language' might seem something quite alien to reality; no speaker will speak it over any length of time because every speaker has mastered different 'functional languages' between which he is accustomed to switch back and forth. For instance, when a speaker from Southern Germany uses standard German, he distinguishes between *Fuß* ('foot') and *Bein* ('leg'). However, in his regional variety, *Fuß* is sufficient for both functions, without further distinction. In every moment of speaking, the structures of a functional language are something concrete because they guide the speaker in choosing the appropriate means of expression. But these structures are not rigid, they are in constant motion. For the observer who thinks in the categories of the system, any change will therefore be a 'mistake'. But from the point of view of Integral Linguistics, this instability is part of the very essence of language. All this has been dealt with in greater detail elsewhere. I shall now proceed to briefly discussing some of the areas that for Coseriu belong to the tasks of Integral Linguistics (cf. Albrecht 2003: 41–50).

3.1 Coseriu's first desideratum regarding Integral Linguistics is a history of discourses and expressive knowledge. In this context, we need to recall Coseriu's well-known distinction of three levels of language to which three levels of linguistic knowledge correspond (Coseriu 1985; 2007 [1988]: Ch. 2). Speaking in general requires what he calls "elocutional knowledge". Speaking a particular language corresponds to "idiomatic knowledge", while expressing oneself in utterances with which certain purposes are pursued (speech acts, discourses) calls for "expressive knowledge" (cf. the schematic overview in Albrecht 2018: 24). A history of expressive knowledge, i.e. a historical linguistics of texts and discourses, is an enormous task that can only be achieved in parts.

3.2 In various publications, Coseriu points out the importance of a linguistics of "speaking in general", a history of speech in terms of the objects people talk about. A "skeuology" of this kind (from the Greek σκεῦος, respectively plural σκεύη 'utensils, implement, equipment') revolves around elocutional knowledge, which is not bound to any particular language. For instance, in all languages speakers avoid redundancy. One does not usually say *a river with water*, since water belongs to the definition of a river, but one does say *a river with clear, turbid water* etc. (cf., among other articles, Coseriu 1976c).

3.3 In his dialogue *De magistro*, Augustine draws the attention of his son and pupil Adeodatus to the fact that meaning and designation coincide in particular words: *nomen, verbum* or *signum* mean what they are (Coseriu 2015, I: 130–136). According to Coseriu, Integral Linguistics should also include a grammar of metalanguage, i.e. a grammar for speaking about language. Special attention should be paid to those linguistic elements that do not refer to extra-linguistic reality but to language itself, e.g. words such as *word, sentence, text*.

3.4 Another task for Integral Linguistics is to develop a history of repeated discourse (Fr. *discours répété*). Coseriu distinguishes between the free technique of speaking, i.e. the production of spontaneous utterances according to the rules of a particular language, and the recourse to "repeated discourse", i.e. the use of what has already been said. This distinction has no exact equivalent in other linguistic schools or paradigms. Repeated speech includes, for example, quotations, allusions to generally known texts (i.e. what is generally understood by 'intertextuality'), proverbs, fixed idioms, in short, a large part of what is generally regarded as phraseology (Coseriu 1966: 194 ff.; cf. 1967 [1966]). Coseriu's student Harald Thun (1978) took a first step in this direction. But further investigations of this kind on as many languages as possible are called for.

3.5 With his proposal to establish a general historical stylistics, Coseriu invites us to return to the tradition of ancient rhetoric and the work of, e.g., Leo Spitzer and raise it to the technical level of modern linguistics (Coseriu 1988 [1957]; cf. Aschenberg 1984). The aim is to investigate the socio-stylistic linguistic means and patterns of text production which have been considered appropriate in particular contexts and circumstances from antiquity to the present day.

3.6 Coseriu does not refer to the statistical nor to the prescriptive norm in the usual sense but to his own definition of 'norm' (cf. Kabatek 2020) when he writes:

> Finally, there is the need to study every language at the level of the 'norm' and in terms of the frequency of use of items in the lexicon. (Coseriu 1984: 53)

Coseriu's concept of 'norm' (or 'normal language use') correlates with the concept of the language system. The norm is a subset of the system in that it contains only those possibilities provided by the system that are actually common in language use; e.g., *wheelchair-accessible* is common, *wheelbarrow-accessible* would be possible but is uncommon. On the other hand, the system is a subset of the norm because there are many linguistic elements that are common but not necessary for the functioning of the system. The initial plosives in words like Eng. *pan, tan, can* are usually pronounced with aspiration. If the aspiration is missing, this might be perceived as an 'accent' but it does not violate the rules of the English phonological system. Coseriu's reference to different frequencies in the use of lexical items is particularly important in this context. For example, German *plaudern* is a virtual equivalent (listed as such in the dictionary) of French *causer*. However, the French verb is used much more frequently than its German counterpart as it can also be used in low registers simply to mean 'talk'.

3.7 Coseriu's call for extensive contrastive research to be carried out with a view to producing specific dictionaries and grammars for translators shows that he was also concerned about practical linguistic issues. This demand has in the meantime been largely met by the creators of machine translation programs, which rely on extensive aligned corpora of texts for their translations. However, contrastive investigations should now be carried out in order to determine the performance and limitations of such systems and, above all, to identify sources of mistakes. This would provide post-editors of machine-generated translations with useful correction guidelines. For texts that are very different from what is regarded 'ordinary language' (including some, though by no means all, literary texts), machine programs can only be used to a very limited extent.

3.8 Finally, mention must be made of another one of Coseriu's contributions to Integral Linguistics, viz. a manuscript of which so far only a fragment has been published: *El problema de la corrección idiomática* [The problem of language-specific correctness] (Coseriu 1988 [1957] is a fragment in German translation). The objective is to compile an inventory of expressions for evaluating discourse. For example, a speech can be delivered with a "melodious voice" or a "grating voice". Judgments of this kind refer to the purely physiological level of speech. By contrast, a text can be classified as "clear and easy to understand" or as "confused and incomprehensible". Judgments of this kind refer to the level of speaking in general ('elocutional knowledge'). A reviewer can claim that a book is written in "correct and nuanced English" or that the author uses "incorrect and impure English", which relates to the level of the particular language (i.e. 'idiomatic knowledge'). Finally, we can say of a eulogy given at a funeral service that it was "simple and appropriate" or "rhetorically brilliant but embarrassing in the context". These are judgments expressed at the level of discourses in the narrow sense (pertaining to 'expressive knowledge'). There are furthermore evaluations that apply to an utterance together with the intellectual and moral qualities of the author or speaker, e.g. an "intelligent lecture" or "superficial gibberish".

4 Conclusion and outlook

In his reflections on "human nature and human history", Collingwood noted that it has taken a long time to realize that history provides the key the human mind needs in order to have knowledge of itself:

> The really new element in the thought of to-day as compared with that of three centuries ago is the rise of history. It is true that the same Cartesian spirit which did so much for physics was already laying the foundations of critical method in history before the seventeenth century was out; but the modern conception of history as a study at once critical and constructive, whose field is the human past in its entirety, and whose method is the reconstruction of that past from documents written and unwritten, critically analysed and interpreted, was not established until the nineteenth, and is even yet not fully worked out in all its implications. (Collingwood 1993 [1946]: 290)

Collingwood suggests that there are people who, on the basis of this knowledge, concluded that the methods of historical research can help to solve all problems of knowledge, "in other words, that all reality is historical" (ibid.). He considers this to be an error, even though this view may contain "at least one important element of truth" (ibid.). There is a difference between the phenomena investigated by the natural sciences and the nature of the human world:

> The thesis which I shall maintain is that the science of human nature was a false attempt – falsified by the analogy of natural science – to understand the mind itself, and that, whereas the right way of investigating nature is by the methods called scientific, the right way of investigating mind is by the methods of history (ibid.).

There are many parallels between this quote and Coseriu, in particular regarding Coseriu's emphasis on the specificity and legitimacy of the historical sciences at a time when the natural sciences celebrated their greatest triumphs. According to Coseriu, a number of universal dimensions account for the essence of language: formativity (creativity), semanticity, alterity (intersubjectivity), historicity and materiality (cf. Aschenberg 1999: 124; Kabatek and Murguía 1997: 249). Historicity, like materiality, is a consequence of alterity: as speaking (even in the form of a soliloquy) is always addressed to another human being, it is dependent on a material medium, and the creativity inherent in every speech must necessarily be limited by an intersubjectively binding technique that has been handed down in the course of history. It is this technique that linguists investigate by means of appropriate methods. But the structures revealed in the process do not represent the essence of language as a whole, as Jean-Paul Sartre once aptly observed when structuralism was at its height:

> [...] I do not dispute the existence of structures, nor the need to analyse their mechanism. But for me, structure is only an element of the practical-inert. It is the result of a praxis that exceeds its agents. Every human creation has its proper passive dimension: this does not imply that it is entirely subjugated. (Sartre 1966: 70)

Coseriu would hardly have approved of being cited alongside Sartre, whose work did not greatly impress him. But his own opinion comes quite close to Sartre's observation when he remarks:

> Man is only creative to the extent that he stands, as a historical being, in a tradition while at the same time going beyond that tradition. [...] But the share of tradition and creation is different in different human activities and in different human beings. (Coseriu 1979 [1978]: 120)

Thus, despite the creativity inherent in the activity of speaking, the study of language is subject to the primacy of history.

References

Albrecht, Jörn. 1988. "τὰ ὄντα ὡς ἔστιν λέγειν: Über die Schwierigkeit, die Dinge zu sagen, wie sie sind, und andere davon zu überzeugen". In: Jörn Albrecht (ed.), *Energeia und Ergon. Sprachliche Variation – Sprachgeschichte – Sprachtypologie.* Vol. I: *Schriften von Eugenio Coseriu (1965–1987)*, xvii-xlv. Tübingen: Narr.
Albrecht, Jörn. 2003. "El paradigma incompleto de E. Coseriu: Tarea pendiente para la tercera generación". *Odisea* 3, 41–54.
Albrecht, Jörn. 2018. "L'héritage de Coseriu". *Cahiers de lexicologie* 112, 13–31.
Antilla, Raimo. 1993. "Change and metatheory at the beginning of the 1900s: the primacy of history". In: Charles Jones (ed.), *Historical linguistics. Problems and perspectives*, 43–73. London and New York: Longman.
Aschenberg, Heidi. 1984. *Idealistische Philologie und Textanalyse. Zur Stilistik Leo Spitzers.* Tübingen: Narr.
Aschenberg, Heidi. 1999. *Kontexte in Texten. Umfeldtheorie und literarischer Situationsaufbau.* Tübingen: Niemeyer.
Boc, Oana. 2007. *Textualitatea literară și lingvistica integrală.* Cluj-Napoca: Clusium.
Brøndal, Viggo. 1939. "Linguistique structurale". *Acta Linguistica* 1, 2–10.
Collingwood, Robin George. 1993 [1946]. *The idea of history.* Oxford: Oxford University Press.
Coseriu, Eugenio. 1966. "Structure lexicale et enseignement du vocabulaire". In: *Actes du Premier Colloque International de Linguistique Appliquée*, 175–217. Nancy: Annales de l'Est.
Coseriu, Eugenio. 1967 [1966]. "Lexical structure and the teaching of vocabulary". In: *Linguistic theories and their applications.* Strasbourg: The Council of Europe (English translation of Coseriu 1966).

Coseriu, Eugenio. 1968 [1966]. "Der Mensch und seine Sprache". In: Herbert Haag and Franz Peter Möhres (eds.), *Ursprung und Wesen des Menschen*, 67–79. Tübingen: Mohr Siebeck.

Coseriu, Eugenio. 1976c. "Logique du langage et logique de la grammaire". In: Jean David and Robert Martin (eds.), *Modèles logiques et niveaux d'analyse linguistique*, 15–33. Paris: Klincksieck.

Coseriu, Eugenio. 1978 [1958]. *Sincronía, diacronía e historia. El problema del cambio lingüístico* (third edition). Madrid: Gredos.

Coseriu, Eugenio. 1979 [1978]. "Humanwissenschaften und Geschichte. Der Gesichtspunkt eines Linguisten". *Det Norske Videnskaps-Akademi, Årbok 1978* (Oslo), 118–130.

Coseriu, Eugenio. 1980. "Vom Primat der Geschichte". *Sprachwissenschaft* 5, 125–145.

Coseriu, Eugenio. 1983. "Linguistic change does not exist". *Linguistica nuova ed antica. Rivista di linguistica classica medioevale e moderna* 1, 51–63.

Coseriu, Eugenio. 1984. "Fundamentos y tareas de la lingüística integral". In: *Segundo Congreso de Nacional de Lingüística (16 al 19 de Setiembre de 1981)*. Tomo III, Actas I, 37–53. San Juan: R. Argentina.

Coseriu, Eugenio. 1985. "Linguistic competence: what is it really?" *The Modern Language Review* 80:4, xxv-xxxv.

Coseriu, Eugenio. 1988 [1957]. "Die Ebenen des sprachlichen Wissens. Der Ort des 'Korrekten' in der Bewertungsskala des Gesprochenen". Chapter 2 of Coseriu (ms. 1957). German translation by Susanne Höfer. In: Jörn Albrecht, Jens Lüdtke and Harald Thun (eds.), *Energeia und Ergon. Sprachliche Variation – Sprachgeschichte – Sprachtypologie. Studia in honorem Eugenio Coseriu*, Vol. I: *Schriften von Eugenio Coseriu (1965–1987)*, 327–364. Tübingen: Narr.

Coseriu, Eugenio. 1988 [1979]. "Humboldt und die moderne Sprachwissenschaft". In: Jörn Albrecht (ed.), *Energeia und Ergon. Sprachliche Variation – Sprachgeschichte – Sprachtypologie*, Vol. I: *Schriften von Eugenio Coseriu (1965–1987)*, 3–11. Tübingen: Narr.

Coseriu, Eugenio. 1995a. "My Saussure". In: Tullio De Mauro and Shigeaki Sugeta (eds.), *Saussure and linguistics today*, 187–191. Rome: Bulzoni.

Coseriu, Eugenio. 2000 [1992]. "The principles of linguistics as a cultural science". *Transylvanian Review* 9:1, 108–115.

Coseriu, Eugenio. 2007 [1980]. *Textlinguistik. Eine Einführung*. Edited by Jörn Albrecht (fourth edition). Tübingen: Narr.

Coseriu, Eugenio. 2007 [1988]. *Sprachkompetenz. Grundzüge der Theorie des Sprechens*. Edited by Heinrich Weber (second edition). Tübingen: Narr.

Coseriu, Eugenio. 2008. *Lateinisch-Romanisch. Vorlesungen und Abhandlungen zum sogenannten Vulgärlatein und zu den romanischen Sprachen*. Edited by Hansbert Bertsch. Tübingen: Narr.

Coseriu, Eugenio. 2015. *Geschichte der Sprachphilosophie*. Vol. 1: *Von Heraklit bis Rousseau*. Vol. 2: *Von Herder bis Humboldt*. Edited by Jörn Albrecht. Tübingen: Narr & Francke: Attempto.

Feyerabend, Paul. 1970. *Against method*. Minnesota: M. Radner and S. Vinocur.

Guitarte, Guillermo L. 1988. "Dialecto, español de America e historia en Coseriu". In: Harald Thun (ed.), *Energeia und Ergon. Sprachliche Variation – Sprachgeschichte –*

Sprachtypologie. Vol. II: *Das sprachtheoretische Denken Eugenio Coserius in der Diskussion (1)*, 487–500. Tübingen: Narr.
Humboldt, Wilhelm von. 1963 [1829]. *Über die Verschiedenheiten des menschlichen Sprachbaues* (1829). In: Andreas Flitner and Klaus Giel (eds.), *Wilhelm von Humboldt. Schriften zur Sprachphilosophie*. Vol. 3, 144–367. Darmstadt: Wissenschaftliche Buchgesellschaft.
Humboldt, Wilhelm von. 1963 [1836]. *Über die Verschiedenheit des menschlichen Sprachbaues und ihren Einfluss auf die geistige Entwicklung des Menschengeschlechts* (1830–1835). In: Andreas Flitner and Klaus Giel (eds.), *Wilhelm von Humboldt. Schriften zur Sprachphilosophie*. Vol. 3, 368–756. Darmstadt: Wissenschaftliche Buchgesellschaft.
Humboldt, Wilhelm von. 1988 [1836]. *On language. On the diversity of human language construction and its influence on the mental development of the human species*. Edited by M. Losonsky, translated by P. Heath. Cambridge: Cambridge University Press.
Joseph, John. 2018. "'This eternal wanderer': A non-dogmatic reading of Saussure". In: John Joseph and Ekaterina Velmezova (éds.). *Le 'Cours de linguistique générale': réception, diffusion, tradition*, 197–208. (= Cahiers de l'ILSL 57) Lausanne: Université de Lausanne.
Kabatek, Johannes. 2020. "Linguistic norm in the linguistic theory of Eugenio Coseriu". In: Franz Lebsanft and Felix Tacke (eds.), *Manual of standardization in the Romance languages*, 127–144. Berlin & Boston: De Gruyter.
Kabatek, Johannes and Adolfo Murguía. 1997. *"Die Sachen sagen, wie sie sind…". Eugenio Coseriu im Gespräch*. Tübingen: Narr.
Leibniz, Gottfried Wilhelm. 1965 [1684]. "Meditationes de cognitione, veritate, et ideis". In: Carl Immanuel Gerhard (ed.), *Die philosophischen Schriften von Gottfried Wilhelm Leibniz*. Vol. 4, 422–426. Hildesheim: Olms.
Milner, Jean-Claude. 2002. *Le périple structural. Figures et paradigmes*. Paris: Éditions du Seuil.
Munteanu, Cristinel. 2013a. "Influența lui R. G. Collingwood asupra lui Eugenio Coseriu". In: Ana Catană-Spenchiu and Ioana Repciuc (eds.), *Flores philologiae. Omagiu profesorului Eugen Munteanu la împlinirea vârstei de 60 de ani*, 442–460. Iași: Editura Universității.
Munteanu, Cristinel. 2013b. "On the real object of linguistics". *Energeia–Online-Zeitschrift für Sprachwissenschaft und Sprachphilosophie* 3, 43–56.
Paul, Hermann. 1888 [1886]. *Principles of the history of language*. Translated from the second edition of the original [1886] by Herbert A. Strong. London: Swan, Sonnenschein, Lowrey & Co.
Paul, Hermann. 1920 [1880]. *Prinzipien der Sprachgeschichte* (fifth edition). Tübingen: Niemeyer. [First edition: *Principien der Sprachgeschichte*.]
Sartre, Jean-Paul. 1966. "'Jean-Paul Sartre répond'. Interview avec Bernard Pingaud". *L'Arc* 30, 87–96.
Saussure, Ferdinand de. 1975 [1916]. *Cours de linguistique générale*. Edited by T. De Mauro. Paris: Payot.
Schleicher, August. 1977 [1863]. "Die Darwinsche Theorie und die Sprachwissenschaft". In: Hans Helmut Christmann (ed.), *Sprachwissenschaft des 19. Jahrhunderts*, 85–105. Darmstadt: Wissenschaftliche Buchgesellschaft.
Terracini, Benvenuto. 1957. *Conflitti di lingue e di cultura*. Venice: Neri Pozza.

Thun, Harald. 1978. *Probleme der Phraseologie. Untersuchungen zur wiederholten Rede mit Beispielen aus dem Französischen, Italienischen, Spanischen und Rumänischen.* Tübingen: Niemeyer.

Vico, Giambattista. 1971 [1744]. *Princìpi di scienza nuova d'intorno alla comune natura delle nazioni, in questa terza impressione dal medesimo autore in un gran numero di luoghi corretta, schiarita, e notabilmente accresciuta.* In: Paolo Cristofolini (ed.), Giambattista Vico: *Opere Filosofiche*, 377–702. Firenze: Sansoni.

Willems, Klaas. 2003. "Eugenio Coseriu (1921–2002). Versuch einer Würdigung". *Leuvense Bijdragen* 92, 1–25.

Pierre Swiggers (Leuven)
At the roots of linguistic change: the historicity of language

> *If one takes 'language' in the functional acceptation, first as function and then as system – and it is precisely in that way one has to understand it, since language does not function because it is a system, but, quite on the contrary, it is a system in order to fulfill a function, in order to correspond to a purposiveness (Sp. finalidad) –, then it becomes evident that the problem has to be put in opposite terms. Far from functioning only 'while not changing', as it happens in 'codes', language changes in order to keep functioning as such. [...] Language manifests itself only in the speech of individuals, and speaking is always speaking a language. The whole being of language necessarily revolves within this circle.**

1 Introduction

The passage quoted above captures the essence of one of Eugenio Coseriu's major works, viz. *Sincronía, diacronía e historia. El problema del cambio lingüístico* (Coseriu 1978 [1958]; henceforth: *SDH*).[1] More importantly, it expresses the principle that underlies his unitary view of language, hence his conception of what 'general linguistics' should be about, a view he forged during his years

---

* "Si se entiende la lengua funcionalmente, primero como función y luego como sistema – y es así como hay que entenderla, pues la lengua no funciona porque es sistema, sino, al contrario, es sistema para cumplir una función, para corresponder a una finalidad –, entonces resulta evidente que los términos del problema deben invertirse. Lejos de funcionar sólo "en ne changeant pas", como sucede con los "códigos", la lengua cambia para seguir funcionando como tal. [...] La lengua no se da más que en el hablar de los individuos, y el hablar es siempre hablar una lengua. Todo el ser del lenguaje gira necesariamente en este círculo" (Coseriu 1978 [1958]: 30–31).
1 Although in my current research Coseriu's publications in linguistic historiography are more frequently put to use than his early writings on language history, language/speech/norm, etc., I have chosen *SDH* as the subject of the present study, for three reasons. As a student in Romance philology, I became acquainted with the contents of *SDH* through the classes (in historical-comparative Romance) of Joe Larochette. Later I had the opportunity to discuss some of its topics with the late Hans Helmut Christmann and Brigitte Schlieben-Lange. Finally, at the 22nd Congrès international de Philologie et de Linguistique romanes (Brussels, 1998), I had the privilege of exchanging ideas with Coseriu on the insights of Michel Bréal concerning language change (cf. Coseriu 1978 [1958]: 42, 110, 196).

in Montevideo, and which he defended, often in reaction to emergent (at times, ephemeral) currents in linguistic theory, throughout his later career. Coseriu's unitary view of language justifies his conception of *Sprachwissenschaft* as a single discipline in essence. This view of language consists in recognising the full historical spectrum of languages as 'embodied' techniques. In this respect, Coseriu's conception comes close to that of André Martinet (e.g., 1954, 1960).

As concisely stated in the passage quoted, Coseriu saw language as the dynamic architectural system offering the potential for speech activities (carried out by speakers in a wide variety of situations), developing over time and subsuming the speech traditions (i.e. inherited linguistic 'property'; Coseriu [1978 [1958]: 32] speaks of *acervo lingüístico* and refers to Porzig's [1950: 106–107] German term *Sprachbesitz*), and constantly adapting itself to the requirements of expressive and communicative functions. In this characterisation, I have incorporated some key notions that Coseriu integrated in his later work, such as 'architecture of language' (subsuming the variational axes: diastratic, diatopic and diaphasic), and 'traditions of speaking' (G. *Traditionen des Sprechens*; cf. Schlieben-Lange 1983). However, these later terminological additions did not imply a revision of the language view articulated from the early 1950s on; they fitted harmoniously in the mould of a comprehensive theory already in place.

The present contribution analyses Coseriu's language view as it is expounded in relation to the problem of linguistic change (cf. the subtitle of *SDH*). I will not deal with the reception of this work,[2] at times mistakenly viewed as being an analysis of specific language changes, or a proposal for a typology of changes. It should be noted that although *SDH* is a study of the 'problem of linguistic change', only a handful of examples of linguistic change are actually discussed: evolution of *-al* before consonant in Spanish (Coseriu 1978 [1958]: 102–103), the consequences of the weakening or loss of final *-s* in varieties of Spanish (Coseriu 1978 [1958]: 127), palatalisation of velars in Latin (Coseriu 1978 [1958]: 149–150), the evolution of the sibilants in Spanish (Coseriu 1978 [1958]: 153–155 and 204), palatalisation of intervocalic *-ll-* in varieties of Spanish, and – most prominently – the integration of a periphrastic future in the verb system of Late Latin and Early Romance (Coseriu 1978 [1958]: 136 and 157–175). A few examples of "synchronic" variation and analogical levelling are also discussed (e.g. Coseriu 1978 [1958]: 54, 59, 63, 95–97, 125, 146).

---

2 As for reviews (of the first edition), I have consulted: Adrados (1961), Jungemann (1960), Lope Blanch (1960), Pérez Vidal (1959), Roca (i) Pons (1959), Sandmann (1960), Togeby (1960).

Within the limits imposed, it is impossible to discuss the various topics dealt with in *SDH*, a book filled with stimulating – often provocative – ideas, relevant criticisms of competing views[3], and references to philosophical conceptions: apart from Aristotle, W. von Humboldt, G. W. F. Hegel and B. Croce, who figure prominently, Coseriu incorporates insights from a wide variety of philosophers: P. Carabellese, E. Cassirer, J. Dewey, M. Heidegger, I. Kant, A. Marty, M. Merleau-Ponty and G. B. Vico (on Coseriu's philosophical sources, see López Serena 2019). Among the topics I will not deal with here, or only in a cursory way, are Coseriu's extensive critical analysis of Saussure's views on synchrony and diachrony; the author's concept of 'system' and 'norm' as belonging to a historical language (Sp. *lengua histórica*), and his ideas about language-making-itself, language-overcoming-itself, and language-reshaping-itself (Coseriu 1978 [1958]: 108–110). Another topic that would call for a separate study is the influence of Antonino Pagliaro and Vittore Pisani on Coseriu's thinking. As is well known, Pagliaro inspired Coseriu considerably (cf. Coseriu 1994); a major point of divergence, however, as pointed out in *SDH* (Coseriu 1978 [1958]: 77), concerns Pagliaro's (1952) underplaying of the role of communication.

2 A brief presentation of *Sincronía, diacronía e historia*

SDH was written in 1955 and revised in the subsequent year and a half. It was first published in 1957, as an article in the *Revista de la Facultad de Humanidades y Ciencias* [de la Universidad de Montevideo]. In 1958 it was published separately, also in Montevideo (a reprint of this first edition was published in Tübingen in 1969). A second edition appeared in the *Biblioteca Románica Hispánica* (Madrid: Gredos) in 1973; this edition contains revisions of detail, and several new footnotes. In 1978 a third edition appeared in the same collection; it contains minor revisions of the second edition. The book has been translated into Russian (1963), German (1974), Portuguese (1979), Italian (1981), Japanese (1981), and Ru-

---

3 Central stage, of course, is given to the discussion of Saussure's language theory (see also Coseriu 1973 [1952]; for Coseriu's global appraisal of Saussure, see Coseriu 1995a). Note that in *SDH*, Coseriu makes use of the Spanish translation of the *Cours* by Amado Alonso (= Saussure 1945 [1916]). In *SDH* many (constructive) criticisms can be found of various structuralist schools: Geneva structuralism, Praguian structuralism, Copenhagen glossematics, Martinet's functionalism (*SDH* contains many incisive remarks on Martinet 1955), Bloomfieldian linguistics (and its application in Hoenigswald 1960); and also of the French "sociological" school (A. Meillet, J. Vendryes).

manian (1997); an English translation, announced in the foreword of the second edition, did not materialise (but there is a French online translation, see Section 7). For the present contribution the text of the third edition has been used (Coseriu 1978 [1958]).

The book owes its title to the last chapter, "Sincronía, diacronía e historia", essentially a discussion of the famous Saussurean dichotomy. Coseriu's examination of Saussure's dichotomy – although it does not involve a discussion of Saussure's concept of *"idiosynchronie"* (Saussure 1945 [1916]: 115, 125 = 2002: 169, 185) – is important in many respects.

(a) It points to the twofold reduction of 'language': first, its reduction to a 'language state' (Sp. *estado de lengua*), which involves the postulate of rigid systematicity (whereas Coseriu posits language as 'diasystemic', comprising a plurality of systems and norms), and, second, the reduction to a synchronic projection, which involves the corollary of immutability. According to Coseriu, Saussure fell victim (despite his claim of sticking to a 'methodological dichotomy') to turning the linguist's epistemological categories into ontological characteristics (of the language). This *aporia* can only be overcome by recognising the true nature of language, which is *historicity*; Coseriu uses the German term *Geschichte*, i.e., processual development, which he opposes to *Historie*, the historical account or history-writing (Coseriu 1978 [1958]: 89–92; see also Coseriu 1980). A parallel attempt to overcome the Saussurean dichotomy was undertaken by another Romance scholar, viz. Walther von Wartburg (1943), who insisted on the mutual imbrication (G. *Ineinandergreifen*) of description and history.

(b) It brings out Saussure's incapacity of thinking in terms of change-in-progress (Coseriu 1978 [1958]: 256); on the late recognition of the distinction between accomplished change and change-in-progress, see Swiggers (1988).

(c) It shows the Neogrammarian bias (with some traces of naturalism) in Saussure's discussion of *linguistique diachronique* (Coseriu 1978 [1958]: 261).

For the benefit of the reader less familiar with *SDH*, I recall that the book has seven chapters:

I.   La aparente aporía del cambio lingüístico. Lengua abstracta y proyección sincrónica [The apparent *aporia* of linguistic change. The 'abstract language' and synchronic projection]

II. Lengua abstracta y lengua concreta. La lengua como "saber hablar" históricamente determinado. Los tres problemas del cambio lingüístico [The 'abstract language' and the 'concrete language'. Language as historically determined 'knowing (how) to speak'. The three problems of linguistic change]

III. La racionalidad del cambio. Innovación y adopción. Las leyes fonéticas [The rationality of change. Innovation and adoption]
IV. Las condiciones generales del cambio. Determinaciones sistemáticas y extrasistemáticas. Estabilidad e inestabilidad de las tradiciones lingüísticas [The general conditions of change. Systemic and extrasystemic determinations. Stability and instability of linguistic traditions]
V. El cambio lingüístico como problema histórico. Sentido y límites de las explicaciones "generales" [Linguistic change as an historical problem. The significance and the limits of 'general' explanations]
VI. Explicaciones causales y explicaciones finalistas. El estructuralismo diacrónico frente al cambio lingüístico. Sentido de las interpretaciones "teleológicas" [Causal explanations and finalistic explanations. Diachronic structuralism facing linguistic change. Relevance of 'teleological' interpretations]
VII. Sincronía, diacronía, historia [Synchrony, diachrony, history]

Of these, chapters 2 and 6 are, in my view, indispensable reading for historical linguists.

3 Setting things straight

A highly typical feature of Coseriu's writings in general linguistics – e.g., his approach of the status of word classes, of the nature of the proper name, or his reflections on the nature of (linguistic) universals – consists in rigidly defining the frame of the discussion. In doing so, Coseriu applies the Aristotelian principle (*Topics*, I) that before starting a discussion, one does well to circumscribe and define the issue at stake, and complies with the requirements that Nelson Goodman (1978: 109–140) formulated under the heading "rightness of rendering", requirements that involve fixing the frame of reference, defining the categories used in the discussion, and observing coherence.

3.1 In his discussion of the problem of linguistic change, Coseriu starts from the observation that linguists – often structuralist linguists – seem to cherish the ideal of an immutable system, functioning in a balanced way. Moreover, some authors (e.g., Bally 1950: 18) seem to imply that a language can only function properly if it does *not* change. While it may be relevant to reflect on the nature of an ideal system, it is important to face the facts: languages change, they have changed in the past and we witness their changing during the time-span of our individual lives. Here we note Coseriu's realistic stance: it is perfectly legitimate for linguists to construe theories and to entertain speculative views, but

(i) theorisation must not ignore the facts, (ii) theorisation should avoid the leap from thought to reality (this is the well-known scholastic fallacy of *transitus ab intellectu ad rem*). Theorising about language change thus has to start from the fact that languages change, or, more precisely, that languages evolve (cf. Milică, this volume).

3.2 A second, also "realistic", observation – in fact a truism, though often overlooked by theoretical linguists – is that when we address the problem of linguistic change, we have to be conscious that we are dealing with changes in the behaviour and the habits of speakers. Coseriu refers in this respect to a statement of Nicolai Hartmann: "The life of language is not a second, general life next to, or above that of the speakers".[4]

3.3 Facing the problem of linguistic change means facing a theoretical object of enquiry, viz. that of the mutability of language, which is an essential, not an accidental feature.

> Change is not mere accident, but it belongs to the essence of language. As a matter of fact, language *is being made* (Sp. *se hace*) through what is called "linguistic change"; *linguistic change is nothing but the manifestation of creativity of language* (Sp. *lenguaje*) *in the history of particular languages* (Sp. *lenguas*). (Coseriu 1978 [1958]: 108; italics in the original).

To study a theoretical object, it is important to understand its dimensions; these are of course different according to the content-matter that is at stake: in the theory of numbers one does not have to consider the evolution of its content matter, by contrast, the theory of linguistic mutability has to include, crucially, the dimension of change or evolution. With respect to the problem of linguistic change, we can identify three levels, each of which requires an explanation (see Section 4):

I. The *universal* level: this is the problem of the mutability of all languages.
II. The *general* level: the question here is how to explain the general conditions of language change; under what circumstances can (and do) languages change?
III. The *historical* level: here we address the problem of explaining changes, or series of changes, in (a time segment of) a particular language.

---

4 "Das Leben der Sprache ist ja nicht ein zweites, allgemeines Leben neben oder über dem der Sprechenden" (Hartmann 1933: 219). Coseriu could also have referred to the theoretical position of Franz Nikolaus Finck, who defined language as the sum of *Sprechtätigkeiten* (see the introduction to Finck 1909 and 1910; cf. Swiggers and Seldeslachts (in prep.). Coseriu (1978 [1958]: 22) refers to Finck's distinction between *Sprache* and *Sprechen*.

3.4 Coseriu also makes evident the need for a further clarification. It is well known that historical linguists commonly use the term 'cause' in order to explain linguistic change. Change is then conceived as the 'effect' or 'consequence' of a cause. Under 'causes' historical linguists put a wide gamut of heterogeneous facts or situations: substratal, superstratal or adstratal influences; the asymmetry of the vocal apparatus; analogy; the loss of phonetic distinctions; the discrepancy between the linearity of the signifier (Fr. *signifiant*) and the holistic apprehension of the signified (*signifié*); borrowing; prestige, etc. Coseriu does not list, let alone discuss the various sorts of 'causes' appealed to by historical linguists, but he addresses the issue in a more fundamental way, viz. by clarifying the notion of causality. As a matter of fact, causation is a complex phenomenon,[5] as can be seen already from the common distinction between 'direct' and 'indirect' cause. The issue is even more complex, as Coseriu (1978 [1958]: 200–201) points out, drawing on Aristotle's (*Physics*, II,3 and II,7) fourfold distinction between (i) efficient cause, (ii) material cause, (iii) formal cause, and (iv) final cause. All sound changes have of course some articulatory process as their efficient cause, and all involve the vocal apparatus as their material cause, but their formal and final causes may differ in various ways.

Aristotle's distinction applies to causation of physical events, but this 'naturalist' approach is not applicable, according to Coseriu, to linguistic change, since here we deal with facts of cultural history:

> There is no contradiction in saying that linguistic change has 'causes', since, as a matter of fact, it has the four Aristotelian motivations: the new linguistic fact is effected by somebody (efficient cause), with something (material cause), involving the idea of what is made (formal cause), and it is made *for something* (final cause). When we say that linguistic change "has no causes', we only mean that it does not have causes in the naturalist sense, or that – except for the material aspect – it does not have 'objective', natural causes, that are exterior to freedom. (Coseriu 1978 [1958]: 201; italics in the original).

From this theoretical position, two corollaries follow. The first one applies to linguistic theories, and more specifically to structuralist studies: as Coseriu points out, the structuralist view – strictly focusing on the 'system' of language – cannot account for cultural motivations of change [i.e. the *why?*-question], nor for the place in time of a change [i.e. the *when?*-question], since the latter has to be linked to initiatives of the speakers of a language. The second corollary has

---

5 Causation can be multifactorial (e.g., various triggers for a single result), but I have in mind here 'causation' in its various philosophical aspects. For multifactorial causation (or 'multiple causation'), see Malkiel (1967).

a much broader scope: Coseriu posits that linguistics is not, and cannot be, a science of causal laws. Referring to Giambattista Vico, Coseriu (1978 [1958]: 237) argues that the human sciences (Sp. *ciencias del hombre*) are 'exact', achieving something that cannot be attained by the natural sciences: only in the human sciences do truth and certainty (*verum et certum*) coincide (Coseriu's views have been forcefully endorsed by Strunk 1991 in his study of the intricate history of changes in inflectional paradigms).

4 The three explanatory levels exemplified: the case of the Vulgar Latin future

One of the linguistic changes that are discussed in detail by Coseriu is the emergence of a new – 'analytic' or periphrastic – future in Vulgar Latin. Of this phenomenon, with reflexes in all the Romance languages, though not in identical ways (cf. the various auxiliaries combined with the infinitive), basically two explanations have been provided by Romance scholars:[6]

a) The first explanation refers to facts relating to the *signifiant* level; (i) the formation of the future tense in Classical Latin differed between, on the one hand, the first and second conjugation, and, on the other hand, the remaining conjugations; (ii) owing to phonetic developments in (some varieties of) spoken Latin (e. g., merger of intervocalic /-b-/ and /-v-/, and merger of /ē/ and /ĭ/), a number of verbal forms were no longer distinctive.
b) The second explanation, mainly put forward by adherents of Karl Vossler's 'idealistic school', is that the periphrastic forms were created for expressive needs, in order to render a particular 'affective' nuance, such as moral obligation or sense of responsibility.

Coseriu's approach aptly illustrates his stance as a general linguist. Interestingly – with the hindsight of half a century of linguistic research –, in dealing with the problem he uses the terms 'grammaticalisation' (Sp. *gramaticalización*) and 'to be grammaticalised' (*gramaticalizarse*), but at the same time he stresses the insufficiency of an explanation in terms of 'grammaticalisation'. As a matter of fact, if one concedes that the periphrastic forms originally did not have the meaning of a future but were 'grammaticalised', how can one explain that

---

[6] The useful 'fact-based' account by Rohlfs (1922), mentioned by Coseriu (1978 [1958]), offers the essential comparative data. Today, the standard reference work is Fleischman (1982), a comprehensive study from a linguistic, cultural and language-philosophical point of view.

they obtained a temporal value which they initially did not have? Also, how could they be 'grammaticalised' into a category of which one contends that it disappeared in Latin?

According to Coseriu, the issue of the 'new' periphrastic future forms should be addressed in a threefold way. While combining, and refining, the valuable points in the two types of traditional explanation, it is necessary to explain:
(1) the general instability of the forms for the future;
(2) the recurrent replacement of forms expressing the future by forms that originally had a modal or aspectual meaning;
(3) the replacement of the future at some point in the history of Latin.

The first two problems belong to general linguistics, and more particularly to the search for explanatory principles accounting for universal or very general (and hence potentially universal) phenomena. The answer to the first two problems lies in the recognition of the true value of the future. The future has a time reference that is (i) virtual, (ii) uncertain, (iii) mixed with modal connotations. The correct recognition of this multiple load of the forms of the future – as a universal linguistic fact – makes it easy to understand the replacement of synthetic forms by periphrastic forms: this is not a replacement by new *signifiés*, but a substitution of monolexical *signifiants* with bilexical ones, involving a shift in weight between temporal and modal values.

Still, this is only part of the explanation for the first two problems: so far, we have explained how such a substitution takes place. If we ask the 'ultimate' question: "why does the future involve a twofold dimension, viz. a temporal and a modal one?", then we have to turn to the speaker's experience of time and existence. Here, Coseriu refers to two philosophers, viz. Pantaleo Carabellese (1940) and Martin Heidegger (1927), who recognised the 'duplicity' of the future: the future is 'co-present' in the subject's conscience, but it is also a projection, tied up with our will or intention. The latter dimension is what Coseriu (1978 [1958]: 172) calls the 'exteriority' (Sp. *exterioridad*) of the future.

What remains to be explained is the third problem, viz. the historical replacement in the history of Latin of the synthetic forms of the future by periphrastic forms. This 'historical' problem – which in the terminology of Weinreich, Herzog and Labov (1968: 186–187) would be called the 'actuation problem' – is of course not one that calls for a universal explanation: as it relates to historical data, it has to be explained by a particular 'condition' (Coseriu eschews the term 'cause' in dealing with the explanation of specific changes).

At this point, Coseriu brings in what at first sight may seem a farfetched (cf. Togeby 1960: 161–162), or at least vague, explanation, in that he points to Chris-

tianity as the 'historically determining circumstance' (Sp. *circumstancia históricamente determinante*). However, the arguments he advances are compelling:
a) the substitution took place in the wake of the expansion of Christian religion; some authors – e.g., Bertoldi (1946: 259–261) and Muller (1945: 188–191) – have identified it as a typical phenomenon of early Christianity;
b) the periphrastic future forms express modal connotations that were pervasive in the Christian world view, and its conception of human existence; this is evident from the fact that the periphrastic forms are frequently used – in *written* Latin – by Christian authors;
c) in the writings of Augustine, we find an explicit testimony regarding the duplicity of the future, viz. as 'co-present experience' and as 'projective expectation':

> Tempora sunt tria, praeteritum, praesens et futurum, sed fortasse proprie diceretur: tempora sunt tria: praesens de praeteritis, praesens de praesentibus, praesens de futuris. Sunt enim haec in anima tria quaedam et alibi ea non video, praesens de praeteritis memoria, praesens de praesentibus contuitus, praesens de futuris expectatio (*Confessiones* XI, 20). [There are three tenses, preterite, present, and future. But perhaps it might be properly said: there are three tenses, the present of things past, the present of things present, and the present of things future. These three indeed somehow exist in the soul and otherwise I do not see them: the present of things past, i.e. memory; the present of things present, i.e. sight; the present of things future, i.e. expectation.]

As a result, Coseriu is able to account for the substitution in Vulgar Latin of synthetic future forms with periphrastic forms in terms of a particular, historically bound, 'expressive' solution to a universal problem of 'expressibility'.

5 Questions and answers

In Sections 3 and 4 the gist of chapters II, III, IV and V of *SDH* has been taken into account: the notion of causality, and the three explanatory levels (the rational problem of linguistic change as a universal phenomenon; the rational and descriptive problem of the conditions for language changes; the descriptive-historical problem of determining the specific conditions of particular changes). Sections 3 and 4 have thus dealt with Coseriu's answer to the question "What does a theory of language change have to account for?". Chapters VI and VII of *SDH* have been briefly dealt with in Section 2.

In this section, I take a brief look at Coseriu's answers to two overarching questions in the study of language history, viz.: "What does the process of language change consist in?", and "What is (being) changed?".

To answer the first question, Coseriu uses the concepts 'innovation' and 'adoption': change is the diffusion or generalisation of an innovation, or, more precisely, of a series of successive adoptions (Sp. *una serie de adopciones sucesivas*; Coseriu 1978 [1958]: 80; in Coseriu 1980, the processes of 'diffusion' and 'selection' receive a more autonomous status). We can speak of change only at the stage of adoption. Coseriu's discussion of the two phases can be represented as in the following schema:

innovation	intrasystemic	± conscious	individual	speech (*habla*)	use (*uso*)
adoption	diasystemic	conscious	social	language (*lengua*)	knowledge (*saber*)

Contrary to many linguists, Coseriu considers innovation not (simply) as an unconscious process; it may involve borrowing or a selection between isofunctional variants (Coseriu 1978 [1958]: 79). I have not included in the schema the dimensional features 'expressive' and 'communicative'. Coseriu posits innovation as motivated by expressive and communicative conditions, but considers adoption to be an answer to an expressive need (Coseriu 1978 [1958]: 87). In my view, adoption should also be linked to communicative needs (this would also be more coherent with Coseriu's view of language as 'dialogical' and 'intersubjective').

Innovation and adoption are phases of change, seen from the speakers' (and hearers') point of view. From the point of view of the language forms, change is the course of a generalisation process, and this generalisation has two 'faces' (cf. Kuryłowicz 1945):
a. an 'intensional' face: the spread of the generalisation through the overall structure of the language;
b. an 'extensional' face: the spread of the generalisation through the speech habits of the members of the linguistic community.

While (a) is an object of study for historical(-comparative) grammar, (b) is a matter of (historical) sociolinguistics – I am aware of using the term anachronistically with regard to *SDH*, which was published in 1958. As to intensional generalisation, it should be noted that Coseriu (1978 [1958]: 93–94) defends an 'abruptness' view of language change, a view that later sociolinguistic work has forced us to rectify (cf. Labov 1981; Wang 1969, 1978).

> If the innovation adopted affects a phoneme, it is adopted (as a possibility) for the same phoneme in whatever word and in whatever position; and if it affects a phoneme in a cluster or in particular position, it is adopted for all the words that contain the same phoneme in the same cluster or in the same position. (Coseriu 1978 [1958]: 94)

As to the second question – "What is (being) changed?" –, Coseriu answers that language, understood as historical language, *is not changed:* rather, it changes all the time, or, better, it is in a constant process of creation. In this process the rules or procedures of the language system and technique are put to application. This term, 'application', refers to the use made by (generations of) speakers of the principles and procedures underlying the system, and yielding new norms and new relationships within the system. In using the possibilities of the language system and language type, speakers realise an 'interpretation', which in some cases can involve a 'reinterpretation', with a reorganisation of structural relationships (cf. Coseriu 1983: 63; for a related view, see Itkonen 1984, who however stresses the 'subconscious rationality' of speakers).

It is in the light of this that we have to understand Coseriu (1983) with its provocative title: "Linguistic change does not exist". What Coseriu means, is that 'linguistic change', understood as 'change *of* a language (as a reified entity)' does not exist, because there is only change *within* the language, which itself is a historical-cultural sum of traditions.

> So, linguistic change is the historical process by which language disappears or arises, by which linguistic traditions die out or come into being, and by which often new traditions partially or wholly take the "place" of those dying out in the system of traditions which we call a language. Certainly, what becomes different through change is the specific language itself as a historical product, as a set of traditions; and in this sense we can speak of "linguistic change", i.e. of change in a language or in languages. But properly speaking this does not mean that language as an objective product (*ergon*) changes: it means that a language is produced. In the right perspective, languages are not continually changing: they are continually being produced, being done. (Coseriu 1983: 55; it seems to me that the end of the quotation would be more appropriate if it said: "[are] being made" [G. *werden gemacht*], in line with Coseriu's [1978 [1958]: 65, 109; 275] notion of "la lengua se hace/se rehace".)

6 Final thoughts

SDH ranks among the major contributions to the theory of linguistic change. Nonetheless, the book has not received due recognition from historical linguists[7]

---

[7] Coseriu's ideas as expressed in *SDH* are not dealt with in the manuals of Arlotto (1972), Bynon (1977), Jeffers and Lehiste (1979), nor in the contributions to Joseph and Janda, eds. (2003). The book is in the bibliography of Anttila (1989) but it is not mentioned in the systematic reference lists at the end of the separate chapters (in Section 23.3. "The primacy of history", Anttila summarises the ideas put forward in Coseriu 1980, which is a reformulation of the fundamental claim made in Coseriu [1978] 1958). Joseph and Janda in their introduction (eds. 2003: 43–44)

and theoretical linguists. Apart from being accessible for a long time only in its original Spanish version and in a Russian translation – as yet there is no English translation (a French online translation, prepared by Thomas Verjans in 2007, can be consulted on: http://www.revue-texto.net/Parutions/Livres-E/Coseriu_SDH/Sommaire.html) –, a number of other reasons explain the book's fate. On the one hand, theoretical linguists have until recently bypassed publications that deal with language history and with issues of historical-comparative linguistics. On the other hand, historical linguists interested in theory have focused either on the explanation of a number of paradigmatic cases of linguistic change or on possible models for their professional practice. An additional reason is the fact that work on Romance languages was not particularly favoured by theoretical linguists; vice versa, Romance scholars have shied away from theoretical linguistics (see Malkiel 1964).

In retrospect, *SDH*, published at a time when sociolinguistics started to receive professional recognition and (generative-)transformational grammar entered the stage, can be read as a critical examination of pre-structuralist and structuralist linguistics. But it was and still is much more than that: it was the first comprehensive theoretical discussion of linguistic change (far superior to Paul 1920 [1880]), involving a refined notion of 'phonetic law' (Coseriu 1978 [1958]: 101–106) and a clear differentiation of innovation and adoption. In addition, *SDH* admonished historical linguists to reflect upon what should be considered an 'explanation'.

The book also has weaker points. For instance, it misses explanatory principles such as 'linguistic traffic' (Gauchat's *Sprachverkehr*), 'diffusion of forms through specific social groups', and one also regrets that phenomena such as lexically bound generalisation of alterations (metaphorically: 'lexical contagion') are not considered. With the rediscovery of the work of Louis Gauchat (cf. Swiggers 2019) and Jules Gilliéron (cf. Swiggers 1999; Lauwers, Simoni-Aurembou and Swiggers, eds. 2002) the importance of these phenomena has been recognised. Sociolinguistic work – adumbrated in Gauchat's and Gilliéron's writings – has also shown the relevance of 'generational convergence patterns', across dialect boundaries; and, more importantly, sociolinguistics has established the undeniable fact of gradual changes.[8] In *SDH*, Coseriu instead adheres to the 'abrupt-

---

briefly discuss the contents of Coseriu (1983), referring to its presentation at the Los Angeles conference on 'Causality and linguistic change' (May 1982).

8 See already the critical remarks in Jungemann (1960: 95). For a discussion of, and further references on the contrasting views ('abrupt' vs. 'gradual') of linguistic change, see Swiggers (2013).

ness' view of linguistic change, and the 'social motivation' of linguistic changes is insufficiently elaborated.

All in all – again in retrospect – *SDH* remains a strikingly "modern" book: it discusses, in a critical manner, 'grammaticalisation', insists on the role of intersubjective relations and the 'dialogical' nature of language (Coseriu 1978 [1958]: 77–79). And it urges scholars in the humanities to value, not to depreciate, their research questions, methodology, principles, and not in the least their object: *language*.

References

Adrados [Rodríguez Adrados], Francisco. 1961. Review of E. Coseriu. 1958. *Sincronía, diacronía e historia. El problema del cambio lingüístico* (Montevideo). *Emerita* 29, 152–153.
Anttila, Raimo. 1989. *Historical and comparative linguistics* (first edition 1972). Amsterdam & Philadelphia: John Benjamins.
Arlotto, Anthony. 1972. *Introduction to historical linguistics.* Boston: Houghton Mifflin.
Bally, Charles. 1950. *Linguistique générale et linguistique française.* Bern: Francke.
Bertoldi, Vittorio. 1946. *La parola quale mezzo d'espressione.* Napoli: Pironti.
Bynon, Theodora. 1977. *Historical linguistics.* Cambridge: Cambridge University Press.
Carabellese, Pantaleo. 1940. *Critica del concreto.* Roma: Signorelli.
Coseriu, Eugenio. 1958. *Sincronía, diacronía e historia. El problema del cambio lingüístico.* Montevideo: Universidad de la República, Facultad de Humanidades y Ciencias.
Coseriu, Eugenio. 1973 [1952]. "Sistema, norma y habla". In: Eugenio Coseriu, *Teoría del lenguaje y lingüística general. Cinco estudios*, 11–113. Madrid: Gredos.
Coseriu, Eugenio. 1978 [1958]. *Sincronía, diacronía e historia. El problema del cambio lingüístico* (third edition). Madrid: Gredos.
Coseriu, Eugenio. 1980. "Vom Primat der Geschichte". *Sprachwissenschaft* 5, 125–145.
Coseriu, Eugenio. 1983. "Linguistic change does not exist". *Linguistica nuova ed antica. Rivista di linguistica classica medioevale e moderna* 1, 51–63.
Coseriu, Eugenio. 1994. "My Pagliaro". In: Tullio De Mauro and Lia Formigari (eds.), *Italian studies in linguistic historiography*, 39–44. Münster: Nodus.
Coseriu, Eugenio. 1995a. "My Saussure". In: Tullio De Mauro and Shigeaki Sugeta (eds.), *Saussure and linguistics today*, 187–191. Rome: Bulzoni.
Finck, Franz Nikolaus. 1909. *Die Sprachstämme des Erdkreises.* Leipzig & Berlin: Teubner.
Finck, Franz Nikolaus. 1910. *Die Haupttypen des Sprachbaus.* Leipzig & Berlin: Teubner.
Fleischman, Suzanne. 1982. *The future in thought and language. Diachronic evidence from Romance.* Cambridge: Cambridge University Press.
Goodman, Nelson. 1978. *Ways of worldmaking.* Indianapolis: Hackett.
Hartmann, Nicolai. 1933. *Das Problem des geistigen Seins. Untersuchungen zur Grundlegung der Geschichtsphilosophie und der Geisteswissenschaften.* Berlin: de Gruyter.
Heidegger, Martin. 1927. *Sein und Zeit.* Halle an der Saale: M. Niemeyer.

Hoenigswald, Henry M. 1960. *Linguistic change and linguistic reconstruction*. Chicago: University of Chicago Press.
Itkonen, Esa. 1984. "On the rationalist conception of linguistic change". *Diachronica* 1, 203–216.
Jeffers, Robert and Ilse Lehiste. 1979. *Principles and methods for historical linguistics*. Cambridge, Mass.: MIT Press.
Joseph, Brian D. and Richard Janda (eds.). 2003. *The handbook of historical linguistics*. Oxford: Blackwell.
Jungemann, Frederick. 1960. Review of E. Coseriu. 1958. *Sincronía, diacronía e historia. El problema del cambio lingüístico* (Montevideo). *Modern Language Notes* 75:1, 93–96.
Kuryłowicz, Jerzy. 1945. "La nature des processus dits 'analogiques'". *Acta Linguistica* 5, 15–37.
Labov, William. 1981. "Resolving the Neogrammarian controversy". *Language* 57, 267–309.
Lauwers, Peter, Marie-Rose Simoni-Aurembou and Pierre Swiggers (eds.). 2002. *Géographie linguistique et biologie du langage: Autour de Jules Gilliéron*. Leuven, Paris & Dudley: Peeters.
Lope Blanch, Juan M. 1960. Review of E. Coseriu. 1958. *Sincronía, diacronía e historia. El problema del cambio lingüístico* (Montevideo). *Nueva revista de filología hispánica* 12, 397–402.
López Serena, Araceli. 2019. "La interrelación entre lingüística y filosofía en *Sincronía, diacronía e historia* de Eugenio Coseriu". *Onomázein. Revista de lingüística, filología y traducción de la Pontificia Universidad Católica de Chile* 45, 1–30.
Malkiel, Yakov. 1964. "Distinctive traits of Romance linguistics". In: Dell H. Hymes (ed.), *Language in culture and society: a reader in linguistics and anthropology*, 671–686. New York: Harper & Row.
Malkiel, Yakov. 1967. "Multiple versus simple causation in linguistic change". In: *To Honor Roman Jakobson*, vol. 2, 1228–1246. The Hague: Mouton.
Martinet, André. 1954. "The unity of linguistics". *Word* 10, 121–125.
Martinet, André. 1955. *Économie des changements phonétiques. Traité de phonologie diachronique*. Berne: Francke.
Martinet, André. 1960. *Éléments de linguistique générale*. Paris: A. Colin.
Muller, Henry François. 1945. *L'époque mérovingienne: essai de synthèse de philologie et d'histoire*. New York: S. Vanni.
Pagliaro, Antonino. 1952. *Il linguaggio come conoscenza*. Roma: Ed. Studium.
Paul, Hermann. 1920 [1880]. *Prinzipien der Sprachgeschichte* (fifth edition). Tübingen: Niemeyer. [First edition: *Prinzipien der Sprachgeschichte*.]
[Pérez Vidal, José] "J.P.V." 1959. Review of E. Coseriu. 1958. *Sincronía, diacronía e historia. El problema del cambio lingüístico* (Montevideo). *Revista de dialectología y tradiciones populares* 15, 184–185.
Porzig, Walter. 1950. *Das Wunder der Sprache*. Bern: Francke.
Roca-Pons ("Roca i Pons"), Josep. 1959. Review of E. Coseriu. 1958. *Sincronía, diacronía e historia. El problema del cambio lingüístico* (Montevideo). *Estudis Romànics* 6, 171–172.
Rohlfs, Gerhard. 1922. "Das romanische *habeo*-Futurum und Konditionalis". *Archivum Romanicum* 6, 105–154.

Sandmann, Manfred. 1960. Review of E. Coseriu. 1958. *Sincronía, diacronía e historia. El problema del cambio lingüístico* (Montevideo). *Zeitschrift für romanische Philologie* 76, 138–141.
Saussure, Ferdinand de. 1945 [1916]. *Curso de lingüística general*. [Spanish translation by Amado Alonso]. Buenos Aires: Losada. [Reedition: Oviedo: Losada, 2002]
Schlieben-Lange, Brigitte. 1983. *Traditionen des Sprechens*. Stuttgart: Kohlhammer.
Strunk, Klaus. 1991. *Zum Postulat "vorhersagbaren" Sprachwandels bei unregelmäßigen oder komplexen Flexionsparadigmen*. München: C.H. Beck.
Swiggers, Pierre. 1988. "Le problème du changement linguistique dans l'œuvre d'Antoine Meillet". *Histoire, Épistémologie, Langage* 10:2 (= *Antoine Meillet et la linguistique de son temps*), 155–166.
Swiggers, Pierre. 1999. "La géographie linguistique de Jules Gilliéron: Aux racines du changement linguistique". *Cahiers Ferdinand de Saussure* 51, 113–132.
Swiggers, Pierre. 2013. "*Aspectos* del desarrollo de la lingüística histórica en los siglos XIX y XX". In: Ricardo Gómez, Joaquín Gorrochategui, Joseba A. Lakarra and Céline Mounole (eds.), *Koldo Mitxelena Katedraren III. Biltzarra / III Congreso de la Cátedra Luis Michelena / 3rd Conference of the Luis Michelena Chair*, 467–509. Vitoria-Gasteiz: Servicio Editorial de la Universidad del País Vasco/Euskal Herriko Unibertsitateko Argitalpen Zerbitzua.
Swiggers, Pierre. 2019. "Louis Gauchat: la voie vers une conception dynamique du changement linguistique". In: Antonio Briz, María José Martínez Alcalde, Nieves Mendizábal, Mara Fuertes Gutiérrez, José Luis Blas and Margarita Porcar (eds.), *Estudios lingüísticos en homenaje a Emilio Ridruejo*, 1353–1364. Valencia: Publicacions de la Universitat de València.
Swiggers, Pierre and Herman Seldeslachts. In prep. "Hat die Sprache ein von den sprechenden Subjekten unabhängiges Dasein? Eine Karte von F. B. Finck an A. Meillet".
Togeby, Knud. 1960. Review of E. Coseriu. 1958. *Sincronía, diacronía e historia. El problema del cambio lingüístico* (Montevideo). *Romance Philology* 14, 159–162.
Wang, William S. Y. 1969. "Competing changes as a cause of residue". *Language* 45, 9–25.
Wang, William S. Y. 1978. "The three scales of diachrony". In: Braj Kachru (ed.), *Linguistics in the seventies: directions and prospects*. Special issue of *Studies in the Linguistic Sciences* 8:2, 63–75.
Wartburg, Walther von. 1943. *Einführung in die Problematik und Methodik der Sprachwissenschaft*. Halle an der Saale: Niemeyer.
Weinreich, Uriel, William Labov and Marvin I. Herzog. 1968. "Empirical foundations for a theory of language change". In: Winfred P. Lehmann and Yakov Malkiel (eds.), *Directions for historical linguistics. A symposium*, 97–195. Austin & London: University of Texas Press.

Ioan Milică (Iaşi)
Coseriu's journey to the realm of linguistic change

> Let us, for example, consider the fact that the sciences of man do not possess a proper term to replace the inconvenient and inadequate term evolution: *unlike natural objects, cultural objects undergo historical development, not 'evolution'*.*

1 Preliminaries

The present paper discusses Coseriu's philosophical model of linguistic change and explores the assumption that causal language-centred evolutionary models should be replaced with a finalistic speaker-centred dynamic model. Throughout his work, Coseriu emphasized that, from the standpoint of the speaker's consciousness and communicative actions, change is inherent to language insofar as the historical tradition of language use is a perpetual competition among speech acts. Due to the speakers' free and creative linguistic activity, languages change systematically for as long as they are spoken. Therefore, linguistic evolution cannot be accounted for by exploring the external factors which cause languages to change.

At a closer look, Coseriu's speaker-centred model of linguistic change should be interpreted in the light of the intense research carried out in linguistics after World War II, on the one hand, and the growing prestige of quantitative approaches in science, on the other. Unlike many of his fellow linguists who sought to solve the puzzles of language by adopting the concepts and methods of sciences like biology, sociology and psychology, Coseriu believed that any excessive borrowing of this sort is detrimental to linguistics. Instead he defended the creed that the most rewarding path to follow was the centuries-old intellectual course laid down in the philosophy of language. According to Coseriu, linguistics would gain far more benefits from exploring its own tradition than by dissolving itself in the matrices of other sciences. This 'inward' archaeology of knowledge would ultimately confirm that the language sciences did not require any 'outward' imports concerning various conceptual, methodological and terminologi-

---

* "Considérese, por ej., el hecho de que las ciencias del hombre no disponen aún de un término propio para sustituir el molesto e inadecuado *evolución:* los objetos culturales tienen *desarrollo histórico,* y no 'evolución' como los objetos naturales" (Coseriu 1978 [1958]: 181; italics in the original).

cal matters. This is not to say that Coseriu distrusted or altogether rejected any collaboration among sciences and scientists. On the contrary, he argued that linguistics, as a historical science, should recognize its place among the humanities in harmony with the neighbouring scientific enterprises, just like physics and chemistry value the ideals of objectivity and precision, provided that they are grounded in causality (Coseriu 1978 [1958]: 235–236). However, as a cultural science, "linguistics must give up the irrational goal of uncovering causal laws in the realm of freedom" (Coseriu 1978 [1958]: 236–237).

Coseriu's monograph *Sincronía, diacronía e historia. El problema del cambio lingüístico*, first published in 1958, was welcomed as a thorough critique of Saussurean structural linguistics (Togeby 1960: 159–162), but, as Coseriu would later explain, the synthesis sought to reconcile important philosophical ideas with major linguistic theories in order to integrate them into a unitary conception of language (Coseriu 1995a: 188) (cf. Swiggers, this volume). More importantly, Coseriu highlighted the crucial role played by speakers' intuitions and creativity in the dynamic making of language as a historical and cultural system of signs. From the perspective of both the philosophy of language and the philosophy of science, it was a fair and legitimate point to make, considering the author's academic background and the dominant trends in post-war linguistics.[1] Ever since linguistics emerged as a modern science in the beginning of the nineteenth century, its object was, in theory, clearly identified, i.e. the study of language. In reality, the nature of the object fuelled metalinguistic disputes: What exactly is language? In this respect, is it wrong to presume that the leading figures in the field imagined, to a certain extent, what the object of enquiry ought to be? Whereas some of the leading theories in linguistics displayed a language-centred design, others featured a speaker-centred design. Coseriu's philosophical perspective endeavoured to bridge the gap:

> 'What makes language a language' is not simply its structure (which stands only as the condition for the functioning of language), but the linguistic activity that creates language and maintains it as tradition. Therefore, if change is understood as systematic language in the making (Sp. *hacerse sistemático de la lengua*), then it is obvious that there can be no contradiction between 'system' and 'change' and that there is no need to speak of 'system' and

---

[1] By the time of his arrival in Montevideo, Coseriu held a doctorate in linguistics (Rome) and a doctorate in philosophy (Milan). He would warmly recall the formative years spent in Italy between 1940 and 1950: "Thanks to a vigorous humanistic tradition, still more vivid in Italy than elsewhere, and thanks to the great Italian philosophical movement of our century, contemporary Italian linguistics [1957] is free from the confusion rooted in sociology and physics as well as from the naive errors and absurdities of mathematization" (Coseriu 1978 [1958]: 52).

'movement' (Sp. *movimiento*) – as two opposite things –, but only of the 'system *in* movement' (Coseriu 1978 [1958]: 271–272).

As the reader of the present paper is about to find out, the conclusion that "language functions synchronically and forms diachronically" (Coseriu 1978 [1958]: 272) covers ideas with distinct backgrounds. It is therefore important to appeal to tradition in order to get a more refined understanding of Coseriu's outlook on 'evolution'. Section 2 hints at the hybridisation of the dominant theoretical outputs in linguistics by the middle of the twentieth century. Section 3 dwells on the divided legacy of nineteenth-century linguistics and signals some conspicuous inconsistencies in the design of evolution with regard to linguistic change. Section 4 briefly approaches the Saussurean paradigm set by Coseriu as the starting point in the quest to reconcile the classical philosophy of language with modern linguistic theories. The closing remarks ponder on the conceptual and terminological importance of evolution in linguistic research.

2 A sea journey without a compass

Twentieth-century linguistics mirrored the growing entropy of various schools of scientific thought. In Europe, the birthplace of the science of language, the fall of the Iron Curtain split the continent between Structural Linguistics, in the West, and Marxist Linguistics, in the East. In North America, the influence of behaviourism and the development of anthropological linguistics were about to compete with the tenets of generativism and to confront the experimental approaches carried out in pragmatics. If one adds to the count the wide scope of interdisciplinary research of the time, ranging from computational linguistics and corpus linguistics to psycholinguistics and sociolinguistics, then one is not mistaken to assume that, at the end of the 1950s, what was by tradition referred to as 'linguistics' had already given way to a lively competition among various linguistic trends. It was a period of lively scrutiny and vivid debate, which undoubtedly left its mark on the contemporary language sciences.

To gain a better understanding of this post-war intellectual revolution, one must simply remember that, at the beginning of the twentieth century, scientists like Ferdinand de Saussure believed that linguistics should privilege abstract rigorous modelling by focusing on the "faculty of constructing a language, i.e. a system of distinct signs corresponding to distinct ideas" (Saussure 1959 [1916]: 10). This was the spirit of the age: to set forth new principles and guidelines that challenge the traditional ones and render them obsolete. In resonance with the Neogrammarian matrix, which distinguished between the language system and its use, Saussure's view on language was conceived as an axiological enterprise. This ambitious theoretical design, defined as *la linguistique de la langue* ['linguistics of language', i.e. the scientific focus on the language system], was envisaged as proper linguistics, in contrast with the usage-oriented field called *la linguistique de la parole* ['linguistics of speech'] (cf. Saussure 1959 [1916]: 18–19).

Less than half a century later, the ideal of uncovering a powerful and generally acknowledged theoretical model appeared even more remote as the analytic and experimental approaches gained the upper ground of scientific enquiry. To paraphrase the leaders of the Neogrammarian movement, the entire linguistic undertaking of the time looked like a sea journey without a compass (Osthoff and Brugmann 1878, in Lehmann 1967: 219). After more than a hundred years, the same elusive question was waiting for an answer: What kind of science is linguistics? Some of the founders, like August Schleicher, did not hesitate to include linguistics among the natural sciences. Others, like Saussure, replied that linguistics was, from the moment of its conception, a historical science. Furthermore, revered anthropologists such as Claude Lévi-Strauss proclaimed that "linguistics occupies a special place among the social sciences, to whose ranks it unquestionably belongs" (Lévi-Strauss 1963: 31). Even ruthless dictators like Stalin had something to say about linguistics, as a matter of state and politics. No further examples are required to grasp the fact that, in the late 1950s and the early 1960s, the panorama of reflections on language was eclectic and provocative. The mosaic-like picture of various language theories were to face further challenges.

In 1958, when the first edition of Coseriu's *Sincronía, diacronía e historia* appeared in Montevideo, the international scientific community of the time prepared to celebrate the centennial publication of Charles Darwin's *On the Origin of Species* (1859). Regarded as the most influential academic work of the nineteenth century, Darwin's research shed new light on a core concept in science: 'evolution'. The book brought forth a simple, yet striking idea, namely that life on Earth reflects the principle of natural selection and this great active force drives the survival of the fittest. From the moment of its birth, the idea sparked controversy and has continued to fuel debate.

Leaving aside the seemingly unending quarrel that still antagonizes creationists and evolutionists, after World War II, the realm of natural sciences became the field of ground-breaking discoveries and the stage of controversy. As evolutionary biology established itself at the forefront of sciences, this complex wave of change extended Darwin's legacy far beyond the epistemological boundaries of natural sciences. However, as some of the approaches claimed Darwinian descent, there were voices, mostly from the humanities, arguing that the concepts and methods of biology had proven inadequate when adopted and adapted to explain phenomena that do not fall under the scope of natural sciences. To put it simply, biology was not credited to hold the golden key that would unlock all possible explanations concerning everything a scientist could study or think of.

On a more general standpoint, if one is to interpret such disputes as collateral evidence of the Post-Renaissance paradigm shift that gradually moved the prestige from the sciences of culture, such as theology and philology, to the sciences of nature, such as physics, chemistry and biology, then any controversy that occasionally divides humanists and naturalists also signals the circulation of ideas between arts and sciences. As Stevick puts it, one should not forget that the answers of science improve by time: "Just as language history has excised false formulations, many of them from biology (and its enthusiastic imitators), so evolutionary theory has purified itself from the crudities of extrascientific notions" (Stevick 1963: 160).

To resume, at the middle of the twentieth century, the scientific context welcomed new ideas while disrupting the old ones. Coseriu approached the cornerstone issue of linguistic change and, to cross the seemingly widening gap between linguistics and philosophy, he focused on Wilhelm von Humboldt's seminal work.

3 The divided Humboldtian legacy

In nineteenth-century linguistics, Wilhelm von Humboldt, a brilliant scholar and liberal statesman, was a towering figure. In 1821, he appointed Franz Bopp, a close and lifelong friend, professor in linguistics at the University of Berlin. This founding act would set comparative grammar on the course of modern science. As a loyal reader of Aristotle's, Coseriu found in Humboldt's work the open intellectual background that he would constantly value in building his own vision. Since Humboldt developed a keen affinity with classical antiquity and with Aristotle's works in particular, it is no wonder that Coseriu regarded Humboldt's cultural edifice as a strategic inflection point in the history of ideas. More precisely, Coseriu believed that Humboldt's legacy stood as a pivotal synthesis that bridged the classical philosophy of language and modern linguistic theories (cf. Trabant, this volume; see also Trabant 1992). To support this interpretation, Coseriu reviewed the Aristotelian and Humboldtian notional constructs and stated that the main fallacy of modern theories of linguistic change has consisted in approaching language as a mechanical communicative product shaped by some blind laws of change, instead of regarding it as a typically human creative activity. Coseriu writes:

> language functions and enacts itself as *speaking* (Sp. *se da concretamente en el hablar*). To take this fact as the foundation of the entire theory of language means to start with Humboldt's familiar statement that language is not ἔργον, but ἐνέργεια. This idea is often cited but, in most cases, quickly discarded by those who take refuge in language as ἔργον. Instead, one must first of all take Humboldt's assertion seriously, and that is to consider it as foundational, since the statement is neither a paradox nor a metaphor, but the very truth. Language is really, and not metaphorically, *activity*, not *product*. [...] Secondly, ἐνέργεια ought to be understood in its precise and fruitful meaning. To do so, one needs to consider that Humboldt followed Aristotle in order to set out the distinction between ἐνέργεια and ἔργον. Consequently, his ἐνέργεια (*Tätigkeit*) should not be taken in the common meaning, as any activity or simple 'action' (*Handlung*), but with reference to Aristotle's ἐνέργεια (for he coined both the concept and the term): as a free and finalistic activity that comprises in itself its goal (Sp. *fin*) and that is the realization of that very goal, and that, ideally, is prior to the 'potential' (Coseriu 1978 [1958]: 44–46; italics in the original).[2]

Herein lies Coseriu's novel, yet at the same time classical perspective on linguistic change: languages are permanently being used by their speakers and therefore display a dynamic though fragile equilibrium between what has just been said and what is about to be said. In other words, the definite language of the past meets the indefinite language of tomorrow. This interplay among various traditions of language use reveals not only the speakers' creativity, but also the historical transformations brought about, as Humboldt (1988 [1836]: 49) stated, by the enduring, yet *"transitory"* nature of language. In Humboldt's view, the approach on language as *activity*, not as *product*, dwells on a dynamic modelling of speech. More precisely, speaking is defined as the "ever-repeated mental labour" (ibid.) of expressing thoughts by strings of articulated sounds. Thus, the essence of language consists in being produced. The linguistic activity brought forth by the act of speaking, albeit neither general, nor "complete" (ibid.), sustains and reveals the workings of the interconnected parts that make up the semiotic network of language.[3] By habit and by tradition, language is actively con-

---

[2] As Coseriu explains, Aristotle envisages a threefold understanding of activity: a) the activity as such, κατ' ἐνέργειαν, b) the activity as potential, κατὰ δύναμιν, and c) the activity as product, κατ' ἔργον (Coseriu 1978 [1958]: 45). If one is to illustrate this threefold understanding of activity with reference to the linguistic activity of man, then it is important to note that a) the activity of speaking as such and b) the ability to speak or the "idea" that one can speak do not coincide with c) language as realized speech.

[3] "Language can be compared to an immense web, in which every part stands in a more or less clearly recognizable connection with the others, and all with the whole. Whatever his point of

veyed and transformed from individual to individual, from one generation to another. In Coseriu's own words (1978 [1958]: 272), "language functions synchronically and forms (Sp. *se constituye*) diachronically", by virtue of the speakers' communicative abilities and expressive needs. Therefore, linguistic changes should not be viewed as phenomena shaped by external causes and laws, but as a flow of speech acts created within the communicative possibilities systematically entailed by language.

"Language is one of the fields whence the general mental power of human beings emerges in constantly active operation", wrote Humboldt (1988 [1836]: 27). He subsequently explained that "[t]he proper evolution of language is in natural accord with that of the *intellectual capacity* as such" (Humboldt 1988 [1836]: 144; italics in the original). Here, as elsewhere, Humboldt sets forth one of his key concepts: G. *Entwicklung* 'development', which according to Alexander von Humboldt in the preface to his brother's posthumously published work, sheds light on another important philosophical concept, viz. the 'organism of language'. From the standpoint of the human spirit, languages are developing organisms ceaselessly shaped by creativity.

The Enlightenment laid the foundations of modern scientific thought. There is no reason to believe otherwise if, following Cassirer (1975 [1923]: 153–154), the seminal conceptual legacy of the Romantics must also be acknowledged. At a closer look, Humboldt's vision on language exerted its influence on both sides of the nineteenth-century linguistic turn, the naturalists and the culturalists. As Cassirer argues, Humboldt's "new philosophical view of language demanded and made possible a new approach to linguistic science" (Cassirer 1975 [1923]: 162), and comparative linguistics answered the call by defining its functions in line with Humboldt's 'organism of language'. However, this new course induced a shift:

> the concept of the 'organic' retained its central position; but its meaning changed radically once the biological concept of development prevailing in modern natural science was opposed to the concept of development dominant in Romantic philosophy. In the field of biology, the speculative concept of organic form was gradually replaced by its purely scientific concept, and this immediately affected the study of language (Cassirer 1975 [1923]: 163–164).

---

departure, man always makes contact in speaking with a merely isolated portion of this fabric, but invariably does so, instinctively, as if everything that this one portion must necessarily agree with were simultaneously present to him at the same moment." (Humboldt, 1988 [1836]: 69).

This change of tide needed a manifesto, and August Schleicher would be its author. Revered by many (cf. Koerner 1989: 325–375), secretly belittled by others (cf. Saussure 2006: 142), Schleicher claimed that the evolutionary theory had already been of current use in German linguistics by the time Darwin published his world-famous book. There can be no doubt that Schleicher explored Humboldt's ideas and tuned them to fit his own views on language. More precisely, he "saw the Humboldtian language types as successive stages in a *systema linguae* formed on the analogy of the *systema naturae* of the natural science of his time" (Bynon 2001: 1225; italics in the original). Prior to 1859, Schleicher had defined linguistics as a natural science and subsequently introduced "some basic methodological innovations: the phonological reconstruction of Indo-European, the family-tree model of language descent, and the insistence on the importance of establishing regular sound laws" (Morpurgo Davies 1998: 167). "Observation is the foundation of modern knowledge", he wrote in his assessment of Darwin's work, and to this statement he added an unequivocal comment: "nothing else is acceptable but the necessary conclusions arrived at through that channel" (Schleicher 1869: 25–26).

Schleicher's naturalism had an ideological core that would not only blend linguistics with biology, but it would also rely on a projection that was to become the Achille's heel in other studies on linguistic change, viz. the assimilation of the speaker to a talking mechanical puppet, due to the fact that the physiology of speaking is, by nature, independent of the will of man. If one leaves aside the hindering detail that it is rather difficult to make accurate observations on the true nature of speaking by looking at it through the lenses of written documents, one cannot overlook the keystone of the naturalist paradigm: "Languages are organisms of nature; *they have never been directed by the will of man*" (Schleicher 1869: 21; my emphasis, I.M.). With one stroke of the brush, the speaker's activity and the progressive differentiation of languages become segregated landscapes. Consequently, the external factors that shape linguistic change build up an evolutionary force that eludes the speaker.

Following Pisani (1954: 345), who concluded that it was only after 1880 that the Neogrammarian scholars acknowledged that language existed only by virtue of individual speech acts, Coseriu (1973 [1954]: 212) argues that Schleicher's theoretical design insulates the historical course of language from the speakers' communicative activity. It therefore does not reflect the Humboldtian creative language-in-the-making model, since the speaker is attributed a decorative, mechanical status. In the quest for a solid theory of language evolution through gradual variation, Schleicher casts the speaker in a weak role.

Interestingly, whereas linguistic naturalism would be met with scepticism by the following generations of linguists, Darwin's theory of natural selection would reach increasingly wider audiences. That was in no small part due to the skilfully crafted style that would set the rhetorical standards of science for the years to come. As shown by various researchers (Tort 1979, Bergounioux 2002, Mendivil-Giro 2006), Darwin "recognized the basic affinities between evolutionary biology and historical linguistics" (Harmon 1996: 90). He drew several parallels between natural organisms and natural languages in order to defend the idea of natural selection in analogy with linguistic phenomena. This persuasive strategy mainly supports the evolutionary succession of species, but it also illustrates the prestige of the historical linguistics of the time. For instance, when Darwin (1909: 363) invokes the geological history of life on Earth, he solves the puzzle of evolution and the weakness in the argument by shrewdly projecting the lack of fossil records into the metaphorical frame of philology. On another instance, Darwin argues that the genealogical classification of life forms mirrors the hierarchy of language trees and, even if he barely mentions the "illustrious Humboldt" (Darwin 1909: 419), his descriptions of the web of complex relations which binds together plants and animals remind us of a Humboldtian vision of nature.[4]

On the other side of the story, Heymann Steinthal, a fervent admirer of Wilhelm von Humboldt[5] and the founder of psycholinguistics, took on the task to revive the idea that language reveals the speaker's inner self. We are still a long way from Coseriu's dynamic speaker-centred model of linguistic change, but, among the mid-nineteenth-century linguists, Steinthal clearly states that language is the medium that allows humans the freedom to express their mind. Unlike Schleicher's rather mechanical conception of the speaker, Steinthal insisted on a language-in-the-mind design which favoured the definition of linguistics as a science akin to history, philosophy, aesthetics, rhetoric, and, last but not least, psychology. To speak, Steinthal (2013: 195) argues, is to fulfil an activity that circumscribes linguistics to the circle of psychology, since the linguistic material itself is the product of the human spirit.

Steinthal's emphasis on the speaker's perception and communicative ability is undoubtedly a step closer to the complex reality of human speech acts. However, as Coseriu (1978 [1958]: 64) points out, the risk of this line of argument resides in the focus on an imaginary, abstract speaker, a blueprint-like prototype

---

4 Cf. Wulf (2015) for an outline of the major part played by Alexander von Humboldt in the development of evolutionary biology in the first half of the nineteenth century.

5 According to Koerner (1989: 33), Steinthal was "probably the most influential champion of Wilhelm von Humboldt in the 19th century". His work instilled a 'mentalist' research tradition respected not only by some prominent Neogrammarians, such as Hermann Paul, but also by the forerunners of linguistic idealism such as Georg von der Gabelentz. Unlike Schleicher, Steinthal had no affinity with evolutionary biology.

with little or no connection to reality. In fact, Steinthal's 'mentalism' illustrates the open rejection of any mechanistic naturalism in linguistics. It also entertains a view of language as product, in spite of the claim that "language is not a stable product, but pure activity" (Steinthal 2013: 437). Moreover, the Humboldtian key concept of development plays in Steinthal's conception of language a rather marginal and fuzzy role. The notion covers neither the given process or activity and its outcome, as Humboldt believed, nor the progressive differentiation of forms, as Schleicher thought, but refers to various stages in the cultural and historical development of humanity. This chain-like view of evolution is undoubtedly 'static', with its 'dynamic' counterpart in the natural sciences.

To sum up, Schleicher fostered an evolutionary model of linguistic change nurtured by the strong belief that linguistics is a natural science, and yet, his model relied on a weak role attributed to the speaker. Steinthal's approach (2013: 203) strongly called for an active view on language by projecting the speaker's consciousness at the heart of the model, but the explanatory power of the theory was unfortunately undermined by a 'passive', picture-like conception of evolution. As the two proponents of the main trends in nineteenth-century linguistics, viz. naturalism and psychologism, placed Humboldt's philosophical umbrella concepts such as development, evolution and organism in different orbits, the language science of the next century would inherit this divided legacy. As Coseriu points out, this puzzling course unveils the gap created in time between the sciences of nature and the sciences of culture:

> For natural phenomena, it is undoubtedly adequate to seek for an external necessity, or *causality*; by contrast, for cultural phenomena what should be sought after is an internal necessity, or *purposiveness* (Sp. *finalidad*). Therefore, a conception of language that is really positive (and not 'positivist') must constantly take into account and always remember that language pertains to the realm of freedom and purposiveness, and that consequently facts of language cannot be interpreted and explained in causal terms (Coseriu 1978 [1958]: 193–194; italics in the original).

4 The evolution of *evolution*

Joseph (2012) offers an excellent view on the atmosphere in linguistics towards the *fin de siècle*. It also clearly outlines Saussure's evolutionary model and his understanding of the key concepts 'diachrony' and 'synchrony' in relation to history. In Joseph's words, the problem Saussure

> saw with 'history of the language' is that it embraces much more than the changes within the system of *langue* from one point in time (one synchronic state) to another. Indeed, it

tends not even to view the evolution of a language in that way, but rather to imagine that it has a continuous existence across time periods, with particular elements regenerating but the system as a whole remaining in effect the same. Saussure's view was the opposite: the elements persist over time and are simply rearranged, with each rearrangement introducing a new system (Joseph 2012: 514).

The *Cours de linguistique générale* (1916) led Coseriu (1978 [1958]: 42) to presume that Saussure translated in sociological terms Schleicher's naturalist model, when, in fact, it has never been so (cf. Saussure 2006: 102). What Saussure had in mind points to a different understanding of evolution: if synchrony were a picture, diachrony would be the moving picture of language evolution. Today, it is beyond any doubt that, for Saussure, linguistics was a historical science:

> any language has in itself a history which unfolds ceaselessly, made up of a succession of *linguistic events*, which have had no external echo, nor have ever been engraved in the annals of history; and by the same token they are themselves also quite independent in general of external events. Rather like the great moraines visible at the foot of glaciers, all languages bear the marks of a huge collection of things carried along down the centuries, but these things *have* dates, and *very different dates*, just as the glacial deposits of my comparison show that a given piece of granite comes from a distance a few leagues from the highest peaks of the mountain range, while another block of quartz is from scarcely further than its first foothills... So language *has a history:* that is a constant characteristic. (Saussure 2006: 98–99; italics in the original).

This geological analogy supports the view that the course of natural languages varies across time and space and their incessant flow is shaped by two dialectic forces, the continuity of transmission from one generation to another and the ceaseless transformation or movement over time, which "coexist in a necessary balance" (Joseph 2012: 379). In other words, Saussure was fully aware of the fact that "in reality there is never equilibrium, or a permanent, stable point in any language" (Saussure 2006: 105). Conceived as a continuous and dynamic series of transformations, the Saussurean evolutionary model foreshadows Coseriu's language-in-the making design. What sets the two visions apart is the difference of perspective on the nature of speech acts. "Can linguistic facts be said to be the result of acts of will?", Saussure wonders, before adding that, to this question, "the science of language gives a positive answer". However, of all human acts of will, "the linguistic act, if I might call it that, is characterized as being the least reflected on, the least premeditated, as well as the most impersonal of all" (Saussure 2006: 99). This portrayal of individual speech reveals that Saussure built a remarkable evolutionary language-centred model which, in turn, downplayed the speaker's creative role. This shortcoming is mainly due to Saussure's Neogrammarian restrictive conception of linguistic creativity (cf. Saussure 2006: 107).

To conclude, let us rephrase the opening question: What do great linguists mean by evolution? Is it the development of language organisms in the mirror of the human mind? Is it the progressive differentiation of linguistic forms hinting at the *Ursprache?* Is it the speaker's active consciousness embroidered in the semiotic fabric of language? Is it the ever-changing series of transformations in the abstract picture of the language system? Or perhaps the perpetual interplay between what speakers want to say and what language by tradition has to offer?

Each of the already mentioned points of view deserves further thoughtful reconsideration if one is to deal with the history of linguistic theories in terms of the motion picture analogy imagined by Saussure (2006: 104) to explain linguistic change. In fact, following Coseriu's distinction (1978 [1958]: 19) between '(primary) language' and 'metalanguage', nothing prevents us from thinking that the concept of evolution concerns not only the complex realm of language *per se*, but also the scientific metalanguage traditionally used to refer to speech acts and facts of language. Whenever the studied object and the methodology overlap, the stemming confusion undermines the conclusions and sets science off course. Therefore, it is equally important to explore the reality of language without prejudice while acknowledging that the core concepts of one science do not necessarily solve the difficult issues of another. Secondly, multifarious concepts like evolution, language or organism ought to be understood in line with the views expressed by their proponents in order to assess whether such flexible constructs of the mind should be deemed weak or strong. Coseriu's principled discontent with the term evolution, which he would otherwise sparsely and cautiously use in his work, was primarily a warning against the lack of clarity, coherence or precision evidenced by various linguistic studies. For the benefit of future research, it is undoubtedly commendable to eschew the flaws of previous research. Even at a glance, the rich array of semantic cognates used in linguistics to refer to evolution – 'development', 'differentiation', 'transformation', 'modification', 'succession', 'process', 'adaptation', 'drift' or 'fluctuation' – ultimately reveals that no science purges its conceptual and terminological heritage.

References

Bergounioux, Gabriel. 2002. "La sélection des langues: darwinisme et linguistique". *Langages* 36 (146), 7–18.
Bynon, Teodora. 2001. "The synthesis of comparative and historical Indo-European studies: August Schleicher". In: Sylvain Auroux, E. F. Konrad Koerner, Hans-Josef Niederehe and

Kees Versteegh (eds.), *History of the language sciences. An international handbook on the evolution of the study of language from the beginnings to the present.* Vol. 2, 1223–1239. Berlin & New York: De Gruyter.

Cassirer, Ernst. 1975 [1923]. *The philosophy of symbolic forms.* Vol. 1: *Language.* Translated by Ralph Manheim. New Haven & London: Yale University Press. (German original 1923.)

Coseriu, Eugenio. 1973 [1954]. "Forma y sustancia en los sonidos del lenguaje". In: Eugenio Coseriu, *Teoría del lenguaje y lingüística general. Cinco estudios*, 115–234. Madrid: Gredos.

Coseriu, Eugenio. 1978 [1958]. *Sincronía, diacronía e historia. El problema del cambio lingüístico* (third edition). Madrid: Gredos.

Coseriu, Eugenio. 1995a. "My Saussure". In: Tullio De Mauro and Shigeaki Sugeta (eds.), *Saussure and linguistics today*, 187–191. Rome: Bulzoni.

Darwin, Charles. 1909. *On the origin of species by means of natural selection, or the preservation of favoured race in the struggle of life.* New York: P. F. Collier & Son.

Harmon, David. 1996. "Losing species, losing languages: connections between biological and linguistic diversity". *Southwest Journal of Linguistics* 15:1–2, 89–108.

Humboldt, Wilhelm von. 1988 [1836]. *On language. On the diversity of human language construction and its influence on the mental development of the human species.* Edited by M. Losonsky, translated by P. Heath. Cambridge: Cambridge University Press.

Joseph, John E. 2012. *Saussure.* Oxford: Oxford University Press.

Koerner, Konrad. 1989. *Practicing linguistic historiography. Selected essays.* Amsterdam & Philadelphia: John Benjamins.

Lehmann, Winfred P. 1967. *A reader in nineteenth-century historical Indo-European linguistics.* Bloomington: Indiana University Press.

Lévi-Strauss, Claude. 1963. *Structural anthropology.* Translated by Claire Jacobson and Brooke G. Schoepf. New York: Basic Books.

Mendívil-Giró, José-Luis 2006. "Languages and species: limits and scope of a venerable comparison". In: Joana Roselló and Jesús Martín (eds.), *The biolinguistics turn. Issues on language and biology*, 82–118. Barcelona: Promociones y Publicaciones Universitarias.

Morpurgo Davies, Anna. 1998. *History of linguistics.* Vol. 4: *Nineteenth-century linguistics.* London & New York: Longman.

Pisani, Vittore 1954. "August Schleicher und einige Richtungen der heutigen Sprachwissenschaft". *Lingua* 4, 337–368.

Saussure, Ferdinand de. 1959 [1916]. *Course in general linguistics.* Translated by Wade Baskin. New York: Philosophical Library.

Saussure, Ferdinand de. 2002. *Écrits de linguistique générale.* Texte établi par Simon Bouquet et Rudolf Engler. Paris: Éditions Gallimard.

Saussure, Ferdinand de. 2006. *Writings in General Linguistics.* English translation of Saussure (2002) by Carol Sanders and Matthew Pires. Oxford: Oxford University Press.

Schleicher, August. 1869. *Darwinism tested by the science of language.* Translated by Alex V. W. Bikkers. London: John Camden Hotten.

Steinthal, Heymann. 2013. *Ermeneutica e psicologia del linguaggio.* A cura di Davide Bondì. Milano: Bompiani.

Stevick, Robert. 1963. "The biological model and historical linguistics". *Language* 39:2, 159–169.

Togeby, Knud. 1960. Review of E. Coseriu. 1958. *Sincronía, diacronía e historia. El problema del cambio lingüístico* (Montevideo). *Romance Philology* 14, 159–162.
Tort, Patrick. 1979. "L'Histoire naturelle des langues. De Darwin à Schleicher". *Romantisme* 25–26, 123–156.
Trabant, Jürgen. 1992. "Du travail de l'esprit a la danse de la coordination". *Histoire Épistémologie Langage* 14:2, 231–244.
Wulf, Andrea. 2015. *The invention of nature. Alexander von Humboldt's new world*. New York: Alfred A. Knopf.

Angela Schrott (Kassel)
Eugenio Coseriu and pragmatics

Speaking is a universal and general human activity, which is realized individually in specific situations by individual speakers as representatives of language communities with shared traditions of speaking a particular language.*

1 Introduction: why pragmatics?

Eugenio Coseriu's linguistic thinking is essentially based on the concept of speaking as activity. This understanding is absolutely central to Coseriu's system of linguistic competence, whose core are the rules and traditions that govern language use (Coseriu 1955–1956, 1985, 2007 [1988]). The quote I have chosen as the starting point for my contribution summarizes his concept of language in a nutshell. The dynamic concept of activity (G. *Tätigkeit*) is very close to the perspective of pragmatics, which focuses on language use as an activity that takes place in individual environments of speaking. Pragmatics is thus not a discipline focused on the analysis of specific linguistic structures of the language system (*langue*), but rather a perspective on language (Verschueren 1995: 11, 2009: 14–16) that explores its use and its potential in speaking as an activity and form of human behavior. Thus, linguistic phenomena are analyzed with a focus on speakers and language use. Since this perspective includes the interlocutors and the situation in which they speak to each other, pragmatics is interdisciplinary in its design, also encompassing cognitive, semiotic, historical, and cultural dimensions (Verschueren 1995: 13, Escandell Vidal 2004: 348–350). This wide scope of the pragmalinguistic perspective is implied in Coseriu's definition quoted above, which encompasses the universal dimension of speaking, the common traditions of speaking particular languages in language communities, and the individuality of speaking in specific situations. Coseriu's definition therefore has the merit of not only embracing all the dimensions of the pragmatic perspective, but also of providing the necessary categories to distinguish them. The understanding of language expressed in the quote is further developed by Coseriu into an elaborate system of linguistic competence (1955–1956, 1985,

---

* "Das Sprechen ist eine universelle allgemein-menschliche Tätigkeit, die jeweils von individuellen Sprechern als Vertretern von Sprachgemeinschaften mit gemeinschaftlichen Traditionen des Sprechenkönnens individuell in bestimmten Situationen realisiert wird" (Coseriu 2007 [1988]: 70) (translation A.S.).

2007 [1988]). The distinctions of this system can be applied to distinguish the dimensions of pragmalinguistics mentioned by Verschueren – cognitive, semiotic, linguistic, historical, and cultural – and thus provide the outline of an integrated theory of pragmalinguistics.

In several publications I have developed a model for pragmalinguistic research based on Coseriu's system of language as an activity which extends his original system of linguistic competence and opens it up to current topics of pragmatics (Schrott 2014, 2015, 2017a, 2020). This article summarizes these publications and develops them further.

2 Coseriu's system of linguistic competence (G. *Sprachkompetenz*)

The cited definition contains three basic characteristics. Speaking has universal qualities; it has the historical characteristics of the particular language used by the speakers and it is an individual activity because human beings always speak as individuals. The triad of universal activity, historical languages and individual realization is reflected in three levels and three types of knowledge (Coseriu 2007 [1988]: 69–75; on the development and history of the model see Coseriu 1955–1956: 31–34, 1973 [1955–1956]: 285–291, Kabatek 2017).

Table 1: The levels of linguistic competence (Coseriu 2007 [1988]: 75; slightly modified, translation A.S.)

Level	Point of view		
	Activity (*enérgeia*)	Knowledge (*dýnamis*)	Product (*érgon*)
Universal level	Speaking in general, in all languages	Universal principles and rules (elocutional knowledge)	–
Historical level of languages	Speaking a particular language	Linguistic traditions (idiomatic knowledge)	–
Individual level of discourse	Discourse as speaking in a particular situation	Discourse traditions (expressive knowledge)	Text

The universal level is formed by the universal principles and rules that apply to speaking in all languages, regardless of the structures of different languages and also regardless of the cultures in which the speakers live (Coseriu 2007 [1988]:

74–75). Coseriu calls this universal layer of speaking the *elocutio* and refers to it as 'elocutional knowledge'. In the reception of the model it has become more common to speak of universal principles and rules, since in this way the universal status of this knowledge becomes clear. The universal principles include fundamental cognitive and communicative-semiotic abilities, such as a basic coherence of speech (Coseriu 2007 [1988]: 106). The 'alterity of speaking' which implies that people speak to others and for others in order to be understood and make an effort to understand their interlocutors is also a universal principle of speaking (Coseriu 2007 [1988]: 79, 89–90, 192–193). This concept is closely related to the idea of the cooperative principle that Grice (1989) established in pragmatics: In a certain way, cooperation and 'alterity' are two sides of the same coin.

The historical level of languages refers to historicity as a characteristic of all languages that are subject to linguistic change and therefore have a historical dimension (Coseriu 2007 [1988]: 107–109). By 'idiomatic knowledge', Coseriu understands the mastery of languages, i.e., the ability to express oneself and communicate correctly in one or more languages (G. *Sprechenkönnen*), be they native or foreign languages. The concept of linguistic knowledge not only relates to languages of the present but also to earlier time periods, for example when someone learns Old English, Middle High German, or Old Spanish in order to read the texts of these periods. The term 'linguistic traditions', which I have chosen for this knowledge type, implies that linguistic knowledge is passed from generation to generation as a tradition (Schrott 2015: 121, Lebsanft and Schrott 2015: 24–25). The concept of tradition is already present in the Coserian system of language competence (cf. the quote chosen for this contribution and also 2007 [1988]: 81). As Coseriu defines 'culture' as the ability to produce traditions (1974 [1958]: 92), the idea of tradition is central for his understanding of linguistic competence as a cultural competence (2007 [1988]: 65). For Coseriu, the concept of tradition combines firmness and flexibility, as each tradition offers space for variation and change and thus makes possible the creation of something new that can be learned and transmitted (Coseriu 1974 [1958]: 92, 2007 [1988]: 69; on the influence of Menéndez Pidal on the Coserian idea of tradition cf. Lebsanft and Schrott 2015).

The individual level refers to discourse as an activity performed in a specific speech situation by an individual speaker who takes responsibility for his words. In addition to the universal principles and the mastery of a particular language, this level hosts a third knowledge type that enables speakers to adapt their speech acts to different speech situations, interlocutors and topics of conversation. This cultural knowledge – Coseriu calls it 'expressive knowledge' – allows the speaker to adapt his discourse to the speech situation and act appropriately and successfully (Coseriu 2007 [1988]: 74, 86–88). Here, too, it makes sense to speak of 'traditions', as this knowledge type is also of historical nature and is passed on from generation to generation as a cultural tradition (Coseriu 2007 [1988]: 81, cf. Schrott 2015: 117–118, 120–125). In Romance linguistics, the concept of discourse tradition is central to linguistic approaches that understand language as a cultural competence and analyze the design of discourses and texts embedded in their social and cultural environments (cf. Schlieben-Lange 1983, Koch 1997, Oesterreicher 1997, Lebsanft 2005, Schrott 2015, 2017a, Kabatek 2015, 2018a).

Linguistic traditions and discourse traditions have in common the character of habitualized knowledge. They differ in that the former refer to the mastery of languages, whereas the latter are cultural models of verbal interaction that show how to use a language not only correctly but also appropriately in different speech situations in order to successfully implement one's communicative intentions (Coseriu 2007 [1988]: 88–89).

As a concept, discourse traditions cover wide-ranging cultural traditions of interaction. A very insightful case of discourse-traditional knowledge are communicative routines, e. g., how to start or end a conversation, how to write a private letter, or how to phrase a polite request. However, as cultural patterns of speaking, discourse traditions also include certain styles of verbal interaction, such as modern small talk or the art of gallant speech in the eighteenth century. Moreover, text types or genres can also be understood as discourse traditions or combinations of discourse traditions, for the successful writing of a short story or a leading article is also based on the mastery of the corresponding discourse traditions. Finally, discourse traditions also include literary forms: Coseriu (2007 [1988]: 171–172) cites the sonnet as an example of a cultural tradition of writing that can be translated and thus transferred from one language to another.

Coseriu's system differentiates analytically between three types of principles, rules and traditions which, together, always shape the discourse and at the same time presents them in their interconnectedness. Linguistic traditions and discourse traditions enter into a particularly close connection as discourse traditions select the linguistic means that are used in a situation and are thus the regulating factor (Koch 2005: 231–232). At the same time, discourse traditions only become visible when realized in speech; they need the linguistic material to take shape (Kabatek 2015: 58). The two types of tradition are therefore interdependent, but this interdependency is asymmetrical, the dependencies are of different kinds.

The three sets of knowledge are the core of the Coserian model, but the tripartite system goes beyond the field of knowledge. For integrated into the model are three points of view: language can be conceived as an activity (*enérgeia*), as knowledge underlying this activity (*dýnamis*) and as its product (*érgon*) (Coseriu 2007 [1988]: 71–72). I have already discussed the aspect of *dýnamis*, i.e., the three sets of knowledge, in detail. These three types of rules and traditions have their origin in speaking as a creative activity (*enérgeia*) which generates new rules and traditions beyond the already existing knowledge. The creative force of *enérgeia* is the motor for change in linguistic traditions as well as in discourse traditions and drives language change and the transformation of cultural models of speaking. The product of this activity (*érgon*) are the texts (spoken or written) which can be recorded, passed on, or remembered as something that has been produced in verbal interactions (Coseriu 2007 [1988]: 72). The product manifests itself vividly and clearly above all on the individual level, because products always arise from a specific situation and have an individual speaker as their author.

3 A new system for pragmatics: three levels, three fields, three perspectives

The desideratum of a comprehensive systematization has been brought up several times in pragmatics. A quotation from Escandell Vidal (2004), which is still relevant, may serve as an illustration:

> Pragmatics has reached an outstanding level of development, both in social and inferential approaches; now it is time to work out an integrated theory [...]. Only in this way will we be able to account at the same time for what is universal and what is culture-specific; only in this way will we be able to edge closer to a better, fuller, and richer understanding of human communication. (Escandell Vidal 2004: 366)

The model of the three levels based on Coseriu not only fulfils the requirement of separating universal rules and culture-specific norms of speaking, but goes even further. Coseriu's tripartite system separates universal rules, linguistic traditions and discourse traditions, thus making a clear distinction between universal rules and traditions as well as between two types of tradition. The main potential for pragmatics lies in the cross-classification offered by the model, i.e., the clear distinction between universal knowledge and traditional knowledge on the one hand (universal rules vs. linguistic traditions and discourse traditions) and the differentiation between linguistic knowledge (linguistic traditions) and nonlinguistic knowledge (universal rules, discourse traditions) on the other. In addition, these rules and traditions are systematically recorded in their interactions and dependencies. Thus, linguistic traditions are the material through which discourse traditions as cultural knowledge take shape in discourse. As for the non-linguistic sets of knowledge, the universal principles set a general framework of cooperation to which the discourse traditions add their cultural imprint (Schrott 2015: 129–130, 2020: 25, 27–28).

Both differentiations – cultural vs. universal, linguistic knowledge vs. cultural knowledge – are present in pragmalinguistic research. Thus, Coseriu's model does not bring entirely new categories to pragmatics as such; its power rather lies in its explicit distinctions and systematic cross-references. Thanks to the three types of knowledge Coseriu's system also explains the interdisciplinary nature of pragmatics: the universal rules capture cognitive and semiotic bases of communication, the linguistic traditions include the mastery of languages, and the discourse traditions embrace the cultural models of interaction. Therefore, Coseriu's model offers pragmatics a system that does justice to the nature of pragmalinguistic research which goes far beyond an approach of language restricted to idiomatic knowledge. On the basis of the three levels of linguistic competence, a model of three levels and perspectives of pragmatics can be developed that starts from the point of view of *dýnamis* and focuses on the knowledge of rules and traditions that are effective in speaking (cf. Schrott 2014, 2017a, 2020):

Table 2: Three levels, three fields and three perspectives of pragmatics

Level	Universal level	Historical level	Individual level
Rules and traditions	Universal principles and rules	Linguistic traditions	Discourse traditions
Fields	Universal pragmatics	Language pragmatics	Discourse-traditional pragmatics
Perspectives	Universal	Historical	Historical and cultural

Based on the levels and types of knowledge, three fields and perspectives of pragmatics emerge. The universal principles and rules form the central object of investigation of universal pragmatics, which focuses on fundamental cognitive and communicative-semiotic abilities and aims to explore universal rules and units of speech. The perspective on speaking is universal; the aim is to find universal rules, units and categories of speaking that are valid in all languages and cultures. Examples of the approach of universal pragmatics are the theory of universal speech act types (Searle 1969) and the cooperative principle (Grice 1989). Another example are studies of verbal politeness which examine different languages and cultures in search of universal principles (cf. Brown and Levinson 1987). Universal pragmatics is thus concerned with rules and principles that take shape in particular languages, but are not part of these languages (cf. Coseriu's statement on the scope of pragmalinguistics in Kabatek and Murguía 1997: 159–160).

At the historical level, the focus of language pragmatics is on the forms and structures of particular languages and their potential for verbal interaction. Language pragmatics is dedicated to the study of particular languages, such as English, Spanish, or French. It covers semasiological studies that start from certain elements or structures (e.g., modal particles or tense forms) and examines their functional profiles; it also includes onomasiological studies that investigate the linguistic means which realize cognitive concepts (e.g., modalization or succession in time). Incidentally, this field is the only one in which designations such as 'Spanish pragmatics' or 'English pragmatics', which presuppose reference to particular languages, are justified (cf. Coseriu's statement in Kabatek and Murguía 1997: 159–160). The perspective is historical, since a particular language is examined as it is at a certain time, e.g., the German language spoken at present, the Spanish of the Middle Ages or the French of the seventeenth century.

On the individual level, the discourse traditions as cultural models that shape and guide speech are at the center of attention. Here, the branch of discourse-traditional pragmatics examines cultural traditions that enable successful linguistic interaction by guiding the speaker to select from his or her linguistic repertoire those means that are appropriate and promising in a speech situation. For instance, if a speaker wants to make a request, the discourse traditions valid in his or her cultural community guide the speaker to formulate the request in such a way that it appears neither too submissive nor too demanding and reaches its goal in an appropriate manner; if a private letter is written to a friend, the mastery of the relevant discourse traditions ensures that the writer can create the desired closeness by greeting and addressing the friend in an appropriately warm manner. Discourse-traditional pragmatics has a historical perspective as it explores traditions that are the result of historical developments, and it has at the same time a cultural perspective as it is focused on the cultural knowledge embraced by the very discourse traditions.

Since all three sets of knowledge are present in speech, the three perspectives also merge and overlap, depending on the object of investigation and the research questions. When it comes to the relatedness of universal principles and discourse traditions, this means that even pragmalinguistic research aiming at universal principles must always consider the cultural influence of discourse traditions and that pragmalinguistic approaches concerned with historical and cultural phenomena must always bear in mind the influence of universal rules. In the same way, language pragmatics is not a discipline strictly limited to linguistic structures, because a linguistic element and its functions can only be studied in depth if one considers the universal principles and culture-specific discourse traditions that guide its use.

Close connections also exist between linguistic traditions and discourse traditions which merge in language use, as all speaking is a cultural activity. A central task of language pragmatics and discourse-traditional pragmatics is to recognize how both types of traditions interact in concrete verbal interaction. If, for example, imperative forms in different languages are used in a different way in order to express volitions, the reasons for the divergent use may be at different levels. The imperatives can have different functional profiles in the languages in question which imply that the imperative forms are used in different ways. However, it is also possible that the functional profiles are more or less identical and that the difference can be traced back to divergent cultural discourse traditions of expressing requests. In the first case, the difference lies in the language traditions, i.e., in the different linguistic systems, and the varying imperative use distinguishes the speakers of different language communities. In the second case, the difference lies in the discourse tradition. While the discourse traditions used in one language favor direct volitions with the imperative, the discourse traditions used in the other language prefer indirect requests and avoid using imperatives. In the latter case, the different way of expressing volitions characterizes cultural communities that apply different discourse traditions of requesting. The Coserian system thus provides clear, analytically linked categories that precisely describe the interaction of linguistic traditions and discourse traditions.

In order to have a full understanding of both types of traditions, it is useful to take a closer look at the groups that practice them (Coseriu 2007 [1988]: 86). Language traditions create a community that is constituted through language: people belong to one or more language communities because they speak these languages. Language communities have relatively clear boundaries and their history can be written as the history of well identifiable communities (Coseriu 2007 [1988]: 86–87). Discourse traditions are also practiced by individuals who belong to groups. These groups may be identical with the language communities, but they are usually not (ibid.). Thus – returning to the examples already mentioned – literary forms like the sonnet are mastered by only a relatively small group in a language community. However, discourse traditions with limited accessibility can be present in several language communities, which is the case with sonnets, which have been appropriated as a discourse tradition by small groups of speakers of different languages, so that sonnets exist in Italian, French, German and many other languages. On the other hand, discourse traditions can have an extremely wide range and encompass several language communities; this is the case with certain communicative routines (cf. Schrott 2014, 2017b). The cultural communities that carry traditions of discourse can thus be smaller or larger than a single language community, and they can also embrace smaller groups in several language communities. This differentiation implies that the speakers of a language community may differ considerably in their cultural traditions, while, conversely, speakers with very similar cultural discourse traditions can belong to different language communities.

Both traditions also differ in the type of community they form. Since the average speaker can usually only master a very limited number of languages, he or she belongs to only a few language communities which strongly shape his or her identity. By contrast, the vast majority of speakers practice a far greater number of discourse traditions than languages. This differentiation implies that both types of tradition influence individuals in different ways and shape their identity to different degrees. Regarding the level of particular languages, speakers are closely connected with their languages in all their verbal interactions, whereas discourse traditions are options for the speakers between which they always make new choices when entering a new speech situation.

The model of the three levels, three fields and three perspectives of pragmatics presented above (Table 2) applies to different directions in pragmalinguistic research and can be adapted to the profiles and research questions of these directions. In the following, I will focus on historical and contrastive pragmatics.

4 How to use the model: historical pragmatics and contrastive pragmatics

4.1 Historical pragmatics and the history of language

As linguistic traditions and discourse traditions change over time, the historical dimension is inherent in the model and allows it to be adapted to the topics of historical pragmatics. As a discipline historical pragmatics deals with speaking in former linguistic and cultural communities, analyzing communicative tasks and their solutions in earlier times (cf. Cruz Volio 2017, Iglesias Recuero 2010, 2016, 2017, Schrott 2016, 2020, Taavitsainen and Jucker 2008, 2010, Held 2006, Jung and Schrott 2003). The challenge of historical pragmatics lies in the fact that the discourses, seen as *enérgeia*, belong to the past and that the interactions of earlier times are only accessible as products (*érgon*) created according to traditions of the past that no longer exist or have at least changed significantly. Therefore both types of tradition can only be reconstructed as fragments.

Historical pragmatics can set two different priorities here: it can primarily aim to recover the functional profiles of linguistic structures and thus choose the historical level of particular languages as the focal point, or it can be mainly dedicated to the individual level and the discourse traditions that guided verbal interaction in the past. Nevertheless, historical pragmatics must always take both types of tradition into account, a necessity that is illustrated by the research on verbal politeness (cf. Iglesias Recuero 2017, 2016, 2010, Nevala 2010, Jucker 2012, Schrott 2020). A clear example within this field are requests, which in present-day languages and cultures are frequently expressed through question acts that open up an option – *Can you pass the bread? ¿Puedes pasarme el pan? Tu peux me passer le pain?* – whereas the imperative as a direct way of expressing volition is much less frequent (cf. Brown and Levinson 1987, Lara Bermejo 2018, Siebold 2008, Díaz Pérez 2003, Kerbrat-Orecchioni 2001, van Mulken 1996). Historical studies on English, Spanish and French indicate that in the Middle Ages and early modern times the imperative was the most common form, whereas requests realized with interrogative sentences represent a much more recent development (cf. Frank 2011: 63–65, Kohnen 2008: 27, Schrott 2020: 36–38).

The key question is what exactly has changed. On the one hand, of course, the linguistic traditions have changed. However, linguistic change is not the crucial factor here. What is decisive is that the discourse traditions of polite speech and the associated cultural values have undergone change. Nowadays, polite requests avoid imposing actions on the addressee, instead giving the addressee (at least superficially) options for action. By contrast, the findings in medieval corpora of English, French and Spanish indicate that giving options was not a central value and that volitions were expressed clearly and plainly (cf. Culpeper and Archer 2008: 74–76, Frank 2011: 446–447). The added value of politeness came from expressions of appreciation that accompanied direct volitions (Frank 2011: 173). Therefore, it is reasonable to assume that in English, French and Spanish verbal politeness in the Middle Ages was aimed at the 'positive face' as a desire for appreciation and closeness, whereas verbal politeness today aims to satisfy the 'negative face' as a need for self-determination and freedom of choice (Frank 2011: 446–447, Kohnen 2008: 41–42).

The example of verbal politeness illustrates the advantages of the model of pragmalinguistics inspired by Coseriu. For the question of whether a change affects the linguistic traditions or the discourse traditions is already contained in Coseriu's system and its distinction of the three levels. The same applies to the issue of the universal principles, as the connection to possible universal foundations of polite speech is already given in the system. Furthermore, the Coserian system allows us to fundamentally reflect on the scope of language history. The case of verbal politeness shows that the history of language and speech can only be grasped by an entangled history of language which does not focus solely on linguistic structures, but includes the impact of discourse traditions and thus conceives the history of language as a cultural history (Gardt 2011). The difference between a language history focused on language change and a language history understood as cultural history can be accommodated by Coseriu's model of the three levels. Thus, a history of language that is limited to language change as a change in linguistic structures is situated exclusively on the historical level of languages, whereas an extended history of language, which understands language and speech as cultural phenomena, operates on two levels: on the historical level of languages and on the individual level of discourse traditions.

4.2 Contrastive pragmatics

Another branch of pragmatics that gains from the three-level model is contrastive pragmatics, which explores speaking in different cultural environments and focuses on the diversity of cultural imprints that characterize language use (cf. Díaz Pérez 2003, Jung and Schrott 2003, Siebold 2008, Trosborg 2010, Wierzbicka 2003, 2010). As a discipline, contrastive pragmatics can focus on different language systems, i.e. their structures and functional profiles, which are situated on the historical level of languages, or it can operate primarily on the individual level in order to highlight cultural contrasts in discourse traditions. When exploring cultural differences and similarities, contrastive pragmatics is confronted with the question of whether these common features could possibly constitute a universal rule of speech (Trosborg 2010: 9–10). Another central research question is whether empirically established differences in verbal interaction are caused by different linguistic traditions on the historical level of languages or by different discourse traditions on the individual level of discourse.

To illustrate these research topics, I refer once again to the example of the polite request expressed by interrogative structures as a question act (Schrott 2014, 2017b). As mentioned above, this communicative routine is widely known to speakers of different languages. Such a wide distribution suggests that it is worth examining whether it might represent not a limited cultural tradition, but a universal rule of speech. From this perspective, an indirect request of the type *Can you pass the bread?* would be explained as the universal rule of avoiding potentially impolite directness and using instead an indirect expression that respects the 'negative face' of the addressee. However, evidence against the hypothesis of universality can be found if one expands the spectrum of languages and cultures studied. Thus, research on Polish or Russian shows that these speaker communities have a clear preference for direct requests which are often accompanied by expressions of appreciation and affection which are directed to the 'positive face' of the interlocutor (Wierzbicka 1985: 154–156, 2003: 33–37, 2010: 46–48). The case study of the polite request shows that the widespread technique of realizing polite requests through questions has no universal status but has to be considered as a cultural discourse tradition. If a technique of requesting is the same in several cultures, it must be examined whether a universal principle is effective in such a case or, rather, whether the speaker communities in question share the same cultural patterns and discourse traditions of interaction (Schrott 2014).

The example of verbal politeness shows that studies on contrastive pragmatics are also permanently confronted with the question to what extent verbal interactions in different languages and cultural areas are shaped by the linguistic traditions of the historical level of the individual languages or by the discourse traditions of the individual level. Here, too, the system already takes into account the necessity of this differentiation and, in addition, shows how both types of tradition interact. The methodological necessity, always present in contrastive pragmatics, of examining cultural discourse traditions for their universal part also finds clear guidance in Coseriu's system. In the field of tension between universality and cultural diversity Coseriu's model is able to create a balance, since it shows that universal rules and cultural discourse traditions are always co-present in speaking as an activity (*enérgeia*). To sum up, analogous to historical pragmatics, it also applies to contrastive pragmatics that the Coserian model offers a coherent system that points out clearly the different types of knowledge as well as their complex interdependencies.

5 An open system

Coseriu's linguistics is based on speaking as an activity (*enérgeia*). The sets of knowledge that go into speaking are born out of this activity; they constantly change and renew themselves through the creative power of *enérgeia*. The conceptual proximity of the concept of *enérgeia* to the pragmalinguistic perspective on language as an activity has become clear in the preceding presentation of the three levels of language and language use. Therefore, the interpretation of the Coserian model as a blueprint for pragmatics is not to be considered as a reinterpretation that changes the system, but rather as a creative development which preserves the spirit of the Coserian system while opening up to new research questions that were not originally linked to the model. Under this premise, the distinctions between universal rules, language traditions and discourse traditions can not only enrich pragmalinguistic research but also offer a coherent system for the topics of research as well as for the different fields of pragmatics. The model provides categories that not only give clear distinctions for the three sets of knowledge, but also indicate the complex interdependencies between them. Universal rules are specified culturally and historically by discourse traditions, and discourse traditions choose linguistic traditions for discourse and regulate which linguistic structures are included in the discourse. At the same time, linguistic traditions are always the material in which discourse traditions take shape, so they are in a sense second-order traditions (Kabatek 2015: 57–58).

A great strength of Coseriu's model lies in its integrative power, for it not only provides systematic linking at the level of the objects to be researched, but also organizes various branches of pragmatics (and linguistics in general). Thus, linguistic lines of study dealing with basic cognitive and semiotic abilities operate on the universal level, while culture-oriented branches of linguistics have their focus on the level of discourse traditions. Another important strength is that the model, which is absolutely coherent in itself and therefore in a certain sense self-contained, is at the same time characterized by openness and freedom for further development. This is the concluding thought for a readership that may be getting to know Coseriu's work for the first time: Coseriu's linguistics is a productive system that allows and stimulates innovation. In this way, the concept of *enérgeia* also applies to the system itself.

References

Brown, Penelope and Stephen C. Levinson. 1987. *Politeness. Some universals in language usage.* Cambridge: Cambridge: University Press.
Coseriu, Eugenio. 1955–1956. "Determinación y entorno. Dos problemas de una lingüística del hablar". *Romanistisches Jahrbuch 7*, 29–54.
Coseriu, Eugenio. 1973 [1955–1956]. "Determinación y entorno. Dos problemas de una lingüística del hablar". In: Eugenio Coseriu, *Teoría del lenguaje y lingüística general. Cinco estudios* (third edition), 282–323. Madrid: Gredos.
Coseriu, Eugenio. 1974 [1958]. *Synchronie, Diachronie und Geschichte. Das Problem des Sprachwandels.* München: Fink.
Coseriu, Eugenio. 1985. "Linguistic competence: what is it really?" *The Modern Language Review* 80, 25–35.
Coseriu, Eugenio. 2007 [1988]. *Sprachkompetenz. Grundzüge der Theorie des Sprechens.* Edited by Heinrich Weber (second edition). Tübingen: Narr.
Cruz Volio, Gabriela. 2017. *Actos de habla y modulación discursiva en español medieval: representaciones de (des)cortesía verbal histórica.* Frankfurt am Main: Peter Lang.

Culpeper, Jonathan and Dawn Archer. 2008. "Requests and directness in Early Modern English trial proceedings and play texts, 1640–1760". In: Andreas H. Jucker and Irma Taavitsainen (eds.), *Speech acts in the history of English*, 45–84. Amsterdam & Philadelphia: John Benjamins.

Díaz Pérez, Francisco Javier. 2003. *La cortesía verbal en inglés y en español. Actos de habla y pragmática intercultural*. Jaén: Universidad de Jaén.

Escandell-Vidal, María Victoria. 2004. "Norms and principles. Putting social and cognitive pragmatics together". In: Rosina Márquez Reiter and María Elena Placencia (eds.), *Current trends in the pragmatics of Spanish*, 347–371. Amsterdam & Philadelphia: John Benjamins.

Frank, Birgit. 2011. *Aufforderung im Französischen. Ein Beitrag zur Geschichte sprachlicher Höflichkeit*. Berlin & New York: De Gruyter.

Gardt, Andreas. 2011. "Sprachgeschichte als Kulturgeschichte. Chancen und Risiken der Forschung". In: Péter Maitz (ed.), *Historische Sprachwissenschaft. Erkenntnisinteressen, Grundlagenprobleme, Desiderate*, 289–300. Berlin & Boston: De Gruyter.

Grice, Herbert Paul. 1989. "Logic and conversation". In: Herbert Paul Grice, *Studies in the way of words*, 22–40. Cambridge: Harvard University Press.

Held, Gudrun. 2006. "Schwerpunkte der historischen Pragmalinguistik: Exemplarische Fallstudien". In: Gerhard Ernst, Martin-Dietrich Gleßgen, Christian Schmitt and Wolfgang Schweickard (eds.), *Romanische Sprachgeschichte. Ein internationales Handbuch zur zeitgenössischen Forschung*. Vol. 2, 2302–2318. Berlin & New York: De Gruyter.

Iglesias Recuero, Silvia. 2010. "Aportación a la historia de la (des)cortesía: las peticiones en el siglo XVI". In: Franca Orletti and Laura Mariottini (eds.), *(Des)cortesía en español: espacios teóricos y metodológicos para su estudio*, 369–396. Roma & Estocolmo: Università degli Studi Roma Trè-EDICE & Universidad de Estocolmo.

Iglesias Recuero, Silvia. 2016. "Otra cara de la pragmática histórica: la historia de los actos de habla en español. Peticiones y órdenes en las *Novelas ejemplares* de Cervantes". In: Araceli López Serena, Antonio Narbona Jiménez and Santiago del Rey Quesada (eds.), *El español a través de los tiempos. Estudios ofrecidos a Rafael Cano Aguilar*. Vol. 2, 971–994. Sevilla: Universidad de Sevilla.

Iglesias Recuero, Silvia. 2017. "Mecanismos de atenuación en las peticiones de ayer a hoy". *Lingüística española actual* 39, 289–316.

Jucker, Andreas H. 2012. "Changes in politeness cultures." In: Terttu Nevalainen and Elizabeth Closs Traugott (eds.), *The Oxford handbook of the history of English*, 422–433. Oxford: Oxford University Press,.

Jung, Verena and Angela Schrott. 2003. "A question of time? Question types and speech act shifts from a historical-contrastive perspective. Some examples from Old Spanish and Middle English". In: Kaszia M. Jaszczolt and Ken Turner (eds.), *Meaning through language contrast*. Vol. 2, 345–371. Amsterdam & Philadelphia: John Benjamins.

Kabatek, Johannes. 2015. "Warum die 'zweite Historizität' eben doch die zweite ist – von der Bedeutung von Diskurstraditionen für die Sprachbetrachtung". In: Franz Lebsanft and Angela Schrott (eds.), *Diskurse, Texte, Traditionen. Modelle und Fachkulturen in der Diskussion*, 49–62. Bonn & Göttingen: Bonn University Press & Vandenhoeck & Ruprecht.

Kabatek, Johannes. 2017. "Determinación y entorno: 60 años después". In: Gerda Haßler and Thomas Stehl (eds.), *Kompetenz – Funktion – Variation. Linguistica Coseriana V*, 19–37. Frankfurt am Main: Peter Lang.

Kabatek, Johannes. 2018a. *Lingüística coseriana, lingüística histórica, tradiciones discursivas*. Edited by Cristina Bleorțu and David Gerards. Madrid & Frankfurt a. M.: Vervuert – Iberoamericana.

Kabatek, Johannes and Adolfo Murguía. 1997. *"Die Sachen sagen, wie sie sind…" Eugenio Coseriu im Gespräch*. Tübingen: Narr.

Kerbrat-Orecchioni, Catherine. 2001. *Les actes de langage dans le discours. Théorie et fonctionnement*. Paris: Nathan.

Koch, Peter. 1997. "Diskurstraditionen: zu ihrem sprachtheoretischen Status und ihrer Dynamik". In: Barbara Franz, Thomas Haye and Doris Tophinke (eds.), *Gattungen mittelalterlicher Schriftlichkeit*, 43–79. Tübingen: Narr.

Koch, Peter. 2005. "Sprachwandel und Sprachvariation". In: Angela Schrott and Harald Völker (eds.), *Historische Pragmatik und historische Varietätenlinguistik in den romanischen Sprache*, 229–254. Göttingen: Universitätsverlag Göttingen.

Kohnen, Thomas. 2008. "Directives in Old English: beyond politeness?" In: Andreas H. Jucker and Irma Taavitsainen (eds.), *Speech acts in the history of English*, 27–44. Amsterdam & Philadelphia: Benjamins.

Lara Bermejo, Víctor. 2018. "Imperativos y cortesía en las lenguas romances de la Península Ibérica". *Bulletin of Hispanic studies* 95, 1–24.

Lebsanft, Franz. 2005. "Kommunikationsprinzipien, Texttraditionen, Geschichte". In: Angela Schrott and Harald Völker (eds.), *Historische Pragmatik und historische Varietätenlinguistik in den romanischen Sprachen*, 25–44. Göttingen: Universitätsverlag Göttingen.

Lebsanft, Franz and Angela Schrott. 2015. "Diskurse, Texte, Traditionen". In: Franz Lebsanft and Angela Schrott (eds.), *Diskurse, Texte, Traditionen. Modelle und Fachkulturen in der Diskussion*, 11–46. Bonn & Göttingen: Bonn University Press & Vandenhoeck & Ruprecht.

Nevala, Minna. 2010. "Politeness". In: Andreas H. Jucker and Irma Taavitsainen (eds.), *Historical pragmatics*. Berlin & New York: Mouton de Gruyter, 419–450.

Oesterreicher, Wulf. 1997. "Zur Fundierung von Diskurstraditionen". In: Barbara Frank, Thomas Haye and Doris Tophinke (eds.), *Gattungen mittelalterlicher Schriftlichkeit*, 19–41. Tübingen: Narr.

Schlieben-Lange, Brigitte. 1983. *Traditionen des Sprechens. Elemente einer pragmatischen Sprachgeschichtsschreibung*. Stuttgart & Berlin: Kohlhammer.

Schrott, Angela. 2014. "Sprachwissenschaft als Kulturwissenschaft aus romanistischer Sicht: Das Beispiel der kontrastiven Pragmatik". *Romanische Forschungen* 126, 3–44.

Schrott, Angela. 2015. "Kategorien diskurstraditionellen Wissens als Grundlage einer kulturbezogenen Sprachwissenschaft". In: Franz Lebsanft and Angela Schrott (eds.), *Diskurse, Texte, Traditionen. Modelle und Fachkulturen in der Diskussion*, 115–146. Bonn & Göttingen: Bonn University Press & Vandenhoeck & Ruprecht.

Schrott, Angela. 2016. "Dunkle Rede, helle Köpfe: Historische Dialogforschung in der Romanistik". In: Elmar Eggert and Jörg Kilian (eds.), *Historische Mündlichkeit. Beiträge zur Geschichte der gesprochenen Sprache*, 77–100. Frankfurt am Main: Peter Lang.

Schrott, Angela. 2017a. "Las tradiciones discursivas, la pragmalingüística y la lingüística del discurso". *Revista de la Academia Nacional de Letras* 10, 25–57

Schrott, Angela. 2017b. "Cortesía verbal y competencia lingüística: la petición cortés como tradición discursiva". *Normas: revista de estudios lingüísticos hispánicos* 7, 188–203.

Schrott, Angela. 2020. "Regeln, Traditionen, Urteile: Verbale Höflichkeit und wie sie gelingt". In: Angela Schrott and Christoph Strosetzki (eds.), *Gelungene Gespräche. Literatur, Sprache, Gesellschaft*, 23–54. Berlin & New York: De Gruyter.

Searle, John R. 1969. *Speech acts. An essay in the philosophy of language.* Cambridge: Cambridge University Press.

Siebold, Kathrin. 2008. *Actos de habla y cortesía verbal en español y en alemán. Estudio pragmalingüístico e intercultural.* Frankfurt am Main: Peter Lang.

Taavitsainen, Irma and Andreas H. Jucker. 2008. "Speech acts now and then: Towards a pragmatic history of English". In: Andreas H. Jucker and Irma Taavitsainen (eds.), *Speech acts in the history of English*, 1–23. Amsterdam & Philadelphia: John Benjamins.

Taavitsainen, Irma and Andreas H. Jucker. 2010. "Trends and developments in historical pragmatics". In: Andreas H. Jucker and Irma Taavitsainen (eds.), *Historical pragmatics*, 3–30. Berlin & New York: Mouton de Gruyter.

Trosborg, Anna. 2010. "Introduction". In: Anna Trosborg (ed.), *Pragmatics across languages and cultures*, 1–39. Berlin & New York: Mouton de Gruyter.

van Mulken, Margot. 1996. "Politeness markers in French and Dutch requests". *Language Sciences* 18, 698–702.

Verschueren, Jef. 1995. "The pragmatic perspective". In: Jef Verschueren (ed.), *Handbook of pragmatics*, 1–19. Amsterdam & Philadelphia: John Benjamins.

Verschueren, Jef. 2009. "Introduction: The pragmatic perspective". In: Jef Verschueren and Jan-Ola Östman (eds.), *Key notions for pragmatics*, 1–27. Amsterdam & Philadelphia: John Benjamins.

Wierzbicka, Anna. 1985. "Different cultures, different languages, different speech acts". *Journal of Pragmatics* 9, 145–178.

Wierzbicka, Anna. 2003. *Cross-cultural pragmatics. The semantics of human interaction* (second edition). Berlin & New York: De Gruyter.

Wierzbicka, Anna. 2010. "Cultural Scripts and international communication". In: Anna Trosborg (ed.), *Pragmatics across languages and* cultures, 43–78. Berlin & New York: Mouton de Gruyter.

Johannes Kabatek (Zürich)
Eugenio Coseriu on immediacy, distance and discourse traditions

> *The interesting aspects of the expressive competence are those that in both senses present a certain degree of generality. Such aspects may be 'historical' or 'universal'. They are universal if they have to do with the nature of humans or with human experience in general, and they are historical if they depend on historically determined spheres of experience or culture. This means that expressive competence has its own universality and its own historicity.**

1 Introduction

Peter Koch (1951–2014) and Wulf Oesterreicher's (1942–2015) concepts of 'immediacy' and 'distance' (Koch and Oesterreicher 1985, English translation 2012), as well as Koch's closely related notion of 'discourse traditions' (Koch 1987), are probably the most successful and frequently cited in Romance linguistics in recent decades. They have also been adopted in other disciplines, thus becoming part of the linguistic canon (Feilke and Hennig 2016, Gruber, Grübl and Scharinger 2020). This "canonization" (Kabatek 2000a) might be seen, for example, in the fact that they are often mentioned without explicit reference to the sources, as if it is supposed that they are common knowledge. These concepts are explicitly built on Coseriu's theory of language and are envisaged as filling gaps and covering areas not taken into account by Coseriu. There are only a small number of explicit comments by Coseriu himself on Koch's and Oesterreicher's proposals. However, I believe that it is possible, at least in part, to infer from Coseriu's

---

* "[L]os aspectos interesantes del saber expresivo son los que presentan, en ambos sentidos, cierto grado de generalidad. Tales aspectos pueden ser 'universales' o 'históricos'. Son universales los que se relacionan con la naturaleza propia del hombre y con la experiencia humana general; son históricos los que dependen de ámbitos históricamente determinados de experiencia o de cultura. Es decir que el saber expresivo posee su propia universalidad y su propia historicidad." (Coseriu, *El problema de la corrección idiomática*. Unpublished manuscript, Montevideo 1957). All translations of quotes in this article are mine. I would like to thank the editors, the anonymous reviewers as well as the participants of an Academia.edu discussion forum for their valuable comments on an earlier draft of this paper. Thanks also to Araceli López Serena and Ursula Schaefer for the English versions of Fig. 1 and Fig. 2.

https://doi.org/10.1515/9783110712391-014. The original version of this chapter has been revised: the labeling of Figure 5 on page 238 (left column) has been corrected. An Erratum is available at DOI: https://doi.org/10.1515/9783110712391-024

work his view on the issues they raised, even if to do so entails going back as far as his work from the 1950s, when his theory of language was first outlined. The following pages will begin with some biographical remarks (Section 2) and then briefly present the proposals of Koch and Oesterreicher (Section 3). Section 4 will discuss some explicit reactions by Coseriu, and finally, Section 5 will outline his 'anachronistic reaction' to the proposals found in a still unpublished manuscript on 'linguistic correction' written in Montevideo in the 1950s.

2 Biographical background

The lives of both Wulf Oesterreicher and Peter Koch intersect with that of Eugenio Coseriu. Oesterreicher studied German and Romance Philology in Tübingen from 1962 to 1969 and attended Coseriu's classes. Even if in 1971, he moved to Freiburg im Breisgau as a PhD student and assistant of Hans-Martin Gauger, Coseriu used to consider him a disciple. Oesterreicher's supervisor Gauger had also studied in Tübingen, but he had finished his PhD before Coseriu's arrival in 1963 and, as a disciple of Mario Wandruszka (1911–2004), he partly supported ideas that differed from those of Coseriu, even if he knew well and was influenced by the latter's work. After his appointment as a professor in Freiburg in 1969, Gauger had two assistants who were originally from Tübingen; first, Brigitte Schlieben-Lange (1943–2000), who had finished her PhD under Coseriu's supervision in 1970 before starting to work with Gauger, and second, Wulf Oesterreicher. In Romance linguistics, Freiburg evolved in the 1970s and 1980s, especially after the appointment of Wolfgang Raible (b. 1939) in 1978, into an alternative centre to the almighty Tübingen, adopting new tendencies such as sociolinguistics, pragmatics and text linguistics. It was Brigitte Schlieben-Lange who introduced the young student Peter Koch to Hans-Martin Gauger, suggesting that he should be offered a position as assistant to Gauger's chair. Oesterreicher and Koch became friends and colleagues and jointly discussed current issues in linguistics (see Oesterreicher and Koch 2016). In 1985, the same year in which the collaborative research project 'Transitions and tensions between Orality and Literacy' began its productive activity in Freiburg, they published the seminal paper "Sprache der Nähe – Sprache der Distanz" [Language of immediacy, language of distance] in the journal *Romanistisches Jahrbuch*, a critical and constructive discussion of Coseriu's conception of variational linguistics (see the following section). In 1987, Peter Koch defended his habilitation thesis on Italian medieval traditions of dictating letters, an unpublished work where "immediacy" and "distance" as well as "discourse traditions" are presented exhaustively as crucial concepts (Koch 1987). In 1988, Peter Koch and Wulf Oesterreicher both contributed to the Coseriu Festschrift *Energeia und Ergon* with papers which mention the term "discourse tradition" and thus present it in public for the first time (Koch 1988, Oesterreicher 1988). Ten years later, the two authors published comprehensive papers on the issue in a collective volume (Koch 1997, Oesterreicher 1997).

After Coseriu's retirement, Brigitte Schlieben-Lange was appointed as his successor. A few years later, following the death of Hans-Helmut Christmann (1929–1995), Peter Koch was appointed to the other chair of Romance linguistics at Tübingen, and thereafter Koch and Coseriu would meet regularly in the Romance department. On the occasion of Koch's fiftieth birthday, in 2001, Coseriu called Koch and Oesterreicher's 1990 book in which the conception of immediacy and distance is discussed and illustrated in a comprehensive way a "masterpiece". However, he also reacted somewhat sceptically to their criticism to his theory, as we will see in Section 4.

3 Koch and Oesterreicher's development of Coseriu's theory of language variation

3.1 Based on Ludwig Söll's (1985) observation that "spoken" and "written" are ambiguous terms in that they refer to a purely medial difference, on the one hand, and to different "conceptions", on the other, Koch and Oesterreicher propose for the latter the terms "immediacy" and "distance" in order to take into account a universal continuum along which language is realized. The terms correspond roughly to 'informal' and 'formal' speech. This continuum is not limited to societies with literacy, yet when writing systems do exist, a strong correlation can be observed between written language and 'distance' as well as between spoken language and 'immediacy'.[1] But this is not a causal relationship, and 'distant' texts can be spoken while 'immediate' texts can be written, although this is more exceptional and writing is more likely to be used for texts of distance. Koch and Oesterreicher develop a list of parameters that allow them to situate an utterance or text along the continuum. Essentially, their contribution seeks to identify the particularities of the universal continuum that they establish and its relationship to written and spoken communication. The reference to Coseriu's theory is given at two points. First, the authors adopt Coseriu's three-level distinction between the universal, historical and individual levels (see below). Second, they draw on Coseriu's conception of linguistic varieties

---

[1] This correlation has been empirically demonstrated by Douglas Biber in several works, see e.g. Biber (1988). As for Koch and Oesterreicher and Biber, see Raible (2019).

and the interdependency of these. In the 1950s, Coseriu adopted Leiv Flydal's distinction of 'diatopic' and 'diastratic' varieties and added the 'diaphasic' dimension as a third one in a 'diasystem'.[2] Coseriu had mentioned in several places that there is an ordered relationship between the different dimensions of variation: a dialect may function as a sociolect, and a sociolect as a style, but not vice-versa, as in the case of France, where speakers of *patois* are associated with lower classes and informal speech. Koch and Oesterreicher adopt this idea and call it the "chain of varieties" (G. *Varietätenkette*), and they relate the whole diasystem to the ordering principle of immediacy and distance and to the diasystematic "markedness" of utterances, which can be strong or weak. This leads them to add two further dimensions to Coseriu's 'architecture' of the language: a fourth, idiomatic dimension of immediacy and distance not included in the traditional three, and a universal dimension determining the whole 'building' (to continue the architectural terminology). The difference between the universal and the idiomatic dimensions of immediacy and distance is that the former is the leading principle of all the other dimensions, whereas the latter refers to elements that are related to the difference between written or spoken varieties of a particular language and that are not covered by the other dimensions. The whole system is represented schematically as in Fig. 1:

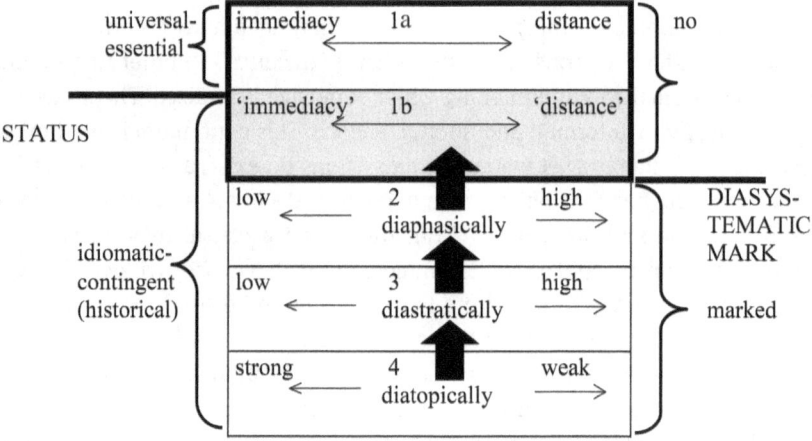

Figure 1: Linguistic varieties between immediacy and distance (Koch and Oesterreicher 1990: 15)

---

[2] The term 'diasystem', used by Coseriu in several works alongside 'architecture', a term he adopts from Flydal (1952), was originally coined by Uriel Weinreich (1954).

3.2 In another scheme (Fig. 2), the authors describe the continuum between immediacy and distance. In the original version of this scheme,[3] Koch and Oesterreicher (1985: 23) describe the aforementioned parameters and their respective two poles (e. g. "private" vs. "public", with or without emotion, physically close or physically distant, etc.). They also introduce examples (the roman numbers in the scheme) for oral or written texts at different points along the continuum, texts such as a family conversation, a private telephone call, a private letter, a scientific talk or a legal text. In later versions, they call these examples of texts, adopting Koch's term, "discourse traditions" (G. *Diskurstraditionen*).

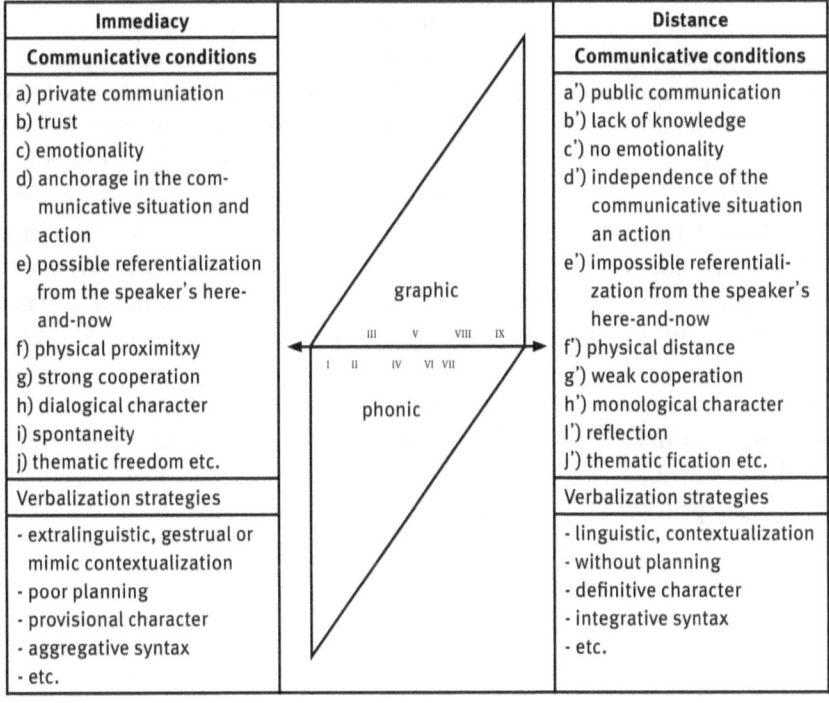

Figure 2: The continuum between immediacy and distance with its conceptional-medial affinities according to Koch and Oesterreicher (1990: 12)

---

3 Dürscheid (2016: 359) relates the success of Koch's and Oesterreicher's proposal to the catchiness of this graph.

As already mentioned, the term "discourse traditions" was introduced publicly by Koch and Oesterreicher in two contributions to a Coseriu Festschrift in 1988. As a term, it goes back to Koch's 1987 habilitation thesis, and as a concept, to Brigitte Schlieben-Lange's 1983 book *Traditionen des Sprechens*, where the term "Texttraditionen" [textual traditions] is used. In the theoretical introduction to Koch's comprehensive empirical study on medieval Italian, he discusses Coseriu's distinction between the universal, historical and individual levels. This distinction was introduced by Coseriu in his paper "Determinación y entorno" (Coseriu 1955–1956), and developed in later publications, when he combined the three levels with the three aspects of *érgon*, *dýnamis* and *enérgeia* (cf. Coseriu 1985: 29). As it allowed for a clear location of the different fields of linguistics, Coseriu (1985: 25) himself believed the three-level distinction (with all its implications) to be his most important contribution to linguistics. Since Koch's aim was to study the tradition of dictating letters in medieval Italian, he discussed where to locate such traditions of texts within Coseriu's scheme. Whereas in Coseriu's conception the historical level is limited to a language's grammar and lexicon, and the individual level seems to be limited to the individual and unique utterance, Coseriu's view, according to Koch, lacks the traditionality of texts; that is, the idea that an utterance might repeat previous utterances or previous forms of utterances, e.g. the form of a letter. This observation led Koch to postulate a twofold distinction of the historical level: to speak or to write is not only to produce a text or utterance following the rules of a language (its grammar and lexicon), but also to refer to previously uttered texts, repeating or altering them. Koch offers two versions of the modified scheme, which also include the individual dimension of the "idiolect", a term explicitly criticized by Coseriu (1974 [1958]: 54–55): one going from the intention to the result, and a second one describing the path from the utterance to its universality:

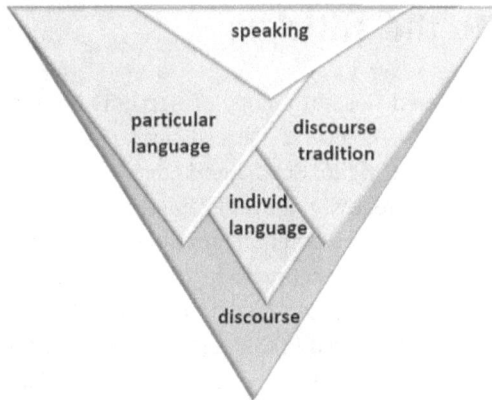

Figure 3: From the speaking activity to discourse (Koch 1987)

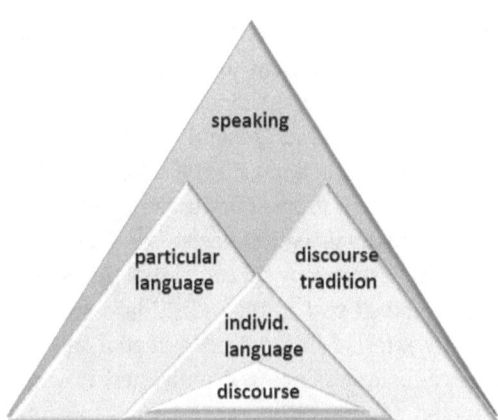

Figure 4: From discourse to speaking activity (Koch 1987)

Koch's criticism touched on an aspect of language that seemed absolutely crucial and that allowed the combination of phenomena like 'intertextuality' or Bakhtin's 'discourse genre' with Coseriu's three-level distinction. The concept of discourse traditions was successfully applied above all in historical linguistics, where it served to offer a differentiated view of the diachrony of a language when combining the traditional notion of historical grammar with that of textual traditions (see e.g. Jacob and Kabatek 2002, Kabatek 2008 and 2018).

4 Coseriu's reaction to the criticism

4.1 When Brigitte Schlieben-Lange offered Coseriu a copy of her 1983 book on historical pragmatics (Schlieben-Lange 1983), Coseriu thanked her for the "excellent book on an issue that does not exist" (Brigitte Schlieben-Lange, p.c.). Coseriu in most cases respected the individual creativity of his disciples, and he knew that Brigitte Schlieben-Lange had, through her popular introductions to pragmatics and sociolinguistics, made parts of his theory widely known in circles where hitherto it had been largely ignored (Schlieben-Lange 1973, 1979). And Coseriu obviously saw that the phenomena described in that later book touched on something that historical linguistics had neglected for a long time. But he was sceptical about the concept of 'historical pragmatics'. In fact, he almost avoided the term 'pragmatics'; in any case 'pragmatics' was for him incompatible with history: what was commonly called pragmatics was about the individual level, the individual utterance and its uniqueness, but above all about the universal level of what he called in Spanish *lingüística del hablar*, 'linguistics of speaking', and universality has no history. In a discussion with Brigitte Schlieben-Lange and Harald Weydt on the historicity of speech acts (Schlieben-Lange and Weydt 1979), Coseriu denies the historicity of speech acts (in the sense of universal acts), distinguishing three kinds of historicity: the historicity of language, historicity in the sense of "tradition" or "repetition", and "general" historicity in the sense of uniqueness in history. The historicity of language is the historicity of the language system itself: languages are historically grown entities, and their speakers grow into the language and grow the language within themselves. This means that the history of a particular language is assumed by the individual through the process of acquisition: the language becomes part of the individual's self, and thereby the assumed history is not an external one but an essential, internal one. In this sense, language seems 'a-historic' since the individual is within this history and may create an unlimited number of utterances out of this interiorized and history-independent competence. The second kind of history is the history of repetition of texts or text forms (forms, formula, genres): of *érga*. And the third one is the 'general historicity' of any historical event and its uniqueness. All three historicities are of course separable only methodologically and appear as co-present in any concrete text or utterance. In this sense, this sentence is part of a unique text, it represents a scientific essay and it is written in English.

Coseriu's distinction of three historicities is not a reaction to Koch's introduction of the concept of discourse traditions, but the aforementioned discussion takes place in a context that is close to the Freiburg discussions of the early

1980s. And Coseriu's distinction seems, at first glance, to be absolutely compatible with Koch's scheme: the historicity of language would be the one of the 'left' historical level in Koch's scheme, the secondary historicity of tradition would be the one of the 'right' historical level and, finally, the 'general belonging to history' would be the unique place in history of the individual utterance, thus the individual level. But, as we will see, this is not exactly Coseriu's view, and I will return to a discussion of the locus of secondary historicity within the three-level distinction in Section 5.

4.2 In the case of the distinction between immediacy and distance, there is a direct reaction by Coseriu to the model. During the interviews I had with Coseriu together with my colleague Adolfo Murguía in 1994 and 1995 (Kabatek and Murguía 1997: 153), Coseriu answered the following question:

> JK: From time to time, people say that Coseriu has not taken into account or has not been aware of this or that, and there are people who say "the building is lacking a window" or "there is a door missing". Do these criticisms touch on real limitations? Would you say that the critics have not looked at the entire building or that they tend to add something where it is not sufficiently well developed? For example, in the context of research into orality and literacy over recent years the criticism has arisen that the "central dimension oral-written" has not been taken into account when describing linguistic varieties.
>
> C: These are often misunderstandings. For example, the distinction between written and spoken is by no means the central one for me when we distinguish varieties. These are different realizations that can have their own traditions but that do not correspond to a general type of varieties in the sense of spatial, socio-cultural or stylistic varieties, first of all because there are no different communities. I consider the spoken language as a "group of language styles", what I call "register". This is explicitly described in *La corrección idiomática* but it was not further developed. The difference is similar to the one we find in language styles. Here, however, there are several styles becoming one register, and even another language may become a register. We can, for example, have Latin for a series of uses and another language, a Romance language or German, for other purposes etc. But it is something different to say that I have not developed this further, and in a way I am glad that others are doing it and that now the Italians also talk about "diamesic" varieties etc. [...]

The situation here is that of an interview, and thus the answer is spontaneous and somewhat incomplete; it is evidently not a fully-fledged response to Koch and Oesterreicher's theory. On other occasions, Coseriu made very positive comments about their contribution, and he had great respect for the fact that they had opened up an important field for linguistic investigation. However, what is important in his comment here is that he identifies his manuscript on linguistic correctness as the place where he discusses in a comprehensive way the questions raised by Koch and Oesterreicher, and that he did not have time to elaborate further on these issues. In the following section, I will take a look at this manuscript and see if it helps us to clarify Coseriu's views.

5 Coseriu on immediacy, distance and discourse traditions 'avant la lettre'

5.1 Up to this point, the picture still seems to be vague: Koch and Oesterreicher criticise Coseriu's theoretical views in a 'sympathetic', constructive way, adding several concepts while appearing to confirm and validate the basic variational theory proposed by Coseriu. Coseriu, on the other hand, shows a positive attitude towards this constructive elaboration, as well as some clear signs of rejection. The rejection in the interview is a spontaneous one, with few details. A consideration of the earlier manuscript on linguistic correctness by Coseriu may, however, yield some 'anachronistic' answers to the questions raised by Koch and Oesterreicher. Let us begin with the notion of discourse tradition and then move on to the more general conception of immediacy and distance.

5.2 For Koch, the basic argument for the need of the concept of discourse tradition is that, in Coseriu's terms, there is only linguistic historicity of a language (a grammar and a lexicon); that is, there is no historicity of texts or discourses. There is, of course, traditionality in the sense of habitual realizations of the system (Coseriu's 'norm'), and there is also what Coseriu calls "repeated discourse", the possibility of the insertion of fixed textual fragments or phraseologisms.[4] But there seems to be no place for the overall present historicity of texts in the second sense. A text or discourse is a unique event and "by definition", as Koch states, it only has a unique history in the aforementioned third sense. For Koch, the individual level is indeed the level of this third sense, and Coseriu's secondary historicity is not included in the three-level distinction. Koch therefore postulates the addition of discourse traditions parallel to linguistic historicity on the same level (for the following, see also Kabatek 2018: 14–18).

---

4 I would like to thank an anonymous reviewer for pointing out that Coseriu considers the competence of "repeated discourse" as an "idiomatic textual competence" (alongside with an idiomatically determined knowledge of 'things') located at the historical level: "On the historical level we must distinguish between *extralinguistic competence* (Sp. *saber idiomático extralingüístico*) (the traditional knowledge about the 'things' that also includes the traditional ideas and beliefs about the things), *idiomatic 'textual' competence* (*saber idiomático 'textual'*) (knowledge of 'texts' transmitted as such in a language community, e.g. proverbs, sayings, idioms, etc.) and the *traditional technique of speaking* (*técnica tradicional del hablar*) ('language' *sensu stricto*)" (Coseriu 1991 [1977]: 258; italics in the original).

> On the other hand, expressive competence is neither actual nor individual. The [...] rules of discourse, this is what we must specify now, offer patterns to the speaker for adequately designing the actual discourse. They indicate *discourse traditions:* styles, genres, text types, discourse universes, speech acts, etc., each of them gathering together classes of discourses. Given that this knowledge is historically marked all the way through, expressive knowledge must be part of the same level as idiomatic knowledge. (Koch 1987: 31; italics in the original)

Koch's argumentation is convincing if we start out from the idea that the individual level is purely 'actual' and 'individual': mere actuality can only be historical in an *a posteriori* sense of the 'third' historicity, and as mere actuality it does not even correspond to 'competence' or 'knowledge', given that these imply a 'background', a certain historical stability. But if we take a closer look at Coseriu's texts, above all at the unpublished manuscript on linguistic correctness,[5] we can see not only that Coseriu was wholly aware of the historicity of texts, but that he also included it in his general view on language. He explicitly mentions textual tradition and talks about "expressive historicity", the historicity of the individual level, alongside the "expressive universality" ("expressive" is here referring to the individual, the textual level). The first example of textual traditionality offered by Coseriu is the one in formulaic language such as Eng. *good morning, good evening,* Sp. *buenos días, buenas tardes,* Fr. *bonjour* etc. He argues that regarding the translation of these forms, it is not a matter of translating language but rather translating a text: Sp. *buenos días* is not 'good days' in English but rather 'good morning' (cf. Coseriu 1985: xxx). Coseriu explicitly discusses the issue of the existence of a linguistic competence on the individual level:

> At the same time, we must observe that – even if it's true that the level of language to which expressive competence belongs is 'particular' in the sense that it deals with individual, concrete and occasional realizations of linguistic activity – this does not imply that such competence is particular in its content and its sphere of application. It is not even necessarily individual in its extension in linguistic communities.
>
> The content of the individual competence applies to *types* of circumstances and of discourses. It does not refer, for example, to 'how to talk to this child, here and now', but rather to how to talk to children in general, or at least to 'how to talk to this child in several situations': otherwise it would not be a competence (Sp. *de otro modo, no sería un saber*). And in its extension, this competence may in some aspects belong to very limited communities and

---

5 In his reflections, Koch refers to Coseriu (1973 [1972]) and (1981 [1980]) even if he must have known the unpublished manuscript on linguistic correction since he refers to it in Koch (1987). Some of the relevant passages of the manuscript were published in German translation in the 1988 Festschrift for Coseriu, cf. Coseriu (1988 [1957]). As for criticism of Koch's restricted view of the individual level, see Lebsanft (2015).

even to one single individual, but it also presents aspects of a much larger extension. For example, only the best friends of Juan Pérez Alonso might know how you have to speak with him when he is angry after having lost a bet, and maybe only his best friend José Sánchez knows how, but to know how to speak with a friend is a competence of an indefinite number of individuals. However, apart from some special cases, the interesting aspects of expressive competence are those that in both senses present a certain degree of generality. Such aspects may be 'historical' or 'universal'. They are universal if they have to do with the nature of humans or with human experience in general, and they are historical if they depend on historically determined spheres of experience or culture. *This means that expressive competence has its own universality and its own historicity.* There are, in fact, universal (non-idiomatic) ways of speaking in certain circumstances and universal ways of structuring certain types of discourse (e.g. narrative discourse) [...], and, by analogy, historical modes of both species (Coseriu, ms., emphasis mine, J.K.).

What Koch calls "discourse tradition" is thus part of Coseriu's three-level distinction: it is the level of the historicity of texts.[6] Given that Coseriu not only mentions the historicity of texts but also the universality of texts, we can infer that there are aspects of each higher level on each lower level, and that there must also be universality of the historical level. This means that a more complete scheme of the three-level distinction would be as follows:[7]

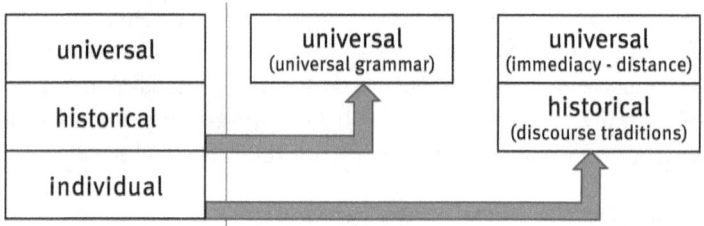

Figure 5: Coseriu's three-level distinction with the addition of higher-level aspects of the lower levels

---

6 This view is also clearly expressed in Coseriu's theory of text linguistics (Coseriu 1981 [1980]). In the introduction to the Spanish edition of this book (Coseriu 2007 [1980]), Óscar Loureda Lamas emphasises the three-level distinction of the individual level. Other scholars have also insisted on the necessity of locating the traditionality of texts on the individual level (see Lebsanft and Schrott 2015: 22).

7 Schlieben-Lange (1990: 115), Loureda Lamas (2005) and López Serena (2012: 270; see also López Serena, in press) offer similar schemes for the individual level derived from Coseriu's observations in his book on text linguistics, as well as from the unpublished *El problema de la corrección idiomática*.

The three levels on the left (which, as the whole scheme, should in fact be considered adding a third dimension with the three aspects of *enérgeia*, *dýnamis* and *érgon*) can be read from the universal to the individual level. The universal level refers to universal linguistic facts, the language faculty prior to the distinction of languages, the axiomatic fact that a language is a system of abstract arbitrary signs created as interindividual conventions and that these systems are being built up in communication among human groups. The historical level refers to historical systems and norms, to take an example, the grammar of modern standard Spanish. This grammar includes e.g. rules for nominal determination such as the rule that a common noun in subject position cannot appear without a determiner under normal conditions of stress, so I must say *la casa es grande* 'the house is big' or *esta casa es grande* etc. but I cannot simply say **casa es grande* 'house is big'. The individual level is the one of unique individual utterances based on that grammar, and it includes individual deviations. To continue with nominal determination: if in a concrete situation someone says e.g. in Spanish *este Pablo es increible* ('this Pablo is incredible') and not *Pablo es increíble* ('Pablo is incredible'), then the hearer is invited to interpret the nuance expressed by that concrete utterance in a concrete situation (in the sense of the meaning *here*, the 'meaning of the meaning' in a concrete setting). If an individual 'pragmatic' need is repeated and creates a tradition, we arrive at the level of discourse traditions, e.g. if there is a tradition of omitting determiners in newspaper headlines or in telegrams due to the lack of space. This means that the historicity of individual utterances is the tradition of texts, i.e. discourse tradition. Finally, immediacy and distance would be the universal principles underlying all textual productions (see the next section).

The universality that derives from the historical level is (to continue with the example of nominal determination) a general or 'universal' conception of grammars of determination, e.g., in a generative framework, the DP-Hypothesis and the idea that there is a universality that can be derived from the determiner systems in languages. Of course, the idea of UG in generative grammar is considered to be top-down and not bottom-up, but this is only a matter of a subjective point of view and not of empirical evidence. In my view, the universality of the historical level is derived, that is, it does not arise from principles prior to the distinction of particular languages; rather, it extracts universality from particular languages.

5.3 This brings us to the second point, the distinction between 'immediacy' and 'distance'. Two issues need to be discussed here: the universal dimension of immediacy and distance as well as its language-specific dimension. As for the universal dimension, immediacy and distance are the two poles that universally determine the making of a text: reference to objects in a speech event or the creation of a reference in a written text (and all the dimensions listed by Koch and Oesterreicher in Fig. 2) are matters of a concrete text, but the dimensions as such are universal. This means that in Coseriu's scheme, 'immediacy' and 'distance' would be categories of the universality of texts or utterances, and both 'discourse traditions' and 'immediacy and distance' identify and develop necessary distinctions that take their starting point in the individual level.

But what about the language-specific dimension of 'immediacy' and 'distance' as a fourth dimension of language variation? In Kabatek (2000a), I questioned the need for a fourth dimension, claiming that what had been offered by Koch and Oesterreicher to illustrate the need for it (e.g. the *passé simple* in French as an almost exclusively written form) could simply be interpreted as phenomena of a diaphasic variety situationally limited to certain forms of written texts (this has previously been observed in a similar way by Albrecht 1986–1990).

5.4 Having identified the historicity and the universality of the individual level, the question that remains is whether there is still a need for the historical and the universal level in the left-hand column of our scheme (Fig. 5). Several scholars have proposed to prioritize the level of the text, and to consider the remaining dimensions to be mere instances of this basic dimension.[8] We could say that Coseriu postulates a historical level of the language because the historical situation of the 1950s prompted him to look at language from a structuralist point of view. This is probably true, but it does not mean that such a view is outdated or obsolete. Of course, Coseriu's aim was basically to identify the necessary distinctions of dimensions in the architecture of a language that could be the loci of structurally different varieties. And the architecture of a language, that is, its varieties, reflect those systems that have historically arisen in different places, among different groups, and in different situations. They are, then, the historical result of systematization that emerged from communicative situations and, at the same time, the basis for communication in different situations. This is also true for the textual traditions that are the historical result of communicative needs between immediacy and distance. Yet the basic difference between a variety (a dialect, a sociolect or a style) and a textual tradition is that the latter depends on concrete models, on *erga*, whereas the former is a system independent of its concrete realizations, a system of rules that allow for the creation, *enérgeia*, of an unlimited number of concrete texts, including the creation of new rules.[9]

---

[8] See, e.g., the tradition of textual grammar in the line of Harald Weinrich or, in a different framework, some more recent constructionalist approaches.
[9] It should, however, be added that the repetition of texts is also a creative act, it includes innovation, deviation or simply the creativity of repetition. In this sense, it is *érgon in enérgeia*.

6 Conclusions

Koch and Oesterreicher introduced new terms and concepts that made it possible to focus on two fundamental dimensions of human language: the 'universality' and the 'historicity' of texts or utterances between immediacy and distance. Both dimensions are considered to be amplifications or corrections of Coseriu's three-level model of language. However, as we have seen, the two phenomena were not ignored by Coseriu: as well as accommodating the universality of the text in the context of his *lingüística del hablar*, he describes in his unpublished book on linguistic correction the traditionality or historicity of texts or utterances as a historical dimension of the individual level. Thus, instead of duplicating the historical level and adding the historicity of the texts as a parallel historicity of language, and instead of postulating the centrality of immediacy and distance in variational linguistics, Fig. 5 combines Coseriu's model with Koch's and Oesterreicher's additions. The result is somewhat different from what Koch and Oesterreicher proposed. But the phenomena that they were focusing on are real, and their identification as such dovetails with Coseriu's postulate to "say things as they are".

References

Albrecht, Jörn. 1986–1990. "'Substandard' und 'Subnorm'. Die nicht-exemplarischen Ausprägungen der 'Historischen Sprache' aus varietätenlinguistischer Sicht". In: Günter Holtus and Edgar Radtke (eds.), *Sprachlicher Substandard*, 65–88, Tübingen, Niemeyer (1986), and in: Günter Holtus and Edgar Radtke (eds.), *Sprachlicher Substandard III*, 44–127. Tübingen, Niemeyer (1990).

Biber, Douglas. 1988. *Variation across speech and writing*. Cambridge: Cambridge University Press.

Coseriu, Eugenio. 1955–1956. "Determinación y entorno. Dos problemas de una lingüística del hablar". *Romanistisches Jahrbuch 7*, 29–54.

Coseriu, Eugenio (ms. 1957). *El problema de la corrección idiomática*. Unpublished manuscript, Montevideo 1957. Transcription by Johannes Kabatek and Reinhard Meisterfeld, Tübingen.

Coseriu, Eugenio. 1973 [1972]. *Die Lage in der Linguistik* (= *Innsbrucker Beiträge zur Sprachwissenschaft*, Vorträge 9). Innsbruck: Universität Innsbruck Institut für vergleichende Sprachwissenschaft.

Coseriu, Eugenio. 1974 [1958]. *Synchronie, Diachronie und Geschichte. Das Problem des Sprachwandels*. München: Wilhelm Fink. (German translation of Coseriu 1958.)

Coseriu, Eugenio. 1978 [1958]. *Sincronía, diacronía e historia. El problema del cambio lingüístico* (third edition). Madrid: Gredos.

Coseriu, Eugenio. 1981 [1980]. *Textlinguistik. Eine Einführung*. Edited by Jörn Albrecht (second edition). Tübingen: Narr.
Coseriu, Eugenio. 1985. "Linguistic competence: what is it really?" *The Modern Language Review* 80:4, xxv–xxxv.
Coseriu, Eugenio. 1988 [1957]. "Die Ebenen des sprachlichen Wissens. Der Ort des 'Korrekten' in der Bewertungsskala des Gesprochenen". Chapter 2 of Coseriu (ms. 1957). German translation by Susanne Höfer. In: Jörn Albrecht, Jens Lüdtke and Harald Thun (eds.), *Energeia und Ergon. Sprachliche Variation – Sprachgeschichte – Sprachtypologie. Studia in honorem Eugenio Coseriu*, Vol. I: *Schriften von Eugenio Coseriu (1965–1987)*, 327–364. Tübingen: Narr.
Coseriu, Eugenio. 1991 [1977]. *El hombre y su lenguaje. Estudios de teoría y metodología lingüística* (second edition). Madrid: Gredos.
Coseriu, Eugenio. 2007 [1994]. *Lingüística del texto*. Edited by Óscar Loureda Lamas. Madrid: Arco/Libros. (Spanish translation of Coseriu 1981 [1980].)
Dürscheid, Christa. 2016. "Nähe, Distanz und neue Medien". In: Helmuth Feilke and Mathilde Hennig (eds.), *Zur Karriere von 'Nähe und Distanz'. Rezeption und Diskussion des Koch-Oesterreicher-Modells*, 357–385. Berlin & Boston: De Gruyter.
Feilke, Helmuth and Mathilde Hennig (eds.). 2016. *Zur Karriere von 'Nähe und Distanz'. Rezeption und Diskussion des Koch-Oesterreicher-Modells*. Berlin & Boston: De Gruyter.
Flydal, Leiv. 1952. "Remarques sur certains rapports entre le style et l'état de langue". *Norsk Tidsskrift for Sprogvidenskap* 16, 241–258.
Gruber, Teresa, Klaus Grübl and Thomas Scharinger (eds.). 2020. *Was bleibt von kommunikativer Nähe und Distanz? Mediale und konzeptionelle Aspekte von Diskurstraditionen und sprachlichem Wandel*. Tübingen: Narr.
Jacob, Daniel and Johannes Kabatek (eds.). 2001. *Lengua medieval y tradiciones discursivas en la Península Ibérica: descripción gramatical – pragmática histórica – metodología*. Madrid & Frankfurt: Iberoamericana & Vervuert.
Kabatek, Johannes. 2000a. "L'oral et l'écrit – quelques aspects théoriques d'un 'nouveau' paradigme dans le canon de la linguistique romane". In: Wolfgang Dahmen, Günter Holtus, Johannes Kramer, Michael Metzeltin, Wolfgang Schweickard and Otto Winkelmann (eds.), *Kanonbildung in der Romanistik und in den Nachbardisziplinen. Romanistisches Kolloquium XIV*, 305–320. Tübingen: Narr.
Kabatek, Johannes. 2018a. *Lingüística coseriana, lingüística histórica, tradiciones discursivas*. Edited by Cristina Bleorțu and David Gerards. Madrid & Frankfurt a. M.: Vervuert – Iberoamericana.
Kabatek, Johannes (ed.). 2008. *Sintaxis histórica del español y cambio lingüístico: Nuevas perspectivas desde las tradiciones discursivas*. Madrid & Frankfurt: Iberoamericana & Vervuert.
Kabatek, Johannes and Adolfo Murguía. 1997. *"Die Sachen sagen, wie sie sind…". Eugenio Coseriu im Gespräch*. Tübingen: Narr.
Koch, Peter. 1987. *Distanz im Dictamen. Zur Schriftlichkeit und Pragmatik mittelalterlicher Brief- und Redemodelle in Italien*. Unpublished habilitation thesis, Freiburg im Breisgau.
Koch, Peter. 1988. "Norm und Sprache". In: Jörn Albrecht, Jens Lüdtke and Harald Thun (eds.), *Energeia und Ergon. Sprachliche Variation – Sprachgeschichte – Sprachtypologie. Studia in honorem Eugenio Coseriu*, Vol. II: *Das sprachtheoretische Denken Eugenio Coserius in der Diskussion (2)*, 327–354. Tübingen: Narr.

Koch, Peter. 1997. "Diskurstraditionen: zu ihrem sprachtheoretischen Status und ihrer Dynamik". In: Barbara Frank, Thomas Haye and Doris Tophinke (eds.), *Gattungen mittelalterlicher Schriftlichkeit*, 43–79. Tübingen: Narr.

Koch, Peter and Wulf Oesterreicher. 1985. "Sprache der Nähe – Sprache der Distanz. Mündlichkeit und Schriftlichkeit im Spannungsfeld von Sprachtheorie und Sprachgeschichte". *Romanistisches Jahrbuch* 36, 15–43

Koch, Peter and Wulf Oesterreicher. 1990. *Gesprochene Sprache in der Romania: Französisch, Italienisch, Spanisch*. Tübingen: Niemeyer (second edition: Berlin & New York: De Gruyter, 2011).

Koch, Peter and Wulf Oesterreicher. 2012. "Language of inmediacy – language of distance: orality and literacy from the perspective of language theory and linguistic history". In: Claudia Lange, Beatrix Weber and Göran Wolf (eds.), *Communicative spaces: variation, contact, change. Papers in honour of Ursula Schaefer*, 441–473. Frankfurt: Peter Lang. (English translation of Koch and Oesterreicher 1985.)

Lebsanft, Franz. 2015. "Aktualität, Individualität und Geschichtlichkeit. Zur Diskussion um den theoretischen Status von Diskurstraditionen und Diskursgemeinschaften". In: Franz Lebsanft and Angela Schrott (eds.), *Diskurse, Texte, Traditionen. Methoden, Modelle und Fachkulturen in der Diskussion*, 97–113. Bonn: Bonn University Press.

Lebsanft, Franz and Angela Schrott. 2015. "Diskurse, Texte, Traditionen". In: Franz Lebsanft and Angela Schrott (eds.), *Diskurse, Texte, Traditionen. Methoden, Modelle und Fachkulturen in der Diskussion*, 11–46. Bonn: Bonn University Press.

López Serena, Araceli. 2012. "Lo universal y lo histórico en el saber expresivo: variación situacional vs. variación discursive". *Analecta Malacitana*, Anejos 86, 261–281.

López Serena, Araceli. In press. "La tradicionalidad discursiva como materia y las tradiciones discursivas como objeto de estudio". *Verba*.

Loureda Lamas, Óscar. 2005. "El texto según Coseriu". In: Jesús Martínez del Castillo (ed.), *Eugenio Coseriu in memoriam*, 101–122. Granada: Granada Lingüística.

Oesterreicher, Wulf. 1988. "Sprechtätigkeit, Einzelsprache, Diskurs und vier Dimensionen der Sprachvarietät". In: Jörn Albrecht, Jens Lüdtke and Harald Thun (eds.), *Energeia und Ergon. Sprachliche Variation – Sprachgeschichte – Sprachtypologie. Studia in honorem Eugenio Coseriu*, Vol. II: *Das sprachtheoretische Denken Eugenio Coserius in der Diskussion (2)*, 355–386. Tübingen: Narr.

Oesterreicher, Wulf. 1997. "Zur Fundierung von Diskurstraditionen". In: Barbara Frank, Thomas Haye and Doris Tophinke (eds.), *Gattungen mittelalterlicher Schriftlichkeit*, 19–41. Tübingen: Narr.

Oesterreicher, Wulf and Peter Koch. 2016. "30 Jahre 'Sprache der Nähe – Sprache der Distanz'. Zu Anfängen und Entwicklung von Konzepten im Feld von Mündlichkeit und Schriftlichkeit". In: Helmuth Feilke and Mathilde Hennig (eds.), *Zur Karriere von 'Nähe und Distanz'. Rezeption und Diskussion des Koch-Oesterreicher-Modells*, 11–72. Berlin & Boston: De Gruyter.

Raible, Wolfgang. 2019. "Variation in language: how to characterise types of texts and communication strategies between orality and scripturality. Answers given by Koch and Oesterreicher and by Biber". *International Journal of Language and Linguistics* 6, 157–174.

Schlieben-Lange, Brigitte. 1973. *Soziolinguistik. Eine Einführung*. Stuttgart: Kohlhammer.

Schlieben-Lange, Brigitte. 1979. *Linguistische Pragmatik*. Stuttgart: Kohlhammer.

Schlieben-Lange, Brigitte. 1983. *Traditionen des Sprechens. Elemente einer pragmatischen Sprachgeschichtsschreibung*. Stuttgart: Kohlhammer.
Schlieben-Lange, Brigitte. 1990. "Normen des Sprechens, der Sprache und der Texte". In: Werner Bahner, Joachim Schildt and Dieter Viehweger (eds.), *Proceedings of the Fourteenth International Congress of Linguists, Berlin, GDR, August 10 – August 15, 1987*. Vol. I, 114–124. Berlin: Akademie-Verlag.
Schlieben-Lange, Brigitte and Harald Weydt [mit Beiträgen von Eugenio Coseriu und Hans-Ulrich Gumbrecht]. 1979. "Streitgespräch zur Historizität von Sprechakten". *Linguistische Berichte* 60, 65–78.
Söll, Ludwig. 1985. *Gesprochenes und geschriebenes Französisch* (third edition). Berlin: Schmidt.
Weinreich, Uriel. 1954. "Is a structural dialectology possible?" *Word* 10, 388–400.

Andreas Widoff (Lund)
System, norm and meaning

> Whereas the norm includes everything that is traditional realisation in a language, the system is restricted to the functional oppositions, that is, everything that is distinctive in the technique of a particular language [...].*

1 Introduction

The distinction between system and norm, which was first proposed in 1952 (Coseriu 1975 [1952]), suggests that a language cannot be characterised as a uniform structure that unambiguously prescribes and proscribes certain linguistic expressions. System and norm are different levels of linguistic organisation that correspond to different fashions in which linguistic manifestations belong to a language. The norm is the established tradition and comprises what is common and proper in a language. The system is the functional structure and comprises the oppositions that delimit the possibilities of a language. The system provides the speakers with the means to transcend, and possibly transform, normal language use. Speakers who use a language in a deviant manner are therefore not necessarily in violation of the system, although they will be in breach of the norm. For example, the sentence *I have a hunger* is possible and comprehensible in English (cf. *I have a headache, I have a sensation*), but it is not in accordance with the norm if the speaker wishes to express his desire for food. In that case, the norm prescribes *I'm hungry*. The system permits more than is tolerated by the norm.

The distinction between system and norm should not be entirely alien to contemporary linguistics. It strikes a note that I believe is intuitively understood and appreciated in many quarters of the discipline. Coseriu (1992 [1988]: 293) himself remarks that proponents of generative grammar refer to a similar fact about linguistic structure with the notion of "degrees of grammaticality". One

---

Acknowledgements: This research was supported by *Vetenskapsrådet* (The Swedish Research Council), grant 2020–00252. I am grateful for comments on a previous draft from Johan Blomberg, Göran Sonesson, Jordan Zlatev, two anonymous reviewers and the editors. I also thank Miklas Scholz and Simon Devylder for indispensable aid with the uses of *mit* and *avec*.

* "Während die Norm all das beinhaltet, was traditionelle Realisierung ist, enthält das *System* nur die funktionellen Oppositionen, nämlich alles, was in einer einzelsprachlichen Technik distinktiv ist [...]" (Coseriu 1992 [1988]: 298).

https://doi.org/10.1515/9783110712391-015

might add that it also bears a resemblance to the distinction between grammaticality and acceptability (Chomsky 1965), although such comparisons should not be drawn too far. The distinction between system and norm, however, is not in common use and is little known outside the circles where Coseriu's work already exerts an influence.

The purpose of the present article is to introduce the concepts of system and norm to a wider audience, to demonstrate their utility and to discuss their application in semantics. The next section places the concepts in the context of their inception and provides examples of how they apply to different phenomena. The remainder of the article is devoted to a matter that is scarcely treated in Coseriu's own work: how the distinction applies to the semantic interpretation of roots. For reasons that will become clear, roots are an interesting case where one consequence of the distinction is especially radical and revealing, namely that roots have deviant uses that are permitted by the system. I will propose that *married with him* is one such use of *with* in English.

2 Refining the Saussurean dichotomy

Coseriu's concepts of system and norm spring from the concern that Saussure's (1916) concepts of *langue* and *parole* are rather too coarse. As such, the concern is not original, and it did in fact unite many linguists in the decades following the publication of Saussure's *Cours de linguistique générale* (cf. Saussure 2011 [1916]). There were many proposals on how to improve the Saussurean concepts, put forward by scholars like Jespersen (1925), Bally (1926), Gardiner (1932), Bühler (1934), Brøndal (1937), Trubetzkoy (1958 [1939]), Sechehaye (1940), Hjelmslev (1942, 1943), von Wartburg (1943), Martinet (1948), Møller (1949) and Flydal (1952). In this row of contributions, Coseriu's (1975 [1952]) is the last, and it drew substantially on earlier work. One would be amiss not to mention the similarity with ideas of Trubetzkoy and Hjelmslev. While the distinctive phonemes of the system are his main concern, Trubetzkoy (1958 [1939]: 42) recognises that the choice between variants may constitute a 'norm' in itself, namely if the choice is socially relevant, such as is the case if only one variant is normal, whereas others are seen as regional, social, affectatious, or pathological deviations. Such deviant variants are permitted by the 'system' but breach the strictures of the norm. Hjelmslev (1942) distinguishes between 'schema', language as pure form, 'norm', language as material form, and 'usage', language as the sum of habits. Roughly speaking, 'schema' and 'norm' correspond to Coseriu's 'system', and 'usage' to Coseriu's 'norm'. The main difference is that Hjelmslev separates the purely relational structure of language (schema) from the positive content of structure (norm), such as meanings and phonemes, whereas Coseriu treats these two aspects together, so that he, for example, does not abstract the relational definition of a phoneme (e.g. by means of commutation) from its articulatory definition in terms of distinctive features (cf. Jensen, this volume).

From this historical perspective, system and norm divide *langue* into two parts: a 'functional' part, comprising the distinctive invariants of a language, and a 'traditional' part, comprising the normal, recurring variants of a language. In lack of such a distinction confusion arises as to where normal, recurring variants belong. Trubetzkoy, for instance, understands the abovementioned norm in regard to variants of phonemes as a norm of *parole*, so that these variants are, in fact, not part of *langue* at all. But it is a mistake, Coseriu argues, to simply relegate such variants to *parole*, since normal variants are representative of a language rather than of utterances. The concept of parole is better reserved for the purely momentary and occasional manifestations of language. Neither would it be appropriate to include them in the system, since normal variants are merely recurring units, not functionally distinctive ones (Coseriu 1975 [1952]: 56–64). Thus arises the need for an intermediary region, a region that lacks the structural properties of the system but retains its constancy. This region is the norm.

Coseriu (1975 [1952], 1970 [1966/1968], 1973, 1992 [1988], 2007 [1988]) provides examples of the distinction from the fields of phonology, morphology, syntax and lexicology. The perhaps simplest application of the distinction is the one already mentioned, the difference between phonemes and their normal variants. For example, the phoneme /b/ in Spanish is [+ oral], [+ bilabial], and [+ voiced]. No other features are distinctive. The additional features [+ occlusive] and [+ fricative], one of which the phoneme would have when realised, merely define two normal variants that stand in complementary distribution (Coseriu 1992 [1988]: 298f.). Although not stated explicitly, it follows from Coseriu's description that the phoneme in principle could be realised as [+ trill] but that this would diverge from the norm.

In lexical morphology, the distinction corresponds to the difference between the productivity of word-formation, which is part of the system, and the inventory of established formations, which is part of the norm. Coseriu (1992 [1988]: 300) exemplifies this with long, awkward derivations in Italian, which are possible but not present in the norm. Let me provide a simpler example. In English, nominalising *-ness* is highly productive with few restrictions, but it does not attach to verbs or bound bases (Bauer et al. 2013: 245f.). Thus, *sayness and *ducedness are excluded from the system. New formations such as *sayingness* and *introducedness*, on the other hand, are not. These are simply unfamiliar to the norm. Another illuminating divergence is formations that are disfavoured by the norm because of competing words: the only two things standing in the way of *arrogantness* and *strongness* are *arrogance* and *strength*. While rare in use, they are still permitted by the system.[1]

Of particular interest for the purpose of the present article are applications of the distinction in semantics. The phenomenon of relevance here is traditional interpretations, i.e. conventional limitations of the possibilities inherent in the system. In many cases, the limitation affects the product of word-formation, so that it specifies a compositionally underdetermined meaning. Coseriu (2007 [1988]: 272) cites the German compounds *Hauptmann* ('captain [rank]') and *Hauptstadt* ('capital'), which have the indicated senses in the norm. From the point of view of the language system, they may just as well be interpreted as 'most important man' and 'most important city' in analogy with *Hauptsache* ('main matter'). We can add to Coseriu's examples the observation that the invariant meaning of the words becomes evident in certain other formations, for instance *Kulturhauptstadt* ('cultural capital'). In some cases, the cause of the limitation is an affective variation, such as in Bally's (1935) *croire en Dieu* ('believe in God') and *croire au diable* ('believe in the devil'). Custom has it that belief in a divine being involves faith and that belief in a diabolic one does not, a difference that is marked in French by *en* (for trust and hope, i.e. faith) and *à* (for plain cognitive belief). This gives rise to certain collocations in the norm. Another kind of limitation pertains to constructions. Coseriu (1970 [1966/1968]: 42) illustrates this with nominalised adjectives signifying nations in German, which by default are interpreted as designating the corresponding language: *das Englische* (the English) has as its normal sense 'the English language'. Other nominalised adjectives, such as *das Wahre* (the true) and *das Schöne* (the beautiful), receive more general interpretations: 'that which is true', 'that which is beautiful', etc. Such interpretations are in contrast to the interpretation of *das Englische* not limited by the norm.

3 Monosemy and polysemy

Coseriu strongly favours a monosemist approach to meaning, a view that he derives from the structuralist notion of the solidarity between signifier and signified. The constitutive properties of a linguistic system are those that are delineated on both planes of the linguistic sign, or in other words, that are functionally distinctive. Signifier and signified are thus articulated in a parallel fashion, paired with one another one-to-one. From this structure follows an assumption

---

[1] *Strongness* occurs fewer than 0.01 times per million words. *Arrogantness* is even rarer (OED).

of monosemy: each signified is assumed to correspond to one invariant, unitary meaning that is present throughout all possible uses. Only if the assumption proves to be obviously false is it abandoned, as it would be in cases of unrelated meanings that happen to share the same expression (Coseriu 1992 [1988]: chap. 7). Polysemy for Coseriu therefore tends to coincide with what a polysemist approach classifies as homonymy. This stance in favour of monosemy is strictly speaking not required for the arguments pursued in the present article. All that is required is that system and norm are kept apart, and that the former is more general than the latter. To keep things simple, I will adhere to the monosemist view.

The possible uses of a unitary meaning are, first of all, merely possible and therefore not necessarily normal, and since their character is one of possibility, and not of normality, they are also infinite in number. Unitary meanings belong to the system, not to the norm, a fact that when overlooked leads to confusion. Critics of structural semantics, Coseriu remarks, have proven to be unaware of the distinction between system and norm, "and therefore their analysis is restricted to the level of normal language use" (Coseriu 2000 [1990]: 29). On such a norm-centred view of language, to know the meaning of a word is not to apply a unitary meaning: it is to conform with tradition and normality. It is, as expressed by a proponent of the view, to be "able to use the word appropriately, in conformity with the norms of the language, in ways that are accepted by other speakers of the language" (Taylor 2017: 260). Unitary meanings, by contrast, are far removed from normal standards of appropriateness.

Previous research on the monosemist side has made the case that the polysemist approach assumes unnecessarily restricted meanings, which on closer scrutiny turn out to be overdetermined (e.g. Dietrich 1997, Coene and Willems 2006, Van der Gucht et al. 2007, De Cuypere 2013, Willems 2013). Attention has also been brought to the importance of distinguishing system from norm, especially so in Willems (2013). In accordance with Coseriu's (e.g. 1970 [1969], 1979, 1992 [1988]) theory of meaning, these contributions have mainly argued that presumed polysemy is in fact polyvalence (sense variation subsumed under an invariant meaning) and that combinations that have been deemed ill-formed are perfectly fine given an appropriate context. One example is Pustejovsky's (2001: 98) *good rock*, which he claims to be anomalous on the grounds that a rock has no inherent purpose (and thereby nothing it is naturally good for), but this seems like an unhappy conclusion, since the combination is not too rare in actual language use (Willems 2013: 279). A more precarious task is it to invoke the distinction in cases of possible uses that are not merely unusual or unfamiliar, but patently deviant. In such cases, one must assert the possibility of uses that are rejected by speakers of the language.

By 'deviant' uses I shall understand cases that are on the far end among norm-diverging uses. There are different aspects to the norm, not all of which have the same importance in the present context. In part, the norm is a matter of frequency, as Coseriu (1975 [1952]: 64) illustrates with the Spanish *Artajo trajo la valija abajo* ('Artajo took down the suitcase'), which exhibits a disproportionate number of occurrences of the phoneme /x/. The sentence is 'unusual', makes an odd stylistic impression, but it is in no way wrong. In Swedish, it is common to say *en gång i månaden* ('once a month'), not so common to say *en gång per månad* ('once per month').[2] The latter is not wrong, but it is less usual, and a speaker would diverge from the norm if she consistently chose the latter over the former. In part, the norm is also a matter of what has been done before: a word such as *introducedness* is 'unfamiliar' to the norm because it is not recognised as an established word-formation. As such it might bother speakers, but it is not necessarily deemed to be wrong. Finally, the norm is also a matter of proper language use. It is a normative force. Uses that diverge from the norm in this sense are 'deviant'. For example, the English system provides the means for the weak inflection *drink–drinked–drinked*, which is proscribed by the norm in favour of *drink–drank–drunk* (see Coseriu 1975 [1952]: 69f., for other examples of this sort). Similarly, *arrogantness* is rejected in favour of *arrogance*, although this might not be felt to be quite as bad as the weak inflection. Clearly, deviance is a matter of degree, but this does not prevent us from recognising obvious cases. The crucial point is that a semantic description of the system must include possibilities that lie outside the appropriate range of uses and that are rejected by speakers of the language. It must include also that which is at odds with proper language use.

This is curiously not a point that Coseriu appears to have been eager to stress. It should be worthwhile, however, since a common charge against the monosemist stance is that it leads to the adoption of overly general meanings (e.g. Wierzbicka 1980, Lakoff 1987, Langacker 1988, Allwood 2003, Tuggy 2003, Tyler and Evans 2003, Taylor 1999, 2006). From this perspective, unitary meanings that include deviant uses are blatant overgeneralisations that fail the requirement of making accurate predictions. This reasoning follows from the assumption that a description of meaning should be an account of normal language use, or as it is expressed in Goddard (2011: 37): "we are entitled to expect that an accurate definition [...] will predict the appropriate range of use of a word". Because of this assumption, proponents of polysemy come to expect that also monosemist accounts of meaning should delimit normal language use.

---

[2] 40 995 instances (91%) against 3903 (9%) in the Swedish *Korp* (all open corpora).

Sometimes they even expect it to be supplemented with a theory of use that accounts for individual senses, so that it should be able to both delimit and detail normal language use (i. e. to both define the boundaries and describe the content within those boundaries of normal language use). Since this is a much more extensive task than the polysemist task of individuating senses, it puts the monosemist approach at a disadvantage in regard to its possible success (as has previously been pointed out by Riemer 2005: 124 ff.).

In order to treat this matter in as pure a form as possible, I shall have to limit the object matter to roots. Thereby do I exclude the effects of word-formation, an area where the productive capacity of language is not in dispute (cf. Dietrich, this volume). More importantly, I also exclude the semantic corollaries of word-formation and do therefore not engage in arguments to the effect that a word like *Hauptmann* has a unitary meaning that is much broader than its normal sense. This might be more contentious, but it shall be of no concern here. I concentrate on the argument that also roots have unitary meanings that include more uses than are part of the norm. What is more, I limit the argument to uses that are not merely unusual or unfamiliar but also deviant. These restrictions, which condense the matter to its core, should make the argument sufficiently radical to demonstrate the unique and far-reaching consequences of employing the concepts of system and norm in semantics.

4 Prepositions of concomitance

As examples of roots I will use simple prepositions. A suitable starting point is German *mit*, a recurring example in Coseriu's work. The preposition has a wide range of uses, including instrument (*mit dem Messer* 'with the knife'), comitative (*mit einem Freund* 'with a friend'), sentiment (*mit Freude* 'with joy'), and material (*mit Mehl* 'with flour').[3] Coseriu proposes that the unitary meaning is 'und x ist dabei' ('and x is present', Coseriu 1970 [1969]: 117), or in more condensed terms, 'copresence' or 'concomitance' (Coseriu 1987: 8; cf. 1989: 9). On Coseriu's ac-

---

[3] A reviewer believes 'sentiment' is too narrow a category and suggests 'circumstantial' instead. I have described these four uses so that they agree with Coseriu's paraphrases (1970 [1969]: 15), which in the present case is *bei Empfindung von Freude* ('with a feeling of joy'). It also agrees with Coseriu's (1989: 9) description of French *avec* as being able to designate "un sentiment ou une attitude concomitante de l'action" ('a sentiment or an attitude concomitant with the action'). With this said, there is no degree of granularity that is perfect for all purposes, so 'sentiment' might very well be a variant of 'circumstantial'. In what follows, I provide descriptions that are granular enough to reveal relevant patterns of language use.

count, this meaning is not a lexical meaning but an instrumental meaning, a meaning that can only occur in combination with lexical meanings, i.e. as *mit x*. In this respect, it is similar to a plural affix, which can only be interpreted as such in combination with a lexeme (Coseriu 1972 [1971], 1992 [1988]: 149 f.). Interestingly, Coseriu (1989: 9–10) has proposed the same unitary meaning for French *avec*, a preposition with a comparable range of uses. Similar meanings have also been suggested by other linguists – apparently independently of each other – for corresponding prepositions, although mostly in passing and not as the main point of analysis. Ralph (1984: 12) describes the general meaning of Swedish *med* as 'association (simultaneous occurrence)' (in Swedish: 'förknippning (samtidig förekomst)'), and Haug (2009: 339) the meaning of Norwegian *med* as "'concomitance' in a wide sense". Rapoport (2014: 160) proposes that partial dictionary definitions of English *with* can be "condensed into a single definition of accompaniment or simultaneousness". These are all very similar, if not identical, notions of the prepositional meaning. For the sake of argument, I will assume it is exactly 'concomitance' in all cases, barring for the moment the possibility of interlingual differences.

Given the polysemist requirement that meanings provide an account of normal language use, one would now expect these prepositions to be used in an identical manner. The expectation is of course not borne out. While there indeed are considerable overlaps, there are also noticeable differences.

Table 1 shows a partial comparison (not including all common uses) of English *with*, German *mit*, Swedish *med* and French *avec*. (Norwegian *med* has not been included.) The first four uses are taken from Coseriu's (1970 [1969]) discussion of *mit*. The other uses have been selected to demonstrate differences between the languages. The first two uses, instrument and comitative, exemplify the preference in European languages to express both senses by the same morpheme (Stolz et al. 2006, 2013). Corresponding uses of the four prepositions are also seen for 'sentiment' and 'material'. The remaining eight uses illustrate differences in various constellations. German and Swedish agree for 'means of transportation', 'object of cessation', and 'content of container', whereas English and French have other prepositions or none at all. English and French agree for 'part of meal', whereas German and Swedish have *zu* and *till*. German, Swedish and French agree for 'object of marriage', whereas English has *to*. Only English uses its preposition of concomitance for 'manner or cause of action' and 'object of emotion', and only Swedish uses its corresponding preposition for 'pertaining to'. These discrepancies show that the unitary meaning of concomitance is an overgeneralisation from the point of view of normal language use. The question is how to respond to this apparent problem.

Table 1: Prepositions of concomitance in English, German, Swedish, and French. Exclamation marks and shading indicate deviation from at least the norm with respect to the specified designation. Norm-conforming expressions are given within parentheses.

Use / Designation	English *with*	German *mit*	Swedish *med*	French *avec*
instrument	cut with the knife	mit dem Messer schneiden	skära med kniven	couper avec le couteau
comitative	go with a friend	mit einem Freund gehen	gå med en vän	aller avec un ami
sentiment	do it with joy	mit Freude machen	göra det med nöje	le faire avec plaisir
material	sprinkle with flour	mit Mehl bestreuen	strö med mjöl	saupoudrer avec la farine (more common: saupoudrer de farine)
means of transportation	!go with train (go by train)	mit dem Zug fahren	åka med tåg	!aller avec train (aller en train)
part of meal	serve biscuits with the coffee	!Kekse mit dem Kaffee servieren (Kekse zum Kaffee servieren)	!servera kakor med kaffet (servera kakor till kaffet)	servir des biscuits avec le café
object of emotion	be angry with you	!wütend mit dir sein (wütend auf dich sein)	!vara arg med dig (vara arg på dig)	!être en colère avec toi (être en colère contre toi)
object of marriage	!be married with him (be married to him)	mit ihm verheiratet sein	vara gift med honom	être mariée avec lui
object of cessation	!quit with tobacco (quit tobacco)	mit dem Tabak aufhören	sluta med tobak	!arrêter avec le tabac (arrêter le tabac)
manner or cause of action	scream with pain	!mit Schmerz schreien (vor Schmerz schreien)	!skrika med smärta (skrika av smärta)	!hurler avec douleur (hurler de douleur)
pertaining to	!like everything with Berlin (like everything about Berlin)	!alles mit Berlin mögen (alles an Berlin mögen)	gilla allt med Berlin	!aimer tout avec Berlin (aimer tout de Berlin)

Table 1: Prepositions of concomitance in English, German, Swedish, and French. Exclamation marks and shading indicate deviation from at least the norm with respect to the specified designation. Norm-conforming expressions are given within parentheses. *(Continued)*

Use / Designation	English *with*	German *mit*	Swedish *med*	French *avec*
content of container	!a glass with beer (a glass of beer)	ein Glas mit Bier (more common: ein Glas Bier)	ett glas med öl (more common: ett glas öl)	!un verre avec bière (un verre de bière)

Broadly speaking, there are three possible responses. The first response is to maintain the assumed meaning and to invoke the distinction between system and norm: the differences are due to different norms; unitary meanings belong to the system. The second response is to take the impression of overgeneralisation at face value and to insist on the particularity of each language: it was a mistake to assume the same unitary meaning for all languages; the meaning must be adjusted to better fit each one of them. The third response is to take the apparent overgeneralisation as evidence against the monosemist approach itself: 'concomitance' is not merely an erroneous description in this particular case; it is a mistake in principle to assume a unitary meaning like this. Of these responses, the first and second are committed to monosemy, whereas the third is not. The second and third response have another notion in common, however, namely that no deviant uses should be subsumed under the description. Whereas the second response, in contrast to the third, does not subscribe to the idea that a semantic description must detail normal language use, it does assume that it must delimit normal language use. To the best of my knowledge, there are no linguists who actually endorse this position, but it represents what critics of monosemy tend to expect from a monosemist account. For this reason, it is worth considering in relation to the position of the first response.

It is of course possible that the unitary meanings of *with*, *mit*, *med* and *avec*, contrary to my assumption, are slightly different and that this is reflected in different usage patterns. There are also grammatical differences between the languages that provide the prepositions with different material for their complements. But it is unlikely that such semantic and grammatical differences could account for all of the observed differences. Hence, we have reason to believe that some deviant uses are permitted by the system. A closer look at a few examples will reinforce this point. For the sake of brevity, I will concentrate on English *with*.

In the examples provided above, German and Swedish use *mit* and *med* for 'object of cessation', while English and French have expressions with a direct object. English has *quit tobacco*, not *quit with tobacco*. Of importance is that English does not in general disallow *with* in objects of cessation. Expressions like *quit with the lies* or *stop with the false advertising* are perfectly fine. The similar *quit with the job*, however, is not. To all appearances, this variation is due to constructional restrictions that relate to the semantics of the complement of *with*. Whatever the precise conditions for the use of *with* in objects of cessation might be, they must be rather specific, more so than could be accounted for by a unitary meaning. In other words, a meaning like 'concomitance', which is meant to cover all possible uses of *with*, cannot reasonably be expected to discriminate between expressions like *quit with tobacco* and *quit with the lies*. Not even polysemic descriptions would normally make such minute distinctions.

In contrast to German, Swedish, and French, English does not use *with* but *to* in objects of marriage: *be married to him*, not *be married with him*. The same use of *to* is seen in a few other expressions for nuptial relationships, such as *be engaged to him* and *be betrothed to him*, and in some expressions for other family relationships, such as *be related to him*. In expressions for personal relationships, *to* is used in some cases, such as *be a good friend to him, be like a sister to me*, and *with* in other cases, such as *be friends with him, be associated with him*. Also the marital *become joined with him in marriage* and the general *be involved with him* have *with*. Other constructions permit both prepositions with little to no difference in the resulting designation: *be allied with him* or *be allied to him, be connected with him* or *be connected to him*. More generally, if we consider a broader spectrum of uses, English has a number of expressions where *to* and *with* alternate in the same fashion: *compared with/to, conform with/to, connection with/to, similarity with/to, talk with/to* and so forth. In some such cases, the choice between *with* and *to* is at most vaguely distinctive, which stands in stark contrast to other pairs, such as *go to him* and *go with him*, which are clearly distinct. Sometimes the resulting sentences are entirely equivalent, e.g.: *he was connected with the mafia* or *he was connected to the mafia*.

As we can see, there are circumstances where the opposition between the two prepositions does not yield a substantial difference at the level of designation. This sporadic affinity between *with* and *to* is an *irregular equivalence*, i.e. an occasional identity of designation that does not in general hold for the items in question. Such equivalences cannot readily be accounted for in terms of polysemy, or so I have attempted to show in previous work. They require an analysis based on more general meanings (Widoff 2018). To make sense of this particular case of irregular equivalence, we must briefly consider *to*. In a study of *to, towards, until, into, in* and *at*, De Cuypere (2013) proposes that the meaning of *to* is 'establisher of a relationship between X and reference point Y', which is a feature of the meaning of the other prepositions as well, but for *to* it is the only necessary feature. In other words, *to* has a very general meaning, even as prepositions go. Assuming this meaning for *to* and 'concomitance' for *with*, the cause of such equivalences must be that certain states of affairs are insensitive to the distinction between the mere establishment of a relationship and the concomitance of the relationship. If we transpose this observation to an object of marriage, there appears to be no systemic reason to choose *to* over *with*. One could think of the two-place predicate of being married in terms of the establishment or in terms of the concomitance; it does not yield a substantial difference. Adding these things together – that irregular equivalences require unitary meanings and that there appears to be no systemic reason for the norm – we can deduce the need for an analysis in terms of unitary meanings that include deviant uses. The strong preference for *to* over *with* in expressions for nuptial relationships, such as *married to him* and *engaged to him*, is merely a rule of the norm.

As a final note, it is worth mentioning that *with* occurs in common expressions where the prepositional phrase does not designate an object of marriage, but instead other family members or an object of action, as in *married with two kids* or *engaged with the task*. It is possible that the preference for *to* in the nuptial category is reinforced by such expressions. The combination *married with him* would then be similar to *arrogantness* not only in that both are deviant, but also partially in the cause of the deviance, namely the existence of a competing expression. While this suggests that *married with him* is in accordance with the norm under a different interpretation (i.e. 'accompanying family member' instead of 'object of marriage'), such an interpretation is not easily conjured in the present expression: *married with him* strongly indicates that the complement is to be interpreted as an object of marriage. For the phrase to actually designate family members other than the spouse a complement that unequivocally designates such family members appears to be required.[4] To accurately assess the precise interaction between different designations of *with x*, a more extensive investigation of the preposition is required.

5 Methodological concerns

The analysis in the previous section suggests that some deviant uses of *with* are in accordance with the system. Opponents to the structural disposition inherent

---

[4] Among 177 instances of *married with* in the BNC, there is not a single instance of *married with* where a personal pronoun or a proper name in itself makes up the complement. Typical instances are *married with three children*, *married with two daughters*, and the like.

in this analysis might see a methodological danger in the tolerance for deviant uses. It could, they might worry, lead to an overly lenient attitude that leaves language description without a sound foundation in evidence. The linguist might, as it were, mould the evidence to fit the description, because what is to decide which usage is and which is not permitted by the system? I propose to continue with a few clarifications to calm the worst concerns.

The assertion that a deviant use is permitted by the system is relative to a description. It is not an immediate judgement over the appropriateness of an expression. It is based on an explication of the linguistic system and it is as such inaccessible to the naive knowledge of the ordinary speaker. In the case of *married with him*, the assertion crucially rests on the assumption that the unitary meaning of *with* is 'concomitance'. In addition, it has been guided by an assumption that is helpful but dispensable: the heuristic of using comparisons with other languages to gauge the limits of English *with*. If the crucial assumption is in doubt, there are the standard ways to substantiate it: investigation of the usage of *with* and investigation of the paradigmatic neighbours of *with x*, i.e. other prepositions in similar combinations (cf. Coseriu 1989: 21). The former checks if all extant uses are compatible with the assumed meaning (thereby assessing its invariance), the latter if the semantic integrity of each term in the paradigm is upheld (thereby assessing their distinctiveness). The present context has not permitted an extensive investigation of this sort.

The assertion itself is also open to scrutiny on the basis of what it entails: a deviant use that is permitted by the system must be interpretable in a manner compatible with the proposed unitary meaning. In the present example the requirement is satisfied: *married with him* is comprehensible and receives an interpretation that is equivalent to *married to him*, an affinity that is not found in expressions such as *married of him, married in him, married at him, married about him, married over him* or *married through him*, which are either incongruent or understood differently. If in doubt, this claim is open to experimental testing, for instance by sense similarity and sensicality judgement tasks.

6 Conclusion

The import of the structural stance expounded in this article is that the system permits deviant uses of roots. This follows from a consistent application of the distinction between system and norm. To say that *married with him* is permitted by the system is analogous to saying that *arrogantness* is. The basic notion underlying this line of thought is that a language is organised as a system of oppositions. The semantic potential of a root is therefore not exhausted by its normal use. There are infinite possibilities within the space circumscribed by the system. Semantic descriptions of the system can accordingly not be expected to delimit normal language use or to account for all of its variants. Serious attention to the system sets a rather different goal for semantic descriptions: to state the general scope of unitary meanings, regardless of the particular facts of normal language use. This difference is not always appreciated in other strands of linguistics. In this article, I have therefore sought to clarify some part of what a semantic description of the system is actually supposed to be.

References

Allwood, Jens. 2003. "Meaning potentials and context: some consequences for the analysis of variation in meaning". In: Hubert Cuyckens, René Dirven and John R. Taylor (eds.), *Cognitive approaches to lexical semantics*, 29–66. Berlin: Mouton de Gruyter.
Bally, Charles. 1926. *Le langage et la vie*. Paris: Payot.
Bally, Charles. 1935. "En été: au printemps; croire en Dieu: croire au diable". In: *Festschrift für Ernst Tappolet*, 9–15. Basel: Schwabe.
Bauer, Laurie, Rochel Lieber and Ingo Plag. 2013. *The Oxford reference guide to English morphology*. Oxford: Oxford University Press.
BNC = The British National Corpus. Accessed at <www.english-corpora.org/bnc/> on 2020–09–24.
Brøndal, Viggo. 1937. "Langage et logique". In: *La grande encyclopédie française*. Paris. (Reprinted in Brøndal 1943. *Essais de linguistique générale*. Copenhague: Munksgaard.)
Bühler, Karl. 1934. *Sprachtheorie. Die Darstellungsfunktion der Sprache*. Jena: Gustav Fischer.
Chomsky, Noam. 1965. *Aspects of the theory of syntax*. Cambridge: M.I.T. Press.
Coene, Ann and Klaas Willems. 2006. "Konstruktionelle Bedeutungen. Kritische Anmerkungen zu Adele Goldbergs konstruktionsgrammatischer Bedeutungstheorie". *Sprachtheorie und germanistische Linguistik* 16:1, 1–35.
Coseriu, Eugenio. 1970 [1966/1968]. *Einführung in die strukturelle Betrachtung des Wortschatzes*. Tübingen: Narr.
Coseriu, Eugenio. 1970 [1969]. "Bedeutung und Bezeichnung im Lichte der strukturellen Semantik". In: Peter Hartmann and Henri Vernay (eds.), *Sprachwissenschaft und Übersetzen*, 104–121. München: Max Hueber.
Coseriu, Eugenio. 1972 [1971]. "Semantik und Grammatik". In: Hugo Moser (ed.), *Neue Grammatiktheorien und ihre Anwendung auf das heutige Deutsch*, 77–89. Düsseldorf: Schwann.
Coseriu, Eugenio. 1973. *Probleme der strukturellen Semantik*. Edited by Dieter Kastovsky. Tübingen: Narr.
Coseriu, Eugenio. 1975 [1952]. "System, Norm und Rede". In: Eugenio Coseriu, *Sprachtheorie und allgemeine Sprachwissenschaft. 5 Studien*, 11–101. München: Fink.
Coseriu, Eugenio. 1979. "'τὸ ἓν σημαίνειν'. Bedeutung und Bezeichnung bei Aristoteles". *Zeitschrift für Phonetik, Sprachwissenschaft und Kommunikationsforschung* 32:4 (Festschrift für Georg F. Meier), 432–437.

Coseriu, Eugenio. 1987. "Bedeutung, Bezeichnung und sprachliche Kategorien". *Sprachwissenschaft* 12:1, 1–23.
Coseriu, Eugenio. 1989. "Principes de syntaxe fonctionnelle". *Travaux de linguistique et de philologie* 27, 5–46.
Coseriu, Eugenio. 1992 [1988]. *Einführung in die allgemeine Sprachwissenschaft* (second edition). Tübingen: Francke. (German translation of Coseriu 1981.)
Coseriu, Eugenio. 2000 [1990]. "Structural semantics and 'cognitive' semantics". *Logos and Language* 1:1, 19–42. (English translation of Coseriu 1990.)
Coseriu, Eugenio. 2007 [1988]. *Sprachkompetenz. Grundzüge der Theorie des Sprechens.* Edited by Heinrich Weber (second edition). Tübingen: Narr.
De Cuypere, Ludovic. 2013. "Debiasing semantic analysis: the case of the English preposition *to*". *Language Sciences* 37, 122–135.
Dietrich, Wolf. 1997. "Polysemie als 'volle Wortbedeutung' – gegen die 'Mehrdeutigkeit' der Zeichen". In: Ulrich Hoinkes and Wolf Dietrich (eds.), *Kaleidoskop der Lexikalischen Semantik*, 227–237. Tübingen: Narr.
Flydal, Leiv. 1952. "Remarques sur certains rapports entre le style et l'état de langue". *Norsk Tidsskrift for Sprogvidenskap* 16, 241–258.
Gardiner, Alan. 1932. *The theory of speech and language.* Oxford: Clarendon.
Goddard, Cliff. 2011. *Semantic analysis: a practical introduction.* Oxford: Oxford University Press.
Haug, Dag. 2009. "The syntax and semantics of concomitance in Norwegian". In: Miriam Butt and Tracy Holloway King (eds.), *Proceedings of the LFG09 Conference*, 338–356. Stanford, CA: CSLI Publications.
Hjelmslev, Louis. 1942. "Langue et parole". *Cahiers Ferdinand de Saussure* 2, 29–44.
Hjelmslev, Louis. 1943. *Omkring sprogteoriens grundlæggelse.* Munksgaard: København.
Jespersen, Otto. 1925. *Mankind, nation and individual from a linguistic point of view.* Oslo: Aschehoug.
Korp. Språkbanken. Accessed at <spraakbanken.gu.se/korp/> on 2020–09–24.
Lakoff, George. 1987. *Women, fire, and dangerous things. What categories reveal about the mind.* Chicago: University of Chicago Press.
Langacker, Ronald. 1988. "A view of linguistic semantics". In: Brygida Rudzka-Ostyn (ed.), *Topics in cognitive linguistics*, 49–90. Amsterdam & Philadelphia: John Benjamins.
Martinet, André. 1948. "Où en est la phonologie?" *Lingua* 1, 43–58.
Møller, Kristen. 1949. "Contribution to the discussion concerning 'langue' and 'parole'". In: Louis Hjelmslev (ed.), *Recherches structurales: Interventions dans le débat glossématique* (*Travaux du Cercle linguistique de Copenhague* 5), 87–96. Copenhague: Nordisk sprog- og kulturforlag.
OED = *Oxford English Dictionary.* Available at <www.oed.com>.
Pustejovsky, James. 2001. "Type construction and the logic of concepts". In: Federica Busa and Pierrette Bouillon (eds.), *The language of word meaning*, 91–123. Cambridge: Cambridge University Press.
Ralph, Bo. 1984. *Svenskans grundläggande prepositioner.* Göteborg: Göteborgs universitet.
Rapoport, Tova. 2014. "Central coincidence: the preposition *with*". *Faits de Langues* 44:2, 159–173.
Riemer, Nick. 2005. *The semantics of polysemy: reading meaning in English and Warlpiri.* Berlin: Mouton de Gruyter.

Saussure, Ferdinand de. 2011 [1916]. *Course in general linguistics*. Translated by Wade Baskin. New York: Columbia University Press.

Sechehaye, Albert. 1940. "Les trois linguistiques saussuriennes". *Vox Romanica* 5, 1–48.

Stolz, Thomas, Cornelia Stroh and Aina Urdze. 2006. *On comitatives and related categories: a typological study with special focus on the languages of Europe*. Berlin & New York: Mouton de Gruyter.

Stolz, Thomas, Cornelia Stroh and Aina Urdze. 2013. "Comitatives and instrumentals". In: Matthew S. Dryer and Martin Haspelmath (eds.), *The World Atlas of Language Structures Online*. Leipzig: Max Planck Institute for Evolutionary Anthropology. Available online at <http://wals.info/chapter/52>.

Taylor, John R. 1999. "Cognitive semantics and structural semantics". In: Andreas Blank and Peter Koch (eds.), *Historical semantics and cognition*, 17–48. Berlin & New York: Mouton de Gruyter.

Taylor, John R. 2006. "Polysemy and the lexicon". In: Gitte Kristiansen, Michel Achard, René Dirven and Francisco J. Ruiz de Mendoza Ibañez (eds.), *Cognitive linguistics: current applications and future perspectives*, 51–80. Berlin & New York: Mouton de Gruyter.

Taylor, John R. 2017. "Lexical semantics". In: Barbara Dancygier (ed.), *The Cambridge Handbook of Cognitive Linguistics*, 246–261. Cambridge: Cambridge University Press.

Trubetzkoy, Nikolai S. 1958 [1939]. *Grundzüge der Phonologie*. Göttingen: Vandenhoeck & Ruprecht.

Tuggy, David. 2003. "The Nawatl verb *kīsa:* a case study in polysemy". In: Hubert Cuyckens, René Dirven and John R. Taylor (eds.), *Cognitive approaches to lexical semantics*, 323–362. Berlin & New York: Mouton de Gruyter.

Tyler, Andrea and Vyvyan Evans. 2003. *The semantics of English prepositions: spatial scenes, embodied meaning, and cognition*. Cambridge: Cambridge University Press.

Van der Gucht, Fieke, Klaas Willems and Ludovic De Cuypere. 2007. "The iconicity of embodied meaning. Polysemy of spatial prepositions in the cognitive framework". *Language Sciences* 29, 733–754.

Wartburg, Walther von. 1943. *Einführung in Problematik und Methodik der Sprachwissenschaft*. Halle: Niemeyer.

Widoff, Andreas. 2018. *Hermeneutik och grammatik: Fenomenologiska undersökningar av språket som tal och teknik*. [Hermeneutics and grammar: Phenomenological investigations into language as speech and technique]. Lund: Lunds universitet.

Wierzbicka, Anna. 1980. *Lingua mentalis: the semantics of natural language*. Sydney: Academic Press.

Willems, Klaas. 2013. "The linguistic sign at the lexicon-syntax interface: assumptions and implications of the Generative Lexicon Theory". *Semiotica* 193, 233–287.

Dagobert Höllein (Kassel)
Coseriu, significative semantics and a new system of semantic roles

> Expressions such as [...] I cut the bread with a knife ~ I cut the bread by using a knife ~ I cut the bread, while I am using a knife as an instrument *etc. are considered as 'synonymous', as 'identical in meaning', as going back to the same deep structure in the transformationalist literature, whereby it becomes obvious that what is meant is not the language-specific signified, but the designation, i.e. the relation of these expressions to the extralinguistic world, or rather, the corresponding states of affairs themselves.*

1 Introduction

Shortly after Fillmore developed role semantics, Coseriu (1970 [1969], 1970, 1972 [1971]) criticised this type of semantics in a series of articles. More than half a century after Fillmore's *The case for case* (1968), mainstream denotative role semantics still struggles with the same difficulties in the analysis of abstract events, prepositional objects, sentential arguments etc. Even though Coseriu did not address all the problems in detail, his differentiation between signified (G. *Bedeutung*) and designation (G. *Bezeichnung*, or 'denotation') plays a key role in solving the difficulties with which role semantics is confronted.

The aim of this article is to discuss Coseriu's distinction between signified and designation with regard to role semantics and to align the distinction with the new significative-semantic approach to roles that is currently being developed. I will first address the main problems of role semantics in Section 2. Coseriu's solution to these problems is presented in Section 3. A new approach to semantic roles, which is informed by Coseriu's distinction and developed in order to solve the problems described in Section 2, is then presented in Section 4. Section 5 rounds off the article with a brief summary.

---

* "Ausdrücke wie [...] *Ich schneide das Brot mit dem Messer ~ Ich schneide das Brot, indem ich dafür ein Messer benutze ~ Ich schneide das Brot. Dabei verwende ich als Instrument ein Messer* usw. werden nämlich in der transformationalistischen Literatur jeweils als 'synonym', als 'gleichbedeutend', als auf dieselbe Tiefenstruktur zurückgehend betrachtet, wobei offensichtlich wird, daß es sich nicht um die einzelsprachliche Bedeutung, sondern um die Bezeichnung handelt, d. h. um den Bezug dieser Ausdrücke auf das Außersprachliche, besser gesagt, um die jeweils gemeinten Sachverhalte selbst" (Coseriu 1970: 56; italics in the original).

2 Current problems of role semantics

Fillmore's (1968) major achievement was to analyse sentence parts not only syntactically but semantically, which provides the background for the idea of role semantics. Nevertheless, denotative role semantics was not able to provide a definitive list of roles which would help to analyse all sentences in a satisfying way. Moreover, while the model was successfully applied to constructed examples, it failed with regard to the analysis of texts. The problem has been addressed since the 1970s by various scholars, e.g. Starosta (1978), but the core of Fillmore's theory largely remained unchanged, as recent publications on role semantics such as Levin and Rappaport Hovav (2005) show. Instead, new roles have been suggested to conceal the problem, as Lakoff (1977: 244) and Dowty (1991: 554) explained, with the exception of Dowty (1991) (cf. below).

After many adjustments to his initial set of roles, Fillmore finally stopped creating new lists. In 2006, he contended: "Moreover, the goal of limiting the number of semantic roles to a roster of reusable universal role names lost its importance" (Fillmore 2006: 616). As a result, role list approaches – as Levin and Rappaport Hovav (2005: 35) call them – were eventually abandoned altogether. However, this entails that the main merit of semantic role analysis has also been eliminated, viz. to make texts analysable by means of a limited set of roles. The current situation in role semantics becomes apparent if an analogy is made with the study of syntactic relations: a syntactic theory struggles to analyse syntactic relations, but the core of the theory remains the same, the only thing that has changed is the number of syntactic relations – or it is maintained that it is not important to know the complete set of syntactic relations.

Dowty (1991: 553–559) undertook a detailed analysis of the problems the theory of semantic roles encounters and developed a program which was meant to solve these problems. Dowty's approach is widely accepted today. He reduces the large number of roles to only two: 'Proto-Agent' and 'Proto-Patient'. Dowty is not interested in an exhaustive semantic analysis and uses semantic roles mainly as a tool to assign syntactic relations to roles:

> With a three-place predicate, the nonsubject argument having the greater number of entailed Proto-Patient properties will be lexicalized as the direct object and the nonsubject argument having fewer entailed Proto-Patient properties will be lexicalized as an oblique or prepositional object (and if two nonsubject arguments have approximately equal numbers of entailed P-Patient properties, either or both may be lexicalized as direct object). (Dowty 1991: 576)

In the linguistic literature, e.g. Primus (1999: 33–47), Dowty's approach is considered a theory of semantic roles, but in fact it only assigns syntactic relations to phrases.[1] This becomes obvious when Dowty analyses trivalent predicates (Dowty 1991: Section 9.3).

(1) He gave him a suitcase with $3 million to $5 million. (https://apnews.com/6bded47517cdbe70929f74c13fe7e69c)

In (1), *He* is a Proto-Agent and *a suitcase with $3 million to $5 million* probably Proto-Patient since it has more Proto-Patient properties than *him*, as is shown in Table 1:

Table 1: Checklist for P-Patient (Dowty 1991: 572)

P.-Patient-properties	*a suitcase [...]*	*him*
a. undergoes change of state	+	–
b. incremental theme	+ (?)	+ (?)
c. causally affected by another participant	+	+ (?)
d. stationary relative to movement of another participant	+	–
(e. does not exist independently of the event, or not at all)	–	–

The question marks in lines b. and c. in Table 1 are indicative of the problem that interests me here: applying Dowty's (1991: 572) model entails that signifieds and designation are mixed up. The implications deriving from this confusion will be discussed in detail in the next section. Note that the third complement *him* is not analysed semantically, but only negatively in terms of a non-Proto-Patient and hence as an oblique object. Dowty's model helps us in distinguishing the subject and the direct object and in additionally determining a second object syntactically, viz. as the phrase that remains. However, this is not, by any standards, what might be called a semantic role theory. It does not allow us to make any statements about the semantic function of indirect objects or prepositional objects – it only provides evidence that both are no direct objects.

---

[1] Based on Dowty (1991), Primus (1999: 47–55) created her own semantic proto-role-theory, which still follows the idea of denotative semantics as her examples show: "(29) *Peter gave Mary an apple.* $\forall x \forall y \forall z[\text{GIVE}(x, y, z) \rightarrow \text{P-CONTROL}(x, \text{BECOME}(\text{POSS}(y, z)))]$" vs. "(30) *Peter took the apple from Mary.* $\forall x \forall y \forall z[\text{TAKE}(x, y, z) \rightarrow \text{P-CONTROL}(x, \text{BECOME}(\neg\text{POSS}(y, z)))]$" (Primus 1999: 54). Primus explains: "the participant y is a Proto-Recipient" (Primus 1999: 55). However, the y-participants *Mary* in (29) and *from Mary* in (30) are an indirect and a prepositional object, but because the Proto-Patient-role pertains to designation, not the signified, it can be called synonymous in the two sentences.

The basic problem thus remains unsolved in denotative semantics: the approach has not been able to present a set of semantic roles that allows us to provide complete analyses of sentences. The difficulty is not a matter of individual counter-examples against available sets of semantic roles, it is about substantial problems that arise when the proposed roles are applied to texts. Ágel and Höllein (2021) argue that these difficulties derive from the basic theoretical assumptions of denotative semantics.[2] Here, I only discuss some of the issues that are central to the remainder of the article. Ágel and Höllein analysed a German newspaper article in terms of denotative semantics and significative semantics with a view to establishing a set of roles that can be found in naturally occurring data. The use of corpus data is necessary because in studies of denotative semantics only simple, constructed examples are considered. It proved impossible to analyse the underlined elements in the sentences below by means of the set of denotative-semantic roles proposed by Fillmore (2003: 464) (the original German sentences are provided in parentheses; I will return to the outcome of an analysis in terms of significative semantics in Section 4.2 below):

(2) The slogan that concentrates her fears [?] is hotspot school. (Das Schlagwort, das ihre Ängste konzentriert, lautet: Brennpunktschule.)

(3) The slogan concentrates her fears [?]. (Das Schlagwort konzentriert ihre Ängste.)

(4) An initiative is trying to fight against this [?]. (Eine Initiative versucht dagegen anzukämpfen.)

(5) They don't know it [?] any other way from their family. (Sie kennen es nicht anders aus ihrer Familie.)

(6) An initiative fights against this [GOAL] (Eine Initiative kämpft an dagegen.)

(7) So many people in Neukölln have to live on welfare [?]. (So viele Menschen in Neukölln müssen von Sozialhilfe leben.)

(8) It [?] was Ylva's first day at school. (Es war Ylvas erster Schultag.)

(9) [2nd person plural] [?] Create more good offers! ([2nd person plural] Schafft mehr gute Angebote!)

(10) Children are aggressive or violent [?]. (Kinder sind aggressiv oder gewalttätig.)

(11) I think everyone should search for the right school for his child [?]. (Ich denke, jeder sollte für sein Kind die richtige Schule suchen.)

---

[2] Ágel and Höllein (2021) present a complete set of significative-semantic roles for German along with the concept of "sign-shaped sentence pattern", which – simply put – are significative-semantic argument structure patterns and in this sense close to Goldberg's (2019) construction grammar.

The following observations are in order:
1. Denotative-semantic analysis is no longer precise when things become abstract: the subject in (2) and the direct object in (3) are so abstract that no role can be assigned. Neither the role definitions nor the concrete example sentences provided in Fillmore (2003: 464) are of any help with regard to the analysis.
2. Denotative-semantic analyses usually do not assign semantic roles to subject or object subordinate clauses or infinitive constructions as in (4). This also applies to propositional uses of *it* (G. *es*) as in (5). The corresponding categories therefore remain empty.
3. Since there are no specific prepositional object roles in denotative-semantic terms, provisionally the role GOAL is chosen for type (6). For other prepositional objects, e.g. in (7), no semantic role can be assigned.
4. In studies of denotative semantics no indications of how to interpret so-called formal subjects as in (8) (or even formal objects) can be found.
5. With imperative clauses such as (9), which are ACTION clauses (see Section 4.2) and whose direct object is a PATIENT in terms of denotative semantics, it is unclear whether Fillmore would propose something like a deep structure AGENT or whether he would assume subjectlessness. The latter solution would imply that ACTION clauses do not necessarily have an AGENT.
6. A further limitation of denotative-semantic analyses is obscured by the grammatical analysis: According to Ágel (2017: 358–394), predicatives form the predicate together with a copular verb. However, denotative semantics would probably prefer a formal grammatical analysis with predicatives construed as independent sentence elements. As a result, these independent predicatives would need to be assigned semantic roles. It is unclear what these roles might be. The assignment of roles is particularly problematic in the case of adjectival predicatives as in (10), which do not indicate circumstances or facts.
7. In the case of grammatically underspecified objects as in (11), no role can be assigned according to Fillmore (2003: 464).[3]

The aforementioned problems the denotative-semantic approach runs into are serious, yet denotative semantics has not offered any solutions. This is astonishing, all the more so if one considers that Coseriu already identified the core prob-

---

[3] If the roles STIMULUS and EXPERIENCER are chosen and modelled as in Van Valin (2007: 54–55), the problem of synonymy again arises because the same role is assigned to more than one syntactic relation (see also Section 3).

lem of role semantics at an early stage, some fifty years ago. Against this background it is even more regrettable that representatives of denotative semantics have not taken note of his writings. Likewise, publications of other scholars who also criticized Fillmore's model – e.g. Susov (1973), Starosta (1978, 1988), Fleischmann (1985) and Welke (2019, 2011), among others – have unfortunately not been taken into account in the discussion of role semantics.[4]

3 Coseriu's solution: signified and designation

Central to the understanding of Coseriu's theory of semantics (and, by extension, of significative semantics) is the difference between signified and designation. To be more precise, Coseriu makes a distinction between 'designation' (G. *Bezeichnung*), language-specific 'signified' (G. *Bedeutung*) and 'sense' or 'text meaning' (G. *Sinn*):

> Designation is the relation to extra-linguistic objects or to the extra-linguistic reality itself [...]. Meaning [i.e. signified] is the linguistically-given content in a particular language, the particular form of the possibilities of designation in a given language. Sense is the particular linguistic content which is expressed by means of designation and meaning and which goes beyond designation and meaning in a particular discourse, such as a speaker's attitude, intention, or assumption. (Coseriu 1985: xxx)

With Willems (2011: 43), this three way-split is simplified for the purpose of this study and only the distinction between signified and designation is taken into account. (Terminology is not consistent in Coseriu's English publications. While in Coseriu and Geckeler (1981 [1974]: 30), language-specific meaning is termed 'signification', it is simply called 'meaning' in Coseriu (1985: xxx). To avoid any misunderstandings, and in accordance with the standardised terminology used in the present volume, I use the term 'signified' to refer to *Bedeutung*.)

The distinction between signified and designation is central to solving the main problem of role semantics outlined in the previous section. The distinction is known "since the Stoics", but it is unfortunately "disregarded over and over again" (Coseriu and Geckeler 1981 [1974]: 54). To make it clear: the Saussurean

---

[4] If critical scholars are quoted at all, then the main criticism is not addressed. For instance, Starosta (1978) is quoted by Levin and Rappaport Hovav (2005: 42–43), but they do not discuss the critical remarks Starosta raises from a significative-semantic perspective. Starosta (1978) criticizes role semantics in a similar way as Coseriu, without however being familiar with Coseriu's approach.

sign consists of the acoustic image (Fr. *signifiant*) and the meaning (Fr. *signifié*). The bilateral sign is also where Coseriu situates *Bedeutung*: the signified is language-internal, hence to be defined in terms of semasiological relations.[5] By contrast, *Bezeichnung* or designation is a relation of language-external reference. Designation "is the relation of whole linguistic signs to 'objects' of extralinguistic reality" (Coseriu and Geckeler 1981 [1974]: 54). English role semantics in general and Fillmore (2003) in particular mix up signifieds and designation in the ambiguous use of the term "meaning" (Coseriu 1970 [1969]: 107). Coseriu (1970 [1969]: 109) explains the problem by discussing Fillmore's examples:
(12) John broke the window.
(13) A hammer broke the window.

According to Fillmore, *John* is an AGENT in (12), whereas *a hammer* is an INSTRUMENT in (13). Coseriu challenges this analysis and points out that the subjects in both sentences code the same semantic role (CARRIER OF ACTION in terms of a significative-semantic role, see Section 4.2) since both code the same signified. Moreover, despite being centred on designation, Fillmore's analysis of *John* as AGENT in (12) and of *a hammer* as INSTRUMENT in (13) is misleading even from a language-external point of view, because "it is possible to break a window with John as an instrument" (Coseriu 1970 [1969]: 109). Coseriu's criticism is all the more striking because denotative semantics has still not recognised the importance of the difference between signified and designation (Willems 2019: 476–477). Coseriu further illustrates the difference with examples such as the following (Coseriu 2007 [1988]: 84):
(14) Caesar Pompeium vicit.
(15) Pompeius a Caesare victus est.
(16) Victoria Caesaris.

It is, of course, justified to call the entity designated with *Caesar* in (14)–(16) an AGENT. However, then AGENT does not refer to a semantic role, but it is a description of the Roman statesman mentioned in the sentences. But the fact that the extralinguistic entity Caesar is understood to be the AGENT (designation) is expressed by three entirely different "language-specific functions" (Coseriu 2007: 84). To describe the signifieds of these language-specific functions is the goal of significative semantics. Denotative semantics bypasses the signifieds and

---

5 According to Saussure (2003: 129–131), a sign's signified can only be defined by means of negative "differences", whereas according to Coseriu (1992 [1988]: 68–78) there is a "positively understood value" (Coseriu 1992 [1988]: 74) in addition to the negative differences; see Willems (2019: 480–487), Belligh and Willems (2021: 8) and Höllein (2019: 25–26).

amalgamates meaning that is internal to language and meaning that is external to language. Coseriu writes:

> the whole signified of the sentence (G. *Satzbedeutung*) is simply reduced to the designation. Hence the many 'deep' similarities between different languages and the many alleged universals that transformational grammar repeatedly finds: in reality, these are very often radically different structures of signifieds (G. *Bedeutungsstrukturen*), which however are equivalent in designation and therefore considered 'identical in deep structure'. The 'identity' meant here, however, is basically an extralinguistic (G. *außersprachliche*) one, it is simply the IDENTITY OF THE WORLD AS SUCH and by no means an identity of the languages under consideration. (Coseriu 1970: 57; emphasis in the original)

Coseriu and Geckeler (1981 [1974]) also provide cross-linguistic examples that illustrate the importance of the distinction. For instance, English, German and French represent extralinguistic reality in identical ways by means of the words *ladder – Leiter – échelle* and *stairway – Treppe – escalier*. By contrast, the fact that the relation between signifieds and designation is not the same in all languages is illustrated by the following languages, which only have one word for both referents in the extralinguistic reality: "Italian (*scala*), Spanish (*escalera*), Portuguese (*escada*), Romanian (*scară*)" (Coseriu and Geckeler 1981 [1974]: 49), "while in German, English and French the distinction is made linguistically" (Coseriu and Geckeler 1981 [1974]: 50). The alternative, viz. that an Italian or Spanish speaker would not be able to make a distinction between the two referents, can be ruled out.

One wonders whether the shortcomings not only of role semantics but of semantics in general are not to a considerable extent due to the problem of terminology pointed out above. While in German, the distinction between *Bedeutung* (signified) and *Bezeichnung* (designation) is readily available, in English both are understood as *meaning* and therefore oftentimes mixed up. Unfortunately, this confusion has also affected German semantics through the reception of linguistic literature published in English (see Höllein 2019, 5–7). However, with Coseriu (1972 [1971]: 78) the basic problem can be formulated as follows: Role semantics is about signifieds, not designation.

4 An outline of significative semantics and the set of semantic core roles

Independently from Coseriu, but around the same time, Susov (1973) established a significative-semantic system of semantic roles based on the same criticism. Susov's approach was extended to a new semantic theory especially by Welke

(1988, 2011, 2019), but also by Ágel (2017), Ágel and Höllein (2021) and Höllein (2017, 2019). The result is a theory that takes into account the aforementioned problems of current semantics and opens up new perspectives. Significative semantics is able to fulfil the general goal of role semantics to describe sentences with a limited set of properly defined semantic roles. Programmatically, this implementation would have been possible 50 years ago since Coseriu's account laid the groundwork for significative semantics. At that time, the possibilities of extensive corpus research were very limited. Corpora are the missing link to significative semantic investigations, even of rare syntactic phenomena such as prepositional objects.

4.1 Principles of significative semantics

Significative semantics is based on six principles, which are basically designed in response to denotative role semantics. As these principles have already been introduced in Höllein (2019), they are only briefly presented below.

1. Language-specific determination of roles. Denotative semantics is based on the universality of roles. Fillmore refers to a "universal system of deep-structure cases" (Fillmore 1968: 21) but defines the roles in terms of particular languages. Whether semantic roles are universal concepts or not has to remain unresolved until every language is described with regard to its own system of roles. Denotative semantics justifies this procedure by arguing that the roles are gained language-externally (Fillmore 1968: 25, Levin and Rappaport Hovav 2005: 11). Extralinguistic reality thus becomes the source from which all languages derive their roles in an identical manner. From the perspective of significative semantics, the problem is that extralinguistic reality can only be obtained through the mediation of particular languages (Welke 2002: 96). There are at least as many language-external realities as there are languages: "the signified is by definition language-specific" ("da die Bedeutung per definitionem einzelsprachlich ist", Coseriu 1987: 8). The scope of significative semantics and any set of significative-semantic roles are therefore by definition limited to a particular language (which also raises specific problems, cf. Section 4.2). This may be illustrated by pointing out that different languages differ considerably with regard, e.g., to prepositions, compare:

(17) count/rechnen, lean/(sich) stützen, rely/(sich) verlassen → on/auf
(18) wait/warten, hope/hoffen, long/sinnen → for/auf
(19) work/arbeiten, strike/streiken, write/schreiben → for/für
(20) ask/bitten, beg/betteln, plead/anflehen → for/um

The examples in (17)–(20) are taken from Engelen (1970: 16–17) and illustrate the differences between English and German regarding the prepositions that are governed by semantically similar verbs in different languages. Verb classes with the same prepositional object in English have only limited counterparts in German, and vice versa.

2. Language-specific definition of roles. Coseriu's criticism regarding denotative semantics has been outlined in Section 3. Again independently from Coseriu, Fleischmann expressed the leading idea of significative semantics as follows: "For [significative semantics] […], ontological conditions are irrelevant while the chosen linguistic representation is decisive" (Fleischmann 1985: 104). Significative-semantic roles are therefore defined and determined according to language-specific criteria, i.e. without reference to extralinguistic situations. Accordingly, a significative-semantic syntactic analysis does not access language-external knowledge domains. In this regard, significative-semantic analysis differs drastically from denotative semantic analysis (see Section 4.2).

3. Direct analysis of roles. The starting point of this principle is the procedure of denotative semantics which has been shown to be problematic from a significative-semantic perspective. The procedure does not actually analyse external situations but explains a number of linguistic realisations as default cases. It remains unclear for what reason a sentence is declared as default. Compare the following sentences (Fillmore 1977: 75):
(21) I hit Harry with the stick.
(22) I hit the stick against Harry.

According to Fillmore, (22) is derived from (21), because "we will find, I believe, that it is in some sense more natural to say [(21)] than [(22)]" (Fillmore 1977: 75). (22) is therefore also analysed in the same denotative-semantic terms as (21). This approach is not viable in terms of significative semantics, and significative-semantic roles must be analysed independently in each sentence. Thus, no propositions are considered default cases only in order to derive roles of other propositions from them (for further discussion see Höllein 2019: 13–16).

4. Prototypical determination of roles. Significative-semantic roles have prototypical properties. From the perspective of significative semantics, "clearcut" (Dowty 1991: 574) distinctions are not suitable to describe languages adequately. This principle of significative semantics is the only one which is shared with parts of denotative semantics. As a matter of fact, prototype theory is the only substantial change achieved by Dowty (1991) with regard to the theory of denotative-semantic roles, given that Dowty, too, abandons the assumption of semantic invariance (cf. the discussion in Section 2).

5. 'One-per-sent'. Each semantic role may only occur once in a sentence. This principle goes back to the so-called "one-per-sent solution" of Starosta (1978, 1988: 138). It was later adopted by Chomsky ('theta criterion') and then became famous. With regard to significative semantics it was first formulated by Ágel (2017: 49). The principle states that it should be impossible that one sentence contains several AGENTS or PATIENTS.

6. No synonymy. In accordance with Goldberg (1995: 67), there are no synonymous pairs of syntactic relations and semantic roles in significative semantics. The principle of no synonymy is a reaction to denotative-semantic analyses which have to assume synonymy on a massive scale since their point of comparison are (language-external) situations and not (language-internal) events. The distinction between situations and events stems from Welke (2002: 96), who defines situations (G. *Situationen*) as language-external and events (G. *Sachverhalte*) as language-internal in order to avoid confusion. Consider the two sentences below (Fillmore 1968: 25):
(23) John opened the door.
(24) The door was opened by John.

In denotative semantics, both the direct object *the door* in (23) and the subject in (23') are analysed as PATIENT. Denotative semantics thus indirectly assumes that in this case the subject and the direct object are synonymous. Obviously, this is not intended, but a denotative-semantic analysis is forced to draw this conclusion because the analysis is based on designation. Synonymy is then a derivative effect that has to be accepted. The massive synonymy of Fillmore's INSTRUMENT role, which is analysed in Höllein (2020), is surpassed by Shamsan (2018: 49), who assumes nine (!) synonymous roles for the subject relation in Arabic passive sentences. Common to all these analyses is the muddling-up of designation and signifieds that was already criticised by Coseriu (1970 [1969]: 105) (see Section 3). In terms of significative semantics, the principle of no synonymy is reflected in semantic analysis: "If two constructions are syntactically distinct, they must be semantically [distinct]" (Goldberg 1995: 67), i.e. they must be analysed in terms of different semantic roles.

4.2 Significative-semantic roles

According to the first principle of significative semantics, semantic roles have to be established for every particular language separately. Since there is as yet no generally accepted set of significative-semantic roles for English, the roles described here are only preliminary suggestions for roles connected to predicates, subjects, direct objects and indirect objects. More specific roles like those for prepositional complements are disregarded because of the difficulties described in Section 4.1.

Table 2: significative-semantic core roles

predicate	subject	indirect object	direct object
action	carrier of action	affected by action	matter of action
activity	carrier of activity	affected by activity	
process	carrier of process	affected by process	
state	carrier of state	affected by state	

The set of core roles in Table 2 is based on the idea that there are four types of events and roles that depend on these event roles. The event roles ACTION, ACTIVITY, PROCESS and STATE are significative-semantic event roles in the tradition of Saussure's (1997) semasiological approach to semantics. Below are four basic examples (SYN = syntactic relations, SIG = significative-semantic roles):

(24)	He	gave	him	the suitcase.
SYN	subject	predicate	indirect object	direct object
SIG	CARRIER OF ACTION	ACTION	AFFECTED BY ACTION	MATTER OF ACTION

(25)	I	run.
SYN	subject	predicate
SIG	CARRIER OF ACTIVITY	ACTIVITY

(26)	He	was knocked out.
SYN	subject	predicate
SIG	CARRIER OF PROCESS	PROCESS

(27)	This rose	is beautiful.
SYN	subject	predicate
SIG	CARRIER OF STATE	STATE

Transitive structures as in (24) are ACTIONS. Intransitive structures in active voice like the example in (25) are prototypically ACTIVITIES. Intransitive structures in passive voice as in (26) (which may be accompanied by a prepositional phrase) are PROCESSES and predicative structures with the copular verb *be* as in (27) are STATES.[6]

Recall that these roles are proposed only tentatively, because the significative-semantic roles that have thus far been identified are developed for German and only tested in German corpora. A complete set of significative-semantic roles for German is meanwhile available and will be published in Ágel and Höllein (2021). However, in accordance with the first principle of significative semantics, this set is not automatically transferable to English. The core roles might nevertheless be suitable for English as well. Conversely, a completely different set has to be developed with regard to prepositional objects in English, which differ dramatically from German as the contrastive study of Engelen (1970: 16–23) showed.

An analysis of the examples (2)–(11) in terms of denotative-semantic roles was provided in Section 3. Below I provide the alternative analysis in terms of significative-semantic roles.

(2) The slogan that concentrates her fears [CARRIER OF STATE] is hotspot school.
(3) The slogan concentrates her fears [MATTER OF ACTION].
(4) An initiative is trying to fight against this [MATTER OF ACTION].
(5) They don't know it [MATTER OF ACTION] any other way from their family.
(6) An initiative fights against this [?].
(7) So many people in Neukölln have to live on welfare [?].
(8) It [CARRIER OF STATE] was Ylva's first day at school.
(9) [2nd person plural] [CARRIER OF ACTION] Create more good offers!
(10) Children are aggressive or violent [STATE].
(11) I think everyone should search for the right school for their child [MATTER OF ACTION].

The significative-semantic analysis of the examples demonstrates that the problems caused by denotative semantics disappear. Only the roles of prepositional objects are missing. In German, these roles have already been elaborated in Höllein (2019) on the basis of Lerot (1982), Ágel (2017) and Rostila (2005, 2007). Significative-semantic roles of prepositional objects are not "familiar semantic roles like AGENT, PATIENT, RECIPIENT, which only emerge from higher-level generalizations producing more grammaticalized a[rgument]-constructions like the German transitive construction" (Rostila 2018: 424). With regard to English, the elaboration of these roles is a task for the future. In the next section, I

---

[6] For a semantic description of significative-semantic predicate/event roles, see Höllein (2017).

briefly present the significative-semantic method, which has already been tested for German.

4.3 The method of significative semantics

From the discussion in the previous section, it has become evident that adopting significative-semantic roles solves central problems of denotative semantics. While for German a set of such roles has meanwhile been established and tested on large corpora, this work is still pending for English.[7] By way of example, I briefly discuss in this section how the significative-semantic role ACTION can be obtained. The method was introduced in Höllein (2019: 138–162) and consists of five steps. The first step is to choose a role, in this case the significative-semantic predicate role ACTION. The second step consists in collecting corpus data. In the third step, the data has to be analysed and sorted (there may be one group or several groups). This can be done intuitively at first and does not have to follow precise rules. The fourth step is to establish a paraphrase that reflects the meaning of the group or groups formed in the third step. The final step is the most important one: productive examples have to be found to back up the group or groups. If there are no such examples in the corpus, the groups should be sorted differently. Productive examples are sentences in which the phenomenon appears, although it is not expected in this particular environment; compare:

(28) OH MY! I met @snoopdogg and he instagrames our pic! (https://twitter.com/santaron916, 10. Dez. 2015)

(29) He posts our picture | He loads up our picture | He publishes our picture […]

In (28), the new English verb *to instagram* acts as if it was a transitive predicate with a CARRIER OF ACTION (*he*) and a MATTER OF ACTION (*our pic*). The verb is coerced into the transitive construction (for a detailed explanation of coercion see Höllein 2019: 41–50). This example of linguistic productivity corroborates the significative-semantic role ACTION because the verb *instagram* operates similarly to the verbs listed in (29), which are default instances of the role ACTION. The significative-semantic role can eventually be adequately defined. The above

---

[7] The set of significative-semantic roles was tested on a sub-corpus of DeReKo (The Mannheim German Reference Corpus) (see Höllein 2019: 138–162) and is currently being tested on diachronic New High German data in the project *Syntaktische Grundstrukturen des Neuhochdeutschen* [Basic syntactic structures in New High German] at the Universities of Gießen and Kassel. The project is supported by the German Research Foundation (DFG).

example is only tentative and would have to be replicated with regard to larger corpora and systematically collected productive examples. Moreover, the method is not limited to the identification of significative-semantic roles but can also be used for the significative-semantic modelling of other entities on other levels such as, for example, prefix verbs.

5 Conclusion

This article has dealt with the problems of denotative role semantics and how to solve them by drawing on Coseriu's early criticism, which is of particular importance for the theory of significative semantics. However, although Coseriu's criticism strikes at the core of the problems of denotative semantics, his thoughts are still not widely received. He made his critical remarks half a century ago, but his arguments continue to be valid given that denotative-semantic theory has largely remained the same.

Based on Coseriu's criticism, significative semantics has been developed for German. In this article, the new model was introduced and briefly applied to English by way of illustration. The transfer to English has been carried out cautiously because significative semantics is based on meanings (signifieds) that differ from one language to another and therefore requires an approach in which roles are established on a language-specific basis. The case of prepositional objects has shown that a simple translation across languages is not possible. At the same time, an outline of the method has been provided by means of which significative-semantic roles can be established with regard to English (and possibly also other languages). Following Coseriu's ideas, an extension of significative semantics to other languages would also be desirable because this would allow us to demonstrate the importance of the distinction between signifieds and designation on a much larger scale. It would also be particularly useful to develop a system of significative-semantic roles based on corpus-linguistic research of other languages than German and English.

References

Ágel, Vilmos. 2017. *Grammatische Textanalyse: Textglieder, Satzglieder, Wortgruppenglieder*. Berlin & Boston: De Gruyter.

Ágel, Vilmos and Dagobert Höllein. 2021. "Satzbaupläne als Zeichen: Die semantischen Rollen des Deutschen in Theorie und Praxis".

Belligh, Thomas and Klaas Willems. 2021. "What's in a code? The code-inference distinction in Neo-Gricean Pragmatics, Relevance Theory, and Integral Linguistics". *Language Sciences* 83, 1–22. In: Anja Binanzer, Jana Gamper and Verena Wecker (eds.), *Prototypen. Schemata. Konstruktionen. Untersuchungen zur deutschen Morphologie und Syntax*. Berlin & Boston: De Gruyter.

Coseriu, Eugenio. 1970 [1969]. "Bedeutung und Bezeichnung im Lichte der strukturellen Semantik". In: Peter Hartmann and Henri Vernay (eds.), *Sprachwissenschaft und Übersetzen Symposium an der Universität Heidelberg 24.2.–26.2.1969*, 104–121. München: Hueber.

Coseriu, Eugenio. 1970. "Semantik, innere Sprachform und Tiefenstruktur". *Folia Linguistica* 4:1, 53–63.

Coseriu, Eugenio. 1972 [1971]. "Semantik und Grammatik". In: Institut für Deutsche Sprache (ed.), *Neue Grammatiktheorien und ihre Anwendung auf das heutige Deutsch: Jahrbuch 1971*, 77–89. Düsseldorf: Schwann.

Coseriu, Eugenio. 1981. *Lecciones de lingüística general*. Madrid: Gredos.

Coseriu, Eugenio. 1985. "Linguistic competence: what is it really?" *The Modern Language Review* 80:4, xxv–xxxv.

Coseriu, Eugenio. 1987. "Bedeutung, Bezeichnung und sprachliche Kategorien". *Sprachwissenschaft* 12:1, 1–23.

Coseriu, Eugenio. 1992 [1988]. *Einführung in die allgemeine Sprachwissenschaft* (second edition). Tübingen: Francke (German translation of Coseriu 1981).

Coseriu, Eugenio. 2007 [1988]. *Sprachkompetenz. Grundzüge der Theorie des Sprechens*. Edited by Heinrich Weber (second edition). Tübingen: Narr.

Coseriu, Eugenio and Horst Geckeler. 1981 [1974]. *Trends in structural semantics*. Tübingen: Narr.

Dowty, David R. 1991. "Thematic proto-roles and argument selection". *Language* 67, 547–619.

Engelen, Bernhard. 1970. "Das Präpositionalobjekt im Deutschen und seine Entsprechungen im Englischen, Französischen und Russischen". In: Ulrich Engel (ed.), *Forschungsberichte des Instituts für Deutsche Sprache*. Vol. 4, 3–30. Tübingen: Narr.

Fillmore, Charles J. 1968. "The case for case". In: Emmon Bach and Robert T. Harms (eds.), *Universals in linguistic theory*, 1–88. New York: Rinehart and Winston.

Fillmore, Charles J. 1977. "The Case for Case Reopened". In: Peter Cole and Jerrold M. Sadock (eds.), *Syntax and semantics*. Vol. 8: *Grammatical relations*, 59–81. New York: Academic Press.

Fillmore, Charles J. 2003. "Valency and semantic roles: the concept of deep structure case". In: Vilmos Ágel, Ludwig M. Eichinger, Hans-Werner Eroms, Peter Hellwig, Hans-Jürgen Heringer and Henning Lobin (eds.) *Dependenz und Valenz: Ein internationales Handbuch der zeitgenössischen Forschung*, 457–475. Berlin & New York: De Gruyter.

Fillmore, Charles J. 2006. "Frame semantics". In: Keith Brown (ed.), *Encyclopedia of Language & Linguistics*, 613–620. Amsterdam: Elsevier.

Fleischmann, Eberhard. 1985. *Kasustheorie und Translationslinguistik: Dissertation zur Promotion B.* Karl-Marx-Universität Leipzig.

Goldberg, Adele E. 1995. *Constructions. A Construction Grammar approach to argument structure*. Chicago: University of Chicago Press.

Goldberg, Adele E. 2019. *Explain me this: creativity, competition, and the partial productivity of constructions*. Princeton, N. J.: Princeton University Press.

Höllein, Dagobert. 2017. "Gibt es Handlungs-, Tätigkeits-, Vorgangs- und Zustandsverben: Ein Vorschlag für signifikativ-semantische Rollen von Prädikaten". *Zeitschrift für germanistische Linguistik* 45:2, 286–305.

Höllein, Dagobert. 2019. *Präpositionalobjekt vs. Adverbial: Die semantischen Rollen der Präpositionalobjekte*. Berlin & Boston: De Gruyter.

Höllein, Dagobert. 2020. "Verbund von Valenztheorie und Konstruktionsgrammatik am Beispiel produktiver Präpositionalobjekte". *Linguistische Berichte. Sonderheft* 28, 83–112.

Lakoff, George. 1977. "Linguistic gestalts". In: Samuel E. Fox, Woodford A. Beach and Shulamith Philosoph (eds.), *Papers from the Thirteenth Regional Meeting of the Chicago Linguistic Society*, 236–287. Illinois: University of Chicago Press.

Lerot, Jacques. 1982. "Die verbregierten Präpositionen in Präpositionalobjekten". In: Werner Abraham (ed.), *Satzglieder im Deutschen: Vorschläge zur syntaktischen, semantischen und pragmatischen Fundierung*, 261–291. Tübingen: Narr.

Levin, Beth and Malka Rappaport Hovav. 2005. *Argument realization*. Cambridge: Cambridge University Press.

Primus, Beatrice. 1999. *Cases and thematic roles: ergative, accusative and active*. Berlin & New York: De Gruyter.

Rostila, Jouni. 2005. "Zur Grammatikalisierung bei Präpositionalobjekten". In: Torsten Leuschner, Tanja Mortelmans and Sarah de Groodt (eds.), *Grammatikalisierung im Deutschen*, 135–168. Berlin & New York: De Gruyter.

Rostila, Jouni. 2007. *Konstruktionsansätze zur Argumentmarkierung im Deutschen*. Tampere: Tampere University Press.

Rostila, Jouni. 2018. "Argument structure constructions among german prepositional objects". In: Hans C. Boas and Alexander Ziem (eds.), *Constructional approaches to argument structure in German*, 406–446. Berlin & Boston: De Gruyter.

Saussure, Ferdinand de. 1997. *Linguistik und Semiologie: Notizen aus dem Nachlass, Texte, Briefe und Dokumente*. Edited by Johannes Fehr. Frankfurt a. M.: Suhrkamp.

Saussure, Ferdinand de. 2003. *Wissenschaft der Sprache: Neue Texte aus dem Nachlass*. Suhrkamp. Frankfurt a. M.: Suhrkamp.

Shamsan, Muayad. 2018. "Theta roles assigned to subject argument in Arabic and English passive voice". *International Journal of Applied Linguistics and English Literature* 7:7, 47–51.

Starosta, Stanley. 1978. "The one per sent solution". In: Werner Abraham (ed.), *Valence, semantic case, and grammatical relations*, 439–576. Amsterdam: Benjamins.

Starosta, Stanley. 1988. *The case for lexicase: an outline of lexicase grammatical theory*. London & New York: Pinter.

Susov, Ivan P. 1973. *Semantičeskaja struktura predloženija: Na materiale prostogo predloženija v sovremennom nemeckom jazyke*. Leningrad.

Van Valin, Robert D. 2007. *Exploring the syntax-semantics interface*. Cambridge: Cambridge University Press.
Welke, Klaus. 1988. *Einführung in die Valenz- und Kasustheorie*. Leipzig: Bibliographisches Institut.
Welke, Klaus. 2002. *Deutsche Syntax funktional: Perspektiviertheit syntaktischer Strukturen*. Tübingen: Stauffenburg.
Welke, Klaus. 2011. *Valenzgrammatik des Deutschen: Eine Einführung*. Berlin & New York: De Gruyter.
Welke, Klaus. 2019. *Konstruktionsgrammatik des Deutschen: Ein sprachgebrauchsbezogener Ansatz*. Berlin & Boston: De Gruyter.
Willems, Klaas. 2011. "Meaning and interpretation: The semiotic similarities and differences between Cognitive Grammar and European structural linguistics". *Semiotica* 185, 1–50.
Willems, Klaas. 2019. "Eugenio Coserius Sprachzeichentheorie und der Prager Strukturalismus". In: Tomáš Hoskovec (ed.), *Travaux du Cercle linguistique de Prague. Nouvelle Série* 8 (*Expérience et avenir du structuralisme*), 469–503. Kanina: OPS & Praha: PLK.

Wolf Dietrich (Münster)
Coseriu's approach to word formation as an illustration of his theory of meaning

> *Semantically, with regard to content, word formation corresponds to a grammaticalization of the 'primary' lexicon, i.e. the lexicon that is the starting point of word formation processes.**

1 Introduction

In his discussion of Generative Grammar, Coseriu was among the first to make the claim that everything in language is semantic. There is no contradiction whatsoever between semantics and (a-semantic) syntax as assumed by transformational grammar (Coseriu 1975 [1971]: 113). Grammatical semantics (tenses, moods, aspectual functions, number, etc.) as well as syntactic functions (active, passive, ergative constructions, nominal cases, word order determined by focus, etc.) cannot be accounted for without reference to meaning. Even word classes or parts of speech such as nouns and verbs have their specific meaning as 'moulds' of a particular lexical meaning (Coseriu 1974; cf. 1977 [1974]). For example, *fish* as a noun expresses 'fish' as a substance (thing or class of things), *to fish* as a verb means an action ('to do something with *fish* as a noun', especially 'to catch fish').

The general English term 'meaning' is much too vague and not suitable to be used in linguistic analysis. Therefore, Coseriu's distinction between three kinds of 'meaning' is of key importance to the study of grammar, syntax and the lexicon: the signified (G. *Bedeutung*, Fr. *signifié*) (and the corresponding verb 'signify', G. *bedeuten*, Fr. *signifier*) is the lexical or grammatical contents given in a particular language. Designation (G. *Bezeichnung*) (corresponding verb: 'designate') is the semantic relation between a linguistic sign made up of a form and a signified and its reference to an extralinguistic object or concept in a specific text. Finally, 'sense' or 'text meaning' (G. *Sinn*) refers to the meaning of a whole text or piece of utterance (compare, e.g., "what is the sense of your question?") (Coseriu 1985, 2007 [1988]).

In his theory of word formation, Coseriu is anxious to avoid the traditional mixture of morphological and semantic categories, e.g. prefixation, suffixation

---

* "In inhaltlicher, bedeutungsbezogener Hinsicht entspricht die Wortbildung einer Grammatikalisierung des 'primären', d.h. den Wortbildungsverfahren jeweils zugrunde liegenden Wortschatzes" (Coseriu 1977a: 52).

as well as diminutives, collective formations or 'nomina agentis'. In Section 2, I will show that, e.g., modification is a functional category of word formation in Romance languages as well as English, but in some cases it is expressed by means of suffixation while in others by means of prefixation. The specific signified, i.e., the kind of modification, is provided with the individual suffix or prefix. On the other hand, suffixes also occur to form 'developments', as I will explain in Section 3. Morphological instruments such as prefix and suffix, derivation and composition are not themselves semantic, they do not express any functional category. Moreover, the distinction between signifieds, which is inherent in a lexeme or a grammatical morpheme, and designation, which relates to a specific situation or kind of context, is important because linguistic description does not refer to individual situations or specific persons or objects mentioned in a text (Coseriu 1977a: 49). Linguistic description is concerned with linguistic structures, abstract morphosyntactic functions, and so on. Therefore, in a coherent linguistic analysis it is imperative not to confuse grammatical signifieds such as 'collective modification' (see Section 2) or 'generic composition' (see Section 3) with specific designations. A Spanish derivation such as *álamo → alam-eda* may apply to several types of designation that can be specified as 'avenue planted with poplars', 'poplar forest' or 'smaller poplar grove'. However, the language-specific signified of the derivation is only 'collective modification with regard to *álamo* 'poplar''. Similarly, the signified of a French derivation such as *cuisine → cuisinière* is '[generic composition] with regard to kitchen', regardless of the designation of a person ('female cook') or an instrument ('kitchen stove'). Hence, designations are not included in signifieds. We generally identify designations by virtue of our world knowledge, not on the basis of language-specific linguistic categories.

In contrast to traditional theories of word formation, Coseriu proposes purely semantic categories such as 'modification' (of an existing primary word or lexeme), 'development' of a primary word into a new, derived word by adding a syntactic function, which can either be predicative or attributive, and 'composition' (cf. Coseriu 1977a for an overview). Composition is the combination of two lexemes (just as in traditional composition) or of a lexeme and a generic element such as 'someone' or 'something'. For example, *teach-er* is a generic compound of 'someone' + 'teach': 'someone who teaches'. In Coseriu's approach, word formation is 'grammar in the lexicon' (see Laca 1986). Since Coseriu has often been very succinct in his own writings, many of his insights have been developed by his students in full-length studies (see Laca 1986, Lüdtke 1978, 2005, Staib 1988). Geckeler (1981a, 1988) published a number of seminal articles in English on Coseriu's studies in semantics, especially lexical semantics.

In this article, I discuss Coseriu's theory of word formation against the background of his distinction between the 'signified' (*Bedeutung*) and 'designation' (*Bezeichnung*). I will draw on English, French and Spanish examples and pay special attention to grammatical meanings as they appear in word formation. Although semantics is the primary subject of the article, it is important to keep in mind that word formation is a synchronic process according to Coseriu. A derivation is only possible in a language when it is formed from an existing word, the so-called 'base', resulting in a derived word that has a different meaning compared to the base. The same is true of composition. Compositions made with elements that no longer exist in the language or that do not have the meaning they have in the compound are at least partially opaque and not analysable as results of word formation, e. g. *cran* in *cranberry* or *dog* in *hot dog*. On the other hand, shortenings like *admin* for *administration* or *lab* for *laboratory*, *sitcom* for *situation comedy* etc. do not belong to word formation because their meaning is not different from their base. The same is true for abbreviations such as *USA*, *UNO*, *WHO*, etc. Conversely, if the clipped form possesses a new meaning, there is no longer any morphological connection between the base and the clipped form and it has become lexicalized; compare, e. g., the example of *vamp* and its historical base *vampire* (Marchand 1969: 441). 'Lexicalization' is defined as the loss of transparency between a derived form and its base whenever the semantic relation between both no longer exists. For example, French *fourchette* 'fork' is no longer understood as a diminutive of *fourche* 'pitchfork', Spanish *tenedor* 'fork (as a tableware)' is no longer understood as derived from *tener* 'to hold', i. e. as if it were still meaning 'holder'. In synchronic linguistics, these are lexicalized forms and therefore morphologically unanalysable.

2 Modification

Modification, in Coseriu's theory of word formation, is the derivation process by which the signified of the base is merely semantically modified, the base's word class remaining unaltered. In many languages, there is a wide range of subcategories of modification such as diminutive, augmentative, approximative, intensifying formation, collective, negative, aspectual functions such as iterative, frequentative, and situating formations. 'Motion' (G. *Movierung*) is the kind of modification by which feminine names of persons or animals are formed from masculine nouns (Latin *equ-us* 'horse' → *equ-a* 'mare'[1], Spanish *suegr-o* →

---

[1] Structurally, Latin hierarchy is different from English: while *equus/equa* are basic terms that

suegr-a 'mother in law'), names of fruit from nouns for fruit trees (Spanish *manzan-o* 'apple tree' → *manzan-a* 'apple', *cerez-o* 'cherry tree' → *cerez-a* 'cherry')², an objective quantification from a base which means a 'normal' size of the object (Spanish *jarr-o* 'jug' → *jarr-a* 'bigger jug'). If we accept that *manzana* 'apple' is a modification of *manzano*, we have to interpret *manzana* as a plentiful shape of *manzano*, which denotes 'apple' as a tree, just as *jarra* means the plentiful shape of *jarro* 'jug'.

Diminutives and augmentatives are not objective quantifications of a given base but affective modifications. They may express familiarity and tenderness in the case of diminutives (e. g. Spanish *mi hij-it-a* 'my dear daughter', *tu cas-it-a* 'your appreciable home', *el Princip-it-o* 'the (kind) little Prince') and a pejorative attitude (e. g. Spanish *puebl-o* 'village' → *pobl-ach-o* 'miserable village') or intensification (e. g. *beso* → *bes-uc-o* 'big kiss', *hombr-az-o* 'big man' or 'fine fellow') in the case of augmentatives. However, familiarity, tenderness and pejorative attitude are no language-specific signifieds of these modifications but context-induced values based on designation. While such values always depend on context and may be positive or negative, the invariant language-specific signified is 'affective modification' without further qualification.

The result of a diminutive or augmentative formation may be an intensifying one if the word class or the context favours such an effect. For example, American Spanish diminutives of adverbs like *ahor-a* 'now' → *ahor-it-a* 'just now' and adjectives like *car-o* 'expensive' → *car-it-o* 'a bit too expensive', *fresqu-it-o* 'rather fresh' are used in order to express this effect, just as do Spanish augmentatives like *bes-uc-o*, *bes-uch-o* 'big kiss', *dulc-e* 'sweet' → *dulz-ón* 'nauseatingly sweet', *amig-o* → *amig-ote* 'family friend (which may be nasty or disagreeable)'. Purely intensifying meanings may occur in other languages as well, for example with the Guarani suffix *-ite*, *-ete* (*i-porã-ite* 3-good-INT 'it is very good', *h-epy-ete* 3-price-INT 'its price is too high, it is too expensive'; see Estigarribia 2020: 250, 253).

Collective modifications are made by *-al* or *-edo/-ado* in Spanish (*manzan-o* → *manzan-al* 'collective formation of apples', *almendr-o* → *almendr-al* 'almond grove', *robl-e* → *robl-ed-o* 'oak forest', *álamo* 'poplar' → *alameda* 'poplar forest' or 'poplar avenue'). While the signified is 'collective', the designation of a poplar

---

include sex, English *horse* is indifferent with regard to sex, but may be, on a secondary level, differentiated by *stallion* and *mare*.

2 By contrast, French *poir-ier* 'pear tree' does not involve modification because it is formed from *poire* 'pear', a base which denotes the fruit, not the fruit tree (see below Section 3.2). In the same way, English *cherry* is the base of the compound *cherry-tree*. In cases such as these there is an inverse direction of word formation.

avenue or poplar forest, an almond plantation or an almond grove, a rice plantation or a paddy field (compare Spanish *arroz-al*, French *riz-eraie*) again depends on the context and/or world knowledge. The French collective suffix is *-aie* (*hêtr-e* 'beech' → *hetr-aie* 'beech-grove', *oranger-aie* 'orange grove') or *-eraie* when there is no base in *-er* (see *riz-eraie* 'paddy field').

Even negative formations are contrasting modifications of a given base. In English, negative adjectives are formed by means of prefixes, for example *un-necessary*, *im-possible*, *a-historical*. In French, the prefixes are *in-* and its variants: *juste* → *in-juste* 'unjust, unfair', *buvable* → *im-buvable* 'undrinkable', *non-* (*non-violent* 'non-violent'), and so forth. Spanish negative prefixes are *in-* and its variants (*in-válido* 'void, invalid', *ir-regular* 'irregular'), *no* (*no existente* 'unexisting'), and *a-* (*a-histórico* 'unhistorical'). Iterative modification is expressed by *re-* or *ri-* in Romance languages: French *relire le roman* 'to read the novel once more', Spanish *rehacer el trabajo* 'to rework the order', Italian *rileggere il romanzo* 'to read the novel once more'. The prefix can also be found in English (*to reset, retake, revivify*, etc.). The use of *re-*, *ri-* is in many languages subject to restrictions: Spanish *recalcar*, for example, often does not mean 'to tread once more' but 'to tread down', 'to tread down with the feet', 'to press with the feet', a meaning that includes repetitiqn of the activity.

Frequentative modification is not a widespread word formation category in Romance languages. Its Latin origin was much more common than it is in Romance (Lüdtke 2005: 366–367): *legere* 'to read' and its passive participle *lectum* was the base of *lect-it-are* 'to read eagerly', *venire* → *ventit-are* 'to keep coming', *capere* → *capt-it-are* 'to strive eagerly after'. Frequentative modification is an important category in Finno-Ugric languages. In Hungarian, for example, the suffix *-gat-/-get-* regularly forms frequentative verbs: *olvas-ni* 'to read' → *olvas-gat-ni* 'to read about', *kérdez-ni* 'to ask' → *kérdez-get-ni* 'to ask around', *beszél-ni* 'to speak' → *beszél-get-ni* 'to talk', *sétál-ni* 'to go for a walk' → *sétál-gat-ni* 'to walk around' (Kiefer 2000: 199–201).

Situating modification is frequent in Germanic and Slavic languages but less usual in Romance languages. In the latter languages, there are partial processes on account of situating prefixes like French *voir* → *pré-voir* 'to foresee', *voler* → *survoler* 'to fly over', Spanish *categorización* → *subcategorización* 'subcategorization', *vivir* → *sobrevivir* 'to survive'. By contrast, in English phrasal verbs, i.e. verbs followed by a stressed prepositional particle (see Marchand 1969: 19, Lüdtke 2005: 368), constitute a dominant word formation type to achieve situating modification (compare *to sit down, come in, look out, give up* etc.).

3 Development

Coseriu (1977a: 53) defines 'development' as the word formation process by which a syntactic function is included ('developed') into the derivation. Developments often entail change of word class, but this is not necessary. The syntactic function developed with this type of word formation is either of a predicative or an attributive nature. Denominal adjectives such as *health → health-y, brother → brotherly, nation → national* include an attributive function because they mean 'health, brother, nation' as attributes of a noun or nominal expression. By contrast, French *beau* 'beautiful' → *beauté* and Spanish *hermoso* 'beautiful' → *hermosura* include a predicative function because they mean 'to be beautiful'. *Beauty* is equivalent to 'being beautiful', *politeness* to 'being polite'. By nominalizing verbs, the predicative function is preserved, compare English *eating, sleeping, fishing* and French *écrire → écriture* (*l'écriture me coûte* 'writing is painful for me'), *lav-er → lav-age* (*le lavage de la voiture* 'the washing of the car'), *préparer → prépar-ation* (*la préparation du plat* 'the preparation of the dish'), Spanish *clasifica-r → clasifica-ción* (*la clasificación de los nombres* 'the classification of the nouns' (cf. Lüdtke 1978).[3]

Examples of developments that do not include a change of word class may be marginal, but they nevertheless exist: *dean → deanery* and Spanish *decano → decanato* either denote the office of the dean, his charge or the period of his charge, compare Spanish *rector* 'head of a university' → *rectorado*. The signified of *deanery, decanato, rectorado* is 'to be dean/head of a university'. If we say *Tomorrow I'll go to the deanery*, then we mean 'I'll go where the dean is dean', given that *deanery* only signifies 'being dean'. His office, charge or time of charge are designations, not signifieds of the word.

Coseriu (1977a: 55) calls 'topicalization' the fact that developments may convey the topic of place, time or charge. French *entr-er → entr-ée* 'entry', *sort-ir → sort-ie* 'exit' as well as Spanish *entr-ar → entr-ada* 'entry', *sal-ir → sal-ida* 'exit' not only signify 'entering' and 'going out', but also include the materiality of the place, the gate or door where people usually go in and out. In some contexts, these words can refer to the period of time during which one is moving, e.g. *Entering the station I met my friend Harry*, French *A l'entrée de l'hiver* 'at the beginning of winter'. Spanish *parar* 'to stop' → *parada* generally refers to the place where the bus or train stops, although its signified is underspecified, viz. 'stop-

---

[3] Zero morphemes also occur in deverbal nominalizations, as for example in French *marcher* 'to walk' → *la marche* 'the walk', *appeler → appel* 'call', Spanish *comprar → compra* 'buying' (the action or its result, the 'purchase').

ping (action and/or place)'. Similarly, Spanish *bajar* 'to go down, descend' → *bajada* signifies 'going down' but may designate the action itself or a slope or a sloping road that makes it possible to move fast. Spanish *alojar* → *alojamiento* means 'housing', but depending on the context, it can designate the place (house, apartment, room) which serves as lodging. In formations such as French *assemblée* 'meeting, assembly', the action of meeting fades into the background in view of the expression of the result of the action, 'the assembly', i.e. 'people gathered in an assembly'. 'Result' is another typical 'topicalization' of nominalized verbs.

Generally speaking, nominalization of verbs by means of 'development' takes its starting point in existing verbs. Nominalizations of adjectives or developments from nouns (recall the case of *dean-ery*, French *rector-at*, Spanish *rector-ado*) at least include a predicative function, as if, meta-linguistically speaking, they included the copula *to be:* 'being beautiful', 'being dean/head of a university'. Formations arrived at by means of the suffixes French *-ée* and Spanish *-ada/-ida* are among the most interesting in Romance languages. Deverbal nominalizations pose no problem for the analysis. Besides the already mentioned examples of French *entrée, sortie, arrivée* 'arrival' and Spanish *entrada, lleg-ada* 'arrival', *salida* 'exit, departure', we find Spanish *llam-ada* 'call', *jug-ada* 'playing', 'move', *fren-ar* 'to brake' → *fren-ada* 'braking (done but once)', *sacud-ir* → *sacud-ida* 'shaking (done but once)' and so forth. However, the problem is how to interpret formations in Spanish *-ada*, French *-ée* if no corresponding verb exists. Spanish *navaj-ada, martill-ada, cabez-ada, corn-ada, gat-ada, palm-ada, plum-ada* all denote strokes or violent movements with objects such as *navaja* 'pocket-knife', *martillo* 'hammer', *cabeza* 'head', *cuerno* 'horn', and *palma* 'palm (of the hand)', yet there are no verbs **navajar, *cabezar, *cornar, *gatar, *palmar, *plumar*, and they even may seem useless, but all the nominalizations signify 'making something with pocket-knife, hammer, one's head, horn, palm, or a pen'. *Gatada* is what a cat usually does, viz. 'a stroke with a claw'. Coseriu analyses these formations as developments of implicit generic verbs such as 'to do', 'to act' (with regard to Portuguese, see Dietrich 1992). The nominalizations denote strokes, hits, cuts, violent movements, but these are the effects we observe in extralinguistic reality, while, by themselves, the words only signify nominalized actions and their results. Word formation, understood as a grammatical process, does not itself create concrete meanings such as 'stroke' or 'cut', but only general signifieds such as 'relation', 'determination', 'diminutive', 'development', etc.

Dishes like Spanish *riñon-ada* 'kidney dish' (from *riñones* 'kidneys') and beverages like Spanish *naranj-ada* 'orangeade', *limon-ada* 'limonade', *almendr-ada* 'almond milk' may be explained as developments from the implicit verb meaning 'to do (what we normally do with the object)'. The language-specific signified of *naranjada* would then be 'the result of doing what is normally done with oranges', whereas language use fixes the designation of a beverage rather than, e.g., a kind of marmalade or fruit salad. In this case, in French we find the suffix *-ade* borrowed from Italian *-ata*, via an intermediate Occitan form *-ada: orange-ade, limonade, citronnade,* but also *gasconnade* 'action, utterance, or behaviour typical of a Gascon', *fanfarron-ada* 'bragging, action or behaviour of a *fanfarrón*, a bragger'.[4] In the same way, we can interpret Spanish *otoñ-ada* 'autumn time', 'autumnal harvest', *invern-ada* 'winter time', in some regions also 'winter quarters', *veran-ada* 'summer time', *tempor-ada* 'time as it goes by', 'season', as derivations from implicit verbs that refer to typical actions of a season, its products or associated dwellings. These specific designations result from language use and world knowledge, the grammatical meaning of the developments invariably being 'what is going on with regard to time, winter, etc.' or 'actions with regard to the base and their results, products, etc.'. French examples are *jour* → *journ-ée* 'what is done during a day', '(the) day in its course', *soir* → *soirée* (the same with regard to 'evening'), *an* → *année* (the same with regard to 'year').

This kind of development is extremely common in Romance languages, from Italian over Catalan, Spanish and Portuguese to French. Some derivations in Italian *-ata*, Catalan, Spanish, and Portuguese *-ada*, French *-ée* seem to denote meanings like 'what fits into a hand, a mouth, an arm' and so on or 'what fits into an instrument such as a spoon', compare French *poign-ée, bouch-ée, brass-ée, cuiller-ée,* or Spanish *man-ada*,[5] *ded-ada de miel* 'a fingertip of honey', *braz-ada* 'armful', *cuchar-ada* 'spoonful', *carret-ada* 'what is done with regard to a cart', 'cartload'. According to Coseriu's account, these derivations have to be understood as developments of implicit verbs which mean 'the fact of X being/existing with regard to hand/mouth/arm/spoon/cart'. Paraphrases such as these do not intend to be stylistically elegant, their only purpose is to indicate, so to speak as formulas, the grammatical signified of this kind of development.

Within the same range of developments are denominal derivations made by the French suffix *-erie* and the Spanish suffix *-ería*. I do not discuss here the

---

[4] Diachronically, the French suffixes *-ée, -ade,* Spanish and Portuguese *-ada, -ida,* Italian *-ata* and its variants all continue Latin neutral perfect passive participles in *-ata* and its variants, which denoted collective results of actions: *excerpta* 'extract, excerpt', *collecta* 'leftovers', *recepta* 'obligation, guaranty' etc.

[5] Spanish *manada* is a synchronic derivation from *mano* 'hand' in uses such as *¡Cógete una manada de cerezas!* 'Just take a handful of cherries!', but it is lexicalized as 'herd', 'flock', 'shoal' in, e.g., *una manada de lobos* 'a pack of wolves'.

problem of the origin of the suffix. It is, in any case, an extension of the old French suffix -*ie* (*rêveur* → *reverie* 'dreaming, reverie', *trompeur* → *tromperie* 'deception', *flatteur* → *flatterie* 'flattery') and Spanish -*ía* (*alegre* 'glad, joyful' → *alegría* 'joy, gladness', *caballero* 'knight' → *caballería* 'knighthood'). The French examples all have a predicative base because they are derived from verbs such as *rêver* 'to dream', *tromper* 'to deceive', *flatter* 'to flatter'. Denominal derivations from -*ero* such as Spanish *carnicero* 'butcher' → *carnicer-ía* 'butchery', French *boucher* → *boucher-ie* 'butchery', *chancelier* → *chanceller-ie* 'chancellery' have been listed in older word formation studies as abstract or collective nouns (see Spanish *caballería* 'knighthood' meaning 'the whole of the knights'). However, not all derivations in -*ie*/-*ía* and -*erie*/-*ería* can be qualified as abstract or collective nouns. A more coherent explanation is to construe them as developments created from implicit verbs: 'the working of a butcher/a chancellor', which may include the topicalization of the place/shop/office where the person works.

We may understand the implicit predicative function as a continuous or frequentative signified in the case of the aforementioned examples, and this is also true for derivations that designate a behaviour or its effects, such as French *cochonn-erie* 'piggery, mess, dirtiness', Spanish *mon-ería* 'apishness, mockery', *pordios-ería* 'begging, mendicancy', 'practice of begging'. The vitality of this kind of development is evidenced by a great number of neologisms such as French *shirt-erie*, which denotes a shirt department in a store, but literally signifies 'multiple existence of shirts', Spanish *futbol-ería* 'activities of footballers or their fans', literally 'what generally happens with regard to football'.

Deverbal adjectives that are developments and not only share the syntactic function of being attributes but also include 'possibility', are formed in English and in Romance languages: *to attribute* → *attributable*, French *attributable*, Spanish *atribuible*; *to eat* → *eatable*, French *manger* → *mangeable*, Spanish *comer* → *comible*; French *punir/puniss-* → *punissable* 'punishable'. In older studies it is occasionally claimed that adjectives derived by means of -*able*/-*ible* include passive voice, but this is an unnecessary assumption. The signified of the derivations can be adequately paraphrased by 'susceptible to attributing/eating/punishing'. Syntactic categories such as voice generally are indifferent with regard to word formation. English and French *changeable*, *variable*, *perishable*, French *périssable*, for example, have to be understood without any reference to passive voice because the base is an intransitive verb: 'susceptible to change', 'likely to rot quickly' (cf. Marchand 1969: 231).

4 Composition

There are two kinds of composition in Coseriu's theory of word formation, viz. compounds consisting of two existing lexemes and compounds of a lexeme and a generic element signifying 'someone' or 'something'. In European languages, the generic element is expressed by a suffix. Here again, Coseriu is anxious to avoid morphological classifications, in particular in terms of suffixation on the one hand and composition on the other. His aim is instead to show that both lexical and lexico-grammatical composition constitute a single word formation process. Composition is different from modification because it does not entail a modified base but a new lexical unit; and it is different from development because it does not develop a new syntactic function, but rather produces a compound in which either a lexical head is specified by a lexical determination (e. g. *housewife* is a kind of wife) or a grammatical head is specified by a lexical element, for example *-er* 'agent' is specified by *teach* in *teach-er* 'the one who teaches'.

4.1 Lexical composition

There are three points of interest in a description of lexical composition in English and Romance. The first point is a delimitation of what belongs to composition and what to free syntax. The semantic criterion of a new semantic unit formed by composition is not always decisive. In Germanic languages such as English and German, a rather reliable criterion is accent: compounds have one accent, generally on the first, determinative part (*wáterproof, bláckbox* versus *bláck bóx, gréenhouse* versus *gréen hóuse*; but see Marchand 1969: 21–29). In Romance languages, besides the semantic criterion, there is only the criterion of syntactic determination in the whole compound: Spanish *ciudad dormitorio* 'dormitory town' is a compound because a determinative adjective can only be that of the head of the whole: *esta ciudad dormitorio* 'this dormitory town', *una ciudad dormitorio aburrida* 'a dull dormitory town'. Spanish *mesa de madera* as well as French *table de bois* 'wooden table' are compounds because only their heads *mesa* and *table* can be determined by adjectives or determiners (articles, possessive adjectives or demonstrative adjectives).

Secondly, with the exception of determiners and classifying adjectives that indicate a general quantity or quality (*grand(e)* 'big', *bon, bueno* 'good'), the normal position of determinative adjectives in Romance languages is after the substantive. This is also the word order with determinative nouns in compounds:

Spanish *esposa modelo* 'exemplary wife', *salario base* 'minimum wages', French *prison juvénile* 'youth prison', *boîte à lettres* 'letter box' etc.

The third point refers to scholarly compounds with elements of Greek and Latin origin, for example *herbivore*, French *herbivore*, Spanish *herbívoro*; English and French *hypotension*, Spanish *hipotensión*; *geography*, French *géographie*, Spanish *geografía*, etc. In traditional studies of word formation these compounds are treated as prefix formations, at least when the head is an existing word in the corresponding language. By contrast, in Coseriu's account, prefixes are grammatical morphemes and therefore cannot express concrete meanings such as 'plants', '(too) low', 'referring to earth' and so forth. As a consequence, if we accept words such as these as analysable or partly analysable in terms of synchronic word formation, then we must construe them as compounds. We must realise, however, that they have been formed in Greek and Latin or according to rules of Greek and Latin. The order of elements they show, therefore, is that of Ancient Greek, which means that the determinative element does not follow but precedes the head.

4.2 Generic composition

As pointed out above, generic composition is semantically composition, in spite of its form, which is derivation. Derivation, is not a functional category in Coseriu's semantic theory of word formation. Most of the generic compounds have been listed, in traditional word formation studies, as *nomina agentis*, *nomina loci* or *nomina instrumenti*, sometimes in two or more different classifications whenever a derivation such as English *cleaner* 'person or thing that cleans', *cracker* 'kind of firework', 'kind of biscuit', 'installation for cracking hydrocarbons', Spanish *joyero* 'jeweller', 'jewel box', French *cuisinière* '(female) cook', 'cooker' etc. refers to a person (agent) or an instrument, receptacle, or vehicle (or ship), according to the context. French *cerise* 'cherry (as a fruit)' → *ceris-ier* may refer to a tree ('cherry tree') or its wood ('cherry wood'). Such an approach is in stark contrast to Coseriu's account. First of all, instruments, vehicles and trees are extralinguistic objects, not grammatical functions. Secondly, linguistic analysis should not classify designations but establish the function of a morphological form or category, or a syntactic construction, in terms of what they signify. When there is only one form, i.e. one morpheme and its variants, the linguistic analysis should assume the existence of only one signified. In the light of the above examples, this means that the generic composition in Spanish *joy-ero*, for instance, has a single, unitary signified, independently of its reference to a person or a receptacle. This signified may be paraphrased as 'someone or something with regard to jewels'.

In this short contribution, I can only give some illustrative examples of generic composition, not an exhaustive account. Such an account is provided in Staib (1988) for French and Spanish.

An important and rather productive suffix that forms agentive generic compounds is French *-eur*, Spanish *-or*. It generally forms deverbal nouns denoting persons, with some variation and restrictions in the formation of female nouns: French *chass-er* → *chass-eur* 'hunter', *chass-euse* (obsolete, now usually *chass-eresse* 'huntress'); *imprim-er* → *imprim-eur*, *imprim-euse* 'printer'; Spanish *caz-ar* → *cazador*, *-a* 'hunter, huntress'; *jug-ar* → *jug-ador*, *-a* 'player', 'gamer', 'gambler'. Many forms are inherited from Latin and therefore not easily analysable in a synchronic account: French *accus-er* 'to accuse', but *accus-ateur, accus-atrice* 'accuser', *construire* 'to build, construct', but *construc-teur* 'constructor', Spanish *escribir* → *escritor* 'writer'. In other cases, we have a generic compound inherited from Latin but no existing verb, compare, e.g., Spanish *espect-ador* 'spectator'. The agent of a compound formed with this suffix generally is someone who acts frequently, professionally, not accidentally.

The same French and Spanish suffixes also form generic compounds that denote utensils, tools, or machines that are understood as mechanical agents: French *séch-euse* 'dryer', *tond-euse (à gazon)* 'lawnmower', *lav-euse* 'washing machine'; Spanish *calcul-ador-a* 'calculating machine', *seg-ador-a* 'mowing-machine'.

Another common suffix is French *-ier*, *-ière*, Spanish *-ero*, *-a*. It forms deverbal and denominal generic compounds which only express an underspecified relationship between the base and the preceding lexical unit, without any agentive feature. Formations with this suffix denote the characteristics of a person (Spanish *pesc-ar* → *pesqu-ero* 'who has to do with fishing, fisherman', *jardín* → *jardin-ero*, French *jardin-ier* 'who has to do with garden(ing), gardener'), a receptacle (French *cendr-es*, Spanish *ceniz-a* 'ashes' → *cendr-ier, cenic-ero* 'ashtray'), *cafet-ière, cafet-era* 'coffee pot, coffee machine'), a tree (French *poire* 'pear' → *poir-ier* 'pear (as a tree)', Spanish *hig-o* 'fig' → *higu-era* 'fig tree') or also a kind of ship: Spanish *pesqu-ero* 'fishing boat, trawler', 'fisherman'; *ballen-ero*, just as English *whaler*, a 'whaling ship' or a 'seaman engaged in whaling'.

Deverbal French *-oir, -oire* and Spanish *-adero* (by suffix accumulation from *-ad(or)* + *-ero*) form generic compounds that denote places where some action is habitually executed: French *abatt-oir*, Spanish *mat-adero* 'slaughterhouse', literally 'which has to do with slaughtering'; *fum-oir* 'smoking chamber' or 'room, compartment, or place where smoking is allowed', Spanish *bail-adero* 'ballroom, locality for dancing'.

4.3 Romance verb-substantive compounding

The widespread type of composition exemplified by the type French *lave-vaisselle*, Spanish *lavaplatos* 'dishwasher' has been widely discussed in many word formation studies. Putting aside previous discussions, I only refer to Coseriu (1977a: 57–60) and the account he gives within his framework of generic composition. Firstly, Coseriu insists on the fact that, according to his experience with word formation, word formation processes often are 'cumulative', i.e. several processes occur concomitantly. Secondly, he rejects traditional explanations according to which either the verbal form that appears in this kind of compounds is an inflectional form (3rd person singular indicative or an imperative) or the attached noun is the direct object of a transitive verb. Coseriu's account is again firmly based on semantics: these compounds (French *coupe-papier* 'letter opener', 'paper cutter', *tire-bouchon*, Spanish *sacacorchos* 'corkscrew'; *cuentapasos* 'pedometer') signify what generic compounds such as *opener, cutter, washer* signify: 'something that opens, cuts, washes', and nothing more. The verbal elements of these compounds are generic compounds formed by a zero morpheme: *coupe-* + ø 'what cuts', *lave-/lava-* + ø 'what washes', *tire-/saca-* + ø 'what draws out'.

In these cases, the compound consisting of a verb and a noun is actually the outcome of a double process of composition. It is, first of all, a generic compound formed from a verbal root and a zero morpheme. The generic compound then enters into a composition with a noun. The noun is not the object of the verb, but a nominal determination of what already is a nominal compound. The resulting signifieds may be paraphrased by formulas such as 'cutter with regard to paper', 'washer with regard to dishes', 'drawer of corks', and so on.

With regard to this type of compounds, Romanian is strikingly different from other Romance languages; it is not productive and limited to antonomastic and pejorative terms (cf. Coseriu 1977a: 59, Munteanu and Windisch 2016).

5 Conclusion

In this article I have shown to what extent Coseriu's theory of word formation, as an example of his studies on grammar, is based on semantics. According to this theory, it is functional distinctions in a particular language that must be differentiated, not reference to extralinguistic objects or these objects themselves. Modification, development and composition are the processes established in word formation. Other functional categories, including diminutive, augmentative, collective, intensifying, negative, but also development categories such as the predicative function and the attributive function have been described in this article. Coseriu's account of generic compounding is perhaps one of his most conspicuous contributions to the theory of word formation. Even though Coseriu's account does not resolve all existing problems in the analysis of word formation, his consistent functionalist point of view is arguably an excellent basis for future research in this field.

References

Coseriu, Eugenio. 1974. "Les universaux linguistiques (et les autres)". In: Luigi Heilmann (ed.), *Proceedings of the Eleventh International Congress of Linguists*. Vol. I, 47–73. Bologna: il Mulino.

Coseriu, Eugenio. 1975 [1971]. *Leistung und Grenzen der Transformationellen Grammatik*. Tübingen: Narr.

Coseriu, Eugenio. 1977 [1974]. "Linguistic (and other) universals". In: Adam Makkai, Valerie Becker Makkai and Luigi Heilmann (eds.), *Linguistics at the crossroads*, 317–346. Padua & Lake Bluff, Ill.: Liviana & Jupiter Press (English translation of Coseriu 1974).

Coseriu, Eugenio. 1977a. "Inhaltliche Wortbildungslehre am Beispiel des Typs *coupe-papier*". In: Herbert E. Brekle and Dieter Kastovky (eds.), *Perspektiven der Wortbildungsforschung. Beiträge zum Wuppertaler Wortbildungskolloquium vom 9.–10. Juli 1976. Anläßlich des 70. Geburtstages von Hans Marchand am 1. Oktober 1977*, 48–61. Bonn: Grundmann.

Coseriu, Eugenio. 1985. "Linguistic competence: what is it Really?" *The Modern Language Review* 80, xxv–xxxv.

Coseriu, Eugenio. 2007 [1988]. *Sprachkompetenz. Grundzüge der Theorie des Sprechens*. Edited by Heinrich Weber (second edition). Tübingen: Narr.

Dietrich, Wolf. 1992. "Problemas dum estudo funcional da formação de palavras em português. O exemplo dos sufixos *-ada* e *-aria*". *Actas do III Congresso Internacional dos Lusitanistas*, 807–816. Coimbra: Associação Internacional de Lusitanistas.

Estigarribia, Bruno. 2020. *A grammar of Paraguayan Guarani*. London: UCL Press.

Geckeler, Horst. 1981a. "Structural semantics". In: Hans J. Eikmeyer and Hannes Rieser (eds.), *Words, worlds and contexts*, 381–413. Berlin & New York: de Gruyter.

Geckeler, Horst. 1988. "Major aspects of the lexematics of the Tübingen School of semantics". In: Werner Hüllen and Rainer Schulze (eds.), *Understanding the lexicon: meaning, sense and world knowledge in lexical semantics*, 11–22. Tübingen: Niemeyer.

Kiefer, Ferenc (ed.). 2000. *Strukturális magyar nyelvtan. 3. kötet: Morfológia*. Budapest: Akadémiai Kiadó.

Laca, Brenda. 1986. *Die Wortbildung als Grammatik des Wortschatzes. Untersuchungen zur spanischen Subjektnominalisierung*. Tübingen: Narr.

Lüdtke, Jens. 1978. *Prädikative Nominalisierungen mit Suffixen im Französischen, Katalanischen und Spanischen*. Tübingen: Niemeyer.

Lüdtke, Jens. 2005. *Romanische Wortbildung. Inhaltlich – diachronisch – synchronisch*. Tübingen: Stauffenburg.

Marchand, Hans. 1969. *The categories and types of present-day English word-formation. A synchronic-diachronic approach* (second, completely revised and enlarged edition). München: Beck.

Munteanu, Cristinel and Rudolf Windisch. 2016. "Züge sui generis der rumänischen Komposita des Typs frz. *coupe-papier*". *Romanistisches Jahrbuch* 67, 67–102.

Staib, Bruno. 1988. *Generische Komposita. Funktionelle Untersuchungen zum Französischen und Spanischen.* Tübingen: Niemeyer.

Brenda Laca (Montevideo)
The categories of the Romance verb

> But the basic organization of the verb is more or less the same in all Romance languages, and this allows us to speak of a Romance 'verbal system', not only from a historical but also from a synchronic point of view.*

1 Introduction

Coseriu's analysis of the categories of the Romance verb is based on two fundamental assumptions. The first one, expressed in the quotation above, is that the Romance languages, in spite of considerable micro-variation and the lack of strict one-to-one translation equivalents, share a common tense-aspect system. The second assumption is that cross-linguistic variation in the temporal domain concerns first and foremost the expression of aspect and its relation to tense. In this article, I will first show how Coseriu resorts to the methods available to him at the time, those of classical European structuralism, in order to turn these intuitions into a full-fledged systematic account of the Romance verb, which is still, to a large extent, compatible with the knowledge accumulated in the field over the past half century. After introducing this account, I will discuss two original ideas advanced in the analysis which find unexpected echoes in contemporary work on tense and aspect categories: (i) the idea that Romance 'imperfect' morphology, far from being aspectual, expresses a modal-temporal category, viz. 'non-actuality', and (ii) the idea that some periphrastic expressions are syncretic in as far as they correspond to different layers of aspect.

Note: This article is partly based on Laca (2017). I gratefully acknowledge support from the ANI Uruguay through the *Sistema Nacional de Investigadores* and from the CSIC-Universidad de la República (Uruguay) through the project *Variación y semántica de los tiempos verbales*, ID 54.

* "Aber die Grundlage der Organisation des Verbs ist in allen romanischen Sprachen ziemlich dieselbe, und das berechtigt uns, von einem romanischen 'Verbalsystem' nicht nur historisch, sondern auch synchronisch zu sprechen" (Coseriu 1976 [1968–1969]: 91).

https://doi.org/10.1515/9783110712391-018

2 *Das romanische Verbalsystem* (Coseriu 1976 [1968–1969])

For reasons of space, I will concentrate on Coseriu's main publication on the categories of the Romance verb, which appeared first in German in 1976 and was only translated into a Romance language, Spanish, twenty years later. This publication was not literally written by Coseriu himself but compiled by one of his students, Hansbert Bertsch, from the notes of a series of lectures Coseriu delivered in the sixties, mainly at the University of Tubingen. This reflects a central feature of the way Coseriu chose to proceed in developing and disseminating his ideas, which has been aptly characterized by Dietrich (2003: 7) as follows:

> although in the course of time he published a great number of articles, Coseriu privileged the Socratic way of oral presentation – at home and in meetings all over the world – over the elaboration of substantial monographs (my translation, B.L.).

A second important characteristic of Coseriu's work is that it is closely linked to the work of some of his students. The development and dissemination of his views on the categories of the Romance verb would have been to my mind unthinkable without the participation of at least three of his direct disciples: Brigitte Schlieben-Lange, who devoted her dissertation to the verbal system of Catalan and Occitan (Schlieben-Lange 1971), Wolf Dietrich, who more or less at the same time explored the issue of the periphrastic expression of verbal aspect in an outstanding dissertation (Dietrich 1973), and, some time later, Nelson Cartagena, who, in a series of papers on Spanish tense and aspect, contributed to refine and disseminate the main tenets of Coseriu's analysis (Cartagena 1976, 1977).

2.1 The underlying intuitions

The intuition as to the existence of a common tense-aspect system shared by the Romance languages which is amenable to analysis with structural-functional methods is paradoxical against the background of the rest of Coseriu's teaching at the time. The notion of system is being applied not to a particular language, but to a set of linguistic varieties. By contrast, in most of Coseriu's work the notion of system is explicitly restricted to what he called a 'functional language', ideally homogeneous and not interfered by variation (Coseriu 1976 [1968–1969]: 30). This paradox is, I think, indicative of the level at which Coseriu implicitly situated the unity of the categories of the Romance verb. In some of his writings (see in particular Coseriu 1968 [1965], 1971, 1988 [1971]), he defended the thesis that the Romance languages are not only representatives of a language family, but also of a 'linguistic type', i.e. a set of abstract principles that determine the organization of the individual systems and thus justify parallel developments even centuries after the effective separation of the individual languages. It is probably at this more abstract level of linguistic type that the basic organization of the verb is said to be more or less the same accross the Romance languages.

The second intuition, viz. that the main locus of crosslinguistic variation concerns the expression of aspect and the way aspectual distinctions are related to tense, is undoubtedly based on Coseriu's extraordinary multilingual competence, which comprised both practical competence and in-depth knowledge of the philological traditions of most Romance languages, as well as with Greek and Latin and Slavic and Germanic languages. His first-hand experience of this array of languages led him to recognize that, notwithstanding some degree of overlapping and the existence of partial translation equivalences, the Romance imperfect cannot be assimilated to the past of imperfective verbs in Slavic, nor to the Greek imperfect, nor to the English past progressive. The reason is, in his view, that languages differ in the way in which temporal location, aspectual viewpoint and the temporal structure of the described situations are interwoven.

2.2 Analytical tools: form-meaning relations and privative oppositions

In analyzing the semantic organization of the Romance verbal system, Coseriu resorts to the methods of classical European structuralism, more specifically to the application of two postulates. The first one concerns the relation between forms and meanings, the second one the formal type of contrast which should be privileged in the feature analysis of grammatical meanings.

The relation between forms and meanings is interpreted in such a manner that form guides the analysis of meaning in at least two basic ways. The first one is dictated by the postulate of unitary meaning (see Coseriu 1999 [1981]: 200–208), explicitly formulated as follows:

> Several material categories (types of expression, G. *Ausdruckstypen*) may correspond to a single functional meaning category [...]. The opposite, that is to say, that a morphological category corresponds to different values, does not occur as a matter of principle. (Coseriu 1976 [1968–1969]: 15)

In this version of the one form-one meaning principle, there is room for allomorphy, but not for irreducible polysemy of grammatical categories. The postulate of unitary meaning is developed into an approach which searches for an abstract common denominator for the different meaning effects associated with a given formally identified morphological category. As we will see below, this plays a central heuristic role in the analysis of the Romance imperfect.

The second way in which form guides the analysis of meaning is via a kind of compositional approach in which formal analogies are interpreted as indications for analogies in meaning. This compositional approach is not made explicit, but it is rather clear that several of the proposed semantic categories for the Romance verb are built on the basis of a shared formal component. Thus, the category of 'partializing view' – corresponding to the first level of aspect in the system – comprises expressions consisting of a spatial or motion semi-auxiliary verb and a gerund, as in It. *stare/andare/venire facendo*, lit. 'be/go/come doing'. Likewise, the category of 'prospective secondary perspective' – a sort of non-indexical or relative future – comprises combinations of an allative semi-auxiliary verb and an infinitive, as in Fr. *je vais/j'allais faire* 'I am/was going to do'. Finally, the existence of a morphological element common to the imperfect, the conditional and the pluperfect – as in Span. *hacía/haría/había hecho* 'I did/would do/had done' – is one of the arguments adduced in favour of the hypothesis that the Romance languages distinguish a 'non-actual temporal plane', whose centre is the imperfect, from an 'actual temporal plane', whose centre is the present.

As for the type of contrast which should be privileged, the analysis is guided by the idea that the direct oppositions out of which the semantic features defining the categories are obtained are always privative oppositions. A privative opposition is a binary contrast between a marked and an unmarked term. The marked term is specified for a given semantic feature (thus, for instance, in the contrast between *rectangle* and *square*, *square* is specified as [+equilateral]), whereas the unmarked term is not. The unmarked term appears to have two contextual values: a general unspecified value (as in *rectangle:* 'quadrilateral with four right angles'), and a polar value, which is interpreted as expressing the negation of the feature carried by the marked term (as in *rectangle:* 'non-equilateral quadrilateral with four right angles'). Coseriu exploits the principle of privative oppositions in order to defend the most innovative and controversial assumption of his analysis of the Romance verbal categories, viz. that there is no direct opposition between the simple past and the imperfect, and that the imperfect is not an imperfective past tense.

2.3 The systematics of the Romance tenses

In Coseriu's account, the basic categories of the Romance verb are not aspectual but temporal in nature: those that are obligatorily expressed on the finite verb correspond to distinctions in the temporal location of the situation denoted by the verb, and not to the partial (imperfective) or global (perfective) view superimposed on the situation, nor to the temporal structure of the situation. Aspectual distinctions are only expressed secondarily, either as values associated with the obligatory time-locational features or by means of an optional array of categories with a periphrastic expression.

As summarized in Figure 1, in which examples for the categories are provided in the 3rd person singular of the Spanish verb *cantar* 'sing', temporal location is defined by means of three relations, anteriority ('retrospective perspective'), simultaneity ('parallel perspective') and posteriority ('prospective perspective'). These relations are directly anchored to Speech Time in the case of the 'primary perspective', or to a time that is itself anterior, simultaneous or posterior to Speech Time, in the case of the 'secondary perspective'. Shaded cells indicate non-parallel primary perspectives.

ACTUAL PLANE			PRIMARY PERSPECTIVE				
	RETROSP *cantó* 'sang'			**PARALLEL** *canta* 'sings'			**PROSP** *cantará* 'will sing'
			SECONDARY PERSPECTIVE				
RETROSP hubo cantado 'had sung'		*PROSP* fue a cantar 'went to sing'	*RETROSP* ha cantado 'has sung'		*PROSP* va a cantar 'is going to sing'	*RETROSP* habrá cantado 'will have sung'	*PROSP* irá a cantar 'will be going to sing'
NON-ACTUAL PLANE			PRIMARY PERSPECTIVE				
				PARALLEL *cantaba* 'sang'			**PROSP** *cantaría* 'would sing'
			SECONDARY PERSPECTIVE				
			RETROSP había cantado 'had sung'		*PROSP* iba a cantar 'was going to sing'	*RETROSP* habría cantado 'would have sung'	*PROSP* iría a cantar 'would be going to sing'

Figure 1: The temporal categories of the Romance verb
(PROSP = prospective, RETROSP = retrospective)

This part of the analysis, which can be reformulated as the assumption that there are three absolute tenses as regards orderings directly anchored to Speech Time and two types of relative tenses, anteriors and posteriors, is not particularly innovative. As a general framework for the analysis of temporal systems, it has recurrently been proposed by other linguists and philosophers in the tradition of the *Grammaire Générale*, most notably by Beauzée (see de Saussure 1998). In our times, this framework has been generally adopted in the version of it provided in the few pages Reichenbach devotes to the topic in *A system of symbolic logic* (1947). In fact, the notion of primary perspective accounts for the relations between Reference Time and Speech Time in Reichenbach's system, whereas the secondary perspective accounts for the relations between Event Time and Reference Time.

By contrast, the assumption that the Romance tense system is organized on two distinct temporal planes, an 'actual temporal plane' whose center is the present, and a 'non-actual temporal plane' whose center is the imperfect, is the most original and controversial feature of Coseriu's analysis, to which I shall return in Section 3.

2.4 Aspect and temporal structure

Whereas temporal location as expressed by tenses is conceptually relatively straightforward, the notion of aspect is notoriously more elusive and the term itself is still beset by ambiguity after more than thirty years of intensive research. As a minimal – and certainly insufficient – basis for understanding, aspect can be said to specify the temporal structure of the situation described in a sentence radical (the lexical verb with its arguments) or to determine the viewpoint under which this temporal structure is presented.

In Coseriu's analysis of the Romance verb, aspectual categories in Romance are either covert or have an optional expression in verbal periphrases – patterns of monoclausal combinations of an inflected semi-auxiliary with a fixed non-finite form of the main verb. Interestingly, the domain is split into two categories, "view" (G. *Schau*) and "phase". The former term is a rather clear rendition of 'aspect' in its etymological sense, and it is characterized as "the way in which the situation is visualized". Its main subtype, which, as stated above, is established on the basis of a common morphological make-up (locative or motion semi-auxiliary + gerund), is the 'partializing view', in which the situation is visualized between two points of its temporal structure. Phases, by contrast, correspond to the objective parts of the temporal structure of a situation: its initial and final boundaries, and its development. They also comprise the time immediately preceding the initial boundary and the time immediately following the final boundary of the described situation. Figure 2 provides a schematic representation of the different phases and illustrates them with some of their periphrastic expressions in French:

	I			F	
inminent	inceptive	progressive		conclusive	egressive
être sur le point de Vinf	se mettre à Vinf	être en train de VInf		finir de VInf	venir de VInf
'be about to V'	'start Ving'	'be Ving'		'finish Ving'	'have just Ven'

Figure 2: Phasal periphrases
(I = initial, F = final)

I think it is not too much of a stretch to interpret the distinction between view and phase, for which Coseriu cites Keniston (1936) as an immediate source, as prefiguring a theoretical distinction between two layers of aspect which took two decades to become more or less established in the formal linguistics tradition since it was explicitly formulated by Carlota Smith (1991). It is the distinction between "viewpoint aspect" and "situation aspect shift". Situation aspect shift effectively changes the temporal structure of the basic described situation: for instance, the onset of an activity predicate, as in *She started singing at 5pm*, is not itself an activity predicate, since it involves a definite change of state. *Starting to sing* is a different type of event than *singing*. Viewpoint aspect, by contrast, does not in principle alter the temporal structure of the described situation but presents it through the lens of an interval of visibility which may, for instance, render the initial or final points inaccessible to temporal location. Thus, the situation described in the sentence *She was singing an aria* has the same temporal structure as that in *She sang an aria*, but the imperfective viewpoint aspect in the former sentence renders both the initial and the final points of the situation inaccessible to temporal location, and precludes among other things any inference as to the actual culmination of the event. The interval of visibility has been variously called the Topic or Assertion Time (Klein 1994) or the Reference Interval, and its introduction has contributed to clarify the notion of viewpoint aspect as a time-relational category. At the time Coseriu formulated his views on the Romance verb, the powerful analytic tools provided by interval semantics and event semantics were not even present as distant possibilities. Nonetheless, by building on both the formal make-up of expressions and his own keen semantic intuitions, Coseriu managed to formulate an extremely fruitful and, to my mind, essentially correct idea, viz. that Romance verbal periphrases distribute over at least two semantically distinct layers of aspect (Laca 2004).

3 The Romance imperfect and the non-actual temporal plane

As pointed out above, the most innovative feature in Coseriu's analysis of the Romance tenses is the distinction between an actual and a non-actual temporal plane. It is also the most controversial and the most difficult to understand. The introduction of the non-actual temporal plane is meant to account for the common formal element in imperfect and conditional forms as well as for parallels in their meaning and distribution. The latter involve most notably the counterfactual or 'irrealis' uses which are attested to a different degree in all Romance varieties. The result of this analysis is that the imperfect does not belong to the inventory of past tenses in Romance. Since this goes against the predominant view in the descriptive tradition, Coseriu (1976 [1968–1969]) devotes a whole chapter to arguing in favour of this novel account. I here summarize the main semantic phenomena he intends to capture, over and above the formal parallels.

In its so-called temporal uses, the imperfect is known to require a past reference time supplied by the context, often by means of a verb in the simple past tense (*salieron* resp. *dijo* in 1a–b), to which the situation described in the imperfect is simultaneous:[1]

(1) a. Salieron a la calle. **Nevaba** y el pavimento **estaba** resbaloso.
 'They went out to the street. It was snowing and the pavement was slippery.'
 b. Dijo que se **sentía** mal.
 'He said he was feeling unwell.'

This requirement of anchoring to a past reference time is nowadays generally taken to mean that the imperfect is anaphoric in nature (see, among many others, Berthonneau and Kleiber 1993, Leonetti 2004).

But next to its temporal uses, the imperfect has several uses in which it is not anaphoric to a past reference time and/or does not locate the situation in the past. They are traditionally called "modal uses" of the imperfect and comprise its occurrence in certain communicative situations as a politeness strategy de-

---

[1] All examples are given in Spanish for the sake of consistency. The same uses are well documented accross the Romance languages. The imperfect verb forms in the following examples are in bold.

signed to modulate potentially face-threatening speech acts, such as requests (2a) or in the planning of role-playing by children (2b):

(2) a. Lo **llamaba** para pedirle un favor.
 'I'm calling to ask you a favor.'
 b. Tú **eras** el ladrón y yo el policía. Tú **asaltabas** un banco y yo te **perseguía**.
 'Let's pretend you are the thief and me, the policeman. You'll rob a bank and I'll chase you.'

According to the postulate of unitary meaning introduced above (Section 2.2), this apparent temporal-modal ambiguity of the imperfect should not be taken at face value but reduced, if possible, to a semantic common denominator. That this is not a case of accidental homophony is suggested by the regularity of this polysemy accross the Romance languages. Moreover, an analogous problem arises with the Romance conditional, which next to its temporal uses as a Future of the Past (3 a-b) prominently exhibits modal uses as a politeness strategy (4a) and, even more importantly, in the consequent of counterfactual conditionals (4b).

(3) a. Se pusieron de acuerdo: se **encontrarían** en la estación y **harían** el viaje juntos.
 'They agreed that they would meet at the station and make the trip together'
 b. Dijo que **llegaría** esta tarde.
 'He said he would arrive this evening.'

(4) a. ¿Me **haría** el favor de callarse?
 'Could you please be quiet?'
 b. Si tuviera dinero, me **compraría** ese cuadro.
 'If I had money, I would buy this painting.'

The search for a semantic element shared by the imperfect and the conditional is not only motivated by the coexistence of analogous temporal and modal values. Coseriu also remarks that the contexts in which an imperfect may appear instead of the conditional are an indication that both forms are in a privative opposition and thus must share a common semantic basis. This is the case in the consequent of counterfactual conditionals (5a-b) and also in sequence of tense contexts (6a-b). In the latter, the use of an imperfect instead of a conditional mirrors present *pro futuro* uses (7a-b).

(5) a. Si tuviera dinero, me **compraba** ese cuadro.
'If I had money, I would buy this painting.'
b. Si se lo hubieras pedido, seguro te lo **daba**.
'If you had asked him, he would have given it to you.'

(6) a. Se pusieron de acuerdo: se **encontraban** en la estación y **hacían** el viaje juntos.
'They agreed that they would meet at the station and make the trip together.'
b. Dijo que **llegaba** esta tarde.
'He said he would arrive this evening.'

(7) a. Mañana nos encontramos en la estación.
'Tomorrow we will meet at the station.'
b. Dice que llega esta tarde.
'He says he'll arrive this evening.'

A proportional opposition is thus established, in which the imperfect relates to the present as the conditional relates to the future: the members of each pair share a common temporal orientation, the parallel perspective in the former case, the prospective perspective in the latter. They differ in the temporal plane. The actual temporal plane is organized around Speech Time. Situations in the non-actual temporal plane are located either relatively to a past anchor or in a temporal line which is distinct from the actual temporal line which contains Speech Time.

Coseriu's conception of the non-actual temporal plane thus clearly entails that there is more than one temporal line, an idea which, at the time it was formulated, could only be met with skepticism. Interestingly, nowadays this idea receives unexpected support from formal semantic analyses of temporality, whose models usually integrate more than one temporal line. One of the distinctive properties of human language is that of 'displacement', which allows speakers to talk and reason not only about what is the case here and now, but also about what has been, what could be and what is necessarily the case. Contemporary formal semantics has stressed the idea that the two dimensions of displacement, that of temporality and that of modality, cannot be treated independently of one another because of the manifold regular interactions between them (Thomason 1984, Steedman 1997, Kaufmann, Condoravdi and Harizanov 2006). In these approaches, it has become standard practice to work with two-dimensional matrices such as the one schematically represented in Figure 3. In this matrix, the horizontal lines represent time, the succession of situations and changes that constitute a 'history'. The vertical dimension is a set of possible worlds, alternative circumstances which build a set of 'alternative histories'. Among these histories, there is a privileged segment which corresponds to what is and what has been in the history of the actual world, identified as w_0, which contains Speech Time (S).

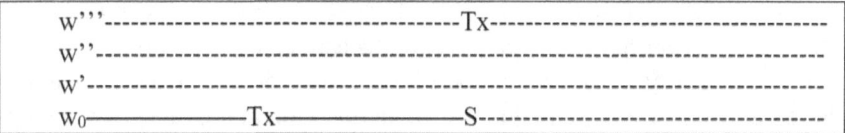

Figure 3: Two dimensional temporal-modal matrix

Coseriu's notion of a non-actual temporal plane may perhaps be made more clear by reformulating it in terms of the anchoring time for the tenses he classifies as non-actual. Unlike the tenses on the actual temporal plane, imperfect and conditional are not anchored to Speech Time, but to a time represented as Tx in Figure 3: a time that has to be recovered from context and is distinct from Speech Time, either because it is located in the past in the temporal dimension, or because it does not belong to the actual history w_0. In the former case, we obtain the anaphoric readings as a Present or, respectively, a Future of the Past, in the latter, the modal readings as counterfactuals or 'irrealis' (see Iatridou 2000 for a very similar interpretation of the counterfactual uses of past tenses). Coseriu's intuition as to the necessity of assuming more than one temporal line in order to capture the organization of the Romance tense system is thus perfectly compatible with contemporary theories of modal-temporal interactions.

4 Syncretism and grammaticalization

Although the postulate of unitary meaning guides Coseriu's analysis, the possibility of a form being associated with two distinct categories in a non accidental way is explicitly acknowledged. This situation arises when two grammatical categories which have different expressions elsewhere in the same language are formally undistinguishable in some cases. Coseriu (1976 [1968–1969]: 107–108) borrows from historical linguistics the term 'syncretism' for this situation, and applies it explicitly to the categories of view and phase. According to him, expressions for the partializing view coincide most of the time with the expression of the progressive phase. But he also implicitly recognizes a different instance of syncretism, this time between secondary and primary perspective, when he discusses the Romance varieties in which the analytic forms expressing the secondary perspective fully replace the corresponding synthetic forms of the primary perspective (Coseriu 1976 [1968–1969]: 146–147), as attested by the *passé composé* forms replacing the simple past forms in spoken French, in Northern Italian varieties and in Romanian, and by the periphrastic future replacing the simple future in spoken American Spanish varieties and in Brazilian Portuguese. As he notes elsewhere (Coseriu 1976 [1968–1969]: 32), the meaning of Fr. *j'ai chanté* 'I have sung' is not the same in a system in which it contrasts with *je chantai* 'I sang' and in a system that does not possess the latter form. Although he does not himself draw this conclusion, it follows from the setup of the categories and oppositions that analytic forms which have fully replaced the corresponding synthetic forms give rise to a syncretism between primary and secondary perspective.

I believe it is rather telling that Coseriu should adopt a term which originally names the result of a diachronic process in order to describe the association of two different categories with the same form. Syncretism is the trace in synchrony of a change in the way forms are associated with meanings. In the light of the current findings of research on grammaticalization, it is to be expected that it will arise as new grammatical expressions are recruited, at first with meanings that specify a particular temporal structure or a phase, then for the expression of a non-deictic temporal relation (view or secondary perspective), and eventually as the expression of a deictic temporal relation. Since each new stage in this process does not necessarily erase the previous form-meaning associations, syncretic expressions are bound to emerge. This is the line of resoning followed by Squartini (1998: 73–91), for whom the differences in semantics and distribution between the contemporary Italian and the Ibero-Romance periphrases descended from STARE + Gerund indicate that, whereas the Italian periphrasis has specialized as a time-relational aspectual category, the Ibero-Romance periphrases retain some of the original actionality characteristics, which were also attested in Italian in previous diachronic stages. The Ibero-Romance periphrases are thus syncretic between durativity and imperfective progressivity (Squartini 1998: 75).

By introducing the notion of syncretism, Coseriu provides an appropriate tool for capturing the traces of diachronic change in a synchronic state. At the same time, this tool makes it possible to correct a number of shortcomings in the analysis of particular forms, which arise when the analysis leans too unilaterally on formal analogies and glosses over important semantic and distributional differences (see Cartagena 1976, 1977).

Thus, for instance, the cell in the system assigned to the *passé antérieur* (HABERE + Participle with the auxiliary in the simple past) corresponds to a form with a retrospective primary and a restrospective secondary perspective (see Figure 1 above). But the *passé antérieur* in all Romance varieties exhibits distributional and semantic restrictions which show that it is not simply a temporal form, a Past of the Past. It selects for telic temporal structures, and it entirely lacks inceptive or simultaneous readings, in contrast to pluperfects (see Bertinetto 1986: 467–482, Laca 2005). These properties fall out naturally from an analysis of the construction HABERE + Participle as an expression for an eggressive or resultative phase when the auxiliary is in the simple past, thus retaining the etymological meaning of the construction.

In the same vein, the cell assigned to the periphrases of the type IRE + Infinitive with the auxiliary in the simple past is that of a retrospective primary perspective and a prospective secondary perspective. But forms as Span. *fue a cantar*, Port. *foi cantar* 'he/she was about to sing' are not simply a Future of the Past. They are restricted to agentive situations and require the intention of an agent to bring about an event (see Laca 2005). They are therefore more accurately classified as the expression of a subtype of the inminence phase, reflecting one of the probable earlier semantic stages in the grammaticalization of the construction.

Whatever these suggestions may be worth, the point I would like to stress is that applying the notion of syncretism to the categories of the Romance verb offers a concrete means of reconciling the way the system functions at a synchronic stage and the traces this system bears of the diachronic developments affecting it.

5 Concluding remarks

Das romanische Verbalsystem (1976 [1968–1969]) shows us a facet of Coseriu which is, as far as I can see, less well represented in the rest of his work. Even if clearly guided by theoretical interests, this is comparative description of the Romance languages at a level of detail which is not pursued in Coseriu's more theoretically oriented writings. In the latter, empirical data are usually presented as illustration or support for theoretical claims, as examples. By contrast, in the study of the categories of the Romance verb, empirical data constitute the problem to be solved by an in-depth analysis. The solutions proposed, based on structuralist methods, still retain their interest and fruitfulness, and are, as I have tried to show, compatible with the wealth of knowledge accumulated in the field in the more than fifity years that have elapsed since the Tubingen lectures.

References

Berthonneau, Anne-Marie and Georges Kleiber. 1993. "Pour une nouvelle approche de l'imparfait: l'imparfait, un temps anaphorique méronomique". *Langages* 112, 55–73.
Bertinetto, Pier-Marco. 1986. *Tempo, aspetto, azione nel verbo italiano. Il sistema dell'indicativo*. Florence: Accademia della Crusca.
Cartagena, Nelson. 1976. "Estructura y función de los tiempos del modo indicativo en el sistema verbal del español". *Revista de Lingüística Teórica y Aplicada* 14–15, 5–44.
Cartagena, Nelson. 1977. "Acerca de las categorías de tiempo y aspecto en el sistema verbal del español". *Revista Española de Lingüística* 8, 373–408.
Coseriu, Eugenio. 1968 [1965]. "Sincronía, diacronía y tipología". In: Antonio Quilis, Ramón Blanco Carril and Margarita Cantarero (eds.), *Actas del XI Congreso Internacional de Lingüística y Filología Románicas, Madrid 1965*. Vol. I, 269–281. Madrid: Revista de Filología Española.
Coseriu, Eugenio. 1971. *Essai d'une nouvelle typologie des langues romanes Sinaia 1971*. Bucarest: Univ. de Bucarest.
Coseriu, Eugenio. 1976 [1968–1969]. *Das romanische Verbalsystem*. Edited by Hansbert Bertsch. Tübingen: Narr.
Coseriu, Eugenio. 1988 [1971]. "Der romanische Sprachtypus: Versuch einer neuen Typologisierung der romanischen Sprachen". In: Jörn Albrecht (ed.), *Energeia und Ergon. Sprachliche Variation – Sprachgeschichte – Sprachtypologie*, Vol. I: *Schriften von Eugenio Coseriu (1965–1987)*, 207–224. Tübingen: Narr.
Coseriu, Eugenio. 1999 [1981]. *Lecciones de lingüística general* (second edition). Madrid: Gredos.
Dietrich, Wolf. 1973. *Der periphrastische Verbalaspekt in den romanischen Sprachen*. Tübingen: Niemeyer.
Dietrich, Wolf. 2003. "Nachruf auf Eugenio Coseriu". *Mitteilungen des Deutschen Hispanistenverbandes* 20 (Februar 2003), 6–8.
Iatridou, Sabine. 2000. "The grammatical ingredients of counterfactuality". *Linguistic Inquiry* 31, 231–270.
Kaufmann, Stefan, Cleo Condoravdi and Valentina Harizanov. 2006. "Formal approaches to modality". In: William Frawley (ed.), *The expression of modality*, 72–106. Berlin & New York: Mouton De Gruyter.
Keniston, Hayward. 1936. "Verbal aspect in Spanish". *Hispania* 19, 163–176.
Klein, Wolfgang. 1994. *Time in language*. London: Routledge.
Laca, Brenda. 2004. "Romance 'aspectual' periphrases: eventuality modification versus 'syntactic' aspect." In: Jacqueline Guéron and Jacqueline Lecarme (eds.), *The syntax of time*, 425–440. Cambridge, Mass.: MIT Press.
Laca, Brenda. 2005. "Périphrases aspectuelles et temps grammatical dans les langues romanes". In: Hava Bat Zeev Schyldkrot and Nicole Le Querler (eds.), *Les périphrases verbales*, 47–66. Amsterdam & Philadelphia: John Benjamins.
Laca, Brenda. 2017. "Tradición y novedad en 'El sistema verbal románico'". *Revista de la Academia Nacional de Letras* 13, 119–135.
Leonetti, Manuel. 2004. "Por qué el imperfecto es anafórico". In: Luis García Fernández and Bruno Camus (eds.), *El pretérito imperfecto*, 481–508. Madrid: Gredos.
Reichenbach, Hans. 1947. *Elements of symbolic logic*. New York: Macmillan

Saussure, Louis de. 1998. "L'approche référentielle: de Beauzée à Reichenbach". In: Jacques Moeschler (ed.), *Le temps des événements. Pragmatique de la référence temporelle*, 19–44. Paris: Kimé.

Schlieben-Lange, Brigitte. 1971. *Okzitanische und katalanische Verbprobleme*. Tübingen: Niemeyer.

Smith, Carlota. 1991. *The parameter of aspect*. Dordrecht: Kluwer.

Squartini, Mario. 1998. *Verbal periphrases in Romance. Aspect, actionality and grammaticalization*. Berlin & New York: Mouton de Gruyter.

Steedman, Mark. 1997. "Temporality". In: Johann van Benthem and Alice ter Meulen (eds.), *Handbook of logic and language*, 895–939. London: Elsevier.

Thomason, Richmond. 1984. "Combinations of Tense and Modality". In: Dov Gabbay and Franz Guenthner (eds.), *The handbook of philosophical logic*. Vol. 2, 135–165. Dordrecht: Reidel.

Elena Faur (Cluj-Napoca)
The crux of metaphor: between Cognitive and Integral Linguistics

> *We are here dealing with attempts to classify reality, not by means of rational categories, but by means of images, and with analogies established not from a strictly formal point of view, between words, but in a poetic manner, between 'visions' that must have arisen at a specific moment from someone's creative imagination. We are dealing with what, in a very broad sense, we call metaphor, which we do not understand here as a simple verbal transposition, as an 'abbreviated comparison', but as a unitary, spontaneous and immediate expression (that is, without any mediating 'as') of a vision, of a poetic intuition.**

1 Introduction

In the introduction to her recently edited volume, Hampe (2017: 4) notes: "it is high time for metaphor theory to integrate major insights" from "yet largely separate, but ultimately complementary strands of inquiry". Needless to say, her remark eventually refers to the integration of diverging strands of metaphor studies. This flourishing field of research currently shows a strong polarization, as reflected in the so-called "metaphor wars" (Gibbs 2017a). But what about an integration of more widely divergent traditions of research? The present article addresses this question and considers the tradition of research that originates from Coseriu's Integral Linguistics, on the one hand, and Conceptual Metaphor Theory (CMT) and associated trends, on the other. I will argue that Coseriu's Integral Linguistics is in some aspects convergent with the central position attributed to

---

Acknowledgements: I wish to thank Mircea Borcilă for his constant and constructive support. I also thank Göran Sonesson, Jordan Zlatev, Simon Devylder, Georgios Stampoulidis, the editors of this volume and an anonymous reviewer for their useful comments, suggestions (and patience), which have helped improve this text.

* "[N]os encontramos frente a intentos de clasificar la realidad, ya no mediante categorías de la razón sino mediante imágenes, y frente a analogías establecidas, no desde un punto de visto estrictamente formal, entre vocablos, sino poéticamente, entre 'visiones', que deben haber surgido, en cierto momento particular, de la fantasía creadora de alguien. Nos encontramos frente a lo que, en un sentido muy amplio, llamamos *metáfora*, que no entendemos aquí como simple transposición verbal, como 'comparación abreviada', sino como expresión unitaria, espontánea e inmediata (es decir, sin ningún 'como' intermedio) de una visión, de una intuición poética" (Coseriu 1956: 16, 1985 [1956]: 81).

the metaphorical process within a largely 'cognitively' oriented trend in present-day metaphor studies. At the same time, Coseriu's principled position – as already advanced in his article "La creación metafórica en el lenguaje" as early as 1956 – presents itself as being based on a distinctive theoretical perspective, which is grounded in the major European tradition in the philosophy of language and culture (Aristotle, Vico, Hegel, Humboldt). Coseriu takes as a starting point for his account Ernst Cassirer's notion of cultural activity such as it is manifested through the "symbolic forms" of language, art, myth and science. However, Coseriu emphasizes that "the adjective 'symbolic' [...] does not tell us what type of activity language is but only characterizes language, indicates the nature of its elements and the instants in which it articulates itself" (Coseriu 1956: 9, 1985 [1956]: 71). Thus, "symbolic" stands for "a secondary moment" in the delimitation of "language as activity", which necessarily implies "a preceding moment" (ibid.), i.e. the moment of acknowledging that "language is a modality specific to man to get in touch with the world, to know reality, *his* reality" (Coseriu 1956: 9, 1985 [1956]: 72; emphasis in the original). Based on this "more comprehensive concept" ("[un] concepto más amplio"), language is defined as "essentially *cognitive activity:* a *cognitive activity that is realized by means of symbols* (or *symbolic signs*)" (Coseriu 1956: 9, 1985 [1956]: 72; emphasis in the original).

As suggested by several authors (Sanchez de Zavala 1982: 23–24, Caamaño 1993: 158–159, among others), Coseriu here takes an important step towards introducing a 'cognitive' perspective on language, which is noteworthy because of the fact that Cognitive Linguistics has established itself as an important research paradigm in the second half of the twentieth century. What is of special significance here is the role Coseriu attributes to the metaphorical creation in language in terms of a "free activity of imagination" ("actividad libre de la fantasía") (1956: 27, 1985 [1956]: 95). For Coseriu this activity is much more than the "infinite" but superficial occurrences of jocular expressions common in everyday language use. He considers metaphors "at a much deeper level" ("mucho más profundamente"), where they are motivated by their primal function of "distinguishing, classifying and initially denominating that which can be known, that which presents itself as reality to man's intuition – creator of his specific world and of his language (an activity that situates itself as a mediating bridge between consciousness and the world" (Coseriu 1956: 28, 1985 [1956]: 97).

Of crucial theoretical importance is that Coseriu, in clear distinction from E. Cassirer, situates metaphor within the primary "signifying function" of language. This signifying function is in turn explicitly situated within the basic cognitively creative dimension of all "cultural" (or "intellectual") activities of human beings. In later studies, Coseriu further developed this point of view, both with respect to its theoretical implications and its roots in the history of the language sciences (cf. in particular Coseriu 1995, 2000 [1990], 2007 [1988], 2015, I: 312–313).

It is worthwhile to consider the question how Coseriu's point of view can be integrated with current dominating trends in metaphor studies, similarly to what has become known as a relationship of "mutual enlightenment" in Gallagher's terms (1997). This is explained by Zahavi (2019: 13) as being "not a question of simply importing and applying readymade ideas from one side to another; [...] not a one-way street [...], but a two-way exchange, where both sides could profit from the interaction". I suggest that this kind of interaction, far from going against Coseriu's own position, is actually convergent with his project of an 'integral' science of language. However, the present article is not intended as an 'exegesis' of a particular part of Coseriu's Integral Linguistics, viz. his approach of metaphor, but as a contribution to the advancement of the theory of metaphor along the lines of a research program at the Babeş-Bolyai University in Cluj-Napoca, whose main objective consists in developing, in "a creative and original" way, "the perspective opened up by Coseriu in the domain of the language sciences as well as in adjacent disciplines" (Bojoga, Boc and Vilcu 2013: 6).

2 The relationship between integralist studies and alternative trends in current metaphor studies

I will first consider the question how integralist studies of language relate to alternative trends in metaphor studies. Are there significant advancements in current metaphor research from which the integralist theory of metaphor might benefit? If so, can they be accommodated within the integralist framework for the study of metaphor? And what can other trends in exchange learn from the integralist theory of metaphor?

Current metaphor research appears to be quite diverse. A first major strand, mainly represented by G. Lakoff and J. Grady, assumes a "neural theory of metaphor". The neural theory of metaphor has been criticized in many respects. A strong objection to CMT's neural explanation of metaphor stability has recently been raised by Zlatev, Jacobsson and Paju (in press). The authors ask: "[W]here is this 'conceptual system' located, and if in 'the brain', given that Conceptual Metaphor Theory has been aiming to become a 'neural theory of metaphor' (Lakoff 2009): whose brain, and how can they remain there indefinitely?" A number of arguments against a "neural foundation" of metaphor theory have previously been presented from the integralist point of view in a number of studies (Borcilă

2003; see also Faur 2013a, 2013b). The main error of the neural theory consists in the misinterpretation of the inherent semantic-creative nature of metaphors. If the explanatory principle of metaphorical creativity is to be sought and found beyond and before the cognitive-creative activity itself in which metaphor is supposed to emerge ("we are pre-wired to have associated experiences" and hence metaphors, Grady and Ascoli 2017: 30), then metaphor ceases to be itself a creative phenomenon. It instead becomes a phenomenon that is conditioned by something of a different nature. Grady's most recent position goes even further and assumes the "innateness" of our conceptual system story ("primary source and target concepts are grounded in experiences that are, in some meaningful sense, part of humans' innate cognitive repertoire", Grady and Ascoli 2017: 29–30), thus projecting a double constraint on metaphorical creativity. It is clear that Lakoff's and Grady's causal interpretation of metaphors cannot be in any way accommodated within the integralist approach to metaphor. The rationale of this disagreement consists in the fact that the latter is based on an entirely different explanatory principle of semantic creativity. This principle originates in Coseriu's concept of *enérgeia*, a concept he situates at the basis of all human cultural activities.

There is currently a lively debate between scholars approaching metaphor from opposing perspectives, either from a "social-discursive perspective", "i.e. metaphor as primary belonging to language or social interaction", or from a "cognition-based perspective", "i.e. metaphor as primary belonging to (or originating from), the individual's conceptual system" (Jensen 2017: 258). The "cognition-discourse divide" (Hampe 2017: 4) in present-day metaphor research can be further subdivided according to more fine-grained dichotomies: (1) universalist vs. culture-specific-oriented approaches, (2) cognition-based vs. communication-based perspectives, (3) stable vs. dynamic views (for a presentation of these subdivisions with regard to current debates, see Zlatev, Jacobsson and Paju, in press). However, there are also attempts to integrate insights from conflicting perspectives into comprehensive models. One of the most comprehensive models which offers a promising theoretical solution of how opposed perspectives can be negotiated and integrated with each other is the "Motivation & Sedimentation Model". This model has been developed within a cognitive-semiotics framework (see Zlatev, Jacobsson and Paju, in press; cf. also Devylder and Zlatev 2020, Stampoulidis, Bolognesi and Zlatev 2019). The authors present a three-levelled metaphor model, which has been inspired by Coseriu's three levels of language, viz. the universal, the historical and the individual level (Coseriu 2007), and the phenomenology of M. Merleau-Ponty. It is beyond the scope of this paper to give an extensive account of this model. I will instead confront a number of landmark ideas in current metaphor research with similar insights in the integralist theory of metaphor and show how both traditions of research can benefit from each other.

An interesting discussion regarding the problem of the directional relation between source and target is raised from the cognition-based perspective by Shen and Porat (2017). The authors point out that new psycholinguistic evidence raises questions about the assumed unidirectionality of metaphorical mappings in CMT. If conceptual metaphors are based on co-activation of heterogeneous domains as a result of their repeated conflation in early experience of the infant (for example, between the feeling of affection and the physical warmth of the caretaker's body), and if conceptual metaphors are supposed to emerge through the process of projection or mapping from one domain to another, from source to target domains, then the following 'discrepancies' remain to be explained: How can the bidirectionality involved in the neural process of co-activation of domains be maintained if the process of projection or mapping is supposed to be unidirectional? What is the relation between both processes, and if there is a shift from one process to another, what lays at the basis of this shift? And, more importantly, why do linguistic metaphors seem to show unidirectionality rather than bidirectionality as far as the process of projection is concerned?[1] Shen and Porat (2017) argue in favour of a solution based on the distinction between two "types" of – or rather two "phases" in – metaphor processing: (1) conceptual and bidirectional and (2) linguistic and unidirectional. The first refers to an "initial phase of metaphor formation and comprehension" (2017: 68), where the domains are "simply 'associated' and which involves no attribution of 'target' and 'source'" (67). The second refers to a "full-blown" linguistic metaphor in which aspects of the source domain are projected or mapped onto aspects of the target domain, where the unidirectionality process is required by the "assignment of the grammatical function" and thus by the "allocation" of either "target" or "source" role to the metaphorical terms (71).

Even if I do not agree with Shen and Porat's (2017) proposed solution of the issue, the authors' insistence on the need to discuss the issue of unidirectionality, in relation to the notions of 'source' and 'target', as well as their suggestion that the connection between the two domains should be understood as a "bare association", with "no attribution of 'target' or 'source'" in the first type of metaphor, represent a welcome starting point for discussion. The same issue has been critically addressed from the perspective of Cognitive Poetics by Stockwell (1999:

---

[1] Shen and Porat (2017) analyze examples like *An anchor is a friend* and (the already famous) *This butcher is a surgeon* and show that while a bidirectional process of projection remains possible in such cases, changing the source and target role will lead to entirely different metaphorical interpretations.

129), who proposes that *"rather than being unidirectional*, it would seem that conceptual metaphor [...] *might be interanimating"* (emphasis mine, E.F.). According to Stockwell, what happens when conceptualizing new experiences through metaphor is not a matter of projection from a target to a source, but a process which supposes the "mutual influence" and permeation of both terms involved in the metaphorical process. Using various examples, he argues that the terms 'source' and 'target' are inappropriate and should be abandoned. Following the model from mathematics, he proposes that the 'equation' of the metaphor's terms should stand for the asymmetric relation between source and target. Stockwell explains that if "the cognitive equation" does not "allow each side of the mapping to influence the other side in a two-way flow", it is difficult to understand how we arrived at conceiving, e. g., an ordinary experience like an argument in terms of a "remote experience" like a war, in the case of the conceptual metaphor ARGUMENT IS WAR. To overcome this difficulty, Stockwell suggests to treat "the cognitive equation" as a "mathematical equation": WAR=ARGUMENT would thus best "account for the points of similarity in the mapping ARGUMENT IS WAR/ WAR IS ARGUMENT" (1999: 134). A similar viewpoint is found, e. g., in Sonesson (2015) with regard to visual semiotics and the parallel concepts 'topic' and 'vehicle' that circulate in rhetoric. Sonesson argues that, in pictorial metaphor, "it is often impossible to decide which term is the 'vehicle' and which 'the tenor'" and that "the direction of comparison" is made clear only "by the larger context" (Sonesson 2015: 99–100).

Shen and Porat as well as Stockwell and Sonesson arrive at a similar conclusion, even if they start from distinct positions and put forward very different arguments. They propose to abandon the directional relation between 'source' and 'target' (or 'vehicle' and 'tenor') and point out that the linkage between domains is not necessarily asymmetrical. The integralist perspective is close to Stockwell's and Sonesson's positions. In line with the Humboldtian assumptions underlying the integralist theory of metaphor, the cross-domain transfer does not take place between two 'passive' lexical entities, where the first (the source) would have the role of assuring the structure of the second (the target). Instead the contents of both terms fuse and contribute, in different proportions and with a specific content, to the metaphorical process. In other words, both lexical items contribute actively to the emergence of the metaphorical entity, created on the basis of the 'vision' of the unitary aspect of the two different contents, which has been grasped and expressed within and through the semantic metaphorical act.[2] In

---

[2] Note that this perspective on the metaphorical process does not adopt Max Black's interactionist view on metaphor. The main disagreement between the two perspectives lies in their in-

line with CMT's assessment from the integralist point of view, Stockwell (1999: 140) points out that the concepts 'source' and 'target' have undermined from the beginning "the perception of metaphor as creative", "condemning us to see things only in the way that we have always seen them". Sonesson's (2015, 2019) evaluation from a cognitive-semiotic perspective demonstrates in turn that what Lakoff and Johnson call metaphors are at best diagrams, in the Peircean sense, and not metaphors as such. Similar to Stockwell's argument, Sonesson argues that as diagrams, CMT's metaphors focus rather on the "static equivalences" which are taken for granted in the "lifeworld", and not on the similarities that are "created anew" by means of metaphors.

Nevertheless, the integralist theory of metaphor may accommodate the concepts 'source' and 'target', but only "from a functional perspective" and without assuming the guiding role assigned by CMT to the image-schematic structure of an experiential content (Borcilă 2013). At first glance, the integralist solution seems to be to some extent convergent to Shen and Porat's (2017) perspective, particularly in considering the asymmetric relation between the terms in linguistic metaphors from a functional perspective. The difference, consists in the fact that, while Shen and Porat restrict the functional perspective to the source and target role within a clause or phrase, in the integralist theory of metaphor this perspective is understood in relation to the cognitive nature of metaphor and thus to the referential dimension of speaking ('designation'): metaphor is the creation of cognitive contents of speaking with the aim of "classifying reality" ("intentos de clasificar la realidad") (Coseriu 1956: 16, 1985 [1956]: 81). Thus, if one considers the integralist perspective of "metaphorical creation in language" and the newest developments in the cognitive paradigm from a functional perspective, the supposed "division of labor" (Shen and Porat 2017: 71) between two very different, and perhaps irreconcilable, 'types' of metaphorical processes – conceptual and linguistic – does no longer seem necessary.

In contrast to the cognition-oriented approach to metaphor, scholars who adopt the social-discursive perspective have spent many efforts over the past years to revive the interest in the socio-cultural and communicative dimensions of metaphor. Scholars such as Leezenberg (2013), Caballero and Ibarretxe-Antuñaño (2013), Forceville (2017), Winter and Matlock (2017), among others, have reconsidered the role of language and culture(s), on the one hand, and of social interaction and public practices, on the other hand, as equally constit-

---

compatible theoretical backgrounds: While Max Back's interactionist metaphor theory is based on logical semantics, integralist metaphor theory is grounded in Coseriu's concept of the intuitive semantic contents of the two lexical items.

utive of mental structures and cognitive processes. Meanwhile, scholars who adopt the communication-based approach (Müller 2010, 2017, Deignan and Cameron 2013, Deignan 2017, Jensen 2017, among others) instead pay specific attention to the dichotomy between stable and dynamic aspects of metaphor.

There is a growing interest in current metaphor research for the study of 'metaphor in the wild':

> My personal preference is to see butterflies in the wild, even if this makes them more difficult to study compared to dead specimens in a laboratory. [...] We can, of course, still examine metaphors 'under glass' as when placed individually down on paper, to better understand their structure and possible meanings. (Gibbs 2017a: 320)

It is thus supposed that observing metaphors in the wild, i.e. as "a matter of use" in various communicative contexts, might provide insights into "aspects of discourse dynamics and embodied meaning-making" (Müller 2017: 297).

While there is a rather general agreement that metaphors arise "in language use to address particular and often specific communicative needs and functions" (Evans 2013: 75), there are few studies that question the so-called communicative function of metaphor. Perhaps the study that stands out in this respect is Jensen (2017). The author explicitly disagrees with the treatment of metaphor as a matter of communication and explains that usually the term "communication [...] entails an idea of two separate interlocutors that send something (thoughts, ideas, feelings, directives, metaphors, etc.) back and forth" (Jensen 2017: 260). It thus presupposes an instrumental use of language, by means of which metaphorical meanings, reified under the form of the product of one's individual mind, are sent to another individual to serve specific "communicative needs". Jensen instead proposes a shift from metaphor as a product used in communication to "metaphor as a process of creating and enacting some kind of metaphorical, i.e. double meaning" (2017: 259) in the "'inter-world' of dialogue". It is this emphasis on metaphor as something "we 'do'" (i.e. activity, process) "in our active and explorative sense-making" (261), as opposed to something "we have" (i.e. product) and can communicate, that is also suggested by Gibbs (2017a: 320) in his dynamic account of metaphor: "I purposely talk about 'metaphor performance' rather than 'metaphor use', because 'performance' gives proper attention to the fact that metaphors are enacted and not simply selected for use from a mental thesaurus". However, in contrast to Gibbs, Jensen appears to envisage a reconceptualization of the communicative dimension of metaphor, elaborating on the idea that these cognitive metaphorical meanings are created in an "inter-personal ecology" (Jensen 2017: 257), and thus that metaphor emerges as a shared or common achievement in human interaction. Unlike other authors who approach metaphor as a dynamic-creative process but consider this dynamicity and creativity of language and metaphor as phenomena that pop up exclusively in language use, thus becoming a "function of discourse", Jensen takes the opposite view and considers creativity and "alterity" (or intersubjectivity) as essential dimensions that mutually concur to "the metaphorical conceptualization process". At first glance, this approach seems close to Coseriu's cardinal concept of (linguistic and metaphoric) creativity, i. e. *enérgeia*, the origins of which can be traced back mainly to its first conceptualization in Aristotle's ontology and later on its conceptual enrichment with the dimension of intersubjectivity in Humboldt's anthropology. Without going into details, it seems be very difficult to consider Coseriu's notion of *enérgeia*, "creativity within and through alterity" (Borcilă 2002), capable of accommodating Jensen's view. Coseriu's and Jensen's perspectives are built on distinct traditions of research: Coseriu's understanding of creativity unfolds ideas that originate in philosophy (Aristotle, Humboldt, Heidegger, Dewey, Merleau-Ponty, Pagliaro), whereas Jensen grounds his view on dynamic systems theory. Adopting the perspective of dynamic systems, Jensen is compelled to see the dialogical and creative dimension of metaphor "as embedded in *supra-individual dynamics* arising from the constant change and reorganization of the system (of interaction)" (Jensen 2017: 262, italics in the original). One feels compelled to ask in this context: "whose creativity?" and "whose alterity?" – and also why metaphor emerges in the first place.

Moving on to the third strand of research, there are also attempts of providing a unified view of the interdisciplinary study of metaphor. Representatives of unifying accounts in cognitive science are Raymond W. Gibbs and Mark Johnson. In a recent interview, Gibbs admits that his "research has been devoted to showing the connections between many diverse theories of metaphor and to not simply favor one view to the exclusion of all other" (Rasulíc 2017: 140–141). Rather than adopting "resistant" "rhetorical stances" to other perspectives, which will keep the "metaphor wars" alive in unproductive ways, scholars should accept that perspectives are complementary and their interaction may enhance our knowledge of the phenomenon (Gibbs 2017a, Gibbs 2017b). Gibbs therefore proposes a view in which various levels of analysis – evolutionary, historical, sociocultural, discourse, linguistic, cognitive, psychological, embodied, neural – are considered "interactive". It remains unclear, in his work, how all these levels can be related to each other without elaborating a unitary framework on the basis of which various approaches can be reinterpreted and integrated.

The second ambitious unifying perspective stems from Mark Johnson, who proposes an integrative theory of "meaning and thought", which he calls "the aesthetics of embodied meaning".[3] He understands the term 'aesthetics', in accordance with Dewey's tradition, "not just as theoretical exploration of the nature of art [...], but rather as pertaining to all the processes by which any aspect of our experience can be meaningful" (Johnson 2018: 24). If 'aesthetics' thus refers to the way meaning emerges, the components of this meaningful experience are constituted by images, image-schemas, qualities, emotions and feelings. The cardinal role assigned to the emotional dimension of meaning is perhaps Johnson's most important achievement both in relation to his previous work and to other studies within CMT. One can find among cognitive scholars occasional references to this dimension, but Johnson has elaborated it to a considerable extent. In contradistinction to Johnson's definition, scholars adopting a communication-based approach have claimed that "[m]uch metaphorical meaning seems to occur in semi-fixed expressions, with relatively stable syntactic and lexical patterns and specific affective and pragmatic meanings" (Deignan and Cameron 2013: 227). It is current practice in many linguistic approaches to treat the expressivity of language, and particularly its emotional dimension, as part of the 'vivid' interaction between speakers. In contrast to such accounts, Johnson's approach to this phenomenon is essentially based on a different tradition of research and considers ideas originating in the work of William James, John Dewey and Antonio Damasio. He notices that both "traditional philosophy of language" and language science

> have tended to either downplay or entirely dismiss the emotional dimension of meaning. C.K. Ogden and I. A Richards (1923) set the stage for this when they distinguished 'descriptive' from 'emotive' meaning, and then concluded that only the former has significant cognitive content relevant to understanding and knowing our world. The unfortunate result of this illegitimate bifurcation of thought and feeling, reason and emotion, has been, until quite recently, the ignoring of emotions in mainstream accounts of language (Johnson 2017: 32).

Particularly with Damasio's "grand" discovery of emotion playing a central role in human thought and meaning, a whole tradition based on Cartesian dualism and on the refutation of emotion fell into disgrace, according to Johnson. Starting from Damasio's breakthrough, and using James' insight about the "thought-

---

[3] Interestingly, Johnson does not treat metaphor in his approach to "meaning and thought" (Johnson 2017, 2018). However, his notion of image schema (Johnson 1987) has been foundational to the development of CMT, as are the components of meaningful experiences, in more recent terms, for "human cognition as a whole", including art, philosophy, science and morality (see the title of Johnson's 2018 book: *The aesthetics of meaning and thought: the bodily roots of philosophy, science, morality, and art*).

feeling" ("all thought has a feeling dimension that includes both a felt sense of the horizon or fringe of meaning surrounding a particular term, and also a feeling of the direction of our thinking", Johnson 2017: 32) and Dewey's notion of "the felt quality as demarcating and pervading the whole situation at a given moment" (2017: 65), Johnson argues that emotion and feeling lie "at the heart of our ability to conceptualize and reason" (2017: 33). Importantly, there is a crucial difference between Johnson's approach and the more common accounts of this issue in Cognitive Linguistics. For the latter, affectivity emerges as a result of language use, in the sense that language itself is put into the service of, i.e. is instrumentally used for, expressing one's feeling and emotions. By contrast, for Johnson emotions and feelings are foundational for human cognition as a whole, and in this sense, they 'permeate' all meaning.

The way Johnson conceptualizes this phenomenon is akin to Coseriu's approach to emotion and affectivity as intrinsic dimensions of the linguistic sign and metaphor. In his theory of metaphor, Coseriu (1956; 1985 [1956]) discusses Bühler's 'Organon model' with its three functions of *Kundgabe* or *Ausdruck* (the indication or expression of the speaker's feelings and attitudes), *Darstellung* (the representation of objects and state of affairs) and *Auslösung* or *Appell* (the influencing of the listeners' attitudes, the 'appealing' function) (Bühler 1990 [1934]: 35). Coseriu points out that the subjective aspects and everything pertaining to the domain of emotions have in general been associated with creativity. It was only one step from here to the conclusion that the creative aspect of language 'exclusively' belongs to certain functions of language use: "there is a tendency to identify 'language' with the informative function (or with 'enunciative language') and, as a result, to claim that creativity is a phenomenon that belongs exclusively to the functions of expression and appealing" (Coseriu 1956: 14, 1985 [1956]: 79). The breakthrough in relation to this view has been accomplished by Coseriu through his elaboration of the notion of creativity. In Coseriu's concept of *enérgeia* (i.e. "creativity within and through alterity"), the creative aspect is not separated from the emotive-affective aspect, because it is in the nature of creativity to be triggered by a speaker's needs of sharing *with* and *for* another person a lived and felt content. Coseriu adopts this view from Humboldt's linguistic anthropology, which says that all as yet undivided powers of man (emotion, intellect, sensibility) fuse into and participate together in language's *enérgeia*. Subjectivity, emotion and affectivity therefore characterize the human activity of speaking in its entirety.

I would like to argue that Johnson's concept of 'emotion' is compatible with the integralist theory of metaphor. According to Coseriu's framework, any attempt to integrate different perspectives conceptually requires that specific concepts and theoretical claims are reinterpreted on the unitary basis his perspective is able to provide. It is worth mentioning in this context that the integralist metaphor theory has already taken advantage of another innovation proposed in the cognitive framework, viz. the concept of 'image schema'. Following Coseriu's own suggestions (Coseriu 1990, 1992 [1989–1990], 2000 [1990]: § 7.1.), the cognitive assumption that in the process of categorization of experience there is a 'mental schema' or 'an image-schematic structure' which emerges in our experience of the world and which is 'associated' to a conceptual content has been reinterpreted with regard to the metaphorical process as follows: 'the mental schema' or 'image schema' cannot be conceived as a representation drawn from the pre-verbal realm, where it was supposed to emerge, but rather as a spontaneously created image in the metaphorical process itself and in 'association' with a lexical meaning (Borcilă 2003, 2013, Faur 2013a, 2013b). Johnson's new concept of 'emotion' can also help to enrich our knowledge about the conceptual content of 'affective schemas' (Borcilă 2013) that emerge in the act of metaphorical designation.

Consider, for instance, the metaphor *threatening sky* (the example is taken from Brandt 2013: 40). The lexical items involved in the metaphorical process are represented by *sky* (term A) and *threatening* (term B). Based on our world knowledge about how the sky may be – blue, silver-blue, blood-red, dark, cloudy, cloudless, calm, clear, infinite, immense etc. – the grasped quality of the sky in this particular moment represents a novel perceptual experience. Having the characteristics of presenting itself in an unexpected new way for the speaker, the novel perceptual aspect cannot be integrated with the other possible *designata* of A (*sky*), toward which it might be oriented through a process of direct determination (for the notion of 'determination', see Coseriu (1973 [1955–1956]: 282–323). As a result, a cross-domain determination is called for, by means of which the novel perceptual aspect captured in relation to A (*sky*) is seen in the perspective of the associated image expressed by B (*threatening*). The image of a powerful and devastating natural force pops up spontaneously in the moment when the speaker has the 'vision' of the novel quality of the sky. The image is subsequently transferred from the domain of the lexical item *threatening* to the domain of the lexical item *sky*, together with an affective schema triggered by the felt sense of fear and anxiety caused by the imminent danger manifested by a force of nature. Thus, in order to capture and express intersubjectively the 'vision' of the perceived peculiarities of the sky, the speaker proceeds to a cross-domain transfer of the image belonging to the domain of B (*threatening*) to the domain of A (*sky*). The novel aspect grasped in relation to the sky is spontaneously expressed through both the image of a forceful and dangerous power of nature and the negative feelings associated to this image and to the lexical item *threatening*. The metaphor *threatening sky* thus emerges through the cross-domain transfer and identification of two lexical items belonging to heterogeneous domains, which have been brought together on the basis of the 'vision' of the felt unitary aspect established between the two lexical items.

This account contrasts with respect to the role the cognitive account assigns to the notions 'image schema' and 'emotion'. Whereas in the cognitive framework, these notions are purely psychological pre-verbal phenomena, in the integralist framework they are reinterpreted as semantic phenomena that emerge in the act of designation. Johnson's concepts of image, image schema, qualities, emotion and feeling are conceived of as pre-existing entities in relation to the activity of speaking; they are stored in pre-linguistic spaces of one's cognitive unconscious, which may become active in conceptualizing 'new realities' through conceptual metaphors. Whereas Johnson conceives of emotions as felt qualities that are associated to pre-linguistic structures of experience, or image schemas, in the integralist theory of metaphor they cannot be felt qualities recruited from the pre-verbal realm but are understood as emergent felt qualities in the metaphorical process itself by means of their 'association' with a lexical meaning.

3 Conclusion

So far the integralist theory of metaphor has successfully exploited some of the innovations introduced in CMT (Lakoff and Johnson 2003 [1980], Lakoff 1987, Johnson 1987), pinpointing its contribution to the description of the mechanism of metaphorical designation (cf. Borcilă 2003, 2013, Faur 2013a, 2013b). I strongly believe that the dialogue between representatives of the integralist approach, developed on the basis of Coseriu's Integral Linguistics approach to language, and other traditions of research should continue and that it is one of the prime tasks of scholars adhering to Coserian Integral Linguistics to carry on the work he initiated around the middle of the twentieth century. In exchange, it is time for alternative trends to pay close attention to achievements of Integral Linguistics, not only with regard to various strands of inquiry within cognitive science but also solutions coming from other traditions. The integralist theory of metaphor may help present-day metaphor research to solve some of its controversial issues, and this dialogue cannot but contribute to an enriched perspective in the understanding of metaphor as a fundamental resource of human creativity.

References

Bojoga, Eugenia, Oana Boc and Cornel Vîlcu. 2013. "Introduction". In: Eugenia Bojoga, Oana Boc and Cornel Vîlcu (eds.), *Coseriu: Perspectives contemporaines*, Vol. I, 5–7. Cluj-Napoca: Presa Universitară Clujeană.

Borcilă, Mircea. 2002. "Eugeniu Coșeriu, fondator al lingvisticii ca știință a culturii". *Limba Română* 10, 48–55.

Borcilă, Mircea. 2003. "Lingvistica integrală și fundamentele metaforologiei". *Dacoromania. Serie nouă* 7–8, 47–77.

Borcilă, Mircea. 2013. *Paradigme contemporane în cercetarea lingvistică*. Prelegeri doctorale, Universitatea "Babeș-Bolyai".

Brandt, Line. 2013. "Metaphor and the communicative mind". In: Riccardo Fusaroli and Simone Morgagni (eds.), *Cognitive Semiotics: Conceptual Metaphor Theory: thirty years after*, 37–72. Berlin & Boston: Mouton de Gruyter.

Bühler, Karl. 1990 [1934]. *The theory of language: the representational function of language*. Translated by Donald Fraser Goodwin. Amsterdam & Philadelphia: John Benjamins (English translation of Bühler 1934).

Caamaño, Antonio Vilarnovo. 1993. *Lógica y lenguaje en Eugenio Coseriu*. Madrid: Gredos.

Caballero, Rosario and Iraide Ibarretxe-Antuñaño. 2013. "Ways of perceiving, moving and thinking: re-vindicating culture in Conceptual Metaphor Research". In: Riccardo Fusaroli and Simone Morgagni (eds.), *Cognitive Semiotics: Conceptual Metaphor Theory: thirty years after*, 268–290. Berlin & Boston: Mouton de Gruyter.

Coseriu, Eugenio. 1956. *La creación metafórica en el lenguaje*. Montevideo: Universidad de la República, Facultad de Humanidades y Ciencias.

Coseriu, Eugenio. 1973 [1955–1956]. "Determinación y entorno". In: Eugenio Coseriu, *Teoría del lenguaje y lingüística general. Cinco estudios*, 282–323. Madrid: Editorial Gredos.

Coseriu, Eugenio. 1985 [1956]. "La creación metafórica en el lenguaje". In: Eugenio Coseriu. 1985. *El hombre y su lenguaje. Estudios de teoría y metodología lingüística*, 66–102. Madrid: Gredos.

Coseriu, Eugenio. 1990. "Semántica estructural y semántica cognitiva". In: *Homenaje al Profesor Francisco Marsá / Jornadas de Filología*, 239–282. Barcelona: Universidad de Barcelona.

Coseriu, Eugenio. 2000 [1990]. "Structural semantics and 'cognitive' semantics". *Logos and Language* 1:1, 19–42 (English translation of Coseriu 1990).

Coseriu, Eugenio. 1992 [1989–1990]. *Strukturelle und kognitive Semantik*. Transcript by Ulrike Maier und Heinrich Weber. Unpublished manuscript. University of Tübingen.

Coseriu, Eugenio. 1995. "Von den *universali fantastici*". In: Jürgen Trabant (ed.), *Vico und die Zeichen – Vico e i segni*, 73–80. Tübingen: Narr.

Coseriu, Eugenio. 2007 [1988]. *Sprachkompetenz. Grundzüge der Theorie des Sprechens*. Edited by Heinrich Weber (second edition). Tübingen: Narr.

Coseriu, Eugenio. 2015. *Geschichte der Sprachphilosophie*. Vol. 1: *Von Heraklit bis Rousseau*. Vol. 2: *Von Herder bis Humboldt*. Edited by J. Albrecht. Tübingen: Narr & Francke: Attempto.

Deignan, Alice. 2017. "Mappings and narratives in figurative communication". In: Beate Hampe (ed.), *Metaphor: embodied cognition and discourse*, 200–219. Cambridge: Cambridge University Press.

Deignan, Alice and Lynne Cameron. 2013. "A re-examination of UNDERSTANDING IS SEEING". In: Riccardo Fusaroli and Simone Morgagni (eds.), *Cognitive Semiotics: Conceptual Metaphor Theory: thirty years after*, 220–243. Berlin & Boston: Mouton de Gruyter.

Devylder, Simon and Jordan Zlatev. 2020. "Cutting and breaking metaphors of the self and the Motivation & Sedimentation Model". In: Annalisa Baicchi (ed.), *Figurative meaning construction in thought and language*, 253–281. Amsterdam & Philadelphia: Johns Benjamins.

Evans, Vyvyan. 2013. "Metaphor, lexical concepts, and figurative meaning construction". In: Riccardo Fusaroli and Simone Morgagni (eds.), *Cognitive Semiotics. Conceptual Metaphor Theory: thirty years after*, 73–107. Berlin & Boston: Mouton de Gruyter.

Faur, Elena. 2013a. "Integral Semantics and Conceptual Metaphor: rethinking Conceptual Metaphor within an Integral Semantics framework". In: Riccardo Fusaroli and Simone Morgagni (eds.), *Cognitive Semiotics. Conceptual Metaphor Theory: thirty years after*, 108–139. Berlin & Boston: Mouton de Gruyter.

Faur, Elena. 2013b. *Semantica cognitivă și emergența studiilor elocuționale*. Teză de doctorat, Universitatea Babeș-Bolyai.

Forceville, Charles. 2017. "From Image Schema to metaphor in discourse: the FORCE schemas in animation films". In: Beate Hampe (ed.), *Metaphor: embodied cognition and discourse*, 239–257. Cambridge: Cambridge University Press.

Gallagher, Shaun. 1997. "Mutual enlightenment: recent phenomenology in cognitive science". *Journal of Consciousness Studies* 4:3, 195–214.

Gibbs, Raymond W. 2017a. "The embodied and discourse views of metaphor: why these are not so different and how can they be brought closer together". In: Beate Hampe (ed.), *Metaphor: embodied cognition and discourse*, 319–334. Cambridge: Cambridge University Press.

Gibbs, Raymond W. 2017b. *Metaphor wars: Conceptual Metaphors in human life*. Cambridge: Cambridge University Press.

Grady, Joseph and Giorgio A. Ascoli. 2017. "Sources and targets in Primary Metaphor Theory: looking back and thinking ahead". In: Beate Hampe (ed.), *Metaphor: embodied cognition and discourse*, 27–45. Cambridge: Cambridge University Press.

Hampe, Beate. 2017. "Embodiment and discourse: dimensions and dynamics of contemporary metaphor theory". In: Beate Hampe (ed.), *Metaphor: embodied cognition and discourse*, 3–25. Cambridge: Cambridge University Press.

Jensen, Thomas W. 2017. "Doing metaphor. An ecological perspective on metaphoricity in discourse". In: Beate Hampe (ed.), *Metaphor: embodied cognition and discourse*, 239–257. Cambridge: Cambridge University Press.

Johnson, Mark. 1987. *The body in the mind. The bodily basis of meaning, imagination and reason*. Chicago & London: The University of Chicago Press.

Johnson, Mark. 2017. *Embodied mind, meaning, and reason. How our bodies give rise to understanding*. Chicago & London: The University of Chicago Press.

Johnson, Mark. 2018. *The aesthetics of meaning and thought. The bodily roots of philosophy, science, morality, and art*. Chicago & London: The University of Chicago Press.

Lakoff, George. 1987. *Women, fire and dangerous things. What categories reveal about the mind*. Chicago & London: The University of Chicago Press.

Lakoff, George and Mark Johnson. 2003 [1980]. *Metaphors we live by*. Chicago & London: The University of Chicago Press.

Leezenberg, Michiel. 2013. "From Cognitive Linguistics to social sciences: thirty years after *Metaphor we live by*". In: Riccardo Fusaroli and Simone Morgagni (eds.), *Cognitive Semiotics. Conceptual Metaphor Theory: thirty years after*, 140–152. Berlin & Boston: Mouton de Gruyter.

Müller, Cornelia. 2010. "The dynamics of metaphor: foregrounding and activating metaphoricity in conversational interaction". *Cognitive Semiotics* 10:6, 85–120.

Müller, Cornelia. 2017. "Walking metaphors: embodied cognition in multimodal discourse". In: Beate Hampe (ed.), *Metaphor: embodied cognition and discourse*, 297–317. Cambridge: Cambridge University Press.

Ogden, Charles K. and Ivor A. Richards. 1923. *The meaning of meaning*. London: Routledge & Kegan Paul.

Rasulić, Katarina. 2017. "A metaphor biangle: Raymond W. Gibbs and Gerald Steen". *Metaphor and the Social World* 7:1, 130–151.

Sánchez De Zavala, Victor. 1982. *Funcionalismo estructural y generativismo*. Madrid: Alianza.

Shen, Yeshayahu and Roy Porat. 2017. "Metaphorical directionality: the role of language". In: Beate Hampe (ed.), *Metaphor: embodied cognition and discourse*, 62–81. Cambridge: Cambridge University Press.

Sonesson, Göran. 2015. "Bats out of the belfry: the nature of metaphor, with special attention to pictorial metaphors". *Signs and Media* 11, 74–104.

Sonesson, Göran. 2019b. "Two models of metaphoricity and three dilemmas of metaphor research". *Cognitive Semiotics* 12:1, 1–17.

Stampoulidis, George, Maria Bolognesi and Jordan Zlatev. 2019. "A cognitive semiotic exploration of metaphors in Greek street art". *Cognitive semiotics*, 12:1. DOI: https://doi.org/10.1515/cogsem-2019–2008.

Stockwell, Peter. 1999. "The inflexibility of invariance". *Language and literature* 8:2, 125–142.

Winter, Bodo and Teenie Matlock. 2017. "Primary metaphors are both cultural and embodied". In: Beate Hampe (ed.), *Metaphor: embodied cognition and discourse*, 99–116. Cambridge: Cambridge University Press.

Zahavi, Dan. 2019. "Applied phenomenology: why it is safe to ignore the epoché?" *Continental Philosophy Review* (Online Publication).

Zlatev, Jordan, Göran Jacobsson and Liina Paju. In press. Desiderata for metaphor theory, the 'Motivation and Sedimentation Model' and motion-emotion metaphoremes. In: Augusto Soares da Silva (ed.), *Figurative language. Intersubjectivity and usage*. Amsterdam & Philadelphia: John Benjamins.

Thomas Belligh (Ghent)
Language as activity, linguistic knowledge and cognitive psychology: a Coserian perspective

> *The biologically conditioned mechanisms underlying the activity of speaking are not directly the object of linguistics as a cultural science. They are the object of branches of physiology, psychology and medicine, including psychiatry.**

1 Introduction

Integral Linguistics (henceforth: IL), the school of thought developed by Coseriu (1974 [1958], 1975 [1962], 1985, 1992 [1988], 2000 [1990], 2001, 2007 [1988], among many other publications) and his followers, remains to this day one of the most well-developed and conceptually coherent frameworks in the functional tradition of linguistics. In addition to being an attractive framework in its own right, it constitutes an interesting point of comparison to reflect on the specific traits of other contemporary linguistic schools. Furthermore, IL can often serve as a source of inspiration to help remedy conceptual confusions that can be found in other linguistic frameworks.

Over the past twenty years there has been substantial work in meta-linguistics, mostly written from an IL perspective, specifying how and why IL differs from one of the most dominant contemporary linguistic schools of thought, viz. Mainstream Cognitive Linguistics (henceforth: MCL).[1] MCL is a framework that has been developed since the 1980s as a reaction against the then overall dominance of Generative Grammar in American linguistics and its tendency to reduce linguistics to the formal study of syntax, morphology and phonology. MCL has put emphasis on describing the rich semantics and pragmatics not only of words, but also of larger constructions in grammar, with a focus on

---

* "Die biologisch bedingten Mechanismen des Sprechens sind nicht unmittelbar Gegenstand der Linguistik als Kulturwissenschaft. Sie sind Gegenstand von Formen der Physiologie, der Psychologie und der Medizin einschließlich der Psychiatrie" (Coseriu 2007 [1988]: 69).
1 As will become clear throughout the paper, Cognitive Linguistics (CL) is a very broad school of thought that is characterized by considerable internal heterogeneity. I use the term 'Mainstream Cognitive Linguistics' to differentiate CL as it has been conceptualized by its founding fathers from the distinctly different forms of CL that can be found nowadays (cf. Section 5).

key notions such as subjectivity, embodiment, construal, prototypicality, metonymy and conceptual metaphor. Various scholars, first in the United States and later also in Europe, have been crucial in the emergence of Cognitive Linguistics, most notably 'the founding fathers' Langacker (1987, 1990, 1991, 2007), Lakoff (1987), Lakoff and Johnson (1999), Talmy (2000) and Geeraerts (1993, 2010, Geeraerts and Cuyckens 2007).

IL and MCL have hitherto been compared on several fronts, including the strengths and shortcomings of the encyclopaedic prototype semantics typical of MCL vs. the unitary, paradigmatically delimited, language-specific semantics typical of IL (cf. Coseriu 2000 [1990], Taylor 1999, Kabatek 2000b), the radically different treatment and conceptualization of monosemy and polysemy in the two frameworks (Van der Gucht 2005, Van der Gucht et al. 2007), the different treatment of the function or meaning of case marking (Willems 1997), and the specific nature of the linguistic sign in the two approaches (Willems 2011). Other scholars have put effort into conceptually enriching MCL with categories borrowed from IL, especially regarding the distinction between language-specific meanings and universal aspects of language use (Zlatev 2007a, 2011).

In this contribution, I focus on a further important difference between IL and MCL that has to my knowledge hitherto not received the same attention as the aforementioned differences. I will be concerned with the different conceptualization, in IL and MCL, of the nature of language and, hence, of the object of study of linguistics and how this object of study relates to other scientific disciplines that belong to the language sciences broadly construed, in particular cognitive psychology and neuroscience. In addition to favouring different kinds of analyses for various specific linguistic phenomena, the two schools of thought also differ with regard to how they view the very nature of linguistic phenomena and the scope of linguistic analyses. My comparison of IL and MCL will mainly focus on their different conceptualizations of the ontology of the human mind and the epistemological and methodological consistency in approaching the mind in both approaches.

The paper is structured as follows. Section 2 outlines the IL view on the nature of language and the object of linguistics and specifies how this view is intimately related to a specific conception of the human mind. In Section 3, the approach typical of MCL is presented, with a focus on how it differs from IL. Section 4 presents two lines of thought from the philosophy of cognitive science that are both in their own way highly problematic for the view endorsed by MCL and more consistent with the view advocated in IL. Section 5 puts forward two possible solutions to define the object of study of MCL in a more coherent manner and discusses some recent developments within the broad field of Cognitive Linguistics that dovetail with this proposal. Section 6 concludes the article.

2 Integral Linguistics: language as a conscious human activity

In IL, language is considered to be a creative human cultural activity and the most predominant and fundamental form of creating culture. Coseriu (1974 [1958], 1975 [1962], 1985, 2001, 2007 [1988]) repeatedly stressed that a language exists in reality only inasmuch as language users make use of – or better still: continuously create – language in the activity of speaking, writing, or by any other means. It is true that in order to carve out an object of linguistic enquiry it is fruitful, and arguably even necessary, to make abstraction of some aspects of these creative acts of language use and to focus, for example, solely on the 'systems' or the 'norms' of specific languages that permeate linguistic activity. However, the systems and the norms that are the legitimate focus of most linguistic research, including that of many specific IL analyses, remain at any given time abstractions which can only be said to exist in reality insofar they are manifested in language use. In fact, Coseriu explicitly rejects the view that language systems and norms would exist at some level beyond the acts of language use performed by individuals. Both the assumption that language systems inhabit a kind of immaterial Platonic realm, most notably favoured by Katz (1972), and the assumption that a language system exists as a social entity over and beyond all language users taken together, as arguably held by Saussure (1968) under the influence of Durkheim, are explicitly dismissed as erroneous by Coseriu (1974 [1958], 1975 [1962], 2001).

Within the overall (Humboldtian) view held by IL that language is ultimately a human activity, a number of specific perspectives are further distinguished by Coseriu (1985, 2007 [1988]). In particular, inasmuch as language is a productive human cultural activity, it can be viewed as dynamic creative activity itself (*enérgeia*), as the products of that activity (*érgon*) or as the knowledge that not only enables linguistic activity, but which is also formed by it (*dýnamis*). Although both the *érgon* and *dýnamis* perspective constitute relevant and even indispensable points of view, they always remain in a certain sense secondary to the true primary nature of language as *enérgeia* (Coseriu 1974 [1958], 2001, 2007 [1988]). The products of an activity (*érgon*) are created by undertaking that activity (*enérgeia*) and in a logical sense the activity also precedes the knowledge that is formed by partaking in that activity (*dýnamis*).

It is crucial to note that viewing language primarily as a human activity does not entail that linguistics needs to be reduced to the study of materialized human behaviour. Language as a human activity manifests itself both in physically observable ways, for example in the airwaves produced in speech and in the coloured dots produced in writing, and mentally, i.e. in the conscious experience accompanying both language production and comprehension. On the one hand, it is fair to say that IL shares with behaviourism a certain focus on what human beings actually do, rather than on speculating about hypothetical psychological processes that lead to behaviour. On the other hand, the behaviourist tendency to reduce the study of human behaviour to its materialized aspects, which are empirically observable from a third-person's point of view, is an unproductive and unnecessary reduction from a Coserian perspective. In fact, the most crucial aspects of language relate to what is going on in the consciousness of language users in terms of meaning making and understanding.

When zooming in on the *dýnamis* aspect of language, it becomes clear that the crucial IL concepts 'system' and 'norm' have an ideal reality for Coseriu. This takes these concepts beyond the status of being merely useful conceptual tools that the linguist puts to use to understand linguistic activity. Building on scholars such as Hegel, Humboldt and Husserl, Coseriu takes systems and norms to be indispensable parts of the overall linguistic knowledge that enables language users and linguists alike to recognize systems and norms in the overwhelming totality of language use. Although the specific characteristics of the ideal nature of 'system' and 'norm' differ to some degree, they are both essential parts of the knowledge of language.

On the basis of the preceding comments, it is clear that Coserian analyses which pertain to knowledge and the human mind should not be interpreted as hypotheses about unconscious mental representations and processes that are put forward to account for linguistic behaviour. Rather, they are insightful *explications* of aspects of conscious phenomena. Consciousness plays a crucial role in the IL framework, as it is the locus of all meaningful phenomena that are the focus of IL investigations (Coseriu 2007 [1988]). While stressing the non-deniable nature of consciousness, Coseriu also emphasizes that recognizing the existence and primacy of consciousness does not entail accepting dualist or idealist metaphysical views. Establishing consciousness as a legitimate object of study does not entail believing that consciousness belongs to a different metaphysical order of a non-physical nature (Coseriu 1975 [1954]).[2]

In IL analyses, the focus is therefore always on the conscious human mind. Analyses of the semantics and pragmatics of words, such as Coseriu's (1989: 9) analysis of the French preposition *avec* ('with'), or Coseriu's (2000 [1990]: 28)

---

[2] It is interesting to note that Coseriu, building on Husserl, put forward this fundamental insight already in 1954. Searle's (1992, 1997) highly influential claim in Anglo-American philosophy that consciousness can perfectly be considered to be of a physical nature is thus anticipated by Husserl and Coseriu several decades earlier in continental philosophy.

analysis of the verb *to climb*, are in fact analyses of the conscious mental phenomena that accompany the production and/or interpretation of these words. However, the direct link between human conscious experience as lived in the Lifeworld (*Lebenswelt*, to use the Husserlian term) of daily experience and the outcome of IL analyses is not always obvious, because IL analyses go beyond the description of experience as it manifests itself directly in our consciousness and strive to reveal the essence of conscious experiences (Willems 1994). IL analyses are thus akin to the practice of eidetic reduction that is the hallmark of Husserlian (1981 [1913], 1989 [1952], 2001 [1913]) phenomenology. Given that IL analyses of, for example, the structurally encoded meanings of words do not focus on what is directly given in conscious experience, IL has to concede that structurally encoded meanings of words are often not as directly accessible to consciousness as the particular senses one finds in usage. For example, Coseriu's (1989: 9) claim that the structurally encoded meaning of *avec* ('with') amounts to nothing more than 'co-presence of' (cf. also Widoff, this volume) is not something that is directly given in our conscious experience, but something that can only be attained by a form of reduction and by focusing on some of the aspects that constitute our conscious experiences in using this particular word. However, given that it is possible to bring paraphrases of structurally encoded word meanings to explicit consciousness, word meanings are considered in IL to be 'implicitly conscious' and 'pre-theoretically known' rather than unconscious. If structurally encoded word meanings were truly unconscious, it should not be possible to bring them to consciousness in the first place.

Coseriu (2007 [1988]: 65) explicitly recognizes that the study of psychological mechanisms and the study of brain states are part and parcel of a complete theory of linguistic competence. Neural mechanisms and the psychological functions that are presumably executed by the human brain enable human language activity to take place. However, Coseriu (2007 [1988]: 69) is at the same time adamant that the study of these psychological and neural mechanisms falls outside the purview of linguistics as a cultural science, as evidenced by the introductory quote of this contribution. For IL both the cultural-hermeneutic investigation of linguistic activity in all its meaningful facets and the neuroscientific or psychological investigation of the relevant mechanisms enabling language activity are important endeavors, but they should be neatly distinguished.

In sum, according to IL, linguistic analyses provide in essence an explication, i.e. an insightful description, of linguistic activity and knowledge, both regarding its materialized aspects and, especially, its conscious mental aspects (cf. Belligh and Willems 2021). Studying what kind of biological and psychological mechanisms enable linguistic activity is an intriguing and legitimate question, but one that belongs to the field of cognitive psychology and neuroscience rather than to the field of linguistics. Purely linguistic analyses, with their hermeneutic focus on understanding conscious meaningful states, are not able to directly reveal the workings of bio-psychological mechanisms that might operate below the threshold of consciousness.

3 Mainstream Cognitive Linguistics: language as an unconscious subpersonal capacity

In contrast to IL, MCL considers linguistics not to be primarily the study of linguistic activity, but rather to have the human mind as its primary object of study (Lakoff 1987, Lakoff and Johnson 1999, Langacker 1987, 1990, 1991, 2007, Geeraerts 2010, Taylor 2002, 2012). The adoption of the term 'cognitive' in the very name of the framework also indicates that the cognitive dimension of language is its primary object of investigation.

Before delving into the problematic aspects of how MCL envisages its cognitive commitment, it is important to note that MCL is unproblematically cognitive with regard to several other aspects. MCL is unproblematically cognitive in the sense that it explicitly situates meaning and conceptualization in the embodied human mind, rather than in a philosophically constructed external possible world, as is the case in formal truth-conditional semantics. As a consequence, linguistic meaning is considered a matter far broader and more diverse in MCL than the kinds of meaning that can be captured by means of the apparatus of formal truth-conditional semantics. In addition, MCL also considers phenomena such as subjectivity, construal, reference points, metonymy and metaphor indispensable parts of linguistic meaning (Langacker 1987, 1990, 1991, 2007). Regarding this particular aspect, IL and MCL are quite similar and both can be considered to be equally 'cognitive', given that IL too construes linguistic meaning as something that is much more diverse than truth-conditional meaning and as something that is fundamentally related to the human mind. In fact, also for IL the human mind is crucial in understanding language, since linguistics is conceived as the study of a human activity that involves an indispensable mental component, rather than as only the science of overtly perceivable materialized language behaviour.

IL and MCL differ drastically with respect to their specific views on the ontology of the human mind. For IL, the unitary conscious human mind is central to its account of language (cf. Section 2), but this is not the case for MCL as it is found in the writings of its founding fathers, especially Lakoff (1987) and Lakoff and Johnson (1999), and in the majority of the work of its contemporary adherents, e.g. Taylor (2002, 2012). The view held in MCL is that linguistic analyses do not provide insights that relate to linguistic activity and to the conscious human mind, but rather insights that pertain directly to hypothesized cognitive unconscious mechanisms. These mechanisms are taken to enable conscious language use while themselves operating below the level of consciousness:

> As a cognitive linguist, I am mainly interested in that aspect of cognition that is unconscious, automatic, and apparently effort-free and independent of skill. Language has this character. (Lakoff 1987: 446)

> The cognitive unconscious [...] consists of all those mental operations that structure and make possible all conscious experience, including the understanding and use of language. [...] The detailed processes and structures of the cognitive unconscious (e.g. basic-level categories, prototypes, image schemas, nouns, verbs, and vowels) are hypothesized to make sense of conscious behaviour. (Lakoff and Johnson 1999: 103–104)

> Lakoff, Langacker and other self-styled Cognitive Linguists would certainly want to maintain that the goal of linguistics is a description of the mental structures which underlie linguistic activity. The aim is not to describe the properties of utterances, but to infer the cognitive reality which gave rise to these properties. (Taylor 2012: 6)

In a similar vein, MCL claims to be 'cognitive' in the same way as cognitive psychology (CP) is:

> Cognitive linguistics is the study of language in its cognitive function, where *cognitive* refers to the crucial role of intermediate informational structures in our encounters with the world. CL is cognitive in the same way that CP is: by assuming that our interaction with the world is mediated through informational structures in the mind. (Geeraerts and Cuyckens 2007: 5; italics in the original)

Since the emergence of modern cognitive psychology in the 1950s it has been commonplace in CP to study the human mind exclusively in material terms and to conceptualize it as a set of computational mechanisms, similar to a kind of software, which is somehow implemented in the human brain, which is in turn supposed to be comparable to some extent to a kind of hardware (cf. Marr 1982, Rumelhart and McClelland 1986, Dennett 1987, 1991, Jackendoff 1987, 2002, Fodor 2000, 2008, Clark 2001, Bechtel 2008, among others). Although cognitive psychology and neuroscience still can be said to have different objects of enquiry, viz. the computations taken by themselves and the physical matter actually carrying out the computations (cf. Brysbaert and Rastle 2013), they ultimately both provide descriptions of the brain. The specificity of modern CP resides, then, in the study of the kind of software that is, by hypothesis, run by our brains, rather than in the study of conscious mental phenomena. Given that these postulated mental computational mechanisms operate below the unitary conscious experience of a person, they have been called 'subpersonal mechanisms' (Dennett 1987, 1991). Human behaviour is considered as an *explanandum* that needs to be explained by proposing a set of computational subpersonal mechanisms that serve as *explanans*. These mechanisms have thus a theoretical status that is somewhat similar to the postulated theoretical entities that serve to explain phenomena in the natural sciences. In this spirit it is maintained that hypotheses about subpersonal computational mechanisms can be tested and falsified on the basis of experiments that tackle perceivable behaviour (De Houwer 2011, Brysbaert and Rastle 2013, De Houwer et al. 2017).

MCL analyses thus seem to target directly the level of the subpersonal cognitive mechanisms that are assumed to account for language activity, rather than providing explications of linguistic activity. IL, on the other hand, refrains from drawing conclusions about the human brain and subpersonal cognitive mechanisms on the basis of linguistic evidence. MCL is arguably very ambitious in its definition of the object of linguistics, but it encounters two major problems in doing so. First, by conceptualizing the object of linguistics as a set of subpersonal computational mechanisms, MCL adopts an object of study whose ontological status and conceptual coherence is highly controversial and which has been heavily criticized (Section 4.1). Second, even when assuming that the conceptualization of the mind in terms of subpersonal computational mechanisms is justified, MCL runs the risk of jumping to epistemologically unwarranted conclusions about these mechanisms (Section 4.2).

4 Two lines of insights from the philosophy of cognitive science

4.1 The controversial ontology of the subpersonal computational mind

The conception of the human mind in terms of subpersonal computational mechanisms has been heralded as the scientific way to study the mind (Churchland 1981, Dennett 1987, 1991) and has proven to be extremely influential in cognitive science. Although much has changed in the paradigm shift from the so-called first wave of cognitive science with its focus on higher-level cognitive computations (Jackendoff 1987, 2002, Fodor 2000, 2008) to the second wave centred on connectionism and parallel distributed processing (Rumelhart and McClelland 1986), both waves have supported the same subpersonal computational software conception of the human mind (Clark 2001, Thompson 2007).

Notwithstanding its overall dominance, the subpersonal computational conception of the mind has not only ardent supporters, but also fervent critics. It has been argued that only the conscious mind has any ontological reality and that the concept of a subpersonal computational unconscious mind is merely a hypothetical construct that lacks any coherent ontological basis (Searle 1983, 1992, 1997, Zlatev 2007b, 2008, 2010). Critics of this conception of the mind have put forward a number of arguments against it, in particular: the argument that computation is not intrinsic to the brain but rather attributed to it metaphorically by conscious agents; the argument that the computational approach is unable to tell apart mental states from non-mental states without ultimately relying on consciousness; the argument that it conflates into one level both inherently conscious phenomena and completely unconscious brain characteristics; and the argument that the approach is unable, as a matter of principle, to deal with crucial mental notions such as representation, normativity, conventionality, common knowledge and intersubjectivity.

Due to space limitations, I cannot discuss these arguments in any detail, but for my purposes here it suffices to highlight that if this line of arguments is valid, then the central object of investigation of MCL turns out to be simply non-existent. IL, on the other hand, does not run into similar problems, as it does not adopt subpersonal computational mechanisms as its object of enquiry. On the contrary, Coseriu's introductory quote to this contribution clearly shows that the outcomes of IL analyses do not pertain to psychological mechanisms and that, as a consequence, IL definitely does not subscribe to viewing these mechanisms in computational terms.

4.2 Epistemological issues in the study of the subpersonal computational mind

Studies that accept the subpersonal computational conception of the human mind commonly adopt a full-fledged 'objective', third-person's perspective to study the mind. In CP it is maintained that the study of computational subpersonal mechanisms necessarily falls outside the purview of conscious introspection and that it can only be addressed by using behavioural or neuroscientific experiments (Sandra 1998, Bechtel 2008, De Houwer 2011, Brysbaert and Rastle 2013, De Houwer et al. 2017). A person's mental life qua first-person consciousness has thus no privileged status in the description of the human mind. The difference between the explication of conscious phenomena and hypotheses about computational subpersonal mechanisms has been emphasized in particular by Bechtel (2008), who points out that the two phenomena are, epistemologically speaking, different kinds of 'decomposition', viz. 'phenomenal decomposition' and 'mechanistic decomposition'. While 'phenomenal decomposition' aims to understand a phenomenon by decomposing it into its relevant aspects, 'mechanistic decomposition' tries to reveal the mechanisms and processes that cause a certain phenomenon.

Furthermore, many accounts that propose models of specific computational subpersonal mechanisms offer results that have little or nothing in common with conscious experience (Churchland 1981, Dennett 1987, 1991, Clark 2001). This is especially evident for the 'neural network models', which have been proposed within the context of connectionism or parallel distributed processing (Rumelhart and McClelland 1986). In these analyses, a set merely consisting of input nodes, hidden layer nodes and output nodes can be trained by changing the connections and the weight of the connections between the nodes to compute all kinds of outcomes. It is obvious that in terms of basic characteristics a model consisting of a set of interacting nodes is fundamentally different from the qualia, concepts and language-mediated thinking that are typical of human conscious experience. The latter properties are within connectionism considered as emergent properties of the computational subpersonal mechanisms that have no place in the mechanisms themselves (Rumelhart and McClelland 1986).

Herein lies a major difficulty that severely threatens the epistemological coherence of MCL. While MCL analyses of the semantics and pragmatics of words, for example Lakoff's (1987) analysis of *over* or Langacker's (1990) analysis of *ring*, are necessarily and inevitably based on an analysis of conscious phenomena, i.e. the thoughts, images and associations that occur in our consciousness when producing or interpreting these words, it is nevertheless claimed that they pertain to unconscious mental representations and processes (Lakoff 1987, Lakoff and Johnson 1999, Taylor 2002, 2012). For example, the typical polysemic analyses proposed by MCL are not only assumed to be explications of language use and linguistic knowledge, but to reveal the nature of mental representations in the cognitive unconscious (Lakoff 1987). This problematic issue has been pertinently raised by Sandra (1998) who, from a psycholinguistic point of view, demonstrated why the view that (cognitive) linguists are in a position to make claims about mental representations in the cognitive unconscious on the basis of introspective analyses of conscious phenomena is flawed. MCL, as any other linguistic framework, is able to provide phenomenal decompositions of meaningful phenomena, but it cannot directly engage in mechanistic decomposition. The position adopted by IL, on the other hand, is again much more in line with the view outlined in this Section, as IL upholds the view that analyses that describe aspects of the phenomenal structure of conscious experience cannot directly shed any light on the structure and working of psychological or neural mechanisms.

The preceding observations should not be interpreted in the sense that linguistics cannot contribute anything at all to the branch of cognitive science that studies the mind in terms of subpersonal computational mechanisms. While linguistic analyses cannot directly elucidate the computations and mental representations used in the subpersonal mechanisms, they can definitely contribute to specifying the kind of tasks which those mechanisms should be able to compute (Marr 1982, Jackendoff 1987, 2002). The level of analysis that is centred on the specification of tasks is a level of analysis that is commonly referred to in cognitive psychology as the computational level (Marr 1982) or as a theory of competence (Jackendoff 1987, 2002). Although the computational level plays an important role in specifying what subpersonal cognitive mechanisms should be able to carry out, it only specifies what the mechanisms should be able to produce, without addressing the actual subpersonal cognitive mechanisms themselves (Marr 1982, Rumelhart and McClelland 1986, Clark 2001, Bechtel 2008).

From this perspective, one can maintain that MCL jumps in an unwarranted manner from analyses that are at most relevant for the computational level to claims about mental representations on the level of the mechanisms of the unconscious subpersonal mind. By contrast, IL makes, to the best of my knowledge, no reference to Marr's (1982) idea of the computational level. This is hardly surprising, as relating linguistic analyses to cognitive science is from a Coserian point of view altogether not the primary goal of linguistics. However, given that any well-executed linguistic analysis provides us with more insight into the nature of linguistic phenomena, all linguistic analyses are relevant to gain a better understanding of what kind of phenomena the subpersonal mechanisms that underlie language use must be able to compute. This is equally true with regard to linguistic analyses conducted in the context of MCL as with regard to IL analyses. For example, if an IL analysis reveals that the Dutch preposition *over* has various uses, including, but not limited to, 'on the other side of', 'transfer', 'completion', 'covering' and 'repetition' (Van der Gucht et al. 2007), this finding only establishes that the subpersonal cognitive mechanisms in the human mind must be able to cover all of these uses. The mere linguistic finding that the preposition *over* has various uses by itself does not shed any light on the kind of unconscious mental representations and computations that generate these various uses as their (conscious) outcome.

5 Two possible avenues for Cognitive Linguistics

As pointed out in the introduction, IL can often help remedy conceptual confusions that are found in other linguistic frameworks. In this section, I build on IL and on the two lines of thought from the philosophy of cognitive science discussed in the previous section to propose two possible avenues for MCL to create a more coherent conception of the object of linguistics. There are basically two options open to CL in order to specify in a more consistent way not only the nature of the object of linguistics but also what the outcomes of CL analyses are supposed to relate to.

A first option for CL is to incorporate the criticism of the incoherent status of subpersonal computational mechanisms (Section 4.1) and to give pride of place to the central role of consciousness rather than targeting the unconscious subpersonal mind and the brain as objects of investigation. When overviewing the broad field of CL, there seem to be at least two major approaches that differ considerably from MCL and that have taken this option. The first one is the approach to CL favored by Leonard Talmy (2000), who explicitly sees the conscious mind as the object of study of CL rather than the unconscious subpersonal computational mind:

> For cognitive semantics, the main object of study itself is qualitative mental phenomena as they exist in awareness. Cognitive semantics is thus a branch of phenomenology. (Talmy 2000: 5)

While Talmy thus entertains a conception of the mind that is similar to the one of IL, there remain substantial differences in the kind of analyses that are favoured in the two approaches (cf. Section 1). Furthermore, IL favours semantic analyses that reduce conscious phenomena to those constitutive aspects that are intersubjectively shared by relying on phenomenological techniques such as eidetic reduction (Willems 1994). Talmy, on the other hand, proffers analyses that tackle conscious phenomena without engaging in similar kinds of reductions and that describe these phenomena in a more 'subjective' and heterogeneous form. As has been noted by both Itkonen (2008) and Zlatev (2010, 2016), Talmy makes the classical mistake of conflating introspection and intuition and in so doing misconstrues the true nature of phenomenology (cf. Husserl 1981 [1913], 1989 [1952], 2001 [1913], Sokolowski 2000).

The second approach within the broadly construed field of CL that has argued for an explicit shift away from subpersonal computational mechanisms and towards the conscious mind as the central object of investigation for the language sciences is the approach known as Cognitive Semiotics (henceforth: CS)

(Sonesson 1989, 2006, Zlatev 2007a, 2007b, 2008, 2010, 2011, 2012, 2016, Zlatev and Blomberg 2019). Inspired by phenomenology (Husserl 1981 [1913], 1989 [1952], 2001 [1913]; cf. Sokolowski 2000), the work of Esa Itkonen (Itkonen 1978, 1983, 1997, 2008, 2016) and the so-called third wave of Cognitive Science (Thompson 2007), CS stresses the centrality of the conscious mind, while at the same time criticizing MCL's commitment to the subpersonal computational mind (Zlatev 2007b, 2008, 2010). In comparison to Talmy's CL approach, CS is far more similar to IL in its treatment of consciousness. The analyses put forward by CS take into account those phenomenological aspects that are intersubjectively shared and that are found in intuition, rather than focusing only on the subjective aspects of experience that are found in introspection (Itkonen 2008, Zlatev 2008, 2010, 2016).

Furthermore, CS acknowledges various distinctions typical of IL that are ignored in MCL, such as the distinction between universal aspects of language use and the semantics of specific languages (Zlatev 2007a, 2011). Finally, CS offers a possible way for CL to live up to its goal of not only explicating linguistic phenomena but of also investigating psychological mechanisms that account for language use. In addition to the explication and conceptual analysis of conscious phenomena, the use of intuition and introspection, referred to in CS as "first person methods", CS aims to take into account the outcomes of participant observation by means of empathy and imagination, referred to as "second person methods", and experimental work more similar to the natural sciences, referred to as "third person methods" (Zlatev 2012, 2016). This approach could potentially allow CL to study some of the psychological mechanisms that account for (the possibility) of language use without having to conceptualize these mechanisms in subpersonal computational terms.

A second, quite different, possible avenue for MCL is to retain the subpersonal computational mind as its favored object of enquiry, while changing its epistemology and methodology accordingly. If the aim of MCL is to become a full-fledged part of the cognitive sciences that conceptualize the mind in subpersonal computational terms, it must abandon its hermeneutic interpretative linguistic analyses and shift to cognitive psychological experimentation (Sandra 1998, Itkonen 1997, 2016) or at least reinterpret the results of linguistic analyses with due caution. Stefanowitsch (2011) has succinctly pointed out that for MCL to become a full-fledged part of cognitive science, CL must overcome a mere "Import Strategy" from CP and adopt the mindset of CP itself. This can consist of conducting behavioural experiments that are sufficiently fine-tuned to falsify hypotheses about the working of the unconscious subpersonal computational mind, or by using linguistic corpora to falsify independently pre-established psycholinguistic hypotheses, rather than using corpora with a focus on describing what one can find in naturally occurring language data (cf. Gries 2003, 2017, Gilquin and Gries 2009 for discussion).

The outcomes of classical cognitive linguistic analyses of the semantics and pragmatics of constructions can nevertheless still provide valuable input to the understanding of the human mind conceived in terms of computational subpersonal mechanisms. In this case, however, their purport needs to be reassessed. Conscious contents that relate to meaning are outcomes of subpersonal processes rather than the mental representations and processes themselves, viz. an *explanandum* rather than an *explanans*. They describe the subpersonal mind on the computational level, which specifies what a computational system should be able to produce, but they are no descriptions of what a cognitive system actually consists of in terms of mental representations and processes.

6 Conclusion

As Coseriu argues in the introductory quote, the biological and psychological mechanisms underlying (the possibility of) language use are no immediate objects of linguistics as a cultural science which aims to explicate the manifold facets of linguistic activity. IL therefore explicitly refrains from making any claims about cognitive psychology or about the brain. Instead, it focuses exclusively on describing and explicating language as an activity which is inherently conscious and observable in its materialized output. While for some researchers this may amount to a limitation of the framework, I would argue that it is far better to clearly and coherently delineate one's object of enquiry and admit one cannot say anything meaningful about other fields of study than to provide analyses that lack a conceptually coherent delimitation of their research object. For IL, both the study of the meaningful phenomena that constitute language and the study of the biological and psychological mechanisms that enable these phenomena are worthwhile, as long as they are neatly distinguished and investigated by linguistics on the one hand and psychology and neuroscience on the other hand.

By contrast, many studies in MCL suffer from conceptual incoherence to the extent that they aim to reveal characteristics of an unconscious subpersonal computational mind while actually providing accounts of conscious meaningful phenomena. I have argued in this contribution that by enriching CL with some of the insights developed in IL and in the philosophy of cognitive science, it is possible to pinpoint these conceptual shortcomings and to propose possible solutions. In particular, CL can continue to rely on analyses of conscious phenomena, such as the semantics and pragmatics of constructions of natural languages, while redefining its object of investigation as the conscious human mind. This can even go hand in hand with psychological experimentation in the context of a school of thought such as Cognitive Semiotics, which actively tries to combine first person methods and third person methods in a consistent way. Alternatively, CL can continue to focus on the subpersonal computational mind by implementing methods that are suited for the investigation of this research object and by turning to a coherent reinterpretation of the scope of its purely linguistic analyses.

References

Bechtel, William. 2008. *Mental mechanisms: philosophical perspectives on cognitive neuroscience*. New York: Erlbaum.

Belligh, Thomas and Klaas Willems. 2021. "What's in a code? The code-inference distinction in Neo-Gricean pragmatics, Relevance Theory and Integral Linguistics". *Language Sciences* 83.

Brysbaert, Marc and Kathy Rastle. 2013. *Historical and conceptual issues in psychology*. Harlow: Pearson.

Churchland, Paul. 1981. "Eliminative materialism and propositional attitudes". *The Journal of Philosophy* 78:2, 67–90.

Clark, Andy. 2001. *Mindware: an introduction to the philosophy of cognitive science*. New York: Oxford University Press.

Coseriu, Eugenio. 1974 [1958]. *Synchronie, Diachronie und Geschichte. Das Problem des Sprachwandels*. München: Wilhelm Fink.

Coseriu, Eugenio. 1975 [1954]. "Form und Substanz bei den Sprachlauten". In: Eugenio Coseriu, *Sprachtheorie und allgemeine Sprachwissenschaft. 5 Studien*, 102–209. München: Fink.

Coseriu, Eugenio. 1975 [1962]. *Sprachtheorie und allgemeine Sprachwissenschaft. 5 Studien*. Edited by Uwe Petersen. München: Fink.

Coseriu, Eugenio. 1985. "Linguistic competence: what is it really?" The Presidential Address of the Modern Humanities Research Association. *The Modern Language Review* 80:4, xxv–xxxv.

Coseriu, Eugenio. 1992 [1988]. *Einführung in die allgemeine Sprachwissenschaft* (second edition). Tübingen: Francke. (German translation of Coseriu 1981.)

Coseriu, Eugenio. 2000 [1990]. "Structural semantics and 'cognitive' semantics". *Logos and Language* 1:1, 19–42. (English translation of Coseriu 1990.)

Coseriu, Eugenio. 2001. *L'homme et son langage*. Edited by Hiltraud Dupuy-Engelhardt, Jean-Pierre Durafour and François Rastier. Louvain: Peeters.

Coseriu, Eugenio. 2007 [1988]. *Sprachkompetenz. Grundzüge der Theorie des Sprechens*. Edited by Heinrich Weber (second edition). Tübingen: Narr.

De Houwer, Jan. 2011. "Why the cognitive approach in psychology would profit from a functional approach and vice versa". *Perspectives on Psychological Science* 6:2, 202–209.

De Houwer, Jan, Dermot Barnes-Holmes and Yvonne Barnes-Holmes. 2017. "What is cognition? A functional-cognitive perspective". In: Steven C. Hayes and Stefan G. Hofmann (eds.), *Core processes of cognitive behavioral therapies*, 119–136. Oakland, CA: New Harbinger.
Dennett, Daniel. 1987. *The intentional stance*. Cambridge, Mass.: MIT Press.
Dennett, Daniel. 1991. *Consciousness explained*. London: Penguin Books.
Fodor, Jerry. 2000. *In critical condition: polemic essays on cognitive science and the Philosophy of Mind*. Cambridge, Mass.: MIT Press.
Fodor, Jerry. 2008. *LOT2: The Language of Thought revisited*. Oxford: Oxford University Press.
Geeraerts, Dirk. 1993. "Vagueness's puzzles, polysemy's vagaries". *Cognitive Linguistics* 4, 223–272.
Geeraerts, Dirk. 2010. *Theories of lexical semantics*. Oxford: Oxford University Press.
Geeraerts, Dirk and Hubert Cuyckens. 2007. "Introducing Cognitive Linguistics". In: Dirk Geeraerts and Hubert Cuyckens (eds.), *Oxford handbook of Cognitive Linguistics*, 3–21. Oxford: Oxford University Press.
Gilquin, Gaetan and Stefan Gries. 2009. "Corpora and experimental methods: A state-of-the-art review". *Corpus Linguistics and Linguistic Theory* 5:1, 1–26.
Gries, Stefan. 2003. *Multifactorial analysis in corpus linguistics: a study of particle placement*. New York: Continuum.
Gries, Stefan. 2017. *Ten lectures on quantitative approaches in Cognitive Linguistics: corpus-linguistic, experimental, and statistical applications*. Leiden: Brill.
Husserl, Edmund. 1981 [1913]. *Ideas pertaining to a pure phenomenology and to a phenomenological philosophy, first book*. The Hague: Martinus Nijhoff.
Husserl, Edmund. 1989 [1952]. *Ideas pertaining to a pure phenomenology and to a phenomenological philosophy, second book*. Dordrecht: Kluwer.
Husserl, Edmund. 2001 [1913]. *Logical investigations*. London: Routledge.
Itkonen, Esa. 1978. *Grammatical theory and metascience: a critical investigation into methodological and philosophical foundations of autonomous linguistics*. Amsterdam & Philadelphia: John Benjamins.
Itkonen, Esa. 1983. *Causality in linguistic theory: a critical investigation into the philosophical and methodological foundations of non-autonomous linguistics*. London: Croom Helm.
Itkonen, Esa. 1997. "The social ontology of meaning". *SKY 1997. Yearbook of the Linguistic Association of Finland*, 49–80.
Itkonen, Esa. 2008. "Concerning the role of consciousness in linguistics". *Journal of Consciousness Studies* 15:6, 15–33.
Itkonen, Esa. 2016. "An assessment of (mentalist) cognitive semantics". *Public Journal of Semiotics* 7:1, 1–42.
Jackendoff, Ray. 1987. *Consciousness and the computational mind*. Cambridge, Mass.: MIT Press.
Jackendoff, Ray. 2002. *Foundations of language. Brain, meaning, grammar, evolution*. New York: Oxford University Press.
Kabatek, Johannes. 2000b. "Einheitlichkeit der Bedeutung, Designat und Integrale Linguistik". In: Bruno Staib (ed.), *Linguistica romanica et indiana. Festschrift für Wolf Dietrich zum 60. Geburtstag*, 187–205. Tübingen: Narr.
Katz, Jerrold. 1972. *The philosophy of linguistics*. Oxford: Oxford University Press.

Lakoff, George. 1987. *Women, fire, and dangerous things: what categories reveal about the mind*. Chicago: The University of Chicago Press.
Lakoff, George and Mark Johnson. 1999. *Philosophy in the flesh: the embodied mind and its challenge to Western thought*. New York: Basic Books.
Langacker, Ronald. 1987. *Foundations of Cognitive Grammar*. Vol. 1: *Theoretical prerequisites*. Stanford: Stanford University Press.
Langacker, Ronald. 1990. *Concept, image, and symbol: the cognitive basis of grammar*. Berlin & New York: Mouton de Gruyter.
Langacker, Ronald. 1991. *Foundations of Cognitive Grammar*. Vol 2: *Descriptive application*. Stanford: Stanford University Press.
Langacker, Ronald. 2007. "Cognitive Grammar". In: Dirk Geeraerts and Hubert Cuyckens (eds.), *The Oxford handbook of Cognitive Linguistics*, 421–462. Oxford: Oxford University Press.
Marr, David. 1982. *Vision*. San Francisco: W. H. Freeman and Company.
Rumelhart, David and James McClelland. 1986. *Parallel Distributed Processing: explorations in the microstructure of cognition*. London: MIT Press.
Sandra, Dominiek. 1998. "What linguists can and can't tell you about the human mind: A reply to Croft". *Cognitive Linguistics* 9:4, 361–378.
Saussure, Ferdinand de. 1968. *Cours de linguistique générale*. Édition critique par R. Engler. Wiesbaden: Otto Harrassowitz.
Searle, John R. 1983. *Intentionality: an essay in the Philosophy of Mind*. Cambridge: Cambridge University Press.
Searle, John R. 1992. *The rediscovery of the mind*. Cambridge, Mass.: MIT Press.
Searle, John R. 1997. *The mystery of consciousness*. London: Granta Books.
Sokolowski, Robert. 2000. *Introduction to phenomenology*. New York: Cambridge University Press.
Sonesson, Göran. 1989. *Pictorial concepts*. Lund: Lund University Press.
Sonesson, Göran. 2006. "The meaning of meaning in biology and cognitive science". *Sign Systems Studies* 34:1, 135–214.
Stefanowitsch, Anatol. 2011. "Cognitive Linguistics as cognitive science". In: Marcus Callies, Wolfram Keller and Astrid Lohöfer (eds.), *Bi-directionality in the cognitive sciences*, 295–310. Amsterdam & Philadelphia: John Benjamins.
Talmy, Leonard. 2000. *Toward a cognitive semantics*. 2 vols. Cambridge, Mass.: MIT Press.
Taylor, John. 1999. "Cognitive semantics and structural semantics". In: Andreas Blank and Peter Koch (eds.), *Historical semantics and cognition*, 17–48. Berlin & New York: Mouton De Gruyter.
Taylor, John. 2002. *Cognitive Grammar*. Oxford: Oxford University Press.
Taylor, John. 2012. *The mental corpus: how language is represented in the mind*. Oxford: Oxford University Press.
Thompson, Evan. 2007. *Mind in life: biology, phenomenology and the sciences of mind*. Cambridge, Mass.: Harvard University Press.
Van der Gucht, Fieke. 2005. *Het "polysemie-monosemie"-debat: contrastieve analyse van de cognitieve en de structureel-functionele semantiek*. PhD Ghent University.
Van der Gucht, Fieke, Klaas Willems and Ludovic De Cuypere. 2007. "The iconicity of embodied meaning. Polysemy of spatial prepositions in the cognitive framework". *Language Sciences* 29:6, 733–754.

Willems, Klaas. 1994a. *Sprache, Sprachreflexion und Erkenntniskritik.* Tübingen: Narr.
Willems, Klaas. 1997. *Kasus, grammatische Bedeutung und kognitive Linguistik. Ein Beitrag zur allgemeinen Sprachwissenschaft.* Tübingen: Narr.
Willems, Klaas. 2011. "Meaning and interpretation: the semiotic similarities and differences between cognitive grammar and European structural linguistics". *Semiotica* 185:1, 1–50.
Zlatev, Jordan. 2007a. "Spatial semantics". In: Dirk Geeraerts and Hubert Cuyckens (eds.), *Oxford handbook of Cognitive Linguistics*, 318–350. Oxford: Oxford University Press.
Zlatev, Jordan. 2007b. "Embodiment, language and mimesis". In: Tom Ziemke, Jordan Zlatev and Roslyn Frank (eds.), *Body, language and mind.* Vol 1: *Embodiment*, 297–337. Berlin & New York: Mouton de Gruyter.
Zlatev, Jordan. 2008. "The dependence of language on consciousness". *Journal of Consciousness Studies* 15:6, 34–62.
Zlatev, Jordan. 2010. "Phenomenology and Cognitive Linguistics". In: Shaun Gallagher and Dan Schmicking (eds.), *Handbook on phenomenology and cognitive science*, 415-446. Dordrecht: Springer.
Zlatev, Jordan. 2011. "From Cognitive to Integral Linguistics and back again". *Intellectica* 56, 125–147.
Zlatev, Jordan. 2012. "Cognitive Semiotics: An emerging field for the transdisciplinary study of meaning". *Public Journal of Semiotics* 4:1, 2–24.
Zlatev, Jordan. 2016. "Turning back to experience in Cognitive Linguistics via phenomenology". *Cognitive Linguistics* 27:4, 559–572.
Zlatev, Jordan and Johan Blomberg. 2019. "Norms of language: What kinds and where from? Insights from phenomenology". In: Aleksi Mäkilähde, Ville Leppänen and Esa Itkonen (eds.), *Norms and normativity in language and in linguistics*, 69–101. Amsterdam & Philadelphia: John Benjamins.

Bibliography

Cited publications by Coseriu

All publications by Eugenio Coseriu can be accessed, with the exception of books, via the website of the Coseriu Archives in Tübingen (www.coseriu.com).

Coseriu, Eugenio. 1952. *Sistema, norma y habla*. Montevideo: Universidad de la República, Facultad de Humanidades y Ciencias. (Also in Coseriu 1973 [1962].)

Coseriu, Eugenio. 1954. *Forma y sustancia en los sonidos del lenguaje*. Montevideo: Universidad de la República, Facultad de Humanidades y Ciencias. (Also in Coseriu 1973 [1962].)

Coseriu, Eugenio (ms. 1955). *Teoría lingüística del nombre proprio*. Unpublished manuscript, Montevideo 1955. Partly available as a typescript.

Coseriu, Eugenio. 1955. "La geografía lingüística". *Revista de la Facultad de Humanidades y Ciencias* (Montevideo) 14, 29–69.

Coseriu, Eugenio. 1955–1956. "Determinación y entorno. Dos problemas de una lingüística del hablar". *Romanistisches Jahrbuch* 7, 29–54.

Coseriu, Eugenio. 1956. *La creación metafórica en el lenguaje*. Montevideo: Universidad de la República, Facultad de Humanidades y Ciencias.

Coseriu, Eugenio (ms. 1957). *El problema de la corrección idiomática*. Unpublished manuscript, Montevideo 1957. Transcription by Johannes Kabatek and Reinhard Meisterfeld, Tübingen.

Coseriu, Eugenio. 1958 [1957]. "Discussion". In: *Actes du Huitième Congrès International des Linguistes (1957)*, 697–699. Oslo: Presses Universitaires d'Oslo.

Coseriu, Eugenio. 1958. *Sincronía, diacronía e historia. El problema del cambio lingüístico*. Montevideo: Universidad de la República, Facultad de Humanidades y Ciencias.

Coseriu, Eugenio. 1964. "Pour une sémantique diachronique structurale". *Travaux de linguistique et de littérature* (Strasbourg) 2:1, 139–186.

Coseriu, Eugenio. 1966. "Structure lexicale et enseignement du vocabulaire". In: *Actes du Premier Colloque International de Linguistique Appliquée*, 175–217. Nancy: Annales de l'Est.

Coseriu, Eugenio. 1967 [1966]. "Lexical structure and the teaching of vocabulary". In: *Linguistic theories and their applications*. Strasbourg: The Council of Europe (English translation of 1966).

Coseriu, Eugenio. 1967a. "L'arbitraire du signe. Zur Spätgeschichte eines aristotelischen Begriffes". *Archiv für das Studium der neueren Sprachen und Literaturen* 204, 81–112.

Coseriu, Eugenio. 1967b. "François Thurot". *Zeitschrift für französische Sprache und Literatur* 77, 30–34.

Coseriu, Eugenio. 1967c. "Georg von der Gabelentz et la linguistique synchronique". *Word* 23, 74–100 (*Linguistic Studies Presented to André Martinet*, I).

Coseriu, Eugenio. 1967d. "Zur Vorgeschichte der strukturellen Semantik: Heyses Analyse des Wortfeldes 'Schall'". *To Honor Roman Jakobson. Essays on the Occasion of His Seventieth Birthday*. Vol. I, 489–498. The Hague & Paris: Mouton.

Coseriu, Eugenio. 1967e. "Lexikalische Solidaritäten". *Poetica* 1, 293–303.
Coseriu, Eugenio. 1968 [1965]. "Sincronía, diacronía y tipología". In: Antonio Quilis, Ramón Blanco Carril and Margarita Cantarero (eds.), *Actas XI Congreso International de Lingüística y Filología Románicas (Madrid 1965)*. Vol. I, 269–281. Madrid: Revista de Filología Española.
Coseriu, Eugenio. 1968 [1966]. "Der Mensch und seine Sprache". In: Herbert Haag and Franz Peter Möhres (eds.), *Ursprung und Wesen des Menschen*, 67–79. Tübingen: Mohr Siebeck.
Coseriu, Eugenio. 1968. "Les structures lexématiques". In: Wilhelm Theodor Elwert (ed.), *Probleme der Semantik* (Zeitschrift für französische Sprache und Literatur, Neue Folge, Beiheft 1), 3–16. Wiesbaden: Steiner.
Coseriu, Eugenio. 1969–1972. *Die Geschichte der Sprachphilosophie von der Antike bis zur Gegenwart. Eine Übersicht*. Vol. I: *Von der Antike bis Leibniz*. Edited by Gunter Narr and Rudolf Windisch. Vol. II: *Von Leibniz bis Rousseau*. Edited by Gunter Narr. Tübingen: Narr.
Coseriu, Eugenio. 1970 [1968]. *Einführung in die transformationelle Grammatik*. Tübingen: Narr.
Coseriu, Eugenio. 1970 [1969]. "Bedeutung und Bezeichnung im Lichte der strukturellen Semantik". In: Peter Hartmann and Henri Vernay (eds.), *Sprachwissenschaft und Übersetzen Symposium an der Universität Heidelberg 24.2.–26.2.1969*, 104–121. München: Hueber.
Coseriu, Eugenio. 1970. "Semantik, innere Sprachform und Tiefenstruktur". *Folia Linguistica* 4:1, 53–63.
Coseriu, Eugenio. 1971 [1966]. "Der Mensch und seine Sprache". In: Eugenio Coseriu, *Sprache. Strukturen und Funktionen. XII Aufsätze*, 109–124. Tübingen: Narr.
Coseriu, Eugenio. 1971 [1967]. "Das Phänomen der Sprache und das Daseinsverständnis des heutigen Menschen". In: Eugenio Coseriu, *Sprache. Strukturen und Funktionen. XII Aufsätze*, 131–155. Tübingen: Narr.
Coseriu, Eugenio. 1971. *Essai d'une nouvelle typologie des langues romanes Sinaia 1971*. Bucarest: Univ. de Bucarest.
Coseriu, Eugenio. 1971 [1973]. "The situation in linguistics". In: *Collection of papers commemorating the 50th birthday of the Korean Language Research Society*, 483–492. Seoul. (English translation of: Coseriu, Eugenio. 1973. *Die Lage in der Linguistik*. Innsbruck: Institut für Sprachwissenschaft der Universität Innsbruck.)
Coseriu, Eugenio. 1972 [1955]. "Sobre las categorías verbales ('partes de la oración')". *Revista de lingüística aplicada* [Concepción/Chile] 10, 7–25.
Coseriu, Eugenio. 1972 [1971]. "Semantik und Grammatik". In: Institut für Deutsche Sprache (ed.), *Neue Grammatiktheorien und ihre Anwendung auf das heutige Deutsch: Jahrbuch 1971*, 77–89. Düsseldorf: Schwann.
Coseriu, Eugenio. 1973 [1952]. "Sistema, norma y habla". In: Eugenio Coseriu, *Teoría del lenguaje y lingüística general. Cinco estudios*, 11–113. Madrid: Gredos.
Coseriu, Eugenio. 1973 [1954]. "Forma y sustancia en los sonidos del lenguaje". In: Eugenio Coseriu, *Teoría del lenguaje y lingüística general. Cinco estudios*, 115–234. Madrid: Gredos.

Coseriu, Eugenio. 1973 [1955]. "El plural en los nombres propios". In: Eugenio Coseriu, *Teoría del lenguaje y lingüística general. Cinco estudios* (third edition), 261–281. Madrid: Gredos.
Coseriu, Eugenio. 1973 [1955–1956]. "Determinación y entorno. Dos problemas de una lingüística del hablar". In: Eugenio Coseriu, *Teoría del lenguaje y lingüística general. Cinco estudios* (third edition), 282–323. Madrid: Gredos.
Coseriu, Eugenio. 1973 [1957]. "Logicismo y antilogicismo en la gramática". In: Eugenio Coseriu, *Teoría del lenguaje y lingüística general. Cinco estudios* (third edition), 235–260. Madrid: Gredos.
Coseriu, Eugenio. 1973 [1962]. *Teoría del lenguaje y lingüística general. Cinco estudios* (third edition). Madrid: Gredos.
Coseriu, Eugenio. 1973. *Probleme der strukturellen Semantik*. Edited by Dieter Kastovsky. Tübingen: Narr.
Coseriu, Eugenio. 1973 [1972]. *Die Lage in der Linguistik* (= *Innsbrucker Beiträge zur Sprachwissenschaft*, Vorträge 9). Innsbruck: Universität Innsbruck Institut für vergleichende Sprachwissenschaft.
Coseriu, Eugenio. 1974 [1958]. *Synchronie, Diachronie und Geschichte. Das Problem des Sprachwandels*. München: Fink.
Coseriu, Eugenio. 1974. "Les universaux linguistiques (et les autres)". In: Luigi Heilmann (ed.), *Proceedings of the Eleventh International Congress of Linguists*. Vol. I, 47–73. Bologna: il Mulino.
Coseriu, Eugenio. 1975 [1952]. "System, Norm und Rede". In: Eugenio Coseriu, *Sprachtheorie und allgemeine Sprachwissenschaft. 5 Studien*, 11–101. München: Fink.
Coseriu, Eugenio. 1975 [1954]. "Form und Substanz bei den Sprachlauten". In: Eugenio Coseriu, *Sprachtheorie und allgemeine Sprachwissenschaft. 5 Studien*, 102–209. München: Fink.
Coseriu, Eugenio. 1975 [1955]. *Die Sprachgeographie*. Edited by Uwe Petersen. Tübingen: Narr (German translation of Coseriu 1955).
Coseriu, Eugenio. 1975 [1962]. *Sprachtheorie und allgemeine Sprachwissenschaft. 5 Studien*. Edited by Uwe Petersen. München: Fink.
Coseriu, Eugenio. 1975 [1971]. *Leistung und Grenzen der transformationellen Grammatik*. Tübingen: Narr.
Coseriu, Eugenio. 1976 [1968–1969]. *Das romanische Verbalsystem*. Edited by Hansbert Bertsch. Tubingen: Narr.
Coseriu, Eugenio. 1976a. "Die funktionelle Betrachtung des Wortschatzes". In: Hugo Moser (ed.), *Probleme der Lexikologie und Lexikographie. Jahrbuch 1975 des Instituts für deutsche Sprache*, 7–25. Düsseldorf : Schwann.
Coseriu, Eugenio. 1976b. "L'étude fonctionelle du vocabulaire. Précis de lexématique". *Cahiers de lexicologie* 29, 5–23.
Coseriu, Eugenio. 1976c. "Logique du langage et logique de la grammaire". In: Jean David and Robert Martin (eds.), *Modèles logiques et niveaux d'analyse linguistique*, 15–33. Paris: Klincksieck.
Coseriu, Eugenio. 1977 [1974]. "Linguistic (and other) universals". In: Adam Makkai, Valerie Becker Makkai and Luigi Heilmann (eds.), *Linguistics at the crossroads*, 317–346. Padua & Lake Bluff, Ill.: Liviana & Jupiter Press (English translation of Coseriu 1974).

Coseriu, Eugenio. 1977a. "Inhaltliche Wortbildungslehre am Beispiel des Typs *coupe-papier*". In: Herbert E. Brekle and Dieter Kastovky (eds.), *Perspektiven der Wortbildungsforschung. Beiträge zum Wuppertaler Wortbildungskolloquium vom 9.-10. Juli 1976. Anläßlich des 70. Geburtstages von Hans Marchand am 1. Oktober 1977*, 48–61. Bonn: Grundmann.

Coseriu, Eugenio. 1977b. "Antrittsrede an der Heidelberger Akademie der Wissenschaften". In: *Jahrbuch der Heidelberger Akademie der Wissenschaften*, 107–110. Heidelberg: C. Winter Universitätsverlag.

Coseriu, Eugenio. 1978 [1958]. *Sincronía, diacronía e historia. El problema del cambio lingüístico* (third edition). Madrid: Gredos.

Coseriu, Eugenio. 1978a. "Lo que se dice de Hervás". *Estudios ofrecidos a Emilio Alarcos Llorach* III, 35–58. Oviedo: Universidad, Servicio de publicaciones.

Coseriu, Eugenio. 1978b. "Hervás und das Substrat". *Studii și cercetări linguistice* 29, 523–530.

Coseriu, Eugenio. 1978c. "Falsche und richtige Fragestellungen in der Übersetzungstheorie". In: Lillebill Grähs, Gustav Korlén and Bertil Malmberg (eds.), *Theory and practice of translation*, 17–32. Bern, Frankfurt a.M. & Las Vegas: Peter Lang.

Coseriu, Eugenio. 1979 [1978]. "Humanwissenschaften und Geschichte. Der Gesichtspunkt eines Linguisten". *Det Norske Videnskaps-Akademi, Årbok 1978* (Oslo), 118–130.

Coseriu, Eugenio. 1979. "'τὸ ἓν σημαίνειν'. Bedeutung und Bezeichnung bei Aristoteles". *Zeitschrift für Phonetik, Sprachwissenschaft und Kommunikationsforschung* 32:4 (Festschrift für Georg F. Meier), 432–437.

Coseriu, Eugenio. 1980. "Vom Primat der Geschichte". *Sprachwissenschaft* 5, 125–145.

Coseriu. Eugenio. 1981 [1958] "Los conceptos de 'dialecto', 'nivel' y 'estilo de lengua' y el sentido propio de la dialectología". *Lingüística española actual* 3:1, 1–32.

Coseriu, Eugenio. 1981 [1977]. *Principios de semántica estructural*. Madrid: Gredos.

Coseriu, Eugenio. 1981 [1980]. *Textlinguistik. Eine Einführung*. Edited by Jörn Albrecht (second edition). Tübingen: Narr.

Coseriu, Eugenio. 1981. *Lecciones de lingüística general*. Madrid: Gredos.

Coseriu, Eugenio. 1982. "Naturbild und Sprache". In: Jörg Zimmermann (ed.), *Das Naturbild des Menschen*, 260–284. München: Fink.

Coseriu, Eugenio. 1983. "Linguistic change does not exist". *Linguistica nuova ed antica. Rivista di linguistica classica medioevale e moderna* 1, 51–63.

Coseriu, Eugenio. 1984. "Fundamentos y tareas de la lingüística integral". In: *Segundo Congreso de Nacional de Lingüística (16 al 19 de Setiembre de 1981)*. Tomo III, Actas I, 37–53. San Juan: R. Argentina.

Coseriu, Eugenio. 1985 [1956]. "La creación metafórica en el lenguaje". In: Eugenio Coseriu. 1985. *El hombre y su lenguaje. Estudios de teoría y metodología lingüística*, 66–102. Madrid: Gredos.

Coseriu, Eugenio. 1985. "Linguistic competence: what is it really?" The Presidential Address of the Modern Humanities Research Association. *The Modern Language Review* 80:4, xxv–xxxv.

Coseriu, Eugenio. 1987 [1978]. *Gramática, semántica, universales. Estudios de lingüística funcional* (second edition). Madrid: Gredos.

Coseriu, Eugenio. 1987. "Bedeutung, Bezeichnung und sprachliche Kategorien". *Sprachwissenschaft* 12:1, 1–23.

Coseriu, Eugenio. 1988 [1957]. "Die Ebenen des sprachlichen Wissens. Der Ort des 'Korrekten' in der Bewertungsskala des Gesprochenen". Chapter 2 of Coseriu (ms. 1957). German translation by Susanne Höfer. In: Jörn Albrecht, Jens Lüdtke and Harald Thun (eds.), *Energeia und Ergon. Sprachliche Variation – Sprachgeschichte – Sprachtypologie. Studia in honorem Eugenio Coseriu*, Vol. I: *Schriften von Eugenio Coseriu (1965–1987)*, 327–364. Tübingen: Narr.

Coseriu, Eugenio. 1988 [1971]). "Der romanische Sprachtypus. Versuch einer neuen Typologisierung der romanischen Sprachen". In: Jörn Albrecht, Jens Lüdtke and Harald Thun (eds.), *Energeia und Ergon. Studia in honorem Eugenio Coseriu*, Vol. 1: *Schriften von Eugenio Coseriu*, 207–224. Tübingen: Narr.

Coseriu, Eugenio. 1988 [1979]. "Humboldt und die moderne Sprachwissenschaft". In: Jörn Albrecht (ed.), *Energeia und Ergon. Sprachliche Variation – Sprachgeschichte – Sprachtypologie*, Vol. I: *Schriften von Eugenio Coseriu (1965–1987)*, 3–11. Tübingen: Narr.

Coseriu, Eugenio. 1989. "Principes de syntaxe fonctionnelle". *Travaux de linguistique et de philologie* 27, 5–46.

Coseriu, Eugenio. 1990. "Semántica estructural y semántica cognitiva". In: *Homenaje al Profesor Francisco Marsá / Jornadas de Filología*, 239–282. Barcelona: Universidad de Barcelona.

Coseriu, Eugenio. 1991 [1977]. *El hombre y su lenguaje. Estudios de teoría y metodología lingüística* (second edition). Madrid: Gredos.

Coseriu, Eugenio. 1992 [1988]. *Einführung in die allgemeine Sprachwissenschaft* (second edition). Tübingen: Francke (German translation of Coseriu 1981).

Coseriu, Eugenio. 1992a. "Zeichen, Symbol, Wort". In: Tilmann Borsche and Werner Stegmaier (eds.), *Zur Philosophie des Zeichens*, 3–27. Berlin & New York: De Gruyter.

Coseriu, Eugenio. 1992b. *Competencia lingüística. Elementos de una teoría del hablar*. Madrid: Gredos (Spanish translation of Coseriu 2007 [1988]).

Coseriu, Eugenio. 1994 [1980]. *Textlinguistik. Eine Einführung*. Edited by Jörn Albrecht (third edition). Tübingen: Narr.

Coseriu, Eugenio. 1994. "My Pagliaro". In: Tullio de Mauro and Lia Formigari (eds.), *Italian studies in linguistic historiography*, 39–44. Münster: Nodus.

Coseriu, Eugenio. 1995 [1984/1986]. *Die Sprachwissenschaft im 20. Jahrhundert. Theorien und Methoden*. Transcript by Peter Fink and Heinrich Weber. Unpublished manuscript. University of Tübingen.

Coseriu, Eugenio. 1995a. "My Saussure". In: Tullio de Mauro and Shigeaki Sugeta (eds.), *Saussure and linguistics today*, 187–191. Roma: Bulzoni.

Coseriu, Eugenio. 1995b. "Von den *universali fantastici*". In: Jürgen Trabant (ed.), *Vico und die Zeichen – Vico e i segni*, 73–80. Tübingen: Narr.

Coseriu, Eugeniu. 1996. *Lingvistica integrală*. Interviu cu Eugeniu Coşeriu realizat de Nicolae Saramandu. Bucureşti: Editura Fundaţiei Culturale Române.

Coseriu, Eugenio. 1997 [1980]. *Linguistica del testo. Introduzione a una ermeneutica del senso*. Translated by Donatella Di Cesare. Roma: La Nuova Italia Scientifica.

Coseriu, Eugenio. 1998 [1981]. "Sens et tâches de la dialectologie". In: Eugenio Coseriu and Peter Wunderli (eds.), *Etudes sur la diachronie et la variation linguistique* (= *Les Cahiers διά* 1), 17–56. Gent: Communication & Cognition (French translation of Coseriu 1981 [1958], revised).

Coseriu, Eugenio. 1998. "Editorial. Le double problème des unités 'dia-s'". In: Eugenio Coseriu and Peter Wunderli (eds.), *Etudes sur la diachronie et la variation linguistique* (= *Les Cahiers διά* 1), 9–16. Gent: Communication & Cognition.
Coseriu, Eugenio. 1999 [1981]. *Lecciones de lingüística general* (second edition). Madrid: Gredos.
Coseriu, Eugenio. 2000 [1990]. "Structural semantics and 'cognitive' semantics". *Logos and Language* 1:1, 19–42 (English translation of Coseriu 1990).
Coseriu, Eugenio. 2000 [1992]. "The principles of linguistics as a cultural science". *Transylvanian Review* 9:1, 108–115.
Coseriu, Eugenio. 2001 [1968]. "L'homme et son langage". In: Eugenio Coseriu, *L'homme et son langage*. Edited by Hiltrud Dupuy-Engelhardt, Jean-Pierre Durafour and François Rastier, 13–30. Louvain: Peeters.
Coseriu, Eugenio. 2001 [1982]. "Au-delà du structuralisme". In: Eugenio Coseriu, *L'homme et son langage*, 109–115. Louvain, Paris & Sterling, Virginia: Peeters.
Coseriu, Eugenio. 2001. *L'homme et son langage*. Edited by Hiltraud Dupuy-Engelhardt, Jean-Pierre Durafour and François Rastier. Louvain: Peeters.
Coseriu, Eugenio. 2002. "Prolusione: Orationis fundamenta. La preghiera come testo". In: Giuseppe De Gennaro (ed.), *I quattro universi di discorso. Atti del Congresso Internazionale "Orationis Millenium"*, 24–47. L'Aquilla: Libreria Editrice Vaticana.
Coseriu, Eugenio. 2003. "*Orationis fundamenta*. La plegaria como texto". In *RILCE. Revista de filología hispánica* 19:1, 1–25.
Coseriu, Eugenio. 2004 [1972]. "On parts of speech (word categories, 'partes orationis')". *Logos and Language* 5:2, 47–61 (English translation of Coseriu 1972 [1955]).
Coseriu, Eugenio. 2004. *Der Physei-Thesei-Streit. Sechs Beiträge zur Geschichte der Sprachphilosophie*. Edited by Reinhard Meisterfeld. Tübingen: Narr.
Coseriu, Eugenio. 2005a. "Divergenz, Konvergenz, Parallelismus: Typologie des sogenannten Sprachwandels" In: Thomas Stehl (ed.), *Unsichtbare Hand und Sprecherwahl. Typologie und Prozesse des Sprachwandels in der Romania*, 77–86. Tübingen: Narr.
Coseriu, Eugenio. 2005b. "Dialekt und Sprachwandel". In: Thomas Stehl (ed.), *Unsichtbare Hand und Sprecherwahl. Typologie und Prozesse des Sprachwandels in der Romania*, 111–122. Tübingen: Narr.
Coseriu, Eugenio. 2007 [1980]. *Textlinguistik. Eine Einführung*. Edited by Jörn Albrecht (fourth edition). Tübingen: Narr.
Coseriu, Eugenio. 2007 [1994]. *Lingüística del texto*. Edited by Óscar Loureda Lamas. Madrid: Arco/Libros (Spanish translation of Coseriu 1994 [1980]).
Coseriu, Eugenio. 2007 [1988]. *Sprachkompetenz. Grundzüge der Theorie des Sprechens*. Edited by Heinrich Weber (second edition). Tübingen: Narr.
Coseriu, Eugenio. 2008 [1964]. "Towards a structuralist diachronic semantics". In: Patrick Hanks (ed.), *Lexicology. Critical concepts in linguistics*. Vol. 2: *Lexical semantics and structures*, 140–193. London: Routledge (English translation of Coseriu 1964).
Coseriu, Eugenio. 2008. *Lateinisch-Romanisch. Vorlesungen und Abhandlungen zum sogenannten Vulgärlatein und zu den romanischen Sprachen*. Edited by Hansbert Bertsch. Tübingen: Narr.
Coseriu, Eugenio. 2015. *Geschichte der Sprachphilosophie*. Vol. 1: *Von Heraklit bis Rousseau*. Vol. 2: *Von Herder bis Humboldt*. Edited by Jörn Albrecht. Tübingen: Narr & Francke: Attempto.

Coseriu, Eugenio and Horst Geckeler. 1974. "Linguistics and semantics". In: Thomas A. Sebeok (ed.), *Current trends in linguistics*, Vol. 12, 103–171. The Hague & Paris: Mouton.

Coseriu, Eugenio and Horst Geckeler. 1981 [1974]. *Trends in structural semantics*. Tübingen: Narr (new version of Coseriu and Geckeler 1974, with updated References).

Other cited references

Academia Română, Institutul de lingvistică "Iorgu Iordan – Al. Rosetti". 2004. *In memoriam Eugenio Coseriu*. Extras din "Fonetică și Dialectologie", XX-XXI, 2001–2002. București: Editura Academiei Române.

Adrados [Rodríguez Adrados], Francisco. 1961. Review of E. Coseriu. 1958. *Sincronía, diacronía e historia. El problema del cambio lingüístico* (Montevideo). *Emerita* 29, 152–153.

Ágel, Vilmos. 2017. *Grammatische Textanalyse: Textglieder, Satzglieder, Wortgruppenglieder*. Berlin & Boston: De Gruyter.

Ágel, Vilmos and Dagobert Höllein. 2021. "Satzbaupläne als Zeichen: Die semantischen Rollen des Deutschen in Theorie und Praxis". In: Anja Binanzer, Jana Gamper and Verena Wecker (eds.), *Prototypen. Schemata. Konstruktionen. Untersuchungen zur deutschen Morphologie und Syntax*. Berlin & Boston: De Gruyter.

Agha, Asif. 2007. "The object called 'language' and the subject of linguistics". *Journal of English Linguistics* 35:3, 217–235.

Agud, Ana. 1981. *Historia y teoría de los casos*. Madrid: Gredos.

Agud, Ana. Forthcoming. *Critical philosophy of language and linguistics: a humanistic, historical and comparative approach*.

Albrecht, Jörn. 1986–1990. "'Substandard' und 'Subnorm'. Die nicht-exemplarischen Ausprägungen der 'Historischen Sprache' aus varietätenlinguistischer Sicht". In: Günter Holtus and Edgar Radtke (eds.), *Sprachlicher Substandard*, 65–88, Tübingen: Niemeyer (1986), and in: Günter Holtus and Edgar Radtke (eds.), *Sprachlicher Substandard III*, 44–127. Tübingen: Niemeyer (1990).

Albrecht, Jörn. 1988. "τὰ ὄντα ὡς ἔστιν λέγειν: Über die Schwierigkeit, die Dinge zu sagen, wie sie sind, und andere davon zu überzeugen". In: Jörn Albrecht (ed.), *Energeia und Ergon. Sprachliche Variation – Sprachgeschichte – Sprachtypologie*. Vol. I: *Schriften von Eugenio Coseriu (1965–1987)*, xvii-xlv. Tübingen: Narr.

Albrecht, Jörn. 2003. "El paradigma incompleto de E. Coseriu: Tarea pendiente para la tercera generación". *Odisea* 3, 41–54.

Albrecht, Jörn. 2018. "L'héritage de Coseriu". *Cahiers de lexicologie* 112, 13–31.

Allwood, Jens. 2003. "Meaning potentials and context: some consequences for the analysis of variation in meaning". In: Hubert Cuyckens, René Dirven, John R. Taylor (eds.), *Cognitive approaches to lexical semantics*, 29–66. Berlin: Mouton de Gruyter.

Andersen, Henning. 1990. "The structure of drift". In: Henning Andersen and Ernst Frideryk Konrad Koerner (eds.), *Historical Linguistics 1987. Papers from the 8th International Conference on Historical Linguistics*, 1–20. Amsterdam & Philadelphia: John Benjamins.

Andersen, Henning. 2001. "Markedness and the theory of linguistic change". In: Henning Andersen (ed.), *Actualization*, 21–57. Amsterdam & Philadelphia: John Benjamins.

Andersen, Henning. 2006. "Synchrony, diachrony, and evolution". In: Ole Nedergaard Thomsen (ed.), *Competing models of linguistic change*, 59–90. Amsterdam & Philadelphia: John Benjamins.

Anttila, Raimo. 1989. *Historical and comparative linguistics* (first edition 1972). Amsterdam & Philadelphia: John Benjamins.

Antilla, Raimo. 1993. "Change and metatheory at the beginning of the 1900s: the primacy of history". In: Charles Jones (ed.), *Historical linguistics. Problems and perspectives*, 43–73. London & New York: Longman.

Aristotle. 1997. *De Sophisticis Elenchis. Translatio Boethii, Fragmenta Translationis Iacobi, Et Recensio Guilleimi De Moerbeka (Aristoteles Latinus)*. Leiden: Brill.

Arlotto, Anthony. 1972. *Introduction to historical linguistics*. Boston: Houghton Mifflin.

Arvidson, Sven. 2006. *The sphere of attention: context and margin*. London: Kluwer Academic

Aschenberg, Heidi. 1984. *Idealistische Philologie und Textanalyse. Zur Stilistik Leo Spitzers*. Tübingen: Narr.

Aschenberg, Heidi. 1999. *Kontexte in Texten. Umfeldtheorie und literarischer Situationsaufbau*. Tübingen: Niemeyer.

Bally, Charles. 1926. *Le langage et la vie*. Paris: Payot.

Bally, Charles. 1935. "En été: au printemps; croire en Dieu: croire au diable". In: *Festschrift für Ernst Tappolet*, 9–15. Basel: Schwabe.

Bally, Charles. 1950. *Linguistique générale et linguistique française*. Bern: Francke.

Bartsch, Renate. 1985. *Sprachnormen. Theorie und Praxis*. Tübingen: Niemeyer.

Bartsch, Renate. 1987. *Norms of language. Theoretical and practical aspects*. London & New York: Longman.

Bauer, Laurie, Rochel Lieber and Ingo Plag. 2013. *The Oxford reference guide to English morphology*. Oxford: Oxford University Press.

Bechtel, William. 2008. *Mental mechanisms: philosophical perspectives on cognitive neuroscience*. New York: Erlbaum.

Belligh, Thomas and Klaas Willems. 2021. "What's in a code? The code-inference distinction in Neo-Gricean Pragmatics, Relevance Theory, and Integral Linguistics". *Language Sciences* 83, 1–22.

Benveniste, Émile. 1966. *Problèmes de linguistique générale*. Paris: Gallimard.

Benveniste, Émile (ed.). 1951. *Actes de la conférence européenne de sémantique (Nice 26–31 mars 1951)*. Paris: Société de linguistique de Paris.

Bergounioux, Gabriel. 2002. "La sélection des langues: darwinisme et linguistique". *Langages* 36 (146), 7–18.

Bernardo, José Maria. 1995. *La construcción de la lingüística. Un debate epistemológico*. Valencia: Universitat de Valencia.

Berthonneau, Anne-Marie and Georges Kleiber. 1993. "Pour une nouvelle approche de l'imparfait: l'imparfait, un temps anaphorique méronomique". *Langages* 112, 55–73.

Bertinetto, Pier-Marco. 1986. *Tempo, aspetto, azione nel verbo italiano. Il sistema dell'indicativo*. Florence: Accademia della Crusca.

Bertoldi, Vittorio. 1946. *La parola quale mezzo d'espressione*. Napoli: Pironti.

Biber, Douglas. 1988. *Variation across speech and writing*. Cambridge: Cambridge University Press.

BNC = The British National Corpus. Accessed at <www.english-corpora.org/bnc/>.

Boc, Oana. 2007. *Textualitatea literară și lingvistica integrală*. Cluj-Napoca: Clusium.

Bojoga, Eugenia. 1999. *Receptarea operei lui E. Coșeriu în fosta U.R.S.S.* Universitatea Babeș-Bolyai: Cluj-Napoca (PhD Dissertation).
Bojoga, Eugenia, Oana Boc and Cornel Vîlcu. 2013. "Introduction". In: Eugenia Bojoga, Oana Boc and Cornel Vîlcu (eds.), *Coseriu: Perspectives contemporaines*, Vol. I, 5–7. Cluj-Napoca: Presa Universitară Clujeană.
Borcilă, Mircea. 1986. Review of Eugenio Coseriu, *Más allá del estructuralismo, Tomo I* (San Juan, 1982). *Cercetări de lingvistică – Recherches de linguistique* 31:1, 102–103.
Borcilă, Mircea. 1988. "Eugeniu Coșeriu și orizonturile lingvisticii". *Echinox* 5:1, 4–5.
Borcilă, Mircea. 1997. "Între Blaga și Coșeriu. De la metaforica limbajului la o poetică a culturii". *Revista de filosofie* 1–2, 147–163.
Borcilă, Mircea. 2000. "Eugenio Coseriu and the new horizons of linguistics". *Transylvanian Review* 9:1, 103–107.
Borcilă, Mircea. 2001. "Eugeniu Coșeriu și bazele științelor culturii". *Academica* 9:7–8, 22–23.
Borcilă, Mircea. 2002. "Eugeniu Coșeriu, fondator al lingvisticii ca știință a culturii". *Limba Română* 10, 48–55.
Borcilă, Mircea. 2003. "Lingvistica integrală și fundamentele metaforologiei". *Dacoromania*. Serie nouă 7–8, 47–77.
Borcilă, Mircea. 2013. *Paradigme contemporane în cercetarea lingvistică*. Prelegeri doctorale, Universitatea "Babeș-Bolyai".
Borcilă, Mircea. 2016. "Eugeniu Coșeriu și problema temeiului epistemologic al științei lingvistice". In: Cornel Vîlcu, Eugenia Bojoga and Oana Boc (eds.), *Școala coșeriană clujeană. Contribuții*. Vol. I, 19–28. Cluj: Presa Universitară.
Bouquet, Simon. 2000. "Sur la sémantique saussurienne". *Cahiers Ferdinand de Saussure* 53, 135–139.
Bouquet, Simon and François Rastier. 2002. *Une introduction aux sciences de la culture.* Paris: Presses Universitaires de France.
Brandt, Line. 2013. "Metaphor and the communicative mind". In: Riccardo Fusaroli and Simone Morgagni (eds.), *Cognitive Semiotics: Conceptual Metaphor Theory: thirty years after*, 37–72. Berlin & Boston: Mouton de Gruyter.
Brøndal, Viggo. 1937. "Langage et logique". In: *La grande encyclopédie française*. Paris. (Reprinted in Brøndal 1943. *Essais de linguistique générale*. Copenhague: Munksgaard.)
Brøndal, Viggo. 1939. "Linguistique structural". *Acta Linguistica* 1, 2–10.
Brown, Penelope and Stephen C. Levinson. 1987. *Politeness. Some universals in language usage*. Cambridge: Cambridge: University Press.
Brysbaert, Marc and Kathy Rastle. 2013. *Historical and conceptual issues in psychology*. Harlow: Pearson.
Bühler, Karl. 1933. "Die Axiomatik der Sprachwissenschaften". *Kant-Studien* 38, 19–90. (Commented new edition Frankfurt a.M: Klostermann 1969.)
Bühler, Karl. 1934. *Sprachtheorie: Die Darstellungsfunktion der Sprache*. Jena: Gustav Fischer. (Reprints Stuttgart: UTB 1982, 1999.)
Bühler, Karl. 1990 [1934]. *The theory of language: the representational function of language*. Translated by Donald Fraser Goodwin. Amsterdam & Philadelphia: John Benjamins (English translation of Bühler 1934).
Bülow, Edeltraud and Peter Schmitter (eds.). 1979. *Integrale Linguistik: Festschrift für Helmut Gipper*. Amsterdam & Philadelphia: John Benjamins.

Bynon, Theodora. 1977. *Historical linguistics*. Cambridge: Cambridge University Press.
Bynon, Teodora. 2001. "The synthesis of comparative and historical Indo-European studies: August Schleicher". In: Sylvain Auroux, E. F. Konrad Koerner, Hans-Josef Niederehe and Kees Versteegh (eds.), *History of the language sciences. An international handbook on the evolution of the study of language from the beginnings to the present*. Vol. 2, 1223–1239. Berlin & New York: De Gruyter.
Caballero, Fermín. 1868. *Noticias biográficas y bibliográficas de L. Hervás y Panduro*. Madrid: Sordomudos.
Caballero, Rosario and Iraide Ibarretxe-Antuñano. 2013. "Ways of perceiving, moving and thinking: re-vindicating culture in Conceptual Metaphor Research". In: Riccardo Fusaroli and Simone Morgagni (eds.), *Cognitive Semiotics: Conceptual Metaphor Theory: thirty years after*, 268–290. Berlin & Boston: Mouton de Gruyter.
Caamaño, Antonio Vilarnovo. 1993. *Lógica y lenguaje en Eugenio Coseriu*. Madrid: Gredos.
Carabellese, Pantaleo. 1940. *Critica del concreto*. Roma: Signorelli.
Cartagena, Nelson. 1976. "Estructura y función de los tiempos del modo indicativo en el sistema verbal del español". *Revista de Lingüística Teórica y Aplicada* 14–15, 5–44.
Cartagena, Nelson. 1977. "Acerca de las categorías de tiempo y aspecto en el sistema verbal del español". *Revista Española de Lingüística* 8, 373–408.
Cassirer, Ernst. 1942. *Zur Logik der Kulturwissenschaften: Fünf Studien*. Gothenburg: Göteborgs Högskolas Årsskrift.
Cassirer, Ernst. 1975 [1923]. *The philosophy of symbolic forms*. Vol. 1: *Language*. Translated by Ralph Manheim. New Haven & London: Yale University Press. (German original 1923.)
Chomsky, Noam. 1965. *Aspects of the theory of syntax*. Cambridge: M.I.T. Press.
Chomsky, Noam. 1980. *Rules and representations*. New York: Columbia University Press.
Chomsky, Noam. 1986. *Knowledge of language: its nature, origin, and use*. New York: Praeger.
Chomsky, Noam. 2009 [1966]. *Cartesian linguistics. A chapter in the history of rationalist thought* (third edition). Cambridge: Cambridge University Press.
Churchland, Paul. 1981. "Eliminative materialism and propositional attitudes". *The Journal of Philosophy* 78:2, 67–90.
Cigana, Lorenzo. 2014a. "La notion de 'participation' chez Louis Hjelmslev: un fil rouge de la glossématique". *Cahiers Ferdinand de Saussure* 67, 191–202.
Cigana, Lorenzo. 2014b. "*Sprogsystem og Sprogforandring*: il dinamismo del sistema". In: Lorenzo Cigana and Romeo Galassi (eds.), *Strutturalismo, strutturalismi e loro forme* (Janus, Quaderni del Circolo Glossematico, 13), 45–63. Treviso: ZeL Edizioni.
Cigana, Lorenzo. 2016. "La forma del mondo. L'analisi glossematica del contenuto tra linguistica e filosofia". *Rivista italiana di Filosofia del Linguaggio* 1, 22–36.
Clark, Andy. 2001. *Mindware: an introduction to the philosophy of cognitive science*. New York: Oxford University Press.
Coene, Ann and Klaas Willems. 2006. "Konstruktionelle Bedeutungen. Kritische Anmerkungen zu Adele Goldbergs konstruktionsgrammatischer Bedeutungstheorie". *Sprachtheorie und germanistische Linguistik* 16:1, 1–35.
Collingwood, Robin George. 1993 [1946]. *The idea of history*. Oxford: Oxford University Press.
Condillac, Étienne Bonnot de. 1947–1951. *Œuvres philosophiques de Condillac*. Texte établi et présenté par Georges Le Roy. Paris: Presses Universitaires de France.

Croft, William. 2000. *Explaining language change. An evolutionary approach*. Harlow: Pearson Education.
Croce, Benedetto. 1902. *Estetica come scienza dell'espressione e linguistica generale*. Milano, Palermo & Napoli: Sandrone.
Cruz Volio, Gabriela. 2017. *Actos de habla y modulación discursiva en español medieval: representaciones de (des)cortesía verbal histórica*. Frankfurt am Main: Peter Lang.
Culpeper, Jonathan and Dawn Archer. 2008. "Requests and directness in Early Modern English trial proceedings and play texts, 1640–1760". In: Andreas H. Jucker and Irma Taavitsainen (eds.), *Speech acts in the history of English*, 45–84. Amsterdam & Philadelphia: John Benjamins.
Cusimano, Christophe. 2012. *La sémantique contemporaine. Du sème au thème*. Paris: Pups.
Darwin, Charles. 1909. *On the origin of species by means of natural selection, or the preservation of favoured race in the struggle of life*. New York: P. F. Collier & Son.
De Backer, Maarten. 2009. "The concept of neutralization outside the field of phonology". *Indogermanische Forschungen* 114:1, 1–59.
De Backer, Maarten. 2010. "Lexical neutralisation: a case study of the lexical opposition 'day'/'night'. *Language Sciences* 32:5, 545–562.
De Backer, Maarten. 2013. "Neutralisation and semantic markedness: an inquiry into types of lexical opposition in German". *Sprachwissenschaft* 38:3, 343–382.
De Backer, Maarten. 2014. *Lexical neutralisation: theoretical and empirical perspectives*, Ghent, Belgium: Ghent University. Faculty of Arts and Philosophy.
De Cuypere, Ludovic. 2013. "Debiasing semantic analysis: the case of the English preposition to". *Language Sciences* 37, 122–135.
De Houwer, Jan. 2011. "Why the cognitive approach in psychology would profit from a functional approach and vice versa". *Perspectives on Psychological Science* 6:2, 202–209.
De Houwer, Jan, Dermot Barnes-Holmes and Yvonne Barnes-Holmes. 2017. "What is cognition? A functional-cognitive perspective". In: Steven C. Hayes and Stefan G. Hofmann (eds.), *Core processes of cognitive behavioral therapies*, 119–136. Oakland, CA: New Harbinger.
Deignan, Alice. 2017. "Mappings and narratives in figurative communication". In: Beate Hampe (ed.), *Metaphor: embodied cognition and discourse*, 200–219. Cambridge: Cambridge University Press.
Deignan, Alice and Lynne Cameron. 2013. "A re-examination of UNDERSTANDING IS SEEING". In: Riccardo Fusaroli and Simone Morgagni (eds.), *Cognitive Semiotics: Conceptual Metaphor Theory: thirty years after*, 220–243. Berlin & Boston: Mouton de Gruyter.
De Mauro, Tullio. 1967. *Ludwig Wittgenstein. His place in the development of semantics*. Dordrecht: Reidel.
De Mauro, Tullio. 2007. "Prefazione". In: Eugenio Coseriu, *Il linguaggio e l'uomo attuale. Saggi di filosofia del linguaggio*, ed. by Christian Bota, Massimo Schiavi, Giuseppe Di Salvatore and Lidia Gasperoni, 9–16. Verona: Edizioni Centro Studi Campostrini.
De Mauro, Tullio. 2009. "Eugenio Coseriu". In: Harro Stammerjohann (ed.), *Lexicon Grammaticorum. A bio-bibliographical companion to the history of linguistics* (second edition), 327–330. Tübingen: Niemeyer.
De Mauro, Tullio. 2015. "Indirizzo di saluto di Tullio De Mauro". In: Vincenzo Orioles and Raffaella Bombi (eds.), *Oltre Saussure: L'eredità scientifica di Eugenio Coseriu. Atti del*

IV Convegno Internazionale Università degli Studi di Udine (1–2 ottobre 2013), 15–18. Firenze: Franco Cesati.
Dennett, Daniel. 1987. *The intentional stance*. Cambridge, Mass.: MIT Press.
Dennett, Daniel. 1991. *Consciousness explained*. London: Penguin Books.
Devitt, Michael and Kim Sterelny. 1999. *Language and reality. An introduction to the philosophy of language* (second edetion). Cambridge, MA: MIT Press.
Devoto, Giacomo. 1951. "Cronaca". *Archivio glottologico italiano* 36, 82–84.
Devylder, Simon and Jordan Zlatev. 2020. "Cutting and breaking metaphors of the self and the Motivation & Sedimentation Model". In: Annalisa Baicchi (ed.), *Figurative meaning construction in thought and language*, 253–281. Amsterdam & Philadelphia: Johns Benjamins.
Díaz Pérez, Francisco Javier. 2003. *La cortesía verbal en inglés y en español. Actos de habla y pragmática intercultural*. Jaén: Universidad de Jaén.
Di Cesare, Donatella. 1988. "Die aristotelische Herkunft der Begriffe ἔργον und ἐνέργεια in Wilhelm von Humboldts Sprachphilosophie". In: Jörn Albrecht, Jens Lüdke and Harald Thun (eds.), *Energeia und Ergon. Sprachliche Variation – Sprachgeschichte – Sprachtypologie. Studia in honorem Eugenio Coseriu*. Vol. 2: *Das sprachtheoretische Denken Eugenio Coserius in der Diskussion (1)*, 29–46, Tübingen: Narr.
Di Cesare, Donatella. 1997. "Introduzione". In: Eugenio Coseriu. 1997 [1980]. *Linguistica del testo. Introduzione a una ermeneutica del senso*, 11–24. Roma: La Nuova Italia Scientifica.
Dietrich, Wolf. 1973. *Der periphrastische Verbalaspekt in den romanischen Sprachen*. Tubingen: Niemeyer.
Dietrich, Wolf. 1992. "Problemas dum estudo funcional da formação de palavras em português. O exemplo dos sufixos *-ada* e *-aria*". *Actas do III Congresso Internacional dos Lusitanistas*, 807–816. Coimbra: Associação Internacional de Lusitanistas.
Dietrich, Wolf. 1997. "Polysemie als 'volle Wortbedeutung' – gegen die 'Mehrdeutigkeit' der Zeichen". In: Ulrich Hoinkes and Wolf Dietrich (eds.), *Kaleidoskop der Lexikalischen Semantik*, 227–237. Tübingen: Narr.
Dietrich, Wolf. 2003. "Nachruf auf Eugenio Coseriu". Mitteilungen des Deutschen Hispanistenverbandes 20 (Februar 2003), 6–8.
Di Girolamo, Edoardo. 1978. *Critica della letterarietà*. Milano: Il Saggiatore.
Dowty, David R. 1991. "Thematic proto-roles and argument selection". *Language* 67, 547–619.
Dürscheid, Christa. 2016. "Nähe, Distanz und neue Medien". In: Helmuth Feilke and Mathilde Hennig (eds.), *Zur Karriere von 'Nähe und Distanz'. Rezeption und Diskussion des Koch-Oesterreicher-Modells*, 357–385. Berlin & Boston: De Gruyter.
Ehlers, Klaas-Hinrich. 2010. *Der Wille zur Relevanz. Die Sprachforschung und ihre Förderung durch die DFG 1920–1970*. Stuttgart: Franz Steiner Verlag.
Engelen, Bernhard. 1970. "Das Präpositionalobjekt im Deutschen und seine Entsprechungen im Englischen, Französischen und Russischen". In: Ulrich Engel (ed.), *Forschungsberichte des Instituts für Deutsche Sprache*. Vol. 4, 3–30. Tübingen: Narr.
Escandell-Vidal, María Victoria. 2004. "Norms and principles. Putting social and cognitive pragmatics together". In: Rosina Márquez Reiter and María Elena Placencia (eds.), *Current trends in the pragmatics of Spanish*, 347–371. Amsterdam & Philadelphia: John Benjamins.

Estigarribia, Bruno. 2020. *A grammar of Paraguayan Guarani*. London: UCL Press.
Evans, Vyvyan. 2013. "Metaphor, lexical concepts, and figurative meaning construction". In: Riccardo Fusaroli and Simone Morgagni (eds.), *Cognitive Semiotics. Conceptual Metaphor Theory: thirty years after*, 73–107. Berlin & Boston: Mouton de Gruyter.
Ezawa, Kennosuke, Franz Hundsnurscher and Annemete von Vogel (eds.). 2014. *Beiträge zur Gabelentz-Forschung*. Tübingen: Narr.
Faur, Elena. 2013a. "Integral Semantics and Conceptual Metaphor: rethinking Conceptual Metaphor within an Integral Semantics framework". In: Riccardo Fusaroli and Simone Morgagni (eds.), *Cognitive Semiotics. Conceptual Metaphor Theory: thirty years after*, 108–139. Berlin & Boston: Mouton de Gruyter.
Faur, Elena. 2013b. *Semantica cognitivă și emergența studiilor elocuționale*. Teză de doctorat, Universitatea Babeș-Bolyai.
Feilke, Helmuth and Mathilde Hennig (eds.). 2016. *Zur Karriere von 'Nähe und Distanz'. Rezeption und Diskussion des Koch-Oesterreicher-Modells*. Berlin & Boston: De Gruyter.
Feyerabend, Paul. 1970. *Against method*. Minnesota: M. Radner and S. Vinocur.
Fillmore, Charles J. 1968. "The case for case". In: Emmon Bach and Robert T. Harms (eds.), *Universals in linguistic theory*, 1–88. New York: Rinehart and Winston.
Fillmore, Charles J. 1977. "The Case for Case Reopened". In: Peter Cole and Jerrold M. Sadock (eds.), *Syntax and semantics*. Vol. 8: *Grammatical relations*, 59–81. New York: Academic Press.
Fillmore, Charles J. 2003. "Valency and semantic roles: the concept of deep structure case". In: Vilmos Ágel, Ludwig M. Eichinger, Hans Werner Eroms, Peter Hellwig, Hans-Jurgen Heringer and Henning Lobin (eds.) *Dependenz und Valenz: Ein internationales Handbuch der zeitgenössischen Forschung*, 457–475. Berlin & New York: De Gruyter.
Fillmore, Charles J. 2006. "Frame semantics". In: Keith Brown (ed.), *Encyclopedia of Language & Linguistics*, 613–620. Amsterdam: Elsevier.
Finck, Franz Nikolaus. 1909. *Die Sprachstämme des Erdkreises*. Leipzig & Berlin: Teubner.
Finck, Franz Nikolaus. 1910. *Die Haupttypen des Sprachbaus*. Leipzig & Berlin: Teubner.
Fischer-Jørgensen, Eli. 1995 [1975]. *Trends in phonological theory until 1975. A historical introduction*. (Travaux du Cercle Linguistique de Copenhague, 27.) København: Akademisk Forlag.
Fleischmann, Eberhard. 1985. *Kasustheorie und Translationslinguistik: Dissertation zur Promotion B*. Karl-Marx-Universität Leipzig.
Fleischman, Suzanne. 1982. *The future in thought and language. Diachronic evidence from Romance*. Cambridge: Cambridge University Press.
Flydal, Leiv. 1952. "Remarques sur certains rapports entre le style et l'état de langue". *Norsk Tidsskrift for Sprogvidenskap* 16, 241–258. (Occasionally cited as 'Flydal 1951' due to offprints of the article dated 1951.)
Fodor, Jerry. 2000. *In critical condition: polemic essays on cognitive science and the Philosophy of Mind*. Cambridge: MIT Press.
Fodor, Jerry. 2008. *LOT2: The Language of Thought revisited*. Oxford: Oxford University Press.
Forceville, Charles. 2017. "From Image Schema to metaphor in discourse: the FORCE schemas in animation films". In: Beate Hampe (ed.), *Metaphor: embodied cognition and discourse*, 239–257. Cambridge: Cambridge University Press.
Forster, Michael N. 2017. Review of E. Coseriu, *Geschichte der Sprachphilosophie* (2015). *Historiographia Linguistica* 44:1, 165–171.

Forster, Michael N. 2020. "Philosophy, history of philosophy, and historicism". In: Efraim Podoksik (ed.), *Doing humanities in nineteenth-century Germany*, 19–39. Leiden & Boston: Brill.

Frank, Birgit. 2011. *Aufforderung im Französischen. Ein Beitrag zur Geschichte sprachlicher Höflichkeit*. Berlin & New York: De Gruyter.

Gabelentz, Georg von der. 2016 [1891/1901]. *Die Sprachwissenschaft, ihre Aufgaben, Methoden und bisherigen Ergebnisse*. Ed. by Manfred Ringmacher and James McElvenny. Berlin: Language Science Press.

Gallagher, Shaun. 1997. "Mutual enlightenment: recent phenomenology in cognitive science". *Journal of Consciousness Studies* 4:3, 195–214.

Gardiner, Alan. 1932. *The theory of speech and language*. Oxford: Clarendon.

Gardt, Andreas. 2011. "Sprachgeschichte als Kulturgeschichte. Chancen und Risiken der Forschung". In: Péter Maitz (ed.), *Historische Sprachwissenschaft. Erkenntnisinteressen, Grundlagenprobleme, Desiderate*, 289–300. Berlin & Boston: De Gruyter.

Geckeler, Horst. 1981a. "Structural semantics". In: Hans J. Eikmeyer and Hannes Rieser (eds.), *Words, worlds and contexts*, 381–413. Berlin & New York: de Gruyter.

Geckeler, Horst. 1981b. "Progrès et stagnation en sémantique structurale". In: Horst Geckeler, Brigitte Schlieben-Lange, Jürgen Trabant and Harald Weydt (eds.), *Logos Semantikos. Studia linguistica in honorem Eugenio Coseriu 1921–1981*, Vol. III, 53–69. Berlin & New York: Walter de Gruyter.

Geckeler, Horst. 1988. "Major aspects of the lexematics of the Tübingen School of semantics". In: Werner Hüllen and Rainer Schulze (eds), *Understanding the lexicon: meaning, sense and world knowledge in lexical semantics*, 11–22. Tübingen: Niemeyer.

Geckeler, Horst, Brigitte Schlieben-Lange, Jürgen Trabant and Harald Weydt (eds.). 1981. *Logos semantikos. Studia linguistica in honorem Eugenio Coseriu, 1921–1981*. 5 vols. Berlin: de Gruyter; Madrid: Gredos.

Geeraerts, Dirk. 1993. "Vagueness's puzzles, polysemy's vagaries". *Cognitive Linguistics* 4, 223–272.

Geeraerts, Dirk. 2010. *Theories of lexical semantics*. Oxford: Oxford University Press.

Geeraerts, Dirk and Hubert Cuyckens. 2007. "Introducing Cognitive Linguistics". In: Dirk Geeraerts and Hubert Cuyckens (eds.), *Oxford handbook of Cognitive Linguistics*, 3–21. Oxford: Oxford University Press.

Gibbs, Raymond W. 2017a. "The embodied and discourse views of metaphor: why these are not so different and how can they be brought closer together". In: Beate Hampe (ed.), *Metaphor: embodied cognition and discourse*, 319–334. Cambridge: Cambridge University Press.

Gibbs, Raymond W. 2017b. *Metaphor wars: Conceptual Metaphors in human life*. Cambridge: Cambridge University Press.

Gilquin, Gaetan and Stefan Gries. 2009. "Corpora and experimental methods: A state-of-the-art review". *Corpus Linguistics and Linguistic Theory* 5:1, 1–26.

Goddard, Cliff. 2011. *Semantic analysis: a practical introduction*. Oxford: Oxford University Press.

Goldberg, Adele E. 1995. *Constructions. A Construction Grammar approach to argument structure*. Chicago: University of Chicago Press.

Goldberg, Adele E. 2003. "Constructions: a new theoretical approach to language". *Trends in Cognitive Sciences* 7:5, 219–224.

Goldberg, Adele E. 2019. *Explain me this: creativity, competition, and the partial productivity of constructions*. Princeton, N. J.: Princeton University Press.
Goodman, Nelson. 1978. *Ways of worldmaking*. Indianapolis: Hackett.
Grady, Joseph and Giorgio A. Ascoli. 2017. "Sources and targets in Primary Metaphor Theory: looking back and thinking ahead". In: Beate Hampe (ed.), *Metaphor: embodied cognition and discourse*, 27–45. Cambridge: Cambridge University Press.
Grice, Herbert Paul. 1989. "Logic and conversation". In: Herbert Paul Grice, *Studies in the way of words*, 22–40. Cambridge: Harvard University Press.
Gries, Stefan. 2003. *Multifactorial analysis in corpus linguistics: a study of particle placement*. New York: Continuum.
Gries, Stefan. 2017. *Ten lectures on quantitative approaches in Cognitive Linguistics: corpus-linguistic, experimental, and statistical applications*. Leiden: Brill.
Gruber, Teresa, Klaus Grübl and Thomas Scharinger (eds.). 2020. *Was bleibt von kommunikativer Nähe und Distanz? Mediale und konzeptionelle Aspekte von Diskurstraditionen und sprachlichem Wandel*. Tübingen: Narr.
Guitarte, Guillermo L. 1988. "Dialecto, español de America e historia en Coseriu". In: Harald Thun (ed.), *Energeia und Ergon. Sprachliche Variation – Sprachgeschichte – Sprachtypologie. Vol. II: Das sprachtheoretische Denken Eugenio Coserius in der Diskussion (1)*, 487–500. Tübingen: Narr.
Gurwitsch, Aron. 1964. *The field of consciousness*. Pittsburgh: Duquesne University Press.
Hacker, Peter and Gordon Baker. 1985. *Language, sense and nonsense. A critical investigation into modern theories of language*. Oxford: Blackwell.
Hampe, Beate. 2017. "Embodiment and discourse: dimensions and dynamics of contemporary metaphor theory". In: Beate Hampe (ed.), *Metaphor: embodied cognition and discourse*, 3–25. Cambridge: Cambridge University Press.
Hanks, Patrick. 2013. *Lexical analysis. Norms and exploitations*. Cambridge, Mass. & London: MIT Press.
Harmon, David. 1996. "Losing species, losing languages: connections between biological and linguistic diversity". *Southwest Journal of Linguistics* 15:1–2, 89–108.
Harris, Roy. 1981. *The language myth*. London: Duckworth.
Hartmann, Nicolai. 1933. *Das Problem des geistigen Seins. Untersuchungen zur Grundlegung der Geschichtsphilosophie und der Geisteswissenschaften*. Berlin: de Gruyter.
Haß, Ulrike. 2010. "'Datenverarbeitende Maschinen' und der strukturalistische Diskurs". In: Hans-Harald Müller, Marcel Lepper and Andreas Gardt (eds.), *Strukturalismus in Deutschland. Literaturwissenschaft und Sprachwissenschaft 1910–1975*, 194–216. Göttingen: Wallstein.
Haßler, Gerda. 1991. *Der semantische Wertbegriff in Sprachtheorien vom 18. bis zum 20. Jahrhundert*. Berlin: Akademie-Verlag.
Haßler, Gerda. 2006. "Los conceptos en el período del nacimiento del estructuralismo y su transmisión en España". In: Ricardo Escavy (ed.), *Caminos actuales de la historiografía lingüística*. Vol. I, 81–114. Murcia: Universidad de Murcia.
Haßler, Gerda. 2016. "La historiografía de la lingüística en la obra de Eugenio Coseriu". In: Antonio Salvador Plans, Carmen Galán Rodríguez et al. (eds.), *La Historiografía Lingüística como paradigma de investigación*, 519–531. Madrid: Visor Libros.

Haug, Dag. 2009. "The syntax and semantics of concomitance in Norwegian". In: Miriam Butt and Tracy Holloway King (eds.), *Proceedings of the LFG09 Conference*, 338–356. Stanford, CA: CSLI Publications.
Hegel, Georg Wilhelm Friedrich. 1970 [1832–1845]. *Werke*. 20 vols. Frankfurt a. M.: Suhrkamp.
Heidegger, Martin. 1927. *Sein und Zeit*. Halle an der Saale: Niemeyer.
Heidegger, Martin. 1986 [1927]. *Sein und Zeit* (sixteenth edition). Tübingen: Niemeyer.
Heidegger, Martin. 1959: *Unterwegs zur Sprache*. Pfullingen: Neske.
Held, Gudrun. 2006. "Schwerpunkte der historischen Pragmalinguistik: Exemplarische Fallstudien". In: Gerhard Ernst, Martin-Dietrich Gleßgen, Christian Schmitt and Wolfgang Schweickard (eds.), *Romanische Sprachgeschichte. Ein internationales Handbuch zur zeitgenössischen Forschung*. Vol. 2, 2302–2318. Berlin & New York: De Gruyter.
Hjelmslev, Louis. 1928. *Principes de grammaire générale*. Copenhague: Bianco Lunos Bogtrykkeri.
Hjelmslev, Louis. 1935. *La catégorie des cas. Étude de grammaire générale*. Première partie. Acta Jutlandica 7:1. Aarhus: Universitetsforlaget.
Hjelmslev, Louis. 1937. *La catégorie des cas. Étude de grammaire générale*. Deuxième partie. Acta Jutlandica 9:2. Aarhus: Universitetsforlaget.
Hjelmslev, Louis. 1941. "Et par sprogteoretiske betragtninger". *Årbog for nordisk målstræv* 4, 81–88.
Hjelmslev, Louis. 1942. "Langue et parole". *Cahiers Ferdinand de Saussure* 2, 29–44. Reprinted in: Louis Hjelmslev. 1959. *Essais linguistiques*. Vol. I, 69–81. (*Travaux du Cercle Linguistique de Copenhague* 12.) København: Nordisk Sprog- og Kulturforlag.
Hjelmslev, Louis. 1943. *Omkring sprogteoriens grundlæggelse*. Munksgaard: København.
Hjelmslev, Louis. 1947. "Structural analysis of language". *Studia Linguistica* 1, 69–78.
Hjelmslev, Louis. 1953 [1943]. *Prolegomena to a theory of language*. Baltimore: Waverly Press.
Hjelmslev, Louis. 1961 [1943]. *Prolegomena to a theory of language*. Translated by Francis J. Whitfield (second edition). Madison: The University of Wisconsin Press.
Hjelmslev, Louis. 1958. "Dans quelle mesure les significations des mots peuvent-elles être considéreés comme formant une structure, rapport par Louis Hjelmslev". In: *Actes du Huitième Congrès International des Linguistes (1957)*, 636–654, "Discussion", 666–669, "Conclusion", 704. Oslo: Presses Universitaires d'Oslo. Reprinted as "Pour une sémantique structurale" in: Louis Hjelmslev. 1959. *Essais linguistiques*. Vol. I, 96–112. (*Travaux du Cercle Linguistique de Copenhague* 12.) København: Nordisk Sprog- og Kulturforlag.
Hjelmslev, Louis. 1961. *Prolegomena to a theory of language*. Madison: The University of Wisconsin Press.
Hjelmslev, Louis. 1970a [1939]. "Note sur les oppositions supprimables". *Travaux du Cercle Linguistique de Prague* 8, 51–57. Also in: Louis Hjelmslev. 1970. *Essais linguistiques* (second edition) (Travaux du Cercle Linguistique de Copenhague 12), 82–88. København: Nordisk Sprog- og Kulturforlag.
Hjelmslev, Louis. 1970b [1939]. "La structure morphologique". *Cinquième congrès international des linguistes. Rapports*, 66–93. Bruges: Imprimerie Sainte Catherine. Also in: Louis Hjelmslev. 1970. *Essais linguistiques* (second edition) (Travaux du Cercle Linguistique de Copenhague 12), 113–138. København: Nordisk Sprog- og Kulturforlag.

Hjelmslev, Louis. 1970c. "Observations de L. Hjelmslev (23.04.42)". *Bulletin du Cercle Linguistique de Copenhague 1941–1965*, 8/31, 96–99. Copenhague: Akademisk Forlag.
Hjelmslev, Louis. 1970d. "Language and system (19.09.46)". *Bulletin du Cercle Linguistique de Copenhague 1941–1965*, 8/31, 101–102. Copenhague: Akademisk Forlag.
Hjelmslev, Louis. 1972a. *Sprogsystem og sprogforandring* (Travaux du Cercle Linguistique de Copenhague 15). København: Nordisk Sprog- og Kulturforlag.
Hjelmslev, Louis. 1972b. *La catégorie des cas. Étude de grammaire générale*. Edited by Eugenio Coseriu. München: Fink.
Hjelmslev, Louis. 1973 [1957]. "Introduction à la discussion générale des problèmes relatifs à la phonologie des langues mortes, en l'espèce du grec et du latin". *Acta Congressus Madvigiani. Proceedings of the Second International Congress of Classical Studies*. Vol. 1: *General Part*, 31–33. København: Munksgaard. Also in: Louis Hjelmslev (1973), *Essais linguistiques II* (Travaux du Cercle Linguistique de Copenhague 14), 267–278. Copenhague: Nordisk Sprog- og Kulturforlag.
Hjelmslev, Louis. 1973a. "Structure générale des corrélations linguistiques". In: Louis Hjelmslev (ed.), *Essais linguistiques II* (Travaux du Cercle Linguistique de Copenhague 14), 57–98. Copenhague: Nordisk Sprog- og Kulturforlag.
Hjelmslev, Louis. 1973b. "A causerie on linguistic theory". In: Louis Hjelmslev (ed.), *Essais linguistiques II* (Travaux du Cercle Linguistique de Copenhague 14), 101–117. Copenhague: Nordisk Sprog- og Kulturforlag.
Hjelmslev, Louis. 1975. *Résumé of a theory of language* (Travaux du Cercle Linguistique de Copenhague 16). Copenhagen: Nordisk Sprog- og Kulturforlag.
Hjelmslev Archives, Royal Danish Library, Acc. 1992/5. See also the site: https://cc.au.dk/en/infrastructuralism/about-project-infrastructuralism/.
Hoenigswald, Henry M. 1960. *Linguistic change and linguistic reconstruction*. Chicago: University of Chicago Press.
Höllein, Dagobert. 2017. "Gibt es Handlungs-, Tätigkeits-, Vorgangs- und Zustandsverben: Ein Vorschlag für signifikativ-semantische Rollen von Prädikaten". *Zeitschrift für germanistische Linguistik* 45:2, 286–305.
Höllein, Dagobert. 2019. *Präpositionalobjekt vs. Adverbial: Die semantischen Rollen der Präpositionalobjekte*. Berlin & Boston: De Gruyter.
Höllein, Dagobert. 2020. "Verbund von Valenztheorie und Konstruktionsgrammatik am Beispiel produktiver Präpositionalobjekte". *Linguistische Berichte. Sonderheft* 28, 83–112.
Holt, Jens. 1946. *Rationel semantik (pleremik)*. København: Munskgaard.
Holt, Jens. 1967. "Contribution à l'analyse fonctionnelle du contenu linguistique", *Langages* 6, 59–69.
Humboldt, Wilhelm von. 1903–1936. *Gesammelte Schriften* (17 vols.) Edited by Albert Leitzmann et al. Berlin: Behr.
Humboldt, Wilhelm von. 1963 [1829]. *Über die Verschiedenheiten des menschlichen Sprachbaues* (1829). In: Andreas Flitner and Klaus Giel (eds.), *Wilhelm von Humboldt. Schriften zur Sprachphilosophie*. Vol. 3, 144–367. Darmstadt: Wissenschaftliche Buchgesellschaft.
Humboldt, Wilhelm von. 1963 [1836]. *Über die Verschiedenheit des menschlichen Sprachbaues und ihren Einfluss auf die geistige Entwicklung des Menschengeschlechts* (1830–1835). In: Andreas Flitner and Klaus Giel (eds.), *Wilhelm von Humboldt. Schriften*

zur Sprachphilosophie. Vol. 3, 368–756. Darmstadt: Wissenschaftliche Buchgesellschaft.
Humboldt, Wilhelm von. 1988 [1836]. *On language. On the diversity of human language construction and its influence on the mental development of the human species*. Edited by M. Losonsky, translated by P. Heath. Cambridge: Cambridge University Press.
Husserl, Edmund. 1985 [1939]. *Erfahrung und Urteil. Untersuchungen zur Genealogie der Logik*. Edited by Ludwig Landgrebe. Hamburg: Felix Meiner.
Husserl, Edmund. 1954. *Die Krisis der europäischen Wissenschaften und die transzendentale Phänomenologie: eine Einleitung in die phänomenologische Philosophie* (Husserliana VI). The Hague: Martinus Nijhoff.
Husserl, Edmund. 1981 [1913]. *Ideas pertaining to a pure phenomenology and to a phenomenological philosophy, first book*. The Hague: Martinus Nijhoff.
Husserl, Edmund. 1989 [1952]. *Ideas pertaining to a pure phenomenology and to a phenomenological philosophy, second book*. Dordrecht: Kluwer.
Husserl, Edmund. 1980 [1913]. *Logische Untersuchungen* (first edition 1900–1901). Tübingen: Niemeyer.
Husserl, Edmund. 2001 [1913]. *Logical investigations*. London: Routledge.
Iatridou, Sabine. 2000. "The grammatical ingredients of counterfactuality". *Linguistic Inquiry* 31, 231–270.
Iglesias Recuero, Silvia. 2010. "Aportación a la historia de la (des)cortesía: las peticiones en el siglo XVI". In: Franca Orletti and Laura Mariottini (eds.), *(Des)cortesía en español: espacios teóricos y metodológicos para su estudio*, 369–396. Roma/Estocolmo: Università degli Studi Roma Trè-EDICE & Universidad de Estocolmo.
Iglesias Recuero, Silvia. 2016. "Otra cara de la pragmática histórica: la historia de los actos de habla en español. Peticiones y órdenes en las *Novelas ejemplares* de Cervantes". In: Araceli López Serena, Antonio Narbona Jiménez and Santiago del Rey Quesada (eds.), *El español a través de los tiempos. Estudios ofrecidos a Rafael Cano Aguilar*. Vol. 2, 971–994. Sevilla: Universidad de Sevilla.
Iglesias Recuero, Silvia. 2017. "Mecanismos de atenuación en las peticiones de ayer a hoy". *Lingüística española actual* 39, 289–316.
Itkonen, Esa. 1978. *Grammatical theory and metascience: a critical investigation into methodological and philosophical foundations of autonomous linguistics*. Amsterdam & Philadelphia: John Benjamins.
Itkonen, Esa. 1983. *Causality in linguistic theory: a critical investigation into the philosophical and methodological foundations of non-autonomous linguistics*. London: Croom Helm.
Itkonen, Esa. 1984. "On the rationalist conception of linguistic change". *Diachronica* 1, 203–216.
Itkonen, Esa. 1997. "The social ontology of meaning". *SKY 1997. Yearbook of the Linguistic Association of Finland*, 49–80.
Itkonen, Esa. 2008. "Concerning the role of consciousness in linguistics". *Journal of Consciousness Studies* 15:6, 15–33.
Itkonen, Esa. 2016. "An assessment of (mentalist) cognitive semantics". *Public Journal of Semiotics* 7:1, 1–42.
Jackendoff, Ray. 1987. *Consciousness and the computational mind*. Cambridge, Mass.: MIT Press.

Jackendoff, Ray. 2002. *Foundations of language. Brain, meaning, grammar, evolution*. New York: Oxford University Press.
Jacob, Daniel and Johannes Kabatek (eds.). 2001. *Lengua medieval y tradiciones discursivas en la Península Ibérica: descripción gramatical – pragmática histórica – metodología*. Madrid/Frankfurt: Iberoamericana/Vervuert.
Jakobson, Roman. 1971 [1965]. "Quest for the essence of language". In: Roman Jakobson, *Selected Writings*, Vol. 2: *Word and language*, 345–359. Den Haag & Paris: Mouton.
Jakobson, Roman. 1971 [1969]. "Linguistics in its relation to the other sciences". In: Roman Jakobson, *Selected Writings*. Vol. II: 655–696. The Hague & Paris: Mouton.
Jeffers, Robert and Ilse Lehiste. 1979. *Principles and methods for historical linguistics*. Cambridge, Mass.: MIT Press.
Jensen, Thomas W. 2017. "Doing metaphor. An ecological perspective on metaphoricity in discourse". In: Beate Hampe (ed.), *Metaphor: embodied cognition and discourse*, 239–257. Cambridge: Cambridge University Press.
Jensen, Viggo Bank. 2012. "Eugenio Coseriu, Scandinavian linguists and variational linguistics". *Dacoromania. Serie nouă* 17:2, 154–162.
Jensen, Viggo Bank. 2015a. "Eli Fischer-Jørgensen, Eugenio Coseriu et Louis Hjelmslev: Quelque points d'une correspondance". *Cahiers Ferdinand de Saussure* 68, 27–45.
Jensen, Viggo Bank. 2015b. "Il ruolo della "Scuola di Copenaghen" nel "rimodellamento" coseriano degli assiomi saussuriani". In: Vincenzo Orioles and Raffaella Bombi (eds.), *Oltre Saussure: L'eredità scientifica di Eugenio Coseriu. Atti del IV Convegno Internazionale Università degli Studi di Udine* (1–2 ottobre 2013), 121–132. Firenze: Franco Cesati.
Jensen, Viggo Bank. 2020. "Introduction". In: Viggo Bank Jensen and Giuseppe D'Ottavi (eds.), *From the Early Years of Phonology. The Roman Jakobson – Eli Fischer-Jørgensen correspondence (1949–1982)*, 11–84. Copenhagen: Det Kongelige Danske Videnskabernes Selskab.
Jespersen, Otto. 1925. *Mankind, nation and individual from a linguistic point of view*. Oslo: Aschehoug.
Johnson, Mark. 1987. *The body in the mind. The bodily basis of meaning, imagination, and reason*. Chicago: University of Chicago Press.
Johnson, Mark. 2017. *Embodied mind, meaning, and reason. How our bodies give rise to understanding*. Chicago & London: The University of Chicago Press.
Johnson, Mark. 2018. *The aesthetics of meaning and thought. The bodily roots of philosophy, science, morality, and art*. Chicago & London: The University of Chicago Press.
Joseph, Brian D. and Richard Janda (eds.). 2003. *The handbook of historical linguistics*. Oxford: Blackwell.
Joseph, John E. 2012. *Saussure*. Oxford: Oxford University Press.
Joseph, John E. 2018. "'This eternal wanderer': A non-dogmatic reading of Saussure". In: John Joseph and Ekaterina Velmezova (éds.). *Le 'Cours de linguistique générale': réception, diffusion, tradition*, 197–208 (= *Cahiers de l'ILSL* 57). Lausanne: Université de Lausanne.
Jucker, Andreas H. 2012. "Changes in politeness cultures". In: Terttu Nevalainen and Elizabeth Closs Traugott (eds.), *The Oxford handbook of the history of English*, 422–433. Oxford: Oxford University Press,.
Jung, Verena and Angela Schrott. 2003. "A question of time? Question types and speech act shifts from a historical-contrastive perspective. Some examples from Old Spanish and

Middle English". In: Kaszia M. Jaszczolt and Ken Turner (eds.), *Meaning through language contrast*. Vol. 2, 345–371. Amsterdam & Philadelphia: John Benjamins.

Jungemann, Frederick. 1960. Review of E. Coseriu. 1958. *Sincronía, diacronía e historia. El problema del cambio lingüístico* (Montevideo). *Modern Language Notes* 75:1, 93–96.

Kabatek, Johannes. 2000a. "L'oral et l'écrit – quelques aspects théoriques d'un 'nouveau' paradigme dans le canon de la linguistique romane". In: Wolfgang Dahmen, Günter Holtus, Johannes Kramer, Michael Metzeltin, Wolfgang Schweickard and Otto Winkelmann (eds.), *Kanonbildung in der Romanistik und in den Nachbardisziplinen. Romanistisches Kolloquium XIV*, 305–320. Tübingen: Narr.

Kabatek, Johannes. 2000b. "Einheitlichkeit der Bedeutung, Designat und Integrale Linguistik". In: Bruno Staib (ed.), *Linguistica romanica et indiana. Festschrift für Wolf Dietrich zum 60. Geburtstag*, 187–205. Tübingen: Narr.

Kabatek, Johannes. 2002. "Die unveröffentlichten Manuskripte Eugenio Coserius – eine Projektskizze". In: Adolfo Murguía (ed.), *Sprache und Welt. Festgabe für Eugenio Coseriu zum 80. Geburtstag*, 111–124. Tübingen: Narr.

Kabatek, Johannes. 2005. "Über Trampelpfade, sichtbare Hände und Sprachwandelprozesse". In: Thomas Stehl (ed.), *Unsichtbare Hand und Sprecherwahl. Typologie und Prozesse des Sprachwandels in der Romania*, 155–174. Tübingen: Narr.

Kabatek, Johannes. 2015. "Warum die 'zweite Historizität' eben doch die zweite ist – von der Bedeutung von Diskurstraditionen für die Sprachbetrachtung". In: Franz Lebsanft and Angela Schrott (eds.), *Diskurse, Texte, Traditionen. Modelle und Fachkulturen in der Diskussion*, 49–62. Bonn & Göttingen: Bonn University Press & Vandenhoeck & Ruprecht.

Kabatek, Johannes. 2017. "Determinación y entorno: 60 años después". In: Gerda Haßler, Thomas Stehl (eds.), *Kompetenz – Funktion – Variation. Linguistica Coseriana V*, 19–37. Frankfurt am Main: Peter Lang.

Kabatek, Johannes. 2018a. *Lingüística coseriana, lingüística histórica, tradiciones discursivas*. Edited by Cristina Bleorțu and David Gerards. Madrid & Frankfurt a.M.: Vervuert – Iberoamericana.

Kabatek, Johannes. 2018b. "Lingüística coseriana, lingüística histórica y tradiciones discursivas". *Anadiss* 25, 255–258.

Kabatek, Johannes. 2020. "Linguistic norm in the linguistic theory of Eugenio Coseriu". In: Franz Lebsanft and Felix Tacke (eds.), *Manual of standardization in the Romance languages*, 127–144. Berlin & Boston: De Gruyter.

Kabatek, Johannes. 2021. *Eugenio Coseriu. Beyond structuralism*. Berlin & Boston: De Gruyter.

Kabatek, Johannes and Adolfo Murguía. 1997. *"Die Sachen sagen, wie sie sind...". Eugenio Coseriu im Gespräch*. Tübingen: Narr.

Kabatek, Johannes (ed.). 2008. *Sintaxis histórica del español y cambio lingüístico: Nuevas perspectivas desde las tradiciones discursivas*. Madrid/Frankfurt: Iberoamericana/Vervuert.

Katz, Jerrold. 1972. *The philosophy of linguistics*. Oxford: Oxford University Press.

Kaufmann, Stefan, Cleo Condoravdi and Valentina Harizanov. 2006. "Formal approaches to modality". In: William Frawley (ed.), *The expression of modality*, 72–106. Berlin & New York: Mouton De Gruyter.

Keller, Rudi. 1990. *Sprachwandel. Von der unsichtbaren Hand in der Sprache*. Tübingen: Francke.
Keller, Rudi. 1994. *On language change: the invisible hand in language*. London & New York: Routledge.
Keniston, Hayward. 1936. "Verbal aspect in Spanish". *Hispania* 19, 163–176.
Kerbrat-Orecchioni, Catherine. 2001. *Les actes de langage dans le discours. Théorie et fonctionnement*. Paris: Nathan.
Kiefer, Ferenc (ed.). 2000. *Strukturális magyar nyelvtan*. 3. kötet: *Morfológia*. Budapest: Akadémiai Kiadó.
Koch, Peter. 1987. *Distanz im Dictamen. Zur Schriftlichkeit und Pragmatik mittelalterlicher Brief- und Redemodelle in Italien*. Unpublished habilitation thesis, Freiburg im Breisgau.
Koch, Peter. 1988. "Norm und Sprache". In: Jörn Albrecht, Jens Lüdtke and Harald Thun (eds.), *Energeia und Ergon. Sprachliche Variation – Sprachgeschichte – Sprachtypologie. Studia in honorem Eugenio Coseriu*, Vol. II: *Das sprachtheoretische Denken Eugenio Coserius in der Diskussion (2)*, 327–354. Tübingen: Narr.
Koch, Peter. 1997. "Diskurstraditionen: zu ihrem sprachtheoretischen Status und ihrer Dynamik". In: Barbara Frank, Thomas Haye and Doris Tophinke (eds.), *Gattungen mittelalterlicher Schriftlichkeit*, 43–79. Tübingen: Narr.
Koch, Peter. 2005. "Sprachwandel und Sprachvariation". In: Angela Schrott and Harald Völker (eds.), *Historische Pragmatik und historische Varietätenlinguistik in den romanischen Sprache*, 229–254. Göttingen: Universitätsverlag.
Koch, Peter and Wulf Oesterreicher. 1985. "Sprache der Nähe – Sprache der Distanz. Mündlichkeit und Schriftlichkeit im Spannungsfeld von Sprachtheorie und Sprachgeschichte". *Romanistisches Jahrbuch* 36, 15–43
Koch, Peter and Wulf Oesterreicher. 1990. *Gesprochene Sprache in der Romania: Französisch, Italienisch, Spanisch*. Tübingen: Niemeyer (second edition: Berlin: De Gruyter, 2011).
Koch, Peter and Wulf Oesterreicher. 2012. "Language of inmediacy – language of distance: orality and literacy from the perspective of language theory and linguistic history". In: Claudia Lange, Beatrix Weber and Göran Wolf (eds.), *Communicative spaces: variation, contact, change. Papers in honour of Ursula Schaefer*, 441–473. Frankfurt: Peter Lang (English translation of Koch and Oesterreicher 1985).
Koerner, Konrad. 1989. *Practicing linguistic historiography. Selected essays*. Amsterdam & Philadelphia: John Benjamins.
Kohnen, Thomas. 2008. "Directives in Old English: beyond politeness?" In: Andreas H. Jucker and Irma Taavitsainen (eds.), *Speech acts in the history of English*, 27–44. Amsterdam & Philadelphia: Benjamins.
Korp. Språkbanken. Accessed at <spraakbanken.gu.se/korp/> on 2020–09–24.
Kuryłowicz, Jerzy. 1945. "La nature des processus dits 'analogiques'". *Acta Linguistica* 5, 15–37.
Labov, William. 1981. "Resolving the Neogrammarian controversy". *Language* 57, 267–309.
Laca, Brenda. 1986. *Die Wortbildung als Grammatik des Wortschatzes. Untersuchungen zur spanischen Subjektnominalisierung*. Tübingen: Narr.
Laca, Brenda. 2004. "Romance 'aspectual' periphrases: eventuality modification versus 'syntactic' aspect". In: Jacqueline Guéron and Jacqueline Lecarme (eds.), *The syntax of time*, 425–440. Cambridge, Mass.: MIT Press.

Laca, Brenda. 2005. "Périphrases aspectuelles et temps grammatical dans les langues romanes". In: Hava Bat Zeev Schyldkrot and Nicole Le Querler (eds.), *Les périphrases verbales*, 47–66. Amsterdam & Philadelphia: John Benjamins.
Laca, Brenda. 2017. "Tradición y novedad en 'El sistema verbal románico'". *Revista de la Academia Nacional de Letras* 13, 119–135.
Lakoff, George. 1977. "Linguistic gestalts". In: Samuel E. Fox, Woodford A. Beach and Shulamith Philosoph (eds.), *Papers from the Thirteenth Regional Meeting of the Chicago Linguistic Society*, 236–287. Illinois: University of Chicago Press.
Lakoff, George. 1987. *Women, fire, and dangerous things. What categories reveal about the mind*. Chicago & London: University of Chicago Press.
Lakoff, George and Mark Johnson. 2003 [1980]. *Metaphors we live by*. Chicago & London: The University of Chicago Press.
Lakoff, George and Mark Johnson. 1999. *Philosophy in the flesh. The embodied mind and its challenge to Western thought*. New York: Basic Books.
Langacker, Ronald. 1987. *Foundations of Cognitive Grammar*. Vol. 1: *Theoretical prerequisites*. Stanford: Stanford University Press.
Langacker, Ronald. 1988. "A view of linguistic semantics". In: Brygida Rudzka-Ostyn (ed.), *Topics in cognitive linguistics*, 49–90. Amsterdam & Philadelphia: John Benjamins.
Langacker, Ronald. 1990. *Concept, image, and symbol: the cognitive basis of grammar*. Berlin & New York: Mouton de Gruyter.
Langacker, Ronald. 1991. *Foundations of Cognitive Grammar*. Vol 2: *Descriptive application*. Stanford: Stanford University Press.
Langacker, Ronald. 2007. "Cognitive Grammar". In: Dirk Geeraerts and Hubert Cuyckens (eds.), *The Oxford handbook of Cognitive Linguistics*, 421–462. Oxford: Oxford University Press.
Laplace, Colette. 1994. *Théorie du langage et théorie de la traduction: les concepts – clefs de trois auteurs: Kade (Leipzig), Coseriu (Tübingen), Seleskovitch (Paris)*. Paris: Didier Érudition.
Lara Bermejo, Víctor. 2018. "Imperativos y cortesía en las lenguas romances de la Península Ibérica". *Bulletin of Hispanic studies* 95, 1–24.
Lauwers, Peter, Marie-Rose Simoni-Aurembou and Pierre Swiggers (eds.). 2002. *Géographie linguistique et biologie du langage: Autour de Jules Gilliéron*. Leuven, Paris & Dudley: Peeters.
Lebsanft, Franz. 2005. "Kommunikationsprinzipien, Texttraditionen, Geschichte". In: Angela Schrott and Harald Völker (eds.), *Historische Pragmatik und historische Varietätenlinguistik in den romanischen Sprachen*, 25–44. Göttingen: Universitätsverlag Göttingen.
Lebsanft, Franz. 2015. "Aktualität, Individualität und Geschichtlichkeit. Zur Diskussion um den theoretischen Status von Diskurstraditionen und Diskursgemeinschaften". In: Franz Lebsanft and Angela Schrott (eds.), *Diskurse, Texte, Traditionen. Methoden, Modelle und Fachkulturen in der Diskussion*, 97–113. Bonn: Bonn University Press.
Lebsanft, Franz and Angela Schrott. 2015. "Diskurse, Texte, Traditionen". In: Franz Lebsanft and Angela Schrott (eds.), *Diskurse, Texte, Traditionen. Modelle und Fachkulturen in der Diskussion*, 11–46. Bonn & Göttingen: Bonn University Press & Vandenhoeck & Ruprecht.

Leezenberg, Michiel. 2013. "From Cognitive Linguistics to social sciences: thirty years after *Metaphor we live by*". In Riccardo Fusaroli and Simone Morgagni (eds.), *Cognitive Semiotics. Conceptual Metaphor Theory: thirty years after*, 140–152. Berlin & Boston: Mouton de Gruyter.

Lehmann, Winfred P. 1967. *A reader in nineteenth century historical Indo-European linguistics*. Bloomington: Indiana University Press.

Leibniz, Gottfried Wilhelm. 1965 [1684]. "Meditationes de cognitione, veritate, et ideis". In: Carl Immanuel Gerhard (ed.), *Die philosophischen Schriften von Gottfried Wilhelm Leibniz*. Vol. 4, 422–426. Hildesheim: Olms.

Leibniz, Gottfried Wilhelm. 1990 [1765]. *Nouveaux essais sur l'entendement humain*. Edited by Jacques Brunschwig. Paris: Flammarion.

Leonetti, Manuel. 2004. "Por qué el imperfecto es anafórico". In: Luis García Fernández and Bruno Camus eds.), *El pretérito imperfecto*, 481–508. Madrid: Gredos.

Lévi-Strauss, Claude. 1963. *Structural anthropology*. Translated by Claire Jacobson and Brooke G. Schoepf. New York: Basic Books.

Lepore, Ernest and Barry C. Smith (eds). 2008. *The Oxford handbook of philosophy of language*. Oxford: Oxford University Press.

Lerot, Jacques. 1982. "Die verbregierten Präpositionen in Präpositionalobjekten". In: Werner Abraham (ed.), *Satzglieder im Deutschen: Vorschläge zur syntaktischen, semantischen und pragmatischen Fundierung*, 261–291. Tübingen: Narr.

Levin, Beth and Malka Rappaport Hovav. 2005. *Argument realization*. Cambridge: Cambridge University Press.

Levinson, Stephen C. 2000. *Presumptive meanings. The theory of Generalized Conversational Implicature*. Cambridge, MA: MIT Press.

Lieb, Hans-Heinrich. 2018. "Integrational Linguistics: The approach". Available online: https://www.integrational-linguistics.science/inteling/introAppr.

Locke, John. 1894 [1690]. *An Essay concerning Human Understanding*. Edited by Alexander Campbell Fraser. Oxford: University of Oxford Press.

Lope Blanch, Juan M. 1960. Review of E. Coseriu. 1958. *Sincronía, diacronía e historia. El problema del cambio lingüístico* (Montevideo). *Nueva revista de filología hispánica* 12, 397–402.

López Serena, Araceli. 2009. "Intuition, acceptability and grammaticality: a reply to Riemer". *Language Sciences* 31:5, 634–648.

López Serena, Araceli. 2012. "Lo universal y lo histórico en el saber expresivo: variación situacional vs. variación discursiva". *Analecta Malacitana*, Anejos 86, 261–281.

López Serena, Araceli. 2019. "La interrelación entre lingüística y filosofía en *Sincronía, diacronía e historia* de Eugenio Coseriu". *Onomázein. Revista de lingüística, filología y traducción de la Pontificia Universidad Católica de Chile* 45, 1–30.

López Serena, Araceli. In press. "La tradicionalidad discursiva como materia y las tradiciones discursivas como objeto de estudio". *Verba*.

Loureda Lamas, Óscar. 2005. "El texto según Coseriu". In: Jesús Martínez del Castillo (ed.), *Eugenio Coseriu in memoriam*, 101–122. Granada: Granada Lingüística.

Loureda Lamas, Óscar and Reinhard Meisterfeld. 2007. "Eugenio Coseriu y su legado científico". *Estudis romànics* 29, 269–277.

Lüdtke, Jens. 1978. *Prädikative Nominalisierungen mit Suffixen im Französischen, Katalanischen und Spanischen*. Tübingen: Niemeyer.

Lüdtke, Jens. 2005. *Romanische Wortbildung. Inhaltlich – diachronisch – synchronisch.* Tübingen: Stauffenburg.

Machado, Antonio. 1988. *Poesía y Prosa I-IV.* Ed. by Oreste Macrí. Madrid: Espasa Calpe.

Maldonado García, María Isabel. 2015. "Eugenio Coseriu y su contribución a la lingüística". *Eurasian Journal of Humanities* 1:1, 1–11.

Malkiel, Yakov. 1964. "Distinctive traits of Romance linguistics". In: Dell H. Hymes (ed.), *Language in culture and society: a reader in linguistics and anthropology*, 671–686. New York: Harper & Row.

Malkiel, Yakov. 1967. "Multiple versus simple causation in linguistic change". In: *To Honor Roman Jakobson*, vol. 2, 1228–1246. The Hague: Mouton.

Marchand, Hans. 1969. *The categories and types of present-day English word-formation. A synchronic-diachronic approach* (second, completely revised and enlarged edition). München: Beck.

Marr, David. 1982. *Vision.* San Francisco: W. H. Freeman and Company.

Martinet. André. 1946. "Au sujet des "*Fondements de la théorie linguistique de Louis Hjelmslev*"". *Bulletin de la société linguistique de Paris* 42, 19–42.

Martinet, André. 1948. "Où en est la phonologie?" *Lingua* 1, 43–58.

Martinet, André. 1954. "The unity of linguistics". *Word* 10, 121–125.

Martinet, André. 1955. *Économie des changements phonétiques. Traité de phonologie diachronique.* Berne: Francke.

Martinet, André. 1960. *Éléments de linguistique générale.* Paris: A. Colin.

Mauthner, Fritz. 1982 [1901–1902]. *Beiträge zu einer Kritik der Sprache.* 3 vols. New edition. Frankfurt am Main/Berlin/Wien: Ullstein.

Meillet, Antoine. 1921. *Linguistique historique et linguistique générale.* Paris: Honoré Champion.

Mendívil-Giró, José-Luis. 2006. "Languages and species: limits and scope of a venerable comparison". In: Joana Roselló and Jesús Martín (eds.), *The biolinguistics turn. Issues on language and biology*, 82–118. Barcelona: Promociones y Publicaciones Universitarias.

Milner, Jean-Claude. 2002. *Le périple structural. Figures et paradigmes.* Paris: Éditions du Seuil.

Møller, Kristen. 1949. "Contribution to the discussion concerning 'langue' and 'parole'". In: Louis Hjelmslev (ed.), *Recherches structurales: Interventions dans le débat glossématique* (*Travaux du Cercle linguistique de Copenhague* 5), 87–96. Copenhague: Nordisk sprog- og kulturforlag.

Morpurgo Davies, Anna and Giulio Ciro Lepschy. 2016. *History of linguistics.* Volume IV: *Nineteenth-century linguistics.* London: Routledge.

Müller, Cornelia. 2010. "The dynamics of metaphor: foregrounding and activating metaphoricity in conversational interaction". *Cognitive Semiotics* 10:6, 85–120.

Müller, Cornelia. 2017. "Walking metaphors: embodied cognition in multimodal discourse". In: Beate Hampe (ed.), *Metaphor: embodied cognition and discourse*, 297–317. Cambridge: Cambridge University Press.

Muller, Henry François. 1945. *L'époque mérovingienne: essai de synthèse de philologie et d'histoire.* New York: S. Vanni.

Munteanu, Cristinel. 2013a. "Influența lui R. G. Collingwood asupra lui Eugenio Coseriu". In: Ana Catană-Spenchiu and Ioana Repciuc (eds.), *Flores philologiae. Omagiu profesorului Eugen Munteanu la împlinirea vârstei de 60 de ani*, 442–460. Iași: Editura Universității.

Munteanu, Cristinel. 2013b. "On the real object of linguistics". *Energeia–Online-Zeitschrift für Sprachwissenschaft und Sprachphilosophie* 3, 43–56.

Munteanu, Cristinel and Rudolf Windisch. 2016. "Züge sui generis der rumänischen Komposita des Typs frz. *coupe-papier*". *Romanistisches Jahrbuch* 67, 67–102.

Nevala, Minna. 2010. "Politeness". In: Andreas H. Jucker and Irma Taavitsainen (eds.), *Historical pragmatics*. Berlin & New York: Mouton de Gruyter, 419–450.

OED = *Oxford English Dictionary*. Available at <www.oed.com>.

Oesterreicher, Wulf. 1988. "Sprechtätigkeit, Einzelsprache, Diskurs und vier Dimensionen der Sprachvarietät". In: Jörn Albrecht, Jens Lüdtke and Harald Thun (eds.), *Energeia und Ergon. Sprachliche Variation – Sprachgeschichte – Sprachtypologie. Studia in honorem Eugenio Coseriu*, Vol. II: *Das sprachtheoretische Denken Eugenio Coserius in der Diskussion (2)*, 355–386. Tübingen: Narr.

Oesterreicher, Wulf. 1997. "Zur Fundierung von Diskurstraditionen". In: Barbara Frank, Thomas Haye and Doris Tophinke (eds.), *Gattungen mittelalterlicher Schriftlichkeit*, 19–41. Tübingen: Narr.

Oesterreicher, Wulf. 2001. "Historizität – Sprachvariation, Sprachverschiedenheit, Sprachwandel". In: Martin Haspelmath, Ekkehard König, Wulf Oesterreicher and Wolfgang Raible (eds.), *Language typology and language universals/Sprachtypologie und sprachliche Universalien/La typologie des langues et les universaux linguistiques*. Vol. 2, 1554–1595. Berlin & New York: de Gruyter.

Oesterreicher, Wulf and Peter Koch. 2016. "30 Jahre 'Sprache der Nähe – Sprache der Distanz'. Zu Anfängen und Entwicklung von Konzepten im Feld von Mündlichkeit und Schriftlichkeit". In: Helmuth Feilke and Mathilde Hennig (eds.), *Zur Karriere von 'Nähe und Distanz'. Rezeption und Diskussion des Koch-Oesterreicher-Modells*, 11–72. Berlin & Boston: De Gruyter.

Ogden, Charles K. and Ivor A. Richards. 1923. *The meaning of meaning*. London: Routledge & Kegan Paul.

Pagliaro, Antonino. 1952. *Il linguaggio come conoscenza*. Roma: Ed. Studium.

Pagliaro, Antonino. 1993 [1930]. *Sommario di linguistica arioeuropea*. Palermo: Novecento.

Pareyson, Luigi. 1960 [1954]. *Estetica. Teoria della formatività*. Bologna: Zanichelli.

Paul, Hermann. 1888 [1886]. *Principles of the history of language*. Translated from the second edition of the original [1886] by Herbert A. Strong. London: Swan, Sonnenschein, Lowrey & Co.

Paul, Hermann. 1920 [1880]. *Prinzipien der Sprachgeschichte* (fifth edition). Tübingen: Niemeyer. [First edition: *Principien der Sprachgeschichte*.]

Peirce, Charles Sanders. 1931–1958. *Collected Papers I-VIII*. Edited by Charles Hartshorne, Paul Weiss and Arthur Burks. Cambridge, MA: Harvard University Press.

[Pérez Vidal, José] "J.P.V." 1959. Review of E. Coseriu. 1958. *Sincronía, diacronía e historia. El problema del cambio lingüístico* (Montevideo). *Revista de dialectología y tradiciones populares* 15, 184–185.

Pisani, Vittore. 1954. "August Schleicher und einige Richtungen der heutigen Sprachwissenschaft". *Lingua* 4, 337–368.

Porzig, Walter. 1950. *Das Wunder der Sprache*. Bern: Francke.

Pott, August Friedrich. 1876. *Ueber die Verschiedenheit des menschlichen Sprachbaues und ihren Einfluss auf die geistige Entwicklung des Menschengeschlechts, Von Wilhelm von Humboldt. Mit erläuternden Anmerkungen und Exkursen sowie als Einleitung Wilhelm von Humboldt und die Sprachwissenschaft von A.F. Pott*. Berlin: Calvary.

Prieto, Luis. 1975a. *Essai de linguistique et sémiologie générale*. Genève: Droz.

Prieto, Luis. 1975b. *Pertinence et pratique*. Paris: Minuit.

Primus, Beatrice. 1999. *Cases and thematic roles: ergative, accusative and active*. Berlin & New York: De Gruyter.

Pustejovsky, James. 2001. "Type construction and the logic of concepts". In: Federica Busa and Pierrette Bouillon (eds.), *The language of word meaning*, 91–123. Cambridge: Cambridge University Press.

Raible, Wolfgang. 2019. "Variation in language: how to characterise types of texts and communication strategies between orality and scripturality. Answers given by Koch and Oesterreicher and by Biber". *International Journal of Language and Linguistics* 6, 157–174.

Ralph, Bo. 1984. *Svenskans grundläggande prepositioner*. Göteborg: Göteborgs universitet.

Rapoport, Tova. 2014. "Central coincidence: the preposition *with*". *Faits de Langues* 44:2, 159–173.

Rasmussen, Michael. 1992. *Hjelmslevs sprogteori*. Odense: Odense Universitetsforlag.

Rasulić, Katarina. 2017. "A metaphor biangle: Raymond W. Gibbs and Gerald Steen". *Metaphor and the Social World* 7:1, 130–151.

Reichenbach, Hans. 1947. *Elements of symbolic logic*. New York: Macmillan

Riemer, Nick. 2005. *The semantics of polysemy: reading meaning in English and Warlpiri*. Berlin: Mouton de Gruyter.

Roca-Pons ("Roca i Pons"), Josep. 1959. Review of E. Coseriu. 1958. *Sincronía, diacronía e historia. El problema del cambio lingüístico* (Montevideo). *Estudis Romànics* 6, 171–172.

Rohlfs, Gerhard. 1922. "Das romanische *habeo*-Futurum und Konditionalis". *Archivum Romanicum* 6, 105–154.

Rostila, Jouni. 2005. "Zur Grammatikalisierung bei Präpositionalobjekten". In: Torsten Leuschner, Tanja Mortelmans and Sarah de Groodt (eds.), *Grammatikalisierung im Deutschen*, 135–168. Berlin & New York: De Gruyter.

Rostila, Jouni. 2007. *Konstruktionsansätze zur Argumentmarkierung im Deutschen*. Tampere: Tampere University Press.

Rostila, Jouni. 2018. "Argument structure constructions among german prepositional objects". In: Hans C. Boas and Alexander Ziem (eds.), *Constructional approaches to argument structure in German*, 406–446. Berlin & Boston: De Gruyter.

Rumelhart, David and James McClelland. 1986. *Parallel Distributed Processing: explorations in the microstructure of cognition*. London: MIT Press.

Ruwet, Nicolas. 1991. "À propos de la grammaire générative. Quelques considérations intempestives". *Histoire Épistémologie Langage* 13:1, 109–132.

Sánchez de Zavala, Victor. 1982. *Funcionalismo estructural y generativismo*. Madrid: Alianza.

Sandmann, Manfred. 1960. Review of E. Coseriu. 1958. *Sincronía, diacronía e historia. El problema del cambio lingüístico* (Montevideo). *Zeitschrift für romanische Philologie* 76, 138–141.

Sandra, Dominiek. 1998. "What linguists can and can't tell you about the human mind: A reply to Croft". *Cognitive Linguistics* 9:4, 361–378.

Sartre, Jean-Paul. 1966. "'Jean-Paul Sartre répond'. Interview avec Bernard Pingaud". *L'Arc* 30, 87–96.
Saussure, Ferdinand de. 1945 [1916]. *Curso de lingüística general*. [Spanish translation by Amado Alonso]. Buenos Aires: Losada. [Reedition: Oviedo: Losada, 2002]
Saussure, Ferdinand de. 1959 [1916]. *Course in general linguistics*. Translated by Wade Baskin. New York: Philosophical Library.
Saussure, Ferdinand de. 1968 [1916]. *Cours de linguistique générale*. Édition critique par Rudolf Engler. Wiesbaden: Harrassowitz.
Saussure, Ferdinand de. 1975 [1916]. *Cours de linguistique générale*. Edited by Tullio De Mauro. Paris: Payot.
Saussure, Ferdinand de. 1997. *Linguistik und Semiologie: Notizen aus dem Nachlass, Texte, Briefe und Dokumente*. Edited by Johannes Fehr. Frankfurt a.M.: Suhrkamp.
Saussure, Ferdinand de. 2002. *Écrits de linguistique générale*. Texte établi par Simon Bouquet et Rudolf Engler. Paris: Éditions Gallimard.
Saussure, Ferdinand de. 2003. *Wissenschaft der Sprache: Neue Texte aus dem Nachlass*. Suhrkamp. Frankfurt a.M.: Suhrkamp.
Saussure, Ferdinand de. 2006. *Writings in General Linguistics*. English translation of Saussure (2002) by Carol Sanders and Matthew Pires. Oxford: Oxford University Press.
Saussure, Ferdinand de. 2011 [1916]. *Course in general linguistics*. Translated by Wade Baskin. New York: Columbia University Press.
Saussure, Louis de. 1998. "L'approche référentielle: de Beauzée à Reichenbach". In: Jacques Moeschler (ed.), *Le temps des événements. Pragmatique de la référence temporelle*, 19–44. Paris: Kimé.
Saussure, Louis de. 2003. "Valeur et signification ad hoc". *Cahiers Ferdinand de Saussure* 56, 289–310.
Schleicher, August. 1869. *Darwinism tested by the science of language*. Translated by Alex V. W. Bikkers. London: John Camden Hotten.
Schleicher, August. 1977 [1863]. "Die Darwinsche Theorie und die Sprachwissenschaft". In: Hans Helmut Christmann (ed.), *Sprachwissenschaft des 19. Jahrhunderts*, 85–105. Darmstadt: Wissenschaftliche Buchgesellschaft.
Schlieben-Lange, Brigitte. 1971. *Okzitanische und katalanische Verbprobleme*. Tubingen: Niemeyer.
Schlieben-Lange, Brigitte. 1973. *Soziolinguistik. Eine Einführung*. Stuttgart: Kohlhammer.
Schlieben-Lange, Brigitte. 1979. *Linguistische Pragmatik*. Stuttgart: Kohlhammer.
Schlieben-Lange, Brigitte. 1983. *Traditionen des Sprechens. Elemente einer pragmatischen Sprachgeschichtsschreibung*. Stuttgart: Kohlhammer.
Schlieben-Lange, Brigitte. 1990. "Normen des Sprechens, der Sprache und der Texte". In: Werner Bahner, Joachim Schildt and Dieter Viehweger (eds.), *Proceedings of the Fourteenth International Congress of Linguists, Berlin, GDR, August 10 – August 15, 1987*. Vol. I, 114–124. Berlin: Akademie-Verlag.
Schlieben-Lange, Brigitte and Harald Weydt [mit Beiträgen von Eugenio Coseriu und Hans-Ulrich Gumbrecht]. 1979. "Streitgespräch zur Historizität von Sprechakten". *Linguistische Berichte* 60, 65–78.
Schrott, Angela. 2014. "Sprachwissenschaft als Kulturwissenschaft aus romanistischer Sicht: Das Beispiel der kontrastiven Pragmatik". *Romanische Forschungen* 126, 3–44.

Schrott, Angela. 2015. "Kategorien diskurstraditionellen Wissens als Grundlage einer kulturbezogenen Sprachwissenschaft". In: Franz Lebsanft and Angela Schrott (eds.), *Diskurse, Texte, Traditionen. Modelle und Fachkulturen in der Diskussion*, 115–146. Bonn/Göttingen: Bonn University Press/Vandenhoeck & Ruprecht.

Schrott, Angela. 2016. "Dunkle Rede, helle Köpfe: Historische Dialogforschung in der Romanistik". In: Elmar Eggert and Jörg Kilian (eds.), *Historische Mündlichkeit. Beiträge zur Geschichte der gesprochenen Sprache*, 77–100. Frankfurt am Main: Peter Lang.

Schrott, Angela. 2017a. "Las tradiciones discursivas, la pragmalingüística y la lingüística del discurso". *Revista de la Academia Nacional de Letras* 10, 25–57

Schrott, Angela. 2017b. "Cortesía verbal y competencia lingüística: la petición cortés como tradición discursiva". *Normas: revista de estudios lingüísticos hispánicos* 7, 188–203.

Schrott, Angela. 2020. "Regeln, Traditionen, Urteile: Verbale Höflichkeit und wie sie gelingt". In: Angela Schrott and Christoph Strosetzki (eds.), *Gelungene Gespräche. Literatur, Sprache, Gesellschaft*, 23–54. Berlin & New York: De Gruyter.

Searle, John R. 1969. *Speech acts. An essay in the philosophy of language.* Cambridge: Cambridge University Press.

Searle, John R. 1983. *Intentionality: an essay in the Philosophy of Mind.* Cambridge: Cambridge University Press.

Searle, John R. 1992. *The rediscovery of the mind.* Cambridge, Mass.: MIT Press.

Searle, John R. 1997. *The mystery of consciousness.* London: Granta Books.

Sechehaye, Albert. 1940. "Les trois linguistiques saussuriennes". *Vox Romanica* 5, 1–48.

Shamsan, Muayad. 2018. "Theta roles assigned to subject argument in Arabic and English passive voice". *International Journal of Applied Linguistics and English Literature* 7:7, 47–51.

Shen, Yeshayahu and Roy Porat. 2017. "Metaphorical directionality: the role of language". In: Beate Hampe (ed.), *Metaphor: embodied cognition and discourse*, 62–81. Cambridge: Cambridge University Press.

Siebold, Kathrin. 2008. *Actos de habla y cortesía verbal en español y en alemán. Estudio pragmalingüístico e intercultural.* Frankfurt am Main: Peter Lang.

Smith, Carlota. 1991. *The parameter of aspect.* Dordrecht: Kluwer.

Snell-Hornby, Mary. 1988. *Translation studies. An integrated approach.* Amsterdam & Philadelphia: John Benjamins.

Söll, Ludwig. 1985. *Gesprochenes und geschriebenes Französisch* (third edition). Berlin: Schmidt.

Sokolowski, Robert. 2000. *Introduction to phenomenology.* New York: Cambridge University Press.

Sonesson, Göran. 1978. *Tecken och handling.* Lund: Doxa.

Sonesson, Göran. 1981. "A plea for integral linguistics". In: *Papers from the 5th Scandinavian Conference of Linguistics*, II, 151–166. Stockholm: Almqvist & Wiksell.

Sonesson, Göran. 1989. *Pictorial concepts. Inquiries into the semiotic heritage and its relevance for the analysis of the visual world.* Lund: Aris/Lund University Press.

Sonesson, Göran. 2006. "The meaning of meaning in biology and cognitive science. A semiotic reconstruction". *Sign Systems Studies* 34:1, 135–214.

Sonesson, Göran. 2007. "From the meaning of embodiment to the embodiment of meaning". In: Tom Ziemke, Jordan Zlatev and Roslyn M. Frank (eds.), *Body, language and mind.* Vol 1: *Embodiment*, 85–128. Berlin & New York: Mouton De Gruyter.

Sonesson, Göran. 2009. "The view from Husserl's lectern. Considerations on the role of phenomenology in Cognitive Semiotics". *Cybernetics and Human Knowing* 16:3/4, 107–148.
Sonesson, Göran. 2010. "Semiosis and the elusive final interpretant of understanding" *Semiotica* 179:1/4, 145–258.
Sonesson, Göran. 2012. "Semiotics inside-out and/or outside-in: How to understand everything and (with luck) influence people". *Signata* 2, 315–348.
Sonesson, Göran 2013. "The natural history of branching: approaches to the phenomenology of Firstness, Secondness, and Thirdness". *Signs and Society* 1:2, 297–326.
Sonesson, Göran. 2015. "Bats out of the belfry: the nature of metaphor, with special attention to pictorial metaphors". *Signs and Media* 11, 74–104.
Sonesson, Göran. 2016. "Epistemological prolegomena to the Cognitive Semiotics of evolution and development". *Language and Semiotic Studies* 2:4, 46–99.
Sonesson, Göran. 2018. "Beyond the 'tragedy of culture'. In-between epistemology and communication". *The American Journal of Semiotics* 33:3/4, 141–180.
Sonesson, Göran. 2019a. "The Psammetichus Syndrome and beyond: five experimental approaches to meaning-making". *The American Journal of Semiotics* 35:1/2, 11–32.
Sonesson, Göran. 2019b. "Two models of metaphoricity and three dilemmas of metaphor research". *Cognitive Semiotics* 12:1, 1–17.
Sonesson, Göran. To appear. "Nothing human is alien to me – except some of it. From Integral Linguistics to Cognitive Semiotics by way of phenomenology". *Zeitschrift für Semiotik*.
Squartini, Mario. 1998. *Verbal periphrases in Romance. Aspect, actionality and grammaticalization.* Berlin & New York: Mouton de Gruyter.
Staib, Bruno. 1988. *Generische Komposita. Funktionelle Untersuchungen zum Französischen und Spanischen.* Tübingen: Niemeyer.
Stampoulidis, George, Maria Bolognesi and Jordan Zlatev. 2019. "A cognitive semiotic exploration of metaphors in Greek street art". *Cognitive semiotics*, 12:1. DOI: https://doi.org/10.1515/cogsem-2019–2008.
Starosta, Stanley. 1978. "The one per sent solution". In: Werner Abraham (ed.), *Valence, semantic case, and grammatical relations*, 439–576. Amsterdam: Benjamins.
Starosta, Stanley. 1988. *The case for lexicase: an outline of lexicase grammatical theory.* London & New York: Pinter.
Steedman, Mark. 1997. "Temporality". In: Johann van Benthem and Alice ter Meulen (eds.), *Handbook of logic and language*, 895–939. London: Elsevier.
Stefanowitsch, Anatol. 2011. "Cognitive Linguistics as cognitive science". In: Marcus Callies, Wolfram Keller and Astrid Lohöfer (eds.), *Bi-directionality in the cognitive sciences*, 295–310. Amsterdam & Philadelphia: John Benjamins.
Steinthal, Heymann. 2013. *Ermeneutica e psicologia del linguaggio.* A cura di Davide Bondì. Milano: Bompiani.
Stevick, Robert. 1963. "The biological model and historical linguistics". *Language* 39:2, 159–169.
Stockwell, Peter. 1999. "The inflexibility of invariance". *Language and literature* 8:2, 125–142.

Stolz, Thomas, Cornelia Stroh and Aina Urdze. 2006. *On comitatives and related categories: a typological study with special focus on the languages of Europe*. Berlin: Mouton de Gruyter.
Stolz, Thomas, Cornelia Stroh and Aina Urdze. 2013. "Comitatives and instrumentals". In: Matthew S. Dryer and Martin Haspelmath (eds.), *The World Atlas of Language Structures Online*. Leipzig: Max Planck Institute for Evolutionary Anthropology. Available online at <http://wals.info/chapter/52>.
Strunk, Klaus. 1991. *Zum Postulat "vorhersagbaren" Sprachwandels bei unregelmäßigen oder komplexen Flexionsparadigmen*. München: C.H. Beck.
Subbiondo, Joseph. 2017. "The history of linguistics matters: linguistic relativity and integral linguistics". *US-China Foreign Language* 15:4, 215–221.
Susov, Ivan P. 1973. *Semantičeskaja struktura predloženija: Na materiale prostogo predloženija v sovremennom nemeckom jazyke*. Leningrad.
Swiggers, Pierre. 1988. "Le problème du changement linguistique dans l'oeuvre d'Antoine Meillet". *Histoire, Épistémologie, Langage* 10:2 (= *Antoine Meillet et la linguistique de son temps*), 155–166.
Swiggers, Pierre. 1999. "La géographie linguistique de Jules Gilliéron: Aux racines du changement linguistique". *Cahiers Ferdinand de Saussure* 51, 113–132.
Swiggers, Pierre. 2005. "Formes, fonctions at catégories linguistiques: les *Principes de grammaire générale* de Louis Hjelmslev". *Linguistica* 45:1, 41–52.
Swiggers, Pierre. 2013. "*Aspectos* del desarrollo de la lingüística histórica en los siglos XIX y XX". In: Ricardo Gómez, Joaquín Gorrochategui, Joseba A. Lakarra and Céline Mounole (eds.), *Koldo Mitxelena Katedraren III. Biltzarra / III Congreso de la Cátedra Luis Michelena / 3rd Conference of the Luis Michelena Chair*, 467–509. Vitoria-Gasteiz: Servicio Editorial de la Universidad del País Vasco/Euskal Herriko Unibertsitateko Argitalpen Zerbitzua.
Swiggers, Pierre. 2019. "Louis Gauchat: la voie vers une conception dynamique du changement linguistique". In: Antonio Briz, María José Martínez Alcalde, Nieves Mendizábal, Mara Fuertes Gutiérrez, José Luis Blas and Margarita Porcar (eds.), *Estudios lingüísticos en homenaje a Emilio Ridruejo*, 1353–1364. Valencia: Publicacions de la Universitat de València.
Swiggers, Pierre and Herman Seldeslachts. In prep. "Hat die Sprache ein von den sprechenden Subjekten unabhängiges Dasein? Eine Karte von F. B. Finck an A. Meillet".
Tămâianu, Emma. 2001. *Fundamentele tipologiei textuale. O abordare în lumina lingvisticii integrale*. Cluj-Napoca: Clusium.
Taavitsainen, Irma and Andreas H. Jucker. 2008. "Speech acts now and then: Towards a pragmatic history of English". In: Andreas H. Jucker and Irma Taavitsainen (eds.), *Speech acts in the history of English*, 1–23. Amsterdam & Philadelphia: John Benjamins.
Taavitsainen, Irma and Andreas H. Jucker. 2010. "Trends and developments in historical pragmatics". In: Andreas H. Jucker and Irma Taavitsainen (eds.), *Historical pragmatics*, 3–30. Berlin & New York: Mouton de Gruyter.
Talmy, Leonard. 2000. *Toward a cognitive semantics*. 2 vols. Cambridge, Mass.: MIT Press.
Taylor, John R. 1999. "Cognitive semantics and structural semantics". In: Andreas Blank and Peter Koch (eds.), *Historical semantics and cognition*, 17–48. Berlin & New York: Mouton de Gruyter.
Taylor, John R. 2002. *Cognitive Grammar*. Oxford: Oxford University Press.

Taylor, John R. 2006. "Polysemy and the lexicon". In: Gitte Kristiansen, Michel Achard, René Dirven and Francisco J. Ruiz de Mendoza Ibañez (eds.), *Cognitive linguistics: current applications and future perspectives*, 51–80. Berlin & New York: Mouton de Gruyter.
Taylor, John R. 2012. *The mental corpus: how language is represented in the mind*. Oxford: Oxford University Press.
Taylor, John R. 2017. "Lexical semantics". In: Barbara Dancygier (ed.), *The Cambridge Handbook of Cognitive Linguistics*, 246–261. Cambridge: Cambridge University Press.
Terracini, Benvenuto. 1966. *Analisi stilistica. Teoria, storia, problemi*. Milano: Feltrinelli.
Terracini, Benvenuto. 1957. *Conflitti di lingue e di cultura*. Venice: Neri Pozza.
Thomason, Richmond. 1984. "Combinations of Tense and Modality". In: Dov Gabbay and Franz Guenthner (eds.), *The handbook of philosophical logic*. Vol. 2, 135–165. Dordrecht: Reidel.
Thompson, Evan. 2007. *Mind in life: biology, phenomenology and the sciences of mind*. Cambridge, MA: Harvard University Press.
Thun, Harald. 1978. *Probleme der Phraseologie. Untersuchungen zur wiederholten Rede mit Beispielen aus dem Französischen, Italienischen, Spanischen und Rumänischen*. Tübingen: Niemeyer.
Togeby, Knud. 1960. Review of E. Coseriu. 1958. *Sincronía, diacronía e historia. El problema del cambio lingüístico* (Montevideo). *Romance Philology* 14, 159–162.
Toolan, Michael. 1996. *Total speech. An integrational linguistic approach to language*. Durham & London: Duke University Press.
Tort, Patrick. 1979. "L'Histoire naturelle des langues. De Darwin à Schleicher". *Romantisme* 25–26, 123–156.
Trabant, Jürgen. 1987. "Louis Hjelmslev: Glossematics as General Semiotics". In: Martin Krampen, Klaus Oehler, Roland Posner, Thomas A. Sebeok and Thomas von Uexküll (eds.), *Classics of semiotics*, 89–108. New York & London: Plenum.
Trabant, Jürgen. 1992. "Du travail de l'esprit a la danse de la coordination". *Histoire Épistémologie Langage* 14:2, 231–244.
Trabant, Jürgen. 2003. *Mithridates im Paradies. Kleine Geschichte des Sprachdenkens*. München: Beck.
Trabant, Jürgen. 2015 [2003]. "Vor-Bemerkungen, dreißig Jahre danach". In: Eugenio Coseriu. 2015. *Geschichte der Sprachphilosophie*. Vol. 1: *Von Heraklit bis Rousseau*. Edited by Jörn Albrecht, XVII-XXV. Tübingen: Narr & Francke: Attempto.
Trabant, Jürgen. 2018. "Über Humboldts Trias von Zeichen, Wort und Bild". In: *In memoriam Josef Simon. Alma Mater. Beiträge zur Geschichte der Universität Bonn*. 110. Bonn: Bouvier, 36–54.
Trosborg, Anna. 2010. "Introduction". In: Anna Trosborg (ed.): *Pragmatics across languages and cultures*, 1–39. Berlin & New York: Mouton de Gruyter.
Trubetzkoy, Nikolaj S. 1958 [1939]. *Grundzüge der Phonologie*. Göttingen: Vandenhoeck & Ruprecht.
Tuggy, David. 2003. "The Nawatl verb *kīsa*: a case study in polysemy". In: Hubert Cuyckens, René Dirven and John R. Taylor (eds.), *Cognitive approaches to lexical semantics*, 323–362. Berlin & New York: Mouton de Gruyter.
Turner, Mark. 1996. *The literary mind. The origins of thought and language*. Oxford: Oxford University Press.

Tyler, Andrea and Vyvyan Evans. 2003. *The semantics of English prepositions: spatial scenes, embodied meaning, and cognition*. Cambridge: Cambridge University Press.

Urban, Wilbur Marshall. 1939. *Language and Reality*. London: Macmillan.

Van der Gucht, Fieke. 2005. *Het "polysemie-monosemie"-debat: contrastieve analyse van de cognitieve en de structureel-functionele semantiek*. PhD Ghent University.

Van der Gucht, Fieke, Klaas Willems and Ludovic De Cuypere. 2007. "The iconicity of embodied meaning. Polysemy of spatial prepositions in the cognitive framework". *Language Sciences* 29, 733–754.

Van de Walle, Jürgen, Klaas Willems and Dominique Willems. 2006. "Structuralism". In: Jan-Ola Östman and Jef Verschueren (eds.), *Handbook of pragmatics*, 1–36. Amsterdam & Philadelphia: John Benjamins.

van Mulken, Margot. 1996. "Politeness markers in French and Dutch requests". *Language Sciences* 18, 698–702.

Van Valin, Robert D. 2007. *Exploring the syntax-semantics interface*. Cambridge: Cambridge University Press.

Verschueren, Jef. 1995. "The pragmatic perspective". In: Jef Verschueren (ed.), *Handbook of pragmatics*, 1–19. Amsterdam & Philadelphia: John Benjamins.

Verschueren, Jef. 2009. "Introduction: The pragmatic perspective". In: Jef Verschueren and Jan-Ola Östman (eds.), *Key notions for pragmatics*, 1–27. Amsterdam & Philadelphia: John Benjamins.

Vico, Giambattista. 1971 [1744]. *Princìpi di scienza nuova d'intorno alla comune natura delle nazioni, in questa terza impressione dal medesimo autore in un gran numero di luoghi corretta, schiarita, e notabilmente accresciuta*. In: Paolo Cristofolini (ed.), *Giambattista Vico: Opere Filosofiche*, 377–702. Firenze: Sansoni.

Vico, Giambattista. 1988 [1710]. *On the most ancient wisdom of the Italians, unearthed from the origins of the Latin language*. Ithaca & London: Cornell University Press.

Vîlcu, Dina. 2014. "Pleading for 'Integral Linguistics'". In: Eugenia Bojoga, Oana Boc and Dumitru-Cornel Vîlcu (eds.), *Coseriu: Perspectives contemporaines*. Vol. 2, 165–173. Cluj: Presa Universitară Clujeană.

Vîrban, Floarea. 2020. "Language change *versus* language non-change: the peculiar issue of language identity". Paper presented at the Coseriu conference in Cádiz, Spain, January 2020.

Völker, Harald. 2009. "La linguistique variationelle et la perspective intralinguistique". *Revue de Linguistique Romane* 73, 27–76

Völker, Harald. 2013. "The diasystem and its role in generating meaning: Diachronic evidence from Old French". In: Deborah Artaega (ed.), *Research on Old French: the state of the art*, 187–204. Dordrecht: Springer.

Wang, William S. Y. 1969. "Competing changes as a cause of residue". *Language* 45, 9–25.

Wang, William S. Y. 1978. "The three scales of diachrony". In: Braj Kachru (ed.), *Linguistics in the seventies: directions and prospects*. Special issue of *Studies in the Linguistic Sciences* 8:2, 63–75.

Wartburg, Walther von. 1943. *Einführung in die Problematik und Methodik der Sprachwissenschaft*. Halle an der Saale: Niemeyer.

Weinreich, Uriel. 1954. "Is a structural dialectology possible?" *Word* 10, 388–400.

Weinreich, Uriel, William Labov and Marvin I. Herzog. 1968. "Empirical foundations for a theory of language change". In: Winfred P. Lehmann and Yakov Malkiel (eds.), *Directions*

for historical linguistics. A symposium, 97–195. Austin & London: University of Texas Press.
Welke, Klaus. 1988. *Einführung in die Valenz- und Kasustheorie*. Leipzig: Bibliographisches Institut.
Welke, Klaus. 2002. *Deutsche Syntax funktional: Perspektiviertheit syntaktischer Strukturen*. Tübingen: Stauffenburg.
Welke, Klaus. 2011. *Valenzgrammatik des Deutschen. Eine Einführung*. Berlin & New York: De Gruyter.
Welke, Klaus. 2019. *Konstruktionsgrammatik des Deutschen: Ein sprachgebrauchsbezogener Ansatz*. Berlin & Boston: De Gruyter.
Widoff, Andreas. 2018. *Hermeneutik och grammatik: Fenomenologiska undersökningar av språket som tal och teknik*. [Hermeneutics and grammar: Phenomenological investigations into language as speech and technique]. Lund: Lunds universitet.
Wierzbicka, Anna. 1980. *Lingua mentalis: the semantics of natural language*. Sydney: Academic Press.
Wierzbicka, Anna. 1985. "Different cultures, different languages, different speech acts". *Journal of Pragmatics* 9, 145–178.
Wierzbicka, Anna. 2003. *Cross-cultural pragmatics. The semantics of human interaction* (second edition). Berlin & New York: De Gruyter.
Wierzbicka, Anna. 2010. "Cultural Scripts and international communication". In: Anna Trosborg (ed.), *Pragmatics across languages and cultures*, 43–78. Berlin & New York: Mouton de Gruyter.
Willems, Klaas. 1994a. *Sprache, Sprachreflexion und Erkenntniskritik*. Tübingen: Narr.
Willems, Klaas. 1994b. "Das Unbestimmtheitsprinzip und die Grundformen der Komposition". *Wirkendes Wort* 44, 349–364.
Willems, Klaas. 1996. *Eigenname und Bedeutung. Ein Beitrag zur Theorie des 'nomen proprium'*. Heidelberg: Universitätsverlag C. Winter.
Willems, Klaas. 1997. *Kasus, grammatische Bedeutung und kognitive Linguistik. Ein Beitrag zur allgemeinen Sprachwissenschaft*. Tübingen: Narr.
Willems, Klaas. 2003. "Eugenio Coseriu (1921–2002). Versuch einer Würdigung". *Leuvense Bijdragen* 92, 1–25.
Willems, Klaas. 2011. "Meaning and interpretation: the semiotic similarities and differences between cognitive grammar and European structural linguistics". *Semiotica* 185:1, 1–50.
Willems, Klaas. 2013. "The linguistic sign at the lexicon-syntax interface: assumptions and implications of the Generative Lexicon Theory". *Semiotica* 193, 233–287.
Willems, Klaas. 2016. "The universality of categories and meaning: a Coserian perspective". *Acta Linguistica Hafniensia* 48:1, 110–133.
Willems, Klaas. 2019. "Eugenio Coserius Sprachzeichentheorie und der Prager Strukturalismus". In: Tomáš Hoskovec (ed.), *Travaux du Cercle linguistique de Prague. Nouvelle Série* 8 (*Expérience et avenir du structuralisme*), 469–503. Kanina: OPS & Praha: PLK.
Willems, Klaas. 2020. "Form, meaning, and reference in natural language: a phenomenological account of proper names". *Diacronia* 11, 1–20.
Winter, Bodo and Teenie Matlock. 2017. "Primary metaphors are both cultural and embodied". In: Beate Hampe (ed.), *Metaphor: embodied cognition and discourse*, 99–116. Cambridge: Cambridge University Press.

Wittgenstein, Ludwig. 1963 [1921]. *Tractatus logico-philosophicus*. Frankfurt am Main: Suhrkamp.
Wittgenstein, Ludwig. 1971 [1953]. *Philosophische Untersuchungen*. Frankfurt am Main: Suhrkamp.
Wulf, Andrea. 2015. *The invention of nature. Alexander von Humboldt's new world*. New York: Alfred A. Knopf.
Zahavi, Dan. 2019. "Applied phenomenology: why it is safe to ignore the epoché?" *Continental Philosophy Review* (Online Publication).
Zlatev, Jordan. 2007a. "Spatial semantics". In: Dirk Geeraerts and Hubert Cuyckens (eds.), *Oxford handbook of Cognitive Linguistics*, 318–350. Oxford: Oxford University Press.
Zlatev, Jordan. 2007b. "Embodiment, language and mimesis". In: Tom Ziemke, Jordan Zlatev and Roslyn Frank (eds.), *Body, language and mind*. Vol 1: *Embodiment*, 297–337. Berlin & New York: Mouton de Gruyter.
Zlatev, Jordan. 2008. "The dependence of language on consciousness". *Journal of Consciousness Studies* 15:6, 34–62.
Zlatev, Jordan. 2010. "Phenomenology and Cognitive Linguistics". In: Shaun Gallagher and Dan Schmicking (eds.), *Handbook on phenomenology and cognitive science*, 415-446. Dordrecht: Springer.
Zlatev, Jordan. 2011. "From Cognitive to Integral Linguistics and back again". *Intellectica* 56, 125–147.
Zlatev, Jordan. 2012. "Cognitive Semiotics: An emerging field for the transdisciplinary study of meaning". *Public Journal of Semiotics* 4:1, 2–24.
Zlatev, Jordan. 2016. "Turning back to experience in Cognitive Linguistics via phenomenology". *Cognitive Linguistics* 27:4, 559–572.
Zlatev, Jordan and Johan Blomberg. 2019. "Norms of language: What kinds and where from? Insights from phenomenology". In: Aleksi Mäkilähde, Ville Leppänen and Esa Itkonen (eds.), *Norms and normativity in language and in linguistics*, 69–101. Amsterdam & Philadelphia: John Benjamins.
Zlatev, Jordan, Göran Jacobsson and Liina Paju. In press. Desiderata for metaphor theory, the 'Motivation and Sedimentation Model' and motion-emotion metaphoremes. In: Augusto Soares da Silva (ed.), *Figurative language. Intersubjectivity and usage*. Amsterdam & Philadelphia: John Benjamins.

Author Index

Adrados [Rodríguez Adrados], Francisco 182, 194
Ágel, Vilmos 264f., 269, 271, 273
Agha, Asif 22
Agud, Ana 4f., 10, 13f., 19–21, 24f., 63, 66, 72, 142, 162
Albrecht, Jörn 4–7, 15, 19, 21, 23f., 26f., 29, 41f., 48, 67, 146, 165f., 169–172, 240
Allwood, Jens 250
Alonso, Amado 183
Andersen, Henning 115, 117, 119, 127f.
Anttila, Raimo 169, 192
Archer, Dawn 220
Aristotle 1f., 8, 11, 17, 26, 49, 52–54, 75, 81–83, 85, 93, 139, 142, 158, 169, 183–187, 201f., 312, 319
Arlotto, Anthony 192
Arvidson, Sven 158
Aschenberg, Heidi 173, 175
Ascoli, Giorgio 314

Baker, Gordon 70
Bally, Charles 185, 246, 248
Bartsch, Renate 30
Bauer, Laurie 247
Bechtel, William 333, 335–337
Belligh, Thomas 6, 22, 36f., 42, 267, 327, 331
Benveniste, Émile 12, 51
Bergounioux, Gabriel 205
Bernardo, José Maria 140
Berthonneau, Anne-Marie 302
Bertinetto, Pier-Marco 307
Bertoldi, Vittorio 190
Bertsch, Hansbert 35, 171, 296
Biber, Douglas 229
Blomberg, Johan 339
Bloomfield, Leonard 22, 64, 140, 183
Boc, Oana 171, 313
Bojoga, Eugenia 147, 313
Bolognesi, Maria 314

Borcilă, Mircea 16, 20f., 36, 137, 143, 152, 313, 317, 319, 322f.
Bouquet, Simon 87
Brandt, Line 322
Brøndal, Viggo 166, 246
Brown, Penelope 217, 220
Brugmann, Karl 200
Brysbaert, Marc 333–335
Bühler, Karl 43, 246, 321
Bülow, Edeltraud 154f.
Bynon, Theodora 192, 204

Caamaño, Antonio Vilarnovo 143, 312
Caballero, Fermín 91
Caballero, Rosario 317
Cameron, Lynne 318, 320
Carabellese, Pantaleo 183, 189
Cartagena, Nelson 296, 306
Cassirer, Ernst 11, 52, 155, 183, 203, 312
Chomsky, Noam 13, 16, 22, 30, 51f., 57f., 65, 70, 86, 90, 138–142, 144, 157, 246, 271
Churchland, Paul 334, 336
Cigana, Lorenzo 4, 6, 19, 23, 115, 127, 129
Clark, Andy 333, 335–337
Coene, Ann 249
Collingwood, Robin George 11, 166f., 175
Condillac, Étienne Bonnot de 84–86
Condoravdi, Cleo 304
Coseriu, Eugenio 1–37, 39, 41–44, 47–59, 63–71, 73–77, 81–94, 115–131, 137–147, 151–162, 165–176, 181–194, 197–208, 211–218, 220–223, 227–230, 232–238, 240f., 245–252, 257, 261, 265–271, 275, 279–281, 284–286, 288f., 291f., 295–307, 311–314, 317, 319, 321–323, 327–331, 335, 340, 345
Croce, Benedetto 36, 52, 183
Croft, William 25
Cruz Volio, Gabriela 219
Culpeper, Jonathan 220

Cusimano, Christophe 128
Cuyckens, Hubert 328, 333

Damasio, Antonio 320
Darwin, Charles 26, 155, 200, 204 f.
De Backer, Maarten 115, 121 f., 128 f.
De Cuypere, Ludovic 249, 255
De Houwer, Jan 334 f.
De Mauro, Tullio 1, 10, 51 f.
Deignan, Alice 318, 320
Dennett, Daniel 333 f., 336
Devitt, Michael 12
Devoto, Giacomo 12
Devylder, Simon 314
Dewey, John 11, 143, 183, 320
Di Cesare, Donatella 143, 145 f.
Di Girolamo, Edoardo 125
Díaz Pérez, Francisco Javier 220 f.
Dietrich, Wolf 33–35, 249, 251, 279, 285, 296
Dowty, David 262 f., 270
Durkheim, Émile 120, 329
Dürscheid, Christa 231

Ehlers, Klaas-Hinrich 92 f.
Engelen, Bernhard 270, 273
Escandell-Vidal, María Victoria 211, 215
Estigarribia, Bruno 282
Evans, Vyvyan 250, 318
Ezawa, Kennosuke 18

Faur, Elena 35 f., 147, 152, 311, 314, 322 f.
Feilke, Helmuth 227
Feyerabend, Paul 170
Fillmore, Charles 32 f., 261 f., 264–267, 269–271
Finck, Franz Nikolaus 186
Fischer-Jørgensen, Eli 1, 11 f., 118
Fleischman, Suzanne 188
Fleischmann, Eberhard 266, 270
Flydal, Leiv 1, 4 f., 14, 19, 23, 28, 116, 118, 230, 246
Fodor, Jerry 333 f.
Forceville, Charles 317
Forster, Michael N. 47, 55, 59
Frank, Birgit 220

Frei, Henri 119
Funke, Otto 119

Gabelentz, Georg von der 18, 88 f., 205
Gallagher, Shaun 313
Gardiner, Alan 246
Gardt, Andreas 221
Gauchat, Louis 193
Gauger, Hans-Martin 228
Geckeler, Horst 6, 9 f., 42, 118 f., 121, 127, 266–268, 280
Geeraerts, Dirk 328, 332 f.
Gibbs, Raymond 36, 311, 318 f.
Gilliéron, Jules 193
Gilquin, Gaetan 340
Gipper, Helmut 21, 154–157
Goddard, Cliff 250
Goldberg, Adele 34, 264, 271
Goodman, Nelson 185
Grady, Joseph 313 f.
Grammont, Maurice 119
Grice, Herbert Paul 213, 216
Gries, Stefan 340
Gruber, Teresa 227
Grübl, Klaus 227
Guitarte, Guillermo 165
Gurwitsch, Aron 158

Hacker, Peter 70
Hampe, Beate 311, 314
Harizanov, Valentina 304
Harmon, David 205
Harris, Roy 21 f., 153–158
Hartmann, Nicolai 186
Haß, Ulrike 92
Haßler, Gerda 17 f., 81, 83, 90
Haug, Dag 252
Hegel, Georg Wilhelm Friedrich 2, 4 f., 11, 13, 16, 21, 34, 49 f., 52, 54, 64, 71, 76, 82, 123, 139, 142 f., 158, 183, 312, 330
Heidegger, Martin 13, 52, 55–58, 143, 183, 189, 319
Held, Gudrun 219
Hennig, Mathilde 227
Herzog, Marvin 189
Hjelmslev, Louis 1–14, 18–20, 22, 29, 42 f., 49, 57, 115–131, 156, 246

Hoenigswald, Henry 183
Höllein, Dagobert 32–34, 261, 264, 267–274
Humboldt, Wilhelm von 2, 4, 8, 11, 13, 15f., 18, 20, 22, 26, 47, 49–55, 64, 66, 68, 71, 81f., 85f., 91, 115f., 123, 131, 137, 139f., 142f., 145f., 154, 158, 168f., 171, 183, 201–206, 312, 319, 321, 330
Hundsnurscher, Franz 18
Husserl, Edmund 10f., 42, 139, 157, 159–161, 330, 338f.

Iatridou, Sabine 305
Ibarretxe-Antuñano, Iraide 317
Iglesias Recuero, Silvia 219f.
Itkonen, Esa 73, 192, 338f.

Jackendoff, Ray 333f., 337
Jacob, Daniel 233
Jacobsson, Göran 313f.
Jakobson, Roman 6, 14, 51, 154
James, William 320
Janda, Richard 192
Jeffers, Robert 192
Jensen, Thomas W. 314, 318f.
Jensen, Viggo B. 1, 3f., 9, 11f., 18f., 29, 115f., 118, 127, 131, 247
Jespersen, Otto 119, 246
Johnson, Mark 12, 36, 140, 144, 317, 319–323, 328, 332f., 336
Joseph, Brian D. 192
Joseph, John E. 2, 98, 151, 166, 206f.
Jucker, Andreas 219f.
Jung, Verena 219, 221
Jungemann, Frederick 182, 193

Kabatek, Johannes 3f., 7, 9f., 20, 23, 25, 27–30, 41, 55f., 63, 65f., 69f., 73f., 81, 137, 152f., 157, 159, 173, 175, 212, 214, 217, 223, 227, 233, 235f., 240, 328
Kant, Immanuel 6, 11, 67, 71, 139, 183
Katz, Jerrold 329
Kaufmann, Stefan 304
Keller, Rudi 25
Keniston, Hayward 301
Kerbrat-Orecchioni, Catherine 220
Kiefer, Ferenc 283

Kleiber, Georges 302
Koch, Peter 28f., 214, 227–238, 240f.
Koerner, Konrad 204f.
Kohnen, Thomas 220
Kuryłowicz, Jerzy 191

Labov, William 189, 191
Laca, Brenda 9, 35, 280, 295, 301, 307
Lakoff, George 12, 36, 140, 144, 250, 262, 313f., 317, 323, 328, 332f., 336
Langacker, Ronald 12, 250, 328, 332f., 336
Laplace, Colette 142
Lara Bermejo, Víctor 220
Lauwers, Peter 193
Lebsanft, Franz 213f., 237f.
Leezenberg, Michiel 317
Lehiste, Ilse 192
Lehmann, Winfred P. 200
Leibniz, Gottfried Wilhelm 11, 31, 52, 160, 167
Leonetti, Manuel 302
Lepore, Ernest 12
Lerot, Jacques 273
Lévi-Strauss, Claude 146, 154, 200
Levin, Beth 262, 266, 269
Levinson, Stephen 31, 217, 220
Lieb, Hans-Heinrich 21, 155–157
Locke, John 31, 52, 55, 58, 84
Lope Blanch, Juan M. 182
López Serena, Araceli 183, 227, 238
Loureda Lamas, Óscar 44, 152, 158, 238
Lüdtke, Jens 280, 283f.

Machado, Antonio 72
Maldonado García, María Isabel 152, 158
Malkiel, Yakov 187, 193
Marchand, Hans 281, 283, 287f.
Marr, David 333, 337
Martinet, André 109, 119, 182–183, 246
Marty, Anton 119, 183
Matlock, Teenie 317
Mauthner, Fritz 72f.
McClelland, James 333, 335–337
Meillet, Antoine 119, 183
Meisterfeld, Reinhard 152, 158
Mendívil-Giró, José-Luis 205

Merleau-Ponty, Maurice   183, 314, 319
Milică, Ioan   25f., 186, 197
Milner, Jean-Claude   166
Møller, Kristen   246
Morpurgo Davies, Anna   204
Müller, Cornelia   91, 318
Muller, Henry François   190
Munteanu, Cristinel   1, 166f., 291
Murguía, Adolfo   3, 10, 55f., 64–66, 69f., 73f., 81, 137, 152f., 157, 159, 175, 217, 235

Nevala, Minna   220

Oesterreicher, Wulf   4, 7, 28f., 214, 227–232, 235f., 240f.
Ogden, Charles K.   320
Osthoff, Hermann   200

Pagliaro, Antonino   1, 36, 52, 82, 169, 183, 319
Paju, Liina   313f.
Pareyson, Luigi   51
Paul, Hermann   5, 23, 64, 67, 70, 143, 165, 169, 193, 205
Peirce, Charles Sanders   158, 161
[Pérez Vidal, José] "JPV"   182
Pisani, Vittore   183, 204
Porat, Roy   315–317
Porzig, Walter   182
Pott, August Friedrich   82
Pottier, Bernard   106
Prieto, Luis   155f., 159–162
Primus, Beatrice   263
Pustejovsky, James   249

Raible, Wolfgang   228f.
Ralph, Bo   252
Rapoport, Tova   252
Rappaport Hovav, Malka   262, 266, 269
Rasmussen, Michael   4
Rastier, François   87
Rastle, Kathy   333–335
Rasulić, Katarina   319
Reichenbach, Hans   300
Richards, Ivor A.   320
Riemer, Nick   251

Roca-Pons, Josep   182
Rohlfs, Gerhard   188
Rostila, Jouni   273
Rumelhart, David   333f., 336f.
Ruwet, Nicolas   140

Sánchez de Zavala, Victor   145, 312
Sandmann, Manfred   182
Sandra, Dominiek   335f., 339
Sapir, Edward   13, 63, 119
Sartre, Jean-Paul   175f.
Saussure, Ferdinand de   1–5, 9–12, 14, 18, 22, 26, 42, 48–51, 54, 63, 66, 81, 83, 87–90, 93, 116, 123, 128, 142, 145f., 151, 157, 166, 169, 183f., 199f., 204, 206–208, 246, 267, 272, 300, 329
Saussure, Louis de   83, 300
Scharinger, Thomas   227
Schleicher, August   166, 200, 204–207
Schlieben-Lange, Brigitte   27, 181f., 214, 228f., 232, 234, 238, 296
Schmitter, Peter   154f.
Schrott, Angela   7, 21, 26–28, 211–214, 216, 219–222, 238
Searle, John R.   216, 330, 335
Sechehaye, Albert   123, 246
Seldeslachts, Herman   186
Shamsan, Muayad   271
Shen, Yeshayahu   315–317
Siebold, Kathrin   220f.
Simon, Josef   71
Simoni-Aurembou, Marie-Rose   193
Smith, Barry C.   12
Smith, Carlota   301
Snell-Hornby, Mary   31
Sokolowski, Robert   338f.
Söll, Ludwig   28, 229
Sonesson, Göran   6, 21f., 151, 156–162, 316f., 339
Squartini, Mario   306
Staib, Bruno   280, 290
Stalin, Joseph   200
Stampoulidis, George   314
Starosta, Stanley   262, 266, 271
Steedman, Mark   304
Stefanowitsch, Anatol   339
Steinthal, Heymann   205f.

Sterelny, Kim   12
Stevick, Robert   201
Stockwell, Peter   315–317
Stolz, Thomas   252
Strunk, Klaus   188
Subbiondo, Joseph   155, 157
Susov, Ivan P.   266, 268
Swiggers, Pierre   14, 19, 24 f., 41, 124, 181, 184, 186, 193, 198

Taavitsainen, Irma   219
Talmy, Leonard   328, 338 f.
Tămâianu, Emma   146
Taylor, John R.   12, 249 f., 328, 332 f., 336
Terracini, Benvenuto   51, 168
Thomason, Richmond   304
Thompson, Evan   335, 339
Thun, Harald   173
Togeby, Knud   182, 189, 198
Toolan, Michael   22
Tort, Patrick   205
Trabant, Jürgen   4 f., 12 f., 16, 20, 27, 41, 47, 53, 55, 115, 139, 142, 167, 201
Trosborg, Anna   221
Trubetzkoy, Nikolaj S.   29, 119, 246 f.
Tuggy, David   250
Turner, Mark   12
Tyler, Andrea   250

Urban, Wilbur Marshall   5, 11, 43

Van de Walle, Jürgen   128

Van der Gucht, Fieke   249, 328, 337
van Mulken, Margot   220
Van Valin, Robert D.   265
Vendryes, Joseph   183
Verjans, Thomas   193
Verschueren, Jef   211 f.
Vico, Giambattista   11, 36, 52, 54, 139, 159 f., 168, 183, 188, 312
Vîlcu, Cornel   313
Vîlcu, Dina   152
Vîrban, Floarea   67
Vogel, Annemete von   18
Völker, Harald   4, 115 f., 118

Wandruszka, Mario   228
Wang, William S. Y.   191
Wartburg, Walther von   184, 246
Weinreich, Uriel   10, 189, 230
Weinrich, Harald   240
Welke, Klaus   266, 268 f., 271
Weydt, Harald   27, 234
Whorf, Benjamin Lee   13
Widoff, Andreas   29, 31, 34, 245, 255, 331
Wierzbicka, Anna   221 f., 250
Willems, Klaas   1, 13 f., 29, 35, 42, 74, 119, 170, 249, 266 f., 328, 331, 338
Winter, Bodo   155, 317
Wittgenstein, Ludwig   13, 52 f., 55 f., 58
Wulf, Andrea   205

Zahavi, Dan   313
Zlatev, Jordan   313 f., 328, 335, 338 f.

Subject Index

actual/non-actual (tense)   35, 298–305
adaptation   208
adequacy   8
adoption   1, 18, 24f., 68, 120, 185, 191, 193, 250, 332
Agent (role)   32, 176, 262f., 265, 267, 271, 273, 288–290, 307, 335
alterity   13, 25, 50, 53, 56, 58f., 143, 175, 213, 319, 321
anthropology   4, 20, 44, 63, 154, 156, 319, 321
anti-logicism   12, 50
anti-positivism   6
apophantic   54, 56
appeal (G. *Appell*)   27, 43, 199
apprehensio simplex   34
appropriateness   249, 257
arbitrariness   17f., 83f., 92–94
architecture   1f., 4f., 9, 19, 23, 28, 116, 118, 130, 182, 230, 240
articulation (first ~, phonetic ~)   54, 127
aspect   35, 189, 279, 281, 295–307
aufheben ('sublate'), *Aufheben*, *Aufhebung* ('sublation') (Hegel)   4, 22, 49f., 116, 123
Auslegung   15

Bedeutung (signified, cf. meaning)   8f., 13, 27, 31f., 34, 42, 50, 52f., 58, 83, 143, 261, 266–269, 279, 281
Bezeichnung (designation)   8f., 31f., 34, 42, 44, 83, 261, 266–268, 279–281

Cartesian linguistics   16, 51, 86, 139
case   32–33, 261, 269–275
case grammar   32f.
categories (logical ~, ~ of language)   5, 13, 16, 33, 35, 50, 64, 74f., 77, 82f., 172, 184f., 211, 216, 218, 223, 240, 265, 279f., 287, 291, 295–300, 305–307, 311, 328, 333
causality   6, 117, 119, 187, 190, 193, 198, 206

cause   117, 174, 187, 189, 197, 248, 252f., 256, 336
causes (Aristotle)   6, 26, 68, 117, 120, 160, 168f., 187, 203
change (linguistic)   4, 9, 24–26, 49f., 56, 59, 66–68, 71, 75, 77, 92, 116–124, 127, 140–142, 146f., 158, 172, 181f., 184–193, 197f., 200, 202, 204, 206, 213, 215, 219–222, 263, 270, 284, 287, 301, 304, 306, 319
cognitio clara   160
cognitio obscura   160
Cognitive Linguistics   33, 36f., 140, 144, 312, 321, 327f., 332f., 338
cognitive psychology   12, 36, 327f., 331, 333, 337, 340
Cognitive Semiotics   22, 151, 156, 162, 338, 341
communicate   64, 171, 213, 318
communication   8, 13, 25, 27, 30, 43, 53, 58, 154f., 171, 183, 215f., 229, 239f., 314, 318, 320
community   1, 8, 13, 51, 67–72, 84f., 125, 157, 171, 191, 200, 217–219, 236
competence, linguistic (G. *Sprachkompetenz*)   7, 20f., 26–29, 57, 70, 138, 141, 144f., 211–214, 216, 227, 234, 236–238, 297, 331, 337
composition   33, 84, 280f., 288f., 291
– generic composition   280, 289–291
– lexical composition   288
compound   7, 33, 248, 280–282, 288–291
computation   333–335, 337
conceptual field (G. *Begriffsfeld*)   102–104
Conceptual Metaphor Theory   36, 311, 313
concomitance   31, 251–257
congruence   8f.
connotation   5, 19, 43, 115f., 124–126, 130f., 189f.
connotative semiotics   1, 4f., 14, 19
connotator   125f., 130f.
consciousness   5, 20, 25, 36f., 47, 68, 70f., 75f., 119, 128, 137, 158, 160f.,

165 f., 186, 191, 197, 206, 208, 312, 330–333, 335 f., 338 f.
construction   32, 34, 240, 248, 255, 264 f., 271, 273 f., 279, 289, 307, 327, 340
Construction Grammar   33 f., 240, 264, 271
contensive   129 f.
content   1–3, 5–10, 13 f., 19, 32, 42–44, 47, 50, 53, 59, 70, 82, 89, 125–127, 143–146, 153, 181, 186, 193, 237, 246, 251 f., 254, 266, 279, 316 f., 320–322, 340
contrastive pragmatics   219, 221 f.
cooperative principle   213, 216
copresence   31, 251
correctness   8 f., 82, 174, 235–237
creativity   7 f., 13, 25, 47, 54, 83, 86, 137, 143 f., 146, 155, 175 f., 186, 198, 202 f., 208, 234, 240, 314, 319, 321, 323
critical approach   71, 77
critical rationalism   10
cultural science   10, 15 f., 20–22, 36 f., 137–140, 154 f., 157, 159, 198, 331, 340
culture   6, 10 f., 15, 28, 64, 75, 137, 139, 147, 159, 169, 201, 206, 212 f., 215–218, 220, 222 f., 227, 238, 312, 314, 317, 329

definition of language   7
denotation   5, 59, 125, 261
denotative-semantic roles   264, 270, 273
derivation   33, 247, 280 f., 284, 286 f., 289
designation (cf. *Bezeichnung*)
determination   3, 49, 66, 90, 93, 126, 155, 168, 185, 220, 239, 269 f., 285, 288, 291, 322
development (G. *Entwicklung*)   5, 15–18, 23, 25 f., 33, 66, 93, 102–105, 139, 147, 184, 197, 203, 206–208, 222, 229, 280, 284–288, 300
deviance (semantic)   250, 256
diachrony   3 f., 9, 48–50, 76, 88 f., 116–118, 123, 168, 183, 185, 206 f., 233
diamesic   235
diaphasic   8 f., 23, 182, 230, 240
diastratic   1, 4 f., 8 f., 23, 182, 230
diasystem   4, 19, 23, 118, 172, 230
diatopic   1, 4 f., 8 f., 23, 182, 230
diminutive   33, 280–282, 285, 291

discourse tradition   26, 28 f., 212, 214–223, 227–229, 231–234, 236–240
distance (and immediacy)   8, 14, 28 f., 69, 76, 115, 129, 207, 227–231, 235 f., 239–241
distinctio and *disiunctio*   5
distinctive features   8 f., 160, 247
diversity (G. *Verschiedenheit*)   13, 50, 53, 57, 59, 221 f.
drift   119, 127 f., 208
dualism   53 f., 59, 320
dýnamis   8 f., 58, 143, 212, 215 f., 232, 239, 329 f.

elocutional knowledge   8 f., 141, 144, 172, 174, 212 f.
embodied   182, 318–320, 332
emotion   36, 231, 252 f., 320–323
enérgeia   4, 8 f., 13, 15, 42, 49, 51–53, 58, 71, 117, 140 f., 143, 212, 214 f., 219, 222 f., 232, 239 f., 314, 319, 321, 329
entorno ('setting', 'environment', G. *Umfeld*)   49, 51
epistemology   5 f., 14, 55, 70, 84 f., 139, 159, 339
érgon   8 f., 146, 212, 215, 219, 232, 239 f., 329
essence of language   12, 27, 47–52, 54, 56, 58 f., 143, 169, 172, 175, 186, 202
evocation   5, 43
evolution   2, 25 f., 116, 120, 124, 127, 129 f., 182, 186, 197, 199 f., 203–208
evolutionary   197, 200 f., 204–207, 319
exemplary norm   30, 174
Experiencer   265
explanandum/explanans   37, 334, 340
expression (G. *Kundgabe*)   43, 297, 321
expressive knowledge   8 f., 24, 29, 141, 144, 153, 172, 174, 212 f., 237
extension   58, 141, 237 f., 266, 275, 287

face   220–222, 303
figurative language   36
form (and substance)   18, 34, 49 f., 98–100, 104 f., 108, 116, 123 f., 127, 130, 246–248, 262–268, 279–281, 296–298, 338–341

formativity (G. *Formativität*)   13, 47, 50f., 57, 175
freedom   6, 12, 117, 119f., 187, 198, 205f., 220, 223
functional language   3–5, 9, 13, 23, 117f., 126, 172, 296

generalisation   191–193
Generative Grammar   16, 22, 31f., 65, 151, 156f., 239, 245, 279, 327
German   8, 13, 25, 29, 31f., 41f., 48, 57, 66, 85, 88f., 91–93, 153, 165, 167f., 171f., 174, 182–184, 204, 213, 217f., 228, 235, 237, 248, 251–255, 264, 268, 270, 273–275, 288, 296
Glossematics   1, 4, 13, 19, 49, 115, 124, 131, 183
grammar   8, 28, 33, 50, 57, 63f., 77, 91f., 131, 157, 173f., 191, 193, 201, 232f., 236, 239f., 268, 279f., 291, 327
grammaticalization   279, 305–307
grammatikähnlich   34

hermeneutic   3, 66, 74, 331f., 339
hermeneutics   14f., 73, 146, 160–162
historical   3f., 7–9, 12, 14–17, 19f., 23–29, 47–49, 51, 53, 55, 57–59, 63f., 66f., 70f., 74, 76, 81, 84, 87, 90, 93, 116f., 123, 138f., 141, 143, 145, 147, 165–173, 175f., 181f., 184–187, 189–193, 197f., 200, 202, 204–207, 211–214, 216f., 219–222, 227, 229, 232–241, 247, 281, 283, 295, 305, 314, 319
historical-comparative linguistics   24, 88, 165, 193
historical language   4f., 7, 9, 22f., 28, 34, 57f., 68, 118, 125, 155, 168, 172, 183, 192, 212
historical pragmatics   219f., 222, 234
historicity   13, 23f., 27, 47, 49f., 54–57, 59, 155, 175, 181, 184, 213, 227, 234–241
historiography   16f., 82, 88, 91f., 181
history   1–5, 10f., 13–19, 21–24, 26, 28, 41, 47–50, 52, 59, 64, 66f., 71, 73, 75, 77, 79, 82, 84, 88–93, 130, 138–140, 144, 165f., 168–173, 175f., 184–189, 192, 201, 205–208, 212, 218f., 221, 234–236, 305, 313
history of linguistics   17, 38, 65, 73, 81f., 86–88, 90f., 94, 115, 139, 142f., 146, 169
Humboldtian structuralism   4

iconicity   161
idealism   13, 68, 205
idea of language   47f.
idiomatic knowledge   8f., 27, 30, 144f., 153, 172, 174, 212f., 216, 237
idola fori   55, 58
imagery   12
image schema   36, 320, 322f., 333
imaginative ability (Hegel)   34
immediacy (and distance)   28f., 227–231, 235f., 239–241
inappropriate   9, 316
incongruence   8f.
incorrect   9, 174
individual   7–9, 12, 14f., 25–29, 35, 47, 49, 51, 53, 58, 66–69, 71–77, 119f., 126, 144f., 155, 167f., 171, 181, 185, 191, 203f., 207, 211–213, 215–222, 229, 232, 234–241, 251, 264, 280, 297, 314, 318f., 329
indivisibilium intelligentia   34
innovation   24f., 185, 191, 193, 204, 223, 240, 322f.
instrumental meaning/signified   31, 252
Instrument (role)   9, 12, 32, 52f., 56, 84, 160, 251–253, 261, 267, 271, 280, 286, 289
Integral Linguistics   1, 3–7, 11, 14, 19–22, 24f., 35–37, 69, 135, 137f., 141, 144, 146, 151–158, 162, 170, 172–174, 311, 313, 323, 327, 329
intentionality   25, 33, 68
intertextuality   24, 173, 233
introspection   335, 338f.
intuition   4, 15f., 34, 67, 70, 72, 128, 167, 198, 295–297, 301, 305, 311f., 338f.
intuitive knowledge   10, 15, 36, 144
invisible hand   25
'ipseity'   167

katà synthéken (Aristotle)   54
knowledge   4, 6, 8–10, 15, 28–30, 36, 52–54, 57, 64, 68–70, 73–75, 77, 85, 88, 117, 144 f., 151, 153, 159–161, 167, 170, 172, 175, 191, 197, 204, 212–217, 222 f., 227, 236 f., 250, 254, 257, 270, 280, 283, 286, 295, 297, 307, 319, 322, 327–331, 335–337

language history   5, 23 f., 66, 88, 165, 181, 190, 193, 201, 221
language use   24, 27 f., 36 f., 160, 173, 197, 202, 211, 218, 221 f., 249–251, 286, 312, 318 f., 321, 328–330, 333, 336 f., 339 f.
langue   2–4, 9–12, 22, 24, 29 f., 49, 51, 57 f., 88, 123 f., 141, 151, 158, 200, 206, 211, 246 f.
Latin   24, 122, 172, 182, 188–190, 235, 281, 283, 286, 289 f., 297
Lebenswelt   331
Leistung und Grenzen (Sp. *alcances y limites*)   16
levels of language   7 f., 21, 29, 146, 172, 222, 314
lexematics   42, 145 f.
lexical field (G. *Wortfeld*)   89, 102–104, 106, 121
lexicon   8 f., 28, 33 f., 173, 232, 236, 279 f.
Lifeworld   151, 158–161, 317, 331
linguistic change   3, 9, 14, 19 f., 23–26, 48 f., 67 f., 115–117, 119–121, 126 f., 130, 147, 165, 168, 181 f., 184–188, 190, 192–194, 197, 199, 201–206, 208, 213, 220
linguistic philosophy   12, 54, 85, 139
literacy   228 f., 235
logic   64, 74, 83, 120, 300
logicism   12, 50
lógos   54, 56, 83, 139, 143

markedness   19, 115, 120–122, 124, 128–130, 230
materiality   175, 284
matrix (of linguistic competence)   7, 9, 13, 27–29, 199, 212, 216, 304 f.

meaning (cf. signified, G. *Bedeutung*)   6, 8, 10, 12 f., 17, 20, 22, 25, 27, 29 f., 32–36, 42–44, 50, 53–55, 58, 66, 72, 82–85, 87, 89 f., 93, 122, 153 f., 169, 171, 173, 188 f., 202 f., 239, 245, 247–250, 252, 254–257, 261, 266–268, 274 f., 279, 281–283, 285–287, 289, 297 f., 302, 306 f., 318–323, 328, 330–332, 340
mentalism   206
metachrony   123
metaphor   35 f., 202, 311–323, 328, 332
metaphorical mapping   315
mind   6, 16, 27, 34 f., 44, 52 f., 56, 58, 69, 71 f., 75 f., 128, 147, 175, 187, 205, 207 f., 217, 281, 296, 301, 318, 328, 330, 332–335, 337–341
mistake, error   15, 172, 174, 199, 247, 254, 338
modal-temporal category   35, 295
modification   33, 121 f., 158, 208, 280–283, 288, 291
mondo civile (Vico)   48, 168
monosemy   248 f., 254, 328

'naming' function (ὀνομάζειν)   34
natural science   25, 67, 159–162, 165–167, 175, 188, 200 f., 203 f., 206, 334, 339
necessity   6, 67, 116 f., 125, 206, 220, 222, 238, 305
neurolinguistics   6, 22, 69
neutralisability   122, 129
neutralisation   121, 129 f.
nomen agentis   33
nomen instrumenti   289
nomen loci   289
nominalization   284 f.
non-language-specific (G. *allgemein-sprachlich*)   6–8, 167 f., 184–186, 212–216, 229–239, 262–268
norm, normal language use (Sp. *norma*)   1, 3 f., 8–13, 18 f., 24, 29–32, 35, 49, 69, 76, 115, 117 f., 120, 123–126, 141, 158, 173, 181, 183 f., 192, 215, 236, 239, 245–251, 253 f., 256–258., 329 f.

opposition   4, 8, 14, 30, 48–50, 57, 59, 66, 83, 86 f., 89, 118–124, 128–130,

141, 143, 146, 169, 245, 255, 257, 297 f., 303 f., 306
orality   228, 235
Organon model (Bühler)   43, 321
original knowledge (Sp. *saber originario*)   10, 73, 167

paradigm   9, 17, 63 f., 73, 89, 128, 140, 144, 156, 170, 173, 188, 199, 201, 204, 257, 312, 317, 334
parole en générale (speaking in general, G. *Sprechen im Allgemeinen*)   9, 42, 167, 172 f., 212, 216 f., 236–240
parole (speech, G. *Rede*)   2, 4, 10–12, 29 f., 42, 49, 88, 141 f., 200, 246 f.
pathêmata tês psychês (Aristotle)   54
Patient   262 f., 265, 271, 273
performance   57 f., 142, 174, 318
periphrastic future   182, 189 f., 306
phase   131, 169, 191, 300 f., 305–307, 315
phenomenology   22, 156, 161 f., 314, 331, 338 f.
philosophical   11–16, 21, 24, 48, 50–52, 54–59, 65, 67–69, 73, 81, 139 f., 142 f., 157, 167, 171, 183, 187 f., 197 f., 203, 206
philosophy of language   2, 4 f., 8, 11–15, 45, 47 f., 50–52, 54 f., 57 f., 65, 67, 69 f., 73, 77, 82–85, 137, 143, 197–199, 201, 312, 320
philosophy of science (epistemology)   5, 198, 327–341
phonology   3, 5, 9, 14, 19, 29, 31, 73, 128, 247, 327
phraseology   236
poetic   311, 315
politeness   27 f., 216, 220–222, 284, 302 f.
polysemy   9, 31, 72, 248–250, 255, 298, 303, 328
polysystematicity   119
positivism   6
pragmatics   26–28, 44, 69, 153, 199, 211–213, 215–219, 221–223, 228, 234, 327, 330, 336, 340
prefix   275, 280, 283, 289
preposition   31, 34, 251–257, 269 f., 330, 337

prepositional meaning/signified   31, 252
primary language and metalanguage   9, 208
primary lexicon   33, 279
primary perspective   299 f., 305–307
principle of antidogmatism   10
principle of humanism   10
principle of realism (or absolute objectivity)   10
principle of public responsibility   10
principle of tradition   10, 22
procedure (G. *Verfahren*)   4, 6, 23 f., 27 f., 30, 33, 90, 126 f., 145, 160–162, 192, 269 f.
prospective perspective   299, 304
proto-role   263
prototype   12, 30 f., 33, 205, 270, 328, 333
psycholinguistics   6, 69, 199, 205
purposiveness (Sp. *finalidad*, G. *Finalität*)   6, 19, 115, 117, 119 f., 181, 206

quidditas (pl. *quidditates*)   34

ratio significandi   83
re-create (G. *wiedererzeugen*)   14 f., 25–27, 68, 119
reference (cf. *Bezeichung*, designation)
relation (Fr. *rapport*)   42 f., 89 f., 102–106, 247, 251 f., 268, 299 f.
repeated discourse (Fr. *discours répété*)   9, 28, 173, 236
representation (G. *Darstellung*)   43, 270, 301, 321 f., 330, 335–337, 340
retrospective perspective   299
– secondary perspective   298–300, 306 f.
Romance languages   1 f., 9, 24, 28, 35, 88, 146, 172, 181 f., 188, 193, 214, 227–229, 235, 280, 283, 285–288, 291, 295–298, 302 f., 307
Russian   24, 147, 183, 193, 222

'saying' function (λέγειν)   34
schema   5, 10–14, 77, 85 f., 121, 124 f., 191, 246, 320, 322
sedimentation   161, 314
selection   13, 40, 118 f., 191, 200, 204 f.

semantic   7–11, 13, 18, 23, 31, 33f., 36, 53f., 70, 83, 85f., 121f., 139, 143, 146, 154, 208, 246, 250f., 254, 257f., 261–266, 268–275, 279–281, 288f., 297f., 301–304, 306f., 314, 316f., 323, 338
semanticity   13, 50, 53, 59, 175
semantic role   32–34, 261–265, 267–269, 271, 273f.
semantics   3, 5, 8, 10, 12, 31f., 38, 50–52, 55f., 69, 84f., 145f., 154, 156, 170, 246, 248, 251, 255, 261–275, 279–281, 291, 301, 304, 306, 317, 327f., 330, 332, 336, 338–340
sêmeion   54
semiotic   14, 22, 82f., 125, 127, 144, 155f., 158–162, 202, 208, 211–213, 216, 223, 317
semiotics   21–23, 151, 154, 156–158, 160, 162, 314, 316
'sense' ('text meaning', G. *Sinn*)   8f., 14, 27, 43f., 47, 141, 146, 165, 167, 266, 269, 279
sentence meaning   31
signification (Fr. *signification*)   7f., 42f., 266
significative-semantic roles   33, 264, 269–275
significative semantics   32, 261, 264, 266–271, 273–275
signified (Fr. *signifié*; cf. meaning)   8f., 23, 31–35, 42f., 82f., 84, 87, 143f., 146, 187, 248f., 261, 263, 266–269, 271, 275, 279–282, 284–287, 289–291
Sinn ('text meaning', 'sense')   8f., 14, 27, 43f., 47, 141, 146, 165, 167, 266, 269, 279
'skeuology'   172
sociolinguistics   8, 44, 69, 191, 193, 199, 228, 234
soliloquy   175
Spanish   1f., 8, 24, 35, 41, 50, 74, 91, 153, 168, 172, 182f., 193, 213, 217, 220, 234, 238f., 247, 250, 268, 280–291, 296, 299, 302, 306
speaking (Sp. *hablar*, G. *Sprechen*)   1, 3f., 6f., 9, 12, 14, 20–23, 26f., 30, 42, 47, 49, 57f., 66–68, 70–72, 76, 84, 118, 121, 126f., 137, 141–144, 146, 151, 153, 155, 169f., 172–176, 181f., 192, 202–204, 211–216, 218f., 221f., 233f., 236, 238, 246, 249, 254, 285, 317, 321, 323, 327, 329, 336
speech act   8, 11, 25–27, 30, 158, 171f., 197, 203–205, 207f., 213, 216, 234, 237, 303
speech (Sp. *habla*, G. *Rede*)   1, 3f., 8–11, 19f., 29–31, 36, 42, 49–51, 58, 68f., 71–73, 75f., 87, 89, 139, 141, 144, 157, 172–175, 181f., 191, 200, 202, 207, 213f., 216f., 219–221, 229f., 239, 279, 299f., 304f., 329
"Sprachwissenschaft ist Sprachgeschichte" (H. Paul)   5, 23, 165
stimulus   265
structuralism   2, 4, 14, 64, 67, 69, 73, 76, 116, 119, 130, 140, 142, 145, 151, 155, 158, 165f., 171, 175, 183, 185, 295, 297
structural linguistics   2, 4, 8, 90, 92, 145, 198f.
structural semantics   1, 6f., 9f., 14, 19, 81, 86f., 89f., 121, 145, 249
subpersonal   37, 332, 334–341
substance (and form)   18, 34, 49f., 98–100, 104f., 108, 116, 123f., 127, 130, 246–248, 262–268, 279–281, 296–298, 338–341
suffix   280, 282f., 285–288, 290
symbolic   139, 300, 312
synchrony   3, 9, 48–50, 76, 88f., 116–118, 123, 168f., 183, 185, 206f., 306
syncretism   305–307
synonymy   90, 265, 271
synphasic   3
synstratic   3, 118
syntax   3, 5, 31f., 72, 87, 92, 146, 247, 279, 288, 327
syntopic   3, 118
system (Fr. *langue*)   1, 3–5, 8–14, 18–20, 22–27, 29–32, 35, 49, 55, 66, 69f., 72, 74–76, 85, 89, 91, 115–121, 123–130, 142, 146, 158f., 168, 170–174, 181–185, 187, 192, 198–200, 206–208, 211–216, 218, 220–223, 229f., 234, 236, 239f., 245–251, 254, 256–258,

261, 268f., 275, 295–298, 300, 305–307, 313f., 319, 329f., 340

target   314–317, 334
technique   7–9, 59, 120, 137, 144, 170–173, 175, 182, 192, 222, 236, 245, 338
teleology   19, 115, 121, 124, 127
temporal structure   297, 299–301, 306f.
tense   35, 188, 190, 217, 279, 295–300, 302f., 305
text meaning (G. *Sinn*, Sp. *sentido*, Fr. *sens*)   8f., 14, 27, 43f., 47, 141, 146, 165, 167, 266, 269, 279
textual tradition (G. *Texttradition*)   232f., 237, 240
theory of language   2–5, 11, 14, 18f., 25f., 29f., 35, 37, 41, 49, 66, 81, 90, 93, 124, 145, 190, 202, 204, 227–229
'third-person' perspective   330, 335
thought   5, 8, 11, 13, 17f., 48, 50, 52–56, 58f., 63, 66–68, 73, 75, 82–85, 88, 115, 121, 138f., 154, 166f., 171, 175, 186, 192, 199, 202f., 206, 223, 257, 275, 318–321, 327f., 336, 338, 341
tò prépon   8
tradition   4, 8, 11f., 17, 21, 27, 30, 52, 54f., 57, 64f., 71, 73, 75f., 82, 87f., 90, 92, 115, 117f., 141f., 157, 173, 176, 182, 185, 192, 197–199, 202, 205, 208, 211–223, 228, 232, 234f., 239f., 245, 249, 272, 297, 300–302, 311f., 315, 319f., 323, 327
translation   1, 3, 5, 7, 9–11, 13, 21, 24f., 29, 41f., 44, 81, 91, 147, 152, 174, 183f., 193, 211f., 227, 237, 275, 295–297
truth   5, 15, 56f., 159, 175, 188, 202, 332
type   8f., 13, 18, 24, 27, 30, 32–35, 81, 90, 94, 117f., 122f., 127, 153, 160, 167, 189, 192, 204, 212–216, 218–222, 235, 237f., 261, 265, 272, 280, 283f., 291, 297f., 300f., 307, 312, 315, 317
typology   3f., 121, 146, 182

unconscious   36f., 70f., 119, 128, 191, 323, 330–333, 335–340
underspecified, indeterminate (G. *unbestimmt*)   31, 35, 265, 284, 290
unitary   3, 5f., 8, 23, 31, 75, 151–153, 170, 181f., 198, 289, 311, 316, 319, 321, 323, 328, 332, 334
unitary meaning (signified)   31, 42, 83, 249–252, 254–258, 297f., 303, 305
universal   7–10, 13, 25, 27, 29, 33, 54, 58, 76, 84, 117, 127, 167, 175, 185f., 189f., 211–213, 215–218, 220–223, 227, 229f., 232, 234, 238–240, 262, 268f., 314, 328, 339
universal–historical–individual   7, 29, 229, 232
universality   222, 227, 232, 234, 237–241, 269
Ursprache   208
usage, language use   11–13, 31, 52, 55f., 58, 115, 123–126, 131, 151, 200, 246, 254, 257, 331
utterance token meaning   31
utterance type meaning   31

variation   1, 4f., 7–9, 11, 13, 19, 23, 35, 126, 182, 204, 213, 229f., 240, 248f., 255, 290, 295–297
variational linguistics   4, 14, 28, 228, 241
variety   2, 11, 28, 42, 44, 172, 182f., 240
verb   32, 35, 49f., 71, 174, 182, 247, 265, 270, 272, 274f., 279, 283–287, 290f., 295–302, 307, 331, 333
Verum-Factum principle   159f.
view (G. *Schau*)   300

word formation   3, 33–35, 279–285, 287–289, 291f.
Wortfeld (lexical field)   89, 102–104, 106, 121

Johannes Kabatek

Erratum to: J. Kabatek, Eugenio Coseriu on immediacy, distance and discourse traditions

published in: Klaas Willems/Cristinel Munteanu (eds.), *Eugenio Coseriu: Past, Present and Future*, Berlin/Boston, De Gruyter, 2021, pp. 227–244, ISBN 978-3-11-071233-9

Erratum

Despite careful production of our books, sometimes mistakes happen. We apologize that in the original version of this chapter, there was a mistake in the labeling of Figure 5 on page 238:

The left column reads:

universal

historical

universal

Please note the subsequent correction:

universal

historical

individual

The updated original chapter is available at DOI: https://doi.org/10.1515/9783110712391-014
https://doi.org/10.1515/9783110712391-024

www.ingramcontent.com/pod-product-compliance
Lightning Source LLC
Chambersburg PA
CBHW031750220426
43662CB00007B/341